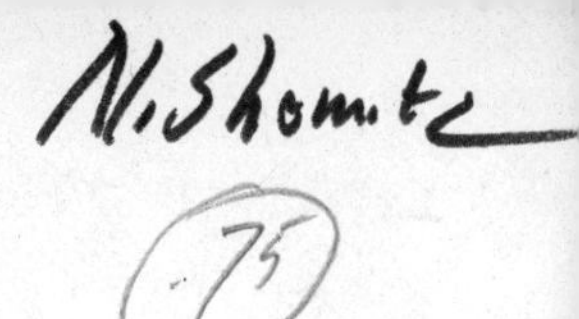

STRATEGY AND STRUCTURE

Chapters in the History of the Industrial Enterprise

ALFRED D. CHANDLER, JR.

STRATEGY AND STRUCTURE

Chapters in the History of the Industrial Enterprise

THE M.I.T. PRESS

MASSACHUSETTS INSTITUTE OF TECHNOLOGY

Cambridge, Massachusetts, and London, England

First M.I.T. Press Paperback Edition, October 1969
Third Paperback Printing, July 1970

ISBN 0 262 03004 7 (hardcover)
ISBN 0 262 53009 0 (paperback)

LIBRARY OF CONGRESS CATALOG CARD NUMBER: 62–11990
PRINTED IN THE UNITED STATES OF AMERICA

To

Frederick Merk

and

Arthur H. Cole

with gratitude

ACKNOWLEDGMENTS

MANY individuals have contributed to this study by providing information, by helping me develop my thoughts about the meaning of the data, by typing and checking the several versions of the manuscript, and finally by making available essential time and money. First of all, I want to thank John McDonald and Catharine Stevens, with whom I started to learn about the workings of big business and to think about the historical development of corporate structure and strategy. I am particularly indebted to Harold G. Mangelsdorf and Dr. George S. Gibb for their valuable assistance in working out the Jersey story, and to James M. Barker, who helped me in much the same way on the Sears experience.

Sidney S. Alexander, Morris A. Adelman, Barry E. Supple, Arthur H. Cole, Fritz Redlich, and Lynwood S. Bryant read all or parts of the manuscript, and I am indeed grateful for their exceedingly useful comments and criticisms. I especially want to thank Dr. Redlich for dragooning me into his campaign against empiricism in the writing of business history and his invaluable assistance in developing useful concepts. Other colleagues and academic neighbors who helped me work out specific ideas were Leland H. Jenks, Walt W. Rostow, Gordon M. Jensen, John B. Rae, and E. Neal Hartley.

I also want to offer my sincere thanks to the many busy corporation executives who were so generous with their time and information and who supplied correspondence, memoranda, and other documents so essential to any historical study. The four case studies particularly depended on company records and interviews with men involved in organizational changes. While voluminous, the record was not always complete. At du Pont and Sears, I examined in detail only the documents dealing with the major administrative reorganizations. However, the information in the records themselves and in available printed sources makes me quite certain that continued investigation in these archives would add little to the stories set forth in Chapters 2 and 5. At Jersey Standard, where I had access to all the available records, I carried the detailed story up to the end of 1927. The history of the organizational changes after 1927 will be described in full in the forthcoming volume III of the *History of the*

Standard Oil Company (New Jersey). I stopped my analysis at this date at the company's request because they did not wish to have this third volume anticipated. In order to indicate the relevance of the structural changes before 1928 to Jersey's present-day organization, I have briefly outlined the story for the years after 1927 from information available in *The Lamp* and *Fortune*. The General Motors story ultimately came to be based on information and materials which had been in the public domain before the summer of 1956. Yet I am confident that should information not yet in the public domain become available, it would not substantially alter the history presented here.

Information on other companies that were studied more briefly came largely from annual and other corporation reports, government documents, magazine articles, and the few pertinent business histories and biographies. For a number of firms such data were supplemented by interviews. As new facts are constantly appearing about these many enterprises and as some of the companies studied are currently undergoing organizational changes, I have arbitrarily set January 1, 1961, as the cutoff date for this historical investigation. Therefore, for the companies described here I have not used information which appeared after that date.

I am grateful to the Sloan Research Fund of the School of Industrial Management at the Massachusetts Institute of Technology and the John Simon Guggenheim Memorial Foundation for providing essential funds to relieve me from teaching time and to cover some secretarial and travel costs. The American Philosophical Society made a small grant that covered expenses incurred in making the study of Jersey Standard, while the Center for International Studies at M.I.T. supported a summer's research on the beginnings of large-scale enterprise in American industry.

I am particularly indebted to Dean John E. Burchard and Professor Howard R. Bartlett of M.I.T.'s School of Humanities for lightening my academic duties so that I could have more time for research and writing and also to E. P. Brooks, Dean Emeritus of the School of Industrial Management, and Howard W. Johnson, the present Dean, for their continuing interest and encouragement of my work. I am also grateful to a number of M.I.T. undergraduates who wrote papers on related subjects and who listened while I tried to work out some of my ideas in class. An excellent undergraduate thesis by Wayne Stuart entitled "The Development of Industrial Organization Theory" was of particular relevance. The ladies who provided secretarial, research, and editorial assistance were all exceedingly helpful, and I want especially to thank Gerta Kennedy, Ruth Roland, Ruth Crandall, and Constance Boyd. Joan Goldberg deserves a special vote of thanks for her hard work and good humor in the typing and retyping, the checking and rechecking of the manuscript's several drafts.

This, as all my other academic endeavors, could hardly have been possible at all without the encouragement and understanding of my wife, who in consequence carried far more than her share of nonacademic responsibilities.

While many contributed, the final product is mine, and for it I take full responsibility.

ALFRED D. CHANDLER, JR.

Brookline, Massachusetts
July, 1961

CONTENTS

STRATEGY AND STRUCTURE

Chapters in the History of the Industrial Enterprise

INTRODUCTION—STRATEGY AND STRUCTURE

Motives and Methods

This investigation into the changing strategy and structure of the large industrial enterprise in the United States began as an experiment in the writing of comparative business history. The initial thought was that an examination of the way *different* enterprises carried out the *same* activity — whether that activity was manufacturing, marketing, procurement of supplies, finance, or administration — would have as much value as a study of how a *single* firm carried on *all* these activities. Such a comparative analysis could permit deeper probes into the nature of the function studied, and so provide more accurate interpretations and more meaningful evaluations of the performance of several different enterprises in that activity than could a whole series of histories of individual firms. It could thus indicate more clearly the ways in which American businessmen have handled that activity over the years.

Of the several activities carried on in American business, that of administration appeared to be among the most promising for such an experiment in comparative history. Business administration has a particular relevance for today's businessmen and scholars. The enormous expansion of the American economy since World War II has led to the rapid growth of a multitude of industrial companies. Their executives are faced with complex administrative problems that before the war concerned only those of the largest corporations. At the same time, the growth of units that carry on political, military, educational, medical, as well as business activities has brought their administration to the attention of sociologists, anthropologists, economists, political scientists, and other scholars. Yet the historians have provided social scientists with little empirical data on which to base generalizations or hypotheses concerning the administration of great enterprises. Nor have the historians formulated many theories or generalizations of their own.

If changing developments in business administration presented a challenging area for comparative analysis, the study of innovation seemed to furnish the proper focus for such an investigation. Historically, administrators have rarely changed their daily routine and their positions of power except under the strongest pressures. Therefore a study of the creation of new administrative forms and methods should point to urgent needs and compelling opportunities both within and without the firm. For a study of such forms, that of the organizational structure used to administer the largest and most complex of American industrial enterprises seemed to offer the widest possibilities.

What then has been the structure used to administer such great enterprises? And who were its innovators? A preliminary survey of the experience of fifty of the largest industrial companies in the United States helped to answer these questions.[1] This survey showed that in recent years what may be called the multidivisional type of organization has become generally used by industrial firms carrying on the most diverse economic activities. In this type of organization, a general office plans, coordinates, and appraises the work of a number of operating divisions and allocates to them the necessary personnel, facilities, funds, and other resources. The executives in charge of these divisions, in turn, have under their command most of the functions necessary for handling one major line of products or set of services over a wide geographical area, and each of these executives is responsible for the financial results of his division and for its success in the market place. This administrative form, often known in business parlance as the "decentralized" structure, is depicted in Chart 1 (page 10).

The first companies to devise this "decentralized" form, according to the preliminary study, included the E. I. du Pont de Nemours & Co., General Motors Corporation, Standard Oil Company (New Jersey), and Sears, Roebuck and Company. Du Pont and General Motors began to fashion their new structure shortly after World War I. Jersey Standard started its reorganization in 1925, and Sears started its in 1929. Five other firms among the fifty studied — United States Rubber, B. F. Goodrich, Union Carbide & Carbon, Westinghouse Electric, and The Great Atlantic & Pacific Tea Co. — initiated comparable changes between 1925 and 1932. Except for the last, the A. & P., these administrative reorganizations proved to be less creative innovations than those in the first group.[2] Therefore du Pont, General Motors, and Jersey Standard were selected for study. And of the two innovators of the new multidivisional form in the merchandising field, Sears was picked instead of A. & P. because its activities were more complex and because information about the company was more readily available.

Possibly, other large corporations not on the list of the top fifty began to set up the "decentralized," multidivisional structure in the 1920's and even earlier. But the four selected—du Pont, General Motors, Jersey Standard, and Sears—were among the very first to initiate major reorganizations of this kind. What is important for this study is that the executives of these four began to develop their new structure independently of each other and of any other firm. There was no imitation. Each thought its problems were unique and its solutions genuine innovations, as brand new ways of administering great industrial enterprises. In time, the innovations became models for similar changes in many American corporations.

As my investigation of organizational innovation in these four companies progressed, several important facts became clear. First, a meaningful analysis of the creation of the new administrative form called for accurate knowledge about the firm's previous organization and in fact about its entire administrative history. Second, changes in organizational structure were intimately related to the ways in which the enterprise had expanded. An evaluation of administrative change, therefore, demanded a detailed understanding of the company's methods of growth. Third, these patterns of growth, in turn, reflected changes in the over-all American economy, particularly those affecting the market or demand for the enterprise's products. Finally, the reorganizations were influenced by the state of the administrative art in the United States at the time they were being carried out. The first two of these points required further investigation into the history of the four companies selected. The third and fourth called for a broader awareness of the history of the American business economy.

This need to enlarge the scope of the study made possible a broadening of its objectives. One way to ascertain the impact of the more general economic and administrative developments on the growth and organization of these industrial enterprises was to compare the experience of the four studied with that of many other similar large corporations. Such an expanded comparison not only could make the process of innovation in the four selected companies more comprehensible, but could also provide information on which generalizations might be made about the history of the industrial enterprise as an institution, and one of the most critically important of modern institutions at that. In this way what began as an experiment in comparative business history was broadened into one in the writing of institutional history.

To carry out these broader objectives, the administrative histories of close to a hundred of America's largest industrial enterprises were briefly examined. The companies included the fifty with the largest assets in 1909 and seventy of the largest by assets in 1948.[3] The latter group consisted of the fifty used in the preliminary study which had determined what was the most modern administrative form and who were its innovators. Twenty of the next largest were added in order to get a wider representation in various industries. These companies and their relative sizes are listed in Tables 1 and 2. (For the second group, size in 1959 as well as in 1948 is indicated.)

The information on these many companies came primarily from readily available materials such as annual and other company reports, government publications, articles in periodicals, and occasionally business histories and biographies. In eighteen of the more significant of these companies, interviews with senior executives helped supplement the printed record. The far more detailed analyses of organizational innovation at du Pont, General Motors, Standard Oil (New Jersey), and Sears, Roebuck were based, on the other hand, largely on internal company records—business correspondence, reports, memoranda, minutes of meetings, and the like. These historical documents were supplemented by interviews with men who had participated in the organizational changes.

Using these data, I have attempted to say something about the history of the large industrial enterprise as a basic, modern American institution. In so doing, this book also provides information about the history of business administration in the United States and about changes in the larger American economy. It tells still more about the history of the individual companies examined. The book attempts to provide this information by focusing on the innovation and spread of the modern "decentralized" form of organization in American industry. The major portion of the work is devoted to the administrative histories of the four companies that first created the new form. As studies in organizational innovation, these stories indicate why du Pont, General Motors, Standard Oil (New Jersey), and Sears, Roebuck enlarged their business, took on new functions, moved into new lines of businesses, and why each such move required a new design for administration. They trace the way in which busy executives worked out, often slowly and painfully, new methods and means for coordinating, appraising, and planning the effective use of vast and varied assortments of men, money, and materials. To make the case studies more meaningful, they are preceded by a broad survey of changing patterns in the growth and administration of the large enterprise in the United States, based on the experience of many of the largest companies. The case studies are then followed, first by a comparative analysis of organizational innovation in the four companies, and then by an extensive investigation into what other industrial enterprises accepted or rejected the new "decentralized" structure, and why and how they did so.

The story of how each of the four innovators met its changing admin-

TABLE 1

The Largest Industrials—1909

Numbers indicate relative size according to 1909 assets. Adapted from A. D. H. Kaplan, *Big Enterprise in a Competitive System* (Washington, 1954.)

I.

	Steel		*Nonferrous*
1	U. S. Steel	5	Amalgamated (Anaconda) Copper
17	Colo. Fuel & Iron	11	American Smelting & Refining
20	Lackawanna Steel	14	Pittsburg Coal
25	Republic Steel	19	American Can
28	Bethlehem Steel	23	Consolidation Coal
31	Cambria Steel	27	International Paper
37	Crucible Steel	34	Calumet & Hecla
38	Lake Superior Corp.	39	U. S. Smelting, Refining, & Mining Co.
46	Jones & Laughlin	40	United Copper
		41	National Lead
		43	Phelps, Dodge
		44	Lehigh Coal & Navigation
		48	American Writing Paper
		49	Copper Range Consolidated

II.

	Agricultural Processing		*Oil*		*Rubber*
3	American Tobacco	2	Standard Oil	10	U. S. Rubber
6	Central Leather	33	Associated Oil		
8	Armour & Co.				
9	American Sugar Refining				
13	Swift & Co.				
18	Corn Products Refining Co.				
21	American Woolen Co.				
30	National Biscuit				
33	Distillers Securities Corp.				
50	United Fruit				

III.

	Electrical		*Machinery*		*Miscellaneous*
15	General Electric	4	International Harvester	24	Du Pont (Explosives)
22	Westinghouse	7	Pullman	26	Va.-Carolina Chem. (Fertilizer)
		12	Singer Mfg. Co.	35	Am. Agri. Chemical (Fertilizer)
		16	American Car & Foundry	42	Sears, Roebuck
		29	American Locomotive	51	Eastman Kodak
		36	Allis-Chalmers		
		45	International Steam Pump		
		47	Baldwin Locomotive Works		

TABLE 2

Seventy Largest Industrials—1948 and 1959

Numbers indicate relative size according to 1948 and 1959 assets. Data for 1948 adapted from A. D. H. Kaplan, *Big Enterprise in a Competitive System* (Washington, 1954), and data for 1959 from *Fortune*'s "Directory of the 500 Largest Industrial Corporations."

I.

1948	*Steel*	*1959*
3	U. S. Steel	3
12	Bethlehem Steel	12
29	Republic Steel	26
35	Jones & Laughlin	42
43	National Steel	33
49	Armco Steel	27
50	Youngstown	55
53	Inland Steel	43

1948	*Nonferrous*	*1959*
20	Anaconda	25
24	Kennecott Copper	47
28	Aluminum Company of America	22
44	International Nickel	
45	International Paper	30
54	American Smelting and Refining	86
57	American Can	36
58	Phelps Dodge	89
70	Pittsburgh Plate Glass	61

II.

1948	*Agricultural Processing*	*1959*
18	American Tobacco	46
26	R. J. Reynolds	40
27	Swift	68
30	Armour	92
31	Liggett & Myers	91
38	Distillers-Seagrams	85
41	Schenley Industries	77
46	United Fruit	
47	National Dairy Products	58
48	Procter & Gamble	35
73	General Foods	80
67	Borden	101
	[General Mills]	

1948	*Oil*	*1959*
1	Standard Oil (N. J.)	1
4	Standard Oil (Ind.)	9
5	Socony-Vacuum	7
6	Texaco	6
7	Gulf Oil	5
11	Standard Oil (Calif.)	10
16	Sinclair Oil	18
21	Shell Oil	14
22	Phillips Petroleum	16
34	Atlantic Refining	45
61	Continental Oil	48
69	Standard Oil (Ohio)	90

1948	*Rubber*	*1959*
32	Goodyear	28
37	U. S. Rubber	57
39	Firestone	39
62	B. F. Goodrich	66

1948	*Mass Merchandising*
13	Sears, Roebuck
23	Montgomery Ward
36	A. & P.
40	F. W. Woolworth
60	J. C. Penney

III.

1948	*Electrical and Electronics*	*1959*
9	General Electric	11
17	Westinghouse Electric	17
66	RCA	44
68	IBM	20

1948	*Auto and Power Machinery*	*1959*
2	General Motors	2
10	Ford Motor	4
19	International Harvester	24
25	Chrysler	21
63	Deere	60
65	Allis-Chalmers	72

1948	*Chemical*	*1959*
8	Du Pont	8
15	Union Carbide	15
33	Eastman Kodak	32
42	Allied Chemical & Dye	50
52	Dow Chemical	37
64	Celanese	93
71	American Viscose	129
86	Monsanto Chemical	54
	[Hercules]	

istrative needs and problems which resulted from the expansion of its business has been told as though it were a chapter in the company's history. Each case study presents the events from the point of view of the busy men responsible for the destiny of their enterprise. Only by showing these executives as they handled what appeared to them to be unique problems and issues can the process of innovation and change be meaningfully presented. Only in this way can the trials of harassed executives faced with novel and extremely complex problems be clearly pictured, and the impact of specific personalities and of historical or accidental situations on over-all change be adequately presented. Moreover, if the chronological development of the story is kept intact and if it can be presented as it appeared to the actors in the story, the data should have more value to businessmen and scholars interested in the growth and government of the great industrial corporation than if they were selected and arranged to develop or illustrate one particular historian's theses.

At the same time, by carefully and explicitly comparing the separate chronological stories with one another and then with similar developments in other great industrial companies, these stories can become more than mere case studies in the meeting and solving of administrative problems resulting from growth. They can provide otherwise unobtainable information essential to the understanding of the history of one of the most significant of today's institutions. Such a comparative and institutional study of American business would seem to have some real advantages over the more traditional histories of individual firms or the more general surveys of the American business economy. Not only does it permit an analysis of significant decisions in far greater depth and detail than is possible even in a multivolume history of a single great company, but it also makes it possible to relate these detailed analyses more clearly and more precisely to broader historical developments.[4] On the other hand, complex decisions, actions, and events are not taken out of context and presented as mere illustrations as they would have to be in a general history of American business or of the American economy. They are not used to illustrate generalizations; they are the data from which the generalizations are derived.

Some General Propositions

If useful comparisons are to be made among four companies and then fourscore more, and if decisions and actions in these firms are to indicate something about the history of the industrial enterprise as an institution, the terms and concepts used in these comparisons and analyses must be carefully and precisely defined. Otherwise comparisons and findings can be more misleading than instructive. The following set of general or theoretical propositions attempts to provide some sort of conceptual precision. Without reference to historical reality, they try to explain in fairly clear-cut, oversimplified terms how the modern, "decentralized" structure came into being.

Before developing these propositions, the term *industrial enterprise* needs to be defined. Used in a broad sense, it means here a large private, profit-oriented business firm involved in the handling of goods in some or all of the successive industrial processes from the procurement of the raw material to the sale to the ultimate customer. Transportation enterprises, utilities, or purely financial companies are not then included in this study, while those firms concerned with marketing and with the extraction of raw materials as well as those dealing with processing or manufacturing do fall within this definition. An industrial enterprise is thus a subspecies of what Werner Sombart has described as the capitalistic enterprise, which as "an independent economic organism is created over and above the individuals who constitute it. This entity appears then as the agent in each of these transactions and leads, as it were, a life of its own, which often exceeds in length that of its human members." [5]

While the enterprise may have a life of its own, its present health and future growth surely depend on the individuals who guide its activities. Just what, then, are the functions of the executives responsible for the fortunes of the enterprise? They coordinate, appraise, and plan. They may, at the same time, do the actual buying, selling, advertising, accounting, manufacturing, engineering, or research, but in the modern enterprise the execution or carrying out of these functions is usually left to such employees as salesmen, buyers, production supervisors and foremen, technicians, and designers. In many cases, the executive does not even personally supervise the working force but rather administers the duties of other executives. In planning and coordinating the work of subordinate managers or supervisors, he allocates tasks and makes available the necessary equipment, materials, and other physical resources necessary to carry out the various jobs. In appraising their activities, he must decide whether the employees or subordinate managers are handling their tasks satisfactorily. If not, he can take action by changing or bringing in new physical equipment and supplies, by transferring or shifting the personnel, or by expanding or cutting down available funds. Thus, the term, *administration,* as used here, includes executive action and orders as well as the decisions taken in coordinating, appraising, and planning the work of the enterprise and in allocating its resources.

The initial proposition is, then, that administration is an identifiable activity, that it differs from the actual buying, selling, processing, or transporting of the goods, and that in the large industrial enterprise the concern of the executives is more with administration than with the performance of functional work. In a small firm, the same man or group of men buy materials, sell finished goods, and supervise manufacturing as well as coordinate, plan, and appraise these different functions. In a large company, however, administration usually becomes a specialized, full-time job. A second proposition is that the administrator must handle two types of administrative tasks when he is coordinating, appraising, and planning the activities of the enterprise. At times he must be concerned with the long-run health of his company, at other times with its smooth and efficient day-to-day operation.[6] The first type of activity calls for concentration on long-term planning and appraisal, the second for meeting immediate problems and needs and for handling unexpected contingencies or crises. To be sure, in real life the distinction between these two types of activities or decisions is often not clear cut. Yet some decisions clearly deal very largely with defining basic goals and the course of action and procedures necessary to achieve these goals, while other decisions have more to do with the day-to-day operations carried out within the broader framework of goals, policies, and procedures.

The next few propositions deal with the content of administrative activities handled through the different types of posts or positions in the most complex administrative structures. The executives in a modern "decentralized" company carry out their administrative activities from four different types of positions (see Chart 1). Each of these types within the enterprise has a different range of administrative activities. Normally, each is on a different level of authority. At the top is a *general office.* There, general executives and staff specialists coordinate, appraise, and plan goals and policies and allocate resources for a number of quasi-autonomous, fairly self-contained divisions. Each division handles a major product line or carries on the firm's activities in one large geographical area. Each division's *central office,* in turn, administers a number of departments. Each of these departments is responsible for the administration of a major function — manufacturing, selling, purchasing or producing of raw materials, engineering, research, finance, and the like. The *departmental headquarters* in its turn coordinates, appraises, and plans for a number of field units. At the lowest level, each *field unit* runs a plant or works, a branch or district sales office, a purchasing office, an engineering or research laboratory, an accounting or other financial office, and the like. The four types of administrative positions in a large multidivisional enterprise are thus: the field unit, the departmental headquarters, the division's central office, and the general office. These terms are used throughout this study to designate a specific set of administrative activities. They do not, it should be stressed, refer to an enterprise's office

CHART 1

The Multidivisional Structure

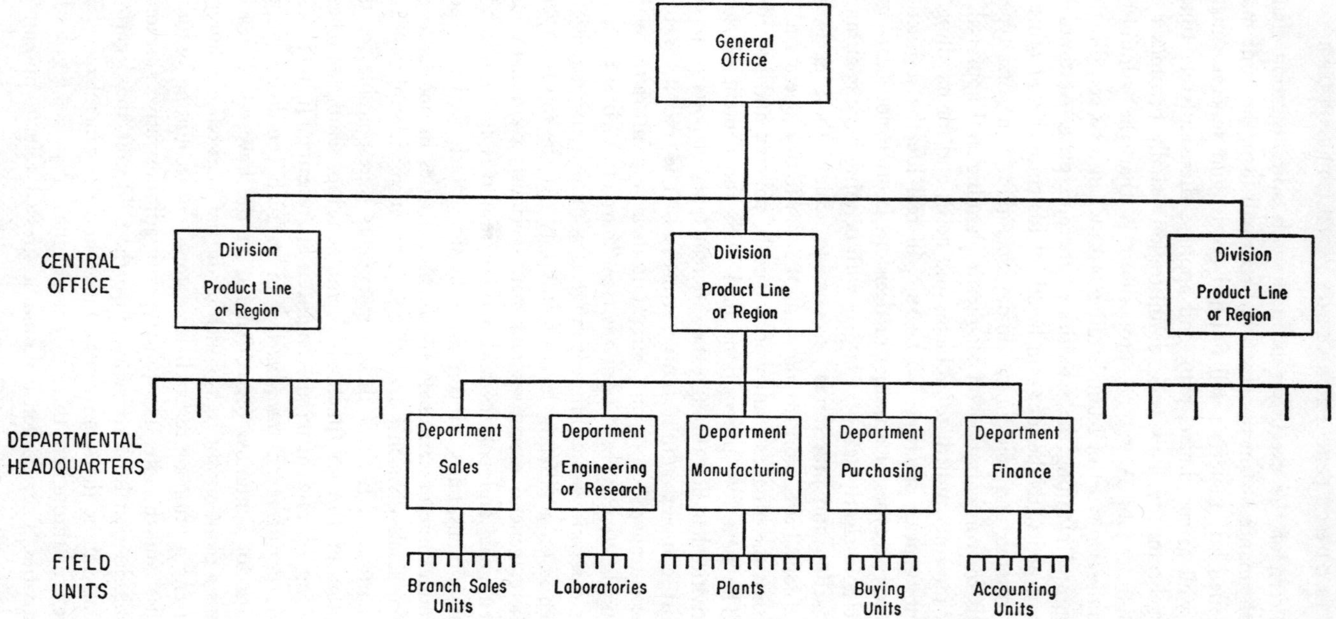

buildings or rooms. One office building could house executives responsible for any one of the positions or conceivably those responsible for all four. Conversely, the executives in any one of the posts could be housed in different rooms or buildings.

Only in the first, the field unit, are the managers primarily involved in carrying on or personally supervising day-to-day activities. Even here, if the volume of activity is large, they spend much of their time on administrative duties. But such duties are largely operational, carried out within the framework of policies and procedures set by departmental headquarters and the higher offices. The departmental and divisional offices may make some long-term decisions, but because their executives work within a comparable framework determined by the general office, their primary administrative activities also tend to be tactical or operational. The general office makes the broad strategic or entrepreneurial decisions as to policy and procedures and can do so largely because it has the final say in the allocation of the firm's resources — men, money, and materials — necessary to carry out these administrative decisions and actions and others made with its approval at any level.[7]

It seems wise here to emphasize the distinction between the formulation of policies and procedures and their implementation. The formulation of policies and procedures can be defined as either strategic or tactical. *Strategic* decisions are concerned with the long-term health of the enterprise. *Tactical* decisions deal more with the day-to-day activities necessary for efficient and smooth operations. But decisions, either tactical or strategic, usually require *implementation* by an allocation or reallocation of resources — funds, equipment, or personnel. Strategic plans can be formulated from below, but normally the implementation of such proposals requires the resources which only the general office can provide. Within the broad policy lines laid down by that office and with the resources it allocates, the executives at the lower levels carry out tactical decisions.

The executives who actually allocate available resources are then the key men in any enterprise. Because of their critical role in the modern economy, they will be defined in this study as entrepreneurs. In contrast, those who coordinate, appraise, and plan within the means allocated to them will be termed managers. So *entrepreneurial* decisions and actions will refer to those which affect the allocation or reallocation of resources for the enterprise as a whole, and *operating* decisions and actions will refer to those which are carried out by using the resources already allocated.

Just because the entrepreneurs make some of the most significant decisions in the American economy, they are not all necessarily imbued with a long-term strategic outlook. In many enterprises the executives responsible for resource allocation may very well concentrate on day-to-day operational affairs, giving little or no attention to changing markets, technology, sources of supply, and other factors affecting the long-term health of their company. Their decisions may be made without forward planning or analysis but rather by meeting in an *ad hoc* way every new situation, problem, or crisis as it arises. They accept the goals of their enterprise as given or inherited. Clearly wherever entrepreneurs act like managers, wherever they concentrate on short-term activities to the exclusion or to the detriment of long-range planning, appraisal, and coordination, they have failed to carry out effectively their role in the economy as well as in their enterprise. This effectiveness should provide a useful criterion for evaluating the performance of an executive in American industry.

As already pointed out, executives in the large enterprise work in four types of offices, each with his own administrative duties, problems, and needs. The four types operate on different scales, and their officers have different business horizons. The managers in the field unit are concerned with one function — marketing, manufacturing, engineering, and so forth — in one local area. The executives in the departmental headquarters plan, administer, and coordinate the activities of one function on a broad regional and often national scale rather than just locally. Their professional activities and their outside sources of information concern men and institutions operating in the same specialized function. The divisional executives, on the other hand, deal with an industry rather than a function. They are concerned with all the functions involved in the over-all process of handling a line of products or services. Their professional horizons and contacts are determined by industry rather than functional interests. Finally, executives in the general office have to deal with several industries or one industry in several broad and different geographical regions. They set policies and procedures and allocate resources for divisions carrying out all types of functions, either in different geographical areas or in quite different product lines. Their business horizons and interests are broadened to range over national and even international economies.

While all four types of offices exist in the most complex of industrial enterprises, each can of course exist separately. An industrial enterprise can include one, two, three, or all four of these offices. Many small firms today have only a single office managing a single plant, store, laboratory, financial operation, or sales activity. Larger companies with a number of operating units carry out a single function — such as sales (wholesale or retail), manufacturing, purchasing, or engineering. Their over-all administrative structure comprises a headquarters and field offices. So also today there are integrated industrial enterprises that handle several economic functions rather than just one. Finally, there are the great diversified industrial empires, carrying on different functions and producing a variety of goods and services in all parts of the globe.

Since each type of position handles a different range of administrative activities, each must have resulted from a different type of growth. Until the volume or technological complexity of an enterprise's economic activities had so grown as to demand an increasing division of labor within the firm, little time needed to be spent on administrative work. Then the resulting specialization required one or more of the firm's executives to concentrate on coordinating, appraising, and planning these specialized activities. When the enterprise expanded geographically by setting up or acquiring facilities and personnel distant from its original location, it had to create an organization at a central headquarters to administer the units in the field. When it grew by moving into new functions, a central office came to administer the departments carrying on the different functions. Such a central administrative unit proved necessary, for example, when in following the policy of vertical integration a manufacturing firm began to do its own wholesaling, procuring of supplies, and even producing raw materials. Finally, when an integrated enterprise became diversified through purchasing or creating new facilities and entered new lines of business, or when it expanded its several functional departments over a still larger geographical area, it fashioned a number of integrated divisional units administered by a general office.

The thesis that different organizational forms result from different types of growth can be stated more precisely if the planning and carrying out of such growth is considered a *strategy,* and the organization devised to administer these enlarged activities and resources, a *structure. Strategy* can be defined as the determination of the basic long-term goals and objectives of an enterprise, and the adoption of courses of action and the allocation of resources necessary for carrying out these goals. Decisions to expand the volume of activities, to set up distant plants and offices, to move into new economic functions, or become diversified along many lines of business involve the defining of new basic goals. New courses of action must be devised and resources allocated and reallocated in order to achieve these goals and to maintain and expand the firm's activities in the new areas in response to shifting demands, changing sources of supply, fluctuating economic conditions, new technological developments, and the actions of competitors. As the adoption of a new strategy may add new types of personnel and facilities, and alter the business horizons of the men responsible for the enterprise, it can have a profound effect on the form of its organization.

Structure can be defined as the design of organization through which the enterprise is administered. This design, whether formally or informally defined, has two aspects. It includes, first, the lines of authority and communication between the different administrative offices and officers and, second, the information and data that flow through these lines of communication and authority. Such lines and such data are essential to assure the effective coordination, appraisal, and planning so necessary in carrying out the basic goals and policies and in knitting together the total resources of the enterprise. These resources include financial capital; physical equipment such as plants, machinery, offices, warehouses, and other marketing and purchasing facilities, sources of raw materials, research and engineering laboratories; and, most important of all, the technical, marketing, and administrative skills of its personnel.

The thesis deduced from these several propositions is then that structure follows strategy and that the most complex type of structure is the result of the concatenation of several basic strategies. *Expansion of volume* led to the creation of an administrative office to handle one function in one local area. Growth through *geographical dispersion* brought the need for a departmental structure and headquarters to administer several local field units. The decision to expand into new types of functions called for the building of a central office and a multidepartmental structure, while the developing of new lines of products or continued growth on a national or international scale brought the formation of the multidivisional structure with a general office to administer the different divisions. For the purposes of this study, the move into new functions will be referred to as a strategy of *vertical integration* and that of the development of new products as a strategy of *diversification*.

This theoretical discussion can be carried a step further by asking two questions: (1) If structure does follow strategy, why should there be delay in developing the new organization needed to meet the administrative demands of the new strategy? (2) Why did the new strategy, which called for a change in structure, come in the first place?

There are at least two plausible answers to the first query. Either the administrative needs created by the new strategy were not positive or strong enough to require structural change, or the executives involved were unaware of the new needs. There seems to be no question that a new strategy created new administrative needs, for expansion through geographical dispersion, vertical integration, and product diversification added new resources, new activities, and an increasing number of entrepreneurial and operational actions and decisions. Nevertheless, executives could still continue to administer both the old and new activities with the same personnel, using the same channels of communication and authority and the same types of information. Such administration, however, must become increasingly inefficient. This proposition should be true for a relatively small firm whose structure consists of informal arrangements between a few executives as well as for a large one whose size and numerous administrative personnel require a more formal definition of relations between offices and officers. Since expansion created the need for new administrative offices and structures, the reasons for delays in developing the new organization rested with the executives responsible for the enterprise's long-range growth and health. Either these administrators were too involved in day-to-day tactical activities to appreciate or understand the longer-range organizational needs of their enterprises, or else their training and education failed to sharpen their perception of organizational problems or failed to develop their ability to handle them. They may also have resisted administratively desirable changes because they felt structural reorganization threatened their own personal position, their power, or most important of all, their psychological security.

In answer to the second question, changes in strategy which called for changes in structure appear to have been in response to the opportunities and needs created by changing population and changing national income and by technological innovation. Population growth, the shift from the country to the city and then to the suburb, depressions and prosperity, and the increasing pace of technological change, all created new demands or curtailed existing ones for a firm's goods or services. The prospect of a new market or the threatened loss of a current one stimulated geographical expansion, vertical integration, and product diversification. Moreover, once a firm had accumulated large resources, the need to keep its men, money, and materials steadily employed provided a constant stimulus to look for new markets by moving into new areas, by taking on new functions, or by developing new product lines. Again the awareness of the needs and opportunities created by the changing environment seems to have depended on the training and personality of individual executives and on their ability to keep their eyes on the more important entrepreneurial problems even in the midst of pressing operational needs.

The answers to the two questions can be briefly summarized by restating the general thesis. Strategic growth resulted from an awareness of the opportunities and needs — created by changing population, income, and technology — to employ existing or expanding resources more profitably. A new strategy required a new or at least refashioned structure if the enlarged enterprise was to be operated efficiently. The failure to develop a new internal structure, like the failure to respond to new external opportunities and needs, was a consequence of overconcentration on operational activities by the executives responsible for the destiny of their enterprises, or from their inability, because of past training and education and present position, to develop an entrepreneurial outlook.

One important corollary to this proposition is that growth without structural adjustment can lead only to economic inefficiency. Unless new structures are developed to meet new administrative needs which result from an expansion of a firm's activities into new areas, functions, or product lines, the technological, financial, and personnel economies of growth and size cannot be realized. Nor can the enlarged resources be employed as profitably as they otherwise might be. Without administrative offices and structure, the individual units within the enterprise (the field units, the departments, and the divisions) could undoubtedly operate as efficiently or even more so (in terms of cost per unit and volume of output per worker) as independent units than if they were part of a larger enterprise. Whenever the executives responsible for the firm fail to create the offices and structure necessary to bring together effectively the several administrative offices into a unified whole, they fail to carry out one of their basic economic roles.

The actual historical patterns of growth and organization building in the large industrial enterprise were not, of course, as clear-cut as they have been theoretically defined here. One strategy of expansion could be carried out in many ways, and often, two or three basic ways of expansion were undertaken at one and the same time. Growth might come through simultaneous building or buying of new faciliities, and through purchasing or merging with other enterprises. Occasionally a firm simultaneously expanded its volume, built new facilities in geographically distant areas, moved into new functions, and developed a different type of product line. Structure, as the case studies indicate, was often slow to follow strategy, particularly in periods of rapid expansion. As a result, the distinctions between the duties of the different offices long remained confused and only vaguely defined. One executive or a small group of executives might carry out at one and the same time the functions of a general office, a central office, and a departmental headquarters. Eventually, however, most large corporations came to devise the specific units to handle a field unit, a functional department, an integrated division, or a diversified industrial empire. For this very reason, a clear-cut definition of structure and strategy and a simplified explanation or theory of the relation of one to the other should make it easier to comprehend the complex realities involved in the expansion and management of the great industrial enterprises studied here, and easier to evaluate the achievement of the organization builders.

A comparative analysis of organizational innovation demands, however, more than an explanation of the terms, concepts, and general propositions to be used in assessing comparable experiences of different enterrises. It also calls for an understanding of the larger historical situation, both within and without the firm, during which strategic expansion and organizational change took place. The executives at du Pont, General Motors, Jersey Standard, and Sears, Roebuck did not solve their administrative problems in a vacuum. Other large enterprises were meeting the same needs and challenges and seeking to resolve comparable administrative problems. Their responses had an impact on the history of these four companies, just as the experience of the four affected that of many others.

The administrative story in each of the case studies falls into two basic parts: the creation of the organizational structure after the enterprise's first major growth or corporate rebirth, and then its reorganization to meet the needs arising from the strategies of further expansion. In developing their early administrative structures, these four firms were following accepted practices in American industry. Here the organization builders could learn from others. In fashioning the modern, multidivisional structure, they were, on the other hand, going beyond existing practices. Here others learned from them. An evaluation of the measures each took to improve the administration of its business requires therefore some knowledge of the methods and practices of business administration at the time when each built its major structure and began the reorganization that led to the fashioning of the multidivisional form.

One way to provide such a historical setting is to present a brief review of the growth of large-scale business enterprise in the United States. As the following survey is based only on readily available printed material supplemented by some interviews for only about a hundred of the nation's largest companies, its findings must be considered preliminary and tentative.[8] Much more detailed study will be necessary before the history of the administration or government of American industry can be accurately and fully explained. Nevertheless, even such a preliminary study indicates significant trends in the growth and administration of industrial corporations. An awareness of these trends is essential for the understanding of the more detailed case studies presented in this volume and of the subsequent changes in the structure and strategy of the large American industrial enterprise.

1 HISTORICAL SETTING

BEFORE 1850 very few American businesses needed the services of a full-time administrator or required a clearly defined administrative structure. Industrial enterprises were very small, in comparison with those of today. And they were usually family affairs. The two or three men responsible for the destiny of a single enterprise handled all its basic activities — economic and administrative, operational and entrepreneurial. In the agrarian and commercial economy of ante-bellum America, business administration as a distinct activity did not yet exist. In mining, manufacturing, marketing, and even transportation, the largest firms were directed by a general superintendent and a president or treasurer.[1] The general superintendent personally supervised the laboring force, whether miners, operators, engineers, conductors, or station agents. In the bigger textile and other manufacturing companies, the president or the treasurer usually handled the finances and arranged for the purchasing of materials and the sale of finished products from and to commissioned agents or other middlemen. On the railroad, the general superintendent carried on the commercial transactions of the company, setting rates, making contracts with shippers, buying materials and equipment, as well as scheduling trains and keeping track and equipment in good condition.

In the marketing and distribution of goods, merchants did most of their own buying and selling. When they were unable to carry on their business directly, they had agents who handled their accounts as well as those of other mercantile enterprises. If the amount of business was large enough, these agents sometimes became partners in the firm, particularly when the enterprise dealt with the transportation and sale of goods between distant commercial centers. Merchants, manufacturers, or railroad officers spent nearly all their time carrying on functional activities — the actual buying and selling or the personal supervision of the operations of a mill or a railroad. Only occasionally were they obliged to consider long-term plans such as the adoption of new machinery, taking on another line of merchandise, or the finding of a new partner or agent.

The Beginnings of Business Administration in the United States

Yet before 1850, a very few of the very largest American economic enterprises did develop embryonic administrative structures. John Jacob Astor's American Fur Company, Nicholas Biddle's Second Bank of the United States, and the state boards of public works or boards of directors of private corporations that built the major canals and first railroads, all these had field units and a headquarters. Astor's American Fur Company managed its virtual monopoly of the fur trapping and trading business in the vast region west of the Mississippi River and the Great Lakes through its Western and its Northern Departments.[2] The departmental headquarters administered a number of "outfits," each headed by a "trader" who supervised the work of the clerks at the trading posts and the *engagés* who did the actual trapping. The two department heads, both veteran fur traders, were partners in the company. Besides supervising the work in their departments, they did most of their own buying of supplies and marketing of furs and, in correspondence with Astor, decided on over-all policies. Astor's work as senior partner in the Fur Company was not sufficiently time consuming to keep him from managing personally many other profitable ventures.

Biddle's Bank of the United States was large and powerful enough to become a major political issue during the age of Jackson simply because it had branches throughout the Union. Each branch office had a cashier appointed by headquarters in Philadelphia and a president elected by a local board of directors.[3] The cashiers, as salaried employees of the bank, devoted their full time to its affairs, while the bank presidents were usually local leaders with extensive outside businesses of their own. To assure a steady flow of information between headquarters and twenty-five branches in the field, Biddle devised an elaborate and detailed system of reports which were supplemented by inspection trips from the Philadelphia office. The work at headquarters was voluminous enough to require one officer to concentrate his full time on supervising the transactions between the branch offices and another to look after the two million dollars' worth of real estate and nine million dollars' worth of bad or suspended debts. Biddle, therefore, spent much more of his time in appraising, coordinating, and planning the activities of his widespread enterprise than Astor ever did in managing the American Fur Company.

Although they were the largest business enterprises of their day, the Bank and the Fur Company had little, if any, impact on the later development of administrative organization in the large industrial firms in this country. The Fur Company was virtually dissolved when Astor withdrew from the partnership in 1834, and Biddle's bank lost its branches in 1836 after Andrew Jackson vetoed the bill for its recharter. More significant for the later story was the construction of the Erie Canal and other large transportation works during the 1820's and 1830's. During construction, the line of the canal or road was divided into a number of "divisions," each in charge of an "assistant engineer" who was responsible for surveying the route and then for inspecting the progress of construction.[4] At headquarters, a chief engineer supervised the work of his assistants in the field. The task of this organization, however, was more technical than administrative: it was only to lay out the line and then to see that the contractors carried out plans. A board, public or private, provided the funds and made the final major decisions as to the termini and general location. Until the 1850's, the contracting firms which actually built the transportation works remained small. Since such a contractor rarely built more than a few sections of a road, he could easily supervise the job by himself.

The *operation* of a railroad or canal called for more administration than its *construction*. Often the chief engineer who planned the work became the general superintendent.[5] On a canal, where he had no responsibility for operating the carriers or for the movement of passengers and freight, he could easily supervise personally the employees who operated the locks, collected the tolls, and handled maintenance and repair. Even on a railroad, which before the 1850's was rarely more than fifty or a hundred miles in length, the general superintendent had little difficulty in keeping close contact with the division engineers and all the employees carrying out the road's business. Such enterprises had as yet little need for a systematic organizational structure.

But with the completion of the great east-west trunk lines early in the 1850's administration became a full-time task in American business. The Erie, the New York Central, the Pennsylvania, the Baltimore & Ohio, and the western roads completed in that same decade, such as the Illinois Central, the Michigan Central, and the Michigan Southern, immediately became and long remained the largest business enterprises in the nation, and their operation demanded wholly new methods of management. As the General Superintendent of the Erie, Daniel C. McCallum, pointed out in 1855:

> A Superintendent of a road fifty miles in length can give its business his personal attention and may be constantly on the line engaged in the direction of its details; each person is personally known to him, and all questions in relation to its business are at once presented and acted upon; and any system however imperfect may under such circumstances prove comparatively successful.
>
> In the government of a road five hundred miles in length a very

different state exists. Any system which might be applicable to the business and extent of a short road would be found entirely inadequate to the wants of a long one; and I am fully convinced that in the want of a system perfect in its details, properly adapted and vigilantly enforced, lies the true secret of their [the large roads'] failure; and that this disparity of cost per mile in operating long and short roads, is not produced by a difference in length, but is in proportion to the perfection of the system adopted.[6]

To McCallum the new system meant, first, the careful and detailed definition of the lines of authority and communication between headquarters and the five divisions in the field. These lines he illustrated in what must have been one of the very first organizational charts ever printed by an American company. Second, the new system required a constant flow of detailed reports, daily, weekly, and monthly, from the division superintendents to the general superintendent as well as inspection visits from headquarters to the divisions. Before the end of the decade, the Pennsylvania, the Baltimore & Ohio, and undoubtedly other roads, had modeled their operating organization on the one first outlined by McCallum. Their superintendents, concentrating on coordinating, appraising, and planning the work of the operating divisions on the basis of statistical data and reports, spent far more time in administrative activities than even Nicholas Biddle had spent. Their whole attention, moreover, was directed to operating decisions. The presidents and the boards of directors of these large roads continued, for a relatively short time at least, to determine major strategic policies of expansion and competition.

As the roads grew in mileage and as their volume of traffic expanded rapidly, the number of their administrative personnel increased and their operating structure had to be redefined. The work involved in accounting and in the handling of passengers and freight grew so large as to call for separate offices for its supervision. At the same time, those activities related more directly to the movement of trains, such as the maintenance of way and of motive power and rolling stock, underwent a comparable departmentalization. Where McCallum of the Erie had innovated in the building of a structure for the administration of field units by departmental headquarters in the 1850's, the managers of the Pennsylvania Railroad pioneered in the 1860's and 1870's in working out a more extensive structure that defined the relations between departments. They spelled out the lines of communication and authority between the major and ancillary units within the transportation department and also between the transportation and the other major departments — the traffic and the accounting or financial departments.[7] The Pennsylvania also created a central office group consisting of department heads who worked with the president to coordinate, appraise, and plan the activities of all the departments in the interest of the enterprise as a whole. Because they were full-time employees and had far more detailed knowledge, understanding, and information about the affairs of the road than the members of the board of directors, the president and the functional vice-presidents soon took over the making of long-term entrepreneurial decisions on the Pennsylvania and other railroads.

As the first private enterprises in the United States with modern administrative structures, the railroads provided industrialists with useful precedents for organization building when the industrial enterprises grew to be of comparable size and complexity. More than this, the building of the railroads, more than any other single factor, made possible this growth of the great industrial enterprise. By speedily enlarging the market for American manufacturing, mining, and marketing firms, the railroads permitted and, in fact, often required that these enterprises expand and subdivide their activities. Such subdivision or specialization, in turn, called for a concentration of effort on coordinating, appraising, and planning the work of the specialized units. Expanding markets also encouraged the use of more complex machinery in manufacturing establishments. This new and increasingly complicated machinery in turn spurred further increases in output and so provided another pressure for expansion and continued growth.

As railroad construction boomed after the Civil War, the national market increased very rapidly in both the urban East and the agricultural West. During the 1870's and 1880's, most of the arable land in the West was settled quickly. Far more significant was the swift growth of commercial and industrial centers, old and new, particularly after 1880, for the new city dwellers and industrial workers required more food, clothing, housing, heat, light, and other products than did the farmers. Between 1840 and 1880, the urban population grew from 11 per cent of the total population in the United States to 28 per cent, or 4 per cent a decade.[8] In the years from 1880 to 1900, it rose from 28 per cent to 40 per cent, or 6 per cent a decade. During the later period, each per cent of growth added many more customers than it had earlier. In 1880, the rural population stood at 36.0 million and the urban at 14.1 million. By 1900, the figures were 45.8 million and 30.2 million, and by then agricultural income was estimated at only $3,034 million out of a total national private production income of $14,550 million.

In meeting the needs and seizing the opportunities created by the new national and increasingly urban market, many an American factory, mining, or marketing firm began to expand by multiplying the volume of output. Very quickly, these enterprises started to buy or build other units distant from their original locations. Soon, too, they were moving into new economic functions. These strategies of geographical dispersion and vertical integration had their beginnings before the depression of the 1870's dampened industrial growth for several years. Only after that depression, in the 1880's and early 1890's, did the great impersonal corporate enterprises appear in any numbers in American industry. Again during the 1890's a severe economic depression slowed growth. Then came the years of high prosperity after 1896 which saw the crest of the first great wave of industrial empire building in the United States. From the 1890's on, one of the basic challenges facing American industrialists was how to fashion the structures essential for the efficient administration of newly won business empires. These enterprises, far too large to be managed by small family groups, came quickly to be administered by full-time professional managers.

In forming these administrative structures, many organization builders first concentrated on the field unit, and on the factory rather than on the sales or purchasing office or the mine. It was on this level that Frederick W. Taylor, Harrington Emerson, and the other advocates of "scientific management" expended nearly all their energies. Even before the writings of these men became well known, industrialists in the steel, meat packing, electrical manufacturing, and agricultural-implement industries had begun to work out systematic designs for the administration of single plants or sales offices. Leaders in these fields had also begun by the 1890's to build departmental structures for the administration of a number of field units and to set up central offices for the management of the company as a whole. By the outbreak of World War I, scholars and analysts were publishing books and articles on industrial organization, writings that dealt with the structure of the large-scale enterprise as well as with that of a factory or branch office.

The Coming of the Integrated, Multidepartmental Enterprise

The coming of the first great integrated enterprises during the 1880's and 1890's brought entirely new problems of industrial management and led to the building of the first sizable administrative structures in American industry. The new administrative needs came less from an increase in volume of output than from the taking on of new functions. In the 1870's, nearly all American industrial enterprises only manufactured. They bought their supplies and sold their finished products through commissioned agents, wholesalers, and other middlemen. Mining enterprises operated in similar fashion; while mercantile firms nearly always handled a single activity, either retailing or wholesaling. By the end of the century, however, many American industries had become dominated by a few great enterprises that, beside manufacturing goods, sold them directly to retailers or even to the ultimate consumer, and purchased or even produced their own essential materials and other supplies. By now, too, a few merchandising companies were beginning to carry on both retail and wholesale functions, to buy directly from the manufacturer, and even to control manufacturing plants.

In manufacturing, the large multifunction enterprise sprang from two quite different strategies of growth. By one strategy, a single company began to expand and integrate through creating its own marketing organization. By the other, a number of manufacturing companies which had joined together in a horizontal combination — a trade association, pool, trust, or holding company — consolidated their manufacturing activities and then quickly moved forward into marketing or backward into purchasing. Firms making products based on new technological processes specifically for the growing urban markets usually found existing marketing channels unsatisfactory and so turned to the first of these strategies. The second type of strategy was employed much more often in industries producing the more staple commodities by an older and less complex technology. In these latter industries, expanded output often led to overproduction and then to combination. Both strategies were responses to the opportunities and pressures developing out of a rapidly growing national market. Both were also occasionally carried out by ambitious mining or marketing firms.

The story of Gustavus Swift provides an excellent example of an enterprise that grew through vertical integration by the creation of a marketing organization. A New England wholesale butcher, Swift moved to Chicago in the mid-1870's.[9] Coming from Massachusetts, he was aware of the growing demand for fresh meat in the eastern cities. After the Civil War, Boston, New York, Philadelphia, and other urban areas were calling for much more meat than could be supplied locally. At the same time, great herds of cattle were gathering on the western plains. Swift saw an opportunity to bring together the new supply and the new demand by exploiting the new technology of refrigeration. In 1878, shortly after his first experimental shipment of refrigerated meat, he formed a partnership with his younger brother, Edwin, to market fresh western meat in the eastern cities.

For the next decade, Swift struggled hard to put into effect his plans for building a nationwide distributing and marketing organization. From the start, he realized that the refrigerated car could meet only part of his needs. There had to be a refrigerated storage plant or warehouse with a distributing and marketing organization in each major city. District offices or "branch houses," beside operating the warehouses, controlled wholesale and occasionally retail outlets in smaller towns and villages as well as in the major cities. Such outlets often came to be operated by Swift's own salaried representatives. The branch managers thus administered the different marketing activities within one area. By advertising and other means, they had to break down the prejudice against eating meat killed more than a thousand miles away and many weeks earlier and to defeat the concerted efforts of local butchers, who had recently created the National Butchers Protective Association to prevent the sale of fresh western meat in the eastern urban markets. At the same time, Swift had to combat the boycotts that the railroads had placed on his refrigerator cars.

By the end of the decade, Swift's initial strategies had proved eminently successful. His fast-growing distributing organization constantly called for more and more supplies. Between 1888 and 1892, Swift, who had incorporated his enterprise in 1885, set up meat-packing establishments in Omaha and St. Louis, and, after the depression of the 1900's, three more in St. Joseph, St. Paul, and Fort Worth. At the same time, the company systematized the buying of cattle and other products at the stockyards. It expanded its marketing facilities abroad as well as in the United States. Before the end of the 1890's, Swift had created a huge vertically integrated industrial empire.

Other packers quickly followed his example. To compete effectively, Armour, Morris, Cudahy, and Schwarzschild & Sulzberger had to build similarly integrated organizations. Those companies that did not follow the Swift model were destined to remain small, local ones. Thus, by the middle of the 1890's, with the rapid growth of these vertically integrated firms, the meat-packing industry had become oligopolistic. The "Big Five" had the major share of the market, each with its field units, functional departments, and central office.

Then, as each firm systematized the administration of its functional activities and devised techniques to coordinate the flow of products through the different departments, it also turned to developing goods that could further employ the vast resources it had collected. To beef, these firms quickly added a full line of meat products, including lamb, veal, and pork. To make better use of their branch-house network, they began to market poultry, eggs, and dairy products. To obtain more profit from their "disassembling" and other processing operations, they went into the leather, soap, fertilizer, and glue businesses.

The meat packers paid much less attention to the administration of their by-product operations than to their main line. Where the market for by-products was close to that for the primary products, the new businesses — such as poultry and eggs — were administered through the existing functional structure. Where the markets were very different, as in the case of leather and fertilizer, they were managed through subsidiaries or divisions to which the central office gave little direction. A senior executive was often responsible for a function and for one or two by-products and, at the same time, helped to make strategic decisions for the enterprise as a whole.

In the same years, Swift's story was paralleled by other agricultural-processing industries whose products were destined for many urban consumers. In the tobacco industry, James B. Duke was the first to appreciate fully the growing market for cigarettes, a new product sold almost entirely in the cities.[10] In 1881, he applied to the manufacturing of cigarettes a recently developed machine. Once he had adapted the new technology to the new demand, he concentrated on expanding his market by extensive advertising and by building up a national and international sales and distributing organization. By 1884, he had left Durham, North Carolina, for New York City, where he set up new factories, sales headquarters, and his central administrative offices. New York, closer to his markets, was a more logical place from which to run his world-wide industrial domain. As he continued to expand his distributing, marketing, and advertising organizations, he also set up a network of warehouses and purchasing offices in tobacco-growing areas. In 1890, Duke merged his company with five smaller concerns. Five years later, the activities of all these had been consolidated into the centralized, functionally departmentalized organization with marketing, manufacturing, purchasing, and financial departments that Duke had fashioned earlier. He then went on to obtain control, through purchases and mergers, of the producers of every other type of tobacco product except cigars. These later acquisitions were not all brought into the existing structure. Some remained integrated subsidiaries loosely administered from American Tobacco's offices at 111 Fifth Avenue.

What Duke and Swift did for their respective industries, James S. Bell and Andrew Preston did for flour and for bananas.[11] In 1889 Bell took on the presidency of the Washburn-Crosby Company in Milwaukee and soon became known as "the greatest merchant miller in the world." He created a large marketing and distributing organization to sell to urban bakeries and retail stores high-grade flour made from spring wheat raised in the recently opened agricultural areas of the Northwest and processed by the new automatic-roller, gradual-reduction milling process. Similarly, in the banana industry, Preston fashioned the organization with its headquarters in Boston which in 1890 became the Boston Fruit Company and in 1899 the United Fruit Company. Preston, like Swift, made use of the new refrigerator technology in his ships, freight cars, and warehouses.

In developing new consumer durables, innovators also found it necessary to create their own marketing and distributing organizations. Both Cyrus McCormick, pioneer harvester manufacturer, and William Clark, the business brains of the Singer Sewing Machine Company, first sold their products through commission agents. Clark soon discovered, however, that salaried men working out of branch sales offices displayed, demonstrated, and serviced sewing machines more effectively and cheaply than did the agents.[12] And just as important, the branch offices could provide the customer with essential credit. Then McCormick, while using the franchised dealer to handle the final sales, came to realize the need for a strong selling and distributing organization with warehouses, servicing facilities, and a large salaried force to stand behind the dealer.[13] Thus in the years following the Civil War, both the McCormick Reaper and the Singer Sewing Machine companies concentrated on building up first national and then world-wide sales departments. Since they purchased their raw materials from only a few industrial companies rather than from many individual farmers, their purchasing problems were less complex and required less attention than those of firms processing agricultural products. But the net result was the creation of a very similar type of organization.

Enterprises developing technologically advanced durable products for producers' markets also became dissatisfied with the existing sales channels. The most significant of these enterprises, in the 1880's, were in the new electrical field. Within a decade after Thomas Edison's proof of the practicality of an incandescent lighting system, two great corporations—General Electric and Westinghouse—came to dominate the industry. By that time, both firms were developing electrical machinery as a source of power for industrial and transportation businesses as well as for the generation of light.[14] The marketing of electric lighting, power machinery, and traction equipment was so complicated technologically that it demanded highly trained salesmen who understood the power and transportation needs of their customers even more thoroughly than the customers themselves did. As the specifications for heavy equipment were very precise and varied with the needs of individual customers, the salesmen had to be in close contact with the manufacturing departments. Moreover, since the technological competition between the two firms was very intense, coordination between marketing, designing, and engineering personnel was essential.

The resulting departmental structure reflected the types of markets in which the products were sold. General Electric and Westinghouse each had a manufacturing department to administer a number of scattered works or factories, a sales department to supervise a nationwide spread of district offices, an engineering department responsible for design, and a finance department. The sales and engineering headquarters included suboffices to handle the major products, for there were basic differences in the designing and marketing of heavy equipment and apparatus which were made to detailed customer specifications, such as large generators, motors, and switch gear, and lighter products which were made in volume ahead of orders, such as lamps, watt meters, and small motors and generators.

To some extent, steel manufacturers began to take over their own marketing because they too had technologically advanced products and an increasingly broadening market. Steel came to be produced on a large scale only in the 1870's, and at that time practically all the steel produced went into rails. In the next decade, as the basic railroad network was completed, structural steel for the new urban market became a major product. Carnegie's decision to use the steel produced at the Homestead works, one of the first great open-hearth works in the United States, for structures rather than rails symbolizes the change in both market and technology.[15] Selling steel to contractors and builders as well as to the growing manufacturing companies in the machinery, agricultural-implement, and other industries required a larger sales force than selling to the relatively few railroads. As in the case of heavy electrical equipment, each order had its own specifications and so required close coordination between sales and manufacturing. Some companies also found it more satisfactory to distribute and market the more standard items made in advance of sale through their own "warehousing" organizations rather than through outsiders.[16] As a result, the largest steel companies, like Carnegie, Illinois Steel, and Jones & Laughlin, by the 1890's had their own marketing organizations.

In the decade before the depression of the 1890's, Carnegie, and apparently the other firms, had obtained control of their supplies of coke and coal, though not yet of ore. Most of the smaller makers of steel and those still manufacturing iron, however, remained essentially single-function enterprises, buying their raw materials from others and selling their products through middlemen. It should be noted, parenthetically, that the experience of the large electrical and steel companies was to provide examples for the organization builders at the du Pont Company, whereas the creators of the early automobile firms which became part of General Motors learned more from McCormick and Clark.

Integration via Combination and Consolidation

The more common road to the formation of the vertically integrated enterprise was by way of horizontal combination and consolidation. The threat of excess capacity appears to have been a primary stimulus to initial combinations in most American industries. But why did factories have difficulty in using fully their available resources in a period of swiftly growing markets? The answer seems to be that the rapid increase in the output of many small enterprises exceeded immediate demand. Each firm expanded because its executives hoped, particularly during the boom periods after the Civil War and again after the depression of the 1870's, to profit thereby from the new markets. Then, as the market became glutted and prices dropped, the many manufacturers became more and more willing to combine in order to control or limit competition by setting price and production schedules. So from the mid-1870's on, many small producers of leather, salt, sugar, whisky and other products made from corn, linseed and cotton oil, biscuit, fertilizer, petroleum, explosives, rope, and rubber joined in large horizontal combinations. Yet, such federations were usually short-lived. Production or price schedules were hard to enforce, even after the combinations became legal entities in the form of trusts or, after the passage of the New Jersey law in 1889, of holding companies. Another reason why they were unsuccessful was simply that they failed to employ fully and effectively the existing resources of their members.

Occasionally a federation dissolved into its original parts. More often it consolidated. And here the distinction between legal and administrative developments must be kept clear. The truly consolidated enterprise operating on a national scale required both new legal and new administrative forms. Legally, it called for an instrument that would permit it to operate in many different states. Administratively, it demanded a structure to provide for centralized coordination, appraisal, and planning for its extended plant and personnel.

Once the opportunity for nationwide operations appeared, the necessary legal instruments were not long in coming. The Standard Oil Company of Ohio formed the first trust in 1882, and by 1889 New Jersey had amended her general incorporation law to permit one corporation to purchase stock of another. Of these two legal innovations, the general incorporation law for holding companies was the most significant. Since the 1850's, railroads and occasionally other utilities (the American Bell Telephone Company, for example) had held stock in other companies, but such action was normally authorized by a special charter of incorporation, or an amendment to it, passed by a state legislature. Before the New Jersey amendment, no general incorporation law explicitly allowed a corporation to hold stock of other corporations. Some state laws, in fact, specifically forbade it. Moreover, many states penalized out-of-state corporations by prohibiting them from owning real estate in the state or subjecting them to special taxes. The provisions for general incorporation of holding companies, which other states soon borrowed from New Jersey, permitted a single parent company to hold the majority of the stock of locally chartered subsidiaries and so provided an inexpensive and easy way for enterprises operating over a wide area to avoid these obstacles and still to retain legal control over their geographically dispersed activities.

After the 1890's, administrative innovations were much more important to the development of American business than legal ones. A combination became administratively a consolidation only after its executive office began to do more than merely set price and production schedules. It remained a combination as long as decisions on how to produce or market and how to allocate resources for the present and in the future were left to the constituent enterprises. It became administratively consolidated when the small executive office was transformed into a centralized headquarters that determined nearly all the activities of the enterprise's plants or marketing units. The factories or sales offices, formerly managed by the heads of member firms, became operated by salaried plant managers or sales representatives.

The transformation of a loose alliance of manufacturing or marketing firms into a single consolidated organization with a central headquarters made possible economies of scale through standardization of processes and standardization in the procurement of materials. Of more significance, consolidation permitted a concentration of production in a few large favorably located factories. By handling a high volume of output, consolidated factories reduced the cost of making each individual unit. They could specialize further and subdivide the process of manufacturing and also were often able to develop and apply new technological improvements more easily than could smaller units. To a lesser extent, consolidations of marketing firms offered comparable advantages.

Horizontal consolidation and centralization immediately created much more pressure for vertical integration than did mere combination. The heavy fixed costs of enlarged plants or, in the case of a marketing firm, enlarged distribution facilities demanded a continuing high volume of output. A manufacturing company found it no longer safe to rely wholly on outside wholesalers or commission agents who also sold goods of competitors. The interests of these agents differed from those of the manufacturer. The wholesaler was often less concerned with increasing the volume necessary for reducing unit manufacturing costs than with obtaining a satisfactory "markup" or commission. He had no particular reason for pushing the products of one client more than those of another. On the other hand, the manufacturer was unable to build up his own special market through brand names and advertising. Moreover, coordination between the marketers and the manufacturers and designers of products proved difficult. As a result, potential savings in cost were lost, and the development of products more nearly fitted to the customers' wants was inhibited. In time, too, many producers became convinced that they could distribute their wares more cheaply than their agents did. A manufacturer could assure himself of these advantages, however, only if his volume was large enough to support a national distributing system.

For these reasons, many consolidated firms, though certainly not all, began to do their own wholesaling and, occasionally, even retailing. They carried out this strategy by creating their own selling organizations or, more often, by combining with or buying existing large nationwide marketing enterprises. At the same time, many set up their own purchasing organizations. Only a few combinations, such as Standard Oil and United States Rubber, had embarked on this strategy of consolidation and integration before the depression of the 1890's. A much larger number did so in the years immediately following 1896.[17] These included firms in different industries, such as The Distillers Securities Company (the lineal descendant of the Distillers and Cattle Feeders Trust), National Biscuit, Pittsburg Coal, International Paper, Allis-Chalmers, International Harvester, American Smelting & Refining, and the du Pont Company.

The story of the du Pont Company in the next chapter describes the processes and shows the reasons for them. It might be well, however, to give here two contemporary comments on why certain enterprises moved from combination or federation to consolidation and integration. The first comes from the *Annual Report of the National Biscuit Company for 1901:*

> This Company is four years old and it may be of interest to shortly review its history. . . . When the Company started, it was an aggregation of plants. It is now an organized business. When we look back over the four years, we find that a radical change has been wrought in our methods of business. In the past, the managers of large merchandising corporations have thought it necessary, for success, to control or limit competition. So when this Company started, it was believed that we must control competition, and that to do this we must either fight competition or buy it. The first meant a ruinous war of prices and a great loss of profits; the second, constantly increasing capitalization. Experience soon proved to us that, instead of bringing success, either of those courses, if persevered in, must bring disaster. This led us to reflect whether it was necessary to control competition. . . . We soon satisfied ourselves that within the Company itself we must look for success.
>
> We turned our attention and bent our energies to improving the internal management of our business, to getting full benefit from purchasing our

> raw materials in large quantities, to economizing the expenses of manufacture, to systematizing and rendering more effective our selling department, and above all things and before all things to improving the quality of our goods and the condition in which they should reach the customer.
>
> It became the settled policy of this Company to buy out no competition. . . .[18]

While building up its distributing organization, the company changed its policy from selling to wholesalers in bulk to marketing small packages to retailers. It developed the various "Uneeda Biscuit" brands. "The next point," the same *Annual Report* continued, "was to reach the customer. Thinking we had something that the customer wanted, we had to advise the customer of its existence. We did this by extensive advertising." Since flour could be easily and quickly bought in quantity from large milling firms, the purchasing requirements were less complex than those of marketing and called for a smaller organization. On the other hand, the company spent much energy after 1901 in bettering plant layout and manufacturing processes in order to cut production costs and to improve and standardize quality. Throughout the first decade of its history, National Biscuit continued its basic policy of "centralizing" manufacturing operations, particularly in its great New York and Chicago plants. At the same time that its executives were systematizing the operations of its functional activities, they were also setting up a central office for the management of the business as a whole. In this way, National Biscuit quickly transformed itself from a combination or federation to a consolidated firm and then to an integrated, multidepartmental enterprise, similar to Swift, Singer Sewing Machine, or General Electric.

The second comment comes from Charles R. Flint, an organizer of the United States Rubber Co. and other new consolidations. When asked in 1899 to describe "the benefits of consolidated management," he replied:

> The answer is only difficult because the list is so long. The following are the principal ones: raw material, bought in large quantities is secured at a lower price; the specialization of manufacture on a large scale, in separate plants, permits the fullest utilization of special machinery and processes, thus decreasing costs; the standard of quality is raised and fixed; the number of styles reduced, and the best standards are adopted; those plants which are best equipped and most advantageously situated are run continuously in preference to those less favored, in case of local strikes or fires, the work goes on elsewhere, thus preventing serious loss; there is no multiplication of the means of distribution — a better force of salesmen takes the place of a larger number; the same is true of branch stores; terms and conditions of sales become more uniform, and credits through comparisons are more safely granted; the aggregate of stocks carried is greatly reduced,

> thus saving interest, insurance, storage and shop-wear; greater skill in management accrues to the benefit of the whole, instead of the part; and large advantages are realized from comparative accounting and comparative administration. . . . The grand result is, a much lower market price. . . .[19]

During these years, some enterprises went still further. Beside handling their own marketing and manufacturing, they took over the production—and often the transportation—of their raw materials. This expanded form of vertical integration usually occurred in those enterprises whose raw materials came out of the ground and where the limited supply could be controlled by a few firms. Such a situation posed the threat that the manufacturer would be unable to obtain his materials at a satisfactory price. Standard Oil moved into the production of crude oil in the late 1880's largely to gain an assured source of supply.[20] In the late 1890's, the largest combinations, which became consolidations, in the fertilizer industry—the Virginia-Carolina Chemical Company and the American Agricultural Chemical Company—carried out a similar strategy for the same reasons.[21] So too did a third fertilizer combination, the International Agricultural Corporation, somewhat later. After International Paper consolidated its mills and built its marketing organization, it purchased control of large tracts of timber in Maine and Canada.

Such defensive reasons played a particularly critical role in stimulating consolidation and integration in the iron and steel industries. The Carnegie Co., troubled by the concentration of control achieved during the depression of the 1890's in the Lake Superior iron-mining regions, purchased large holdings in the Mesabi Range.[22] Other steel companies quickly followed suit. In 1898, Elbert H. Gary, with capital supplied by J. P. Morgan & Co., formed the Federal Steel Co., which combined Chicago's Illinois Steel Co. and the Lorain Steel Company (with plants in Lorain, Ohio, and Johnstown, Pennsylvania) with the Minnesota Iron Company.[23] The new combination soon had railroads and a fleet of ore boats to provide transportation of the ore to the mills. In the same year, many small iron and steel firms in Ohio and Pennsylvania merged to form the Republic and National Steel Companies.[24] Shortly thereafter, a similar combination in the Sault Sainte Marie area became the Lake Superior Corporation. These combinations began at once to consolidate their manufacturing activities, to set up their marketing organizations, and to obtain control by lease and purchase of raw materials and transportation facilities. By 1900, several small firms making high-grade steel did much the same thing when they formed the Crucible Steel Company of America. About this time, the larger established steel companies like Jones & Laughlin, Lackawanna, and Cambria moved to obtain a more certain control over their supplies of ore and simultaneously altered their manufacturing or marketing organizations. Somewhat the same pattern can be discerned in the copper and other metals industries.

These combinations among the producers of semifinished steel and other metal products brought on, between 1898 and 1900, a wave of mergers among the users of steel, copper, and other semifinished materials. In addition to the threat of buying from a very few recently combined producers, who could set their own prices, the memories of unused capacity and low prices during the depression years of the 1890's and the persuasive arguments of the Wall Street promoters eager for the profits of combination stimulated these mergers. Among the users of iron, steel, and copper these included American Tin Plate, American Steel & Wire, American Steel Hoop, National Tube, American Bridge, American Sheet Steel, Shelby Steel Tube, American Can, National Enameling & Stamping Co., American Car & Foundry, American Locomotive, International Harvester, International Steam Pump, and American Brass Co. Some of these new enterprises were combinations of manufacturing works, but some like International Harvester, International Steam Pump, American Can, and American Brass were combinations of already consolidated, integrated companies.

Whatever their origin, most of these combinations quickly consolidated their constituent companies into single operating organizations. Manufacturing facilities were unified and systematized, over-all accounting procedures instituted, and a national and often world-wide distributing organization formed. Some even began to assure themselves of control of supply by building their own rolling mills and blast furnaces. As the American Steel & Wire and National Tube began to make their own steel, they canceled contracts with Carnegie and other semifinished producers.[25] This development, in turn, led Carnegie to bring forth plans to fabricate his own finished products.

The resulting threat of unemployed resources and price cutting led, as students of American business history know so well, to the formation of the United States Steel Corporation.[26] This billion-dollar merger came to include the Carnegie, Federal, and National Steel companies, and the first six of the fabricating companies listed above. It continued as a combination. Although the activities of the various integrated, multifunction subsidiaries were re-formed and redefined, there was no over-all consolidation. Under the chairmanship of one of its most active founders, Elbert H. Gary, it remained, from an administrative standpoint, a federation of operating divisions loosely controlled by the holding company. Only in the 1930's, well after Gary's death, did the corporation's general offices at 71 Broadway begin effectively to coordinate, appraise, and plan policies and procedures for its numerous subsidiaries, and did so then only after it had taken on a management structure very similar to the one Alfred P. Sloan had installed at General Motors many years earlier.

The years from the end of the depression of the 1870's until the turn of the century witnessed an enormous surge in American industrial output. By 1900, industrial capacity surpassed that of any other nation. During this same period of growth, the most dynamic and most significant of American industries had become dominated by a few great vertically integrated enterprises operating in national and often world markets. Small firms remained in these industries, but to exist they had to concentrate on a specialized product or meeting the needs of a local area.

In the last two decades of the nineteenth century, American industrialists concentrated their imagination and energy on the creation of these industrial empires. They became engrossed in planning the strategies of expansion and in securing the resources — the men, money, and equipment — necessary to meet the needs and challenges of a swiftly industrializing and urbanizing economy. The powerful captains — the Rockefellers, Swifts, Dukes, Garys, and Westinghouses — and their able lieutenants had little time and often little interest in fashioning a rational and systematic design for administering effectively the vast resources they had united under their control. Yet their strategies of expansion, consolidation, and integration demanded structural changes and innovations at all levels of administration.

Organization Building

The organization of these new domains was as difficult and as challenging as their creation. The economic advantages of integration and consolidation outlined by Charles Flint were, in no sense, automatically concomitant with industrial imperialism. As Flint's comments and the 1901 annual report of the National Biscuit Company both suggest, the economies of scale resulted only from careful attention to the administration of marketing, manufacturing, and procurement of raw materials and, above all, from coordinating and integrating these different activities into a unified whole. Such attention was particularly essential in those enterprises which had become large initially through combination and consolidation.

The task appeared so difficult that many doubted the possibility of building efficient consolidated enterprises. After completing in 1914 a study of fourteen financially unsuccessful combinations and consolidations that had been formed in the merger movement at the turn of the century, Arthur S. Dewing listed several underlying reasons for their failure: "Every one of which, in varying degree, showed the difficulty of obtaining a sufficiently high degree of business ability to manage a large consolidation of manufacturing plants."[27] To Dewing and many other business analysts of his day, the problem was one of personal contact and individual ability. Only a man of enormous energy and highest intellect could keep in touch with all the activities of one of these vast new enterprises. Since such talented individuals were rare indeed, few enterprises were able to achieve economies of scale. Dewing was quite right. A large industrial corporation held together only by informal personal contacts could hardly be efficient. However, he gave little thought to the possibility of building a formal structure with carefully defined lines of authority and communication and with detailed, accurate, and voluminous data to flow through these lines. Possibly because many Americans continued to think of business administration purely in terms of personal ability, such attitudes as to the almost inevitable inefficiences or diseconomies of large-scale industrial enterprise persisted long after Dewing wrote and long after this type of industrial organization had proved its profitability in terms of return on investment and its efficiency in terms of cost per unit of output.

The industrialists who met these administrative challenges were rarely the men who had created the great industrial domains. Only occasionally were they even members of the empire builder's family. The formulation of designs for the government of a business empire called for different talents and a different temperament than did its acquisition, as the four case studies so clearly illustrate. These organization builders had a formidable task, not only because they had few precedents to rely on, but because in many cases the initial motives for expansion or combination and vertical integration had not been specifically to lower unit costs or to assure a larger output per worker by efficient administration of the enlarged resources of the enterprise. The strategy of expansion had come, as has been stressed, from the desire to assure more satisfactory marketing facilities or to have a more certain supply of stocks, raw materials, and other supplies in order to employ more fully the existing manufacturing plant and personnel. Even after a combination had consolidated, its managers often continued to think of control of competition as its primary purpose. Finally, many of the later mergers were inspired and carried out by Wall Street financiers and speculators, anxious to profit from promoters' fees, stock watering, and other financial manipulations. While the industrialists and not the financiers initiated the patterns of consolidation and integration in American industry, the financiers, in the years after 1897, often exploited the new situation for themselves as they met the new legitimate financial wants raised by these strategies.

In many of the newly created enterprises where administrative consolidation occurred, the executives responsible for consolidation built the new structure in an informal, unplanned manner. In others, organization builders carried out their tasks more systematically and rationally. In either case, the lines of authority and communication evolved at all levels of business administration. A design, either formal or informal, needed to be framed for the management of enlarged factories, branch offices, and other field units. Functional departments had to be built to manage the field units. Central offices had to be fashioned to coordinate, appraise, and set policies for the functional headquarters and the enterprise as a whole. And, by 1900, some of the very largest of the new enterprises were already responsible for the administration of integrated multifunction subsidiaries as well as single-function departments.

Because the railroads had faced comparable administration problems a generation earlier, they provided these organization builders with their only useful precedents or models. Of all the railroads, the experiences of the Pennsylvania became the best known. By the 1880's, when nearly all the major American railroads went through administrative reorganization, the Pennsylvania had become, in the words of one expert, "in every respect the standard railroad in America."[28]

In building both departmental and central office structures, the Pennsylvania was the first American business to work out fully the line-and-staff concept of departmental organization. Its basic problem here was to define the lines of communication and authority between departmental headquarters and the field divisions in the carrying out of its basic activity — transportation. In Pennsylvania's Transportation Department, the executives directly concerned with moving of trains became line officers and those dealing with auxiliary or service activities, staff ones. The line of authority ran from the president to the general manager to the general superintendents and then to the division superintendents in the field.[29] By the 1880's, the principle had been established that line officers at headquarters and in the local divisions gave the orders and made the decisions dealing with personnel, which included those of discipline, wages, hours, allocation of duties, hiring, and firing. Those executives at headquarters or in the divisions in the field who were concerned with the maintenance of way, motive power, or rolling stock — that is, the staff officials — communicated directly with personnel only on matters of standards and procedures. The line-and-staff concept was further extended to clarify the relations between the older transportation department and the newer traffic and financial departments. Again, the line officers — those directly involved with the railroad's primary function, transportation — dealt with people and the staff officers with things. Station agents, for example, received instructions on the obtaining and forwarding of freight from the traffic department, but the transportation department decided their pay and daily routine.

With continuing expansion, the head of the major departments—transportation, traffic, and finance—became vice-presidents who, with the president, administered the enterprise as a whole. The Pennsylvania was one of the very first American business enterprises to make clear the important distinction between the duties of a vice-president and a general manager in charge of each major activity. The vice-president was to concentrate on broad long-term entrepreneurial activities and the general manager on the day-to-day operation of the department. The Pennsylvania, too, was one of the first to use standing committees of the board, especially the executive and finance committee, as the medium through which the representatives of the large investors maintained some sort of watch over the full-time professional managers in the central office.

Not all the railroads, to say nothing of the newer industrial enterprises, followed the Pennsylvania example. Even the New York Central long retained the practice of having its officials in the auxiliary and service activities report directly on all matters to their seniors at headquarters rather than through the line officers—the division or general superintendents.[30] Only a few roads made the distinction between the duties of the vice-president and general manager. On the Pennsylvania itself, the distinction in time became less clear.

Even where the industrialists looked to the railroad experience, they still had much creative work of their own to do. Their administrative problems were more complex. Their field units were often more scattered and less closely connected than were the contiguous railroad divisions. As the volume of manufacturing and of sales expanded and methods became more complicated, more auxiliary and service units were developed in the field units, departmental headquarters, and even the central office than ever existed on the railroads. Moreover, large integrated industrial enterprises carried on a greater variety of activities. The railroads' primary concern was with a single economic function—transportation—while the new integrated industrial enterprises carried out at least three basic functions, and some oil, steel, and meat-packing firms even took on a fourth by becoming responsible for much of the transportation of their products. Direct marketing and the procurement or production of supplies and materials often called for different talents and training than manufacturing. While each major function came to be managed by a separate department, no one department had distinct priority as did the transportation department on a railroad. As a result, the line-and-staff distinction could not be applied in defining interdepartmental relations.

Not only was coordination of departmental activities harder to work out in the integrated industrial enterprise than on a railroad, but the appraisal and planning of several departments with such disparate activities proved a far more complex task.

As the case studies emphasize, some industrial enterprises met these challenges much more creatively than others. By the 1920's, however, the organization builders had worked out fairly standard designs for administering the several functional activities from departmental headquarters and the enterprise as a whole from a central office. By then, trade journals, handbooks, and even textbooks were beginning to discuss the needs, problems, and methods of managing rationally a large single-function or multifunction industrial enterprise. So, at the close of World War I, most large industrial companies whose executives paid any attention to organizational matters were administered through much the same type of organization — the centralized, functionally departmentalized structure.

Before 1920, however, organization builders had yet to devise a structure by which a general office might effectively administer a number of vertically integrated subsidiaries or divisions. By that time a few very large holding companies did control a number of multifunction as well as single-function subsidiaries and were faced with this administrative problem. Some of these, like United States Steel, did little more than form an office to help set price and production schedules for the many almost completely autonomous divisions. Others, like Swift, Armour, and American Tobacco, had developed carefully defined functional departments and a central office to administer those departments which handled their primary lines. They made little attempt, however, to provide a structure to administer their subsidiaries which handled by-products, allied lines, or the other multifunction enterprises which they had come to control through the holding company device. At Standard Oil, long the largest American industrial enterprise and after 1901 second only to United States Steel, the lines of authority and communication were particularly unclear and confused. At its executives offices at 26 Broadway, no sharp distinctions were made between the functions of a general office and those of a central office or even of a departmental headquarters. Consider the description the historians of the Standard Oil Company of New Jersey give of 26 Broadway shortly after the turn of the century:

> The staff at 26 Broadway, upon which all the executives relied for aid, was an uncommonly heterogeneous mixture. The organization, having developed over a time, continued to reflect the mélange of companies based upon historical precedent, personal predilections, state corporation requirements, and tax laws. Even such an orderly mind as that of S. C. T. Dodd

> [the Company's General Counsel] did not have a complete picture of it. In addition to directors, all the principal manufacturing companies and many of the lesser ones had sales agents at headquarters for refined oil in the domestic trade, for refined oil in the export trade, for lubricating oil in the West, for lubricating oil in the East and for export.[31]

When the managers of a federation or combination of integrated companies decided to coordinate, appraise, and plan systematically the work of their far-flung enterprise, they almost always consolidated these activities into a single, centralized, functionally departmentalized organization. As had the different mergers among the users of steel, such as International Harvester, Allis-Chalmers, American Locomotive, American Car & Foundry, and American Can, so many other combinations quickly disbanded their constituent firms and placed the sales, manufacturing, purchasing, or engineering activities of each within large, single-function departments. By 1909, only two or three of the nation's largest industrial empires remained pure holding companies. More, like Standard Oil, American Tobacco, and the meat packers, continued to be legally both holding and operating companies that administered both functional departments and multifunctional units, the latter usually having the legal form of a subsidiary corporation. The large majority, however, became administered through centralized, functionally departmentalized structures. For until Alfred P. Sloan created a new organization form at General Motors in 1920, this structure appeared to be the only one which could assure effective administrative control over a large industrial consolidation.

Yet the dominant centralized structure had one basic weakness. A very few men were still entrusted with a great number of complex decisions. The executives in the central office were usually the president with one or two assistants, sometimes the chairman of the board, and the vice-presidents who headed the several departments. The latter were often too busy with the administration of the particular function to devote much time to the affairs of the enterprise as a whole. Their training proved a still more serious defect. Because these administrators had spent most of their business careers within a single functional activity, they had little experience or interest in understanding the needs and problems of other departments or of the corporation as a whole. As long as an enterprise belonged in an industry whose markets, sources of raw materials, and production processes remained relatively unchanged, few entrepreneurial decisions had to be reached. In that situation such a weakness was not critical, but where technology, markets, and sources of supply were changing rapidly, the defects of such a structure became more obvious.

Further Growth — The Coming of the Multidivisional Enterprise

The last two decades of the nineteenth century witnessed the initial massive expansion of American industry and with it the building of the first great integrated industrial empires.[32] After 1900, even though the attention of industrial leaders became increasingly concentrated on the organization of such empires, the growth of industry and its great enterprises continued. Further expansion rested fundamentally on basic population and technological changes. Critically important was the continuing rapid growth of the city. Urban population rose from 30.2 million in 1900 to 69.0 million in 1930.[33] Then with the development of the electric trolley and more particularly the automobile came a reverse trend from the city to the suburb. As significant were the great new technologically advanced industries based on the new generators of power — the electric and gasoline engine—and on the systematic application of science to industrial production and products. In these new industries (the electrical, automobile, chemical, and electronic) and in the older industries which were revolutionized by changing population and technology (the rubber, petroleum, agricultural implement and other power machinery, and the chain-store and mail-order businesses), the leading enterprises became faced with increasingly complex administrative problems. And it was in these industries that the leading firms turned to managing their activities through the new multidivisional, "decentralized" structure.

After 1900, the large industrial enterprise met the needs and opportunities of an economy growing more urban and more technologically advanced through three types of strategies. Growth came either from an expansion of the firm's existing lines to much the same type of customers, or it resulted from a quest for new markets and sources of supplies in distant lands, or finally it came from the opening of new markets by developing a wide range of new products for different types of customers. The metals companies and many of those that process agricultural products have held to the first of these strategies. For the past half-century, most copper, zinc, iron, steel, tobacco, meat, sugar, liquor, and banana companies have made much the same type of products for much the same type of user. Thus their expansion has brought few new types of administrative problems. In 1960 most enterprises in these industries continued to be run through the older, centralized, functionally departmentalized form.

In those industries most affected by the new markets and new technology, growth came more by going overseas and still more by diversification. Of these two strategies, diversification was far more responsible for the adoption of the "decentralized" structure than overseas expansion. Diversification came when leading companies in these technologically advanced industries realized that their facilities and the scientific know-how of their personnel could be easily transferred into the production and sale of new goods for new markets. For those enterprises whose energies were concentrated primarily in merchandising, diversification came because of the changing markets in the city and then in the suburbs.

Many chemical companies, for example, became aware in the 1920's of the opportunities that lay in following the route already chartered by the du Pont Company of growth through diversification into new lines of products. In these enterprises, as at du Pont, this strategy became systematized by the building of large research departments whose task was to bring forth new products as well as to improve existing products and processes. United States Rubber, B. F. Goodrich, and other rubber companies, even before most chemical companies, began to diversify their lines and to exploit the potentials of rubber chemistry. After World War II, the rubber companies that had concentrated on the tire also entered into systematic research and development and began to make and market latex, plastics, and other chemical products as well as industrial rubber, flooring, footwear, and so forth. In the postwar years, too, gasoline companies started on comparable strategies of expansion through diversification by developing a wide range of petrochemicals.

The application of science to the development of new products through institutionalized research brought the same strategies of diversification in the electrical, electronics, and, to a somewhat lesser extent, the power machinery and automobile industries. The great electrical companies, General Electric and Westinghouse, began as makers of a full line of producers' goods for the generation and use of electric power and light. In the 1920's, they moved into the mass consumer market by producing and selling washing machines, refrigerators, vacuum cleaners, stoves, and other household appliances. At the same time, the energies of their research laboratories brought these companies into the making of plastics, alloys, and a variety of products based on the vacuum tube and the science of electronics. The automobile companies, in turn, began to produce tractors, diesels, airplane engines, electrical equipment, and even household appliances — all using the new sources of power, particularly the internal-combustion engine. The agricultural implement and other power machinery firms followed much the same road, with the first of them developing construction equipment and diesels and the second moving into agricultural implements as well as heavy electrical equipment.

Somewhat later, the large flour, dairy, and other food processing and marketing companies began to diversify by developing a wide variety of breakfast cereals, prepared mixes, cheeses, and other end products processed out of their original basic product. These, too, began to appreciate the potentials of research and soon had their chemical products and divisions. By mid-century, other processors of agricultural goods whose primary line offered less of a variety of end products, such as the meat packers and the soap manufacturers, moved toward diversification, particularly by emphasizing chemical research and development.

Growth through diversification into several lines increased the number and complexity of both operational and entrepreneurial activities even more than a world-wide expansion of one line. The problems of obtaining materials and supplies, of manufacturing and of marketing a number of product lines for different types of customers or in different parts of the world made the tasks of departmental headquarters exceedingly difficult to administer systematically and rationally. The coordination of product flow through the several departments proved even more formidable. Appraisal came to involve not only a constant intelligent analysis of the operating performance in the different economic functions, including engineering and research as well as production, distribution, transportation, the procurement of supplies, and finance, but the making of these appraisals in several very different industries or lines of business. Long-term strategic planning not only called for decisions and action concerning the future use of existing facilities, personnel, and funds, and the development of new resources in the company's current lines, but also involved decisions on entering into new lines of products and dropping or curtailing old ones.

By placing an increasing intolerable strain on existing administrative structures, territorial expansion and to a much greater extent product diversification brought the multidivisional form. Du Pont, General Motors, Jersey Standard, and Sears, Roebuck first devised the new type in the 1920's. Relatively few other large industrial enterprises followed the example of these pioneers before the massive economic boom that followed World War II. The depression, by cutting sales and forcing a contraction of activity, often postponed the adoption of what seemed to be a more complex and expensive structure. On the other hand, by creating excess capacity, the depression hastened diversification. During the war years, most enterprises were too concerned with the problems of conversion to military production and then reconversion back to their old lines. Then with burgeoning markets and swiftly advancing technology of the postwar years, company after company turned to the new "decentralized" form of organization. In refashioning their administrative structures, many were quite consciously influenced by the example of the four innovators studied here.

As enterprises in the chemical industry began to diversify, they soon met the same sort of administrative strains that du Pont had felt between

1919 and 1921. Before 1940, however, only Hercules Powder, Monsanto, and one or two others had patterned their organizations on the du Pont multidivisional structure. But after the war more and more companies, expanding through diversification, adopted the new form. Some, like Allied Chemical and Union Carbide which began their corporate existence as combinations, were able to consolidate the administration of their activities through this new type without ever having developed a centralized, functionally departmentalized structure. The great majority, on the other hand, followed the du Pont example of transforming their centralized structure into the new decentralized form. The list of chemical firms managed through decentralized divisions and a general office became long. Beside du Pont, Hercules Powder, Monsanto, Allied Chemical, and Union Carbide it included the Celanese Corporation of America, American Viscose, Columbia Carbon, Carborundum, American Cyanamid, Koppers, Pittsburgh Coke & Chemical, Glidden, Heyden Newport Chemical, Stauffer Chemical, Geigy Chemical, Atlas Powder, Diamond Alkali, Food Machinery and Chemical, Eastman Kodak, and even the chemical divisions of Shell Oil and Phillips Petroleum.[34]

The largest rubber companies expanded their resources to overseas areas more than did most chemical firms, but in rubber as in chemicals, diversification rather than world-wide expansion was clearly the primary reason for decentralization. Again the du Pont experience served as a model. Before World War II, United States Rubber and Goodrich had adopted the new form. The changes in the first company were carried out in 1929 and 1930 under the auspices of du Pont-trained executives after the du Pont family had purchased a large block of the company's stock. Goodrich returned, under the impact of the depression, to the older centralized structure, but by 1953 it had come back again to a fully decentralized organization. The two companies which concentrated on tires, Goodyear and Firestone, did not begin to diversify seriously until the military needs of World War II, particularly the synthetic-rubber program, provided them with chemical plants and new, technically trained personnel. In 1956, Goodyear adopted the multidivisional structure to administer its several lines. By 1960, Firestone, the least diversified of the industry's "big four," was the only one that still retained the older centralized, functionally departmentalized structure.

In the automobile and power machinery industries, General Motors has been the organizational example. The multidivisional structure at General Motors did not come as a response to administrative needs resulting from a strategy of diversification. Rather, its innovators saw it as a new way of administering a combination or federation of enterprises. However, its decentralized organization not only helped it it to win the largest share of the automobile market in the United States, but also to expand and administer successfully its overseas manufacuring and marketing activities. Furthermore, because of its administrative structure, it was able to execute brilliantly a broad strategy of diversification into the making and selling of all types of engines, and products using engines, in the years after the automobile market fell off in the late 1920's.

Such outstanding performance brought imitation. Ford and Chrysler both followed the General Motors example after the Second World War had taken them into nonautomotive activities and after their founders or immediate successors had left the scene. At Ford, imitation was the most obvious. There, in 1946 executives recruited from General Motors began, to rebuild the company by, in *Fortune's* words, "clapping the G. M. organizational garment onto the Ford manufacturing frame, trimming the garment here and filling out the frame there. Nobody around Ford makes any bones about this." [35] When the smaller Nash Motors Company merged in 1937 with the Kelvinator Corporation, makers of refrigerators and other household appliances, the new management set up a comparable multidivisional structure to administer the resources of the combined firms.

In 1943, International Harvester, the largest of the agricultural implement and power machinery enterprises, reshaped its management structure along these same modern lines. A new president, who had carefully studied the General Motors experience, did not even allow wartime exigencies to interfere with the much-needed administrative reorganization. In 1954, Allis-Chalmers completed a comparable reshaping of its management structure. By then, a number of other smaller implement and power machinery companies, including Borg-Warner, Cherry-Burrell, Thompson Products, American Machine & Foundry, and the Worthington Corporation (the successor to International Steam Pump), had followed suit.

The General Motors example had less of a direct impact on the large electrical and electronics companies when they, too, turned to refashioning their administrative structures. Again, it was the expansion into very different product lines during the 1920's rather than the administration of their extensive overseas holdings that raised critical management problems and strains at General Electric and Westinghouse. In 1931, Westinghouse began a massive reorganization of its administrative structure. At first, organizational ideas and actions came from within. Only after 1934, when the Westinghouse executives had decided on the multidivisional type of structure, did they begin to look at the experience of General Motors and other companies.

At General Electric, changes came only after the retirement of its brilliant president, Gerard Swope. Then in the year immediately following the Second World War, the company, under the guidance of Ralph Cordiner, set up a structure with autonomous divisions resembling those at Westinghouse or General Motors. When Cordiner became president in 1950, he carried the reorganization much further and by 1952 had created as intricate and as sophisticated an organizational structure as had yet been devised for the large industrial enterprise. In these same postwar years, the Radio Corporation of America and Sylvania Electric Products set up their multidivisional organizations. In 1956, after an extensive diversification program in electronic and electric business machines and after the death of its founder, International Business Machines Corporation also turned to the same type of structure.

Diversification has brought similar administrative changes, though more slowly, in some of the older materials and agricultural processing enterprises, particularly those which concentrated a large portion of their resources in distributing and marketing facilities. Pittsburgh Plate Glass built up its diversified product line around a large distributing organization. American Can and International Paper, too, came to handle a variety of quite different products. By 1960, these three were the only materials and metals firms studied here that had accepted the new structure. In the agricultural processing industries, the flour, dairy, and food firms with large marketing and distributing organizations such as General Mills, General Foods, and The Borden Company were the first to diversify and then to decentralize. Another, National Dairy, came to this form in the same way as General Motors had, as a means to administer more effectively a combination of many separate milk, cheese, and other dairying enterprises. Other agricultural processing firms, like Armour and Procter & Gamble that have diversified even more recently, also turned to the new structure. The effect of the administrative experience of du Pont and General Motors on these companies is by no means as clear from the readily available evidence as it is for the administrative changes in enterprises in other industries. On the other hand, where enterprises, like Swift, Seagrams, American Sugar, United Fruit, or the tobacco companies, have stayed with their primary line, the old structure remains.

In the petroleum industry, world-wide expansion and operation did become as significant a cause for the creation of the multidivisional structure as product diversification. Where administrative complexity resulted from territorial expansion, the autonomous, multidepartmental division became based on a region rather than on a line of products. In the oil industry, the experience of Standard Oil (New Jersey) in fashioning the first of such decentralized structures has been a guide for changes in other companies. Standard Oil of California began to develop similar regional, autonomous operating divisions before the outbreak of the Second World War and in 1954 set up a fully manned general office. Before this second date, Continental Oil had fashioned a full-fledged decentralized structure under the direction of a former Jersey Standard executive. More recently, Socony Mobil, Shell, and Texaco have organized separate autonomous, multidepartmental divisions for their domestic and their foreign business. These companies, together with Gulf and to some extent Standard of Indiana, have redefined the role of their top-executive offices so that they have become quite similar to the general office that Jersey Standard first devised in 1927 and modified during the 1930's.

Yet even in oil enterprises, product diversification has been of major significance in bringing structural change. By the mid-1950's, the move into petrochemicals had caused Shell, Standard of California, Phillips Petroleum, Texaco, Standard (Indiana), Standard of Ohio, and Continental Oil to set up autonomous divisions to administer the development, processing, and marketing of their new chemical products. The creation of these new units did much to bring the senior executives to a rethinking of the role and duties of the company's top administrative offices.

In mail-order houses, chain stores, and other mass-marketing enterprises, territorial expansion and operation have been important causes for decentralization. For one thing, although they have incorporated the functions of both the wholesaler and the retailer, the mail-order houses and food chains still concentrate on one basic economic function, distribution. Thus, they carry a far wider variety of lines than even the most diversified, multifunction industrial enterprise. The reason that the food chains handling highly perishable products have set up a structure with autonomous, multidepartmental divisions seems obvious enough. Their administrative decisions are strongly affected by day-to-day changes in the general market. The Great Atlantic & Pacific Tea Co. decided as early as 1925 to decentralize its administrative decisions into regional divisions that would be in closer touch with local conditions than a single central office could be. In more recent years, other food chains, like the Kroger Company and Safeway Stores, have followed this same organizational pattern.

Nevertheless, it was diversification into a new type of merchandising that turned Sears, Roebuck initially to setting up one of the first modern decentralized structures. Its decision in 1925 to sell directly through retail stores as well as the mail-order catalogue created the administrative strains that led to reorganization. Sears's major competitor, Montgomery Ward, retained the older structure as long as the autocratic Sewell Avery remained in charge. But on his retirement, a new set of executives set up a structure in 1956 and 1957 that was a very close copy of the Sears organizational framework.

In this way, the multidivisional type of administrative structure, which hardly existed in 1920, had by 1960 become the accepted form of management for the most complex and diverse of American industrial enterprises. As the population continues to grow and become more suburban, as technology becomes more intricate and more fruitful, and as demands of the industrial market become more complex, the activities of many large American enterprises should become still more diverse and still more complicated. And so, in order to meet the new needs and opportunities, these companies will undoubtedly adopt some variation of this multidivisional structure.

In other words, expansion and diversification have recently brought and will continue to bring to many enterprises the administrative challenges which du Pont, General Motors, Jersey Standard, and Sears, Roebuck first faced in the 1920's. Although these four firms were, at the time of their reorganization, among the very largest in the nation, there are today many companies that are larger and have more widespread and diversified activities than these had in the 1920's. In 1919, Jersey Standard was second only to United States Steel in the size of its assets. General Motors was already the fifth largest in assets, while du Pont was eighteenth and Sears thirty-third.[36] In 1929, their ranking by the same criterion was 3, 2, 12, and 28, respectively. Other indices of the size of these four firms are given in Table 3. Yet, by 1959, companies of comparable size in dollar value of their assets to Jersey, Standard, General Motors, du Pont, and Sears at the time they began their reorganizations would place 22, 63, 137, and 138 in *Fortune's* list of the five hundred largest industrials.

This brief historical outline of the growth of large-scale industrial enterprises in the United States is in no way intended to be a complete or analytical account. Its purpose is to describe basic historical trends necessary to give relevance to the events and actions in the four case studies, and to provide further meaning to the analysis of organizational changes in seventy of the country's leading industrial enterprises described in the final chapter. The historical record certainly does suggest that structure does follow strategy, and that the different types of expansion brought different administrative needs requiring different administrative organizations. Yet this brief review says very little about *what* were the actual needs created by expansion of volume, geographical dispersion, vertical integration, and product diversification. Nor can it indicate *why* some executives in some enterprises became aware of these needs and others did not. Nor can it tell much about *how* the new structure was devised and worked out and just what was the shape of the new lines of authority and communication and of the types of information developed. Nor can it offer much of a description of the problems and difficulties that arose in putting the new structure into operation. Such an understanding of the why, what, and how of the changes in the government of large industrial enterprises can come only by getting inside the companies themselves and by observing how the empire builders and organization planners defined and executed new strategies and fashioned new structures. The fundamental purpose of the four case studies is to provide such an inside view. Once the story of organizational change and in-

TABLE 3

Size of Companies at Time of Initial Structural Changes

	Assets (millions)	*Net Sales (millions)*	*Net Earnings (millions)*	*Employees*	*Stockholders*
Du Pont					
1920	$ 253.4	$ 94.0	$ 14.6	31,000 est.	9,764
General Motors					
1920	$ 604.8	$ 567.3	$ 43.9	80,612	36,894
Jersey Standard					
1925	$1,369.2	$1,145.5 *total income*	$111.2	103,719 (52,497 in U. S.)	26,829
Sears					
1929	$ 251.8	$ 415.4	$ 30.1	41,751	18,222

Comparative Size of Companies in One Year—1925

Du Pont	$ 305.7	—*	$ 24.0	14,000 est.	13,155
General Motors	$ 703.8	$ 734.6	$106.4	83,278	50,917
Jersey Standard	$1,369.2	$1,145.5 *total income*	$111.2	103,719	26,829
Sears	$ 168.0	$ 243.8	$ 21.0	23,193	5,965

SOURCES: Information on du Pont and General Motors is from their annual reports. Jersey data are from Gibb and Knowlton, *Resurgent Years*, pp. 670, 672–673, 686. Sears information comes from Emmet and Jeuck, *Catalogues and Counters*, pp. 595, 650, 657.

* Information on sales is not given by du Pont in its 1925 annual report. In 1924 the net sales were $90.9 million and net earnings $17.0 million.

novation has been presented, then the reasons for comparable changes or lack of them in other companies can be more clearly explained.

Yet a complete history of the changing strategy and structure in any one of these four firms would be a book in itself. To keep the cases manageable, only the initial innovations and changes involved in setting up the new multidivisional structure are described in detail. The fashioning of the earlier structure and the planning of the strategies leading to the new ways of administration are presented in a more condensed form, as are the accounts of structural changes after the initial reorganization.

Each case not only views structural innovation by enterprises in very different industries but each also concentrates on different aspects of such innovations. The new structure called for the creation of both autonomous operating divisions and a controlling and administering general office. The du Pont and Sears stories focus more on the creation of the divisions and the General Motors more on that of the general office. At Jersey, where both already existed, the primary problem was to make a distinction between the duties of each. These differences result partly because Sears and du Pont had been administered previously through centralized, functionally departmentalized structures, while General Motors was managed by a holding company and Jersey Standard partly by a highly decentralized holding company and partly by a highly centralized operating organization.

The cases further indicate how the different executives and the different companies approached the problems of management. Administrators at General Motors and du Pont provide examples of men who viewed management in a highly rational and systematic manner. These men thought in terms of organization and administrative needs — that is, in terms of coordination, appraisal, and planning. The Jersey executives handled their management problems in a more intuitive and unsystematic manner. They rarely saw their problems as administrative ones, but rather as functional ones — that is, as problems of marketing, manufacturing, or producing. The organization builders at Sears had a rational approach and saw the value of studying management needs as administrative rather than functional ones. But they tended to overlook the value of a substantial administrative staff or a clear-cut structure, both essential to exploit the economies of size. Such internal differences in outlook and approach account, more than any other factor, for the difference in the way the four different industrial empires responded to changing external needs and opportunities.

2 DU PONT—CREATING THE AUTONOMOUS DIVISIONS

The Centralized Structure

During the chill winter days of February, 1902, the affairs of the venerable E. I. du Pont de Nemours & Co. were drawing to a crisis. Plans for celebrating its one hundred years of explosives making were already under way when its president, Eugene du Pont, stricken with pneumonia, suddenly died.[1] The remaining five partners began indecisively to look about for a successor. None of their own group appeared to have the necessary qualifications. Four were either too old or in poor health. The fifth, Alfred I. du Pont, at thirty-seven years of age, seemed too inexperienced and erratic. Perhaps the best thing to do, the elder partners decided, was to sell the company to its ancient and friendly competitor, Laflin & Rand. After all, the du Pont Company owned a sizable amount of its stock and its president, J. Amory Haskell, trained at the du Pont–controlled Repauno Chemical Company, had always been close to their interests.

Alfred du Pont disagreed. Young and energetic, he was shocked at the thought of selling the company, his "birthright," to outsiders. If he could get the support of his cousin Coleman du Pont, once his roommate at the Massachusetts Institute of Technology, he would buy it himself. Coleman immediately gave Alfred his backing, but he insisted that they must get Pierre, another cousin, to "handle the finances." [2] A long-distance telephone call brought Pierre's acceptance. The elder du Ponts, on learning of Alfred's allies, were more than willing to sell out to the three cousins at a quickly agreed upon price of 12 million dollars.

Alfred would have had to look long and hard to find two better-equipped business executives to help him manage the family firm. Coleman, a tall, broad-shouldered man with a wide grin, had the temperament and training to create business empires. Pierre, quiet and studious, had the rational, analytical outlook of an organization builder. Ironically, Alfred, trained in the powder mills and most happy when he was personally supervising work on the production line, was far less prepared to rebuild and administer a great industrial enterprise.

Coleman was a member of the Kentucky branch of the family and had never been involved in the explosives industry. After graduating from M.I.T. in 1885, he started work in the Kentucky coal mines owned by his uncle, Alfred Victor du Pont. In a short time he had taken charge of the coal company, making it one of the largest in the region. Then in 1893, he left the coal company to join two of his uncle's protégés, Arthur J. Moxham and Tom L. Johnson, as general manager of their steel mill in Johnstown, Pennsylvania. These two — the latter was soon to become the famous reform mayor of Cleveland — had built, with du Pont financing, street railways in a number of American cities.[3] They had put up the steel mill at Johnstown to provide themselves with rails. Shortly after Coleman arrived, they began the construction of a second plant at Lorain, Ohio, one of the largest and most modern of its day.

As Tom Johnson began to turn his attention to politics, Coleman took over more of the management of the new Lorain Steel Company. He quickly showed his empire-building tendencies by erecting shops to make streetcars together with all their parts, including bodies, wheels, and electric motors.[4] (This last item was one of the most technologically complex products of the day.) In 1898, Elbert H. Gary, backed by J. Pierpont Morgan, persuaded Coleman and his associates to sell the Lorain Steel Company to the Federal Steel Co., which the two financiers had just formed and which four years later was to become the nucleus for the United States Steel Corporation.[5] After the sale, Coleman and Moxham turned their energies back to building electric street railway systems.

Pierre S. du Pont had joined his cousin in Lorain in 1899. Upon graduation from M.I.T. in 1890, he had returned to the family company to take a job at its first smokeless powder works, then being constructed at Carney's Point across the Delaware River from Wilmington. When the close of the Spanish–American War brought a reduction of activity at Carney's Point, Pierre saw little future in Wilmington as long as old men were continuing to manage the family firm in the same old way. So he resigned from the company to join Coleman. At Lorain he helped transfer the properties to Federal Steel Co., managed those which had been retained, and assisted Coleman in his street railway ventures.

The Strategy of Consolidation

Alfred's decision and determination to hold on to the du Pont company changed more than the course of its history: they revolutionized the American explosives industry. At the time of Eugene du Pont's death, the company and the industry were being managed just as they had been for more than a generation. The du Pont Company itself administered only a few black powder plants and the new smokeless powder works at Carney's Point. Until 1902, it remained a family enterprise. As one du Pont noted: "The business was entirely managed by the senior partner. . . . The head of the firm was *ex officio* head of the family."[6] The other partners and nearly all the supervisory force were du Ponts. However, the du Pont family's control ranged well beyond the company. It held stock in other firms, including the Repauno Chemical Company, which was formed in 1880 by Lammot du Pont, Pierre's father, to manufacture a new type of explosive — dynamite. And, through the Gunpowder Trade Association, the du Pont Company wielded strong influence over the rest of the industry.

The Gunpowder Trade Association had been formed in 1872 when overproduction resulting from an increased output and a surplus of Civil War powder threatened to collapse prices.[7] The Association, with each member having a number of votes according to its size, set price and production schedules. After Henry du Pont, the Company's president from 1850 to 1889, purchased a controlling interest in more than half a dozen of the larger powder companies during the depression of the 1870's, he held a majority of these votes. To assure compliance with the schedules he set, he worked them out in close cooperation with the executives of the other firms and particularly with Solomon Turck, the president of the industry's second largest company, Laflin & Rand. Because of this close cooperation, and because of Henry du Pont's policy of buying a stock interest in most of his major competitors, the Association remained more stable and longer-lived than most combinations in American industry.

Henry du Pont and his successor Eugene, as presidents of the strongest firm in the combination, may have controlled their properties, but they hardly administered them. They had a powerful voice in how much other firms produced and at what price, but they knew almost nothing about how each unit carried on its production and sold its quotas. Nor did they particularly care. Neither the individual companies nor the Association paid much attention to costs, to improving processes, or to developing more systematic purchasing and marketing techniques. There was little coordination between the marketing and selling companies. With only a few notable exceptions, the manufacturing firms sold through agents who handled the output of many companies and who apparently also became members of the Association.[8] Effective administration was impossible because neither the separate firms nor the combination itself had the information or methods to assure an efficient use of existing resources and so to reduce unit costs and increase output per worker.

They did not even have a systematic way of gauging existing or potential demand on which to base their price and production schedules.

The lack of administrative control is suggested by the fact that during nearly all of his tenure, Henry du Pont carried on singlehandedly from a one-room office overlooking the powder mills on the Brandywine most of the business of his company and of the Association. He wrote nearly all of the business correspondence himself in longhand.[9] The administrative state of the du Pont interests is further indicated by Pierre's comments to his brother Irénée in February 1902 concerning Alfred's proposal:

> I think there is going to be some tall hustling to get everything reorganized. We have not the slightest idea of what we are buying, but we are probably not at a disadvantage as I think the old company had a very slim idea of the property they possess.[10]

To Coleman and Pierre, this hustling meant more than reviving the family birthright. Reorganization provided an opportunity to transform this loose federation of many relatively small firms into a consolidated, integrated, centrally managed industrial enterprise. Methodically the two cousins, supported somewhat hesitantly by Alfred, embarked on the strategy of consolidation and centralization. First came a careful inventory of the properties they had acquired. Next, Coleman concentrated his charms on persuading the stockholders in these and many other explosives concerns to turn over their stockholdings to the du Ponts in return for cash or for stock in the new firm — the E. I. du Pont de Nemours Powder Co. — formed to take over the combined properties.[11]

Then Pierre focused his energies on fashioning a structure to administer them. The legal and financial changes were, in his mind, only necessary preliminaries to the operational and administrative ones. As he stressed later:

> At the time we made the purchase of the properties, we realized that if a good investment was to be made for us, it would necessitate a complete reorganization of the method of doing business; that the administrative end would have to be reorganized, numerous selling organizations, or administrative organizations done away with, and we would have to establish a system of costs in order that an economical manufacture could be installed throughout the business. That was prevented, absolutely, by our lack of control of the properties in which we were interested, and we had no means of establishing a new system of organization in any of these companies.[12]

The formation of the Powder Company thus made it possible "to operate the properties in one name, through one set of selling agents, and under one management, or operation." Only in this way could the costly duplication of facilities and personnel be eliminated, the different functions —buying, manufacturing, shipping, and selling—be economically and systematically supervised, and the essential coordination between functions maintained.

In carrying out the strategy of consolidation and in setting up the centralized structure, Pierre and Coleman drew on their experience at Lorain. The customers and competitors of the Lorain Steel Company were among the technologically most advanced and efficiently managed businesses of the day. The improvements in plant layout and manufacturing organization which Henry Clay Frick and Carnegie had recently completed at their works were undoubtedly incorporated in the new steel plant at Lorain.[13] General Electric and Westinghouse, Lorain's competitors in the making of electrical engines, must have suggested much about ways to put together a large centralized sales and engineering organization.

The cousins also had a successful model nearer home. In 1892, the du Ponts placed two energetic young executives in charge of the dynamite works at Repauno—J. Amory Haskell, who at thirty-one had proved himself an able manager of a coal company, and Hamilton M. Barksdale, a trained civil engineer who had worked with the Baltimore & Ohio Railroad.[14] These two decided to build a sales organization of their own. Dynamite was still a relatively new product and dangerous to use. Agents accustomed to handling black powder often failed to explain to contractors, mining companies, and other customers how the new powder should be used. So the new managers appointed Charles L. Patterson, one of the industry's master salesmen, to set up sales offices in different parts of the country. He was also to train a force of salaried men in explosives technique so that they might be able to show customers how to use dynamite efficiently and effectively.[15] As the demand for dynamite grew, Haskell and Barksdale, organized production more systematically by forming a manufacturing, an engineering, and a purchasing department.

In 1903, following this model, the three cousins assisted by Haskell and Barksdale created much the same type of an administrative organization to knit together the resources of nearly two-thirds of the American explosives industry.[16] First they consolidated manufacturing. Production was concentrated in a few of the larger plants located as advantageously as possible to the major markets. They next set up three administrative departments to coordinate, appraise, and plan the work of the plants—one for each of the company's major products: black powder, high explosives (dynamite), and smokeless powder. Then they formed a nationwide marketing organization with the old Repauno sales department serving as a nucleus. The engineering, traffic, and purchasing units of the new

Powder Company also drew on the older dynamite company's personnel and procedures. Still another unit proposed by Coleman and Pierre was the Development Department, which was to concentrate on improving product and processes. As it had no predecessor in the explosives industry, the du Ponts may have been inspired by the recently created research organization at General Electric. Finally, to house the headquarters of these new departments, Coleman ordered the construction of a large, many-storied office building in the center of Wilmington.

The six men most active in creating the new company now took over its major executive posts. Coleman, as President, became responsible for broad policy and over-all company performance. Alfred, as General Manager, was given general supervision of manufacturing activities. Pierre became Treasurer. Haskell had full charge of selling. Barksdale headed the largest manufacturing department — high explosives — while Moxham, who had come from Lorain with Coleman and Pierre, was given general oversight of the Development Department. In carrying out their new duties, these men were not only concerned with assuring effective central office planning, appraisal, and coordination of buying, manufacturing, sales, and other functional activities, but they also saw the need to develop departmental designs for coordinating, appraising, and setting policy for each of the several types of field units. Such a structure was essential, they believed, if the vast resources under their control were to be employed rationally and profitably.

Creating the Multidepartmental Structure

In setting up the centralized structure, Coleman and Pierre clearly distinguished between what has in this study been called entrepreneurial and operational activities. Each major department came to have its Vice-President and its Director. The latter was to be responsible for the smooth day-to-day operations of the department, the former was to concentrate more on the long-term planning and appraisal necessary to keep the company alive and growing. Collectively, the Vice-Presidents with the President, acting as the Executive Committee, were to make broad policy for the enterprise as a whole.

Individually, the Vice-Presidents had full responsibility and authority in managing their units.[17] The three manufacturing departments or, as they were then called, the Operating Departments had been placed under the general supervision of Alfred du Pont as General Manager. But Alfred also took the job of Vice-President in charge of the Black Powder Department and actually continued as *de facto* plant superintendent at the old Brandywine mills. From their headquarters in the large new office building in Wilmington, Alfred and the Vice-Presidents and Directors of the other two Operating Departments—High Explosives and Smokeless Powder—with their assistants and staff officers coordinated, appraised, and planned goals and set procedures for the work carried on at the several plants. These departmental headquarters soon had offices for the recruitment and training of personnel, for the inspection of product and process, for the maintenance of plant, for the improvement of processes, and, for a time, for planning new construction and purchasing supplies other than raw materials and equipment. Before long, however, the engineering and purchasing departments became separate units reporting directly to Alfred as the general executive in charge of manufacturing.

The lines of communication and authority between departmental headquarters and the plants in the field were defined in terms of line and staff. The new departments closely followed the pattern first fully developed in the United States by the Pennsylvania Railroad. The line of authority ran from the Vice-President to the Department Director and his assistants, to the plant or works manager, and then to the supervisors and foremen. The plant executives who handled auxiliary functions such as inspection, personnel, or maintenance were responsible to the works or factory managers for their day-to-day working orders. They looked to their seniors at headquarters only for standards and procedures. Executives at headquarters worked at making more precise the information that flowed through these channels in the form of daily, weekly, and monthly reports and concentrated particularly on deriving more accurate cost figures. Such data not only provided a check on plant performance, but, by permitting comparisons between plants and between subdivisions within plants, made it easier to locate weaknesses and inefficiencies.

To improve communication still further between headquarters and field, each Operating Department held regular meetings of its plant superintendents and headquarters staff where the managers exchanged information on ways to make their activities more efficient and less costly. Papers read at the regular meetings of Barksdale's High Explosives Department, and circulated to all departmental administrative and supervisory personnel, covered such topics as standardization of parts and equipment, new manufacturing procedures, safety measures, customer's complaints, comparative costs and savings made at the different plants, morale, incentives, and so forth.[18]

Sales activities were as systematically organized as manufacturing. The Sales Department's Director, Charles L. Patterson, soon instituted a structure comparable, although on a much larger scale, with the one he had fashioned at Repauno. Here the field units included seventeen sales offices headed by branch managers in different cities in every part of the country. Each manager, assisted by a small staff, supervised the activities of a corps of field men. Most salesmen specialized in one product — black powder, high explosives, or smokeless powder — although there were a few "general" salesmen. A few also sold small lots of solvents, ether, and other chemicals, the by-products of the making of smokeless powder. The salesmen, who were now company employees, completely replaced the old outside agents or jobbers in marketing the company's products to railroads, mines, contractors, and makers of rifle and shotgun ammunition. In addition to the regional branch officers, there were, at headquarters, one office supervising sales abroad and two for handling large customers. Colonel Edmund G. Buckner's Military Sales Division sold smokeless powder to national governments, while the Contractors' Division sold high explosives and some black powder directly to large contractors.

At sales headquarters Patterson had three line assistants and three staff officers.[19] The three Assistant Directors were, at first, responsible for the administration of three geographically defined units — the Eastern, Central, and Western Divisions. Later each came to handle one of the company's three major products. Patterson continued to train his salesmen, as he had done at Repauno, to become experts in the methods of using industrial explosives so that they could work closely with the customer on his special blasting problems. Such training became the responsibility of the Technical Division, which also worked at enlarging the market for explosives by studying possible new uses and applications for its products. The other staff units were the Advertising and Trade Record Divisions. The latter pioneered in compiling statistics on sales made by the du Pont Company and its competitors. This information became increasingly valuable for making estimates of market demand to be used to set production schedules and then to determine what quantities of raw materials and other supplies must be purchased. These statistics also provided data on the changing share of the market held by the company, which executives at headquarters as well as the branch manager themselves used to check on the performance of each sales office and of the department as a whole. In time, a fourth staff office, the Sales Expense Division, was formed to compile figures on sales costs and to work out methods for reducing these marketing expenses.

Here as in manufacturing the relations between headquarters and field were defined on what was essentially a line-and-staff basis. The Director, Assistant Directors, and branch managers had charge of men, while the staff executives at headquarters and in the field were responsible rather for standards and procedures. Advertising was more of a line activity, although the advertising office conferred with the field executives about the nature of their programs. To assist the Director and Vice-President of that department in determining policies and the plans for carrying them out, a Sales Board or Sales Executive Committee, consisting of the Assistant Directors and the heads of staff offices, met regularly to determine price schedules, to approve of advertising programs, and to decide comparable tactical decisions. Also the Sales Department appears to have had meetings of headquarters and field officers similar to those in the manufacturing departments.

The five other functional departments reporting directly to the President — Essential Materials, Development, Real Estate, Legal, and Treasurer's — were somewhat smaller than sales or operations.[20] The first became responsible for the procurement and transportation of raw materials necessary for production. In 1906, after the new structure was in full operation, Pierre purchased nitrate-producing properties in Chile to be assured of supplies of raw materials.[21] But these properties continued to be administered locally, not from Wilmington. The coordination of the flow of supplies from Chile and elsewhere to the du Pont plants became the job of the Essential Materials Department.

The initial responsibility of the Development Department was to supervise the two laboratories set up to improve the company's products and the ways of making them.[22] The Eastern Laboratory, founded at Repauno in 1902, concentrated on developments in dynamite, while the Experimental Station, built the following year on the Brandywine, specialized in black powder and the newer smokeless powder. The latter, it might be pointed out, was not an explosive, as was dynamite or black powder, but rather a propellant used for rifle and shotgun shells or, on a much larger scale, for military projectiles. The Development Department also worked on broad problems concerning markets or sources of supply, usually at the request of the top executives in the central office. It was, for example, on the basis of this department's investigations that Pierre purchased the Chilean nitrate properties.

The Treasurer's Department provided the central office with even more valuable and more regular information. Beside their routine financial activities — the handling and supervision of the myriad financial transactions involved in any great industrial enterprise — the financial executives concentrated on developing uniform statistics essential to determining over-all costs, income, profits, and losses. The Department, at first divided into three major units — the Treasurer's Office and the Accounting and Auditing Divisions — came to have, by the time of World War I, additional units that administered credit and collections, salaries, and forecasts and analyses. The auditing unit gathered information on general external financial and economic conditions as well as on the company's internal performance, while the accounting office continued to develop cost data for production, sales, construction, research, and other activities. The creation of these statistical offices, like those in the sales and manufacturing departments, provided the executives administering the du Pont properties with a steady flow of accurate information. Such data were not and, indeed, could not be assembled until Pierre and Coleman had created this centralized, functionally departmentalized operating structure.

The central office, like other sizable industrial enterprises, was comprised of the functional Vice-Presidents and the President who had one or two assistants. Since the administration of the enterprise as a whole was considered to be the collective task of the senior executives, over-all coordination, appraisal, and planning came to be formally carried out in three committees — Finance, Executive, and Administration. The make-up and duties of the Finance and Executive Committees were similar to those in many of the new consolidated industrial firms. The Finance Committee, at first, included the largest stockholders — the three cousins and the older members of the family who had received stock payment for their holdings.[23] The Executive Committee consisted of the men most responsible for fashioning the new organization and then, as time passed, the President and Vice-Presidents in charge of the functional departments.[24]

From the very first, Pierre and Coleman insisted that the Executive Committee should concentrate on long-term planning and appraisal: it must not become involved in making decisions concerning the operating activities of the different departments. Since planning the future use of current facilities and personnel and the development of new resources involved the allocation of funds for both capital and operating expenses, the Executive Committee increasingly took over the financial duties originally assigned to the Finance Committee. Moreover, as the older members of the Finance Committee had little understanding of the new company's operations and policies, the Committee's active members soon were only Pierre and Coleman du Pont. For all practical purposes the Finance Committee became temporarily defunct.

The coordination of day-to-day activities of the different departments was left to the Administration or "Operative" Committee made up of Departmental Directors. Its weekly meetings not only helped to coordinate plans and procedures, but they also provided a place for the interchange of a great deal of information. The members made proposals to the Executive Committee and discussed ways to carry out the strategies and policies that the senior group had agreed upon.

Structural Modifications — 1903–1919

After its initial shakedown, the structure fashioned in 1903 remained relatively unchanged until after the end of World War I (see Chart 2). The modifications which did occur affected the central office rather than the departmental headquarters. These changes were of three sorts. The most important resulted from shifts in the company's top command which in turn reflected the final transformation of the du Pont Company from a family firm to a professionally manned enterprise. A second type of change was the growth of auxiliary departments at the central office and a third,

CHART 2

Du Pont Structure, *circa* 1911

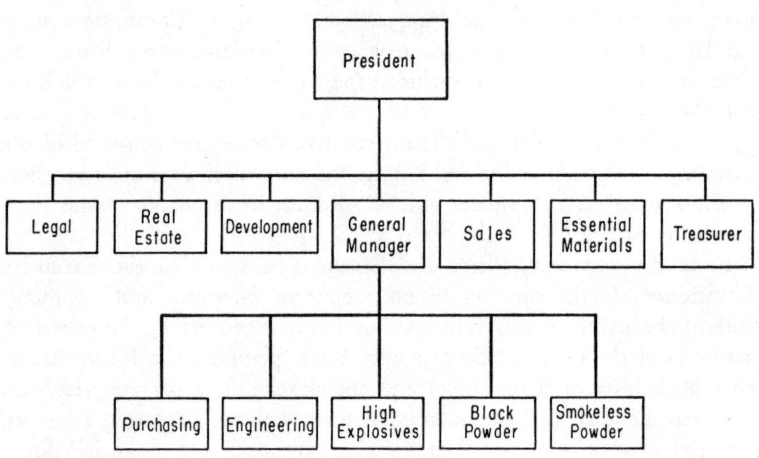

the improvements made in the informational data used to administer the enterprise as a whole.

Of the three cousins who engineered the massive reorganization of the company and the industry, Pierre soon proved himself the most adept in governing it.[25] Alfred preferred to stay close to the black powder operations where he had long worked. Coleman, the empire builder, quickly lost interest in managing the domains he had helped create. Before long he had a controlling interest in the Equitable Life Assurance Society, and, partly as a result of the changes he encouraged there, he had built what was then the largest office building in New York. He turned too to politics, becoming a member of the Republican National Committee in 1908. But Pierre devoted all his energies to the administration of the new du Pont Company. As its first Treasurer, he developed essential statistical data. In 1906, he became the *de facto* head of the company and in 1909, at Coleman's request, took the title of Acting President.

In January, 1911, Pierre, with Coleman's support, relieved Alfred of his duties as General Manager and as Vice-President in charge of the Black Powder Department and a member of the Executive Committee.[26] They retained him as a Vice-President and had him rejoin them on the Finance Committee. Increasing deafness had hindered Alfred's effectiveness. His divorce and remarriage created intense personal and family tensions. But his failure as an administrator was the basic reason for his removal. He was highly competent in supervising personally work in the mills, but he had shown little talent for broader coordination, appraising, and goal setting.

Alfred's removal brought younger men into top management.[27] Barksdale became General Manager and Pierre's brother Irénée, his assistant. The new department heads and members of the Executive Committee — Harry Haskell, the brother of J. Amory Haskell in High Explosives; R. R. M. Carpenter, a brother-in-law of Pierre in Development; Harry Fletcher Brown in Smokeless Powder, Frank L. Connable in Black Powder; and John J. Raskob, Pierre's secretary since the Lorain days, as Treasurer — were experienced and loyal administrators.

In the year following these personnel changes came another reorganization. The Supreme Court, finding that the company had violated the Sherman Antitrust Act, approved a plan to divide its industrial explosives and sporting powder business among three companies — the existing du Pont Company and two new firms, the Hercules Powder Company and the Atlas Powder Company.[28] While this reorganization deprived the du Pont Company of some of its plant and personnel, it had little effect on its basic structure or strategy. These many changes did prove, however, to be too much of a strain on the Acting President.[29] After Pierre's health broke, Barksdale became Acting President as well as General Manager.

Then in 1913, Coleman returned temporarily to oversee the du Pont Company's activities.[30] Pierre, back again in the saddle early in 1914, soon came into conflict with Coleman. At the end of February, shortly after he had received the title of Vice-President, Pierre removed Barksdale and put Irénée in the General Manager's post and, at the same time, asked for the resignation of Moxham.[31] The latter, though still active in the du Pont Company management, had been making plans with two of Pierre's brothers-in-law to consolidate several of du Pont's competitors into a single large firm.

Coleman was apparently disturbed by these changes and other policies that Pierre had instituted, although the evidence available on this controversy is anything but clear. When, in the summer of 1914, Coleman was forced to undergo a serious intestinal operation at the Mayo Clinic in Minnesota, he wrote to Pierre suggesting that the issues be resolved either by letting him buy Pierre out or by having Pierre purchase his shares. Pierre would not hear of the first alternative and hoped to avoid the second. "Before giving further thought to parting, let us take another try at it on the old basis as you suggest," that is, by having Pierre again assume full command.[32] "I will accept the Acting Presidency, or perhaps it will be better to assume your duties under the title of Vice President which I now have." Pierre then suggested changes in the company's top personnel which he hoped Coleman would find satisfactory.

Within a few weeks, Coleman and the Board of Directors had accepted Pierre's proposals with some modifications. Pierre was again to be Acting President and responsible for over-all company policy and performance. Irénée, Pierre's brother, became General Manager. He was to oversee sales as well as operations and also became Chairman of the Executive Committee. Pierre and Irénée would then both be "general" officers responsible for the company as a whole. The rest of the older men in the top command were retired. J. A. Haskell, Barksdale, Moxham, and Patterson (who became a member of the Executive Committee in 1907), relieved of active work, would continue with the company "on salary in advisory capacities" with the title of Vice-President.[33] The new Vice-Presidents, like those appointed in 1911, were young and loyal to Pierre, but also were all experienced and professionally competent.

In carrying out these changes, Pierre deliberately rejected the long entrenched inherited attitude that the firm was managed for the family and the family was to manage the firm. Alfred and even Coleman or Barksdale (who had married a du Pont) should continue in top positions, Pierre clearly believed, only if they continued to be effective administrators. Pierre did appoint family members (two brothers and a brother-in-law) to senior posts in 1911 and 1914, but only after they had proven themselves managerially competent. From this time on, the criterion for promotion was competence rather than family background — universalistic rather than particularistic. Pierre's forceful break with the older tradition, one which in the nineteenth century had been accepted in America as much as in France, was undoubtedly one reason why the du Pont Company proved more of an industrial and administrative innovator than did the few other family-controlled enterprises out of the seventy largest industrial enterprises studied here.

With the changes in top command completed, Pierre carefully defined the duties of the central office. In so doing, he re-emphasized his strong commitment to the delegation of authority and responsibility, and made clear his belief in individual rather than group responsibility for operating administration. The Executive Committee must not interfere with the day-to-day activities of the departments. He insisted that

> Subject to the Board of Directors and Finance Committee, the Executive Committee have full power in the control of the company's affairs. It is desired that this power be used only with discretion in order to:
> (A) Throw responsibility on the heads of departments, where one department alone is interested, and
> (B) Throw responsibility on the heads of two or three departments in matters arising which affect but two or three departments.
>
> In the latter case, should the several heads of departments fail to be unanimous, the decision is to be made by the Chairman of the Executive Committee.
>
> Thus it is expected that the Executive Committee should issue final orders only in cases where more than three departments are interested in the decision and on such other matters as the President asks them to decide for him.[34]

The Committee's job was to consider only problems and policies of the Company as a whole, to set broad goals and policies for the departments, and to coordinate interdepartmental activities in the general interest. Pierre did not expect it to ignore departmental work: "Discussion and criticism of affairs affecting less than four departments is entirely proper," he continued, "so long as discussion and criticism is constructive and given in a spirit to aid the departments interested, but it is not desired that there should be fault-finding where a better solution of a question is not offered."

The Finance Committee, Pierre proposed, was to be returned to "its original position." It would no longer report to the Executive Committee as it had in recent years, but was to be considered equal, and even senior to the latter committee. Still its powers were essentially negative. It would approve the annual and semiannual estimates of appropriations drawn up by the Executive Committee, "thereby authorizing a general financial plan under which the departments may act without further reference to the Finance Committee." Only requests of over $300,000 would be considered in detail. The Committee's approval would also be necessary for appropriations of more than $150,000 not included in the annual budget. Finally, it would approve plans for providing funds for future expenditures and it would recommend dividends. After an exchange of letters, Pierre and Coleman decided the Committee should include themselves, Alfred, and William du Pont, the son of Henry du Pont, the company's domineering president of an earlier generation.

In this way, Pierre permitted the major stockholders to retain a say in company affairs without interfering with major policy decisions. They might, if Alfred and William joined with Coleman, reject important proposals made by the Executive Committee for the allocation of funds and other resources, but even here all the data on which they based decisions were those provided by the more professional managers on that committee. Still, they had general oversight of their investment and could make it clear when they disapproved of important policy. The limits to even these powers are suggested by the fact that only a year later Alfred and William were bringing suit against Pierre and other executives over the sale of Coleman's stock.[35]

Just as Pierre was instituting these changes, came the war in Europe and the enormous expansion of the company's munitions business. The existing organizational structure proved admirably suited to meet the needs of the resulting phenomenal growth. Few organizational adjustments had to be made.[36] Black powder operations, which had become of relatively minor importance, were placed in the High Explosive Department. Plans for postwar product diversification resulted in the creation of a Miscellaneous Manufacturing Department under Lammot du Pont, Pierre's brother.

Of more significance was the growth of the auxiliary or service departments. The Chemical Division came even before the war. It was formed in 1912 to take charge of the research laboratories when the Development Department turned its energies to devising a strategy of diversification. After 1914, the Engineering, Purchasing, and Traffic Departments all grew enormously under the wartime demands. Administratively, these departments became attached to the central office with their Directors reporting directly to the President. So too did the Military Sales Division. The relations between the enlarged auxiliary central office departments and the major Operating, Sales, Treasurer's, and Essential Material Departments were not clearly defined until 1919.

The years just before and during the war saw continued advance in the development of statistical data and of the procedures for its use. Pierre and the financial offices refined the methods used for allocating funds systematically. Procedures for the appropriations of capital expenditures included the use of general forecasts of economic conditions and detailed proposals for individual projects. Well before 1918, the Forecast and Analysis section of the Treasurer's Department was assisting the functional departments and the Executive Committee to allocate rationally funds and other resources by providing "forecasts of probable financial conditions extended twelve months in advance . . . revised every month."[37] Each specific request for capital appropriations had to include the particulars of cost of, need for, and estimated rate of return on investment for the proposed project.[38]

Among the notable advances made during these years in the working out of information so essential for central office planning, coordination, and appraisal were the techniques that F. Donaldson Brown devised for calculating the rate of return on investment. Brown, trained as an electrical engineer at Virginia Polytechnic Institute and Cornell, had joined the du Pont Sales Department in 1908 after serving as general manager of the Baltimore sales office of the Sprague Electric Co.[39] In 1912, he was placed on Barksdale's staff in the General Manager's office and, in 1914, became one of Raskob's assistants in the Treasurer's Department. The techniques which Brown devised and which are still used today at the du Pont Company related the rate of return on capital invested to turnover of capital and to the volume of sales as well as to profit.[40] To do this, Brown broke down costs, investments, sales, and so forth into their component parts. Capital, for example, included funds invested in plant, equipment, and other fixed items and those tied up in working capital such as accounts receivable, finished products, work in process, raw materials, and existing cash balances. The significance of Brown's formula was that it provided executives at both central and departmental headquarters with an accurate standard with which to appraise each operating unit's performance, to locate the sources of deficiencies and inadequacies, and to change and adjust present plans and policies.

Further Centralization — 1919

With the war's end, Pierre became convinced that a new set of executives should take command. Although he was still under fifty, he thought that he and others in top management needed and deserved a rest. More important, new challenges called for young blood and fresh ideas. As Pierre told the Board of Directors in April, 1919: "I am firmly of the opinion that we now have reached another turning point in the conduct of affairs at E. I. du Pont de Nemours & Company; therefore, it would seem wise to place responsibility for future development and management of the business on the next line of men."[41] Pierre had already consulted Irénée, Raskob, Harry Haskell, and one or two others as to possible replacements for the older men.[42] He now proposed that a subcommittee of the Executive Committee, consisting of Donaldson Brown who a year earlier had taken Raskob's place as Treasurer, Frederick W. Pickard who, at the same time, had become Vice-President in charge of sales, Lammot du Pont, chief of the Miscellaneous Manufacturing Department, and

Harry Haskell, as chairman, to study and recommend ways to improve the company's organization.

Haskell was more concerned about structure than personnel, and the changes he favored were essentially those that would strengthen the centralized organization that had worked so admirably during the wartime expansion. As Vice-President in charge of the High Explosives Department he replied to Pierre's proposal for a thorough turnover of top management by saying:

> I quite agree with the principle of advancing the younger men to positions of executive responsibility, for I believe that one reason the Company has been so successful is that for over twenty years the conduct of its [business] is in the hands of young men and this has served to keep off the dry rot of conservatism that sometimes accompanys [*sic*] too unchanging management. On the other hand we have sometimes lost by not geting full value out of experienced men — witness Barksdale and J. A. [Haskell]. Perhaps the new plan will be flexible enough not to repeat the mistakes in the latter respect.[43]

Haskell, recalling earlier changes, added: "I have believed in reorganization by evolution rather than the Company's more usual custom by revolution, but I guess it's a good thing to take a little corporate calomel once in a while and if we get rid of the wheat with the tares, why we never quite know whether we are individually wheat or tare and so can comfort ourselves in the belief that maybe it is the other fellow."

Then Haskell turned to the matter of structure, urging Pierre to simplify and to centralize still further the present organization:

> Regarding manufacturing, I feel very strongly that our present method of splitting operations into their parts without any effective means of coordination of effort is inefficient and indefensible. Instead of creating three brand new operating vice-presidencies, I would strongly advise one over all manufacturing operations, with a very high class assistant, the latter on the Ex. Com. and as many managers or directors as may be found convenient for the specialized operations of different parts of the manufacture. It may be that it would be better for a few years to carry on the dye business as a separate entity. I think it would because it is a developing, unstandardized industry and should merit independent attention just as the Parlin chemical mixtures business was better by itself until standardized — when it was merged with the regular sales and operating departments.

At the end of March, Haskell's subcommittee on organization made its report which spelled out more explicitly the suggestions and implications of what its chairman had written earlier to Pierre.[44] Because of its approach to the problems of organization and because of its arguments on the value of a functionally departmentalized structure, this report is worth some detailed study. Its authors had a highly rational and systematic approach to the problems of administration. They thought in terms of organization needs and, in describing them, used organizational concepts that had only recently been developed. Much more than Pierre du Pont, they wholeheartedly endorsed the dictum Barksdale had made years before on the value and importance of organization: "He performs his duty best when he succeeds in working out an organization — a scheme of organization — and then placing in each position to be filled the best available man and then endeavoring to see that in a general way the objects sought for by the organization and by the personnel are achieved."[45]

Many words and ideas in the Committee's report indicate its awareness of current ideas concerning large-scale organization. Its members, as concerned with practice as with theory, examined the experience of other companies. Beside talking individually to outside executives, they sent an assistant to study four companies with similar problems — Armour, Wilson & Company (both meat packers), International Harvester, and Westinghouse Electric.

The Committee's report began with a careful definition of terms, followed by a lengthy statement of administrative theory. Here the basic points dealt with the purpose of organization:

> The ideal condition is one in which every unit in a group is so coordinated and controlled that each functions to the best advantage with respect to its own work and the work of the whole Company.
>
> The object of organization may be defined as the attainment of maximum of results with a minimum of effort. If we have not enough men of the right sort, maximum results would be impossible. If we have too many men, the results will be obtained at unnecessary expense.[46]

Next came an enunciation of two "principles" based on the company's experience. The first rested on the belief that:

> The most efficient results are obtained at least expense when we coordinate related effort and segregate unrelated effort. For example, purchase of materials is unrelated to the sale of a finished product in a much greater degree than manufacture and sales, or manufacture and purchasing; and legal work is still more unrelated to either of those before mentioned.

This does not mean, the report continued, as "it is so often said, that good organization results from putting like things together." It then gave an example:

> For instance, it is natural to think that all engineers and engineering work should be grouped in one engineering department. Now, surveying a farm,

> designing and building a bridge, running a locomotive, or operating a power house, are all "engineering," but it is quite obvious that they are so unrelated that to group them under one head would be uneconomical. On the other hand, the operation of a boiler house at Carney's Point is similar in name and reality to the operation of a boiler house at Haskell, yet one would not think of grouping them under one head in exchange for the authority exercised over each of them by the plant superintendent.

The basic "principle" was rather "that it is related effort which should be coordinated and not 'like things.' In fact it is often more necessary to combine related efforts which are unlike." For example, the report noted, as had Haskell in his letter, that the present dye-stuff business, like the chemical-mixture business a few years before, was not yet standardized. Therefore it would be wise to have it maintain:

> One individual in control of both production and sales, because the relation of the product and its qualities is so mixed up with the demands of the market for the product that to divorce them and segregate the business into a clearly defined production department and an independent sales department, would be detrimental to the business. Later on when the production of dyes becomes standardized it will no doubt follow the evolution of other portions of the business.

The principle of coordinating "related effort" normally called for placing the different broad functional activities into separate administrative units.

A second underlying principle was that of giving each executive in charge of a set of coordinated or related efforts full authority and responsibility. This was, the Committee stressed, the only way to assure flexibility and adjustment in the face of constant change. Here the report repeated and made more explicit the concept of delegation of individual responsibility and authority which Pierre had so often stressed:

> The principle of individual responsibility and undivided authority has been recognized by the Company and consistently followed in the cases of its established divisions. A unit once defined — for example, the Sales Department or the Development Department — is placed in charge of the best available individual, who as head of that department is held responsible for results, and he can in his official capacity arrange every detail of his department according to his best judgment, subject only to the alternative of having someone replace him if his official judgment is not good. The same principle is followed in turn in the case of branch office managers or plant superintendents, who are individually responsible for the conduct of that part of the Company's business over which they have charge, subject only to the business being conducted according to the principles and methods laid down by the authority next higher up. It is to the recognition of this

principle that we may in large measure attribute the Company's phenomenally successful performance during the recent abnormal years.

This principle had not been fully effective, however, the report continued, for the Executive Committee had tended to make decisions concerning departmental activities despite Pierre's earlier strictures. The result had been a dangerous trend toward committee management and away from individual responsibility. It must be recognized, the report went on, that:

> We have defeated the principle to a partial extent by allowing the Executive Committee to act for the president as the immediate superior in an executive way to whom the department heads are held responsible. The interposition of a committee charged with the duty of performing executive acts better done by an individual is, we believe, responsible for most of the minor inefficiencies, inconveniences, wasted effort and unnecessary duplication, which are matters of common knowledge to those engaged in carrying out the daily routine. These are usually small matters with relation to the business as a whole, and for this reason rarely impose themselves on the attention of the higher officers. Nevertheless, in the aggregate they are of no mean importance.

On the basis of these two principles, the Committee made its recommendations. First, it suggested that most of the company's activities be segregated into four functional "grand divisions"—the Production, Sales, Development, and Treasurer's Departments, each headed by a Vice-President. The Production Department, for example, would include not only manufacturing activities but also purchasing, engineering, construction, research, chemical process control, and a number of other service functions. The remaining few "joint functions, such as traffic, medical, etc. shall be assigned by or on authority of the first Vice-President." In other words, the day-to-day administration of all du Pont activities was to be concentrated in the headquarters of four functional departments. "The objection has been advanced," the report admitted, "that some of the grand divisions are too large and too diversified to be under the control of one individual. The answer is that the controlling individual need not know every detail of the business, but require only a good mind, sound judgment, and knowledge of general business principles." The Committee thus solved the problem of the relations between the auxiliary departments in the central office with the major functional departments by merely incorporating the former into the latter. They would now be staff units at departmental headquarters rather than in the central office.

The central office itself was otherwise little changed. The First Vice-

President (a new position), and not the Executive Committee, was made specifically responsible for appraising and coordinating the work of the major departments and for holding their chiefs accountable for their performance. On this point, Haskell and his colleagues cited the experience of the four companies investigated as well as that of their own company. In all four — Armour, Wilson, International Harvester, and Westinghouse — "executive control was definitely centralized under a general officer," and "in no cases were divisions or departments responsible to a committee." The President's duties were not specifically outlined but they probably remained those of formulating broad policy.

The Executive Committee was to be concerned with policy planning and over-all appraisal. "The proper function of the Executive Committee," the report read, "is to exercise general supervision over the company's affairs; to decide all questions of policy, and in general to act in the Board's stead, and to see that all conduct of business is in accordance with the wishes and policies laid down by the Board." The subcommittee on organization thought "it would be better to start with a small Executive Committee, adding one or two members to it later should it appear that some portions of the four grand divisions were not being adequately represented." The Committee continued to rely on the departments for information on which it based its decisions. Except for the data provided by the financial offices, the central office had no sources of information outside of the department or ways to check their data. Nor did the central office yet have the responsibility for coordinating the forecasts made by the Manufacturing, Sales, and Purchasing Departments even though such coordination was necessary if the movement of product from one department to another was to be smooth and steady.

While the four men signing the report agreed that there should be a Finance Committee, they differed as to its role and make-up. Some, recalling its operations before 1914, thought it again "should be a branch of the Executive Committee." Others held "that matters financial should be segregated from the Company's other activities," and that, as was finally recommended, there continue to be two separate committees. "The opinion was unanimous," the report continued, "on the desirability of having as many members in common as possible on both committees."

The report was then sent to Pierre for study. The President liked its general outlines, but, as he told a special meeting of the Board, "the selection of men must to a certain extent precede the choice of form of organization."[47] The structure should be built around men rather than fitting the men into an ideal structure, as Barksdale had earlier suggested. Pierre recommended the promotion of younger executives and proposed that the present Executive Committee members be moved to the

Finance Committee, where they would serve in a broad advisory capacity. Actually they were to have more of a semiretired position similar to that of J. A. Haskell, Barksdale, and Patterson after the 1914 changes.

Pierre then listed his choices. He would retire as President, becoming Chairman of the Board with nominal duties. Irénée would be President and Lammot, Chairman of the Executive Committee. This Committee would include, besides Donaldson Brown and Frederick Pickard, six relatively young but experienced managers only one of whom was a du Pont or related to the du Pont family. The Executive Committee and then the Board immediately approved Pierre's recommendations.[48]

Within a short time, the new Executive Committee had accepted with some modifications the recommendations of the Haskell report. The major difference was that the Purchasing (including Traffic), Chemical, and Engineering Departments continued as separate units although the single Production Department did have its own large Service Department made up of the Technical, the Welfare, and the Materials and Products Divisions (see Chart 3).[49] This decision left unanswered the nature of the relationship between these more service-like departments and the major operating ones. So the Chemical and the Engineering as well as the new Personnel and the older Legal and Real Estate Departments now became explicitly advisory staff organizations.[50] They worked to develop standards and procedures for the company as a whole and to advise both the departmental and central officers. But their executives were not to give orders to personnel in the line departments. Purchasing, which now handled the procurement of raw materials and the obtaining of supplies for all the company's facilities, continued to make the major buying decisions and so remained, like Production, Sales, and finance, a line rather than staff office.

Once the revised structure had been agreed upon, the new Executive Committee members took up their posts as department heads. William C. Spruance became Vice-President in charge of Production, Walter S. Carpenter, Jr., (R. R. M. Carpenter's younger brother) took over the Development Department, J. B. D. Edge was put in charge of Purchasing, and Brown and Pickard remained the heads of the Treasurer's and the Sales Departments. The staff departments — Chemical and Engineering — were not represented on a committee. The three remaining Executive Committee members had charge of the major subdivisions of the Production Department — Explosives, Cellulose Products, and Paints and Chemicals. This heavy representation of production men on the Executive Committee emphasizes the company's continued concentrated concern with manufacturing and that at du Pont in 1919 production was still looked on as a more basic economic function than marketing.[51]

CHART 3A

Du Pont Structure, 1919–1921

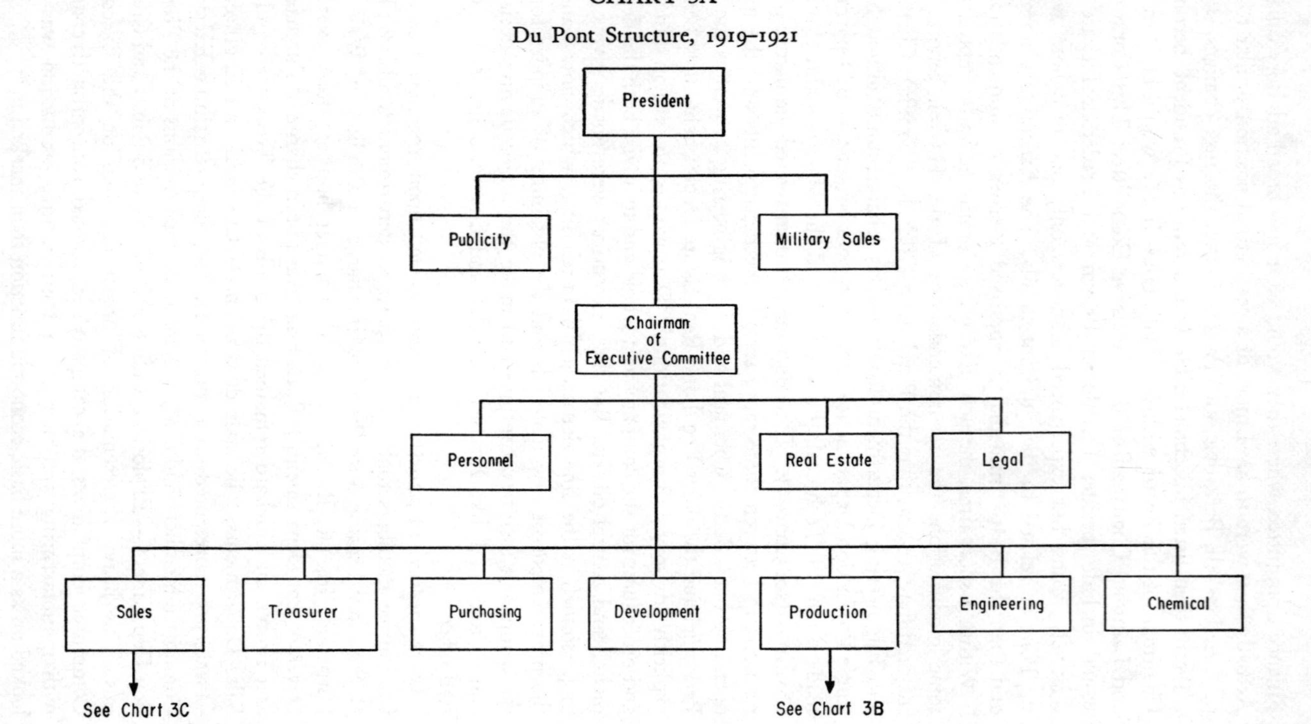

CHART 3B

Du Pont Production Department, 1919–1921

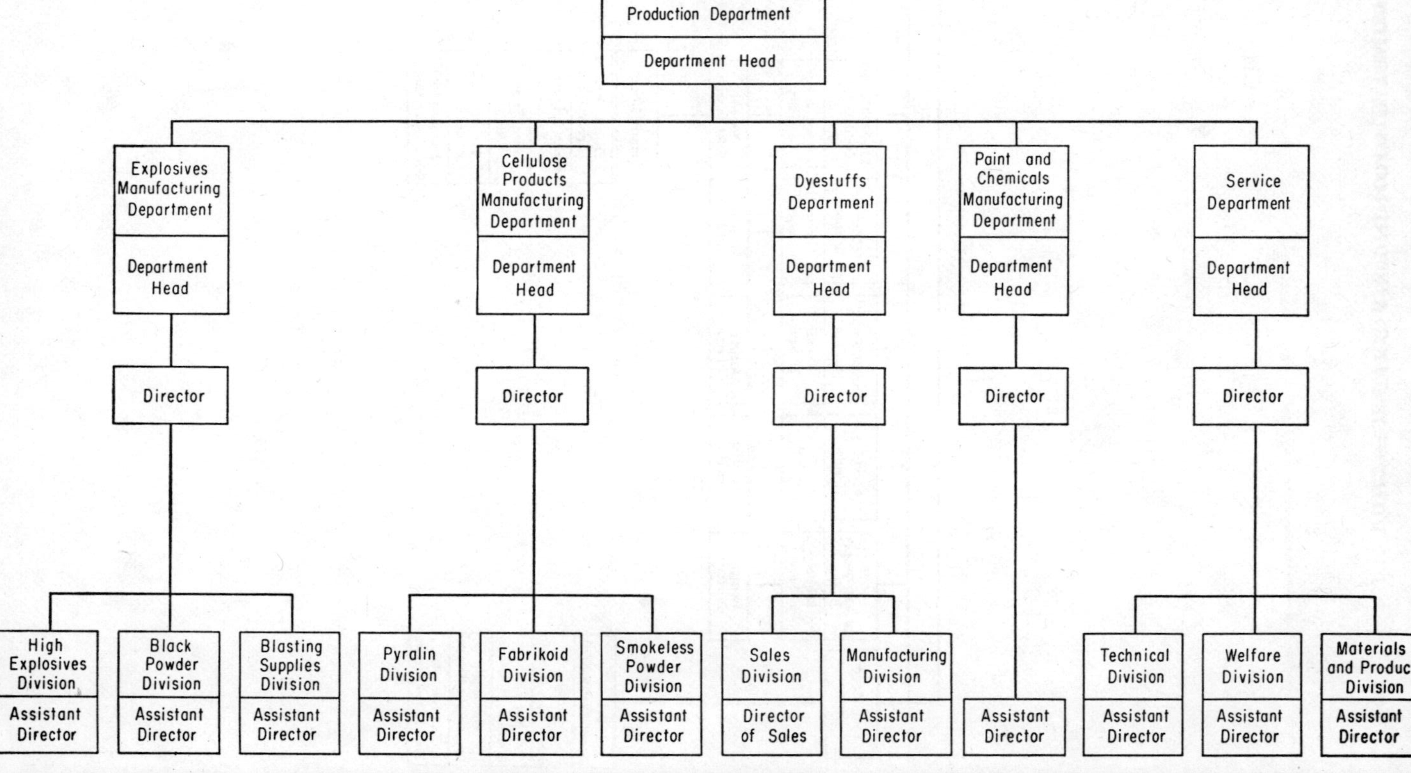

CHART 3C:

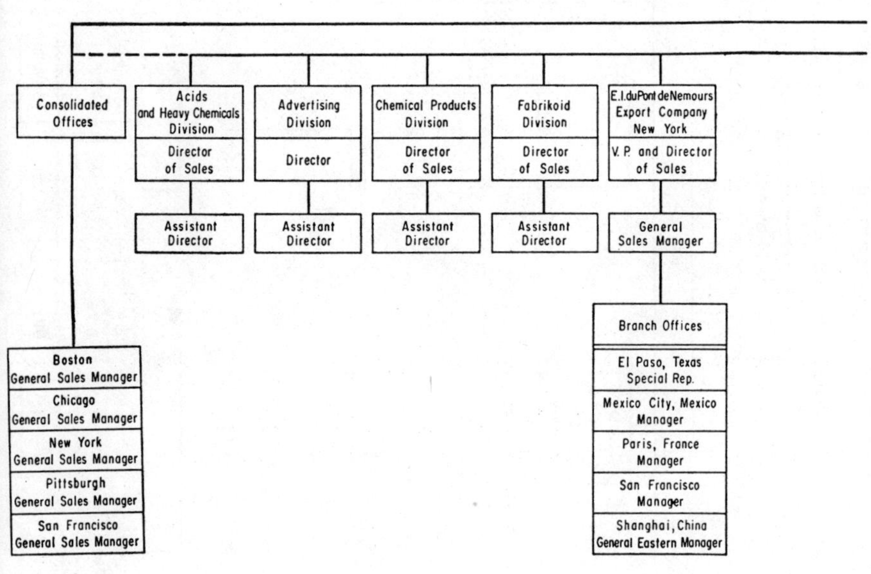

Assistant to Vice President
Consolidated Offices
Acids and Heavy Chemicals Division
Director of Sales
Assistant Director
Advertising Division
Director
Assistant Director
Chemical Products Division
Director of Sales
Assistant Director
Fabrikoid Division
Director of Sales
Assistant Director
E.I.duPont deNemours Export Company New York
V. P. and Director of Sales
General Sales Manager
Branch Offices
El Paso, Texas Special Rep.
Mexico City, Mexico Manager
Paris, France Manager
San Francisco Manager
Shanghai, China General Eastern Manager
Boston General Sales Manager
Chicago General Sales Manager
New York General Sales Manager
Pittsburgh General Sales Manager
San Francisco General Sales Manager

Du Pont Sales Department, 1919–1921

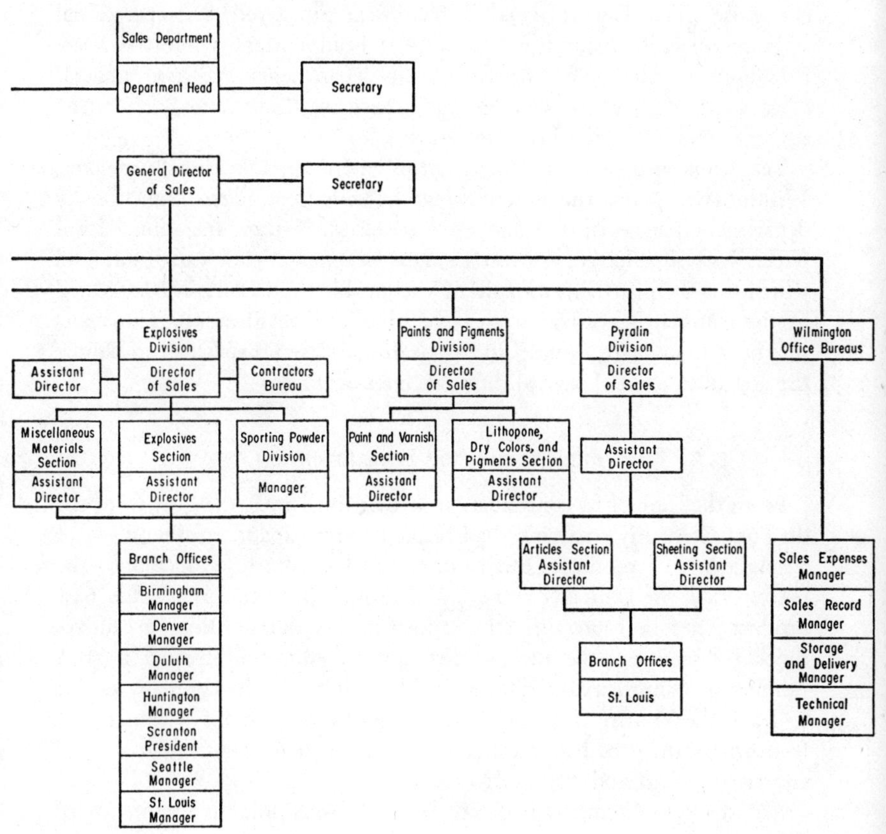

By the summer of 1919, the du Pont Company was ready to meet the postwar world with a new but experienced and seasoned set of top managers and a simplified management structure. Few more rationally planned and thoroughly tested designs existed for coordinating, apprais-ing, and planning the activities of a great vertically integrated industrial enterprise. The Departmental Directors administered the operational activities in each major function at their headquarters, while the Vice-Presidents in charge of the functional departments and two general officers, meeting collectively as the Executive Committee, made the strategic and entrepreneurial decisions.

Yet almost at once the company began having organizational problems. Within two years, the carefully worked-out centralized, functionally departmentalized structure had to be scrapped. The organizational form which had so effectively stood the test of phenomenal expansion and which was then further rationalized was unable to meet the needs created by the company's postwar strategy of product diversification. The struc-ture built to manage a single line of products proved insufficient to handle the administration of several different lines of goods.

The Strategy of Diversification

From the time of its consolidation in 1902 until 1918, the growth of the du Pont Company's activities had resulted from expanding the output of a single line of products. But from the end of World War I until the present day, the company's strategy of growth has been to develop new product lines in quite different industries. As the du Pont executives quickly discovered, the new strategy of diversification created a great number of administrative difficulties. Why then did the company decide to leave the known and well-charted ways of growth for a course that few American firms had yet embarked on? And how was such a novel strategy planned and executed?

The du Pont Company had actually taken some tentative steps toward diversification before World War I. Yet, in 1913, only 3 per cent of its business was outside of explosives.[52] It was the enormous growth of the company's physical, financial, and personnel resources during the war that intensified the search for new lines of business. In planning and carrying out the strategy of moving into industries based on the technology of nitrocellulose chemistry, the bold financial and legal man-euvers of the older empire builders like a Coleman du Pont had rela-tively little relevance. Far more appropriate were the rational, calculating ways of a Pierre du Pont and his technically skilled associates. Moreover, planning and carrying out the new strategy of diversification required more complex and more numerous strategic decisions than did the older one of consolidation, integration, and expansion within a single industry.

Initial Steps Toward Diversification

The du Pont Company had rejected an opportunity to diversify shortly after its rebirth in 1902 and 1903, preferring to concentrate on its primary line. At the time of the consolidation, one of the constituent firms, the International Smokeless Powder & Chemical Co. of Parlin, New Jersey, was carrying on a small business in solvents, ether, and lacquers, largely as a by-product of its smokeless powder manufacturing. The consolidated company continued this mixed chemical business, but looked on it only as a small secondary activity and not as one to be developed into a major new line. As Irénée du Pont later put it: "We made an excellent quality and most attractive material, but the volume was too small to make a good industry out of it." [53]

The first planned move beyond explosives came in 1908 and was initially, like the later developments, a response to a threat of excess capacity.[54] The danger of idle plant and personnel arose when the government temporarily canceled a major part of its orders for military powder. The 1903 consolidation had given the du Pont Company a monopoly of the manufacture of military powder, and political protest was not long in coming. In 1906, Congress provided funds for the Army to build a small plant as a check on the costs of making powder. Two years later, after the government had instituted an antitrust case against the du Pont Company, the House and Senate amended a Naval Appropriations Bill to read that "no part of the appropriations could be spent for the purchase of powder from any trust or combination in restraint of trade or from any corporation having a monopoly of gunpowder in the United States, except in the event of an extraordinary emergency." [55] The Navy then built enlarged facilities at its Indian River plant in Maryland while the Army completed a factory at its Picatinny Arsenal. This construction doubled the country's smokeless powder capacity. In 1908, well before its completion, the du Pont Company closed down one of its three smokeless powder plants and kept the other two running at reduced volume.[56]

"The likelihood of our having a considerable idle capacity at our smokeless powder plants," led the Company's Executive Committee to appoint a subcommittee in December, 1908, to investigate and report on "what steps are already being taken, and what additional steps they would recommend, in the direction of developing further uses for guncotton or any of the other productions of our smokeless powder plants." [57] This loss of orders also turned the company's top executives to a more general review of the value of the government business. If unemployed resources might be turned to new uses, possibly even plant and personnel still operating on government work could be shifted to more profitable activities. As Pierre wrote his cousin William du Pont in the following spring: "Reviewing the whole Government powder business, it has not paid us to go into it but having gone in we can not let it go. The situation has led us to investigate other lines which might occupy the manufacturing capacity which is now occupied in Government business."[58] Thus, while pressures and needs created by changes in the market turned the policy makers to the new strategy, it also made them more aware of the opportunities it offered.

Pierre placed his brother Irénée, who had also received his technical training at M.I.T., in charge of planning the new program by putting him at the head of the Development Department and on the Executive Committee.[59] On the basis of some of the Department's superficial earlier surveys, Irénée decided to concentrate his attention on the potentials of the three industries whose products had nitrocellulose as their basic ingredient—artificial leather, artificial silk, and pyroxylin (Celluloid-type) products including photographic film. According to the Department's reports, the total requirements of these three industries was close to 700,000 pounds of nitrocellulose, or a little more than double the amount normally taken by the Army and Navy in previous years.[60]

Which of these potential fields, then, offered the broadest opportunity to use the company's existing resources? Pyroxylin products enjoyed a large market but their manufacturing raised difficulties. Investigation indicated that "it would be necessary to engage in a great amount of detail manufacture to successfully compete with the large companies at present engaged in this business who sell their products largely in finished forms of combs, collars, knickknacks, etc. or in sheets in hundreds of different thicknesses and color."[61] As was still true of the mixed chemical business at Parlin, the volume of each product was too small to be a profitable business. So instead of attempting to compete with the pyroxylin producers, the Department recommended that the company continue to investigate the possibility of supplying those companies with raw materials by developing "nitrocellulose from short fibre cotton which would be suitable for celluloid manufacture."

A move into the artificial silk industry presented other types of problems. As nothing in this line had as yet been done in the United States, a real opportunity existed. But it dimmed when the Chardonnet Company, successful manufacturers of artificial silk by the nitrocellulose or pyroxylin method in France and Italy, asked too high a price for their patents. Moreover, the company's leading chemists believed that the recently developed viscose process might soon supersede the pyroxylin method of manufacture.[62]

Artificial leather, on the other hand, not only required less initial capital than did artificial silk, but it also provided a field where the company's technological experience, training, and resources could pay off. Since artificial leather had been manufactured in this country from nitrocellulose for only about a decade, it was still, the Development Department reported, "of poor quality although there exists an unsatisfied demand for the high grade article."[63] The company was in an excellent position to improve process as well as product, and also to find technological answers to the industry's major unsolved problem — the efficient recovery of solvents. Moreover, artificial leather, like explosives but unlike pyroxylin articles, was a relatively high volume undifferentiated product that was sold in bulk to other manufacturers for further processing.

To be more certain "whether a satisfactory artificial leather can be produced at a reasonable cost as well as to determine whether the solvents used in the manufacture can be recovered," the Department set up a small pilot plant in the closed-down smokeless powder works in the fall of 1909. The operation proved successful, and on the Department's recommendation, the Executive Committee agreed to go into the business. This decision immediately raised another question. Should the company start by building its own artificial leather plants, close to the existing nitrocellulose capacity, or should it learn more about the business by purchasing a going concern? Deciding on the second alternative, the company in 1910 purchased for $1,195,000 largely in du Pont securities, one of the leading firms in the field, the Fabrikoid Co., which had its main plant in Newburgh, New York.[64]

For a short period after 1910, the Executive Committee did little toward further diversification. Naval expansion plus the lack of inhibiting amendments in later appropriations bills again brought large government orders for smokeless powder. Also as the Fabrikoid venture proved profitable, the Company expanded its output of artificial leather, transferring some of its smokeless powder facilities and personnel to Newburgh. The Development Department continued to work on enlarging the company's line in this field and soon turned over its initial work in patent leathers and one of two other products to the Operating and Sales Departments for further development.[65] Then, in the summer of 1913, excess capacity again became a problem. Government orders dropped off after Congress reduced military appropriations in 1911 and again in 1912. The du Pont Executive Committee again asked the Development Department to investigate "uses, other than those with which we are already familiar, that seem susceptible of development into outlets for material quantities of nitrocellulose in addition to our present sales."[66]

The Development Department in 1913 recommended that the company carry out the plans it had started to work on in 1910 for making pyroxylin from nitrocellulose based on short-staple cotton. The Department had become most enthusiastic about the prospects for such a product.[67] First, the demands for raw materials, for semifinished pyroxylin products (sheets, rods, and tubes), and for finished products were all increasing rapidly. Second, shipping costs kept out foreign competition and so helped provide a protected market. Finally, the company's large operations in nitrocellulose assured it of lower raw materials costs and of production experience that could be concentrated on finding ways to lower cost and improve quality.

Further investigation, however, showed that the company would have difficulty in supplying the existing pyroxylin companies with their nitrocellulose requirements. Young Walter S. Carpenter, Jr., assisting his brother, R. R. M. Carpenter, recently appointed Vice-President in charge of Development, analyzed the problem in this way. The manufacturing firms would not buy from outsiders because "they would sacrifice the perfect control and supervision of their product throughout its manufacture which they now enjoy."[68] The only way to retain such control would be "to instruct us in the details of manufacture or composition of character of their product." As such information was among their most valuable trade secrets, they would hardly give it out to a potential competitor. In other words, by requiring such close coordination between supplier and manufacturer, this process made a policy of vertical integration a business necessity. If the du Pont Company was to develop cellulose on a large enough scale to make it profitable, it would have to move into the making and selling of semifinished and, most probably, finished products.

Once the Executive Committee agreed to go into the pyroxylin business, the next question again was whether to do so by building a plant or by buying out a going concern. On the basis of another of Walter Carpenter's reports, the Committee this time chose the first alternative. The advantage of purchasing the trade, reputation, and "intimate knowledge of the manufacture" of an existing company was outweighed by the benefits of closer integration with the company's present production facilities, more effective use of company-provided raw materials, and technical know-how that would accrue from the building of a new plant at the Haskell Smokeless Powder Works. This plant could use currently idle equipment and personnel. It would "afford an opportunity for employing to good advantage the technical and manufacturing ability of the smokeless powder organization, thus taking advantage of the facilities and capabilities rendered superfluous by decreasing smokeless powder business."[69] Given its lower cost of raw materials, its "probably greater knowledge of cellulose" which would make possible further continued improvement in product and processes, and its large sales force, the company with its new plant could meet "powerful competition" and still make "a generous return of twenty per cent on capital invested," the Committee thought.

The outbreak of the war in Europe modified the pyroxylin program, for in the fall of 1914, the du Pont Company began to receive huge orders for smokeless powder from the Allies. The Executive Committee, as it turned its attention to the new situation, agreed not to abandon plans for a pyroxylin plant but instead to build and operate a small pilot one at the Experimental Station rather than at the Haskell plant.[70] At the same time, the department began its first serious study of the possibilities of a move into photographic film.[71] However, until the late spring of 1915, the company paid little attention to matters other than the construction of the enormous plant and other facilities needed to meet the war orders.

Intensified Pressures for Diversification

Wartime expansion was to increase greatly the problem of excess capacity in the smokeless powder operations, for the giant European orders were largely for smokeless powder to propel shells rather than for high explosives that accounted for the lion's share of the company's normal business. Starting with a capacity of 8,400,000 pounds a year, the three existing plants at Carney's Point, Haskell, and Parlin — all in New Jersey — increased to a production of 200,000,000 pounds a year by the end of 1915.[72] By April 1917, this had reached 455,000,000 pounds a year, or fifty-four times that of the October 1914 rate. Moreover, in 1915, Major William G. Ramsay and his Engineering Department completed in record time the construction of the largest guncotton plant in the world at Hopewell, Virginia. At the same time, at Repauno and other plants devoted to making high explosives for commercial purposes, there was a smaller but by older standards still extremely rapid expansion in the production of T.N.T. and other explosives based on toluene, tetryl, picric acid, ammonium nitrate, and ammonium picrate. Similarly, the output of special explosives and accessories like caps, fuses, and ignition pellets grew enormously.

Also because of the unexpected increase in volume, the du Ponts began to manufacture more of their raw materials than they had in the past. In these years the company produced vast quantities of sulphuric, nitric, and lactic acids, alcohol, toluene, and such new items as diphenylamine, ammonium picrate, and analine, as well as purifying cotton linters and making ice machinery to recover alcohol and acids. The new demand led the company's research laboratories to concentrate on improving its supplies of acids and semiraw materials as well as making its processes more efficient. The need for assured supplies demanded increasing vertical integration.

Almost from the beginning, Pierre du Pont, the company's President, was concerned about the impact of this enormous demand and expansion on the future of the du Pont organization. Writing Coleman shortly after the work on the first war orders had begun, he emphasized:

> We must be careful that our point of view is not entirely warped out of line by this temporary situation. It will take very careful thought and maneuvering to return to former conditions. The Engineering Department has expanded beyond our wildest dream. Those in the Smokeless Operating Department have seized men from other departments in order to quickly meet demands. The other departments all have responded splendidly and have done their utmost to adjust themselves to the new conditions.[73]

Not only did the new demands mean a great expansion in plant capacity but also in the number of trained personnel and in the amount of capital employed.[74] The total number of men working for du Pont rose from 5,300 in the fall of 1914 to over 85,000 in the fall of 1918, while the managerial or administrative group (men receiving salaries of $4,200 or more) grew from 94 to 259. The gross capital employed by the company increased from $83,500,000 in 1915 to $309,000,000 by the end of 1918. Profits—which grew comparably—provided ample funds for any program developed for the postwar use of this greatly enlarged plant and personnel.

The company began to consider the details of such a program as soon as powder-plant construction was far enough along to assure the filling of military orders.[75] An enlarged Development Department had the responsibility for planning the postwar diversification, but the final strategic decisions on where and when to move were those of the Executive Committee. From the first, all agreed that the Department must focus its attention on industries whose processes were based on the science of chemistry. There the company was technologically strong and the market opportunities particularly inviting. "In mechanical manufactures," the Development Department pointed out, "the United States is far in advance at present of any country in the world. In chemical manufacture Germany is undoubtedly in advance of any country in the world." [76] And the war had closed the American market to German goods.

The planning of postwar diversification went through two distinct stages. First, the Department's new Excess Plant Utilization Division concentrated on finding uses for the greatly enlarged smokeless powder facilities, since "only a portion of the present equipment will be useful after the European Wars are settled." [77] Then, in 1917, the Department began to consider its resources as more than physical plant and facilities. Its planners began to think about the use of its laboratories, its sales organization, and particularly its personnel trained in the complex processes of nitrocellulose technology and in the administration of great numbers of men and large amounts of money and materials.

The resulting diversification program into chemical-based industries developed along three lines. First, there was expansion in industries in which the company had already entered — artificial leather (Fabrikoid) and pyroxylin. Growth in the pyroxylin field was hastened when the Arlington Company, makers of Pyralin, a high-grade pyroxylin, approached the du Ponts with an offer to sell.[78] Their management was old and had been troubled by internal dissensions as well as labor and competitive difficulties. The du Pont Company quickly accepted the offer, for the Arlington firm, one of the largest celluloid producers in the country, was an integrated firm with valuable properties and a well-established name. Its plants at Arlington, New Jersey, Poughkeepsie, New York, and Toronto, Canada, were well located for easy coordination with the existing du Pont operations. Moreover, its paper mill in New York and camphor plantation in Florida assured it of supplies which the European war was making difficult to obtain. In the following year, the du Pont Company enlarged its Fabrikoid production through the purchase of the Fairfield Rubber Company in Fairfield, Connecticut, a concern whose major product was rubber-coated automobile and carriage tops.[79] In January, 1917, to assure itself of adequate supplies, it moved further toward vertical integration by purchasing the Marokene Company of Elizabeth, New Jersey, makers of the "gray goods" base for the Fabrikoid products.

Second, the company entered areas where the European war had caused critical scarcities. Of these, the most important was dyes. The du Pont Company went into dyemaking hesitantly even though many of its products, such as diphenylamine and anthracene, were used as "intermediates" in dye manufacturing. Despite urgings of the textile industry, the American government, and the Allied powers, the Development Department as late as December, 1915, made adverse recommendations. The company at the moment had neither the experience nor plant capacity to go into dye production. Walter Carpenter, as Director of Development, noted the specific reasons: "First, as all our plant capacity is fully occupied, we would have to build a complete new plant for the production of intermediates. Second: Due to the scarcity of crude material. Third: Due to the time of our technical men being fully occupied." [80] Carpenter further commented that Pierre du Pont did not altogether agree with his position. A little later, Pierre and the Executive Committee decided that a start should be made. With the assistance of German dye chemists recruited by the State Department, a dye-manufacturing operation was set up at Deepwater, New Jersey, where several new acid plants had been built.[81] The development of a satisfactory product was slow as was the development of plant and personnel. Dyestuffs continued to be a costly drain on the company's treasury until long after the end of the war.

Third, the Development Department continued to study a variety of new products that could use postwar capacity. At first, it hoped to do this by manufacturing chemicals which the company was "making or could make with very slight expenditure" and which should have a wide market as raw materials in the rubber and chemical industries.[82] Quickly it decided that the demand for these could not employ many of the existing resources.

Then it began to investigate individually the smokeless powder plants in order to determine just what were the specific advantages of each in location, equipment, and personnel. After much study, the Development Department experts suggested that the Hopewell plant was entirely too big.[83] While that plant held possibilities for the production of water-soluble chemicals, fertilizers, or paper and other products using wood and cotton pulp, it was almost impossible to find "any one industry capable of using a plant of this size through a long period of time." [84] In May, 1916, the department submitted a detailed report on the future use of the other smokeless powder works. According to this report, the Deepwater Works offered the best combination for the new dyestuffs and allied organic chemical products; facilities and personnel at Carney's Point could be turned to the development of castor, linseed, and other vegetable oils to be used as raw materials for Fabrikoid, paint, and varnish production; and Haskell appeared better suited to the manufacturing of more finished products such as Fabrikoid, pyroxylin, and other plastics.[85] Haskell also might be the place to begin work on artificial silk.

The Parlin works, their report on plant utilization continued, could be used to develop varnishes for which there was a wide and growing market. "Varnish of different kinds is used in large quantities by manufacturers of furniture, leather goods, etc., while there is a similar large consumption of varnish by numerous consumers each requiring relatively small amounts. Varnish is handled by every paint store and used by every painter in the country." Both types of varnish — spirit and oil — would use as raw materials the products of other plants and so provided new outlets for production from existing capacity. Moreover, although they would not use exactly the same equipment, the manufacturing process, the machinery used, and the technical skills needed were close enough to those employed in the plant's current operations to permit the use of surplus equipment and trained personnel.[86]

In this report the Development Department might have paid more attention to marketing, for the selling of small packaged consumer goods was certainly quite different from the type of marketing to which the du Pont Company was accustomed. But it merely noted that:

> Varnish manufacture would give the Company a more complete business which would make it easier to meet trade conditions. The present sales organization could undoubtedly handle the varnishes to a large extent by the same salesmen and force in general as in the case of pyroxylin solutions and thereby reducing the selling expense for both.[87]

Parlin's proximity to New York was a "great advantage," a second report pointed out.[88] Moreover, it was "a logical point for a very small package business and tin can company due to the existing production of ether and pyroxylin solutions." Once Parlin had made good in varnish, it could easily move into the manufacturing of paint.

Since the Executive Committee looked with favor on these proposals, particularly those for the Parlin Works, the Development Department, during the spring and summer of 1916, concentrated on its investigations of varnish and paint with detailed consideration of various products, processes, output and price trends, and technical developments. Later in the year, the Executive Committee decided, on the basis of Development Department studies, to go into the varnish and paint business on a large scale.[89] The move required only a small investment, the Committee agreed, because of anticipated "excess plant." The company enjoyed the advantages of vertical integration since it could supply its own alcohol, pigments, resin, and other materials. Produced on a high-volume basis, they could be delivered to the company plants at a lower price than most existing smaller paint firms currently paid for such supplies.[90] These benefits would be increased when the other plants, particularly those included in the plans for the new Deepwater dyestuff operations, developed raw materials for paints, like linseed oil, chemical colors, and organic chemicals. Such advantages should place the company in a good competitive position and assure a satisfactory return on investment.

The Executive Committee gave even less attention to the problems of marketing than had the Development Department. It did accept the Department's recommendation to "acquire by purchase one or more suitable going concerns, if obtainable at figures indicating a profitable return on investment, with a view to transfer of operations to Parlin at the first opportune moment." Yet, even here, the need to buy experience in manufacturing appears to have been considered much more important than to obtain marketing techniques and facilities. Partly because of this decision and partly because of the continuing need for basic chemicals and other supplies, the du Pont Company, late in 1916, bought the Harrison Bros. & Co., a large integrated concern with plants in Philadelphia, Newark, and Chicago which, besides making paints, had a large sulphuric capacity and also controlled bauxite and sulphur mines in the South. However, the need to assure supplies of essential materials, added to the desire for diversification, gave du Pont personnel and facilities in the paint industry that were too extensive to be easily transferred to the smokeless powder works after the war.

The Final Definition of the Strategy of Diversification

The entry into the paint business helped to bring the Development Department and the Executive Committee to a reappraisal of the objectives of their diversification policies. Up to this time, the emphasis had been on the best use of existing plant capacity. Investigation continued to show the difficulty of finding one product or group of products that could take up the available capacity. Therefore, the Department's senior officers, R. R. M. Carpenter and Walter S. Carpenter, decided that the company should investigate businesses which would put to use all types of resources —talents, equipment, and capital—in the whole du Pont organization rather than primarily the facilities of individual plants. The reasons for the change in policy are best summarized in a resolution which R. R. M. Carpenter recommended and which the Executive Committee passed in February, 1917:

> "WHEREAS, the Development Department has, during the past eighteen months, been engaged in the matter of finding industries allied and otherwise to our organization which will be capable of utilizing our military powder plants after the war, and
>
> WHEREAS, this study develops the fact that there are no industries which will be likely to use more than 25% to 30% of the value (costs) of these plants, and
>
> WHEREAS, it has been developed that there are industries which can utilize much more extensively our organization and at the same time offer good returns;
>
> RESOLVED that it is the sense of the Executive Committee, and that the Development Department be advised as follows:—
>
> That from the studies made and reported in detail to this Committee, the Executive Committee are of the opinion that the energies of the Devel-

opment Department should therefore be in the direction of employing our organization to the full and that their efforts be confined, especially as to future action, to the development of the following industries:—

1 — Dyestuff and allied organic chemicals
2 — Vegetable oil industry
3 — Paint and Varnish
4 — Water Soluble Chemicals
5 — Industries related to Cellulose and Cotton purification.[91]

This new definition of the company's policy of diversification led to the continuing purchase of paint firms during the spring of 1917, firms which included the Becton Chemical Company, manufacturers of lithopone, and Cawley, Clark & Co., both of Newark, and the Bridgeport Wood Finishing Company in Connecticut. Despite low profits and actual losses in the paint business, the Development Department in the spring of 1918 recommended the continuing of building of a full line of paint products; and the Executive Committee approved the purchase of plants at Flint, Michigan, and in Everett, Massachusetts. The first of these concentrated on supplying the automobile trade; the second, like the Bridgeport concern, handled varnishes for interior work. Later in the year, plans for further expansion and consolidation in the paint business were dropped because of increasing marketing difficulties and continuing losses.[92]

Except for expansion in the paint industry, the entry of the United States into the war slowed down the diversification program. Energies were again turned mainly to increasing explosives production. Nevertheless, by November, 1917, the Development Department reported some progress in other areas beside paint.[93] The dyestuffs operations at Deepwater had been transferred from the Development Department to an operating department. New plants had been added at the Deepwater Works. Both the Development and the operating departments were concentrating attention on organic chemicals other than those used specifically for dyes. A cream of tartar plant had been set up at Hopewell. Work had begun on water-soluble chemicals and acids at Hopewell, Harrison, and other recently purchased paint plants. The Department had decided to concentrate its wood-pulp and paper-product development at Hopewell. Only the vegetable-oil group still remained in the investigating stage. The Department also continued its study of the possibilities of moving into artificial silk. Negotiations were opened with the American Viscose Company but were dropped because of the "extraordinary price asked for goodwill and business opportunity."[94] For the time being, the company made no effort to look into other chemically based fields for expansion.

In December, 1917, the du Pont Company purchased 27.6 per cent of the available General Motors stock. The motives for this purchase became a major issue in the recent du Pont-General Motors antitrust suit. Evidence presented at the trial fails to indicate that anyone besides John J. Raskob, the company's Treasurer, saw the matter as more than an investment for war profits and a place to locate some managerial personnel who might not be absorbed by the expansion into chemical-based industries. The suggestion for the purchase of General Motors stock came from Raskob and the Treasurer's Department.[95] The Development Department, which had played the critical role in determining the direction of the diversification program, had no part in this move and, in fact, appears to have been strongly adverse to it.[96]

At the end of the war and with the rapid contraction of the explosive business, the company continued to move into the new industries outlined in the 1917 resolutions. Because utilization of the Hopewell Works continued to present difficulties, the company formed a subsidiary in 1919 to sell its properties there.[97] With that sale, the water-soluble or heavy-chemical program was somewhat curtailed, and the wood-pulp and paper plans dropped. Further investigation indicated that the vegetable-oil industry would not provide a good return on investment. So, by the spring of 1919, the du Pont Company was firmly established in the chemical, paint and varnish, pyroxylin (Celluloid), and artificial leather business as well as explosives. Dyestuffs were still in the development stage. Later in the year, the Executive Committee finally decided to take the plunge into the manufacturing of artificial silk or rayon.[98]

By 1919, then, the du Pont Company was rapidly changing the nature of its business. Where before the war it had still concentrated on a single line of goods, by the first year of peace it was fabricating many different products whose manufacture was closely related to the making of nitrocellulose for smokeless powder but which sold in many very different markets and in some cases used new types of supplies and materials. This strategy of product diversification was a direct response to the threat of having unused resources. The need to find new work for existing resources, beginning with the loss of government orders in 1908 and greatly intensified by the coming of World War I, made senior executives increasely aware of the potentialities of nitrocellulose technology for the development of new products that might employ existing plant and personnel more profitably than the making and selling of explosives. These potentialities became clearer as the company's top command came to realize that their personnel, trained in the techniques of nitrocellulose technology and in the methods of administrating far-flung industrial activities, was an even more valuable resource than their physical plant and equipment. Yet, in carrying out a policy of diversification to assure the long-term use of existing resources, the same executives failed to see a relation between strategy and structure. They realized clearly that structure was essential to combine and integrate these several resources into effective production, but they did not raise the question of whether a structure created to make and sell a single line of goods would be adequate to handle several new and different products for new and different markets.

New Structure for the New Strategy

The essential difficulty was that diversification greatly increased the demands on the company's administrative offices. Now the different departmental headquarters had to coordinate, appraise, and plan policies and procedures for plants, or sales offices, or purchasing agents, or technical laboratories in a number of quite different industries. The development of plans and the appraisal of activities were made harder because executives with experience primarily in explosives were making decisions about paints, varnishes, dyes, chemicals, and plastic products. Coordination became more complicated because different products called for different types of standards, procedures, and policies.[99] For although the technological and administrative needs of the new lines had many fundamental similarities, there were critical dissimilarities.

The central office was even more overwhelmed than the departments by the increased administrative needs resulting from diversification. Broad goals and policies had to be determined for and resources allocated to functional activities, not in one industry but in several. Appraisal of departments performing in diverse fields became exceedingly complex. Interdepartmental coordination grew comparably more troublesome. The manufacturing personnel and the marketers tended to lose contact with each other and so failed to work out product improvements and modifications to meet changing demands and competitive developments. Coordinating the schedules of production and purchasing on the basis of market demand was more difficult for several lines than for one, particularly when the statistical offices at du Pont had no experience in estimating types of markets other than explosives and when little of this sort of analysis had been tried by anyone in the industries du Pont had entered. Also in 1919, no one in the du Pont Company had been assigned the overall responsibility for compiling and acting on these forecasts in order to maintain an even and steady use of company facilities by preventing the piling up of excessive inventories in any one department. Each of the three major departments — Purchasing, Manufacturing, and Sales — made its own estimates and set its own schedules.

New Problems Created by New Strategy

While these administrative strains became quickly apparent, the adoption of a new structure came only when the sharp depression of 1920 and 1921 made its need painfully obvious. The poor performance of some of the company's new ventures provided the first warning of these difficulties. Even in the boom year of 1919, many new products had failed to return the expected profits. Paints were actually showing serious losses. In 1917, the company recorded a loss of $108,720 on a gross sale of $1,265,328 in its paint and varnish business. In 1918, the loss was $321,492 on a gross of $2,958,999, and in 1919, the final reckoning was to show a still larger loss on a larger gross—$489,337 on $4,015,769. "The more paint and varnish we sold," one report wryly noted, "the more money we lost."[100]

Such performance was especially disturbing because the du Ponts had assumed that large volume would bring profits through lowering unit costs. This was indeed one reason why they had moved so readily into the paint business. The industry at that time was made up of many small, nonintegrated, highly competitive firms. Sherwin-Williams was the only large integrated enterprise. Du Pont had anticipated an "opportunity for consolidation and economy in such an industry, as there were no particular secret processes, patents, or other causes which would interfere with a new concern engaging in that business, but that the advantages of careful business management on a large scale would be fully realized." Yet in 1919, when they were losing money, many of the smaller paint companies were enjoying one of their most profitable years.

While the story in other new businesses was less bleak, profits were still well below expectations. Those products which, like paints, were sold in small lots to retailers or ultimate consumers, were turning in the poorest showing. For example, the small return on finished articles helped bring the estimated return on investment in the du Pont's pyroxylin business down from an estimated 21.06 per cent in 1916 to 10.95 per cent in 1917 and 6.60 per cent in 1918.[101]

Selling, nearly all agreed, raised the most difficult problems. The manufacturing of the new lines used many of the same materials and processes as explosives, but there was little similarity in their marketing. Before the end of the summer of 1919, Frederick W. Pickard, the Vice-President in charge of Sales, had already outlined the problem to the Executive Committee. "The expansion of the du Pont organization into various lines of activity logical from the manufacturing standpoint," Pickard wrote, "has produced a sales condition which compels consideration of a wider variety of products which have no logical sales connection with one another."[102]

The greatest problems had resulted, Pickard believed from trying to administer different kinds of marketing activities. "The clearest line of demarcation seems to be between merchandising and tonnage distribution," as "entirely different methods of selling are applied to these two general classes of distribution." Before the war, Pickard continued, "95% of the business was distributed, whether to consumers or dealers, on a tonnage basis." With the move into new lines, particularly through the purchase of the Harrison paint and varnish and the Arlington cellulose products businesses, the company had taken over the selling of a variety of small, packaged goods for use by the ultimate consumer. The result of this "forcible introduction to the merchandising game," the Sales Department chief admitted, "to date has been negative rather than positive." To redress the balance would not be easy. The marketing of consumer goods demanded a new and more extensive type of advertising "with a direct appeal to the customer," and the creation of an enlarged national distributing organization including, possibly, even retail outlets.

Product diversification offered the company three marketing alternatives, Pickard reasoned. It could energetically push the "expansion of merchandising effort on a national scale" for the new lines of consumer goods. It might withdraw and sell out these lines to outsiders, or it might retain its present "'middle of the road' policy, namely; continuing to merchandise those of our lines which are now handled in that way but without extending their scope or endeavoring to develop other lines."

The first course would be expensive. The Vice-President in charge of Sales pointed out that a national advertising campaign alone could run from three to five years at a cost of three to five million dollars a year. In addition, this alternative would "require a large expenditure for special packing plants, storage warehouses, and distributing facilities. The working capital account of the company would be tremendously increased." The second course, a more conservative one, might keep the company from profitable areas and from making the most of its production facilities, its trained personnel, and other resources. The third alternative, Pickard reasoned, could only be temporary: "Like most compromises it is the easiest way, and my personal feeling is that, except as a temporary expedient, it is unsound economically and, if adopted, should be for the purpose of experiment and observation to enable us to reach more accurate conclusions a year or two hence than we can arrive at now."

To decide between such alternatives proved exceedingly difficult. The executives within the Sales Department had been unable to come to a conclusion on a satisfactory course of action. Moreover such a decision was of major significance for the future of the company. Pickard therefore urged the Executive Committee appoint a subcommittee of representatives of the four grand divisions — Production, Sales, Treasurer's, and

Development—to make a thorough study of the problems and possible solutions.

The Problems Analyzed

The Executive Committee immediately formed such a subcommittee of the heads of the Sales, Treasurer's, and Development Departments—Pickard, Donaldson Brown, and Walter Carpenter—and A. Felix du Pont, General Manager of the Explosives Manufacturing Department.[103] These men, too busy to give the necessary attention to the critical problems, then selected a sub-subcommittee of one able representative from each department plus one of the President's assistants. After six months of fairly intensive work, these five men submitted a report to their seniors on March 16, 1920. Their work and the resulting report had an impact far beyond the company's immediate marketing difficulties: for the first time a new form of management structure was proposed.

The investigation had been carried out in the methodical, rational manner that had become a hallmark of the du Pont way of doing business. First, both the subcommittee and its sub-subcommittee were careful to define just what they meant by merchandise, industrial, and jobbers trade. Then they made a detailed study of outside experience. A Mr. Boyd of the Curtis Publishing Company came to Wilmington to give them "a brief dissertation on advertising and merchandising in general." Next, after examining a list of companies with market activities comparable with their own, the members of the sub-subcommittee decided to study the activities and to interview the managers of eight leading industrial enterprises. These included Armour and International Harvester, which the Haskell Committee had looked into the previous winter, and also Johns-Manville, Scovill Manufacturing, Aluminum Company of America, Procter & Gamble, Colgate & Company, and United States Tire Company.

The interviews failed to provide much specific data useful for answering the du Pont Company's immediate problems, for none of these companies had so diversified a product line as du Pont's. But the survey did furnish some useful general information. "In general, we concluded that each company seems to have its own problem and that in management they tend to follow a single controlling head over their manufacturing and sales departments." The sub-subcommittee members also found that those firms which produced both semifinished and finished goods transferred the bulk goods to the finishing division "either at a fixed profit or at market prices." This question had been raised because diversification had made interdivisional billing a much more complex problem at du Pont since the divisions making finished products bought many of their raw materials, such as nitrocellulose and chemicals, from other units within the company. Finally, the managers of the visited companies usually stressed the need for "very careful attention to the minutest detail and the exercise of considerable patience and perseverance in following every item."

With its background studies completed, the sub-subcommittee then turned to considering Pickard's alternatives. In determining whether to expand, contract, or continue the company's merchandising business, it decided to look at the different lines individually and to concentrate on pyroxylin, chemicals, paint, and varnishes. Explosives and Fabrikoid products were currently profitable and were sold almost entirely by bulk, while dyes were still not developed enough commercially to make an investigation worthwhile. In its recommendations on the individual lines, this committee decided that a return of 15 per cent "on total capital invested" was to be considered an "ideal profit." In determining profit, the "transfer of products from bulk to article branches [that is the transfer from raw or semifinished materials to the final manufacturing units] shall be based on the market price with some adjustment." On the basis of the resulting analysis, a number of detailed recommendations were made as to which lines should be maintained, dropped, or expanded.

The more general findings of the committee were of greater significance. First, cost and other statistics clearly demonstrated the critical difference between tonnage and merchandise sales. Nearly all the semifinished products — Pyralin rods and sheets, pyroxylin, pigments, acids and heavy chemicals, and bulk paint shipments — made a reasonable profit, while almost all of the finished packaged products for the ultimate consumer returned less than 15 per cent on investment, many of them even showing a heavy net loss.[104] Second, except for celluloid cuffs and collars, these same finished-goods businesses — paints, varnishes, Celluloid articles, pharmaceuticals, ether and Pyralin chemicals, household cement, and solvents — were at this time prosperous. In other words, where du Pont was losing money, others were making profits.

On the basis of these findings, the sub-subcommittee came to the conclusion early in 1920 that the underlying problem was not one of selling but organization. In the paint and varnish business and in the making of finished Celluloid articles, the company's competitors had "no advantage over us in the purchase of raw materials, and no secret process, no patents preventing us from using the best method of manufacture." Therefore, the sub-subcommittee concluded, "the factor or factors making this great difference between our success in the articles and paint and varnish lines are entirely within ourselves."

"The method of carrying on the business is through its organization," the committee continued in its final report. In the du Pont Company's paint and articles business it found "an excellent line of responsibility for carrying on each of the functions of the business," but "we have been unable to find the exact responsibility for profits." In other words, the activities of each line within each functional department were effectively managed, but no one was responsible for administering them so as to assure a profit on each individual line of products:

> We do not find any competitors who are carrying on these two businesses in this same manner in which we are doing, that is, in no case do they have a divided control, and in all cases have a central control. Are we prepared therefore to say that our method of organization is suitable to these businesses?

In the development within the du Pont Company of new products like dyes and, in the previous few months, artificial silk, responsibility both for manufacturing and sales had been combined in order to meet new and different problems. Were not the paint and articles lines, "although established businesses, somewhat in the same position in respect to the du Pont Company? Will not the same treatment, for a time at least, assist in solving the problem?"

A New Structure Proposed and Rejected

Thereupon, the sub-subcommittee recommended strongly a fundamental change in structure: make product rather than function the basis of the organization; take the offices handling purchasing, manufacturing, marketing, and accounting for paints and varnishes and for Pyralin and Celluloid articles out of existing offices and place each of the two lines under one executive responsible for all four functions as well as for profit and performance. The committee then drew up an organization chart to indicate how these two divisions could be "practically self-contained" units. In each unit, the managing director would have his own purchasing, accounting, manufacturing, and sales departments. The last two offices the committee subdivided into merchandising and bulk operations, each headed by an assistant manager (see Chart 4).

Under the new plan, the Executive Committee would have general supervision over the managers of the proposed divisions. These new units would be line organizations; that is, the line of authority would run from the President to the division's General Manager and then through him and his assistants to the heads of the functional units within the division. The staff departments in the central office would have an advisory relationship to the new divisions. In the words of the report:

> The Managing Director of each of the branches will report directly to the Executive Committee in such manner as they may prescribe; and the

CHART 4

First Proposal of a Decentralized Structure

In report of sub-subcommittee, March 16, 1920

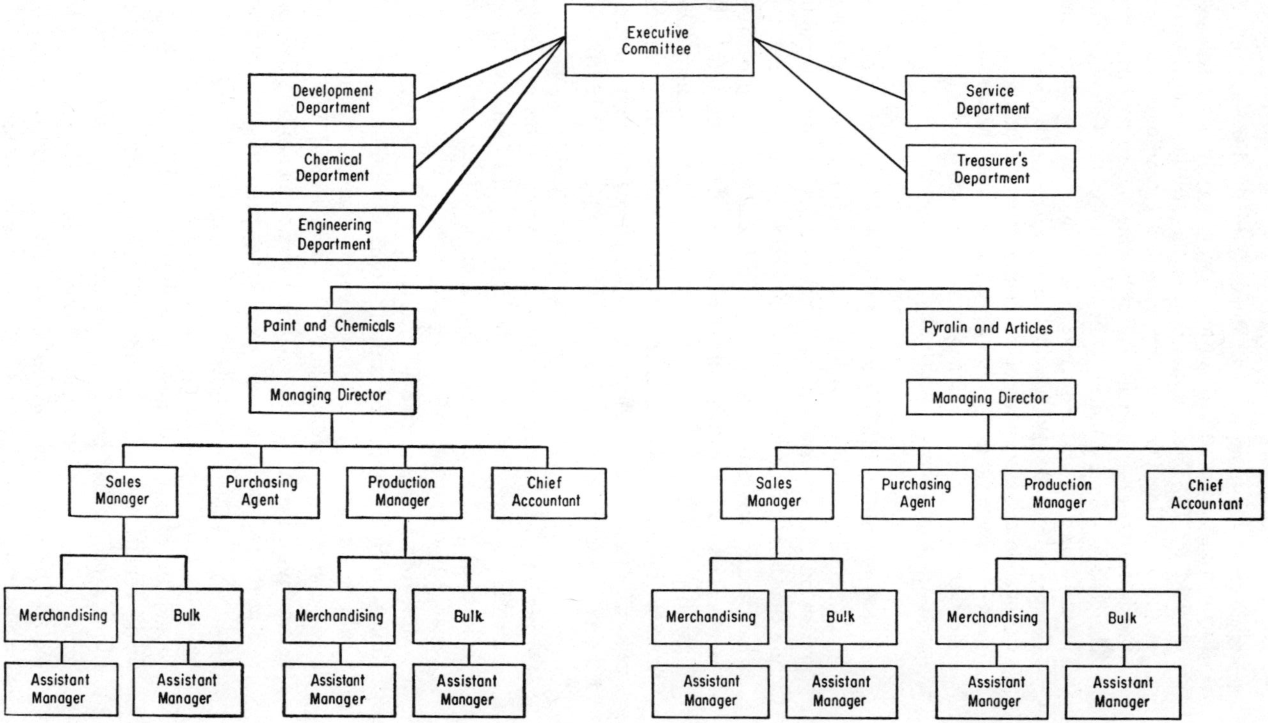

> relations of his Company (or Division) to the Development, Chemical, Engineering and Service Departments will be entirely through the Managing Director and these general departments will be used at the discretion of the Managing Director. Any additional expenditures for the business, that is, further experimental work or looking well to the future, are general charges and will be handled at the discretion of the Committee out of the profits turned in by the particular sub-companies or sub-divisions as the Companies may be. We would like to see as far as possible a monthly compilation of the standing of each business with respect to its own balance sheet if possible, so that within a week or so after the first of each month the General Manager will know the exact condition of his business in respect to the profits for which he is responsible.

These recommendations made by relatively young but experienced departmental executives provided the basic conception not only for the present du Pont management structure but for the multidivisional structure that has become widely used in American industry. But a year and a half had to pass before the proposals were accepted and put into action. Members of both the subcommittee on the marketing problem and the Executive Committee itself had strong objections to them. One senior member made his views clear in penciled notations on the margin of the report. In this critic's opinion, the proposed structure ran counter to "the theory of our present organization," based as it was on functional specialization. Second, the subcommittee had failed to show exactly: "Where is the benefit of the reorganization?" A week later he, or another critic, said: "The report cites the agency for solving ills (namely, change in organization) though does not cite ills or how [they are] to be cured by a change in organization."[105]

Moreover, this executive was certain that the recent losses were the almost inevitable result of moving into new businesses and that they would be rectified with the development of proper administrative procedures and reliable information. "We have carried excessive stock," he noted, "we have made several unfortunate guesses on the purchase of raw materials," or have been "working against orders rather than setting up appropriate stocks." Selling expenses have been too high, the company has taken too many small orders, and "while our business has been large enough for economical business, we have been scattered ver a [*sic*] wide field." Finally, the rationalizing and systematizing of the new manufacturing processes had been expensive and were still not completed. "Our rearrangements, repairs, renewals, and replacements of plants have been high." There were still "miscellaneous shortcomings in factory operations such as poor routing, and inefficient piece-work, pay schedules, short-runs, etc."

The answer was not reorganization but better information and knowledge. It was not the development of new offices and new lines of authority and responsibility but rather the fashioning of more effective inventory controls, or more accurate volumes, sales, and market figures, and of other data to flow through the existing lines of communication. Such information would help prevent unnecessary purchasing and make it possible to find just where the high manufacturing and selling expenses were located. Because of these views, the subcommittee's senior members deleted all of the sub-subcommittee's analyses and recommendations on organization when it forwarded the report to the Executive Committee.[106]

Nevertheless, the suggestions made by the more junior men were discussed among the company's executives, and within a few weeks the Executive Committee appointed another special committee, made up of Donaldson Brown, William S. Spruance — the Vice-President in charge of Production — and Pickard, to study the whole question of organization. By June, these three senior executives had come to substantially the same position as had the sub-subcommittee. On July 8, 1920, they recommended an extension of the early proposals for the paint and pyroxylin businesses to all of the company's lines. Related products in one industry were to be gathered together into self-contained segregated units each under a single general manager who had the authority for all operations and was responsible for profits. This form of organization not only would provide the essential coordination between purchasing, production, and sales, but, as the committee stressed, "affords more direct and logical control of the investment of Working Capital," which could now be separated for each of the major lines.[107]

The new committee on organization also spelled out in more detail the relations between the proposed product divisions and the auxiliary department at headquarters. While the executives in the staff departments were to have no direct authority over divisional activities, they were still to have a part in the administration of the new divisions:

> Directors of staff should be able to establish and maintain general policies, procedures and correlation of the functional activities of like-named units of the departmental organizations to a degree sufficient to insure proper uniformity and efficiency. . . . It is assumed that advisory functional staff officials will employ periodical and special meetings of appropriate officials of the line departments to establish and maintain general policies and procedures, . . . and [will] discuss and advise regarding special major problems.

President Irénée du Pont raised objections to the findings in this report. He disliked abandoning the proven "principle of specialization." [108] The steady growth of the company's efficiency had resulted, he maintained, from "having specialists in charge of the various departments." So he turned the report back to the committee for further study. When that body resubmitted an enlarged report with substantially the same proposals in November, 1920, the President, traditionally having the final say on organizational matters, again vetoed them.

Irénée had strong justification for his position. The old ways had, until very recently, worked exceptionally well. Any professional writer or expert on organization of that day would have endorsed his views completely, as, indeed, did many men in the company, including both his brothers, Pierre and Lammot. Moreover, as President, he, not the men proposing them, would have to carry the responsibility for these fundamental changes.

A Compromise Structure Adopted

Faced with such skepticism about the radical new plan, Pickard and other executives began to seek ways to administer more effectively the activities of those units that handled the same line of products in the different functional departments. During the fall, Pickard and Walter Carpenter had encouraged three men — one from the Sales Department, another from the Manufacturing, and a third from the Development Department — to meet "unofficially and without portfolio" to consider ways of improving the company's performance in the paint business.[109] One of the three, Frank S. MacGregor, had been the Development Department's representative and chairman of the sub-subcommittee that had made the initial proposals for reorganization. This informal "council," as the three called themselves, had worked up some detailed plans by November, 1920. Then, at the Executive Committee meeting of the 23rd of that month, four days after Irénée had turned down for the second time the organization committee's recommendations, Pickard suggested and the Executive Committee agreed to formalization of this paint "council." On December 10, Pickard forwarded the report of the group to the Executive Committee.

The council's report did not concern itself explicitly with organization. Instead it was encouragingly titled "A Plan to Make 10% on Our Paint and Varnish Net Sales." The report began by pointing out that in 1919 the company had "lost nearly $500,000 in actual cash in addition to an expected return on investment of nearly $500,000 which made a total loss of income to the Company of nearly a million," and that most of these losses were on over-the-counter merchandising sales. The performance for the current year was little better, and the forecast for 1921 indicated a probable loss of $800,000. The council then suggested a number of specific ways by which to turn this loss into a profit. It provided excellent detailed figures on the costs of raw materials and production and selling expenses, and indicated just how these might be cut. Such action, however, would require that "the responsibility of profits and the control of the business be in [the] same place," and this place should be "a council composed of the paint sales director, the paint production assistant director, and a neutral member."

The Executive Committee, apparently impressed by the specific nature of the suggestions, approved the plan. It is not surprising that the same men who had written the report were appointed to the new council or, as it came to be called, the Paint Steering Committee. MacGregor, as its chairman, was given full responsibility for du Pont's performance in the paint and varnish business.

Only a week after the Paint Steering Committee had been approved, Pickard and his associate on the subcommittee on organization, William Spruance, broadened the council idea to include most of the company's activities.[110] Again they did not raise the question of organization, but rather made their recommendations in a report on statistical controls. That October (1920), Treasurer Donaldson Brown, the third member of the subcommittee on organization, had pointed out that the growing postwar recession was showing deficiencies in current statistical methods. These had, after all, been developed to meet the requirements of the explosives industry, not those of the new businesses. Inventory control based on three-month forecasts had failed to prevent losses from overbuying of gray goods for Fabrikoid production and from similar overstocking of both raw materials and finished goods in other products. Moreover, several executives had been insisting that the company's present need was for better information rather than for a new organization. At Brown's urging, Spruance and Pickard were assigned to study the existing statistical controls. Brown did not join these men in their final report to the Executive Committee on December 22, for he was then preparing to leave the company to join Pierre du Pont, who three weeks earlier had taken over the presidency of General Motors. As their colleagues undoubtedly expected, Pickard and Spruance insisted that the real problem was not statistics but organization.

The current data were adequate enough, but were not properly utilized. The channels for the flow of this information for the different product lines were not yet clearly defined. This was primarily because each major functional department developed its own statistics.

> The statistical scheme, so far as quarterly forecasts are concerned, rests upon three independent series of calculations, i.e., the sales forecast, the forecast of the manufacturing program, and the estimated cost of materials which

> will be consumed in carrying out the manufacturing program. These calculations are furnished respectively by the Sales, Production, and Purchasing Departments. Your Committee feels that in the absence of any formal and recognized procedure for the consideration of these calculations jointly by the three interested departments there has been, and there is likely to be, a failure on the part of management to forecast or to carry out a unified business program, as well as to take advantage properly of changes in the business situation as they affect the program of one or more of our industries.

Also under the 1919 plan, the Manufacturing Department had been given full responsibility for inventory control, but such control, the report pointed out, must be the joint responsibility of all three departments. Therefore, in order to "obtain the maximum benefit from the statistical scheme," the two men proposed the creation of "industry councils" for each major product similar to the one already started in paints. Each related line of goods would be managed by a Divisional Council that would include the executive in the Sales, Manufacturing, and Purchasing Departments most concerned with that line:

> These Divisional Councils by uniform, proper, and definite delegation of authority by the Heads of these Departments respectively, and without in any way interfering with the functional responsibility or authority of the Departments in their own spheres of action, can exercise the necessary joint control of the business program which is embodied in the quarterly forecasts and harmoniously and effectively carry it out.

To check on the Divisional Councils' work and to resolve any issues arising among the junior executives, Pickard and Spruance further proposed similar councils of Departmental Directors and Vice-Presidents.

The plan for Divisional Councils was thus under attempt to redefine the channels of authority and communication in order to assure more effective administration of the company's diversified product lines. Pickard and Spruance proposed that

> sufficient authority be delegated to the members of the Divisional Councils to permit them, when there is complete agreement, to settle problems concerning the immediate control of the particular industry. In reaching a conclusion it would be their duty to call upon appropriate individuals in other functional departments of the Company, such as the Assistant Treasurer (Forecast and Analysis), the Economic Statistician, the Assistant Director of Materials and Products Division of the Service Department, or the Development, Chemical, or Engineering Department's representatives when these representatives were needed.

Where the members disagreed, after consulting the staff executives, the matter was to go to the Departmental and, if necessary, to the Vice-Presidential Councils. In this way the Councils, in much the same way as the divisions proposed earlier by the sub-subcommittee on marketing problems, were to assure coordination of the different functional activities for each "industry" or major product line. They were to be responsible, for example, for the coordination of product flow through the departments by deciding the level of inventories and volume of orders within each functional department's headquarters.

The Councils were to appraise and to plan as well as to coordinate. They were to develop and apply standards of controls over capital expenditures, apply budget systems for controlling operating expenses, outline plans for chemical and engineering experimental work, and devise "additional plans for expansion of the business." In fact Pickard and Spruance believed the interfunctional product committees could administer all the company's operational activities and make most of its tactical decisions. These committees could handle "nearly all the routine matters concerning immediate control of each industry, with the minimum of delayed decisions or failures to agree on action," and would further "ensure the desirable degree of exchange of ideas and information of mutual direct and indirect interests."

The three members of each Divisional Council were to meet frequently, in fact daily, if possible. A permanent secretary would keep a record of the meetings and make brief monthly reports to the Executive Committee on important decisions taken during the previous months, on general current conditions, and on the outlook for the future. The Councils differed from the Paint Steering Committee and from the divisions proposed earlier in that no departmental representative was made chairman or general manager of the Council, and in that the members were under the supervision of their seniors rather than given full autonomy. The Councils, indeed, would create a type of committee government for most of the du Pont Company's activities.

The Executive Committee immediately accepted the Pickard and Spruance proposals. As 1921 opened, the du Pont Company was beginning to move toward a *de facto* structure based on product divisions rather than functional departments. The senior executives soon came to consider the new Divisional Councils (High Explosives, Blasting Powder, Blasting Supplies, Commercial Smokeless, Colors and Pigments, Pyralin, Acids and Chemicals, Pyralin Chemicals, and Fabrikoid), the Paint and Varnish Steering Committee, and the Dyestuff Department as similar units. For example, in March, 1921, all of these groups were asked to submit the same type of uniform monthly reports.[111]

Of the new coordinating committees, the Paint and Varnish was the most active, and this was because one man alone had full responsibility for its work. MacGregor began by making a number of organization changes—eliminating and combining offices in the sections dealing with paints in the Sales, Production, and Purchasing Departments.[112] Under this control, the paint and varnish business began to improve. At least, the losses lessened. Nevertheless no one suggested, during the winter and spring of 1921, that the example of the paint unit be followed by giving a single executive full responsibility for any one of the nine Councils. In fact, the subcommittee on organization agreed in May that the new Council system was working well, and on its recommendation the Executive Committee voted to continue the current scheme for at least a year.

Crisis and the Acceptance of the Multidivisional Structure

This compromise structure lasted, however, only until September. The company's financial statement for the first half of 1921 provided the shock that finally precipitated a major reorganization. In those six months, as the postwar recession become increasingly severe, the company had lost money on every product except explosives. At the end of the first six months, the profits from explosives had been close to $2,500,000, but the losses for the other products had been over $3,800,000.[113] The largest deficit, over a million, came from the Dyestuffs Department. Paints added a loss of $717,356; cellulose products $746,360; and Fabrikoid $863,904. When other items, such as interest, were taken into account, the total net loss for the six-month period was $2,433,491.

The Executive Committee's regular review of the semiannual operating statistics brought home to it the need for structural changes. Halfway measures were clearly not enough. The six-month performance had been one of the worst in the company's long history. The strategy of diversification seemed to promise little more than difficulties and deficits. Pickard's opening remarks at the Executive Committee meeting of August 2 revealed a sense of crisis. He urged the appointment of a "dictator." [114] He had long been advocating a new long-term scheme of reorganization, the senior sales executive reminded the Committee, but this was no time to make such a complicated change. Rather, the company needed a single man with "absolute jurisdiction over personnel" and with full authority to do what he could to meet the crisis. "What is needed," he insisted, "is decision and action and that you get from an individual and not from an organization of talent such as is seated around this table." The other members agreed. Even Spruance, who felt that the Council system should be given more of a trial, felt that while "it had improved matters, it had fallen short of what should be accomplished by other means." The Committee discussed the alternatives for some time, then decided to take no action until its next regular meeting when the President, who was out of town, would be back in Wilmington.

Before that meeting, however, H. Fletcher Brown, manager of the Smokeless Powder Department from 1911 to 1919, had written a letter based on his second thoughts and probably those of some of his colleagues.[115] His letter, clearly outlining the situation and the alternatives, became a guide for the top committee's major decisions in the following weeks. After going over the company's financial position, Brown emphasized that: "The trouble with the Company is right here in Wilmington, and the failure is the failure of administration for which we, as Directors, are responsible." Du Pont had had little trouble until it began to diversify. After the war it "made money for a year because of a temporary spurt in business. It is now losing money very fast, partly on account of inventory losses which still continue, partly on account of our inexperience in the dyestuffs business, and partly because of the failure of our organization to adjust itself to present conditions." The adjustment, Brown continued, called for two remedies. The centralized functionally departmentalized organization structure should be completely replaced by the one recommended in the previous year. Second, the Executive Committee should not be made up of operating executives.

The Executive Committee was weak, Brown believed, largely because it could not be objectively critical and analytical and because its members were unable to get an over-all picture of the Company's needs and problems:

> The Executive Committee has failed and will continue to fail because, although it is held responsible for results, it is not properly constituted and it lacks authority. With the exception of the Chairman, all members of the Executive Committee are Heads of Departments, and in accordance with custom the members usually refrain from discussing in their meetings the affairs of any one Department. The Committee member at the head of any one Department is moreover in no position to investigate or criticize the work of another Department. It has never been found practicable for this Committee to discuss and control the conduct of affairs of any one Department. Furthermore it is unreasonable to expect that a majority of the members will be able to subject their own Departments to such self-examination and criticism so that the Company as a whole will operate efficiently. The various Departments of the Company lack an adequate directing and co-ordinating force at the present time, without which success is impossible. The Executive Committee furthermore lacks authority. Its careful study of our organization last year resulted in a well thought-out plan for managing the various industries. The plan was vetoed by our President who, according to our custom, exercises the prerogative of decid-

ing all questions of organization. The Executive Committee may well find itself unable to produce satisfactory results under such conditions and limitations.

We have handed over the details of management of this business to the third-line men who form our Divisional Councils. They have come up against the stone wall of excessive cost and extravagance and have appealed to us for help.

The present emergency, Brown concluded, demanded the abolition of the present Finance and Executive Committees and the appointment of a new small combined top committee. This committee should be of five men, "no one whom shall be the Head of any Department of this Company." In this way the Department Head would be able to "give his undivided attention to the details of his own Department," and "the Executive Committee will direct and control the operations of the Company as a whole."

On August 22, 1921, nearly all the senior executives in the company met at a joint meeting of the Executive and Finance Committees. Even Pierre du Pont and Raskob left their busy General Motors affairs to attend.[116] The group quickly agreed on Fletcher Brown's suggestions and then asked him to draw up, with Pickard and Spruance, members of the old subcommittee on organization, plans for a structural reorganization. The three immediately brought forth from the subcommittee's files the earlier proposals for dividing the company into five product or Industrial Departments and eight staff or Auxiliary Departments plus the Treasurer's Department. The only additional change proposed was to reshape the Executive Committee in the way Brown had outlined (see Chart 5).

Their final report fully described the functions of the proposed divisions and the new general office.[117] The report did not follow Brown's suggestion of uniting the Finance and Executive Committees, but rather specifically recommended that they remain separated. This was probably because Pierre, and other du Pont officials and large stockholders no longer actively connected with day-to-day affairs of the company, still wanted to have a place to check on its activities and performance. No department head or other executive with operating responsibilities was to sit on the new Executive Committee for the very reasons Brown had proffered. Nor was any member except for its Chairman to sit on the Finance Committee. The Executive Committee was to concentrate on the administration of the Company as a whole and was to be responsible for its ultimate performance.

While the members of the new committee, with no direct operating duties, were to concentrate on over-all planning, appraisal, and coordination, each was also to help oversee one set of functional activities in all five of the new product division. In carrying out these last duties, the committee members were to act only in an advisory way. In the report's words:

> It is our opinion, furthermore, that no member of the Executive Committee should have the direct individual authority or responsibility which he would if he was in charge of one or more functional activities of the Company. His relations to such functions should be advisory only. For example, our plan provides that one member of the Executive Committee, who may be best fitted by experience for his duty, will co-ordinate the sales function by holding regular meetings with appropriate representatives of the five Industrial Departments. At these meetings, sales policies will be discussed and co-ordinated, subject to the Executive Committee as the final authority.

Beside a member for sales, there would be a second one for purchasing, a third for manufacturing, and a fourth for both chemical and engineering development work. The Executive Committee would therefore take over some of the coordination of functional activities which earlier recommendations had proposed should be given to the staff departments.

The report next took up the duties of the General Managers of the new Departments:

> According to this plan, the head of each Industrial Department will have full authority and responsibility for the operation of his industry, subject only to the authority of the Executive Committee as a whole. He will have under him men who will exercise all the line functions necessary for a complete industry, including routine and special purchasing, manufacture, sales, minor construction, normal and logical chemical and engineer operative and experimental laboratory activities, work supplies, cost-keeping routine and analysis, finished products standards and complaints, orders, work planning, routine traffic, trade records and sales expense.

A General Manager was to report to the Executive Committee, which on a regular schedule would analyze departmental reports and discuss them with the manager and his assistants. The Manager's work was to be evaluated on the basis of financial performance in terms of return on investment as defined by Donaldson Brown's formula. Therefore, interdivisional billing appears to have been based on current market prices as first proposed in the sub-subcommittee's report on "Merchandising versus Tonnage Sales."

With the General Managers handling day-to-day administration and the Executive Committee charged with over-all coordination, appraisal, and policy planning, the duties of the eight more specialized functional departments now became wholly to the provision of advice and services, to both the divisional and general offices. The eight departments included

CHART 5:

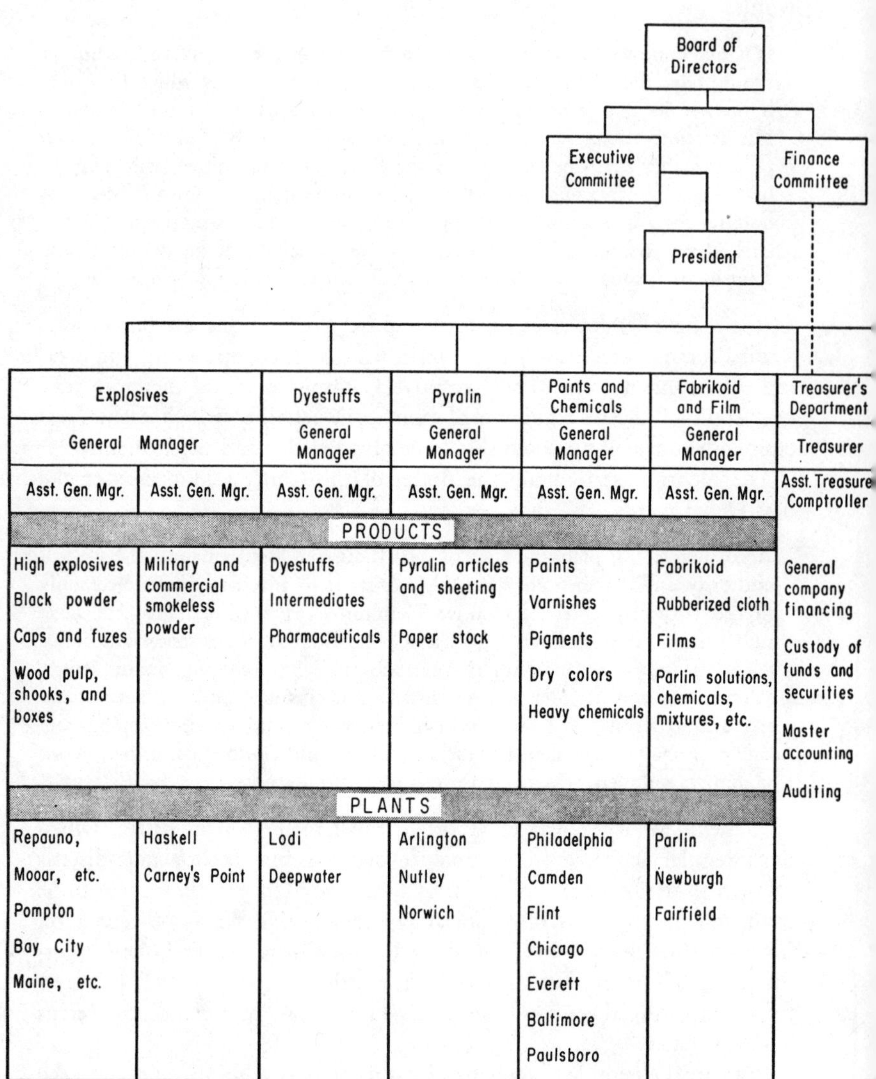
Board of Directors
Executive Committee
Finance Committee
President
Explosives
Dyestuffs
Pyralin
Paints and Chemicals
Fabrikoid and Film
Treasurer's Department
General Manager
General Manager
General Manager
General Manager
General Manager
Treasurer
Asst. Gen. Mgr.
Asst. Gen. Mgr.
Asst. Gen. Mgr.
Asst. Gen. Mgr.
Asst. Gen. Mgr.
Asst. Gen. Mgr.
Asst. Treasure
Comptroller
PRODUCTS
High explosives
Black powder
Caps and fuzes
Wood pulp, shooks, and boxes
Military and commercial smokeless powder
Dyestuffs
Intermediates
Pharmaceuticals
Pyralin articles and sheeting
Paper stock
Paints
Varnishes
Pigments
Dry colors
Heavy chemicals
Fabrikoid
Rubberized cloth
Films
Parlin solutions, chemicals, mixtures, etc.
General company financing
Custody of funds and securities
Master accounting
Auditing
PLANTS
Repauno, Mooar, etc.
Pompton
Bay City
Maine, etc.
Haskell
Carney's Point
Lodi
Deepwater
Arlington
Nutley
Norwich
Philadelphia
Camden
Flint
Chicago
Everett
Baltimore
Paulsboro
Parlin
Newburgh
Fairfield

Proposed Organization for the Du Pont Company, August 31, 1921

AUXILIARY DEPARTMENTS

Legal	Purchasing	Development	Engineering	Chemical	Services	Traffic	Advertising
Chief Counsel	Director of Purchasing	Director	Chief Engineer	Director	Director	Director	Director
Legal and legislative matters	Major purchases and those not special or routine within industrial departments	Expansion and developement studies	Major construction and engineering in the experimental and operative activities	Research laboratory and consulting chemical in the operative and experimental lines	Medical Welfare Real Estate Protection Publicity Salvage and recovery Safety Fire protection General inspection Stationery and printing Mailing	Traffic activities, rate adjustment not carried out within the departments	Advertising

Legal, Purchasing, Development, Engineering, Chemical, Service, Traffic, and Advertising:

> The eight Auxiliary Departments will act as consultants and will also perform staff and service functions for the Company as a whole and for other departments, and in addition will conduct within their departments such activities as may, with the consent of the Industrial Department Heads or the Executive Committee, be so handled in the interests of economy and efficiency. The Executive Committee shall secure proper co-ordination and avoid an unjustifiable degree of specialization in the technical, service, and other functions within the Industrial Departments. Each Auxiliary Department reports individually to the Executive Committee.

Only the Treasurer's Department continued to have some line authority. It would set over-all accounting practices and prescribe the forms for statistical and other regular reports. However, the details of cost accounting were to be left to the General Managers.

The discussion on this report focused on the role of the two departments that could still carry out more than simply service functions—Treasury and Purchasing—and especially on the make-up of the new top committee. Group control, through an Executive Committee of generalists with no operating duties, was a radical departure from past precedents and from the organization theory outlined in the Haskell report of March, 1919. In the discussion over the Executive Committee, there was early agreement that the President and Treasurer, as officers with a general view, should be added to it. The latter, who would still report to the Finance Committee, could supply the statistical and financial information necessary for any major policy decision.[118]

Throughout these meetings in late August and early September, 1921, Irénée du Pont remained skeptical about the underlying concept of the committee. He disliked the abandoning of administration by functional specialists, and he was unhappy about the prospect of group management at the top. "No man on the Executive Committee," he said at one meeting, was "to have individual responsibility." This lack of responsibility would cause difficulties, he felt. Despite this, in deference to the strong opinion of the majority of his colleagues he voted at the same meeting to institute the new committee.[119] Possibly Irénée's protest encouraged the appointment of the President to the Executive Committee, for the President continued to be the individual entrusted with the final responsibility and authority for the company's affairs.

Once the role of the Committee and the Treasurer's Department was decided, the one other point at issue was purchasing. Irénée, Lammot, and most of the other members of the existing top committees agreed that the General Managers should have "full control" over their purchasing. Only Edge, the Vice-President in Charge of Purchasing and Traffic, made a strong plea for continuing centralized purchasing through the existing organization. During a week between meetings on the new plan, he had one of his assistants study the purchasing practices of eleven large companies as well as those of New York City and the federal government. All the institutions investigated, Edge reported, had, or were about to institute, centralized purchasing.[120] Edge's arguments convinced the Committee, and the Purchasing Department was made a separate unit somewhat similar to the Treasurer's Department. However, it was to "close no contract affecting any Department except with the approval of the General Manager and/or the Assistant General Manager."[121] If the department head was certain he could buy to better advantage and was unable to convince the Purchasing Department, then the question would go to the Executive Committee for decision.

Since there was general agreement on all matters except purchasing, the new plan was quickly adopted. The Executive Committee approved it on September 8 and then voted the men for the new posts.[122] Two weeks later the Board of Directors approved all changes. In September, 1921, the du Pont Company put into effect this new structure of autonomous, multidepartmental divisions and a general office with staff specialists and general executives. Each division had its functional departments and its own central office to administer the several departments.

Unencumbered by operating duties, the senior executives at the general office now had the time, information, and more of a psychological commitment to carry on the entrepreneurial activities and make the strategic decisions necessary to keep the over-all enterprise alive and growing and to coordinate, appraise, and plan for the work of the divisions. As the Executive Committee noted in their report to the Board of Directors on the proposed changes, the members of the new committee could "give all their time and effort to the business of the Company as a whole. Being connected with no . . . [division], they will be able to consider all questions or problems without bias or prejudice."[123]

If the general officers were better equipped to handle over-all strategic decisions, the division managers had full authority and the necessary facilities to make the day-to-day tactical ones. As each controlled the functional activities needed for making and selling one major line of products, each could determine, within the framework set and funds allotted by the Executive Committee, the most efficient ways to use the resources at his command. "This type of reorganization fixes responsibility," the final report to the Board continued. "When a man is made responsible for result, his interest is stimulated — hard and effective work follows, which brings success. We believe that the adoption of this plan will bring a tremendous improvement in the morale of the du Pont employees." This was, incidentally, the first time that the planners had suggested that the new type of organization might improve managerial psychology.

The structure accepted in September, 1921, has served the du Pont Company effectively ever since. Losses were soon converted into profits and never again — not even in the middle of the depression of the 1930's — did the company face a crisis as severe as that of 1921. Since that year, new Industrial Departments have been added. There were twelve in 1960, and older ones have been redefined and reshaped. In the last quarter century, only three more Auxiliary Departments have been formed — Employee Relations, Public Relations, and Foreign Relations.[124] As Irénée du Pont and the others had anticipated, purchasing quickly became less centralized and that department's role became increasingly an advisory and service one. The staff also increasingly relieved the Executive Committee of the task of coordinating functional activities in the different product divisions. On the whole, however, there was little change at du Pont after 1921 — much less than occurred after the initial reorganization at General Motors, Jersey Standard, and Sears, Roebuck. The General Managers, the Auxiliary Staff, and the top committees still perform much the same duties and are constituted in much the same form as they were in September, 1921.

At du Pont, then, structure followed strategy. Through a strategy of consolidation and integration, the three cousins had obtained administrative control over their widespread holdings of plants, marketing facilities, and laboratories as well as over a pool of trained personnel. The rational and efficient use of these resources called for the creation of functional departments with headquarters in Wilmington to administer the many units in the field and a central office to coordinate, appraise, and set the goals and policies of the functional departments in the interest of the enterprise as a whole.

The pressure to keep existing resources operating efficiently and steadily also provided a stimulus for the strategy of diversification. With the loss of government orders in 1908 and with the huge expansion of plant and personnel during World War I, the senior officers at du Pont, assisted by the Development Department, worked out a strategy that would assure the continued use of these resources when the demand for their current output declined. At first, they searched for new uses for existing physical facilities, but then decided that finding employment for trained, highly skilled personnel would prove more profitable. Such re-employment of resources in the new lines of business, in turn, often required the accumulation of new plant and personnel.

The strategy of diversification quickly demanded a refashioning of the company's administrative structure if its resources, old and new, were to be used efficiently and therefore profitably; for diversification greatly intensified the administrative load carried by the functional departments and the central office. Once the functional needs and activities of several rather than of one product line had to be coordinated, once the work of several very different lines of business had to be appraised, once policies and procedures had to be formulated for divisions handling a wide variety of products, and, finally, once the central office had to make critical decisions about what new lines of business to develop, then the old structure quickly showed signs of strain. To meet the new needs, the new organizational design provided several central offices, each responsible for one line of products. At the new general office, the Executive Committee and staff specialists concentrated on the over-all administration of what had become a multi-industry enterprise. And in transforming the highly centralized, functionally departmentalized structure into a "decentralized," multidivisional one, the major achievement had been the creation of the new divisions.

In these very same years, organization builders at General Motors had also been pioneering in the creation of the new multidivisional structure although their administrative needs and problems were very different. At General Motors the autonomous, multifunctional divisions had always existed. There, the challenge was not the building of the divisions but the formation of a general office.

3 GENERAL MOTORS—CREATING THE GENERAL OFFICE

The Durant Strategy

On November 19, 1920, the very day that the du Pont Company's Executive Committee sat down to discuss for the second time the proposal to decentralize along product lines, the du Pont Finance Committee was meeting in emergency session in New York City. A few days before, William C. Durant, founder of the General Motors Corporation, had asked Pierre S. du Pont and John J. Raskob, the Chairman of that corporation's Board and its senior financial officer, to confer with him.[1] He was in serious trouble. Stock market prices had been crumbling since summer, and now he owed over $30 million in broker's accounts and loans that he had used in an attempt to maintain the price of General Motors stock. Unless some action was taken quickly, he would be forced into bankruptcy and his great block of General Motors stock would be dumped on the market. To prevent this, Durant, Pierre, and Raskob met with representatives of the other large investor, J. P. Morgan & Co., and together they created a company, financed by the du Ponts and Morgan, to take over Durant's obligations and his General Motors stock.[2] The next day, November 20, Durant resigned as President of General Motors, and ten days later, Pierre du Pont took his place as chief executive of the automobile company.

Shortly after the Executive Committee's meeting on November 19, in Wilmington, Irénée du Pont again turned down the proposal for a multidivisional, "decentralized" structure at the du Pont Company. But within less than a month after the Finance Committee's emergency session in New York, Pierre du Pont adopted for General Motors an organizational plan submitted to him by Alfred P. Sloan, Jr., which had striking similarities to the one Irénée had rejected. Each plan called for autonomous operating divisions and a general office consisting of general executives and staff specialists. Despite the apparent similarities of the proposals, Pierre, as has been pointed out, supported Irénée in his opposition to introducing the organizational changes at du Pont. Actually, it seems quite doubtful that either Pierre or Irénée considered the two plans in any way comparable. Each had been designed to meet specific needs arising from a very different set of management problems. At du Pont, it was the attempt to handle the company's various new product lines within the older centralized functionally departmentalized structure which caused the difficulties. At General Motors, the problem had been the integration and coordination of many almost completely independent operating divisions.

To understand the problems facing Pierre du Pont at General Motors in December, 1920, requires a brief review of the corporation's history; and until 1920, this history was largely the story of its founder's strategy of expansion through combination and integration. Among the early automobile makers, Henry Ford and William C. Durant were the strongest believers in the enormous potential market existing for the moderate-priced car. Whereas Henry Ford, the mechanic, met the market primarily by enlarging his existing industrial plant, Durant, the salesman, did it by combining within a single holding company many scattered facilities for making and selling of automobiles, parts, and accessories. Through this strategy, the combined assets of Durant's General Motors had come to make it the fifth largest of all industrial enterprises in the United States by 1919. Durant had seen his opportunity, and he had moved with speed and decision to create the industrial empire necessary to meet it. But he paid little or no attention to fashioning a structure to govern his sprawling domains.

Before 1920, two groups at General Motors — both representing large investors — had attempted to build some sort of general office to administer this vast collection of men, money, and materials. Neither met with much success. This was partly because nearly all the executives in charge of the many subsidiaries as well as Durant himself saw little value in or need for general administrative control, and partly because no one in either of the two financially interested groups took the time to formulate a realistic administrative structure. Then in 1920 came the sharp postwar depression that made clear the need for over-all administrative supervision and, at the same time, brought a change in command. The new management quickly adopted the structural design Alfred Sloan had already worked out to fill the need.

The Sources of Durant's Strategy

Durant was particularly well equipped to carry out his convictions about the future of the automobile market. In 1908, the year in which he formed General Motors and Henry Ford produced the first Model T,

Durant was already the largest automobile manufacturer in the United States and had long been one of its major carriage makers. The policies he used to build General Motors were those that he had already tested and proved in the carriage business and at Buick.

In 1885, Durant, a twenty-four-year-old insurance salesman in Flint, Michigan, purchased a patent for manufacturing two-wheel carts for $50.[3] He then joined J. Dallas Dort, a young hardware salesman, to form the Durant–Dort Carriage Company, the two partners contracting with a local carriage builder to manufacture the carts. Since Flint, at this time, was already one of the largest centers for vehicle manufacture in the United States, this contracting was easier and required much less capital than building their own works. Instead Durant and Dort concentrated on selling in the expanding national market. Beside making sales themselves, they chose dealers and distributors in all parts of the country to market their products. In rural areas, they relied on men who were already selling farm implements; in the cities, they tended to set up their own dealers.[4]

Their marketing efforts so increased the demand for carts and carriages that Durant and Dort decided to erect their own manufacturing plant, that is, to integrate backward. To meet the volume required, they found it easier and cheaper to build a plant which assembled already finished parts and accessories made elsewhere rather than one which manufactured the carriages from scratch. The new Flint factory, using local suppliers, was soon turning out over two hundred carriages a day, and paying an annual wage roll of over $3 million. But as production expanded, adequate supplies became an increasingly serious problem, and the two partners encouraged the setting up of specialized plants in Flint which made bodies, wheels, upholstery, paint, varnish, axles, and springs. One company built nothing but whip sockets. Durant and Dort not only financed many of these establishments but, according to Carl Crow: "Durant personally organized a number of them in order to make certain that his assembly line would have a dependable supply of parts."[5] He even purchased stands of hickory and hardwood in distant areas. With integration came an increase in Durant's offerings. By the turn of the century, his factories were making a wide variety of buggies, carriages, and spring wagons, all sold under the Blue Ribbon trademark.

Durant's development of this high-volume, integrated business made him a millionaire before he was forty. Little interested himself in the details of operations, he placed competent local men in charge of the carriage company, and before 1900 moved his personal headquarters to New York. There, as he watched J. P. Morgan and other business titans reorganizing American industry, he began to look for new industrial empires to conquer.

The automobile then offered an obvious opportunity for a new business just as it was a threat to his existing one. By 1900, Ransom E. Olds and one or two others had shown automobile manufacturing to be commercially profitable. In that year, a variety of small companies had produced 4,000 cars in the United States. In 1904, one of these tiny ventures, the Buick Motor Co. with a small factory in Flint, failed. Durant needed little urging from its creditors to take over the defunct automobile company.

Returning to Flint in December, 1904, Durant began immediately to plan the creation of an automobile company along lines similar to those of his carriage business.[6] He redesigned the car, built large assembling plants in Flint and then in nearby Jackson. At the same time, he worked hard to build up a national distributing and dealer organization. Selling automobiles was more complex than marketing carriages. The initial demonstration by the dealer meant much more in getting a customer as did efficient servicing in keeping him. The latter required, among other things, that the dealer stock the necessary parts and accessories for repairs and replacements. In the rural areas, especially in the West, Durant granted franchises covering a large territory to distributors, who then put together their own dealer and service systems. In New York and other large cities, he set up his own retail offices to sell directly to the consumer. The major part of Durant's marketing, however, was handled through the company's branch or district offices. These wholesale distributors arranged with the dealers for the number of cars and the parts and accessories each wanted, saw to it that each received what he ordered, and maintained somewhat of a general oversight over the performance of the different dealers. In building both his manufacturing and selling organization, Durant relied heavily on the carriage company's plant and personnel. In moving from carriages to automobiles, Durant was assuring the continued use of many of the resources he had developed in his earlier business.

As sales grew in volume, the automobile maker encouraged the production of parts and accessories in Flint. Manufacturing at Buick, and indeed at nearly all of the automobile companies of the day, was largely an assemblying operation. So in order to assure the necessary supplies for his manufacturing operations, he turned many of the companies he had helped to organize and finance from making parts for carriages to doing automobile work. Durant went even farther afield. For example, he brought Charles S. Mott's Weston-Mott Co., makers of axles and wheels, to Flint from Utica in 1905, and Alfred Champion's spark plug company from Boston in 1908.

Durant's energy and creative ability were reflected in Buick's output. In 1903, the Buick Co. produced 16 cars and in 1904, 31; but in 1906 it made 2,295 and in 1908, 8,487. In four years, Buick became the leading automobile producer in the United States.[7] In 1908, the first year of the Model T, Ford had become the second largest with 6,181 vehicles and Cadillac the third, with 2,380. Arthur Pound gives the most credit for Buick's impressive growth to the creation of a sales organization. "There, perhaps," writes the General Motors' historian, "was Mr. Durant's greatest contribution to the techniques of automobile administration."[8]

Rapid growth whetted Durant's ambitions. As he turned to planning greater automotive enterprises, he left more and more of the administration of Buick in the competent hands of Charles W. Nash, formerly the production manager of the carriage works. Nash and his successor, Walter P. Chrysler, soon worked out a fairly standard centralized structure with manufacturing, sales, engineering, purchasing, and financial departments for the administration of the rapidly growing Buick Co.[9] The sales department with its branches, warehouses, and other distributing facilities came to carry on the wholesale function which included advertising the Buick line. The manufacturing department, operating on a line-and-staff basis, administered the expanding factories. After Chrysler took the helm, he concerned himself largely with obtaining the better cost and other data necessary for the effective administration of manufacturing activities. Apparently neither he nor others at Buick made any concerted effort to compile and analyze the data on sales expenses and market performance. The structure that Nash and Chrysler built at Buick appears to have have been similar to that used at Ford, Studebaker, Franklin, and other rapidly growing automobile concerns in the years just before World War I.[10]

The Creation of General Motors

Durant's immediate success with Buick, coming as it did on top of his earlier experience with the carriage company, further convinced him of the potential market for the horseless carriage. By 1908, he was already predicting the sale of 500,000 cars a year.[11] The exploitation of such a market demanded a massive expansion of facilities and personnel for the making and selling of automobiles. The quickest and probably the cheapest way to obtain the needed capacity was for a number of existing car manufacturers to combine. Early in the summer of 1908, Durant, with Benjamin Briscoe, began to plan along this line.[12] Briscoe, a manufacturer of metal stamping and parts, had been one of the original backers of Buick, but had withdrawn in 1903 to form the Maxwell–Briscoe Motor Co. After obtaining support from partners in J. P. Morgan & Co., the two men tried to get Henry Ford and Ransom E. Olds, now of Reo, to join them. Ford's demand for $3 million in cash defeated that scheme. Briscoe and Durant next pushed forward a plan to combine their own two firms. This proposal came to an end, according to Briscoe, when Francis L. Stetson, Morgan's legal specialist, became convinced that Durant was buying up Buick stock in anticipation of the merger.

Durant then decided to go ahead without Briscoe and the Morgan partners. Frederick L. Smith and his Olds Motor Works, he felt, would do just as well. So, on September 8, 1908, Durant formed the General Motors Company, a holding company, which by the end of the year owned stock in Buick, Olds, and the W. F. Stewart Company, bodymakers in Flint. Within the next eighteen months, largely through exchanging General Motors stock for the stock of the purchased companies, Durant came also to control all or sizable blocks of stock of Cadillac, Oakland, six other automobile companies, three truck firms, and ten parts and accessory companies.

In combining General Motors, Durant followed the same strategy of volume production and vertical integration he had used so effectively at Buick and the carriage company. Only four of the domestic subsidiaries and the one in Canada had major marketing and dealer organizations; and no man knew better than Durant that buying an automobile company without a marketing organization meant buying little more than a patent or plant and equipment. Cadillac and Olds, like Buick, had well-established organizations and reputations. Oakland, owned and managed by Edward M. Murphy, had only just been formed; but Murphy, one of the most successful carriage manufacturers in Pontiac, Michigan, had large manufacturing plants and a good sales organization.[13] The same was true of the McLaughlin Motor Car Co., Ltd., in Canada, another prosperous carriage maker. These five and their extensive resources formed the basis of General Motors. In purchasing the bankrupt Rainier Company and the more solvent Welch and Ewing companies, Durant was buying plant and equipment, while in obtaining the Cartercar and Elmore companies, he appears to have bought little more than patents.

More significant than such minor car companies were the firms making bodies, engines, gears, transmission systems, lamps, rims, and steering mechanisms. Many of these remained operating units in the General Motors Company long after the lesser automobile subsidiaries had disappeared.[14] Durant had purchased them to assure himself of supplies enough to meet the needs of his several assembly plants.

In carrying out expansion by combination and vertical integration, Durant never prepared for nor hardly even considered possible a temporary decline in demand and so failed to build up his cash reserves. He made no attempt to collect information about output and demand in order to make adjustments in production that might prove necessary. Nor was he interested in building an organizational structure to give him information about and control over his operations or to help him achieve potential economies of integration and combination.

As a result, the slight business recession in 1910 forced Durant out of the General Motors management.[15] Between 1908 and 1910, income from sales, and most of these came from Buick, had almost doubled, from over $29 million to $49 million. But when sales, particularly Buick's, dropped below scheduled production, Durant temporarily lacked funds to pay his suppliers and working force. Moreover, much of the inventory that Buick and others had stocked in anticipation of continuing rapid expansion was becoming obsolete because of changes in car design. To meet this emergency, Durant obtained $15 million from a banking syndicate, including Lee, Higginson & Company of Boston, J. &. W. Seligman & Co., and the Central Trust Company, both of New York. In return, Durant had to turn over the management of the company to the bankers, and on November 10, 1910, he signed a five-year voting trust agreement. Under this arrangement Durant remained a Vice-President and Director but had little say in the company's affairs.

The Storrow Regime

The bankers, concerned with steadier present profits rather than with expanding future prospects, paid more attention to internal organization than to external expansion.[16] They moved on two fronts, first the consolidation of many subsidiaries and then an attempt to set up a general office for their administration.[17] In consolidation, the object was to concentrate production in a relatively few large units. They integrated some of the smaller carmaking activities with the larger ones, combined the three truck concerns into the General Motors Truck Company, and united several of the parts and accessory plants. Production of engines, for example, was brought together in the large and highly specialized plant of the Northway Motor & Manufacturing Co. At the same time, General Motors Export Company was set up to handle sales abroad.

In attempting to develop some sort of over-all administrative structure, the banking group and their spokesman, James J. Storrow, new Chairman of the Finance Committee, had no intention of placing all of General Motors' activities within one centralized organization. But it did want more cooperation between and more control over the autonomous subsidiaries. As a first step, Storrow had the general offices moved from New York to Detroit. Then he brought Nash from Flint to Detroit to be the corporation's President. To determine broad policy and to make a beginning of coordination and appraisal, he formed a Board of Managers made up of the heads of the major subsidiaries, a board that met regularly with the President and himself.[18]

Storrow next set up three permanent offices at general headquarters to assist in the over-all administration: a new purchasing office was to achieve some of the economies through buying in large volume for all subsidiaries; an accounting office was to begin at once to standardize accounting procedures throughout the corporation's subsidiaries in order that accurate information on costs, profits, and loss might be developed; and a new production office. While other holding companies, like United States Steel, came to have similar accounting and purchasing offices, Storrow's third office — an engineering or "production" unit — was more of an innovation.

To head this department, the Chairman of the Finance Committee brought to Detroit Tracy Lyon, a senior executive in Westinghouse's Manufacturing Department, as Director of Production "to improve the quality of the materials, the standard of workmanship, and the design of our motor cars." [19] The Director was, according to the Annual Report of 1911, to be given "a general staff of mechanical engineers, gasoline engine engineers, designers, production experts, and other experts not attached to any particular factory, but whose advice and services would always be available, to advise with and assist the necessarily more limited staff of each individual factory." As part of this staff organization, Storrow had the Arthur D. Little, Inc., of Cambridge set up large testing laboratories in Detroit.

To provide for more certain communication and coordination between the many subsidiaries, Storrow and Nash took steps to organize formal interdivisional committees or boards. In May, 1913, Nash brought together the different Purchasing Agents in order to give them "an opportunity to become better acquainted and to discuss topics of common interest relating to their branch of work." [20] The meetings soon became regular monthly affairs where purchasing procedures were outlined for all the subsidiaries and where notes were compared on the price and performance of many articles. This board had a chairman and secretary but no permanent staff, although the secretary did compile a good bit of information on commonly used items. In spite of the fact that the board began working up general contracts for purchases of basic items by the company as a whole, relatively few such contracts had been agreed upon by 1915. Nash may possibly have instituted similar boards for other functions, such as engineering and sales.

Neither the interdivisional groups like the Purchasing Board or the Board of Managers nor the more permanent units in the general office were successful in providing even a modicum of over-all administrative control. The boards remained little more than places to exchange information. Henry G. Pearson, writing on the basis of the Storrow correspondence, suggests the difficulties that were involved in instituting centralized accounting, and describes the strong resistance put up by the carmaking units on "this invasion of their independence."[21] The central Purchasing Office never became more than an information center, and, after two years as Director of Production, Tracy Lyon, returned East a broken but wiser man, according to David F. Edwards, then one of Nash's assistants.[22] Chrysler at Buick, Henry Leland at Cadillac, and other managers were not the type of men to accept the suggestions, or even orders from the general office, particularly when, as in the case of Chrysler and Leland, their operations accounted for nearly all of the company's profits. When Storrow and Nash left General Motors in 1915, the general office, was, despite their efforts, little better equipped to administer the resources of a huge industrial enterprise than that of the ordinary holding company of the day. It did allocate the funds for capital expenditures and distribute the profits made by its subsidiaries, but there is little evidence that even this was done in a very systematic and rational way.

Durant's Return and Renewed Expansion and Integration

Storrow and Nash left because Durant had come back. The story of the founder's return is a complicated one that need not be repeated here.[23] What is necessary for this account is to explain that, before the voting trust agreement with the Boston and New York bankers had expired in November, 1915, Durant had acquired a major integrated, volume-production automobile company in Chevrolet as well as substantial financial allies in the du Ponts of Wilmington. He used both to obtain full control of General Motors. In August, 1916, after the resignation of Storrow and then Nash, Durant became President and Pierre S. du Pont, Chairman of the Board. Since Pierre du Pont was involved so completely in guiding the du Pont Company through its wartime expansion, Durant was left wholly on his own at General Motors.

After his return, structure was forgotten for strategy. Durant carried on even more intensively his basic original policy of producing moderately priced cars for a volume market. He remained convinced of the enormous existing demand for the automobile. In fact, increased volume became, for Durant, an end in itself, more crucial even than profits.[24] Therefore he concentrated on expanding output of existing carmaking units and on providing their plants with the necessary parts, equipment, and materials. Of the score of companies he purchased between 1916 and 1920, only two actually assembled cars and neither of these appears to have had a distributing or a dealer organization of any size. The rest manufactured components, accessories, or materials. As before, Durant paid little attention to developing a line of cars to meet more effectively the different needs and demands of the ever-growing automobile market.

He gave even less thought to effecting an over-all management structure or to building a general office so necessary for coordinating and supervising the activities of his rapidly expanding industrial empire. Durant dropped Storrow's Boards of Managers and Purchasing Agents as well as the general purchasing office, and moved his own office and the company's small financial units back to New York City.[25] His Treasurer and Comptroller made even less effort to standardize accounting and financial procedures than did those of Storrow. Most of the legal work was given to an outside firm, although the corporation did continue to have a patent unit.[26] From 1915 until 1918, the general office at General Motors included little more than Durant and two or three personal assistants.

Durant was able to make a start on his great expansion program before the interruption of America's entrance into World War I. In the spring of 1916, after he had regained control of General Motors, but before Nash and Storrow had resigned, Durant organized a holding company — United Motors Corporation — to buy out several leading parts and accessories companies, including Hyatt Roller Bearing Company and New Departure Manufacturing Co., both major producers of ball bearings, Remy Electrical Company, and the Dayton Engineering Laboratories Company, known as Delco, both makers of starting, lighting, ignition, and other electrical equipment, and the Perlman Rim Corporation.[27] Not only did these purchases help assure a steadier volume of essential supplies from different sources, but they also brought a number of able men into the General Motors orbit. One of these, Alfred P. Sloan, Jr., owner and manager of Hyatt Roller Bearing, Durant made President of the new United Motors Corporation.

Our entry into the war temporarily delayed Durant's plans.[28] Continued automobile production was menaced by military orders, plant conversions, priorities, and the difficulty of obtaining materials. Excess capacity threatened, for the internal-combustion engine had not yet become a vital instrument of war. So the General Motors President turned to developing new products. Like Henry Ford, he began to manufacture tractors. The sudden call for more food had greatly increased the demand for this relatively new agricultural implement. Thus tractor production could continue if automobile building was curtailed, and its manufacture could keep busy some of the assembly plants and, possibly, dealers in rural areas. For similar reasons, Durant decided to buy the Guardian Frigerator Corporation. As one of his assistants later testified, refrigerators could be marketed through the car divisions if automobile production was stopped, and so "keep his dealers alive."[29] After the war, both the tractor and refrigerator operations were retained, the first with Durant's enthusiastic support, the second, rather because of urging by some of his colleagues.

Immediately after the Armistice, Durant finally brought his program into full swing. Not only was there an obvious postwar demand for automobiles, but also the du Ponts and the du Pont Company itself had provided capital by investing over $50 million of their profits in General Motors.[30] The year 1919 was, then, one of massive expansion. Older plants were enlarged, and new ones, particularly assembly plants, were set up in different parts of the country. At the same time, Durant purchased control or a sizable block of stock in many parts and equipment companies. Particularly important was the large investment he made in the Fisher Body, the T. W. Warner (gears), and the Buffalo Metal Goods (brakes) companies.[31] In the early months of 1919, he had studies made of his long-term needs and available supplies in aluminum, leather, plate glass, tires, and petroleum.[32] He also looked into the availability of wheels, storage batteries, magnetos, gears, machine tools, and similar items. After investigation, he decided to sign a contract with the Aluminum Company of America to assure a continuing supply of aluminum. He also made a substantial half-million-dollar investment in the Goodyear Tire & Rubber Company and even still larger ones in the General Leather Company, Doehler Die Casting Company, and the Brown-Lipe-Chapin Co., in order to be certain of his tire, leather, castings, and gear supplies. Other studies were begun on the availability of labor. Durant also spent time and a good sum of money to develop housing facilities at Flint, Detroit, and elsewhere.

In the same year, too, General Motors Acceptance Corporation was formed to assist dealers in the financing of General Motors products and to help customers finance retail sales. To Raskob, rather than Durant, goes the credit of devising this basic innovation that helped make possible the mass marketing of consumer durables by means of installment or carrying payments.[33]

Throughout these years of expansion, Durant continued to show almost no concern for organization structure. In the summer of 1917, he did transform General Motors from a holding to an operating company by turning the various car, accessory, and parts subsidiaries into divisions. The next year, Chevrolet, United Motors, and General Motors of Canada were brought into General Motors and became operating divisions.[34] This was, however, very little more than a legal change. General Motors remained administratively a loosely knit federation of many operating enterprises.

The relations between operating divisions and between the divisions and the general office became more haphazard, less coordinated, and less supervised than they had been under Storrow and Nash. Major decisions, such as plant expansion, capital investment, output, and price, were decided by Durant and the heads of the operating divisions in occasional conferences or in individual talks. Sometimes they were made by Durant with no consultation, at other times by the division manager after only the most casual reference or contact with Durant's office.[35] Furthermore, the organizational status of the many operating units varied. Some accessory and parts divisions were in the United Motors Corporation; others stayed with Chevrolet or Buick; and still others, like Northway and the Champion Ignition Company, remained independent divisions in the larger General Motors Corporation.[36] Again, some were integrated enterprises, others just carried on a single economic function.

Du Pont Contributions to Durant's Organization

Although the lack of any effective over-all administrative structure—clear lines of authority and communication and accurate information about the corporation's operations—failed to disturb Durant, it did trouble the du Ponts. They paid some attention to enlarging the general staff and also appointed the first general officers, in addition to Durant, whose concern should be for the corporation as a whole rather than for any one of its parts. Like the bankers before them, the du Ponts were interested in protecting a sizable investment. Even more than the financiers were they aware of the value of defining clearly the organizational structure.

The du Ponts made their initial move at a Board meeting in February, 1918, a few weeks after the du Pont Company had made its first major investment in General Motors.[37] They then defined the make-up and duties of the top committees in much the same way that Pierre had done earlier for their own company. An Executive Committee, like Storrow's Board of Managers, consisted of the heads of major divisions. But unlike the older board, it was specifically given full authority and responsibility for over-all operating policies and performance. The Committee differed from that of the du Pont Company in 1918 because its members headed multidepartmental product divisions rather than single-function departments.

The Finance Committee, consisting of Irénée and Henry F. du Pont, J. Amory Haskell, Durant, and with Raskob as its Chairman, was to formulate general financial policies such as the amount of dividends to be declared, and to make plans for the issuance and sale of securities and so forth. The Finance Committee would also set the salaries of top executives, approve the annual and semiannual estimates for capital expenditures, and authorize the regular budgets "or plans under which the departments may act without further reference to the Finance Committee." [38] The Committee required detailed accounts of appropriations estimates only on those items that committed the corporation to an expense of more than $300,000.

Next, the du Ponts increased the number of senior officers in the general office. Raskob resigned as Treasurer of the du Pont Company to devote full time to General Motors' finances. At the same time, J. Amory Haskell, who had not really been active in du Pont affairs since 1907, began to pay closer attention to the automobile company's business. He and Durant were the only men on both the Finance and Executive Committees.[39] The coming of these two general officers to General Motors, however, failed to make an appreciable difference in the corporation's basic policies. Raskob, concentrating on finances, was as optimistic about the future of the automobile as was Durant and, like him, was much more concerned with expansion than with systematic organization. Haskell, whose duties were vague and who was now an elderly man, failed to push for organizational improvements. Durant himself, strongly supported by Raskob and Haskell, did take one critical step to enlarge the general office by appointing Chrysler to act as general manager in charge of the car divisions.[40] However, much to Chrysler's annoyance, Durant continued to make nearly all the important decisions concerning these divisions. By the end of 1919, Chrysler, completely frustrated, quit the corporation in anger.

In addition to creating Executive and Finance Committees and to appointing two general officers, the du Ponts, like the bankers before them, had hoped to improve over-all administration by enlarging the staff activities at general headquarters. During 1919 they made their first attempts to better the financial and accounting procedures by adding personnel to the general financial offices and, late in the year, by placing one of their younger executives, John Lee Pratt, as assistant to Durant and as chairman of a new Appropriations Committee.[41]

The du Pont Company also made some of its own staff available to Durant. Early in 1919, the General Motors President, wishing to investigate several parts and accessory plants that he was considering buying and needing information on the availability of materials and fuels, arranged with the du Pont Company to make the necessary studies.[42] The result was the formation of a small Motor Development Section in du Pont's Development Department. As it was placed under Pratt's control, it gave that executive his initial contact with Durant. Similar arrangements for advice and study were made with the du Pont Personnel Department, headed by J. E. Squires.[43] Finally, the services of the large du Pont Engineering Company, which had built the great war plants, were now made available to General Motors. None too satisfied with this arrangement, Durant tried in the spring of 1919 to get Pratt and Squires to come to New York and handle the General Motors work there.[44] The du Ponts, themselves, looked on it only as a temporary proposition.[45] But neither side took steps to change the situation.

Nor did anyone from du Pont succeed in obtaining better administrative control over finances. Pratt described the situation shortly after he arrived to help improve procedures: "No one knew just how the money had been appropriated, and there was no control of how much money was being spent."[46] Durant was largely to blame, Pratt maintained. The Executive Committee consisted of Division Managers and:

> When one of them had a project, why he would get the vote of his fellow members; if they would vote for his project, he would vote for theirs. It was sort of a horse trading. In addition to that, if they didn't get enough money, Mr. Durant, when visiting the plant, would tell them to go on and spend what money they needed without any record of it being made.

Although Pratt's committee was to bring some kind of order into the appropriations procedures, he reported "that during Mr. Durant's regime we were never able to get the thing under control."

The one important addition to the staff before 1921 was the ingenious Charles P. Kettering, the inventor of the self-starter and other automotive innovations, whom Durant and Pierre du Pont prevailed upon to devote full time to technical research.[47] To obtain Kettering's services, the corporation agreed to take over his business interests in Dayton including the Delco–Light Company (farm lighting plants) and the Dayton Wright Airplane Company.

The du Ponts were, therefore, rather more successful than Storrow in providing some sort of organization at the general office to coordinate, appraise, and supervise the divisions. But they failed to make General Motors into more than an expanding agglomeration of different companies making automobiles, parts, accessories, trucks, tractors, and even refrigerators. This failure came largely because no one connected with the du Ponts had the time or the facts or the immediate interest necessary to analyze General Motors' needs and problems. The active du Pont executives were fully involved with the postwar changes in their own company. Pierre, after leaving the du Pont presidency, considered himself in semiretirement and turned to enjoying a less strenuous life at Longwood, his Pennsylvania estate. Raskob, an industrial imperialist, had shown almost as little concern for structure as Durant. Before the end of 1920, the lack of a clearly defined administrative structure was to be proved disastrous. The crisis of 1920, precipitated by the sudden impact of the postwar recession on the corporation not only led to Durant's retirement but made possible the creation of an over-all administrative structure at General Motors.

The Crisis of 1920

The first months of 1920 were still ones of prosperity—the tail end of the war-engendered boom. Both demand and prices were still rising, and new automobiles continued to be in short supply. The division managers, apparently anxious over shortages of materials, inflation, and a growing market, continued to expand their plant, machinery, and other capital equipment. In 1920, the corporation spent $79 million on plant and properties.[48] The managers also stocked up on inventory, to assure themselves of supplies they needed before inflation and scarcities forced prices still higher.[49] Each thought only of his own immediate situation, giving little attention to the problems of the corporation as a whole or possible long-term economic change.

Their calls for money became increasingly strident. So on March 19, 1920, Raskob informed the du Pont Finance Committee that General Motors required $64 million of additional capital.[50] At this time, he seemed little worried about the increasing expenditures and seemed confident of his ability to get the money. J. P. Morgan & Co. and the Nobel's Explosives Trades, Ltd., had shown an interest in the issue. Assuming that the funds would be easily raised and the demand for automobiles would continue, Durant, in the same month, "presented to the Executive Committee a schedule of proposed production made possible by the construction and expansion program then well on towards completion."[51]

By May, Raskob, and possibly Durant, had become much more troubled by the growing expenditures of the divisions. Tightening credit for installment buying indicated a possible decline in demand.[52] Also the Chairman of the Finance Committee was having more difficulty in raising new capital than he had anticipated. On May 13, both the Executive and Finance Committees at General Motors noted the continued increase in the purchasing of inventories.[53] By the end of April these had reached a value of $167,965,646. Raskob then warned the division managers of the need to maintain control over their purchases. At his suggestion, an Inventory Allocation Committee was formed to allot each division its share of the $150 million that Raskob and his associates estimated was available for inventory purchases during the next year. At the same time, the car production schedule for the year August, 1920, to August, 1921, was reduced.

Yet even with smaller production quotas, the division managers made little effort to stay within the limits set by the Inventory Allocation Committee.[54] These executives had full control of the funds in their divisions. They could borrow money as well as place orders for materials and equipment. No one checked to see how they spent the money they received or what materials they purchased and used. While they continued to buy supplies, the demand for their completed products fell off precipitously.[55] By early October, Pratt was appointed chairman of an inventory committee that was to try to gain some control over the situation.[56] With fewer sales, inventories continued to grow, and at the end of October, their value had reached a total of close to $210 million and, as the 1922 Annual Report added, "exceeding by $60 million the allotments of the Executive and Finance Committees. . . . This excess accounted for about 70% of the borrowing at that time."[57]

By then, too, the automobile market had collapsed. To meet the crisis, Ford slashed his prices on September 21 by 20 per cent to 30 per cent.[58] Durant, supported by his division sales managers, attempted for a time to maintain prices.[59] But, by the end of October, the situation had become so serious that many General Motors managers were having difficulty in finding cash to cover such immediate needs as invoices and payrolls. For November, sales dropped below 13,000, one-fourth of what they had been in early summer, and by the next January, production reached a record low of 6,151 vehicles for the month.[60] Before the dust settled, $84 million in inventories and other commitments had to be written off as dead loss.[61]

During the crisis, the price of General Motors stock plummeted. Then came Durant's disastrous attempt to sustain the price by buying General Motors stock on credit, which led to his financial difficulties and to his retirement as President on November 20, 1920. Ten days later, Pierre du Pont took over the presidency. He did so with some reluctance, as he had hoped to continue his more relaxed semiretirement. Yet in this time of crisis it was obvious to his associates in both General Motors and du Pont that only he could command "the respect and confidence of the banks, the investing public and the General Motors Corporation's personnel."[62]

Once he agreed to serve, Pierre acted quickly and firmly. The day after he took office, he began a systematic review of the corporation's position and problems.[63] And one of his very first acts was to approve the plan worked out by Alfred Sloan which defined an organizational structure for General Motors.

The Sloan Structure

Sloan's plan, approved by the Board of Directors on December 29, went into effect immediately.[64] The structure it created remains today as the corporation's basic organization. It lasted because it transformed General Motors from an agglomeration of many business units, largely automotive, into a single, coordinated enterprise. This it did by successfully creating a general office to coordinate, appraise, and set broad goals and policies for the numerous operating divisions.

Sloan had devised his plan some months before the crisis of 1920 demonstrated vividly the essential need for such over-all coordination and control. Durant had reviewed the proposal, but had failed to act on it. To this builder of empires, the details of organization seemed unimportant. But to Alfred Sloan, this lack of attention seemed inexcusable. His rational, precise mind found the promoter's ways of operation wasteful, inefficient, and dangerous.

The Sources of Sloan's Structure

The difference between the approaches of the two men to the problems of administration reflects contrasting personalities, education, and experience. Durant was a small, lively, warm man. Nearly everyone called him "Billy." Mr. Sloan was tall, quiet, and cool. Increasing deafness heightened his reserve. Nearly everyone called him Mr. Sloan. Even his closest associates rarely, if ever, referred to him as "Al" or "Alf."[65]

While Durant went directly from high school into business, Sloan had sought technical training.[66] Like Pierre du Pont and so many of that Delaware family, he attended the Massachusetts Institute of Technology. There he demonstrated his academic ability by completing the course in electrical engineering in three years. Where Durant's initial achievements had been in marketing, Sloan's were in production. In 1899, the M.I.T. graduate, assisted financially by his father, purchased for $5,000 the Hyatt Roller Bearing Company with a plant in Harrison, New Jersey. He had started to work for Hyatt immediately after graduating in 1895, but left it temporarily for an unsuccessful venture in electric refrigerators. On taking over Hyatt, Sloan began immediately to develop the new market for his product which had been created by the infant automobile industry.

Hyatt expanded with the new industry.[67] Volume production, precision manufacturing, and prompt delivery became Sloan's major problems. With such a flourishing demand, marketing took less considered thought. Unlike Durant, Sloan was selling only to other producers, not to the mass consumer market, and his best customers were the largest ones. After 1908, the Ford order alone was apparently large enough to require specialization and subdivision of the manufacturing activities, and with specialization came the need to create a design to coordinate, appraise, and plan for the subdivided units. The result appears to have been the more normal type of centralized structure used in administering enterprises that manufactured goods primarily for a few large customers. The line offices were those directly concerned with manufacturing, and the staff offices were those handling engineering, personnel, and purchasing. Marketing required only a very few men, and most of the selling activities were handled by a partner, Peter Steenstrup, or often by Sloan himself. Still the need to provide dependable service as well as punctual deliveries led Sloan to form an engineering service office in Detroit.

Hyatt grew so rapidly that Sloan was able in 1916 to sell to Durant for $13.5 million the firm that he had purchased for $5,000 in 1899. At Durant's request, Sloan became President of United Motors — the parts and accessories company of which Hyatt became a subsidiary. Here Sloan's managerial duties broadened.[68] His major task now was to build a general office to coordinate and expand the activities of the different operating companies. As each unit was in capable hands, he felt little need to concern himself with detailed administration, except for a continuing interest in Hyatt. Instead, he set up uniform accounting procedures and saw to it that his companies had their records "in proper shape." With the resulting comparable statistics, he was undoubtedly able to evaluate the profitability of his operating divisions and of United Motors as a whole more accurately than the corporation's New York office could do for the major operating divisions. As his subsidiaries were primarily manufacturing organizations like Hyatt, Sloan also concentrated on building a United Motors Service, Inc., to handle sales and service throughout the nation for several of his producing units. This organization assured better coordination between marketing and manufacturing, permitted his divisions to exploit the replacement trade more effectively, and helped provide General Motors' dealers with a reliable supply of parts and accessories. This last factor was an invaluable asset, since the ability to give good, quick servicing and repairing was becoming an increasingly important competitive weapon. With the creation of a large-scale marketing organization, Sloan's office at United Motors took on many of the duties of a central office in a multifunction enterprise. Yet, because of differences and complexities arising from making various products for much the same market, the plants of the several divisions were not combined into a single manufacturing department. Also at United Motors, Sloan had the responsibility of planning expansion. On his initiative this active General Motors' subsidiary purchased enterprises like Harrison Radiator and the Klaxon Company.

While fashioning an administrative office at and setting over-all policy for United Motors, Sloan became increasingly concerned by the lack of structure and system in General Motors' over-all organization.[69] He was not certain just how his own organization fitted into that of the larger corporation, nor just how the different operating divisions and the corporation's general office complemented or supplemented one another. In the summer of 1918, he wrote J. A. Haskell of his worries, pointing out that he had been working on several plans in order to help "keep our organization lined up." [70] As time passed, he became so troubled by the continuing lack of systematic structure at General Motors that he seriously considered resigning from the corporation in order to accept an invitation of Lee, Higginson & Company to become a partner and industrial consultant.[71] But before taking this drastic step, he decided to complete his plans to rationalize the corporation's structure.

Sloan later testified that he received no assistance in drawing up his "Organization Study," [72] insisting that he did it wholly on his own. Certainly no other executive in the corporation — neither Haskell, Raskob, Chrysler, nor the other car division managers, nor even Durant — was in a better position to recognize and understand the corporation's organizational needs. Sloan had built and managed an operating unit, and of more importance, he was the only one of these executives who had created an administrative office for the management of a number of such operating units. Since United Motors sold to nearly all the General Motors' assembling divisions and also to the industry at large, Sloan came to have a more complete view of the over-all situation at General Motors than did any other executive with the possible exception of Durant.

Nor could Sloan have received early in 1920 much help outside of the corporation. The du Pont executives, for example, could have provided little meaningful advice. Only the year before they had attempted to solve their problems by further centralization of an already tightly controlled organization. Any books, and probably any expert, on management would have advocated the same type of functionally departmentalized structure that Harry Haskell had defined for du Pont in 1919 and that Irénée du Pont would continue to maintain until the fall of 1921.

More useful to Sloan would have been a study of the experience of other holding companies, such as United States Steel. But few industrial holding companies had been able to transform their financial offices into general administrative ones, unless they had gone the whole way and created a centralized, functionally departmentalized structure.

For this reason, General Motors' own experience was probably the most valuable source of ideas for Sloan. He was aware of the attempts of Storrow and the du Ponts to set up some kind of a general office to coordinate, appraise, and plan programs and policies for the divisions.[73] His basic aim was to build a general office, or as he called it a "central organization" of general officers and staff executives, to define the lines of authority and communication between this new office and the divisions, and to develop accurate and useful data to flow through these lines. Sloan's objective was a larger and much more active general office than either Storrow or the du Ponts had envisioned. His basic innovations included the formation of a much more comprehensive staff organization and the appointment of general executives to supervise groups of divisions with only advisory and not line authority.

The "Organization Study"

In his analysis of General Motors' organizational needs, Sloan began with the assumption that the operating divisions must retain their autonomy. Obviously, a centralized structure was out of the question. Even the milder type of general supervision which Storrow had attempted had met with great resistance. Moreover, Sloan firmly believed that divisional independence encouraged initiative and innovation. At the same time, the activities of these divisions had to be coordinated and controlled in the interest of the corporation as a whole. A continuation of Durant's almost anarchical decentralization would be even more unsatisfactory than too much central control.

Sloan, therefore, began his proposals by saying: "The object of this study is to suggest an organization for the General Motors Corporation which will definitely place the line of authority throughout its extensive operations as well as to co-ordinate each branch of its service, at the same time destroying none of the effectiveness with which its work has hithertofore been conducted."[74]

The study would then be based on "two principles":

1. The responsibility attached to the chief executive of each operation shall in no way be limited. Each such organization headed by its chief executive shall be complete in every necessary function and enable to exercise its full initiative and logical development.

2. Certain central organization functions are absolutely essential to the logical development and proper control of the Corporation's activities.

With these principles as a basis, Sloan then listed the aims of his study. They were:

1. To definitely determine the functioning of the various divisions constituting the Corporation's activities, not only in relation to one another, but in relation to the central organization.
2. To determine the status of the central organization and to coordinate the operation of that central organization with the Corporation as a whole to the end that it will perform its necessary and logical place.
3. To centralize the control of all the executive functions of the Corporation in the President as the chief executive officer.
4. To limit as far as practical the number of executives reporting directly to the President, the object being to enable the President to better guide the broad policies of the Corporation without coming in contact with problems that may safely be entrusted to executives of less importance.
5. To provide means within each branch whereby all other executive branches are represented in an advisory way to the end that the development of each branch will be along lines constructive to the Corporation as a whole.

Sloan planned to reach these goals by four routes. He would regroup the operating divisions; would include in the general office executives to administer the activities of different groups of divisions; would expand the staff functions in the general office and unite the offices carrying out these functions into a single "Advisory Staff," and finally would enlarge the activities of the financial and accounting units (see Chart 6).

In outlining this program, Sloan began by defining the role and duties of the Finance and Executive Committees. These he left much as they had been outlined by the du Pont Company early in 1918. The first committee would continue to set dividend rates and the salaries of top officials, to raise funds, and to determine other financial policies. It would have "general control" over the corporation's finances and accounting, and would pass on major appropriations recommended by the Executive Committee. The second committee would retain its "entire supervision over the operations side of the Corporation's activities, constituting as a whole practically the entire operating staff." Each operating division would be represented in the Executive Committee, "major operations [car and truck] by a single representative, smaller operations being grouped together, one executive representing several such minor operations." The President's primary role would be to interpret the policies of the top committees and to see that they were carried out. In this, he would continue to have the assistance of his existing personal staff, including the recently created Appropriations Committee, chaired by John L. Pratt.

Sloan, then, stressed the continuing autonomy of the operating divisions whose managers would retain full authority and responsibility:

> The General Manager formulates all the policies of his particular unit subject only to the executive control of the President. The responsibility of the head of each unit is absolute and he is looked upon to exercise his full initiative and ability in developing his particular operation to the fullest possible extent and to assume the full responsibility of success or failure.

Then, to clarify the relations between these autonomous units to each other and to the general office, Sloan assigned each division to one of four "Groups" — Car, Accessory, Parts, and Miscellaneous. Those placed in the Car Group included the divisions "which manufacture and sell complete motor cars — purchasing part of the component parts from outside sources, part from other divisions of the Corporation and manufacturing part with their own facilities." The most important changes came in the organizations of the many accessory and parts divisions and those making allied products. Their organizational status had remained most confused. Some were within the United Motors structure; others were part of Chevrolet or Buick; and still others reported directly to Durant. Sloan placed all these units into either the Accessory or the Parts Group. The first was to include those selling over 60 per cent of their production outside of the corporation and the second, those who turned over at least more than 40 per cent and usually much more of their output to other General Motors divisions. The former had "common problems," Sloan noted, "such as sales and advertising policies, competitive conditions, proper placing of Corporation capital to effect the best results to the Corporation as a whole and many other questions of a Commercial nature which do not enter into the other operations within the Corporation." The fourth group — miscellaneous — included the tractor and refrigerator operations, foreign activities, and the new finance company — the General Motors Acceptance Corporation.

The Accessories Group was to be headed by a "Group Vice-President." His functions were to be "entirely advisory and for the purpose of reflecting to the various operations individually the policy of the President of the Corporation and of the Directors, Finance and Executive Committees." Here for the first time Sloan outlined the duties of a new type of corporation officer — the "Group Executive." Group Executives were to have no specific, day-to-day operating responsibilities. Individually and in an advisory capacity, they supervised the work of several divisions, and collectively they helped set the over-all policies of the corporation. Not only could this new post help to assure more efficient coordination and

CHART 6:

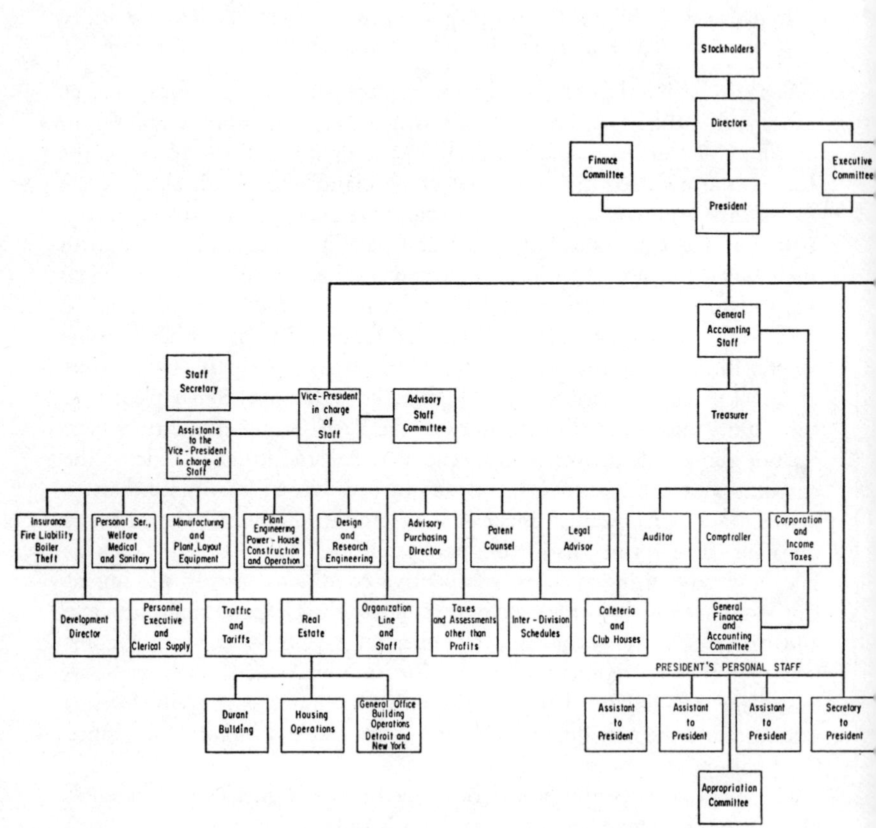
Stockholders
Directors
Finance Committee
Executive Committee
President
General Accounting Staff
Treasurer
Auditor
Comptroller
Corporation and Income Taxes
General Finance and Accounting Committee
Staff Secretary
Assistants to the Vice-President in charge of Staff
Vice-President in charge of Staff
Advisory Staff Committee
Insurance Fire Liability Boiler Theft
Personal Ser., Welfare Medical and Sanitary
Manufacturing and Plant Layout Equipment
Plant Engineering Power-House Construction and Operation
Design and Research Engineering
Advisory Purchasing Director
Patent Counsel
Legal Advisor
Development Director
Personnel Executive and Clerical Supply
Traffic and Tariffs
Real Estate
Organization Line and Staff
Taxes and Assessments other than Profits
Inter-Division Schedules
Cafeteria and Club Houses
Durant Building
Housing Operations
General Office Building Operations Detroit and New York
PRESIDENT'S PERSONAL STAFF
Assistant to President
Assistant to President
Assistant to President
Secretary to President
Appropriation Committee

Sloan's Initial Plan of Reorganization for General Motors, 1920

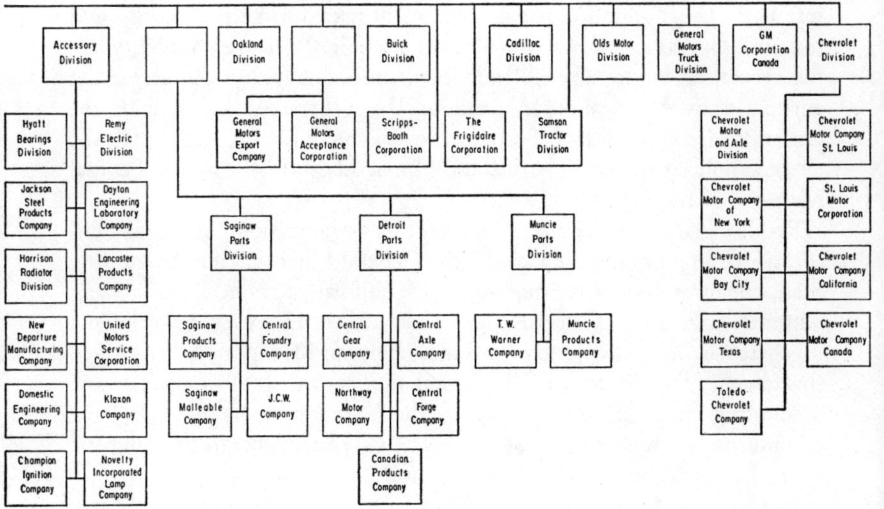

appraisal of the work of a number of divisions, but also it would cut down the number of executives who reported directly to Durant, at that time between thirty and forty. By placing the automobile divisions into one group and by carefully defining the advisory role of the Group Vice-President, Sloan undoubtedly anticipated the position of a Group Vice-President for the automobile divisions. At the time of his report, he envisaged the day when the tractor and agricultural-implement business would so grow as to constitute "one major group, presided over by a Vice-President of the Corporation, reporting to the President."

The single-function units in the Parts Group were, on the other hand, combined into three regionally defined divisions, each under a General Manager. "The divisions in this group are production and manufacturing operations, pure and simple," Sloan pointed out, "and are organized separately, rather than connected with a major division, for the purpose of economy or convenience in manufacture." In combining these plants into three geographical divisions, Sloan still hoped to keep authority and responsibility as far down the line as possible. "The responsibility for the success or failure of each individual operation within the group lies entirely as with every other operation, be it great or small, with the General Manager of that particular operation who formulates all the detailed policies subject only to control in an advisory way by the General Manager of the group."

Besides general executives, "the central organization" required staff specialists. In outlining the work of the General Financial and Accounting Staff, Sloan stressed the importance of uniform accounting as a basic administrative tool, as Storrow had done earlier. However, in order not to encroach on the autonomy of the Division Managers, Sloan added that, while the Financial Vice-President "performs all financial and accounting functions that pertain to the Corporation as a whole," the accounting "within each individual unit [will] be subject to the complete control of the Chief executive of that unit."

In his study, Sloan paid more attention to the creation of an advisory staff of specialists than he did to enlarging and strengthening the financial sections at the proposed new general offices. It was here that he made as important a contribution to the future of the corporation as in the development of the Group Executive. It was the fashioning of these staff facilities and the appointment of the Group Executives that differentiated the general office at General Motors from that at United States Steel, United Copper, Union Carbide, Allied Chemical, and other industrial holding companies of that day, and made possible the transformation of the corporation from a federation into a consolidated enterprise without creating a centralized, functionally departmentalized structure.

> The General Advisory Staff [Sloan wrote] is to constitute in reality a group of organizations or departments, large in some cases, small in others, depending upon the necessity of each individual line of work. The purpose of this staff is to advise the chief executives of the Operation Staff concerning problems of technical and commercial nature which are themselves so broad and require so much study as to be outside of the scope of a single operation and which will be, when developed, of importance to the guidance of all operations.

At this point Sloan stressed that the role of the staff must be only advisory. An operating division is to be, he reminded his readers, "independent and may accept or reject the advice of the Advisory Staff as its judgment may dictate, subject to the general supervision of the President."

Sloan next listed the necessary staff offices and outlined their duties. The new staff included Kettering's Engineering and Research organization and the existing Manufacturing and Plant Lay-out Section, which had its origin in the Technical Laboratory set up by A. D. Little in 1911. In addition, the corporation was to have its own Plant Engineering, Personnel, and Development offices. The function of the last was to study new lines and products that might be developed and new parts and accessory firms that might be purchased. Sloan also recommended the setting up of staff offices or "sections" for three other activities — one for purchasing, similar to the office that had existed in Storrow's time, another for sales, and a third to advise the operating divisions "regarding all matters pertaining to traffic." There was to be a Legal office as well as the existing Patent one. The report further named a number of necessary "housekeeping" sections, including Real Estate, Taxes, General Office, and Insurance.

Finally, Sloan wanted to have two offices to handle his special concerns — organization and interdivisional schedules. The Organization Section was, Sloan wrote:

> To make a study of and at all times to be thoroughly familiar with the Corporation's various organizations; have complete records on hand pertaining thereto including authority charts; to advise when called upon of any operation of the best form of organization for getting certain desired results and do such other development work, referring to form of organization as may be desired.

The second was to help assure an evener flow of product by developing:

> with the cooperation of the individual operations information pertaining to the proposed production schedule to the end that all operations contributing to such schedule are properly advised as to their responsibilities and

to properly distribute the production of the Parts and Accessories Groups to the end that proper provision may be made for all demands and the most effective results thereby obtained.

In this way, Sloan outlined a complete organization structure for the corporation as a whole. He had taken the autonomous parts as given, but after grouping them rationally, he proposed to administer them through "a central organization" of general officers and staff executives. The general officers individually were to supervise and coordinate different groups of divisions and collectively were to help make policy for the corporation as a whole. The staff executives were to advise and serve both the division managers and the general officers and provide business and financial information necessary for appraising the performance of the individual units and for formulating over-all policy.

Minor Modifications

When Pierre du Pont put Sloan's plan into operation, he made only minor modifications. The most important were the enlargement of the Financial Staff and the creation of the Operations Committee.[75] The Financial Staff was to include the Taxes and Insurance Section, which Sloan had placed in the Advisory Staff, and an Employee Bonus and a Statistical Department. Also the Comptroller's office would be divided into three units—General, Cost, and Appropriation Accounting Departments.

The new Operations Committee—a large group made up of managers of the major divisions and the directors of the important staff units—was to advise and assist the Executive Committee, now consisting of only four men, Pierre du Pont, Raskob, J. A. Haskell, and Sloan.[76] Sloan became Vice-President in charge of the Advisory Staff, and Haskell the Vice-President in charge of operations. In a very short time, these positions were reversed, and Sloan became the senior operating officer. The Executive Committee was expected to bring the corporation through its crisis by concentrating attention on making the necessary critical entrepreneurial and strategic decisions that would revive the stricken enterprise. The operating divisions, working through the Operations Committee and with the new general staff, were to take charge of most of the day-to-day work. "It is my belief," Pierre commented in the memorandum announcing the adoption of the new structure, "that 90% of all questions arising will be settled without reference to the Executive Committee and that the time of the Executive Committee members may be fully employed to study general routine and lay down general policies for the Corporation, leaving the burden of management and the carrying out of instructions to the Line, Staff and Financial Divisions."[77]

The year 1921 was one of organization building at General Motors. The new President appointed general officers to supervise two of the groups — the Accessories and the Parts — with Pratt taking charge of the first.[78] Sloan's proposed Miscellaneous Group was dropped, Frigidaire becoming part of the Accessories Group, and the Acceptance Corporation part of the financial staff. In a short time, the Tractor Division was liquidated, while the Export Corporation was enlarged and subdivided, to become the Export Group administered by still another group executive.[79]

The building of the Financial and Advisory Staff called for the opening of still more offices and the appointment of many more executives in the corporation's new general offices. F. Donaldson Brown, the former Treasurer of the du Pont Company, took the post of Financial Vice-President, bringing with him statisticians and economists to staff a new Statistical Department. Assisted by Albert Bradley, a trained economist, as well as by an experienced treasurer and a reliable comptroller, Brown was soon meeting the financial and inventory crisis.[80] John T. Smith, a lawyer, long connected with Durant and his activities, was brought in to set up the Legal Department.[81]

On the Advisory Staff, competent men continued in or were recruited for the different posts. Kettering remained in charge of the Research Section, and the managers of the Manufacturing and Plant Lay-out Section and the Patent Department were unchanged.[82] A. B. C. Hardy, a close associate of Durant since the Carriage Company days, was the chief of the new Advisory Purchasing Section for a short time before he took over the Olds Division. Norval Hawkins, for many years Ford's brilliant sales manager, was appointed the head of the Sales Analysis and Development Section. By the end of the year, other staff offices had been manned.

In these same months, the Executive Committee was making changes in the operating divisions. The managers of Olds, Oakland, Cadillac, and Chevrolet divisions were replaced. The immediate cause for the dismissal of two of these executives was a controversy over the "drawing of money from the Corporation which was not properly authorized."[83] The most important result of the departure of these strong and independent managers, and this result seems to have been quite unintentional, was to make much easier the regaining of control over these divisions and the instituting of uniform accounting and statistical methods. Just as the departure of Alfred and Coleman du Pont had assisted in completing the transformation of the du Pont Company from a family firm into a great impersonal industrial enterprise, manned by professional administrators, so the departure of those executives who had played an important part in the management of the automobile divisions from their earliest years helped to assure the metamorphosis of General Motors from a combination or federation of firms into a single integrated enterprise.

At this time, too, some smaller divisions were consolidated and others dropped.[84] The two car divisions that Durant had purchased after the war — the Sheridan and the Scripps-Booth — were liquidated, as was the Tractor Division, which had suffered heavier losses than any other single unit during the 1920 catastrophe.

By the end of 1921, most of Sloan's proposals had been carried out. Now the general office was much more than the personal headquarters of the President. Now the new general officers, assisted by the staff specialists, had more time to coordinate, appraise, and make policy for the different divisions and for the corporation as a whole. The new and explicit definition of the role of the general office and of the autonomous operating units and of the relations between them made it possible, for the first time, to integrate effectively the resources — managerial and technical as well as physical — of the agglomeration of producing, assembling, marketing, and engineering facilities and personnel that Durant had assembled. Yet the corporation's leaders were still to have a great deal more work to do before the Sloan plan resulted in a smooth-running organization. Not until 1925 did Sloan and his associates feel convinced that they had an efficient and integrated administrative structure at General Motors.

Putting the New Structure into Operation

As the senior executives at General Motors put the new structure into operation during the four years following 1921, they had to devote constant careful thought to three areas: the definition of divisional activities so that the work of each division would more effectively complement that of the others; the development of accurate and effective information to flow through the new structure; and the building of further channels of communication which would bring together more efficiently the efforts of the general staff and the operating executives. In carrying out this work, Sloan with his only superior officer, Pierre du Pont, and his two closest associates, Donaldson Brown and John Lee Pratt, revealed a continuing dispassionate, rational, calculating, and essentially pragmatic approach to the problems of management.

Defining Divisional Boundaries

The first of these broad problems, that of defining the boundaries for the activities of each division, was closely related to market strategy. Concerned primarily with expanding output, Durant had made little attempt to develop a rational product line. The different divisions competed with one another. The corporation as yet had really no low-price car, for Chevrolet was still priced well above Ford.[85] In 1919, Chevrolet sold only 132,170 passenger cars, or 7 per cent of the total market; while Ford's output was 664,482 or 40 per cent of the total.[86] In 1921, the figures were 4 per cent for Chevrolet and 55 per cent for Ford. Buick, a more expensive car, was obviously as much the mainstay of the General Motors line in 1921 as it had been in 1908. In 1921, more Buicks than Chevrolets were sold. Cadillac, while producing the lowest number of cars of the five major divisions, made the most expensive product. It indicated its strength by the relatively small decline in output during the postwar recession. On the other hand, the production of both Olds and Oakland fell in 1921 to less than 1 per cent of the automobiles marketed.

The initial step, then, was to bring the quality of the products of other divisions up to those of Buick and Cadillac and, at the same time, to place the offerings of the different divisions in some kind of rational relationship. This second step was done by formulating a policy of bracketing the market, that is, of having each division produce for a specific price market. As the 1923 Annual Report recorded: "In 1921 a definite policy was adopted. The Corporation should establish a complete line of motor cars from the lowest to the highest price that would justify quantity production."[87] Or, as Sloan later described the strategy:

> The line of products that we had was very defective. General Motors had a line of cars, and of course it was in a highly competitive position. It seemed to me that the intelligent approach would be to have a car at every price position, just the same as a general conducting a campaign wants to have an army at every point he is likely to be attacked.
>
> We had too many cars in some places and no cars in other places.
>
> One of the first things we did was to develop a line of products that met competition in the various positions in which competition was offered.[88]

The same Annual Report noted that by 1923 the product line had been "realigned and adjusted and competition which heretofore existed within the car manufacturing divisions has been largely eliminated. Such a policy makes possible coordination not otherwise practical, in engineering, manufacturing, and particularly in distribution."[89]

The place of the divisions was now pretty well defined. Cadillac sold in the highest-priced position, Buick the next, followed by Oakland and then Olds, with Chevrolet in the largest-volume, lowest-price market. To protect its position and because of "an enormous potential market for a car of quality at a price between that of the Chevrolet and the Oldsmobile," the corporation in 1925 brought out the six-cylinder Pontiac.[90] With the development of the Pontiac, the General Motors basic line was essentially completed. The enterprise was approaching its goal of including in its line "a car for every purse and purpose."

The new management paid close attention to the supporting as well as the front line divisions. By early 1921, it became convinced that General Motors should not extend the old Durant strategy of vertical integration to include ownership or control of sources of the more basic supplies and materials. The Annual Report dated March 26, 1921 put it this way:

> Thus: a comparatively small portion of the total tires produced are consumed by the automobile manufacturer, the larger percentage being sold directly to users of cars for replacement purposes; the greater part of the production of sheets and other forms of steel is consumed by trades other than the automotive industry, therefore investment in these fields has not been made. By the pursuit of this policy, General Motors Corporation has become firmly entrenched in lines that relate directly to the construction of the car, truck or tractor, but has not invested in general industries of which a comparatively small part of the products is consumed in the manufacture of cars.[91]

General Motors explicitly decided not to imitate the strategy Henry Ford was developing, that is, to control and make nearly everything that went into the Model T. There would be no great plant at General Motors comparable to the one then rising on the River Rouge.

Next, a policy on interdivisional billing was established. Whether the products of a division went to other General Motors divisions or outside, they were sold at the going market price. No longer were prices between divisions to be negotiated; insiders would pay the same as outsiders. "Where there are no substantial sales outside," Donaldson Brown pointed out in 1927, "such as would establish a competitive basis, the buying division determines the competitive picture — at times partial requirements are actually purchased from outside sources so as to perfect the competitive situation."[92] Unless such competitive conditions existed, he continued, it would be difficult to evaluate the performance of the parts and accessories divisions. If the price which one division charged another was higher than the price in the open market, it suggested that the selling division was inefficient or that it was increasing its profit at the expense of the buying division. In the latter case, the financial record in terms of return or investment — the basic criterion in appraising divisional performance — would not reflect accurately the use of the resources of either division. As a further check, the Executive Committee as early as October, 1921, asked each division to make a detailed report of its reasons for making outside purchases of items which could have been bought within the corporation.[93]

The Development of Statistical and Financial Controls

Such refinements in the appraisal of divisional performance could only come, however, after the corporation had solved one of its toughest challenges — the development of accurate, uniform data on costs, production, income, and so forth. The man most responsible for mastering this challenge was Donaldson Brown, the former Treasurer of the du Pont Company whom Pierre du Pont had brought with him to General Motors. The builder of many of du Pont's basic financial and statistical controls, Brown in 1921 was probably as well versed as anyone in the United States in the development and use of these new administrative tools. His pioneering achievements at General Motors thus provide a useful illustration of the critical part that reporting and statistical procedures play in the design by which complex, modern industrial enterprises have become administered.

Brown and his general financial staff carried out their work in two stages. In 1921 and 1922, these executives concentrated on developing data and procedures essential to the general office if it was to obtain some sort of administrative surveillance over the many divisions. The lack of such information in both the general office and the divisions had been one cause for the 1920 crisis. To restore order and at the same time to prevent similar dangers in the future, Brown and his assistants began by building informational procedures to control the purchasing and production schedules of each division. Next, they devised methods for the more systematic allocation of capital and other resources and for the more effective use of existing supplies of cash. During this first stage, they were also working actively to institute uniform accounting procedures.

After 1922, the financial staff concentrated more on refining their data and on perfecting their information and methods. During this second stage, they paid more and more attention to the development of data and controls dealing with anticipated conditions rather than to past or current performance. The coordination of product flow from the purchase of supplies to the final sale to the customer, the allocation of resources, the formulation of other policies, and even the appraisal of the performance of the divisions and the corporation as a whole, all rested increasingly on information about estimated or forecasted conditions. General Motors moved from basing administrative decisions and actions on present or past performance to making them on data concerning anticipated conditions in order to integrate its internal activities with changing market and other external conditions with more certainty.

Because an inventory crisis had precipitated the calamities of 1920, Brown's initial move was to improve controls over purchasing and production schedules and to coordinate these more closely with market demand. Even before he and Pierre du Pont had moved to General Motors, steps had been taken to regain control over the inventories. In October, 1920, after the market had disintegrated and when cash supplies of the corporation were becoming dangerously low, John Lee Pratt had been placed in charge of an Inventories Committee.[94] He was given broad powers. His committee was to examine the inventories of all divisions, and if it found any unit with a surplus of goods, that unit was to make no more purchases without the Committee's approval. Pratt had the same authority over payrolls. "The corporation was running short of cash," Pratt later testified, "and we were trying to preserve the cash."

One of Pierre's very first acts after taking the presidency was to enlarge the membership and the duties of Pratt's committee.[95] With Brown and M. L. Prenskey, the General Motors Treasurer, as new members, the Committee was to compute the write-down of existing inventory and to adjust the existing schedules so that each division would purchase only what was immediately necessary. Finally, the Committee was to receive from each division an estimate of sales for the next four months and to review all these estimates each month. These forecasts soon provided the information with which control over inventory could be maintained. This, in turn, permitted the dissolving of Pratt's committee in April, 1921.[96]

Such forecasts, systematically developed, became the basis for a large part of the statistical controls at General Motors. The divisions estimated the sales for each of the next four months and the volume of production and probable expenditures for goods and labor needed to meet these schedules. Only after the general office approved the forecast could the division purchase the necessary supplies. The actual estimating, selection of supplies, and purchasing, like the planning of flow and allocation of stock, remained the responsibility of the division managers. By 1923, these forecasts submitted on the 25th of each month covering the current month and the succeeding three, had come to include "the amount of investment at the end of each month in plant and in capital working items," [97] as well as the estimates of inventory, output, and necessary purchases. To supplement these reports, the divisions were soon submitting others monthly which covered current financial performance.[98]

During these same months, the top executives at General Motors finally put into effect systematic procedures for the allocation of capital funds.[99] Appropriation requests now, as earlier in the du Pont Company, had to include detailed plans of the buildings, equipment, and materials required, the amount of capital needed for, and the estimated savings to be achieved by the request. A General Manager's signature was sufficient authorization for a request below a certain amount. Above that sum the signature of the Group Executive and President as well as the Manager was required. Larger amounts still called for the approval of the Executive Committee and even greater ones that of the Finance Committee. All the large projects were first subject to review by an Appropriations Committee, the direct descendant, undoubtedly, of the Appropriation Committee that Durant had asked Pratt to chair when the latter first came to General Motors. In coming to final decisions, the Appropriation Committee and the general office relied on constantly improved forecasts of the over-all financial and economic situation.

With renewed control over long-term and short-term expenditures came a similar control of the corporation's cash resources. Instead of each division handling its own cash, as it had done before 1921, it now placed incoming receipts in one of more than a hundred banks in which the corporation had placed depository accounts in various parts of the country.[100] The divisions had no control over the depository accounts, and all disbursements from them were handled by the Financial Staff in the general office. Under such a system, the transfer of funds from one part of the corporation and the country to another was extremely easy and almost automatic. Whenever deposits in one bank exceeded a set maximum, the surplus was automatically transferred by telegraph to one of several banks selected to hold these surplus accounts, and whenever a division needed funds it would notify the general office, which would then telegraph a transfer from one of these reserve or surplus accounts. Such a system had several advantages, but the most important was the constant availability of a large pool of cash. At the same time, interdivisional billing was made much easier. One division billed another on a white slip, which the selling division sent to the Comptroller, who charged the buyer and credited the seller. This permitted settlement without any exchange of cash.

The crisis made possible one further advance toward systematic general supervision. At last, uniform accounting procedures were instituted in all parts of the corporation. A Divisional Comptroller, while reporting to his General Manager on routine matters, now followed the guidance of the financial officers in the general office on standards, procedures, and methods.[101] After 1921, the new Cost Accounting Section drew up accounting procedures for all divisions. Data from these procedures gave the division managers as well as the general office a relatively realistic picture of just what were costs and therefore profits. Now, for the first time, the general office had the basic information necessary for determining whether costs were in line with market prices and whether each unit was making a satisfactory return on its investment.[102]

But accurate accounting with its realistic evaluation of profit and loss required more than uniform procedures and improved data. In the automobile industry, with its high volume, its relatively high unit price, and its great plant capacity, the cost of a single unit varied directly with volume of output. Until full capacity was reached, the more cars produced, the lower the unit costs; while the lower the volume, the higher the costs. Costs, and therefore price and profit, were directly tied in with volume. Volume, in turn, was directly related to the demand for automobiles, which fluctuated widely from season to season, and from year to year.

To determine costs in the face of fluctuating demand, Brown used the concept of standard volume or, in his words, "the establishment of a percentage representing an assumed normal average rate of plant operation," over a long period of time.[103]

> This determines [Brown commented early in 1924] the so-called standard volume which is accepted as the basis upon which costs will be measured, and upon which the margin of profit is determined as necessary to afford a given average rate of return on capital employed. The established percentage must reflect the unavoidable fluctuations of business which render an even rate of production impossible, and, as far as practicable, should represent the economic situation of the industry, rather than any abnormal situation which might be recognized as pertaining to a given plant.

At General Motors, Brown continued, standard volume was set at 80 per cent of plant capacity. Manufacturing costs or "standard factory burden," and here the critical costs were those that varied partially with size of output, could be estimated at standard volume. If actual volume was below standard, costs would then be charged against profits as unabsorbed burden. "By this generally accepted method," Brown's assistant, Albert Bradley, wrote in 1926, "there is avoided the distortion of costs and inventory values which would result from spreading a fixed overhead over a fluctuating volume."[104] In 1924, less attention was paid to marketing expenses than to manufacturing costs. Here Brown merely used a standard "allowance for commercial expenses" of 7 per cent of sales, based on past experience.[105] With costs for a standard volume of production and a standard allowance for commercial purposes, Brown and his associates were able to determine for each product a "standard" or "base" price by which to see whether costs were in line with the actual going market price.

Volume affected costs and profits in still another way. It altered the rate of turnover on invested capital. If sales were high, the capital used in the production of each unit could be turned over more rapidly than if the dealers were having difficulties in moving their products. The over-all rate of return depended, as Brown had realized much earlier at du Pont, on both the ratio of sales to profits and the ratio of sales to investment.[106]

In figuring probable income, an accurate estimate of sales had become all important.

Since the planning of financial requirements (the allocation of funds for working and capital expenditures) depended on anticipated income, these factors, like the setting of production schedules, labor needs, the purchasing of supplies, and the allocation of other resources, had come to depend on accurate and long-term forecasting. In early 1924, the long-term estimates at General Motors were still calculated with little precision. Brown described the method in this way in one of a series of articles on the administration of General Motors that he and other executives wrote in 1924 in the periodical, *Management and Administration:*

> In December of every year, each division is required to present an outline of its view of probable operations for the succeeding year, embodying estimates of sales, earnings, and capital requirements. These outlines are in three forms, i.e.: "pessimistic," representing a minimum expectation, "conservative," representing what is considered a likely condition, and "optimistic," representing what the name implies, with production and sales capacity as a limitation.[107]

As the Vice-President in charge of Finances stressed, these annual, like the short-term four months' forecasts, were

> scrutinized by the central office and compared with current and past performance, attention of the proper officials being called to any abnormalities or marked deviations from what might be deemed a conservative sales expectation. Experience has led to the establishment of standards or working capital requirements in relation to volume of business and the forecasted investment in receivables and inventory are carefully checked against such standards, allowance being made for seasonal fluctuations. The tendencies of manufacturing costs and of selling and administrative expenses are observed, and profits are analyzed, with reference to the pricing policy laid down as governing the operations of a given division.

At the very time that Brown was writing his articles, in which the tremendous importance of accurate estimating was emphasized, an unexpected slump in the automobile market indicated a critical weakness in the corporation's forecasting methods. In the spring and summer of 1924, car production dropped off, and more for General Motors than for most companies. The first half of 1923 had witnessed, the corporation's Annual Report for 1924 explained, "an unprecedented demand for the Corporation's products and an inability to meet this demand. This resulted in the loss of sales and some dissatisfaction on the part of the Corporation's dealer organization on account of failure to make adequate delivery."[108] So output was kept high, and sales for 1923 were the largest in General

Motors' history. In anticipation of a large spring demand, production was maintained at capacity during the first quarter of 1924.

As the second quarter passed, Sloan began to suspect that supply was beginning to exceed demand. In May, he decided to investigate by taking a trip west. Crowded dealer lots in St. Louis and then in Kansas City convinced him, and he ordered immediate cuts in production.[109]

The failure to anticipate a drop in demand and then to act quickly on it, a failure threateningly reminiscent of the fall of 1920, brought swift action. On July 2, after reporting on his trip west to a meeting of General Motors purchasing agents, Sloan told them that "machinery is being set up to have the production schedules properly controlled and control insisted upon."[110] The new policy called for ten-day reports from all the corporation's dealers. From these reports, existing forecasts could be quickly appraised and production adjusted to any sudden changes in demand. Sloan provided a further check on the actual performance of the market by obtaining periodic reports from R. L. Polk and Company on new car registrations.[111] By providing registration figures on all makes of new cars, these reports presented a clear picture of just what share of its market each of the different General Motors divisions enjoyed and if and how this share was changing.

This constant flow of accurate information also supplied a more realistic base for subsequent forecasts. In outlining General Motors methods to the American Management Association early in 1926, Albert Bradley, described the new technique succinctly:

> The first and controlling principle in the establishment of General Motors production schedules is that they shall be based absolutely upon the ability of its distributors and dealers to sell cars to the public. Each car division now receives from its dealers every ten days the actual number of cars delivered to consumers, the number of new orders taken, the total orders on hand, and the number of new and used cars on hand. Each ten-day period the actual results are compared with the month's forecast, and each month, as these figures are received, the entire situation is carefully analyzed to see whether the original estimate was too high or too low. If it is decided that the estimate was too high, the production schedule is immediately reduced. If, on the other hand, it is found that the retail demand is greater than had been estimated, the production program is increased, provided the plant capacity permits. In this way the production program is compared month by month, in fact, ten-day period by ten-day period, and the necessary adjustments in the production schedule and in the estimates of the year's volume (i.e., Divisional Index) are made. In other words, instead of attempting to lay down a hard and fast production program a year ahead and stick to it regardless of the retail demand, the Corporation now follows the policy of keeping production at all times under control and in correct

alignment with the indicated annual retail demand, and with the minimum accumulation of finished products in the hands of dealers for seasonal requirements, which the flexibility of the production schedule permits.[112]

Now the general office began to pay closer attention to the validity and accuracy of the long-term divisional forecasts, and to make up indices for the corporation as a whole. By 1925, the divisional and general office staffs were drawing up comprehensive over-all plans for all operating units, plans based on carefully thought-out, long-term forecasts. These annual "Price Studies" soon became one of the most effective ways by which the general office could oversee and check the activities of the division managers without seriously impinging on the latters' authority and responsibility. Again Albert Bradley provides the best description:

> The practice of General Motors Corporation is for each car division, some time prior to the beginning of the sales year, to submit to the Executive Committee a so-called "Price Study," which embodies the Division's estimates of sales in units and in dollars, costs, profits, capital requirements, and return on investment, both at Standard Volume and at the forecast rate of operations for the new sales year, all on the basis of proposed price. This Price Study, in addition to serving as an annual forecast, also develops the standard price of each product; that is, the price which, with the plant operating at standard volume, would produce the adjudged normal average rate of return on capital which has been referred to as the economic return attainable. Proposed prices can therefore be directly compared with the standard prices which express the Corporation's fundamental policy, and a means is thereby provided for the measurement of departures from the policy which are necessitated by competitive conditions and other practical considerations.[113]

As Bradley pointed out the estimate of the year's domestic sales, on which the price studies rested, depended on at least four major factors — the growth of the industry, seasonal variation, the conditions of general business, and activities of competitors. With these factors in mind, the initial sales estimate depended on "the number of cars which are likely to be sold to the public by the entire automotive industry" and this figure was "based primarily upon actual experience for the last three years, after giving careful consideration to the probable number of automobiles needed to replace those which will be worn out or otherwise destroyed during the coming year, and an appraisal of the general business situation for the coming year." Then from this forecast, a "Divisional Index" was drawn up based on the expectations for each division, taking into consideration the total amount of business available within its respective price group and the competitive situation. Thus, Bradley expected that:

> A forecasting program should serve two separate and quite distinct general purposes. In its broadest aspects, the forecast affords a means of gauging an operating program in terms of the fundamental policy of the Corporation regarding the rate of return on capital investment, as related to the pricing of the product, and the conditions under which additional capital will be provided for expansion. The second, and the more frequent, use of a forecast is as a tool for control of current operations.[114]

Because of the heavy investment in inventory, because of the several stages involved in the over-all manufacturing and selling of the mass-produced automobile, and because of the relatively large investment in plant, equipment, and personnel at each stage, scheduling and other decisions concerning the coordination of product flow at General Motors came to rest on anticipated rather than on present conditions, while the actual flow came to be adjusted every ten days to actual market demand. By the same token, the long-term allocation of resources as well as their current use was increasingly set by an estimate of the future situation. Forecasts, therefore, became essential to strategic planning and, at the same time, provided the general office, and the divisional executives, too, with a means to appraise operating activities.

In this way then, between 1921 and 1925, General Motors had worked out highly rational and systematic procedures that permitted it, on the one hand, to coordinate and appraise the operating divisions and to plan policy for the corporation as a whole, and, on the other hand, to assure a smooth product flow from supplier to consumer and a fairly steady use of plants, facilities, and personnel in an industry where the market fluctuated rapidly. Each division's actual costs and profits could be viewed against a standard or average cost and profit, and, with truly comparable figures, the performance of one division could be accurately measured with that of another. Thus the general office was provided with objective criteria by which to evaluate and appraise the work of their division managers. Similarly, as Brown and Bradley indicated, the detailed reports from the divisions, which made possible accurate analyses of the critical revenue and cost factors determining the rate of return on investment, permitted the executives at the top offices to locate sources of strengths and weaknesses of a division. As long as there was a constant flow of such information, there was little need for the general officers to be concerned with the specific detailed work within the divisions.

Beside providing essential data for supervision and appraisal, the new fiscal and financial procedures facilitated forward planning and policy formulation. From this same information the general officers could determine, in broad terms, the price ranges and production schedules within which each division could operate. Of greater significance, a more rational allocation of funds for capital expenditures was made possible, and decisions as to where the corporation should expand, contract, or maintain its activities were make easier.

Finally, these synchronized procedures, by assuring a close coordination of flow from purchasing through production to marketing, helped to increase operating efficiencies. By keeping its varied activities tied together closely and related directly to day-to-day changes in market demand, the corporation was able to make a real reduction in costs. Manufacturing, plant, and sales facilities could be utilized at a fairly even and regular capacity. Both the manufacturing and sales force were assured of steadier employment. Outside suppliers, too, could keep their plants operating more evenly.[115] By reducing the amount of inventory needed, this careful coordination cut down the cost of working capital, lowered expenses of storing, carrying charges, and so forth. It is hard to see how expenses could not have been reduced by such rational control or how, without it, costs could only have increased.

By 1925, the work of the Financial Staff at the central headquarters had become less of a creative and more of a routine activity. The financial executives constantly checked to see whether the reporting and control procedures that had been developed continued to work properly. They made certain that the general executives and the operating managers received information promptly. And they continued to refine and develop the statistical and information controls.

Statistical and financial data and procedure alone, however, did not assure administrative control and coordination. If Sloan and Brown needed any reminder of this fact, the overproduction in the spring of 1924 provided it. The corporation's general officers soon came to spend much time on the road, visiting plants, seeing suppliers, and most of all talking to dealers.[116] Even so Sloan and the other general executives came in time to rely as much on the general staff as on the financial and statistical reports and visits to the field to provide them with essential information. The Advisory Staff played a critical role in permitting the general office to administer the separate divisions and the corporation as a whole.

Defining the Role of the Advisory Staff

The role of the Advisory Staff like that of the Financial Staff was to help coordinate, appraise, and plan policy. The staff carried out these duties partly by providing the division managers and the general officers with expert advice and assistance which was used to improve current operations and to formulate future plans. Kettering's research section worked on improved engines, parts, bodies, fuels, and other technical improvements to better automotive comfort and efficiency.[117] Hawkins' sales unit planned broad advertising campaigns, retail selling programs, showroom displays, and so on. The Factory Section developed and tested new methods of production, cost analysis, waste prevention, salvage, factory layout, design, and so forth. The Purchasing Section advised on work contracts that involved more than one division, assisted in interdivisional buying, and encouraged cooperation between the purchasing departments of the many operating units. In carrying out their advisory duties, the advisory staff was also able to keep a check on the divisions, to suggest ways to improve current methods, and to see how various policies were being followed. In this way they provided the general office with a steady flow of information on operating activities which, like statistical data provided by Brown's financial staff, was relatively free of any divisional bias.

Along with planning and checking activities, staff executives were expected to help coordinate programs and procedures so that the various functional departments in the divisions could perform their routines in approximately the same way. Essentially this meant that the staff assured an exchange of information on sales, production, accounting, engineering, and research, beside often providing data and working up plans to assist the division managers and general officers in outlining more general procedures. By spreading ideas and innovations of both the staff and line executives throughout the organization, Sloan hoped to exploit what might be called the administrative economies of scale — to make the most effective use of the talents and training of this large body of executive and supervisory personnel.

Very soon, Sloan, as Operating Vice-President, found that the staff was having difficulty in carrying out its advisory role effectively. The operating executives often looked on the staff men as interfering outsiders and theorists. For example, Kettering's most important project was the development of a radically new type of engine. According to the 1922 Annual Report, the motor was "cooled by means of copper fins brazed directly to the cylinder walls, thus doing away with radiator, water pump, and water jacket."[118] Not being subject to freezing or overheating, it was lighter, more powerful, and used less fuel than a conventional motor. The operating divisions were far more skeptical about this engine than were Kettering's sanguine staff men. Its introduction would mean production headaches that they preferred to avoid. After millions of dollars had been spent on it, the project was abandoned. Kettering blamed the failure wholly on the resistance of the divisional engineers and production men who failed to see the potentialities of the new design. As Kettering's response suggests, the lines of communication between the staff and operating executives had broken down.

By the time of the rejection of the copper-cooled engine in the summer of 1923, Sloan had begun work on a scheme to reform the lines of communication so that the staff might fulfill its role more effectively. To assure closer contact between line and staff and between divisions themselves, he settled on the interdivisional committee. Like some of the first statistical and financial controls, this committee did not emerge from a long-range plan but rather resulted from the need for meeting immediate problems.

The genesis of the plan was the problem of purchasing, and the first interdivisional committee dealt with that function. When Sloan reviewed the activities of that committee in 1924, he wrote:

> It has shown the way or what I believe to be the way of co-ordinating to the stockholder's benefit the functional activities of our different Operating Divisions without in any sense taking away from those Divisions the responsibility of their individual activities. In other words, expressed otherwise, I feel that in all our functional activities like purchasing, manufacturing, engineering, and sales, a great deal can be accomplished by proper co-ordination and, in my judgment, it is only a question of time when the development of the automotive industry will force us, due to the economics of the future picture, into just such things. The General Purchasing Committee has, I believe, shown the way and has demonstrated that those responsible for each functional activity can work together to their own profit and to the profit of the stockholders at the same time, and such a plan of co-ordination is far better from every standpoint than trying to inject it into the operations from some central activity.[119]

Sloan first turned to the interdivisional committee as a means of improving communication and coordination in the spring of 1922 when the division managers were expressing their skepticism about his suggestion for more centralized purchasing. He believed that the company could save from $5,000,000 to $10,000,000 annually if the purchasing staff in the general office drew up contracts on items that were widely used by the corporation as a whole.[120] The division managers offered many objections.[121] Some feared it would tend to cancel a division's long experience in buying for its particular needs. Others emphasized the diverse requirements of the various operating units. Still others thought that the loss of control over purchasing would seriously infringe on the authority and responsibility of the manager.

As a result of these objections, Sloan proposed that the contracts be drawn by a committee of purchasing agents representing the different divisions.[122] Besides writing specifications, the committee was expected to define broader buying policies and procedures. It had a permanent secretary with an office of his own. His job was to prepare lists and agenda for the meetings and to make detailed studies and reports. The actual specifications of the contracts and their wording were left to the purchasing office at headquarters.

After the discontinuance of the copper-cooled program had made clear the need for better line-and-staff coordination in other areas, Sloan formed a General Technical Committee to coordinate engineering and other technical activities, a Committee for Institutional Advertising, and then a General Sales Committee.[123] Shortly afterward, he added a Works Manager and a Power and Maintenance Committee.

These functional committees, like General Purchasing, had their own secretaries, their own offices and, apparently, their own budgets. In this way, they differed radically from the Purchasing Board set up earlier by Storrow and Nash or the interdepartmental Councils formed at du Pont in December, 1920. They included representatives from the comparable functional departments in each of the five car divisions and occasionally from some of those of other operating units. At first, the staff department heads were just committee members, but soon they became the secretaries of the interdivisional committees dealing directly with their specialties.[124] Thus B. G. Koether headed the Sales Section in the general office and was also Secretary of the Sales Committee. James Lynah, Secretary of the Purchasing Committee, was the manager of the Purchasing Section. Harry Crane, the President's technical adviser, was the Secretary of the General Technical Committee. Under Crane's supervision came Kettering's research laboratories, the Proving Ground, Patents, and Foreign Engineering Liaison Sections. The staff departments not assigned to the interdivisional functional committees — such units as real estate, housing, traffic, industrial relations, office buildings, and so forth — were combined into the General Service Staff under a Vice-President.[125]

General officers sat with staff specialists and operating executives on the interdivisional committees. Sloan, who had become President in May 1923, was on all the committees and was at different times Chairman of the General Technical, the Works Managers as well as the Purchasing Committee.[126] At least one member of the Executive Committee besides Sloan sat on each committee. Brown chaired the General Sales Committee, and Pratt came to head the General Purchasing. The committees, therefore, provided a systematic and regular means by which the line, staff, and general officers could meet monthly or even more often to exchange information and to consider common problems. The spirit of these meetings is caught in a letter from Sloan to Kettering written in July, 1924:

> I greatly regret that you have not been feeling very well and that you were unable to attend the meeting of the Technical Committee in Oshawa last week. We had a splendid meeting not only so far as the meeting itself went

but the boys stayed over Saturday and some of them Sunday and some went fishing and others played golf and that helps a lot in bringing men who are thinking in the same direction, more closely together. I can't help but feel, considering the magnitude of our picture and all that sort of thing, that this cooperation in engineering is working out just splendidly. We must be patient, but I am sure that as time goes on we are going to be fully repaid for the way we have handled it as compared with a more military style which I do not think would ever put us anywhere.[127]

The Role of the Executive Committee

The interdivisional committees' most important functions were to make recommendations to the Executive Committee and to propose new policies and procedures or revisions and modifications of old ones in their major functional area.[128] Except for the Purchasing Committee, none of the committees made final decisions, which were left to the division managers or to the Executive Committee.[129] As individual members of the Executive Committee were also on the interdivisional committees, they took part in the discussions leading to these recommendations and so were able to present the proposals and the reasons for them to their fellow members when decisions were required.

The Executive Committee thus remained the governing body at General Motors. Only on matters of very broad operating policy, particularly if major expenditures were involved, did the decisions of this Committee need the approval of the Finance Committee or of the Board itself. Once the crisis had been surmounted, Pierre had enlarged the small, emergency Executive Committee that he had created in late 1920. Then, after Sloan became President and Pierre, Chairman of the Board, in May, 1923, still other executives were added to the Committee. In 1925, it included ten members.[130] By 1924, the other senior committee — the Operations Committee, consisting of the major operating divisions and staff departments — had been reduced to include only the general managers of the car divisions.[131] Its function appears to have been little more than the discussion of common problems and the exchanging of information. The Executive Committee clearly made the significant entrepreneurial and strategic decisions.

The members of this committee had the time and psychological commitment as well as the necessary information to concentrate on broad strategic matters. Unlike the committee during Durant's regime, nearly all its members were now general officers without any detailed operating duties. Possibly recalling the experience of the Durant period and realizing what had happened at du Pont after he had left the company, Donaldson Brown undoubtedly expressed the feeling of General Motors' top executives when he commented in 1924 on the dangers of management by operating chiefs. Although such committee management did allow the general managers to have a say in basic policy formulation, Brown pointed out that for this very reason the resulting policy was likely to be a compromise between interested parties. Such Executive Committee members could not view problems impartially nor probably look at them in the interests of the corporation as a whole. "Policies should be dealt with from an impartial understanding of the operating aspect," Brown wrote, "and in the exercise of the dual function [as division head and member of the Committee] it is difficult for the individual to divorce himself from the departmental viewpoint."[132] Although there were some exceptions, general officers rather than division managers carried on the basic entrepreneurial activities at General Motors.[133]

The Finished Structure

By 1925 then, the structure, initially designed by Sloan before the crisis of 1920 and put into effect early in 1921, had been worked out so as to assure effective administration of the many and varied industrial resources that Durant had collected (see Chart 7). The organization builders at General Motors had placed the divisions in logical relation to one another. They had instituted a large over-all administrative office with general executives assisted by staff specialists to coordinate, appraise, and set policies for the multifunction autonomous operating divisions. The lines of authority and communication between the general office and the divisions had been carefully defined and then supplemented by the formation of the Interdivisional Committees. Finally, a mass of accurate data, both on internal performance and external conditions, had been developed to flow through these communication channels. Nearly all activities of General Motors had become keyed to forecasted market demand and estimated financial and economic conditions. Such data, compiled regularly by the divisions and then checked and supplemented by the general office, made unnecessary Sloan's original suggestion for a special staff office devoted to interdivisional scheduling.

The new organizational structure served General Motors well. From 1924 to 1927, the Corporation's share of the motor vehicle market rose from 18.8 per cent to 43.3.[134] In the following year, its profits stood at an impressive $276,468,000.[135] From then on, General Motors has maintained the leading position in the industry. The clearly and rationally defined structure became increasingly valuable as the demand for automobiles leveled off and competition intensified. The industry had sold 1.5 million passenger cars in 1921.[136] By 1925, the new passenger cars produced in a year reached 3.7 million, and for the next four years the demand for new cars averaged somewhat under four million a year. Then, with the depres-

CHART 7

General Motors Structure, 1924

C. S. Mott, "Organizing a Great Industrial," *Management and Administration*, 7:525 (May, 1924)

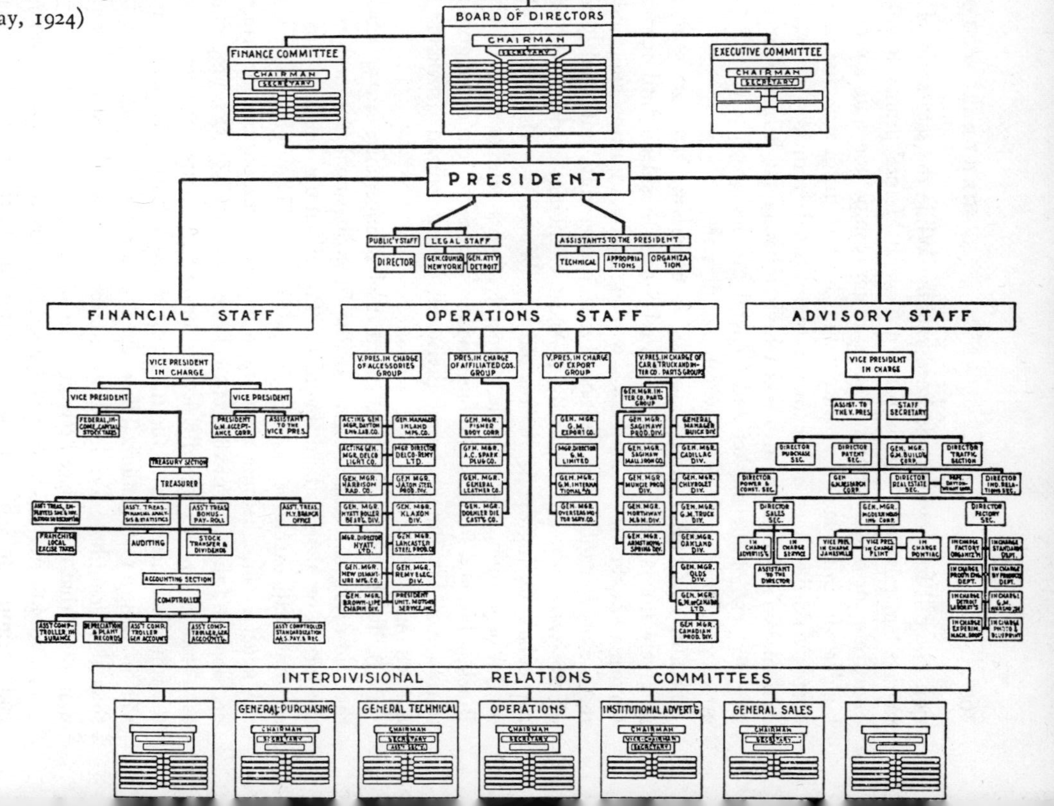

sion, the call for new cars declined rapidly. While the saturation of the market had relatively little impact on General Motors' profits, it proved disastrous for Henry Ford, Sloan's major competitor and an empire builder who in his later years rarely thought in terms of structure or even strategy. Ford's share of the market plummeted from 55.5 per cent in 1921 to 18.9 per cent in 1940 when his sales were far behind Chrysler's 23.7 per cent of the market and General Motors' 47.5 per cent.[137] And after 1926, Ford's profit record was indeed dismal.

Because of General Motors' success, its underlying structure remained relatively unchanged. However, Alfred Sloan, President until 1937 and Chairman of the Board until 1956, was constantly adjusting and modifying the organization. The relations between operating, staff, and general officers were adjusted primarily to meet changing market conditions, particularly during the depression and after World War II. In the middle of the depression, for example, General Motors temporarily combined Buick, Olds, and Pontiac into one division in order to cut down administrative costs.[138] But the multidivisional "decentralized" structure remained intact.

Probably the most significant structural change after 1925 came in the mid-1930's with the abolition of the Inter-divisional Committees and the formation shortly thereafter of the Policy Groups consisting of general and staff executives in the general office.[139] Through these groups, the general office became even more explicitly responsible for strategic decisions and the divisions for tactical ones. The staff grew in importance as it took over the Interdivisional Committees' duties of coordinating the functional activities of the many divisions and began to play a larger role in policy formulation. These changes are too complex to be considered in detail here. While significant, they were much less fundamental than those that took place between 1920 and 1925.

The administrative changes at General Motors between 1920 and 1925 had an importance beyond their contribution to the successful management of the automobile company, for the innovators advertised their accomplishments. Proud of what they had achieved, they described their new organizational methods and techniques in articles appearing in professional journals and in papers delivered at the meetings of the American Management Association. In these essays, they also set forth the new "principles" or "philosophy" of management that they believed their experiences to demonstrate. Donaldson Brown made the most precise statement of this new philosophy of decentralization in a paper on "Decentralized Operations and Responsibilities with Coordinated Control" that he read before the American Management Association in 1927. Here Brown made the distinction between "policy and administrative control."[140] The Executive Committee assisted by a general staff was responsible for settling the long-range policies within which the divisions operated. The heads of the autonomous divisions, responsible for the making and selling of automobiles and other products, enjoyed "administrative control." Brown's statement on the nature of decentralized operating responsibilities and centralized policy formulation marks the real beginning in the United States of the publication of many articles, books, and pamphlets about administrative decentralization. Just because General Motors' executives described so enthusiastically the structure they had built, the corporation became, more than that of any other company, the model for similar structural changes in other large American industrial enterprises.

A Comparison of Organization Building at General Motors and du Pont

The structure that Sloan and his associates developed came to be like the one worked out at du Pont. Yet each was created quite independently of the other and for different reasons. At du Pont, the need to plan for the postwar uses of existing resources led to the strategy of diversification which, in turn, demanded a new structure. At General Motors, the policy of integration and expansion had led to the accumulating of technical and managerial skills, as well as a wide range of physical plant, equipment, and facilities. But these many and varied instruments of production and distribution could not be fully used until a plan to unify them had been worked out.

The new plans of organization at the two companies defined or redefined the lines of authority and communication between the general office and the divisions, and outlined the types of information — detailed reports, statistics, and other pertinent data — that should flow through these channels. The crisis in the affairs of General Motors during the fall of 1920 demonstrated dramatically the dangers inherent in a lack of structural design for over-all administration. The du Pont experience, on the other hand, showed the difficulties resulting from management of several lines of products through a structure in which the channels of authority and communication, though clearly defined, were too long and too complex to assure effective administration — coordination, appraisal, and planning — for the new product lines being sold in very different markets. The reorganization there called less for new kinds of operating reports and data, and more for new channels of communication through which existing procedures for determining costs and profits and for forecasting market and broader economic conditions could be used efficiently.

At both companies, then, structure soon followed strategy. After the du Pont Company, through consolidation, had come first to administer rather than just to control financially the major share of the American explosives industry, it instituted departmental headquarters structured on a line-and-staff basis and a central organization to coordinate, appraise, and set broad policies for the functional departments. Then by greatly increasing the administrative duties of both the departmental headquarters and the central office, the strategy of diversification brought the creation of the new multidivisional "decentralized" structure. With General Motors, the different automotive enterprises that composed it expanded so rapidly to meet the demands of the national market that they too set up functional departments on a line-and-staff basis as well as central administrative offices. Only after the departure of its founder, however, did the corporation acquire a general office to administer the many operating divisions that Durant had collected in his strategy of vertical integration and constant expansion.

The creation of the new forms at du Pont and General Motors sprang from the fact that the senior executives who followed the empire builders, Coleman du Pont and Billy Durant, approached the problems of managing their widespread domains rational and systematically. The definition of the duties of the general officers, the staff specialists, and the division managers, the outlining of the channels of authority and communication, and the development of informational data and procedures did not come automatically but required concentration of thought, time, and energy. Pierre du Pont and his associates, then the next generation of managers at du Pont, Alfred Sloan, and the du Pont-trained Donaldson Brown and John Lee Pratt all focused their attention on these matters. In analyzing their administrative needs, they studied them more as problems of organization than as those of marketing, manufacturing, or engineering. And because they did, structure fairly quickly followed strategy.

Yet the approach of the organization builders at du Pont and General Motors was not necessarily the normal or accepted one in American industry in the 1920's. Their approach must be compared with that of the administrators of one of the oldest and most complex of American industrial enterprises — the Standard Oil Company (New Jersey). There little attention was paid to organization *qua* organization. As a result, structural adjustment and even strategic expansion came in more of an intuitive, unsystematic, *ad hoc* way.

4 STANDARD OIL COMPANY (NEW JERSEY)— *AD HOC* REORGANIZATION

By the mid-1920's, the Standard Oil Company (New Jersey) was facing management problems similar to those that du Pont and General Motors had confronted earlier. Like General Motors, it had been for some time committed to a program of vertical integration. In the same years, it had to meet the demands of the new and rapidly expanding market created by the coming of the automobile. The strategies of vertical integration and the needs of the gasoline business called for the acquisition of new resources and the expansion and reworking of old ones. Vertical integration raised critical problems in the coordination of product flow. The addition of new functions and new products and the growth of old ones intensified the difficulties involved in appraising the performance of the different operating activities and in effectively allocating funds, personnel, and other resources among them.

In responding to the needs created by expansion and vertical integration, the executives at Jersey rarely thought of their problems as organizational ones. With one or two notable exceptions, they worked out no broad studies of organization problems, no detailed reports on organizational needs, no explicit statements of organizational theories or concepts. Authority and responsibility did become more carefully defined and channels of communication and authority more clearly outlined, while detailed and more effective statistical and financial data were developed to assure better communication and administrative control. Still these definitions came more as responses to immediate short-term pressures in the marketing, refining, and producing of oil than from an awareness and understanding of long-term structural needs. Just because of the different approach, the answers came more slowly, less precisely, and less clearly than they did at General Motors and du Pont.

For this very reason, the administrative experience of the Jersey Company demonstrates even more forcefully than that of General Motors or du Pont how the failure to adjust structure to strategy created administrative strains and how the training, temperament, and daily activities of the responsible executives delayed structural adjustment. For Jersey did expand its activities swiftly from 1912 until 1925. The value of its assets — its physical and financial resources — rose almost exactly a billion dollars during those 13 years, from $369,265,000 to $1,369,170,000.[1] Yet until 1925, the Jersey company continued to administer its resources with much the same structure that it had evolved after its dismemberment by the Supreme Court in 1911 for violation of the Sherman Antitrust Act.

Then, between 1925 and 1927, under the pressure of overproduction and falling profits, its senior executives were forced to readjust almost simultaneously the structure of the three major types of administrative offices and their mutual relations. With much stress and strain, departmental headquarters were transformed from a committee type of structure to one based more on a line-of-command concept. New divisions, with their own central offices, were formed to coordinate, appraise, and plan policy for functional departments. Finally, the general office was reshaped to provide more effective administration of all the Jersey properties. The end result of such unplanned, *ad hoc* change was, in time, a multidivisional "decentralized" structure quite similar to that of General Motors or du Pont.

Structure and Strategy before 1925

The administrative history of the modern Standard Oil Company (New Jersey) begins properly in 1912. The changes made in the company's activities after its dismemberment by the Supreme Court ruling was in many ways as sharp a break in its history as the consolidation of the du Pont properties in 1902 and 1903 was in the history of the explosives firm. Unlike the case of the older du Pont Company, however, Standard Oil's predecessor had administered directly rather than merely controlling financially many and various operating organizations. Therefore Standard Oil inherited a wider variety of administrative practices and procedures than did the modern du Pont Company.

The old Standard Oil Company had been an industrial enterprise of great size and diversity. Until the formation of United States Steel, it was the largest in the country and remained the second largest even after 1902. Unlike United States Steel before the 1930's, the old Standard Oil Company was legally both a holding and an operating company, and administratively partly a federated and partly a consolidated enterprise. From its offices at 26 Broadway in New York City it administered both through departments and subsidiaries widely scattered refineries, sales offices, crude oil fields, pipe lines, and tankers in all parts of the world. The senior executives at 26 Broadway had to administer not only the activities of such single-function units but also those of larger multifunction subsidiaries that handled their own marketing, refining, and often transportation facilities. Among the latter were the Standard Oil Companies of Indiana and of New York, Atlantic Refining, Vacuum Oil, and Imperial Oil of Canada. Three more, Standard Oil Companies of California and Louisiana and the Rumanian subsidiary, also produced crude oil.[2] Another subsidiary, Gilbert & Barker, manufactured and sold lamps, pumps, and other equipment to outsiders as well as to Jersey-controlled enterprises.

The design by which this vast empire was administered was anything but clear-cut. As the quotation given in the first chapter indicated, it was the result of historical evolution, personal preferences, legal requirements, and just happenstance. Some attention had been given to Jersey's over-all structure in earlier years, but for more than a decade before 1912 no one had attempted to define in any formal or explicit way the lines of communication and authority within the company. Nor did anyone do so immediately after the dismemberment of the company in 1912.

If a lack of concern for systematic structure was one inheritance from the old company, another and more critical one was the use of committees in administration. Jersey's executives had long administered from 26 Broadway through committees the several units operating within one single function.[3] There were committees for transportation, pipe lines, production, manufacturing, export trade, domestic trade, and for the purchase of supplies. In coordinating, appraising, and making policy for the various units within their functional activity, these committees often became involved in making detailed operating decisions such as the amount of crude oil to run per day in a specific refinery or the amount of kerosene a branch office or sales subsidiary should sell. Committees administered not only these functional units but also the enterprise as a whole. The Directors who devoted their full time to the affairs of the Standard Oil Company met regularly, usually daily, as an Executive Committee that appraised, coordinated, and planned for the different single-function and multifunction units and for the over-all enterprise. Because the lines of authority and responsibility were not clearly defined, that committee often became deeply occupied in operating details of certain activities and paid little or no attention to the administration of others.

After its dismemberment, the Jersey Company continued to be a partly federated and partly consolidated enterprise. Because it also remained a holding as well as an operating company, its multifunction divisions were legally subsidiaries, or in the parlance of the Jersey executives — affiliates. (In this chapter affiliates, then, refer to what were administratively multifunction divisions. Subsidiary refers to what were administratively primarily single-function units with separate legal identities, such as a pipeline or marketing companies.)

Despite legal and administrative similarities, the new company was quite different from the old. Not only was it smaller, but it had lost most of its crude-producing, transportation, and domestic marketing facilities. It became essentially an American refining company that sold its products in foreign markets. In 1912, out of an average of 101.4 barrels run each day by Jersey-controlled refineries, 93.2 were run by refineries in the United States and 8.2 by foreign ones.[4] Most of this output went abroad, as the earnings from marketing activities indicate. In 1913 the return was $10.9 million from sales abroad and only $1.4 million from the domestic market.

The most noticeable change in organization between the old and the new Standard Oil Company was that in the new one the senior executives, that is, the Board of Directors, tended to increase their administrative control over the single-function departments or subsidiaries and to decrease their contact with the integrated multifunction affiliates. The latter included Standard Oil Company of Louisiana, the Imperial Oil Company of Canada (which, through its Latin American subsidiary, the International Petroleum Company Ltd., came to produce crude oil as well as to refine and market), several gas companies that piped and marketed natural gas on a local scale, and Gilbert & Barker, the makers and sellers of burners, tanks, and pumps.[5] At first, Imperial had a direct contact with general headquarters, for Walter C. Teagle, the able, young, and very active Director in charge of Foreign Sales, became its President.[6] But when Teagle took over the presidency of Jersey in 1917, no one at 26 Broadway either in the directorate or in the departmental offices was assigned to watch over the affairs of Imperial or any of the other multifunction subsidiaries except for Louisiana. Frederick W. Weller, the senior executive of Louisiana, remained a Director of the parent company until 1920, but he carried on nearly all his work in Baton Rouge. After 1920, James A. Moffett, Jr., formerly of the Louisiana Company, became the only Board member to oversee directly the activities of that affiliate. Moffett, however, also had the responsibility for the administration of shipping and then of sales.

The New York office received reports from the affiliates, and the Board still held the purse strings. But any allocation of funds or other resources was based on information provided by the affiliates themselves. The parent made little effort to check on the way they employed their resources. Their relations to 26 Broadway came to be much like that of the General Motors' divisions to their general office during Durant's time.

The single-function activities on the other hand, were more closely and formally administered by New York. The Carter Oil Company, whose president had his permanent offices at 26 Broadway, was responsible in 1912 for all the domestic producing activities except those of the Louisiana Company.[7] Pipe lines, again excepting those of Louisiana, soon came to be managed through two subsidiaries, the Oklahoma Pipe Line Company for the lines in the new mid-continent fields and the Tuscarora Company in the older Appalachian fields. As the history of the Jersey Company points out: "The principal officers and several directors of these companies had their offices in New York, however, and top policy was formulated there, where the essential co-ordination with other operations could be most readily worked out." [8]

Marketing was administered by two separate units, a small Domestic Marketing Department and an Export Trade Department. Because the dissolution decree had deprived the company of much of its home market, the Directors decided to drop the old Domestic Marketing Committee. The Marketing Department had a general manager and two branch managers, one who supervised field offices at Newark and the other the one at Baltimore.[9] At headquarters the manager had assistants to handle the main products of kerosene, fuel oil, and gasoline as well as one for specialty products and another for lubricants. Both field offices had a structure comparable with that at headquarters, with the branch manager and his assistants concentrating on the primary products, and the other two executives managing the marketing of lubricants and specialty products. These field men reported directly to their product manager at 26 Broadway. There is little evidence of the development of auxiliary or staff offices as late as 1918, not even for advertising, at departmental headquarters. In 1918, the two field offices administered a total of 80 bulk distributing stations and 180 smaller substations beside a small sales force. As the large number of substations indicates, the distributing organization was still keyed to the sale of kerosene by horse and wagon.

For the administration of foreign marketing, the old Export Trade Committee was retained, but, and this is significant for later developments, the actual administration of its activities came to be almost completely in the hands of the senior departmental executives and not of the Committee. The work of this department differed from that of the domestic marketing, and of the marketing departments in the other companies studied here, in that it supervised a number of subsidiaries, each operating in a different country rather than branch offices within the same nation. Jersey had a marketing subsidiary in nearly every European country as well as two in Latin America and, in time, one in the Far East. Different laws, customs, local needs as well as minority stockholder interests not only made such separate legal organizations necessary but required that their managers be given a fairly free hand in operations.

While the heads of these local subsidiaries managed most of the operational activities, the Export Trade Department and the Director in charge of Marketing appraised and coordinated their work. Coordination included the allocation of supplies from the American refineries. Above all, the home office planned and helped to carry out over-all market strategy. Also because the small output of refineries abroad was marketed through these subsidiaries, the Export Trade Department also administered the European refineries. In 1912, the "Director in charge of Foreign Marketing" was the thirty-four-year-old Walter C. Teagle. Teagle kept in constant contact with Frederick D. Asche, the Manager of the Department, and D. L. Harper, who took over the Department when Asche went on the Board of Directors in 1914. These three men worked closely with one another and with the competent heads of foreign companies, but they rarely met formally as a committee. Here the chain of command, from Teagle to Asche to Harper to the chiefs of the subsidiaries, was clearly defined.[10] As so much of the operational work and the tactical decisions were handled locally, there seemed little need to develop auxiliary or service offices in the headquarters of this department. Advertising, for example, could obviously be taken care of more effectively locally than from 26 Broadway.

If the committee form of management fell away in foreign marketing, it continued to dominate the administration of the Jersey Company's other primary activity — refining. The Manufacturing Committee maintained a tight control over 90 per cent of the company's refining capacity — over the mammoth Bayway, the older Bayonne, and the smaller Eagle refineries, all in New Jersey across the river from New York, over the refineries in Baltimore and Parkersburg, West Virginia, and over small ones in Latin America and later some in the Far East. Its responsibilities were broad. As the Committee itself pointed out, "in the last analysis, all questions of method, of running new products, and equipment, and major problems come before the Manufacturing Committee for determination." [11] It reviewed and recommended to the Board all estimates for running expenses, repairs and new construction, and had the final say on expenditures under a certain limit. These recommendations included, for example, those dealing with when and where to build new refineries. Finally, the Committee was responsible for the coordination of product flow through the major functions — production, transportation, manufacturing, and marketing. It allocated the use of current resources in refining activities and planned for the employment of these and additional resources in the future.

The refining organization at Jersey in these years provides an extreme example of group responsibility in a large-scale industrial enterprise. The department was in reality a federation of refiners who coordinated their activities in the Manufacturing Committee. Each major refinery had its General Manager with an office on the seventh floor at 26 Broadway. Each of these executives was responsible for the operation of his own refinery. Collectively, they made policies and set programs for all matters concerning the manufacturing of Jersey's products. Quite often each tended to put his own needs and interests before those of the Department as a whole. Departmental policy and action was worked out or negotiated in the Manufacturing Committee's Room 707. Executives of Jersey Standard, in fact, referred to the Department's decisions and activities as those of "the Room." "The Room," not the Chairman of the Committee, made the executive decisions, both in theory and in practice.

Only in scheduling and coordinating the flow of petroleum through the refineries did the work of the Manufacturing Committee come to be handled by an individual rather than by a group. Since it was responsible for scheduling runs at all Jersey-controlled refineries, the Committee had to decide on how much would be run, where and when; it also had to be sure that the refineries received deliveries of crude oil and that the two marketing departments were notified of the availability of supplies. This meant that it came to have charge of the allocation to the refineries of crude taken from Carter Oil and purchased from outsiders. In cooperation with the Domestic Trade Department it also allotted refined oil to its own bulk stations and to those of large customers, and through the Export Trade Department to foreign subsidiaries. The immediate day-to-day decisions necessary to keep the flow moving could hardly be handled by a group, and so the Manufacturing Committee's Secretary increasingly took charge of the administration of the coordination of product flow.

The Manufacturing Committee and the other functional units were responsible to the Board of Directors. The Board, like that of the old Jersey Company, consisted largely of full-time executives. The Directors of 1912 had enjoyed long and varied service.[12] Some had helped to build the old company. Others had managed the large multifunction affiliates. These men were generalists rather than functional specialists. Yet because of their long and varied experience, they were old in years. In the period immediately following 1912, they were replaced by younger men whose business experience had been confined to one functional activity.

Teagle, who became President in 1917, set the pattern. In 1912, he was one of the very few Directors specifically in charge of a functional activity. All the Directors who were appointed during the first years of his term, however, were taken from functional departments and each was given the title of Director in charge of his specialty. Such Directors continued to be engrossed in the management of the special activities in which each had so long worked. This was one reason why the Directors of the new company increasingly concentrated on the single-function departments and, by the same token, paid less and less attention to the administration of more distant multifunction affiliates.

In some ways, the structure at Jersey in an unplanned way became similar to that of the du Pont Company before 1921 and, in other ways, like General Motors before its reorganization. The senior officers were responsible individually for the over-all administration of the functional departments whose operating details were handled by a department head, except in the case of the Manufacturing Committee, where the whole committee managed. Collectively with the President and the Chairman of the Board, the senior officer coordinated, appraised, and set policies for the departments and the company as a whole. But unlike the du Pont Executive Committee, they had also to allocate funds to and make decisions (on relatively little information) about a number of multifunction enterprises. Jersey was thus administratively both highly centralized and highly decentralized. Moreover, the channels of authority and communication between the senior executive group and the departments or the multifunction subsidiaries were not defined at all clearly. This lack of an explicit design would probably have caused little difficulty if Jersey's business had remained relatively stable and if the major administrative changes had been only those caused by the normal turnover of top personnel. But these years were ones of rapid growth for Jersey. Growth, in time, forced clarification and redefinition of the structure of the departments and of the company as a whole.

The Strategy of Vertical Integration and Continued Expansion

After 1912, Jersey's strategy of growth came essentially as a response to two pressures. The first, the result of its dismemberment, was the desire to obtain a better balance between the different functions of the oil business. The second was the need to adjust to the rapid changes and expansion of the market caused by the appearance of two of the greatest modern technological innovations, electric power and the gasoline engine.

The coming of these two new generators of power, along with the opening of huge new oil fields in Texas and California, was revolutionizing the patterns of supply and demand in the oil industry even before the breakup of the old Standard Oil Company. By replacing kerosene as the major source of artificial light here and abroad, electricity was rapidly curtailing the demand for the industry's major product. At the same time, the insatiable demand of the automobile for gasoline and lubricants and a somewhat lesser call for fuel oil for ships and in industry more than made up for the decline in the market for kerosene.[13] Gasoline, which had taken 15 per cent of Jersey's deliveries in 1912, in 1927 accounted for 41 per cent. By then, according to Teagle, it provided more than 60 per cent of the industry's return on refined products.[14] For these same years, kerosene had dropped from 44 per cent to 11 per cent of the total refined products that Jersey manufactured. Moreover, while the nature of the market was changing, the over-all demand was quickly increasing. Total deliveries of the company's refined products quadrupled between 1914 and 1927, from just under 40 million barrels to over 170 million.

The ever-expanding demand for petroleum products caused concern for Jersey executives about the availability of supplies at reasonable prices. This concern grew as new competitors, largely producing companies, such as Gulf, the Texas Corporation, and Shell, built refining and marketing organizations. Jersey, with its activities concentrated in refining, had to rely on others for its raw materials and for the marketing of its products. Of the daily average of 96,000 barrels of crude run by its refineries in the United States and Canada in 1912, its domestic subsidiaries and affiliates supplied only 7,500 barrels; while in the years after 1912, one company (Standard Oil of New York) took 40 per cent of the gasoline Jersey sold in the United States.[15] Finally, the dismemberment left Jersey with few transportation facilities. From 1912 until the coming of the great depression of the 1930's, the company's basic objective was to have its resources less concentrated in the manufacturing branch and better deployed in the other sectors of the oil industry.

To carry out this fundamental policy of vertical integration and to meet the demands of the fuel oil and gasoline market, Jersey Standard was forced to add new and to expand existing resources of equipment, plant, and personnel. It had to build new functional departments to administer the new activities. This growth, in turn, brought new tasks and problems to the existing functional units, particularly manufacturing and domestic marketing. It called for increasing specialization and for the fashioning of new service and auxiliary departments. It made more and more complex the coordination, appraisal, and planning of the activities within and between the different administrative units. Finally, expansion led to the purchase of new affiliates and the growth of the older autonomous, multifunction ones, and so raised another range of administrative problems. Yet, despite these steadily mounting pressures, many years were to pass before Teagle and his associates paid serious attention to their company's management structure.

Vertical Integration and the Creation of New Functional Departments

There is no indication in the records in the company's files that Jersey's expansion in the years immediately after 1911 followed any explicitly defined strategic plan. But clearly for many years its directors were more interested in building up their plant, personnel, and other resources in transportation and in the production of crude oil than in developing market facilities. They apparently felt that they could rely on outsiders, particularly the former members of the old company, like Standard Oil of New York, to market their refined products but not to provide them with the necessary crude oil. Initially, one significant reason for integrating backward rather than forward was undoubtedly the rapidly expanding market. Just because the output of the refineries quickly found customers, there was danger that the company could meet this demand only by purchasing crude at seemingly unreasonable prices.[16] Even more serious was the possibility that it might not be able to obtain the desired quantity of supplies when the refineries were ready to process them. However, Jersey's concentration on obtaining crude oil rather than on developing her marketing organization did result in a dangerous delay in finding ways to meet the swiftly growing demand for gasoline.

Two executives, Walter C. Teagle and Everit J. Sadler, the latter one of Jersey's younger and most forceful managers, were particularly concerned over their company's dependence on outsiders for supplies and shipping. They strongly supported the moves made during World War I to expand the output and resources of the domestic affiliates, the Carter Oil Company and Standard Oil of Louisiana.[17] In 1915, Carter moved from the Appalachian to the mid-continent fields and began aggressively to purchase and develop new fields. Simultaneously, the Louisiana Company increased production as large fields were opened up in the vicinity of its refinery. Even before the war, Imperial moved through its subsidiary, International, to production of crude in Peru and, after the war, in Columbia.

Early in 1917, Sadler began to make clear his views on production. What was needed, he insisted, was a precise policy of expansion and then an organization to administer the properties acquired, that is, an explicit strategy and a definite structure for production activities. Rapidly increasing competition for the world's oil supply in the face of an expanding market for refined products made such planning and organization imperative. In March, 1917, Sadler wrote Seth B. Hunt, the Treasurer and Director in charge of producing activities:

> I do not know that a definite policy as to expansion and foreign producing business has ever been decided on by our Company. If it has not, it

would seem to be a very important question which might be better discussed in principle rather than being considered only in cases where isolated fields or propositions are coming up for our consideration. . . .

I feel the real source of power in the oil business is control of production, and it does not seem that our Company is sufficiently fortified in this respect. In the United States possibly we have some protection in production and transportation facilities controlled by friendly concerns. This may or may not be sufficient for our production but, in any event, foreign production is almost exclusively in the hands of our competitors.[18]

One result of Sadler's pleas, supported as they were by Teagle, was a drive after the end of World War I to obtain producing facilities, particularly overseas. By providing new sources of supplies, overseas fields would permit an expansion of the small refining capacity of Jersey's foreign affiliates, since the greater portion of the refined products sold in Europe and Latin America was still exported from Jersey's American refineries.

At home, the most significant move was the purchase in January, 1919, of a controlling interest in Humble Oil & Refining Company, one of the largest producers in Texas. The defensive nature of this acquisition should be stressed. For Humble, the alliance provided useful capital and a friendly customer. As for Jersey, its history points out that "Jersey Standard not only was assured of a greater actual and potential domestic crude production, but obtained the services of an able purchasing organization to remedy that dangerous dependence upon non-Jersey crude suppliers to which Sadler had pointed with alarm a year [*sic*] earlier." [19] Partly because Humble enjoyed an exceptionally able management and partly because of Texas law against outside control, the Jersey Company made no effort to develop any management controls over its Texas affiliate. The purchase of the Humble stock was considered in 1919 as essentially an investment and a form of insurance.[20]

In 1917 Sadler argued further for an organization to carry out the more precisely defined strategy of obtaining and producing crude. By assuring better planning, coordination, and appraisal, proper organization could make production more efficient. As he told Hunt:

It also seems even the work which we are now doing in foreign fields should be handled by a single department, so that each field does not have to do its own experimenting, but can draw from a common clearing house for information. This would prevent competition between the various fields for men and would prevent undesirable men from being employed in one of our foreign fields after another.

A very important advantage in foreign work would be frequent visits to all fields by one or more men from headquarters to get in close touch with the problems to be solved and to carry the best ideas from one field to another . . . I think it no exaggeration to say the difference between the best and the average producing talent may well be 50% on investment in different foreign fields. The ordinary driller, under such conditions, is not competent and must be closely watched.[21]

Two years later, after he repeated his pleas, the Board of Directors set up a Foreign Producing Department and brought Sadler from handling production activities in Mexico to 26 Broadway to become its head. This department coordinated and supervised Jersey's exploration and producing activities in Europe, Asia, the Near East, Africa, and Latin America outside of Peru and Colombia, where Imperial's International operated.[22]

A. F. Corwin, President of Carter, continued to administer domestic production activities from his offices at 26 Broadway. By 1919, Corwin's unit had a clear-cut line-and-staff structure with two operating sections, the Western for the mid-continent fields and the Eastern for the Appalachian fields.[23] The staff at headquarters included a geologist, a statistician, and a financial officer. A Vice-President headed each of the two regional offices. He had under him a General Superintendent with other line assistants and staff officers at the regional headquarters and Division Superintendents who managed the actual operations in the field.

Sadler had a much broader task than Corwin. Not only did he have the whole globe as a field for exploration; but also his field units were, like those of the Export Trade Department, subsidiaries in different countries rather than branch units within the same nation. They had to adjust their internal organization to local differences, both legal and social. But as a whole the structure of Sadler's department was much like that of Corwin's. In 1920, it administered subsidiaries with offices in Venezuela, Bolivia, North Africa, Mexico, and Rumania. In time, the Department set up an office in Paris which helped to handle the production activities throughout most of Europe. At 26 Broadway, Sadler had his line assistants for the supervision of major geographical areas and his small staff offices. He also kept the Board more closely informed of his department's activities than did Corwin. In regular reports, apparently made on his own initiative, he reviewed the existing situation, appraised the effectiveness of current operations, and outlined plans for future expansion. The purpose of this systematic planning was, Sadler explained to his colleagues, "to give an idea of the significance of committing ourselves to a program similar to that outlined, and to provoke general discussion, and eventually a decision as to policy along broad lines."[24] Since he felt it necessary to point out so explicitly the need of thinking in terms of strategy and structure, he was undoubtedly one of the first executives at Jersey to see this need.

In the years following the dissolution, Jersey Standard rapidly expanded its transportation facilities as well as its producing activities.[25] While its foreign affiliates, particularly the German and Italian companies, had small fleets, Jersey had no tankers of its own in 1912. It found chartering ships to be uncertain and often costly for that reason. Even before World War I made imperative the acquisition of new ships, the oil company began to have tankers built. In 1917, Jersey owned 44 ships, over half of which were less than three years old, while its subsidiaries held title to 27.

As the fleet grew, so did the offices and personnel of the new Foreign Shipping Department. The Department arranged that the company and its affiliates had the necessary shipping at the right time and in the right amount. It planned for future as well as current shipping needs, proposing the amount of new tonnage that should be built and the amount to be chartered. After the war, the Department was thoroughly reorganized. Robert L. Hague, former chief of the Construction and Repair Division of the United States Shipping Board, was appointed by the Directors to head what became the Marine Department. Beside improving the morale of the men and officers of the fleet, Hague concentrated on finding ways to make more efficient use of Jersey shipping.

By the mid-1920's, Jersey had moved well along the road to a better balance between functions. Where the total crude production of Jersey affiliates and subsidiaries in 1912 was 11 per cent of total refinery output and only 16 per cent in 1918, it had reached 44 per cent by 1927; while total crude production rose from 11,091 barrels a day in 1912 (7,469 for the domestic units) to 24,166 in 1916, 96,451 in 1920, and 189,911 in 1927.[26] Although the size of Jersey's fleet remained about the same after World War I (38 ships in 1927), the fleets of its affiliates, over which it had general supervision, continued to grow.

Expansion and the Older Departments

As described above, the strategy of vertical integration had led to the addition of new resources and had provided for their administration. The result had been the setting up of two new functional departments and an enlargement of a third, Carter. In all three, the lines of authority and communication were clearly drawn on a line-and-staff basis. At the same time, both the strategy of integration and the exuberant growth of the gasoline market, particularly in the postwar years, were having a powerful impact on the older departments. There, where the lines of authority and communication had never been too distinct, growth led increasingly to administrative confusion and difficulties.

Of the older departments, the Export Trade was the least troubled by the company's rapid expansion. Europe and Latin America were less affected than the American markets by the coming of the internal-combustion engine. Nor did the drive to obtain new sources of crude have too much effect on Europe, for few productive fields had as yet been found there, and refinery capacity had not yet been expanded to use the crude produced elsewhere. Moreover, the competent, energetic, and well-trained executives in the Department and in the foreign marketing subsidiaries were well equipped to meet new changes and challenges. Nevertheless, by 1924, it had become clear that increasing administrative demands called for changes in the overseas sales organization.

The marketing picture at home was far less satisfactory than that abroad. Here less able and less aggressive executives were trying to handle a more complex situation. Not until the expanding demand for petroleum products leveled off in the mid-1920's did the Jersey Board begin to pay serious attention to domestic marketing needs and strategies. Elderly executives in the Domestic Sales Department continued to conduct their business much as they had before the 1911 dissolution. They preferred to concentrate on profitable bulk sales that required much less effort and imagination, and called for fewer rearrangements of existing distributing facilities and for less development of new ones than did the marketing of gasoline or fuel oil for use by the ultimate consumer. Fuel oil continued to be sold in bulk to major shipping and industrial companies, and a large share of Jersey's rapidly growing gasoline production went to former Standard Oil firms that were primarily marketing companies. Between 1912 and 1918, Standard of New York took almost as much gasoline from the Jersey refineries as did the whole of the latter's own Domestic Marketing Department.[27]

In 1919, the Jersey Directors made an initial attempt to improve their American marketing organization. Instead of profiting from the experience of the Export Trade Department, they fell back on tradition and created a Domestic Marketing Committee to appraise and plan policies for the Department. At the same time, they formed a separate unit to administer the facilities and personnel which had grown to meet the greatly enlarged demand for fuel oil which World War I had stimulated. They also appointed two senior sales executives to the Board, one from Jersey and one from Louisiana. These changes had little or no effect on marketing policy. C. E. Young, the new Department Head, made no reports or recommendations as to future plans and programs comparable with those that Sadler was writing as head of foreign production. The new committee, of which Young was Chairman, included able marketing executives — Harper of Export Trade; Moffet, the Director from Louisiana; C. G. Sheffield, the head of the new Fuel Oil Department; Joseph H. Senior, head of the largest Latin American subsidiary; and F. H.

Bedford, Jr., who supervised sales of lubricants abroad.[28] But these men were far too busy with their regular duties in other areas to give domestic marketing much attention. Young, a man in his sixties who had headed the Newark branch office since 1890, was hardly the one to accept new challenges. Nevertheless, it was five years before Teagle and the Jersey Board took further steps to improve domestic marketing strategy and structure.

After World War I, Jersey's rapid expansion created even more strains on its manufacturing than on its marketing organization. In the oil company's oldest and largest department, vertical integration had increased the need for better communication and coordination between its activities and those of the other departments. The unprecedented growth of the gasoline market brought new and more complicated refining processes. It led to such an expansion of refining facilities that total deliveries of refined products rose from 47.7 million barrels in 1916 to 82.7 million in 1920 and to 144.9 million in 1924.[29] Increase in output and technological change also occasioned the growth of service or auxiliary departments, which, in turn, brought new problems of communication and coordination.

As the volume of operations expanded, the Manufacturing Committee's responsibility for the coordination of product flow became increasingly heavy. Crude oil was now available from many more sources, and as the chemical consistency of crude from each new field differed from the others, each called for somewhat different processing. As the Jersey shipping fleet grew, it became even more essential to use the ships steadily and efficiently. As the demand for the different products changed and expanded, so the refineries had to make additional adjustments in their processing operations. Finally, as shifts in demand caused the different marketing units to call for constantly changing amounts and grades from the refineries, other departments beside Manufacturing became concerned with product flow.[30] Domestic Sales, Export Trade, Foreign Producing, and Carter, all appointed executives to be responsible for the flow within their own units. Inevitably, these different departments tended to define product flow in terms of their own immediate and particular needs. Often there was a breakdown of communication between departments concerning current and future requirements and the availability of supplies.

The Growth of Staff Departments

The growth of staff departments brought other difficulties in coordination. These auxiliary and service organizations arose largely from the needs created by the enlargement of refining facilities and personnel.

During the 1920's the domestic marketers began to pay more attention to advertising, but it was many years before they formed additional staff offices to analyze market performance and expenses comparable with the offices set up at du Pont before World War I. The production departments came to have a growing staff of geologists and petroleum engineers to assist in exploration and drilling, but neither they nor the transportation units needed to enlarge auxiliary or staff offices. The greatest proliferation of staff activities come in manufacturing. There expansion and an increasingly complex technology led, in 1919, directly to the formation of the first research and development department in an American oil company, to the enlargement of the engineering activities, to the building of a separate purchasing organization, and, more indirectly, to the establishment of a labor relations office.

The demand for gasoline was responsible for the formation of the Development Department. Until the coming of the automobile, gasoline had been considered only a minor by-product of kerosene. Then, as the first decade of the twentieth century passed, the industry began to concentrate more and more on obtaining a higher portion of these lighter fractions of crude which was used for gasoline. Finally, in 1913, Dr. William M. Burton of Indiana Standard patented a process for cracking a relatively low value of gas oil and other middle distillates into the valuable light fractions. As a result, a much higher amount of gasoline could be obtained from the same amount of crude.[31]

The Jersey Directors were willing at first to pay royalties of 25 per cent of the profit for the use of the Burton process, and during the World War I period Burton pressure stills were being constructed, though rather slowly, at the major Jersey refineries. After Teagle became President, he decided that the time had come for Standard to develop its own processes for cracking gasoline and to improve its automotive lubricants. So, late in 1918, he hired Edgar M. Clark, Superintendent of Indiana Standard's Wood River refinery, to take charge of Jersey's Bayway refinery. Clark, who brought with him able and scientifically trained refiners, began to advocate more long-term planning in manufacturing besides experimenting with new processes.

Unlike the company's older refiners, Clark took a keen interest in developments on petroleum technology.[32] In trying to keep abreast of current trends, Clark wrote regularly to Frank A. Howard, a young Chicago patent lawyer with an engineering degree from George Washington University, who had done some of the legal work on the Burton process. After looking over Clark's correspondence with Howard, Teagle began writing to the young lawyer himself. Before long, at Teagle's request, Clark asked Howard to outline a general plan for carrying on research and development at Jersey.

Teagle, by now strongly committed to the idea, saw the possibilities of using a research department for forward planning in marketing as well as manufacturing. As he wrote A. Cotton Bedford, Chairman of the Board, in June, 1919:

> Since you have been away I have felt more than ever before the need for a thoroughly organized and competent research department under an able executive, such a department not to be confined merely to chemical research, but to general research in connection not only with the production and refining of our products, but with the sales end of the business as well. There are, I am convinced, a number of products that could be manufactured in addition to the lines which we are at present manufacturing, and the manufacture of those products undoubtedly would result in enhanced profits to the company. The General Electric and other concerns of a like character lay a great stress upon their research department. They consider this department on a parity in importance with the maufacturing and sales end of their business. Our research department up to date is a joke, pure and simple; we have no such thing, and on your return here I am anxious to discuss with you this entire question.[33]

As a result of the interest of Clark and Teagle in systematic research, Howard came to Jersey to set up a new department.[34] His Development Department began work by concentrating primarily on improving existing product and processes rather than on developing new ones.[35] The important task, Howard reasoned, was to apply the already known backlog of scientific knowledge to petroleum technology rather than to attempt fundamental research. His unit soon had found a process to take the place of the Burton patents, and by 1927 the Jersey Manufacturing Department was able to get twice as much gasoline from a barrel of crude than it had a decade earlier. Concentrating, as they did, on improving the manufacture of gasoline, neither Howard nor Clark gave any attention to developing market or commercial research. Neither did anyone in the Marketing Department.

Although Howard's organization grew out of the Manufacturing Committee's needs, its administrative relationships with the older unit were confused. Howard became a member of the Manufacturing Committee, and that Committee supplied funds for his construction work and for salaries. However, he reported directly to Teagle and the Board, and Teagle's office supplied the money for special lines of investigation. This lack of a clear-cut connection helped to intensify the conflict between the new staff specialists and the refiners, for several of the latter were skeptical of Howard's rational, scientific approach to what they still considered to be essentially an art.

The relations between the other staff units, Engineering, Personnel, and Purchasing, and the refiners were just as imprecise and unclear. Charles H. Haupt, the manager of the oldest of these offices, the General Engineering Department, was a member of the Manufacturing Committee, but also reported directly to the Board. Since 1913, his department had been responsible for special refinery construction, marketing installations, improvements in apparatus and for necessary tests and experiments.[36] Because Haupt himself was an old-time refiner, he had less trouble with the Manufacturing Department than did Howard. Yet just because of Haupt's conservatism the latter's department had to take over Engineering's role in improving apparatus and processes.

If Haupt paid little attention to forward planning, Clarence J. Hicks, Jersey's labor relations expert, did. Hicks had been brought into the company in 1917 as a result of labor troubles during the previous two years. After 1917, he worked out an industrial representation and joint management-labor conference program, developed annuity and benefits plans, and established a Personnel and Training Department to centralize the hiring and firing of personnel.[37] Hicks' office, which soon had a Medical and Safety Division, was placed directly under Teagle.[38] Hicks, although not a member of the Manufacturing Committee, was able to reduce some of the antagonisms of the refinery superintendents and managers to his program through his extraordinary tact and patience.

After 1921, the Purchasing Department often came into conflict with the manufacturing organization. In that year, the Board decided to take much of the buying of materials and equipment out of the hands of the refineries and to put it into an expanded and reorganized purchasing department. This difficult task was given temporarily to C. G. Sheffield, the competent executive who had been recruited from the Union Oil Company of California in 1919 to take charge of organizing the new Fuel Oil Department.

From the start, the coordination of the work of these new auxiliary and service sections with that of the older operating departments proved difficult. Once acquired, the talents of these staff specialists were not fully or effectively utilized. Normal line-and-staff tensions were intensified at Jersey by the failure to outline precisely the role and duties of the staff specialists. Since Teagle and most of his associates seemed to believe that the conflicts occurred from personality differences alone, they did little to define more clearly the staff executive's position. Another reason that the Board took little action to improve line-and-staff relations was that its individual members tended to be too involved in their own functional duties to think or act about the problems of interdepartmental coordination.

The Board

As has been pointed out already, the Jersey Board during these years was coming to be made up of specialists responsible for the activities of their functional activity. In 1919, two domestic marketers, T. J. Williams and James A. Moffett, Jr., had joined the Board. In 1921, Sadler, Clark, and Charles G. Black (the latter long the Chairman of the Manufacturing Committee) were appointed. Sadler became Director in charge of Production and the other two, Directors in charge of Manufacturing.[39] Two other active directors in the early 1920's were primarily financial men. Between them and A. Cotton Bedford, Chairman of the Board from 1917 to 1925, the Treasurer's post was held from 1910 to 1933.[40] It should be stressed that the offices which these men supervised — the Treasurer's and Comptroller's Departments — were essentially housekeeping units. They had not developed, as had Donaldson Brown's departments at du Pont and General Motors, the financial and statistical data so essential for the administration of a far-flung industrial empire.

Such specialists had little time for, information about, or interest in the administration of the company as a whole. Nor could they fully appreciate the needs and problems of their colleagues on the Board. Only Teagle and possibly A. Cotton Bedford as Chairman of the Board saw the problems from a company rather than a departmental viewpoint. Bedford, however, did little more than look after the company's relations with the public and government.[41] Teagle was constantly on the firing line, helping to meet new situations and challenges in production, refining, and foreign marketing. Deeply committed, preferring action to reflection, Jersey's President concentrated on carrying out the strategies of expansion. Although he often gave too little attention to long-range goals, his talents and temperament were those of a builder of empires rather than organizations.[42] Like Billy Durant and Coleman du Pont, he excelled in the accumulation of resources. Like them, too, he had little interest in erecting the structure necessary to assure the most efficient use of these resources.

By 1924, a rationally defined structure had become a paramount need at Jersey Standard. If the company was to employ its resources, old and new, efficiently, it needed to make structural changes in four areas. The Board members must prevent operating activities from interfering with long-term entrepreneurial planning and appraisal. Better means for coordinating the activities of the different departments were clearly essential. The confused lines of authority and communication within some operating departments demanded redefining. Finally, closer administrative ties with the larger, multifunction affiliates were called for if the over-all resources of all Jersey holdings were to be effectively mobilized.

Initial Awareness of Structural Weaknesses

Although no Jersey executive saw his company's over-all organizational needs in exactly these terms, those who had shown the most concern with structure (Clark, Howard, and Sadler) began by 1924 to point out critical organizational weaknesses. The first two men were disturbed over the internal organization of the most important functional administrative unit, the Manufacturing Committee, while Sadler was aware of the need for closer coordination of all the Jersey activities.

Clark and Howard had become particularly distressed about the difficulties involved in improving the refinery processes and the quality of the finished products. Their problems, they believed, were caused partly by the resistance of the older refiners to new techniques. The company's historians have pointed out how the Manufacturing Committee became badly split in 1922 when the General Superintendent at Baton Rouge continued his own experiments "on batch-type crude distillation stills in almost complete defiance of Clark's contention that effort should be centered in perfecting continuous-process units."[43] Yet Clark and Howard came to blame their problems fully as much on the loose, confused organization of the manufacturing activities. Therefore, in 1923 at Clark's suggestion, Howard made a careful study of the management structure of three other oil companies—Standard of Indiana, Standard of California, and the Union Oil Company of California. Early the next year Clark sent a preliminary report to George W. McKnight, who had been Chairman of the Manufacturing Committee since 1921.[44] A week later, Howard followed up with a more detailed account that analyzed the Manufacturing Committee's organizational defects, suggested reasons for its current difficulties, and proposed solutions.

The defects, Howard began, were threefold. Too much time was spent on operating routine, too much energy in reaching group decisions, and too little use made of staff departments. In Howard's words:

> 1. All responsible executives are badly overburdened with work. This is the real root of most of the troubles met with.
>
> 2. There is a very large and unnecessary amount of paper work—mere passing on of letters and reports through various hands—which takes time very needed from true management functions without accomplishing in itself any useful purpose.

3. In very many matters the Manufacturing Department does not function as a unit, either within itself or in its dealings with outside departments or with the Board of Directors. It functions rather as a loose federation.

4. The mere effort to secure the desired uniformity of policy and of methods requires an undue proportion of the Committee's time.

5. Maximum use is not made of the advice and experience of the technical and operating staffs in aiding one another, and there is in some instances unnecessary friction and resulting waste of energy and time in reconciling conflicting views on technical matters.[45]

Duplication of effort and lack of cooperation, particularly between the refineries in the New York area as well as the loss of valuable time had been the result.

These serious weaknesses were, Howard reasoned:

> The inevitable result of increasing complication of the business of manufacturing management from every angle. Not only have the burdens of the Manufacturing Department on pure manufacturing lines been enormously increased by the Company policy which makes manufacturing act as a flywheel for variations in quantity and quality of crude production, markets, and pipe line and fleet requirements; but on top of these burdens there have come the creation of staff departments required to meet changing conditions. The most important of these staff departments are: industrial relations, engineering, and development. The coordination of policies and functions of these three staff departments with manufacturing proper would have been in itself an enormous burden without the other changing conditions which have been met at the same time.

Howard recommended that the lines of authority and responsibility within the Manufacturing Committee be made clearer and the Committee become in fact a department. At all three of the companies which he had studied, the responsibility for manufacturing activities, in practice, if not in theory, was centralized under a single executive who, with a staff divided along functional lines, administered the refineries in the field. Although Howard agreed that the Manufacturing Committee could not be abolished at Jersey Standard, he did feel its organization could be modified along the lines suggested by the experience of these other three companies.

He proposed first that the Chairman of the Manufacturing Committee "become ex officio General Manager of the Manufacturing Department." Next, he recommended changes in the duties of the Committee members. Instead of representing separate works or refineries, they should take charge of different activities such as employee relations, appropriations, engineering, accounting, development, building and power, processing, and inspection. Thus the position of refinery General Manager with offices in New York would be abolished, and Resident Superintendents would be the senior men in charge of the refineries. These Resident Superintendents as well as the heads of those staff units most closely connected with the details of manufacturing—Plant Engineering, the Experimental Division, and Inspection—would report directly to Room 707. Each Committee member would then have the authority and responsibility for the "active supervision" of one or possibly two specific functions. In other words, Howard proposed to transform this federation of refiners into a department where the field units reported to the department head, and the latter's immediate assistants and the Committee members took charge of specific auxiliary function activities. Howard was not yet proposing a clear-cut line-and-staff departmental structure. The heads of the functional units would have direct contact with their counterparts in the refineries in the field, as Howard had found at Standard of California.

Moreover, the Committee would still have the final say in all manufacturing activities. Therefore, "with a view to the saving of time," in handling the day-to-day decisions, the four senior members of the Committee were to work entirely in New York, meeting daily to take

> care of the bulk of the Manufacturing Department's paper work. The four junior members of the Committee could be relieved from these daily meetings and have time to devote their attention to their several departments and the New York works; to meet with the Manufacturing Committee as a whole, not to exceed one day per week in New York, and perhaps one day per week at works designated by the Chairman.

Howard's plans for converting the Manufacturing Committee into a systematically organized department were undoubtedly discussed by the Board of Directors, but no action was taken at that time. Possibly Teagle and his colleagues thought the plan too radical. More likely they were too busy with other matters to pay much attention to a problem not requiring immediate attention.

Howard made no specific suggestions for changing the Manufacturing Committee's most important single task, that of coordinating product flow, although he did remind McKnight that the allocation of crude oil, assignment of transportation, and distribution of refined products were becoming increasingly complicated. In June, 1924, however, Sadler recommended and the Board agreed that "a definite organization should be established to control this allocation, made up of components representing the producing, pipeline, marine, manufacturing, and marketing interests."[46] Sadler proposed a committee of departmental representatives "to decide questions of grade and quantity of crude to be run at what works, with a comprehensive view of all departments interested and with the minimum of changes, resulting in the economy of the greatest possible uniformity of operation; and in addition it would probably give us a dependable picture to guide us in making the purchases of products." He particularly hoped that its work would result in the "subordination of the departmental interest to the interest of the New Jersey Company as a whole." [47]

The Directors discussed these proposals during the first week of July, debating whether the separate coordinating organization might be made a department rather than a committee. If a committee, should it include senior or second-line executives? Sadler pleaded for the committee rather than departmental type of organization, since he felt that the objection "to the formation of a department is that immediately a department is formed, the contact of the members with the details of the various branches on which they give information is less intimate, so they do not bring to their discussion such clear knowledge of the effect of the changes on the department they represent." Sadler further favored a committee made up of three Directors with three alternates from the Board. He preferred Directors to the more junior men because they would have a broader view of the Company's needs and problems. This new duty, he maintained, should not be too much of a burden on the Directors' time since they, "in the ordinary course of their business, are in close touch with most details which must necessarily be background for an intelligent discussion of the questions involved." This statement, incidentally, reveals how much the Jersey Directors were involved at that time in operational rather than entrepreneurial activities.

Although it discussed thoroughly the proposal for better coordination, the Board took no action. Before a second meeting on the matter, Teagle had already left for Europe to take care of marketing problems. When he returned, there were other matters of more immediate concern. The proposal, like the suggestions of Howard and Clark, would, however, be brought forward again when the need for structural change, created by the strategy of vertical integration and expansion and by the new demand for gasoline, became crystal clear.

The Initial Reorganization — 1925–1926

It took an inventory crisis to provide the needed clarity and so to bring organizational change to Jersey. The series of difficulties resulting from the crisis finally forced Teagle and the Board to pay closer attention to suggestions for organizational improvement made by Sadler and Howard.

Intensified marketing problems made the President and his associates acutely aware of the need for closer coordination between and more effective administrative supervision over the company's different activities as well as for better long-term planning for the present and future use of their many resources. The crisis also brought a realization of the weaknesses in the existing internal structure of two of the major functional departments, Domestic Marketing and Manufacturing. The structural changes initiated by the falling off of demand in 1925 were carried still further in 1927 when the opening of new fields brought forth a deluge of crude oil and so created a second crisis. The threat of idle resources resulting from overproduction of refined products in 1925 started a reorganization of the functional departments. It also led to the creation of new staff offices at 26 Broadway to assist in the short-term coordination of product flow and the long-term allocation of resources. With the overproduction of crude in 1927, departmental reorganization was completed, the major domestic functional departments were combined into a single multifunctional division or affiliate, and a general office was set up to administer this and other regionally defined integrated affiliates. By the end of 1927, Jersey Standard had fashioned a multidivisional structure, comparable with that at General Motors and at du Pont, to administer its vast industrial holdings.

Teagle's Troubles

Teagle's troubles crowded one on another as the demand for gasoline began to slacken. The rapid expansion and then the leveling off of the gasoline and lubricant market followed closely the pattern of new car construction in the 1920's. From the end of the postwar recession of 1921 until 1925, the consumption of refined products, particularly gasoline, grew phenomenally in the American market. In 1922, Jersey delivered 48.7 million barrels to the domestic market. The next year deliveries rose to 68.5 million and in 1924 to a peak of 85.5 million. Then, as production of new automobiles fell off, so did Jersey's output. In 1925, only 78.3 million barrels were delivered, a figure that rose slowly to 85.5 and 89.6, respectively, in the next two years.[48]

The leveling off of demand meant that in 1925 Jersey Standard and the other petroleum companies suffered from excess refining capacity. Advances in manufacturing methods which expanded the amount of gasoline produced from each barrel of crude increased that capacity still further. The problem of the industry was not yet that of having too much crude available. In fact, during most of 1925 Teagle was still concerned with possible crude shortages.[49] In 1926 and 1927, the opening of the great new fields in Oklahoma and Texas would glut the market for crude; but in 1925, the problems were primarily those relating to marketing the refineries' output. Excess refining capacity led to increasing and aggressive competition both here and abroad. At the same time, it intensified the questions about storage and transportation involved in coordinating the flow of petroleum from well to market.

In the summer of 1925, Teagle became aware of long-standing, underlying difficulties. In June, accompanied by young but experienced Orville Harden, Secretary of the Manufacturing Committee, he made an extended tour to view Jersey's holdings in the West and in Canada.[50] On his return to 26 Broadway, he spent several weeks with the Marketing Department, working out a broad, new sales policy to meet the tighter market. By August Teagle fully appreciated the critical need of improving the over-all coordination of product flow and the ability of the Manufacturing and Domestic Marketing Departments to meet rapidly changing conditions.

What had surprised Teagle most on his western trip was the swiftly growing supply of crude stocks despite inadequate storage facilities and a drop in demand at the refineries and from the market. Lack of operational planning within the Jersey group had created excessive inventories all along the line. Carter, Teagle realized, was continuing to produce without a clear understanding of the requirements of the refineries; while the latter were giving too little attention to the needs of the different markets. For these reasons, as Teagle wrote Clark, who was then in Europe, the company had been unsuccessful in curtailing refinery production in the face of a market no longer expanding rapidly. "Unfortunately, we are obligated to run a much larger quantity of sweet Crude than we have any real need for and . . . which we have had to run as we have practically no storage in the field where it can be accumulated." [51]

The conferences that Teagle held on his return from the West to 26 Broadway with the domestic marketers dealt with the problems of stiffening competition and tightening demand. The Jersey President asked not only the members of the Marketing Committee and the top Department executives to attend, but also senior sales executives from the Louisiana Company. The marketers were to study ways and means to ease "the Company's burden of excessive inventories" in the face of falling profits and a declining share of the market.[52] Since the war, competitors, particularly the Texas Corporation and Gulf, had been aggressively building retail distributing facilities and expanding marketing personnel. They had increased their retail outlets through a "lease and license program," by which hitherto independent station owners leased their stations to the company and then operated them under a licensing agreement to sell its products exclusively. To attract dealers, the companies offered to supply gasoline pumps and buildings and to give generous margins below prevailing tank wagon or wholesale prices. Energetic competitors and an apathetic sales department at Jersey caused that company's share of the gasoline business in its relatively small domestic marketing territory to decline from 58 per cent in 1919 to 47 per cent in 1924.[53] In the summer of 1924, Jersey's Marketing Department had made its first move to meet the growing threat, but the Legal Department, fearing the response of the government's Justice Department, refused to let the marketers meet the competition through a lease and license program. The misgivings of the lawyers, however, did not prevent Teagle and the sales executives from expanding the building of company-owned service stations.

The excessive inventories of the following summer emphasized that acquiring retail outlets was not enough. Besides the resulting growing storage problem, there was the fact that the Domestic Marketing Department's profits were falling fast. Where they had been $10.4 million in 1924, the next year they were only $4.4 million.[54] The marketers agreed with Teagle on the need for "an entire change in our methods of arriving at tank wagon and service station prices," and for revamping radically a distribution and storage system still based on horse and wagons rather than on trucks, and on the sale of kerosene rather than gasoline.[55] All realized that they must concentrate more energetically and systematically on the retail sales of gasoline. Yet, as Teagle told Clark, they had to meet "continuously for three weeks in an effort to reconcile the views of all and to decide on an unanimous course of procedure to be effective at once." Agreement was finally reached, and on August 7 the Board approved of a changed price structure, of proposals to develop more efficient distributing methods, and of the expansion of the company's marketing facilities.

The 1925 "Program"

The inability of the existing organization to meet the changing market convinced Teagle of the need for major structural changes. He waited only for the return of key directors before making plans. Writing Clark on July 31, Teagle commented:

> I won't worry you with a recital of all the troubles we are up against here, but there are certainly plenty of them. What we are doing is running too much Crude and selling too little finished products. We have been more or less marking time with the situation awaiting returns of Messrs Bedford and Moffett, who I am glad to say will be back here the first of the week. I feel confident that as a result of their return and the discussion which will then ensue as to our present situation and future policy, that before the end of the week a definite decision can be reached so we can start in doing

these things which are necessary to carry on our business along sound lines.[56]

During August, the Board did reach several important decisions. After reshaping Jersey's marketing policies, it moved to the study of the requirements for a more effective coordination of product flow. This problem of planning and coordination, in turn, led the senior executives to consider explicitly, apparently for the first time in many years, the problems and needs of planning long-term allocation of financial resources. To meet these needs, the Board agreed to create a separate Coordination Committee and Department and to form a new Finance or Budget Committee and Department. Next Teagle and his associates decided on a complete overhauling of the Domestic Marketing Department. Further, they realized that these organizational changes as well as the new operating conditions called for similar alterations in manufacturing, and they now decided to integrate the Louisiana Company's activities more closely with those of the parent company.

These decisions were threshed out at luncheons and in the Board Room during August, 1925. Such decisions on structure were not the result of carefully detailed studies as at General Motors and du Pont. There is no evidence that broad reports were made for the Board or by Board members on Jersey's management structure or even on that of a single department.[57] No fundamental questions appear to have been raised about organization, nor were any set of organizational objectives outlined. As yet no one proposed to change radically the company's over-all structure or its traditional commitment to the administration of operations by committees. The discussion was concerned more with meeting the immediate problems of coordination of product flow and marketing than with dealing specifically with those of over-all organizational structure.

The Coordination Department and Committee

The announcement on September 3, 1925, of the formation of a coordinating unit initiated the new program.[58] Despite Sadler's earlier misgivings, the Board set up a Department, as well as a Committee. The Coordination Committee included senior executives, Teagle, Bedford, Sadler, Clark, and Black. Orville Harden, who as the Secretary of the Manufacturing Committee had been handling coordination of product flow, took charge of the new Coordination Department and soon had it playing a vital role in Jersey's operations. Not only did Harden master efficiently the complex task of guiding product flow, but in doing so he made the department invaluable for the purpose of over-all planning and appraisal.

Harden fully described the functions of the new general office department in a lengthy memorandum written to Clark in October, 1927. He began by defining the Department's major duties: "Primarily it assists in planning and carrying out the activities of the business, from the standpoint of the benefit to the interest as a whole," rather than from the view of any one department, subsidiary or affiliate.[59] This Harden expected to accomplish not by orders, but only by providing essential information. He saw his unit explicitly as a service or staff department without line authority: it could only recommend. But as it promised the producing, refining, and marketing executives information essential for assuring a more rapid turnover of inventory, and a steadier, fuller, and more profitable use of facilities, they were usually only too happy to follow the recommendations.

In Harden's words:

> In general, the Department assists in currently determining the policies to be adopted so far as the activities of the producing, transportation and manufacturing branches of the Company are concerned, and cooperates with the subsidiary companies to see that these policies are carried out. This entails arranging for refinery Crude supplies; Crude transportation and allocation; production, purchases and movements of certain finished products (i.e., naphthas [gasoline], refined oil, gas, and fuel oils); coordination of refining manufacturing operations from the standpoint of Crudes run and products required, stocks on hand, etc., and the allocation of business among the various subsidiary companies.

The report is worth quoting in detail for it shows clearly the complexities involved in carrying out this basic activity in a huge industrial enterprise whose expanded activities cover a large part of the globe. It also indicates how the workings of an essentially operational and tactical activity can assist the senior officers in carrying out entrepreneurial and strategic activities.

In crude oil operations, for example, Harden expected his Department "to assist in determining the most desirable policy as regard Crude inventories, and to cooperate with all the companies, with a view of regulating such inventories." In order to be certain that "supplies be currently available when and as required by our refineries and, on the other hand, that the supplies will not be excessive," the Department not only recommended the allocation of crude to be produced by its affiliates but also supervised purchasing the crude supplies needed for any Jersey refineries here or abroad. All such purchases were cleared through the Department, which also negotiated most of the crude buying contracts.

The task of proposing crude-running programs at the different refineries was particularly complex for:

> This necessarily requires a study of the grades of Crude available, and the desirability for producing the products required for the Trade; the relative

> profits of one Crude against another; also an intelligent distribution of the various grades of Crude as among the Refineries having different market requirements, keeping in mind the relative advantages of one refining point as compared with another for a given grade of Crude; the proper correlation of the various manufacturing plants so that they may be economically operated by taking close advantage of our manufacturing facilities and available storage capacity; producing products at points where the minimum total freight charges to the final destination would prevail.

Like the supplying of the crude, the programming of refinery runs required much accurate information. It further demanded that marine and pipe-line transportation be available. Comparable complex scheduling was necessary to keep the ships and pipe lines operating as close to full capacity as possible and at the same time to prevent overloading of storage facilities at shipping and pipe-line terminals.

The allocation of refined products among the various distribution points was also intricate. As Harden noted:

> The aim, here again, is to do this in the way that would result in the greatest profits to the greatest interests — trying, on the one hand, to minimize freight charges and on the other, to harmonize the situation of the different individual supply points. This problem is one of considerable magnitude, when the volume of our business is considered.
>
> Taking export Naphthas [gasoline], for example, we have certain total requirements — compiled and established by the Department, from information furnished by the sales people — that must be fulfilled, and we have possible supplies available at Baton Rouge, Baytown [Texas], New York, Talara [Peru], California, etc. The Foreign Sales Department looks to the Coordination Department for advice as to the port of loading for each steamer. Working this way we can avoid to a large extent one refiner or terminal of being "long" on a product while another shipping point is "short". It is obvious that this procedure keeps to a minimum outside purchases, by enabling us to ship business to whatever point at which we have supplies, and thus buy only when the interest as a whole is short.

This sort of planning required a great deal of statistical information. In 1921 Harden had made, Clark noted in the forwarding letter, "the first attempt . . . to set up a record of total stocks, Crude oil and products, of the New Jersey Company together with the Louisiana and Humble Companies."[60] As head of the Coordination Department, Harden greatly enlarged these statistics. Besides gathering data on many aspects of crude production, refining, and transportation, Harden developed the "Product Outlook" and "Look Ahead" sheets. The first showed the short-term and the second the long-term total anticipated business for each major product against expected supplies. This over-all picture, regularly revised, would indicate whether refinery operations should be increased or curtailed, and whether crude and refined should be diverted from one place to another. These forecasts, carefully checked against actual operations, were used to find out where and why the estimates were off. It is not surprising that Harden quickly discovered that the lack of accurate market data was the most serious defect in the statistical controls he was developing.

Beside guiding the flow of products, Harden's Department soon became responsible for obtaining uniform figures and determining from them all aspects of refining costs. Such cost data came to include the actual value of the various crudes at the different refineries, the comparative profits of running these crudes at the same and different refineries, the actual profit and loss per barrel based on price paid for crude, and similar statistics. These data were not only "essential to the planning of Crude running programs of the different plants," but also provided a basic tool to the Jersey executives for evaluating current performance and planning future courses of action.[61]

Because of its critical position and of Harden's interest in planning and systematizing, the Coordination office was soon given other duties. For example, it had to approve all changes in product specifications. Even more importantly, it advised the Board on the allocation of resources. All estimates for refinery construction were sent to it for comment. In this last matter, Harden's specific task was to review the requests "from the standpoint of securing the maximum return to the general interests as a whole, rather than merely considering the return to the particular company making the expenditure," and also to avoid any needless duplication of equipment.

The Coordination Department immediately became a vitally important unit in Jersey's general office, partly because it came to meet the real needs and partly because of its manager's drive and ability. The consequent effective coordination of the flow of petroleum from well to market improved Jersey's economic efficiency and made vertical integration more than merely a defensive strategy. With such planning—and *only* with such planning—could integration help make possible lower costs per unit and higher output per worker. The Coordination Department, by providing the information that permitted a more effective linking of the different units within Jersey's management structure, was soon furnishing the data so necessary for planning for the company as a whole.

The development of the basic function did not, of course, come automatically. In forwarding Harden's report to Teagle, Clark emphasized that: "The fault I have to find with this memorandum is that he [Harden] has entirely left out the most important element, and that is his own part in the formation and conduct of the Department." He then continued:

> The work of the Coordination Committee is running along so smoothly, one might be led to believe that it could be conducted by anyone of average intelligence and knowledge of the Company's business. Immediate knowledge of all details of the Company's business, as represented by securing its supplies of crude oil, transportation of it, refining and distribution of products therefrom, and the tact and diplomacy in dealing with the executive heads of the various operating units are qualifications for successful management of the Coordination Committee. The knowledge of the details of the Company's business cannot be acquired in a few months' time, and Orville's versatility with it is the result of his years of work for the Company.[62]

The Budget Department and Committee

The creation of the Coordination Department, as described above, made possible a far more effective mobilization of Jersey resources just by providing an office whose primary task was to reduce costs and assure an evener and steady use of operating plant and personnel. The formation of the Budget Committee and the Budget Department (the second step in the 1925 program) had similar objectives. The aim of this second new staff office was to make more efficient use of Jersey Standard's capital resources and, like the Coordination Department, to provide data essential to more systematic and rational forward planning and other over-all entrepreneurial activities.

Up to this time, the allocation and control of funds for both operating and capital expenses had been haphazard and unsystematic. The regular appropriation requests were defined vaguely and with very little supporting data. Most departments and subsidiaries asked for funds only when a definite and immediate need arose. In reviewing requests and estimates, the Manufacturing Committee and the Board had comparatively few data on which to base decisions, and most of what they did have came from the interested departments and divisions. As a result, the Board had a very incomplete picture of the company's past, present, and future financial commitments. Nor were the Directors able to use financial results as a clear criterion of managerial performance, as did Sloan, Brown, and the du Ponts. Teagle had shown little concern for finding out which operating units were making an effective return on investment. Before the creation of the Coordination Committee, interdepartmental pricing, for example, tended to be handled by negotiation between the organizations involved and was usually worked out on the basis of immediate needs of those producing, refining, or marketing units.[63]

Improvements in financial controls and procedures began immediately after the Board meetings of August, 1925. On September 4, 1925, the day after the announcement of the formation of the Coordination Committee, the Treasurer asked in a circular letter to all department heads that "when application for appropriation and other expenditures are presented to the Board, they should be attached to a statement giving a monthly estimate of the period in which the money will be actually disbursed."[64] This had become necessary if the Treasurer's Department was to "accurately forecast the demands that may be made upon it."

Next, the new Treasurer, Seth B. Hunt, began to develop budgetary procedures. He asked all departments and subsidiaries to present an annual budget of expected expenditures for the coming year which "should show in as few items as possible all cash disbursements whether chargeable to capital account or operating expenses."[65] The budget, he urged, "should be kept at the lowest possible amount consistent with good business, and no item of capital expenditure should be included unless satisfactory earning power can be shown." All budgets were to include estimated gross and net income as well as maintenance, operating, and capital expenditures, and were to be submitted on the same type of form, and forwarded to the office of Wesley Zane.

Then in January, 1926, a Budget Committee and a Budget Department were formally established with Zane as Secretary of the first and Manager of the second.[66] During the two previous years, Zane had been a working member of the Efficiency Committee, a group appointed by the Board in January, 1923, to study ways and means of reorganizing routine office management in order to improve efficiency, avoid duplication, and cut costs.[67] After Zane had returned from a nine months' study of the European offices and had helped the Committee make its report, Teagle immediately put him in charge of compiling and systematizing the Jersey budgets.[68]

Zane's role was a service or staff one.[69] His compilation of uniform data and its presentation to the Board in concise form gave the senior executives, for the first time, a clear over-all picture of the Company's financial commitments and the resources to cover them. Once a department's budget had been approved, Zane's office kept a check on how the funds were being expended, and issued to the Board monthly figures that showed how actual expenditures for each department and subsidiary in the company compared with the budget estimates. During the year, the Department checked requests for money to cover unexpected contingencies and followed them up to see how the funds were being spent. Soon, too, the Department was asking for a careful revision of the annual budget in June of each year.

While the creation of Zane's Department gave the Directors a clearer over-all picture of their financial situation, the data were still crude in comparison to those developed at General Motors after 1921 and at du Pont by World War I. At Standard, there was initially little effort to forecast over-all company financial needs in the light of probable business conditions, or to provide outside checks on any estimates of the operating units. At first, appropriations requests failed to show the need of the expenditure in the unit's over-all program, to say nothing of the need in Jersey's general broad plans. Soon, however, each request came to be accompanied by a good deal of supporting information, which indicated among other things whether and why each request was essential or not so necessary or might even be put off. Very soon, too, Harden's Coordination Department was providing detailed data on current operating costs and on proposed major capital expenditures. Such information provided an excellent check on the reports and budgets of the operating departments and affiliates in much the same way statistics and reports from the general staff did at General Motors and du Pont. Also, the Coordination Department's long-term estimates finally became detailed enough to be used in planning broad policy for the company as a whole.

The creation of the Coordination and the Budget Departments at 26 Broadway was, then, a major step forward in improving communications between the Board, the operating departments, subsidiaries, and the affiliates, and so made possible a more effective mobilization of the Jersey Company's total resources. The formation of Harden's office assured the collection, compilation, and dissemination of a steady flow of reliable data, which could be used for evaluating operating performance as well as for coordinating the rate and direction of product flow. The additional information compiled regularly and systematically by Zane's office gave the Jersey Directors invaluable data for planning the future courses of action for the different operating organizations and for the company as a whole. From this time on, the Jersey Company would have a much clearer picture of where it had been, where it currently stood, and whither it was going.

After 1925, the major work of the two new central office departments was largely that of developing more accurate and sophisticated data and financial and informational procedures and controls. Harden realized, as had earlier senior executives at du Pont and General Motors, that the greatest need was for better information on market prospects. The changing market, after all, determined the volume of each function's activity and the rate of flow through the whole organization. In March, 1929, Harden submitted a perceptive report that stressed the critical need for market analysis, including accurate forecasting and a breakdown of demand. "It is becoming every day more apparent," Harden pointed out, "that we cannot think in terms of raw materials converted into merchandise sold and distributed to possible customers whose taste, buying habits, locations, and ability to purchase are more or less unknown."[70] The more profitable use of Jersey facilities required "co-ordinated and scientific study not only of our present markets, but also our future markets; our present position today in each market; our marketing position as a whole in the industry and what it will probably be next year, the year after, etc." At this time, Harden and others recommended the creation of offices to analyze sales and market conditions. As Harden's report emphasizes, decisions about coordination of product flow and the allocation of funds for capital expenditures were becoming based at Jersey, just as they had been earlier at du Pont and at General Motors on anticipated conditions rather than on past performance.

Reorganizing the Marketing Department

In creating the Coordination and Budgeting organizations, Teagle and his Board were building new and formal lines of communication from general headquarters to all parts of the Jersey domain, and were developing the necessary data to flow through these so that the operating units, new and old, could integrate their resources more productively. The 1925 program also called for change within the structure of the functional departments. Here the first step was the reorganization of the Marketing Department. The lines of authority as well as those of communication between headquarters and the field had to be reshaped if this older unit was to meet more quickly and imaginatively the new needs and challenges.

In reforming the structure of the domestic marketing organization, Teagle's first changes were in top personnel. The current Director in charge of Domestic Sales was replaced by the young and aggressive James A. Moffett, Jr., who had come to 26 Broadway from the Louisiana Company and who had become Director in charge of Foreign Marketing a few months earlier, at Asche's death.[71] Anxious to integrate Louisiana's sales activities with those of the parent company, the Board appointed one of Louisiana's senior marketing executives to a new post, "General Assistant in charge of Marketing Activities." Teagle next selected the new Domestic Sales Committee which, unlike the old, included senior executives in Jersey's domestic marketing organization — the Assistant General Manager for Domestic Sales at 26 Broadway, and the Resident Managers at the two branch offices, Newark and Baltimore. A fourth member, A. Clarke Bedford, had been for some time Moffett's assistant. Teagle then asked these four to suggest how the Sales Department might be reorganized in order to meet more effectively the challenges of the gasoline age.

At a meeting on November 25, 1925, with the members of the new Domestic Sales Committee, the President made clear that he wanted the Louisiana and Jersey marketing organizations to be combined into a single department with headquarters responsible for fewer operating details and, if possible, with fewer administrative personnel.[72] The Committee, in its report of December 4, first recommended the consolidation of some of the branch office activities like accounting. Second, the Department should take over the sales of those fuel oil, gas oil, and miscellaneous asphalt products that sold in relatively small lots through branch offices but which were still "under the direction of Mr. Sheffield," manager of the Fuel Oil Department. The latter would continue to handle only large bulk contracts made directly with shipping companies, road contractors, and similar customers. Next, the New York headquarters would include, beside the four members of the new Committee, assistant managers in charge of marketing what had become the two major sets of products — refined oil and gasoline, and lubricating oils. There would also be an assistant manager to handle service stations and another to supervise the maintenance and repair of the company's automotive equipment, now replacing wagons for gasoline distribution. Apparently these executives were to have direct contact with their counterparts in the branch offices at Newark and Baltimore, which were still to be headed by Branch Managers.

While accepting the general outline, Teagle felt that the recommendations did not go far enough. "It would seem very necessary," he wrote the new marketing Committee, "that you gentlemen should define the exact relationship which you would recommend should exist between you and the Branch Managers in the Field; also your recommendations as to how the work should be handled and divided among you four gentlemen."[73] A lack of such preciseness could lead to difficulties, Teagle stressed in a letter to Moffett. Authority and responsibility should be definitely pinned down:

> You will note that in my letter to these four gentlemen I raise specifically the question as to their relationship to the main station managers. My thought is that the managers should be in charge of and responsible for the entire business in this field, including equipment, construction, service stations, as well as sales, accounting, etc. I am opposed to a division of authority if these local managers are to be held responsible for the entire organization and operations in any particular field, and it seems to me a mistake to have special men for special jobs, as the effect of this would be, in the first place, increased operating cost, and in the second place would make the local

manager feel that he has no responsibility for these special jobs and if anything goes wrong in connection therewith he can pass the blame on to the special man who has been handling it.[74]

What Teagle wanted was to have the lines of authority between the field and headquarters defined on a line-and-staff basis.

These views, however, Teagle did not pass on to the marketers. He let them come up with their own organizational scheme. On December 21, they submitted a second and much more detailed report. The four, each of whom would take the title of General Sales Manager, recommended:

a. That the General Sales Managers, acting as a Committee, shall be held responsible by the Board of Directors for the general management and operation of our domestic marketing business.

b. They shall be held responsible for general selling policies, and shall recommend to the Board such changes as may be necessary from time to time in the general price structure of all products, except that they shall have authority, without reference to the Board, to meet local competitive price conditions, which demand immediate action in order to protect our business, and which do not require general market change.

c. They also shall be held responsible for the expenditure of money in the domestic field, operating under a budget system approved by the Board of Directors, and apportioning these expenditures between the various divisions as may seem advisable from time to time; authority being granted to this Committee to approve estimates without reference to the Board, except in the cases of exceptional expenditures. This Committee will expect to render regular reports at stated periods as to money expended, so that the Board will at all times be posted.[75]

In this way, then, following the old Jersey Standard custom, the Committee would be responsible for making policy under the general supervision of the Board. "This Committee in turn would hold the Branch and Division Manager responsible for the business in his entire field, including carrying out of sales policies as may be laid down by the Committee from time to time, the maintenance of prices, the costs of marketing, selection and operation of service stations, and accounting." But the report did not make clear the relations between the Branch Managers in the field and the product managers at headquarters. To handle the administrative duties and, at the same time, to coordinate the work of the Branch and product managers, the report, as Howard had done earlier for the Manufacturing Department, suggested that two members of the Committee be in the field and the other two in the home office at any given time. In other words, following Teagle's view, the department was to be administered, as at du Pont, with the line of authority from headquarters to the field via the branch manager. The primary difference was that a committee rather than a single individual at headquarters was to be responsible for departmental performance. Domestic sales, like manufacturing, were to be managed by a "Room." The marketers concluded their report by saying that they preferred not to say in advance what the specific duties of each of the four would be and also that they felt that they could begin with the "present Domestic Sales Department organization, making additions to the personnel as may be necessary from time to time."

Except for these last two points, Teagle was quite satisfied. The last sentence particularly disturbed him. It tends, he wrote to the Chairman of the Board from his hunting plantation in Georgia:

> to create the impression that these gentlemen had in mind building up an extensive department in New York. This, I think, is a great mistake. All that the Committee wants to do is to direct the business, leaving all the details and the actual carrying out of the work to the men in the field. If it is agreeable to the Board to delegate to these Sales Managers the additional authority they are asking for, then they, on their part, should, in my opinion, delegate responsibility to the local managers in the Field. If they do this there will be no necessity whatever for them to enlarge in any way the present Sales Department in New York.[76]

The Board in approving of the marketers' recommendations, however, did not require the four executives to define their own duties more specifically.[77]

Teagle's reaction to this report suggests that, when pressed, he could set forth fairly explicit ideas on organization. He saw the need of defining responsibility and authority, and the value of delegating operating responsibility. He advocated a clear line of authority between headquarters and field. And he was troubled by the failure to define the actual duties of the different men within the new Sales Committee itself. Yet apparently it did not occur to him to reject the committee form of administering such operating activities or to clarify the lines of authority within the headquarters office. The relationship between the committee members was just as unclear as between these executives and Moffett and his new assistant. Who really did have responsibility for domestic sales at Jersey Standard in 1926? Teagle would soon have to answer this question of the location of responsibility and authority, not only in marketing but also in manufacturing.

Reorganizing the Manufacturing Department

The reorganization of the Manufacturing Department, like that of the Marketing Department, called for a refashioning of the lines of authority and communication and for changes in personnel. However, the situation was more complex there than in marketing, and so the story of the changes in the manufacturing organization provides a revealing example of the difficulties involved in altering long-established structure. The story is all the more illustrative because both the department involved and the senior executives in the central office failed to study explicitly the organizational needs of the department and its structural relationship with other operating units.

The situation in manufacturing was more complex because, in the first place, the crisis in 1925 was less obvious here than in marketing, and change seemed less imperative. The great expansion of the gasoline business, nevertheless, was creating pressures in the refining as well as in the selling departments. Complaints from customers, both large and small, about variations in the quality and performance of Standard's gasoline emphasized the need to achieve a uniformly refined product from the many different crudes. Complaints, by stressing the continuing necessity of improving existing products and processes, also brought out the importance of a closer liaison between the Development, Manufacturing, and Marketing Departments.

In the second place, Teagle and the Board were less likely to change top personnel in the Manufacturing than in the Marketing Department, because the senior refining executives had long held positions of responsibility. The entrenched and powerful Manufacturing Committee could not be summarily dismissed or reshaped without either depriving the company of able men or causing a breakdown in morale. This was particularly true because, in this oldest of the Jersey departments, length of service was of greater importance for prestige and promotion than in the rest of the Company.

The situation in the Department was further confused by a continuing conflict of attitudes and personalities. This had begun in 1919 when Teagle brought Clark and his lieutenants to head the Bayway plant and to improve and develop better products and processes. The older refiners — like Black, Haupt, and W. C. Koehler who had put Bayway into operation in 1907 — were not only skeptical of the new scientific ways but they also resented the placing of outsiders to senior positions. Clark and his associates on their side failed to hide their impatience at what seemed to them outmoded men using outmoded methods.[78] By keeping the major posts in the Manufacturing Department divided between the two groups, as he did in 1921 when both Clark and Black were promoted to the Board as Directors in charge of Manufacturing, Teagle only assured the continuance of the conflict. On the Manufacturing Committee, Koehler and Haupt were the hard core of the old refineries and Howard the spokesman for the new. The oldest and most senior members (George

W. McKnight, the Committee's Chairman after 1921, and C. E. Graff, Vice-Chairman and Manager of Bayway) usually favored the old Bayway group, while the younger members were more sympathetic to ideas of Clark and Howard.[79]

For both these reasons — the conflict of personalities and the lack of powerful pressures for change — Teagle met with the Committee several times in December, 1925, rather than proposing major changes himself. At these meetings he asked the Committee to suggest ways and means of assuring more uniform quality, of cutting costs, and of standardizing product and processes. He also wanted improved and more systematic methods and a clearer definition of the organization of the Committee and its relations to the Board.[80] Finally, as in the case of marketing, he hoped to bring the Louisiana Company's activities under closer administrative control. Teagle agreed that the Committee should begin its work by having the two senior executives, McKnight and Graff, visit Standard of Indiana, Standard of California, and Union Oil (the same three companies Howard had studied two years before) to examine the way they handled the problems and organized their manufacturing activities.

According to his practice, Teagle left the two men to draft their own detailed plans. Clark, however, thought it best to present his own views. "I have been giving considerable thought to our Manufacturing Committee problems," Clark wrote to McKnight in San Francisco, "and have a 'half-baked' idea. I would like to give you this outline, to be considered by yourself and Mr. Graff at your leisure on the trip."[81] The plan was essentially the one he and Howard had proposed in January, 1924, for a more centralized, departmentalized organization in place of the existing federation of refineries. But as yet neither Clark nor Teagle nor the manufacturers themselves proposed altering the basic committee form of administration.

The recommendations of McKnight and Graff, approved by the Manufacturing Committee on January 29, 1926, did call for more of an allocation of the Committee's work along functional lines.[82] The Department was to have five functional offices. The present Development and Engineering Departments were to be specifically under the Manufacturing Department. The other three dealt with inspection and complaints, quality control, and accounting and cost analysis. The standardization of process and equipment was to be handled by a Standardization Committee. Except in the case of Engineering, the relation between these headquarters offices and the refineries in the field was not made clear. The Engineering Department was to have direct "administrative control" over the Mechanical Departments in the refineries. The administration of the refineries was to be centralized, with Koehler in charge of the two great refineries of Bayway and Bayonne and Thomas R. Parker all the foreign ones. The other domestic refineries, including the Baton Rouge plant, were to continue to have their General Managers on the Committee, with offices at 26 Broadway. The final proposal, then, called for the continuation of a committee or "room"-managed organization but with more clearly defined auxiliary or service units.[83]

The Board accepted most of these recommendations despite strong objections of two of the older refiners, Koehler and Haupt.[84] However, because of the latter protest, the duties of the Engineering Department remained unchanged, and refineries in the New York area kept separate managers. Then, in the following autumn, Teagle agreed on a single management for all three New York refineries, but not under a single manager. The Manufacturing Committee had recommended Frank W. Abrams for the post.[85] Teagle thought the work should be divided between this younger, more imaginative executive and the more experienced Koehler. This, Teagle wrote Graff, "would leave Mr. Abrams free to devote his time and attention to co-ordination of operations and the allocation of Crude between the three plants, as well as questions of method and process, while Mr. Koehler would co-ordinate and adjust labor activities of the three plants in question." [86] This sharp division of responsibility and authority only intensified the conflicts and antagonisms within the Manufacturing Department.

The working out of the program that Teagle and the Board decided on in August, 1925, stimulated other important organizational changes in the following year. Most significant was the consolidation in October, 1926, of the two producing departments into a single one under Sadler's command.[87] On Corwin's retirement from Carter earlier in the year, R. M. Young, the head of its Western Division, became President. Remaining in Tulsa, he reported to 26 Broadway through Richardson Pratt, formerly Corwin's assistant and now one of Sadler's three senior general assistants.[88] The work of Sadler's other two subordinates who supervised foreign production increased rapidly, because in September the personnel of the Paris office had been sharply reduced and the direction of production in Europe transferred back to New York. At the same time, Louisiana's producing activities appear to have come more under the supervision of 26 Broadway.

Sadler now effectively administered all of Jersey's producing activities except those of Humble and Imperial. In spite of his able men in the field, departmental headquarters in New York became deeply involved in operational activities and tactical decisions. He himself kept contact with production in all parts of the world, arranged meetings between producers to exchange information and advice on policies and procedures, set up conferences between the producers and the Board to consider broad production problems, and helped collect, compile, and analyze the necessary statistical data.[89] As a result, Sadler was having less and less time available to carry out his role of a Director in the planning, appraising, and coordinating the activities of the company as a whole.

Interestingly enough, just as the administration of production was becoming more centralized, that of foreign marketing and foreign refining was becoming more decentralized. The postwar expansion of the business of Jersey's subsidiaries, in particular the growing gasoline demand, was forcing the European affiliates to pay closer attention to sales methods and policies. Harper's Export Trade Department was having difficulty in getting agreement on such policies as uniform trade names, prices to be paid the Manufacturing Department for its gasoline and automobile lubricants, the procurement of equipment for service stations, and so forth. The rapid changes in demand were complicating the distribution of refined products to the European affiliates as well as the allocation of European and other crudes to the small continental refineries.

To provide more effective channels of communication between 26 Broadway and the European companies and among the subsidiaries themselves, as well as to reduce the administrative load on the Export Trade Department, Teagle with the senior executives in the Department and the heads of the subsidiaries agreed in the summer of 1924 to set up the European Committee. This Committee, consisting of the chiefs of the major subsidiaries and representatives of the Export Trade Department, was to decide general policies and to standardize procedures.[90] The Committee soon had a permanent staff with headquarters in Paris. This staff acted as a clearing house for information, and checked on how the Committee's policies were being carried out. Although the Paris office assisted in guiding product flow within Europe, it remained primarily concerned with the administration of marketing until 1927.

At the same time, following the suggestion of Clark and Sadler, Teagle transferred the administration of the several small refineries of the European affiliates from the foreign marketing department to the Manufacturing Committee.[91] In the summer of 1925, Clark and Howard traveled through Europe inspecting the refineries to see how they might be improved to meet the growing call for gasoline.[92] Clark was impressed at once by "a very striking need" for better supervision of refining methods and proper product inspection if efficient production of high-quality gasoline was to be achieved. By the end of the trip, he was recommending to Teagle and Moffett the establishment of a separate department to help supervise and coordinate manufacturing in Europe. These suggestions, seconded by the proposals of McKnight and Graff for changes in the

Manufacturing Committee, finally led in the summer of 1926 to the appointment of Thomas R. Parker as the Committee member in charge of European refineries. Parker sailed almost immediately for England, where he began to set up a European manufacturing organization.[93] This regional decentralization of administrative decision making in foreign marketing and manufacturing was more prophetic of the coming organizational changes at Jersey than was the centralization of control in the producing end of the business.

By the end of 1926, much had been accomplished on all three levels of administration. At the general office level the creation of the new Coordination and Budget Departments made possible the more effective administration of the enterprise as a whole. By providing the necessary data and channels of communication, these two units improved the coordination of the flow of product through the vast industrial empire and permitted the Board to carry on more realistic appraisal and planning of the activities of the parts and of the whole. At the central office level, the Directors at 26 Broadway had increased their administrative control over the single-function departments. The new Coordination and Budget Departments assisted here, too, as did the re-forming of the lines of communication and authority in the producing and the foreign and the home marketing departments between the Director in charge and departmental headquarters. Particularly important was the incorporation of Louisiana's activities into the Jersey Company's marketing, manufacturing, and producing organizations. This integration went a step further when Daniel R. Weller, Louisiana's President, was appointed a Director in the Jersey Company in February, 1926, and moved his office from Baton Rouge to 26 Broadway.[94] Finally, on the departmental headquarters level, the two departments most needing reorganization — Manufacturing and Domestic Marketing — had each begun to clarify the lines of authority and communication within departmental headquarters and between headquarters and the field. A third, the Export Trade Department, had strengthened its organization by setting up new lines of communication and new loci for decision making.

Yet many problems still remained. In fact some of the solutions of the previous year were actually creating new difficulties. The increase of administrative control over the functional departments was enlarging the administrative load of the Directors in charge of these activities. Sadler, Black, Clark, Moffett, and even Teagle found themselves so involved in operational activities that they had less and less time to use the information provided by Harden's and Zane's departments for over-all appraisal and planning. Nor were the changes in the departmental organization bringing the expected improvement. Because no really significant alteration had been made in Jersey's basic structure and because of the continued commitment of her executives to committee management of departmental affairs, administrative decision making was still concentrated too on operational activities and tactical decisions, and too little on entrepreneurial and strategic ones.

The Creation of the Multidivisional, "Decentralized" Structure

Teagle himself realized that more needed to be done but did not yet consider the possibility of drastic changes. Only under the pressure of a second crisis, this time resulting from the overproduction of crude, did he go beyond the plans outlined in 1925. By this second reorganization, Jersey's President transformed his company's structure into what was to become the modern multidivisional, "decentralized" type with a general office of general executives and staff specialists and autonomous self-contained operating divisions. The general officers on the Board were to be relieved of operating responsibilities. The Coordination and Budget Department together with parts of other existing auxiliary offices became the new general staff. The functional departments were combined under the administration of regionally defined units. Finally, all the departments themselves came to be administered through a structure that clearly defined responsibility and authority. Yet because the company's reorganizers continued to plan in an informal, *ad hoc* way and also because of the great depression in 1929, the structure outlined in 1927 was not fully worked out until after World War II.

Continuing Difficulties

In a letter to Sadler in October, 1926, Jersey's President reviewed the progress made in the previous year:

> The original program, as you know, provided for the setting up of three main committees, i.e., Co-ordination, Finance and Sales. Up to date we have only had time to really get the first one of these three committees functioning properly. The Finance Committee, based on this year's experience with the Budget, I am quite sure will from the end of this year become almost as active as the Co-ordination Committee, and with these two committees functioning properly we will then have the time necessary to take up and perfect the organization of the Sales Committee.[95]

Furthermore Teagle fully appreciated that more adjustments were called for in the manufacturing as well as in the marketing organization.

Nearly all of Jersey's top executives were at once pleased by the work of the Coordination Committee and Department. "The very wide view obtained by the Co-ordination Committee," noted C. E. Graff, Acting

Chairman of the Manufacturing Committee, "places us in a much better position to decide matters correctly than was possible previously when these questions were submitted to the Manufacturing Committee."[96] "A clearer knowledge of future operations" provided by the new units, Teagle happily reported, was bringing a "uniformity in operations and a clear appreciation of just what capital expenditures are absolutely necessary and those which can be deferred for consideration later."[97] Such data had helped, too, in the more effective allocation and use of personnel. As time passed, the valuable contributions of the Budget Committee and Department also became increasingly appreciated. But if the new staff offices at 26 Broadway were operating effectively, the older functional departments, particularly Manufacturing and Domestic Marketing, were not. The division and diffuseness of responsibility and group decision making kept executive action slow and indecisive, and the Directors in charge of the function were called on to make many operational and tactical decisions.

The new Sales Committee, for example, had discussed many ways to meet Jersey's continuing decline in the domestic gasoline market but had difficulty in agreeing on specific policies. Moffett stressed the need for more effective advertising. Sheffield urged improvements in Jersey's service stations. These should be, the latter advocated, "truly service" rather than just gasoline stations.[98] Sheffield further pointed out the importance of dealer education both as "to service and salesmanship at our stations," and the need for a manual of instruction in "the maintenance of service stations, sales principles and sales arguments." Others favored a plan to form a separate subsidiary to manage the growing number of Jersey and Louisiana service stations.[99] And yet little action had been taken.

Despite its recent changes, the Manufacturing Committee continued to be more divided than the marketers. The old and new schools of refiners were almost immediately involved in a heated controversy over Koehler's plans to cut overhead costs at Bayway.[100] J. R. Carringer, the Resident Manager who had come to the Jersey Company with Clark, defended the existing form of organization at Bayway, which had been set up in 1922 by an expert practitioner of Frederick W. Taylor's brand of scientific management. Significantly, the major issue was over Koehler's plan to eliminate as superfluous the office that was used "to properly plan, schedule and co-ordinate our work." Koehler, the veteran manager, believed that personal supervision of the men in the refineries was all the administration that was needed. To the younger Carringer, the planning office, on the other hand, was a most essential unit in the refinery. Abrams, who with Koehler was responsible for the New York refineries, supported Carringer as tactfully as he could. The issue went to the Board, where

Clark strongly backed Carringer and Black supported Koehler, while Teagle, as before, seemed to feel each side was partly right.

The partial reorganization of the Manufacturing Department not only had failed to end its intramural controversies, but, in Frank Howard's opinion, it had done little to better the liaison between manufacturing, development, and marketing.[101] Continuing losses in refining operations emphasized the need to solve both these problems. By 1927, the Manufacturing Department was, Graff reported, "living in a sea of red figures that threatened to swamp the boat."[102] Teagle's immediate response to this was to cut costs and reduce personnel. He endorsed both Koehler's meat-axe approach and the suggestions of Clark, Howard, and Harden for more sophisticated cost analyses, especially those concerning overhead expenses.[103] Neither action had an immediate effect, for at the end of 1927 domestic refining operations showed a staggering net loss of $36.8 million.[104]

The continuing controversies and the constant involvement of Board members in departmental activities, Teagle increasingly realized, were hampering the Board in determining long-term plans and in carrying the critical negotiations necessary to implement such plans. He found this particularly true in his efforts to obtain oil-producing lands in Poland and the Near East. But it became most apparent in the negotiations over Russian properties and supplies of Russian crude. As early as November, 1924, Teagle was writing to Heinrich Riedemann, head of Jersey's former subsidiary:

> As I look back over what we have done during the past six or eight months, I am rather impressed with the fact that a matter so important as this Russian purchase situation should have been handled by us without really giving the subject the consideration which its importance justified. [J. A.] Mowinckel, [chief of the Italian subsidiary] probably more than anyone else, deserves the credit for really bringing forcibly to our attention in just what direction our present policy would seem to be leading. It is certainly to be regretted that we have so many things to do and our business day is so fully occupied that somehow or other we seem to make mistakes which could have been avoided if we had spent the time necessary to think the matter through to a logical conclusion.[105]

In the following year, Riedemann made the same point, emphasizing the need of focusing on broad strategy. He wrote Jersey's President, "sometimes I have wondered whether it is possible that some of us lose sight of this fact by paying *too* much attention and sacrificing *too* much time to the technical and routine side of our business."[106] A few weeks later, Teagle, then involved in the details of manufacturing and marketing problems as well as those of negotiations with foreign nations and companies, wrote one of his managers: "You Englishmen have a saying that one gets 'fed up'; this is exactly the way I feel about the Russian situation. I have spent more time and thought during the last two years on it than on any other one matter, and so far as I can see now without accomplishing anything." [107] This frustration increased early in 1927 when the complete collapse of these negotiations ended any hopes of accomplishment.

The 1927 Changes

The lack of time for planning and negotiating high-level strategy as well as the continuing failure of the committee-managed Domestic Marketing and Manufacturing Departments to improve their performance were still not enough in themselves immediately to force more major organizational changes at Jersey. Teagle needed the stimulus of an obvious crisis, and one came in the spring of 1927. By the end of 1926, the great new fields in Oklahoma and Texas which were brought in during the previous spring and summer were producing an ever-increasing torrent of crude oil.[108] By April, 1927, Teagle, his associates, and most oil men were anticipating a drop in price below the cost of the production of crude. As this overproduction promised to be longer in duration than any in his memory, Teagle together with Clark and others foresaw a comparable drop in the price of refined products. Such a reduction, they feared, would not bring a sizable increase in volume; in 1927, the market was no longer expanding as it had before 1925.

Not only did the vast flow of crude threaten decreasing prices but also a temporary increase in costs. Clark and Teagle emphasized that the opening of the Seminole and Panhandle fields required large capital expenditures for pipe lines and production equipment.[109] Furthermore, the new crude, heavy in sulphur, demanded changes in the refining equipment which processed it. During 1926 and 1927, the Development Department concentrated on developing new ways and equipment to handle these. As a result, Jersey's profit record for 1927 was the lowest since 1912. Earnings fell from $117.7 million in 1926 to $40.4 million in 1927. Not only did the refining activities show heavy losses, but domestic production reported a small net loss.[110]

Teagle and his associates envisaged two possible courses of action to meet this challenge. One was to control crude oil production either through government regulation or by a voluntary moratorium, with the latter preferred.[111] The second was to explore all possible ways of cutting costs, reducing personnel, and improving efficiency in operations and management. Thus the massive overproduction of crude oil, combined with the already existing problems, finally caused Teagle to decide on a reorganization that went beyond merely patching up existing departments and methods. Assisted by Sadler, he, worked out the over-all structural changes during the spring of 1927.[112] As before, no formal studies or reports were made. At least no evidence of them presently exists in the Jersey files.

The 1927 changes reflect both Jersey's administrative needs and Teagle's increasing awareness of them. The more careful and precise definition of responsibility and authority within the departments reflected the latter's growing skepticism of the value of committee administration of day-to-day operating activities. The placing of the functional departments within a separate, autonomous operating division and the creation of a general over-all administrative office indicated his concern for the increasing centralization of decision making in 26 Broadway.

By the mid-twenties, Teagle had become troubled by the growing size of committees which, he felt, were already too slow in coming to decisions or taking action. In late 1925, he had rejected Clark's recommendation to put Howard on the new Marketing Committee, as Manufacturing's representative. In the following October, he had turned down a similar suggestion by Sadler to have a marketer on the Coordination Committee. Such committees, Teagle had maintained, should only include men from one function. Representatives of others might be brought into the discussion, but should have no say in the final decision. As he told Sadler:

> I have a horror of too large committees as they never accomplish much but spend endless time in talking. A committee of three accomplishes much more than a committee of five, and to add to or bring in to committee discussions any more individuals than is absolutely necessary to obtain the necessary information to intelligent discussions will, I know, only tend to slow up the work actually accomplished, thus reducing the effectiveness of the committee.[113]

Jersey's experience in the years just before 1927 helped confirm Teagle's prejudices. The new departments — Production, Shipping, and Development — which were headed by individuals, ran with much less strain and averaged better profits than did the older committee-managed refining and domestic marketing organizations.[114] In foreign marketing, the Export Trade Department rather than Committee had handled most of the administrative activities since 1912. The new Coordination Committee was meeting less and less often simply because Harden was administering that department's operations so effectively.[115] Moreover, in few other oil companies or even in Jersey's own affiliates were the departmental administrative decisions made in the functional departments by group vote.

Teagle, it should be stressed, was not opposed to group consultation.

A decision maker needed all the advice and information he could get. What Teagle disliked was group responsibility for administrative action. An individual executive, not a "room," should be answerable for departmental decisions; and the line of authority between the different offices at headquarters and those in the field needed to be precisely defined. The history of the Manufacturing and Marketing Departments clearly demonstrated that group responsibility meant slow, indecisive action, based on compromise and negotiation. While such group action might be permissible in working out complicated long-term policies, it was hardly feasible for day-to-day operations. Moreover, unless authority was delegated clearly from headquarters to the field, most decisions soon came to be made at the department offices.

The other aspect of the 1927 reorganization, the creation of multidepartmental units, reflects emphatically Teagle's concern for concentration of decision making at 26 Broadway. In the spring of 1927, he repeatedly emphasized the need to cut down on overhead costs, paper work, and personnel at headquarters.[116] Actually, he had long been troubled by both the centralization of day-to-day administration and the increase of bureaucratic routine in New York. "Ever since I came to New York over seventeen years ago," he had written Black and Clark in March, 1922, "I felt that there was a loss in efficiency and an increase in expense through an effort to centralize too much of our detailed work at 26 Broadway."[117] This was particularly true, he believed, in accounting and marketing. Reduction of paper work and office routine was the primary reason why Teagle created the two "carbon removal committees" — the Statistical Committee and the Efficiency Committee — in 1922 and 1923. Also, as he told the marketers late in 1926, detailed execution of administrative decisions and the carrying out of the actual day-to-day economic activities should be left to executives in the field. If minor operational questions kept coming to 26 Broadway for decision, then the senior officials would inevitably become involved in detail minutiae and so would have little time for more important matters.

The answer to Teagle's problem of pinpointing and clarifying authority and responsibility in the functional departments and, at the same time, of decentralizing administrative decision making may have come from a suggestion made by Frank Howard in February, 1927. The latter was anxious to expand Jersey's research and development activities, yet, like Teagle, he felt this should be done by the operating units, not at 26 Broadway. This expansion might be carried out more efficiently if the difference between the functions of the over-all holding (or parent) company and those of the operating units were clarified. In presenting the Development Department's annual report to Teagle in February, Howard explained:

> My own view of the proper policy for an expansion of research and development work in the Jersey interest, which to my mind is absolutely necessary, is that the next step of the process is to build up a technical staff in subsidiary and affiliated operating companies. It is my sincere conviction that the best interests of Jersey are served by clearly recognizing the distinction between Jersey as an operating Company and Jersey as a holding company. So far, as my limited knowledge of the business goes, there is a failure to observe this distinction in many lines of the Company's business, which is not too helpful, and I would like to report, is perpetuating what I think is an error in the field of research and development.[118]

His Department's Inspection Laboratory and Patent Division were operated, Howard pointed out, "for the benefit of the Jersey interests at large." So, too, was some of the work of the Research Laboratory and the Experimental Division. Therefore these functions could best be handled by the general or parent office. Other activities of the last two Divisions, however, were strictly operating functions and could be better carried out by the operating units using their own technical staffs.

> So far as I can see [Howard concluded], there is no obstacle to putting this plan into effect during the coming year, in a modified form at least. The best development of the plan would require major organization changes which would, of course, have to be considered on their own merits and could not be made to accommodate themselves to the requirements of this relatively small branch of the Company's work.

The value of distinguishing between operating and holding company activities may have increased because of the New York tax laws. According to Howard, Chester O. Swain, the company's General Counsel, pointed out to the Board that until the distinction was made more clearly, the Jersey Company might be unable to qualify for the favorable tax treatment of a holding company under New York law.[119]

In any case, once Teagle had decided on a major reorganization, he followed through with this suggestion. Both legal and administrative distinctions between Jersey's operating and parent organization activities were clarified in a series of organizational changes between May and September, 1927. The Jersey Company divorced itself from operations, and so Standard Oil Company (New Jersey) now became legally only a holding company. Administratively, its functions became specifically to coordinate, appraise, and plan the activities of a number of multifunction divisions and to appraise and plan the work of the enterprise as a whole. The parent organization, legally a holding company and administratively a general office, was to consist of representatives of the major operating divisions as well as general policy-making officers and staff specialists.

Three functional administrative units, the Manufacturing and Domestic

Marketing Departments and Carter Oil, came to be administered by a central office that was legally set up under the name of the Standard Oil Company of New Jersey, incorporated in Delaware — the Delaware Company, as it came to be called.[120] The existing Manufacturing, Domestic Sales, and Export Trade Committees were abolished. The new departments were each headed by a single executive. McKnight had charge of the Manufacturing Department; Sheffield, the Marketing; and Richardson Pratt, the Producing. Each reported to Charles G. Black, the President of the new Delaware Company. Each was held fully responsible for the performance of his department.

The organization of the Manufacturing Department now came to resemble in many ways the one proposed by Howard three years earlier. Graff became McKnight's assistant. Abrams' control over the refineries was tightened, and the Resident Managers reported directly to him. The remaining department offices became functional staff units handling process, quality, and cost control, personnel and development, and so forth.

In Delaware's Marketing Department, members of the former marketing Committee now took charge of major product divisions such as General Sales (gasoline), Lubricating Oil, Fuel Oil, and Asphalt. These product departments and the branch offices in the field reported to Sheffield and his line assistants as did the one major auxiliary unit, the rapidly growing advertising department. Late in 1927, specialties, such as Nujol, Flit, Mistol, and other petroleum by-products that could not be sold effectively through the Department's sales organization, were combined into a separate subsidiary — Stanco, Incorporated — whose President became a Director in the parent company.[121]

Carter became a subsidiary of the Delaware Company. Young remained in Tulsa as Carter's President. Pratt, as head of the new affiliate's Producing Department, continued much as before as the executive responsible for operational contact between the pipe lines, Carter, and the manufacturing organization. But now, instead of reporting to Sadler and the Producing Department, Young and Pratt reported to Black, President of the Delaware Company.

The senior line and staff executives in the Manufacturing and Marketing Departments of the Delaware Company continued to meet in committees to exchange information and occasionally to plan policy and procedures. But there were no more "rooms" with group responsibilities. These same department heads together with Pratt and Young formed the Delaware's Board of Directors and together came to formulate and decide on more general policies and programs for the new affiliate within the framework set by the general office. In this administrative work they were aided by the staff departments that had their nucleus in the old Jersey staff units, including Development, Engineering, Personnel, Purchasing, and Traffic.

Thus the Delaware Company became, in theory at least, an autonomous multifunction operating subsidiary similar in organization to Imperial and Humble. The Louisiana Company, at the same time, returned to its original and quite comparable structure. Daniel R. Weller now returned to Baton Rouge to become again that affiliate's chief executive officer while remaining a Jersey Director.[122] Louisiana's marketing, refining, and producing activities once again reported to Baton Rouge and not to 26 Broadway.

The foreign subsidiaries, except for Imperial, were regrouped for administrative purposes under two officers, one for Europe and one for Latin America. The European Committee was provided with its own producing and enlarged marketing and manufacturing administrative departments. These functional offices were responsible for supervising the execution of policies decided by the Committee and also assisted in coordinating product flow within Europe and its environs.[123] The need for separate subsidiaries in each country, and the minority stockholder interests in these many concerns, made it difficult to form a single European subsidiary with a single head. So the Committee, with supervisory departments, remained the most practical answer. On the other hand, the responsibility for Latin American operations outside of those managed by Imperial's subsidiary, International, was centralized tightly under Joseph H. Senior. That executive, long President of the West Indian Oil Company, maintained offices at 26 Broadway and in his organization had refining and marketing sections. The small natural gas affiliates and the larger pipe-line and shipping units were little changed, remaining relatively independent. The old Marine Department, for example, merely altered its name to the Standard Shipping Company.[124]

The creation of the autonomous operating divisions was a fairly straightforward task. The fashioning of the general office to administer was harder. Most difficult were the decisions as to which of the staff activities properly belonged to the general office and which to the operating divisions. In engineering and development, Teagle and the Board followed Howard's earlier recommendations closely. New research and development laboratories were set up in Louisiana and in the new Delaware Company. So, too, were enlarged engineering facilities. The development and engineering activities concerning Jersey's interests as a whole were placed under the existing Standard Development Company — a subsidiary, set up in 1921 to hold patents — whose name was now changed to the Standard Oil Development Company.[125] As its President, Clark remained, in effect, the Director with supervision over both Engineering and Development, while Howard became the operating head. During September and October, these two men worked out the details of the new subsidiary's organization.[126]

This general staff activity was to serve "along the following lines as may be required or requested by any operating unit of the New Jersey Corporation: chemical and physical research, engineering, testing, inspection and general technical work, patent and trademark work and litigations . . . :" [127] The staff officers were also to assist in the standardization and coordination of manufacturing and technical procedures and policies throughout the Jersey holdings. As one executive noted:

> Under the new form of organization, there will be the endeavor to co-ordinate the refining activities thru the Standard Oil Development Company. This co-ordination will govern only standardization so far as is possible, of equipment and process, and the research and development activities of the different operating units.[128]

To help assure systematic communication between the staff and line organizations, the operating executives most concerned with technical activities became members of the Development Company's Board. This liaison was further encouraged through the continuance of the Standardization Committee set up in 1926, by the formation of a Technical Committee for coordinating research and development, and by the appointment of a third committee which, working with the Development Company's Librarian, facilitated the flow of technical information. A final responsibility of these staff offices was the provision of advice and information to the general executives on the Board which could be used for appraising divisional activities as well as for long-range planning.

The same problem of deciding what belonged to the general office and what to the operating divisions had to be worked out for other offices then at 26 Broadway. Hicks and an industrial relations office remained with the parent company. As Assistant to the President, Hicks and his aides gave advice on broad labor policies and other activities dealing with employee relations and acted as liaison men on these matters between the parent and the operating units.[129] This unit included departments for carrying out the various stock acquisition plans and insurance programs. As Chairman of the Annuities and Benefits Committee, Hicks also supervised and coordinated the pension plans and other employee welfare policies of different divisions. Most of the old Personnel and Training Department now became part of the Delaware Company, and similar organizations were enlarged in other affiliates or subsidiaries. Relations with the press, trade associations, government, and military organizations continued to be handled by another Assistant to the President, as they had been since 1921.[130] Other units dealing with public and employee relations remained with the parent, including *The Lamp,* the Safety Department, and part of the Medical Department.[131] So, too, did the Legal Department and the Secretary's office.[132]

Beside these service departments, the new parent company included offices essential for communication with and administration over the operating affiliates. These were, of course, the recently formed Coordination and Budget Departments, as well as the older Treasurer's and Comptroller's offices — the units that were beginning, among other things, to help develop financial and statistical controls. The manufacturing departments of the integrated affiliates coordinated product flow within the individual divisions, while Harden's unit at the general office helped to guide it between the affiliates. For, while each administrative unit controlled the basic functional activities of producing, refining, and marketing, no unit was fully balanced. Humble remained largely a producer of crude, Delaware was primarily a refining company, while Imperial and the European and Latin American companies still concentrated mostly on marketing.

Also Sadler's Production and Harper's Export Trade Departments stayed on as part of the parent staff. Now much smaller than they had been before, their task was to help coordinate and to advise and provide channels of communication between the functional activities in the different multidepartment divisions. Later, a similar staff department was set up to coordinate foreign refining activities.[133] These staff offices in the new parent company were, then, to assist and advise the operating divisions — Delaware (including Carter), Louisiana, Humble, Imperial, the European and Latin American group, the natural gas affiliates, and Gilbert & Barker — in carrying out their responsibilities and also in aiding the general executives on the Board in over-all supervision and planning.

The creation of a general office also altered the make-up of the Board itself as well as that of the staff. The Board was enlarged to include the representatives of major operating divisions, new and old. G. Harrison Smith of Imperial, William F. Farish, the President of Humble, Heinrich Reidemann and John A. Mowinckel, Chairman and Vice-Chairman of the European Committee, Senior, coordinator of Latin American activities, and Frederick H. Bedford of Stanco, the new marketing subsidiary for specialty products, all became Board members.[134] Weller continued to speak for Louisiana, while Black as President of the Delaware Company and Clark as President of both the Shipping and Development Companies represented their units at Board meetings. Incidentally, by this allocation of duties, Teagle finally solved the problem of the overlapping jurisdictions and the continuing conflict between Black and Clark.

These changes were to provide another important channel of communication and authority between the parent and the operating companies. However, most of the new Directors representing major affiliates continued to work at and live near their local headquarters and to come to New York only a few times a year. Thus the officers who had run the company before 1927 — Teagle, Hunt, Clark, Sadler, Moffett, and Chester O. Swain, the senior Legal Officer — continued to make the significant strategic and enterpreneurial decisions much as they had done before. But now, relieved of day-to-day operating decisions, they had more time for over-all policy planning and appraisal.[135]

By the end of 1927, Teagle and his associates had outlined an over-all management structure that was becoming similar to earlier creations at du Pont and at General Motors. The changes had come as a result of two separate moves, the first in August, 1925, and the second in May, 1927. Together these gave Jersey autonomous, multifunction operating divisions with managers who were responsible for performance and with a general office of general executives and staff specialists, which planned, appraised, and coordinated the activities of the various units and of the enterprise as a whole. Reorganization at Jersey, however, had come in quite a different manner than had those at du Pont and General Motors. It was not the result of a carefully thought-out plan, meeting over-all organization needs, but rather of *ad hoc* answers, arising from functional problems and needs created by Jersey's business strategies. Just because the organization had been shaped in such an *ad hoc,* informal manner, many years had to pass before the duties of the operating officers, staff specialists, and general executives, and the relations between them, were fully worked out.

Working Out the New Structure

The blueprint for Jersey's over-all management structure, at the end of 1927, was then an informal plan in the minds of men rather than written down in manuals, directives, or charts. One reason for the time involved in working out the structure was that different men inevitably read such an informal blueprint differently. Still more significant was the fact that the same executives continued to work in the same offices on much the same type of matters as they had before 1927. Men like Teagle, Hunt, Sadler, and Clark could hardly be expected not to become involved in the affairs of the new Delaware Company.[136]

The evolution of the new structure need not be described here; it will be told in detail elsewhere.[137] All that is necessary now is to indicate how the blueprint of 1927 relates to the company's more formal, carefully rationalized structure of the 1950's. While there were constant minor shifts in organization and personnel, only two series of major changes need be mentioned. The first came in 1933. The continuing contraction of the market, particularly during the great depression, plus the persisting overproduction of crude which so harassed the petroleum industry after 1927, created pressures that helped force the first series of changes. The second set, completed in the years during and after World War II, was a response to the rapid expansion of Jersey's business in the war years and postwar boom.

The 1933 changes had four main aspects.[138] First came the wholesale retirement of top management personnel. The turnover was almost as sweeping as that instituted by Pierre du Pont in his company in 1919. Next, the make-up of the Board was changed to include only policy-making general executives. Third, the activities of the Delaware and Louisiana Companies were reshuffled so that the companies came temporarily to concentrate on the administration of a single function. Finally, the Delaware and Jersey Companies were physically separated by moving the parent company out of 26 Broadway uptown to 30 Rockefeller Plaza.

The onslaught of the depression led to a demand for tighter control and a reduction of administrative personnel. As a result, the administration of all domestic sales, including those of Louisiana and Delaware as well as the new Standard Oil of Pennsylvania, and the recently purchased Colonial Beacon, and excluding only those of Humble, were now "centralized at 26 Broadway." [139] (The Pennsylvania Company had been organized and the Colonial Beacon had been purchased in order to expand Jersey's marketing resources and outlets in the Northeast.) According to *The Lamp,* a new marketing department had been initiated by Robert G. Stewart, recently appointed Director at the Jersey Company in charge of Domestic Sales. This new unit had its senior executive responsible to Stewart for the supervision of day-to-day operations; also its retail, wholesale, tank car, tire, and accessory sections; and its staff offices including an enlarged Advertising Department and the two staff offices recommended earlier by Harden — a Sales Research Department and a Sales Promotion and Training Department. Under the presidency of Frank Abrams, the Delaware Company continued to administer all activities relating to refining, while Carter came to operate quite independently as a producing company. In effect, then, Jersey's domestic petroleum business, outside of Humble, had become defined for administrative purposes along functional lines, with the Carter Company handling production, the Delaware and Louisiana Companies, refining (Louisiana managed production in its own vicinity), and the new sales department, marketing.

However, the managers of these functional units were to have more authority and responsibility than had the executives in the old departments and committees. To help make more certain that the general officers in the parent company would continue to concentrate on over-all entrepreneurial activities while the men in charge of the new functional departments and the other remaining multifunction affiliates focused on operational ones, the reorganizers in 1933 changed the Board's personnel, redefined its duties, and moved the general offices out of 26 Broadway to the new 30 Rockefeller Plaza. A series of resignations reduced the Board from nineteen to thirteen members, and most of these thirteen were new appointments.[140] Except for G. Harrison Smith of Imperial, no Director after 1933 was an officer in, or a representative of, an operating company. The Jersey executives, like those at General Motors and du Pont, finally decided that policy makers ought not to speak from interested or committed positions. In other words, they should not have operating responsibilities and loyalties. At this same time, Farish, formerly Humble's President, became the Chairman of the Board and a new Treasurer was appointed.

The big Board now consisted of full-time executives who devoted their time wholly to over-all coordination, appraisal, and policy planning. An Executive Committee of five directors — Teagle, Swain, Farish, Payne, and Sadler — with a permanent Secretary, met daily as its predecessor had since 1927.[141] In time, each of the five had an alternate to attend when he himself could not be present. Individually, most Directors came to have what was known as "contact" responsibility. Each contact Director was assigned a number of operating subsidiaries to oversee and advise. And, like the Group Executives at General Motors and the members of the Executive Committee at du Pont, these general officers had only an advisory relationship with the heads of the operating units. Collectively, either as the Executive Committee or the Board, they formulated and decided broad policy for the Jersey interests.

These administrative activities included the allocation of Jersey's resources to meet anticipated demands and needs and the appraisal of the effectiveness of the employment of existing resources. Since the market had become more stable than it had been in the early 1920's, Jersey executives were less concerned with strategic planning, in the sense of developing new markets, new refineries, and new shipping and crude producing facilities.[142] *Fortune* described the Committee's duties well:

> But the main business of this executive committee might be divided into two main channels. In the first place it keeps pretty close watch on the flow of oil across the immense Standard map. The Corporation works on a five-year "look-ahead" plan based on estimates of market demands, which

in turn give an idea of necessary refinery output and crude production. For instance, the total flow of gasoline for 1938 was about 116,000,000 barrels to all markets; the projected flow for 1943 is 133,000,000 barrels. This project is of course in constant state of revision, and such revision is carried out by various co-ordinators and the heads of operating companies. . . . The second and much more important function of the committee is to keep a close check on costs of the subsidiaries and their budgets.[143]

The spadework for such long-term coordination and planning continued to be done by the Coordination Department.[144] That Department worked closely with offices in the parent company — with Production, with Foreign Marketing, and with Foreign Refining. One significant change was the revival of the Coordination Committee under the Chairmanship of Sadler. Consisting of two other Board members, Harden and Stewart, and three general staff executives, including Harper and Howard, the Committee became more active, not only in coordinating and appraising operational activities, but in assisting the Board and Executive Committee in long-term planning. Able membership, a reliance on accurate data provided by the Coordination Department, and a concentration on strategic problems helped make this small advisory committee the prime initiator of new projects and new courses of action at Jersey Standard.

If the Coordination Committee or individual Directors proposed a new course of action, the final entrepreneurial decision on the policy came with the act of allocating funds to carry out the plans, primarily through adjusting and finally approving budgets. By systematically appraising the performance, needs, and plans of the many operating units, and by correlating and coordinating them into a broad general scheme for the company as a whole, the policy makers at Jersey were able to chart the course of their vast enterprise far more rationally and efficiently than they had been in the years before the formalizing of budget procedures in 1925.

After 1933, budgets were drawn up by what was called the "group" system. That system, like the Inter-divisional Committees at General Motors, provided a way for bringing general staff and operating executives together regularly and yet avoiding operational bias in top decision making. Budgets from each unit, for example, were thoroughly dissected by a group of specialists. While the executives from the foreign refining, foreign marketing, and producing units of the general office took part, the key men on these groups were operating executives. *Fortune* describes the process as it was carried out in 1940 in this way:

Budgets are made up in the first instance by the subsidiaries. They are then torn to pieces by different "groups," depending on the nature of the appropriation involved. Thus the budget of the Standard Oil Co. of Louisiana will usually involve a decision about expanding or modernizing plant. The "group" that looks at it will include most of Jersey's top U. S. refiners. Where a special problem is involved, Lloyd Smith may be pulled up from Aruba or Leo McCloskey may come down from Imperial Oil in Canada. Similarly when budgets for producing units are involved, a producing "group" will sit in judgement. Thus the budget of Standard's Carter Oil Co., which produces largely in Oklahoma and Illinois, will be scrutinized in New York by a number of men including Gene Holman, President of Lago Petroleum, which operates in Venezuela. In a similar way Lago's budget will be inspected by Leonard McCollum from Carter and other producers. It is only after a budget has passed the approval of the group that it goes up to the executive committee and to the Jersey Board for final review. The point of this "group" system is to bring to bear on every problem all of the talent that the corporation can command, drawn from various parts of the world.[145]

If the 1933 changes brought a more careful definition of the make-up and duties of the Board, the next series of major changes, those that came during and after World War II, resulted rather in formalizing the work of the parent company's staff and in reshaping the domestic operating units.[146] The latter once again became multifunction, regionally defined divisions. The great expansion of the petroleum business in these years undoubtedly made the regional orientation more practical.

In any case, the Louisiana Company was merged with the Delaware Company, whose President soon became fully responsible for marketing as well as refining. After obtaining control over sales, after clearly defining its relations with the parent company, and after acquiring a new name, Esso Standard, to emphasize its independence, the Delaware Company underwent a major internal organizational overhaul.[147] By the end of the war, Carter had also developed refining and marketing organizations and had become an autonomous, integrated unit like Esso and the older affiliates like Imperial and Humble.[148] Other changes, though less significant, took place in many operating affiliates, particularly in those abroad, when Jersey tended to concentrate the expansion of producing, marketing, and even refining facilities.

In the parent company's staff, relatively few new offices were created in the war and early postwar years. The more important structural changes there dealt with the development of more formal and systematic communication between the different staff units. Here the most significant events were the reorganization of the Coordination Committee and the formation of a new Advisory Committee on Human Relations.[149] The financial, legal, and housekeeping sections, most of whose activities had been with the parent company since 1927, were little affected by these two sets of changes.

The reorganization of the Coordination Committee essentially redefined the relationships within the growing staff departments in the general office that dealt with the major functional activities. By this time, the foreign marketing and refining offices (staff offices for liaison with and coordination of foreign marketing and refining) had extended their services to the domestic units, as had the staff production office.[150] An early step in this evolution came in 1943 with the appointment of Frank M. Surface, the head of the Sales Research office, as coordinator of sales research for both foreign and domestic subsidiaries.[151] Departments for pipe-line and shipping coordination were also added. The Coordination Department, whose primary concern continued to be advice on the coordination of product flow, continued as a separate organization; and because of the complex world conditions, a separate Economics Department had been set up by 1940.[152]

After the war, the Coordination Committee came to be made up of the heads of these functional staff departments plus two Jersey Directors, as Chairman and Vice-Chairman, and representatives of affiliates in the New York area. The Committee continued to be, as it had been since 1925, an advisory group only. "Although it makes no decisions," *Fortune* pointed out, "it dissects most problems and propositions before they come to the Board for decision." [153] Although the company had begun to expand its petrochemical lines, the primary concern of these problems and propositions was still the future supply and demand of its basic gasoline, lubricating, and fuel oil lines and the best ways of developing the resources to meet estimated needs. The Committee and the functional coordinating departments also took over the task of reviewing the budgets of the affiliates which had been carried out in prewar years by groups of operating men.

Using the Coordination Committee and its departments as models, the organization builders at Jersey, in 1948, grouped the remaining staff departments — those dealing with people (employees, stockholders, government officials, and the general public) rather than with economic functions—around the Advisory Committee on Human Relations.[154] Most of these units had long been with the company, but their activities had been expanded during the war and postwar period. Working individually or through the new Committee, the executives of these offices continued to advise the Board, often recommending policies and proposals started on their own initiative.

Some Final Considerations

By 1948, the promise of the changes carried out between 1925 and 1927 was fulfilled. Trial and error, often quite painful, led to a clarification of the lines of communication and authority at all three levels of administration. By the end of 1927, the departmental structure had been reshaped, usually on a line-and-staff basis, so that the relationship between the field units and the headquarters as well as the responsibilities for the various duties at headquarters were clearly defined. This clarification made possible the delegation of much administrative work to the field. After 1927, executives at departmental headquarters had no reason to be as overwhelmed with routine work as had been the members of the Manufacturing Committee in 1924.

At the other end of the administrative scale, the duties of the general office were redefined so that the executives responsible for directing the enterprise as a whole had more time to concentrate on broad strategic and entrepreneurial activities. The newly created Coordination and Budget Departments provided them with far more satisfactory data than had previously been available for long-range planning and appraisal. These departments also helped assure more effective coordination of the activities of the operating units.

The operational administration of the functional departments was turned over, as it had been at du Pont, to autonomous, self-contained operating units. These multifunction divisions, the Delaware and Louisiana Companies, administered Jersey's business within specific geographic regions. Since the duties of the executives in the central offices of these divisions were largely operational—that is, keeping the enterprise operating smoothly and efficiently rather than long-term planning, coordination, and allocation of available resources—authority and responsibility were centered in a single officer.

One of the most striking facts about the *ad hoc* structural changes at Jersey was that, almost completely unplanned, the reorganizers in the oil company made the same type of allocation of group and individual responsibility as had those at General Motors and du Pont. Operational administrative activities that required fairly quick action became the responsibility of a single individual, and the more complex, long-range entrepreneurial ones were those of a group. The division or department head consulted his line assistants or staff officers before taking action. But he alone was responsible for the performance of the unit. On the other hand, the Executive or Coordination Committee at Jersey, the Executive Committee at du Pont and at General Motors made their decisions as a group, with each company increasingly accepting group responsibility at the top level. Within the senior decision-making units, the members were considered to be of equal rank. Also, in all three companies, the relation of the individual general officers to the operating executives was an advisory not a line one.

After 1927, two facts brought further modifications in the reorganized structure. The first was the lack of precision in the initial definition of the new organization. The second was the coming of the depression. The first affected the organization of the general office, the second that of the operating divisions.

The initial important structural refinements took place in the development of more accurate and precise information to flow through the new channels of communication and authority. Then the major adjustment in 1933, by further clarifying the role of the general office, completely freed the senior executives from operating activities. With the redefinition of the duties of the Board, with the appointment of a new set of senior executives, with the physical separation of the general office from the central office of the Delaware Company, the senior executives at Jersey came to have a psychological commitment to an over-all or entrepreneurial rather than to a departmental or operating point of view. After 1933, the structural redefinitions in the general office dealt primarily with the duties and responsibilities of the general staff.

The contraction of business caused by the depression led to a temporary abandonment of the regionally defined, multifunction divisions for administering domestic business. The three major domestic operating subsidaries — Delaware, Louisiana, and Carter — became functional rather than regional units, with the general office staff again supervising the coordination of product flow. But, in contrast to the years before 1927, the general executives stayed clear of operating details. Then with the war and postwar boom and the rapid growth of the market, Jersey returned to the multifunction regional divisions. Because the Delaware Company by this time received most of its crude supplies from overseas, it did not take over the control of producing activities but did handle its own procurement, marketing, and refining. At the same time, Carter began to refine and market as well as to produce.

In 1959, as the demand for refined products leveled off once more, Jersey again began to reorganize her operating activities. The need to cut costs, the growing homogeneity of the domestic market, and the desire to move into areas where the Jersey Company had been forbidden to use a Standard Oil trade name since the dissolution of 1911, all helped induce the Board to combine Esso (the old Delaware Company) and Carter with Humble as "the first step in a broad plan for consolidation of producing, refining, marketing and marine activities in the United States in order to achieve nationwide operation under a unified management."[155] Possibly in time Jersey will do as Socony and Shell have already done: form a comparable structure for its foreign business which, particularly with the rise of the new producing areas, is far more complex than in 1927 and during the 1930's. In any case, the formation of such enlarged, multifunction regional units in no way alters the basic structure first outlined in 1927, for the reorganization of that year fashioned for the first time a structure that formally defined the relationship between three basic administrative units — the functional department, the regionally defined multifunctional affiliate, and the general office which coordinated, appraised, and set policy for the autonomous divisions in the interest of the enterprise as a whole.

At Jersey Standard then, structure followed strategy. But there the response was slower, more tentative, and less sure than at du Pont and General Motors. In some ways, this difference was owing to the fact that its problems were more difficult. In 1925, Jersey was at the same time a centralized, functionally departmentalized consolidation, as du Pont had been in 1920, and a loosely held overdecentralized federation like General Motors before its reorganization. Where the problem at du Pont was the formation of the operating divisions and for General Motors that of building the general office, for Jersey it was both, as well as reshaping the organization of some of the functional departments. Moreover, in making its structural changes, Jersey was more encumbered with inherited tradition than General Motors and, thanks to Pierre du Pont, than the explosives company. This inheritance included a commitment to committee management and a lack of concern for organizational problems.

Yet Teagle and his associates did wait a long time before challenging these traditions and adjusting structure to strategy. The delay certainly reflects the personality, training, and daily work of the Jersey executives. With the exception of Sadler and Howard, and possibly of Clark, these men rarely thought in terms of organization. There was little in their training or traditions to develop an awareness of these problems. They focused their day-to-day interests more on the immediate and not on the long-range problems. They preferred action to analysis. They deemed unnecessary the systematic study of the experience of other firms or, in fact, even of their own. As a result, Jersey's organizational structure grew in an essentially unplanned, *ad hoc* way. On the other hand, few, if any, other companies in the oil industry thought more rationally about organization than Jersey. Not only was the Jersey Company the first major oil firm to have fashioned the modern multidivisional structure, but it was also one of the very first American enterprises of any sort to do so.

5 SEARS, ROEBUCK AND COMPANY—DECENTRALIZATION, PLANNED AND UNPLANNED

Changing Strategy and Structure

In 1929, Sears, Roebuck and Company, one of the nation's largest and most profitable marketing companies, was meeting management problems similar to those which du Pont, General Motors, and Jersey Standard had already confronted and for much the same reasons. In 1925, Sears had started on a new strategy. Up to that time, it had sold only through mail-order catalogues. Then a declining market and the resulting threat of excess capacity turned it to retailing through its own stores. This form of expansion required the development of new resources and the reorientation of existing ones. The initial attempt to carry out the new strategy with the older, long-established structure raised innumerable difficulties. As at Jersey and the other companies, the addition of lines of business at Sears demanded a readjustment in the responsibilities of the top executives, a redefinition of the lines of authority and communication, and the development of new types of information to flow through these lines.

Sears's problems were simpler in many ways than those of Jersey Standard. Its growth came from expanding its own resources and by building or buying its own stores, and not from the purchasing and controlling of already large enterprises, as had been largely the case at Jersey, General Motors, and even du Pont. Its activities were not spread all over the world and were confined essentially to one basic activity, marketing. Yet at Sears, as at Jersey, the structure necessary to meet the administrative needs of a new strategy was slow in reaching its final form.

The reasons for the delay, however, were quite different. The executives at Sears, like those at General Motors and du Pont, had a rational, systematic approach to the problem of management. They studied organization for organization's sake as those at Jersey did not. They planned an over-all structure to integrate and mobilize all the resources of the company. But whereas the slow structural adjustment at Jersey resulted from lack of an explicit plan, at Sears it came from the adoption of what was at first an incorrect plan with wrong objectives. The initial structural plan proved ineffective because its framers did not clearly define the channels of authority and communication and did not think through fully the administrative role of the functional departments, the new multifunction divisions, and the general office. Much of this failure, in turn, came because the objective was to reduce costs rather than to maintain and increase the volume of their business.

Initial Strategy and Structure

An understanding of the problems facing Sears, Roebuck in 1929—the year it embarked on the major reorganization of its administrative structure—requires an analysis of both the fashioning of its earlier structure and the development of its new strategy. The real story of the present-day company begins in 1895.[1] Before this, Richard Sears had sold only watches and jewelry by mail order. In that year, Julius Rosenwald and his brother-in-law, Aaron E. Nusbaum, joined the company, providing the capital and executive ability that Sears needed to make the most of the opportunity offered by mail-order selling to American farms and villages. In the following decade, the company's business grew enormously. Sears market was almost wholly in rural America, where the primary retail outlet remained the crossroads general store with its limited stock of relatively high-priced merchandise. In his semiannual catalogue, Sears offered the American farmer a wide variety of goods and, because he purchased in large quantities and often directly from the manufacturer, offered them at a price lower than did the local merchants and storekeepers. Sears was not the first to see the possibilities of mail-order selling. Long before he began to peddle watches, Montgomery Ward & Co. had come to dominate the business. Yet, through his ability to stock and promote goods wanted in the American countryside, Sears was able to surpass his largest competitor in net sales just five years after Rosenwald had joined with him.

Sears's phenomenal success in selling to the American farmer forced his Chicago mail-order enterprise to enlarge its facilities and personnel rapidly and, at the same time, to systematize its buying, distributing, selling, and financial activities. Sears, a brilliant merchandiser, built his business empire by concentrating on sales promotion. In stimulating the demand for offerings in his catalogue, he worked very closely with Louis E. Asher, Manager in charge of the Advertising and Catalogue Department, who became the company's General Manager from 1906 to 1909.[2]

The filling of the orders that he and Asher so effectively generated was left to Rosenwald.

Rosenwald was more interested in system — in administrative structure — than in sales strategy. Of the departments he helped fashion, the buying or Merchandise Department, headed by J. Fletcher Skinner, was the most important. Under Skinner's general direction came a large number of buyers, each handling a major line and each having a great deal of independence in selecting and procuring, at the lowest possible prices, the goods that were then advertised in the catalogue.

Where the Merchandise Department procured the goods, and the Advertising and Catalogue Departments sold them, the Operating Department was expected to get them from the producer or wholesaler to the customer. The needs which arose from the handling of the ever-increasing number of orders pouring into Chicago — sometimes at the rate of a hundred thousand a day — at first brought the company to expanding its physical resources, and in 1905 it began the construction of a huge forty-acre plant on Homan Avenue in West Chicago, a plant that still houses its largest mail-order plant and its general offices. Next came a systematizing of procedures. In 1906 and 1907, the Operating Department's head, Otto C. Doering, assisted by an able staff, worked out a precise, detailed, and very efficient "schedule system" within the mail-order plant.[3] They developed new special machinery to process the orders and made more careful and rational use of the operating personnel. To carry out its "responsibility for handling of in-bound and out-bound orders and merchandise," the Department was given supervision and control over the flow of goods from the producer to the consumer, including transportation and storage.[4] To assist in carrying out these responsibilities, Doering built up a fairly extensive Supply Department and a large one for Traffic.

The equipment and personnel required to handle the ever-increasing volume of business called, in turn, for more working capital. The financial needs could no longer be met by a few individuals or families. So, in 1906 Rosenwald went to a boyhood friend, Harry Goldman, of Goldman, Sachs & Company of New York City. At Goldman's suggestion, the Sears financial structure was re-formed and stock was offered to the public through Goldman, Sachs, and also through Lehman Brothers. The company became capitalized at $40 million, Sears and Rosenwald continuing to control the largest share of the new stock. A Board of Directors was formed, including Sears, Rosenwald, and Albert Loeb. Loeb — originally the firm's lawyer — became one of its three senior executives, first as Secretary, then after 1908 as Treasurer. The other Directors were representatives of the investment houses and two of the company's financial officers.[5] This excursion into public financing led also to the growth of the Treasurer's and Secretary's Departments.

Expansion encouraged vertical integration. When products could not be purchased at a suitable price, the company often bought an interest in a factory that made these goods. By 1906, Sears, Roebuck had a financial investment in at least nine factories, by 1908 more than twenty, and by 1918 over thirty. These not only made durable goods, like farm implements and sewing machines, but also turned out shaped wood, furniture, clothing, and shoes. Shortages during World War I increased the need for control over sources in order to have an assured supply. After the depression of 1921 dramatically ended these shortages and made supplies readily available, the number of factories wholly or partially controlled declined.

Sears's policy towards factory ownership changed little over the years. As Boris Emmet and John E. Jeuck have pointed out in their excellent history of the company:

> In its participation in factory ownership, the company continued to hew closely to the line laid down by Richard Sears: to enter factory ownership only when compelled to and also to restrict its interest to 50 per cent or less wherever feasible. The firm was eager to do as little of its own manufacuring as reasonably possible. It sought instead to "get its foot in the door" in order to insure a supply sufficient for its own needs and to control quality (apparently a secondary consideration for many years) but preferred that the factory sell some of its output to other concerns in order to insure that it would operate on a competitive, economical basis. This was not, however, always possible.[6]

The basic reason then for vertical integration at Sears was, as it had been for Durant and at Jersey Standard, essentially defensive — that is, to have available an adequate supply of stock at a reasonable price.

Shortly after the panic of 1907, Sears resigned. The brief but sharp business depression, coming shortly after the company had been refinanced and its administrative structures organized along the lines of a great modern enterprise, had slowed orders for the first time since 1895. To meet the decline of business, Rosenwald urged a policy of retrenchment, while Sears vigorously demanded increased sales promotion. Troubled by this controversy, suffering increasingly from poor health, and a bit bewildered by the size and complexity of the organization his expansive ideas had encouraged, Sears decided in November, 1908, to retire from active business life. A few months later, his second in command, Asher, also left the company. With his departure, the Advertising and Catalogue Departments were permanently placed under Skinner's Merchandising Department.

Sears, Roebuck, under Julius Rosenwald, the new President, continued to grow rapidly, particularly during the prosperous war years. From 1908 until 1921, each year saw larger volume and profits. Skinner came to have under him more and more buying departments, and the size of these departments grew rapidly as orders trebled and quadrupled during those years. Doering's Operating Department kept apace of its ever-increasing demands. While Skinner and Doering administered the company's day-to-day operations, Albert Loeb, the company's Treasurer, came to make nearly all the entrepreneurial decisions. From late 1916 until 1920 Rosenwald had become almost completely involved in charitable and war work, and the bankers, Goldman and Lehman, appear to have given the thriving company little direct attention.

The most significant development in these years was the geographical expansion to other parts of the country. This growth of plant and personnel brought Sears's first important structural reorganization. The first branch mail-order house was established in 1906 in Dallas, Texas, and the second opened in Seattle in 1910, while a third, placed under the supervision of Julius' son, Lessing J. Rosenwald, was set up in Philadelphia in 1920. The opening of the Philadelphia store led, for the first time, to an evaluation of the relations between the branch houses and the main Chicago plant. The Dallas and Seattle branches had remained quite autonomous. This autonomy, however, was not specifically planned. In the words of Emmet and Jeuck:

> Distance alone tended to allow them [the branches] a freer rein than originally intended, because department heads and other executives in the parent-house simply could not "worry" about branches so far away. There was no system under which the head of, say, the clothing department in Chicago received any credit for the performance of the clothing departments in Dallas or Seattle. Some efforts were made to synchronize procurement, but no steps were taken to make the synchronization really effective.[7]

The loose, informal, decentralized structure had brought some confusion, inefficiencies, and unnecessary competition in procurement of goods. Suppliers were often unable to distinguish between the orders from the different houses. Lack of correlation between catalogues led to errors in description and in the pricing of merchandise.

The need for effective coordination and supervision of the branches led to a clarification and tightening of the lines of communication and authority between the headquarters of the functional departments at Chicago and comparable activities in the field. Rosenwald at first thought that the Philadelphia plant could be managed much like the other two. But the new General Merchandise Manager, who had succeeded to the post on Skinner's death in 1917, strongly disagreed. He submitted a detailed report pointing out the current administrative problems and proposing, as a remedy, the institution of a "central control system." Under this system, which Rosenwald and the other senior executives accepted, the Merchandise Department at Chicago was to have full authority and responsibility for the lines of merchandise in the branches as well as the Chicago house. The merchandise manager in charge of each major line of goods was to control the development of supplies, the buying, and general merchandising and promotional policies. His would be the final say as to quality, price, the source of supply, and catalogue material. The Chicago catalogue editor now became responsible for all catalogues, and Doering's Operating Department received full control over the branch houses' operating procedures and methods. His Supply Departments purchased the equipment and stock needed to operate the houses and his Traffic Department to help guide the flow of goods. The Comptroller's Department was held responsible for all accounting and other financial procedures in the branch houses. The authority of the branch Manager, one executive later pointed out, "applied only to the responsibility for maintenance of inventories and availability of goods for customer orders."[8] By this first definition of the relations between the central office and the branch mail-order houses, supervision and control over the activities of the company's basic functions — purchasing, selling, distribution, and finance — became highly centralized in Chicago.

The year after the different departmental headquarters had gained administrative control over their field activities, the company's central office took steps to acquire somewhat comparable control of the work of the largest, most active, and most complex of its functional units, the Merchandise Department. As the company's business expanded after 1908, the heads of the many buying departments became, almost by necessity, increasingly independent. Skinner and his successor had little time to oversee the myriad transactions that the buyers carried on. The logic of the situation led Rosenwald and Loeb to look on Sears, Roebuck as "a federation of merchants." For all intents and purposes, each buying department became a free agent, as long as it showed a profit. The Merchandise Department made little effort to coordinate, appraise, and plan for its many subdepartments. One executive expressed both the real situation and the way in which it had become defined when he wrote in 1918:

> Another feature is the confidence we place in the leaders of our departments. . . . Each department manager is given a large measure of responsibility in developing his department work according to his ability. The

> business is his business. He is not hedged with limitations, such as dull the initiative. The result is that these men have responded with their best. . . . We have applied the principles of democracy to a commercial enterprise.[9]

About the only significant restraint on the buyers was the testing laboratories. This single important staff organization at Sears, formed in 1912, tried to get the merchandise departments to meet minimum standards and to see that the catalogue claims were verified by actual performance.

The depression of 1921 demonstrated at Sears, much as it did at General Motors, the dangers of the lack of over-all administrative supervision. In both companies, the market collapse created very serious inventory excesses. Anticipating a continued boom after the war, Sears's buyers like the comparably independent Division Managers at General Motors continued to purchase heavily. Inventories, which at the end of 1919 were valued at $42,685,776, rose to $98,264,471 by the following June.[10] Then in the summer and fall came the sharp decline of business and the rapid falling off of prices. By the end of the year, Sears's inventory was valued at $105,071,243. The continued recession in 1921 made the situation even more serious and placed the mail-order firm in as precarious a financial position as General Motors had been a few months before. Only Julius Rosenwald's pledge of $20,000,000 out of his own personal fortune prevented the bankers from taking over the company.

Rosenwald and Loeb responded to the depression by cutting costs wherever possible and increasing the control over the amount of goods the buyers purchased. They appointed a new General Merchandising Manager, Max Adler, who took charge of the program of retrenchment. One activity to fall before Adler's economy axe was the testing laboratories, which were dropped in 1922. Although this removed one restraint on Sears's buyers, Adler's office increased its control over their inventory and financial policies and procedures. The actual historical development of the new inventory controls and budgetary techniques is not clear from existing printed materials, and Emmet and Jeuck say almost nothing on this point.

In these years, however, the Comptroller's duties enlarged increasingly so that well before the end of the decade that executive ranked as the senior financial officer at Sears. Within the Merchandise Department, the General Merchandise Comptroller's office became one of the most important administrative units. Reporting directly to the Vice-President in charge of Merchandise, the General Merchandise Comptroller had, by 1929, become "responsible for all mail order and retail inventories."[11] Working closely with other senior executives at headquarters, he prepared estimates of sales and inventories. Budgets, based on these market estimates, were drawn up by the buying departments and required the approval of both the senior Merchandise officer and his Comptroller. The General Merchandise Comptroller was also responsible "for the watching of surpluses and the discontinuing of merchandise." Thus this office came to provide channels of administrative supervision and control and at the same time developed data to flow through these channels. In these same years, the Operating Department came to be held accountable for drawing up estimates and budgets on operating and capital expenditures.

If the debacle of 1921 was not a direct cause for the development of statistical and financial controls, certainly the lessons it taught played a major part in shaping them. In the 1920's, estimates by buyers and the central office seem to have been educated guesses based on past experience. It was only in the 1930's that Sears began employing trained economists to make careful and more sophisticated analyses of future demand and economic and financial conditions. Nevertheless, this control over inventories meant that the Merchandise Department — its Comptroller working with the buyers — had taken over the function of coordinating the flow of product from producer to ultimate consumer for the many lines handled and that the rate of flow had come to be based on estimated market demand.

By 1924 then, Sears had worked out a centralized, functionally departmentalized structure for its mail-order business. The administration of the purchasing of the merchandise, of its sales promotion, and of its distribution was centralized at Chicago, as was the control over all financial transactions and procedures as well as the supervision of the factories that Sears owned and operated. Within the Merchandise Department, the autonomy of the buyers was limited by the amount of goods they could purchase and the money they might spend. They still had little oversight as to just what they could buy. The Catalogue and Advertising Departments continued to supervise their respective activities in the different mail-order houses. The Operating Department remained accountable for the actual flow of product from the producer to the consumer; while the financial departments, beside being responsible for accounting, credit, and other financial transactions, were beginning to develop the financial and statistical information necessary to assure effective communication and control within the organization.[12] The senior executives must also have found these latter data extremely useful for appraising the performance of the buying and operating departments and in making policy for the company as a whole. Rosenwald and then Loeb, in consultation with the heads of the functional departments, carried out over-all appraisal and set broad policies and procedures.

The New Strategy

In 1925, Sears initiated a strategy that quickly put an excessive strain on the existing structure. The entrance into direct retailing, the most significant single step in Sears's history, was the work of a group of new top managers. After the hard times of 1921, Rosenwald began looking for a successor to take both his place and Loeb's. He himself had lost close touch with the business during the war years, while Loeb suffered from serious heart trouble after 1922. Rosenwald acquired a high respect for the administrative abilities of railroad men and finally asked Charles M. Kittle, Executive Vice-President of the Illinois Central Railroad, to be the new President at Sears. At the same time, he appointed Robert E. Wood a Vice-President.

Wood came directly from Montgomery Ward, where he had taken the post of General Merchandise Manager after leaving the Army in 1918. During the war, this relatively young army officer had built up an impressive record as the director of purchasing and storing all army supplies except ordnance and aircraft. Wood had reached this senior position after a rapid rise from the rank of major to that of acting quartermaster general, handling on the way various supply, purchasing, and transportation duties. A graduate of West Point in 1900, he had had ten years' duty in Panama before the war, helping to build the canal. By 1913, he was a captain and chief quartermaster and "the good right arm" of the canal's builder, George W. Goethals. Leaving the canal in 1915, he worked for a time in a minor executive job at the du Pont Company and then at General Asphalt. The entrance of the United States into the war brought him back to the Army, where he was soon serving again under Goethals, the Army's Director of Purchases, Supplies, and Transportation. War service, in turn, led to the position at Montgomery Ward, for Robert J. Thorne, long one of the leading executives in that mail-order house, had been Goethals' senior civilian assistant.

At Montgomery Ward, Wood began to advocate a new business strategy. More than any other mail-order executive of the time, he was aware of the impact of increasing urbanization and of the coming of the automobile on the national and, particularly, the mail-order market. This awareness apparently came from an odd passion for reading the *Statistical Abstract of the United States,* developed during his off hours in Panama. Such statistics emphasized, Wood told his colleagues at Ward's, that the United States was rapidly becoming an urban nation. Since the mail-order buyers lived in the rural areas, Ward must adjust itself to these changes. Moreover, the mass-produced automobile was making it possible for the farmer to get to town more easily and to buy from a much broader assortment of goods than was available at the crossroads general store. Wood pointed out in October 1921 to Theodore Merseles, Ward's President, that chain stores like J. C. Penney were already beginning to exploit this small-town market.[13] With its existing branch houses as distributing points, its highly developed purchasing organization, and its long-established reputation, Montgomery Ward could easily compete with, Wood insisted, the chain stores in any market.

Merseles paid little attention to Wood's proposals. Earlier in that depression year, Montgomery Ward had set up "outlet stores" in its mail-order plants as a way to reduce inventory. Then, it opened two such stores outside of the mail-order plants. The complete failure of these stores may have turned Merseles against Wood's proposals. In any case, Wood and Merseles continued in conflict over expansion and other policies. So, in 1924, General Wood left Montgomery Ward.

Rosenwald, interested by Wood's ideas on retail activities asked him to join Sears. He would not take any other executive's place, but would come as Vice-President in charge of Factories and Retail Stores. The factories, hitherto under the Merchandise Department, would have their own separate departmental organization. Now Sears had a retail office also, if no retail stores.

Wood began at once to plan Sears's move into the new type of marketing. Again he met with strong opposition from the older mail-order executives, who were more interested in expanding their established business. In the mid-twenties, in fact, Sears opened six more mail-order houses. As he had done at Ward, Wood stressed the significance that the growing city population and the mass-produced automobile would have for their market. The postwar agricultural depression made his arguments still more convincing. Since 1920, farm incomes had dropped from over $17 billion to $11.3 billion.[14] If the new stores were concentrated in large cities, he further argued, they would not cut into the existing mail-order business. Nevertheless, in getting the retail program under way, the strong support of Kittle and Julius Rosenwald were undoubtedly more important to the General than his demonstrated arguments about the potential decline of the mail-order business and the threat of unused resources.

Then in January, 1928, much to his own surprise, Wood found himself running the company with his own hand-picked subordinates. Kittle died suddenly on January 2. When Rosenwald appointed Wood President nine days later, Doering and Adler immediately retired. Each of them had expected to be given the position. Wood and Rosenwald then placed the experienced Donald M. Nelson, a seasoned merchandiser who started in 1912 as a chemist in the testing laboratories, in Adler's job as head of the Merchandise Department and brought in Theodore V. Houser, who had worked with Wood at Montgomery Ward, to be Nelson's assistant.[15] Lessing Rosenwald took Doering's place as the head of Operations. The younger Rosenwald continued to spend most of his time in Philadelphia, where he had been Manager of the branch mail-order house since its opening in 1920. His assistant, Thomas J. Carney, actually handled most of the Operating Department's administration, for Lessing Rosenwald, with Wood, now became concerned with long-term entrepreneurial matters. In the financial departments, Emil J. Pollock became the Comptroller and senior financial officer, while Rosenwald began a search for a new Treasurer. No one took Wood's former post as Vice-President in charge of Factories and Retail Stores. The President's office went on supervising factories, while Wood, as before, concentrated on his campaign of opening retail stores.

Under this new management team, the creation of a nationwide retail chain moved ahead rapidly. 1928 was the year of greatest expansion. In 1925, 8 stores had been opened, 4 located in mail-order plants; in 1926, only one addition was started and 16 in 1927. All 16 were large "A" stores. By the end of 1928, however, Sears had 192 retail stores in operation. Nearly all those opened in that last year were smaller "B" stores.[16] In 1929, the number had grown to 324, and again most of the expansion came with the "B" and still smaller "C" stores. This rapid growth had been paced by a similar expansion at Ward. Merseles, finally convinced of the value of direct retail selling, was determined to keep ahead of Sears. In 1927, Ward had 37 stores; in 1928, 246; and in 1929 as many as 25 a week were opening.

While obviously affected by Ward's expansion, Sears's acquisition of retail stores and personnel followed a fairly specific strategy based on Wood's assumption about the changing nature of the market. In those early years, Wood recalls, the company "made every mistake in the book" in its retail selling and administration.[17] Yet, in the General's opinion, the company's continuing success in retailing can be credited to the original plans. "Business is like war in one respect — if its grand strategy is correct," Wood once wrote, "any number of tactical errors can be made and yet the enterprise proves successful."[18]

The General's basic strategy was to concentrate on the urban market by using three types of stores. Placing his outlets in cities with a population of at least 100,000 should keep the new retail stores from competing closely with his mail-order houses.[19] By having large, medium, and small stores, he hoped to meet the competition of the two primary types of volume marketers in the city — the older department stores and the newer urban chains like Woolworth's, Grant's, or Kresge's.

Against this competition, Wood planned a strategy based on store location and types of lines offered. "Three essential and at that time revolutionary concepts characterized Sears' inauguration of its retail stores," Wood wrote in 1948. "First — location. Second — the character of the stores. Third — mass purchasing and integration of the durable goods lines." The first concept was based explicitly on "the impact of the automobile on the retail business." Retailing had been concentrated in the center of the cities and towns into which all avenues of transportation funnelled. Then, in Wood's words:

> When the automobile reached the masses, it changed this condition and made shopping mobile. In the great cities Sears located its stores well outside the main shopping district, on cheap land, usually on arterial highways, with ample parking space. In the beginning these locations were a source of great amusement and wonderment to the department store world.

As to the second concept, the character of the stores, department and chain stores were largely women's stores, featuring soft lines; and so "Sears, from the beginning, gave its store appeal to the man — the family — the home — the car — and relatively little appeal to style." It concentrated on hard lines like furniture, hardware, tools, guns, fishing tackle, and, most important of all, the durable goods created by the coming of the automobile and of electric power, such as tires, batteries, and other automobile accessories, refrigerators, washing machines, and other electrical appliances.

Finally Wood, as he wrote in 1948, saw the opportunity of lowering unit costs of these new consumer durables or "big tickets," as they had became known in the Sears parlance:

> The volume of Sears and Ward gave opportunity for mass buying, the linking up of mass production and mass distribution. This produced even greater values to the consumer and increased volume. Sears, while remaining primarily a merchant, felt obliged on account of its volume to have manufacturing interests in its volume lines. It owns outright or owns partial interest in thirty manufacturing companies.

Beside providing a renewed interest in factory ownership, the emphasis on consumer durables led to much more "specification buying" or what came to be called "basic buying." The merchandising departments began to design their own products, to determine the best location for production in relation to the market and supplies, and then to go to a manufacturer in the given area with these specifications and negotiate a contract. Specifications, as well as price, became the criteria for purchasing. In this way Sears increased its control over the function of coordinating the flow of product to include every step from the initial design of the product to its sale to the ultimate consumer.

The strategic plans as Wood defined them in 1948 had probably been less clear and precise in the mid-twenties. Nevertheless, there seems little question that these three fundamental concepts provided the basis for planning the expansion of the retail stores between February, 1925 and May, 1929.[20] Policies for carrying out these objectives were often more difficult to determine than was the definition of the grand strategy itself. The location of "A" stores in outlying areas was quite rigorously adhered to, but the location of "B" and "C" stores was a far different matter. The number and variety of lines proved a similarly continuing and vexing problem, and finally the development of specifications and the finding of suitable and willing manufacturers turned out to be no simple task.

In moving into direct retailing, the medium-sized "B" stores raised the most difficulties.[21] In the larger metropolitan areas, location had to be chosen carefully in relation to the existing, or planned, "A" stores and to outside competition. In the smaller cities, where most stores of the "B" type were, the line between downtown and outlying areas was anything but clearly drawn. Nor did their outlying areas offer the same advantages as those of the larger cities. Montgomery Ward's decision to locate in the smaller cities increased these problems further; although Wood had initially planned to locate only in the larger urban areas, he had to follow Ward into the smaller towns, if only to protect Sears's mail-order market.[22]

The type of lines that should be carried in the "B" stores proved particularly difficult to determine. If a primary strategy of concentrating on hard goods was to be followed, what should be the criteria for selecting other lines? The large "A" stores had enough room to handle a variety of soft lines as well as hard. The smallest stores, the "C," could carry hard lines such as tires and auto accessories. But the "B" units needed at least something beside hard lines if they were to use their space and to attract customers. Just what kind of a store a "B" should be, what it should carry, and where it should be located remained continuing questions for the policy makers at Sears for more than a decade. The "B" stores, therefore, created constant pressure for structural as well as strategic adjustment in these years.

Structural Strains Created by the New Strategy

Even after the stores had been located and lines of goods initially decided upon, a clearly defined basic strategy of expansion into this new type of retailing failed to assure effective and profitable operations. Just as at Jersey Standard, General Motors, and du Pont, expansion at Sears demanded the creation of a structure to administer the new facilities. Still more importantly it called for a reorientation of existing resources, just as in the other companies. Unless older plant, procedures, and personnel were integrated closely with the newly acquired resources and unless they were readjusted to meet effectively the needs of the new strategy, growth into the new lines of business could bring only increasing problems, strains, and inefficiencies. These administrative difficulties immediately appeared in three critical areas — the selection and training of personnel, the choice and quality of products carried, and the flow of goods from the mail-order plants to the retail stores.

Yet Wood and his associates at first anticipated no major organizational change. The new stores were to be administered through the existing mail-order structure. The Manager of each of the ten mail-order houses took over the administration of the retail stores that were to be supplied from his plant. Each was given a Regional Retail Manager to handle the day-to-day supervision. The only other organizational modification brought by the new strategy was the formation of a small retail staff unit in the central office at Chicago.[23]

These minor structural adjustments soon proved insufficient to meet the many new administrative problems. Of these difficulties, none appeared more serious than that of personnel. Prior to 1925, the catalogue had sold Sears's vast array of products. People, as well as catalogue descriptions, would now have to make the sales. Direct confrontation with the consumer meant developing a brand new way of merchandising for Sears.

Store managers, their assistants, and other store personnel had to be recruited either from the mail-order plants or from outside.[24] If the new managers came from within, they had little or no training in selling to customers directly over the counter. If they were men experienced in managing small or large retail stores, they had no understanding of the company's mail-order activities and operations nor any appreciation of why they had to fit their work into that of the older operating organization. By 1929, the problem of personnel had become so acute that Wood toyed with the idea of merging with J. C. Penney Company as one way to obtain the necessary trained managers.

By that time, too, Wood realized that the old organizational structure was inhibiting the development of revenue-producing assortments for the stores and complicating the flow of goods to them. The mail-order houses had to supply the new retail stores if Sears was to make full use of its existing buying and distributing facilities and personnel. Such resources, Wood had pointed out to Merseles in 1921, made it possible for the mail-order companies to consider competing successfully with existing volume retailers. Yet the mail-order buyers were completely untrained in purchasing for the new urban market. Nor was the Operating Department much better equipped to distribute the buyers' goods to the new stores. The mail-order personnel, for example, were not used to making adjustments for local and seasonal differences. They shipped skis and other cold-weather sports equipment to southern stores, while store managers in Maine and Minnesota found themselves burdened with bathing suits and other tropical sportswear in the winter months. The buying organization clearly had to be reformed if the stores were to carry the most salable goods, and the Operating Department reorganized if there was to be an efficient "service of supply" from the mail-order distribution system to the retail outlets.

Wood's retail strategy intensified the pressures on its personnel and facilities in other ways. The mail-order houses had been enlarging their lines constantly. By 1925, Sears sold almost everything, but the major proportion of its sales came in clothing and drygoods. As late as 1941, such soft lines still accounted for 56 per cent of Sears's mail-order business. But for the new retail stores, Wood's strategy required a concentration on hard lines and "big tickets." And competing as they did with the established department stores and urban chains rather than with small country crossroads stores, these stores needed to offer a better style of goods of more uniform quality than did the mail-order catalogue. Buying for retail differs so much from that for the mail-order market that Wood for a moment considered the possibility of having two purchasing organizations. He ordered a study of T. Eaton & Company of Canada, a large marketing firm that used two such units.[25] However, he and his associates quickly agreed that such a step would nullify the basic reasons for Sears's move into direct retailing.

Instead Wood encouraged his new managers to reorganize the structure of the existing Merchandise Department. Nelson and Houser started by reviving the testing and inspection laboratories, and at the same time by consolidating and combining the many lines. They fully appreciated that, beside adjusting the buying departments to the new needs of over-the-counter sales, they and their buyers must meet changed conditions in the rural mail-order market which had resulted from the coming of the automobile and the prolonged agricultural depression. The altered market was therefore forcing a much tighter administrative control over the buyers. The old concept of Sears as "a federation of merchants" had become obsolete in the face of new needs and challenges.

Troubled by the increasingly complex administrative problems created by the move into direct retailing, Wood decided, in May, 1929, to defer further expansion.[26] The reason was not because Wood's strategy appeared in any way to be unsuccessful. In just two years, almost 275 stores out of a total of 300 had been opened. Of these, nearly three-fourths were of the "B" type. The retail stores in those prosperous times were showing a good profit. In 1929, only four years after Wood embarked on his new strategy, they already accounted for just under 40 per cent of the company's total sales.[27] With a profit of $30.1 million and a 15.7 per cent rate of return on investment, that year was one of the best in Sears's history. Moreover, Montgomery Ward showed no sign of stopping its expansion; it was to have 500 stores by the end of 1929. But Wood, like Sloan at General Motors, Howard and Sadler at Jersey Standard, and several executives at du Pont, saw the need for action before a crisis had actually arisen. Since he, unlike the more foresighted executives in other companies, was the chief executive officer, he was able to act promptly. He abruptly postponed further expansion until the operations of the existing stores could be improved and until the new line of business could be more effectively integrated with the company's older activities.

The first step Wood took to improve his retail organization was to invite a marketing expert, Alvin Dodd, to come to Sears "to instil some 'retail know-how' into the organization."[28] Dodd was well trained for this task. He had had a long career in industrial education and marketing, including positions like that of Chairman of the War Service Committee of the Retail Research Association, Director of the Retail Research Association, and Manager of the Distribution Department at the United States Chamber of Commerce. In 1929, he was lecturing at Northwestern, University of Chicago, and Stanford on "Trade and Industrial Problems" and was the Director General of the Wholesale Dry Goods Institute.[29] At the same time, too, Wood persuaded General W. I. Westervelt, a West Point classmate, to take charge of the laboratories. He was to give concentrated attention to testing and improving the merchandise that Sears offered.[30]

Before either of these two new executives had time to do more than review their problems, Wood decided on a still broader approach. Sears's difficulties were not to be answered by copying Eaton's or by merging with Penney's. Nor were they to be solved by such piecemeal reorganizations and changes as Houser and Westervelt were making in the Merchandise Department, and as Dodd was beginning to plan in the retail organization. They required an analysis and possible overhauling of Sears's whole management structure. Wood realized, in a way that Walter Teagle at Jersey never did, that the difficulties were more than those of marketing, operations, or buying. The basic problem was organization. For this reason, Sears's President late in August, 1929, asked George E. Frazer, the senior partner of the Chicago firm of Frazer and Torbet, certified public accountants, to take charge of a thorough revamping of Sears's management structure.

The General asked Frazer to chair a Committee of Reorganization which, after careful study, would recommend a new organizational structure to assist the company in realizing three specific objectives.[31] First, the Merchandise Department must be readjusted in order to handle the new needs of the changing mail-order business and the new urban retail markets. Second, "the 'jobbing' end of the business" must be reorganized, that is, the coordination of the flow of supplies from the mail-order houses to the retail stores must be improved. Finally, and most important of all, the structure must provide an effective administration of the plant and personnel of Sears's new retail stores.

Abortive Decentralization

The Frazer Committee's Report remains a landmark in the history of Sears, Roebuck and Company. Its recommendations led to some restructuring of the major functional departments at Chicago, particularly the Merchandise Department, and to the creation of five new territorial divisions for the administration of the mail-order houses and retail stores in the field. Finally, the Committee placed the old functional and the new territorial organization into a larger, over-all structure. However, for two reasons the new design proved ineffective. First, the lines of communication and authority were not defined clearly enough to prevent conflict over the administration of the functional activities within the Territories. Second, the territorial organization did not have the necessary personnel or information to carry out its essential tasks. The distrust of General Wood and George Frazer for large-scale, bureaucratic organization was largely responsible for both these defects.

For the decade after the Frazer Committee had submitted its recommendations, Wood continued to search for a satisfactory structure by which to manage the merchandising empire he had enlarged so greatly between 1925 and 1929. The increasing conflict between the Territories and Chicago over the administration of the new stores and older mail-order houses, as well as the contraction of business caused by the depression, led him to abolish the Territories in 1932 and to return to a functionally departmentalized structure with administrative decision making centralized in Chicago. Then, in 1940, influenced by the unplanned growth of local administrative units and also by the renewed and energetic expansion of Sears's business, the General and his associates began to put into effect a structural design based on the Frazer Committee's original report.

This time the territorial units became full-fledged multifunction, autonomous divisions with the managers responsible for over-all operating performance, and the Chicago headquarters, a general office with staff specialists and general executives.

The Frazer Committee

Wood appointed five experienced executives to the Committee on Reorganization. They were talented, representative, and relatively young. Houser spoke for merchandising; Carney was the acting head of Operations; Pollock, the Comptroller, was the financial and control specialist; while Alvin Dodd was the retail expert. Another member, James M. Barker, was the prospective Treasurer. A graduate and one-time professor of civil engineering at the Massachusetts Institute of Technology, Barker was working for the First National Bank of Boston in Buenos Aires when Lessing Rosenwald asked him to come to Sears. After the banker had accepted the post of Treasurer, Rosenwald suggested that he spend some months learning the business by supervising the Philadelphia mail-order house.[32] The Committee included, then, three men with many years in the mail-order business and three — Barker, Dodd, and Frazer — with broad outside experience. Houser, the youngest, was thirty-seven and Dodd, the oldest, was forty-six.

Chairman Frazer, at forty, was one of the first experts on large-scale administrative organization in the United States.[33] A liberal arts graduate from the University of Iowa, he had gone to Wisconsin in 1910 as an instructor in accounting. There, while taking advanced degrees in law and accounting, he had become enthusiastically involved with Senator La Follette's brand of Progressivism. As Chief Accountant of Wisconsin's Board of Public Affairs, Frazer had set up one of the earliest state budgets in the country. Then, at twenty-three, he went to the Universtiy of Illinois as Professor of Accounting and University Comptroller. In 1915, after having reorganized the university's financial system, he entered the business world as General Auditor at Montgomery Ward. Two years later, he was devising a financial organization for the state of Illinois. With the coming of the war, he went to Washington at the suggestion of R. J. Thorne, the Ward executive who was assisting Goethals, to formulate accounting and other procedures for the Quartermaster Corps. There he was soon working closely with General Wood. Then, after creating a new Financial Department for the Army and renegotiating contracts for the Shipping Board, in 1921 Frazer became chief consultant for the reorganization of Ohio's administrative as well as financial systems. Similar consulting jobs followed, many more in business than in government. Even so, after completing the study at Sears, Frazer wrote Wood that after twenty years of work of this kind, "the suggestions contained in this report are the most important I have been asked to make." [34]

In this same letter, written in early January, 1930, Frazer stated: "Practically every day since September I have been in communication with one or more members of that Committee." Actually, most of the work fell to Houser, Dodd, and Pollock, whose offices were in Chicago.[35] Houser, continuing the work he had started with Nelson, studied and reported on ways to concentrate and regroup the administration of the different lines of merchandise. The Committee had hoped to consolidate all merchandise into twelve basic departments. However, the best Houser could do "and still have what I believe to be practical sized units," was twenty-one.[36] These he classified under three major headings that had been suggested by Dodd: wearing apparel; home furnishings and accessories; and heavy mechanical, farm, and building construction equipment. Houser next worked out organization charts for the departments based on these new groupings and then outlined procedures "with respect to the most important routines." [37]

While Houser was refashioning the buying organization, Dodd was continuing to plan the new marketing one. Everyone agreed that the management of the retail stores from the mail-order houses had proven completely unsatisfactory. After studying the structure of J. C. Penney and other chains, Dodd and the Committee finally decided on a district organization.[38] All retail stores were placed in one of thirty-three geographical districts, each headed by a District Manager with a small staff. The districts, in turn, were put under four territorial offices each of which was to be headed by a Vice-President or Assistant Vice-President. After the general structure had been accepted, Dodd, working closely with Frazer, outlined the duties of the territorial and district officers and defined the boundaries of the districts. The district offices varied in size. The smallest, the Denver district, included one "A" and two "B" stores, while the larger ones included two to four "A"s and up to 15 "B"s. Dodd's and Houser's recommendations were carefully reviewed by financial Vice-President Pollock, who concentrated on improving accounting procedures and statistical information for the retail stores. Next the recommendations were considered by the Committee as a whole and then forwarded to Wood and Lessing Rosenwald.[39]

The Committee's Proposals

The committee's final proposals provided Sears with two organizations, a new territorial one in addition to the older functional one (see Chart 8). The territorial organization was essentially the one Dodd had

CHART 8

Sears Structure as Defined in Frazer Report, January 6, 1930

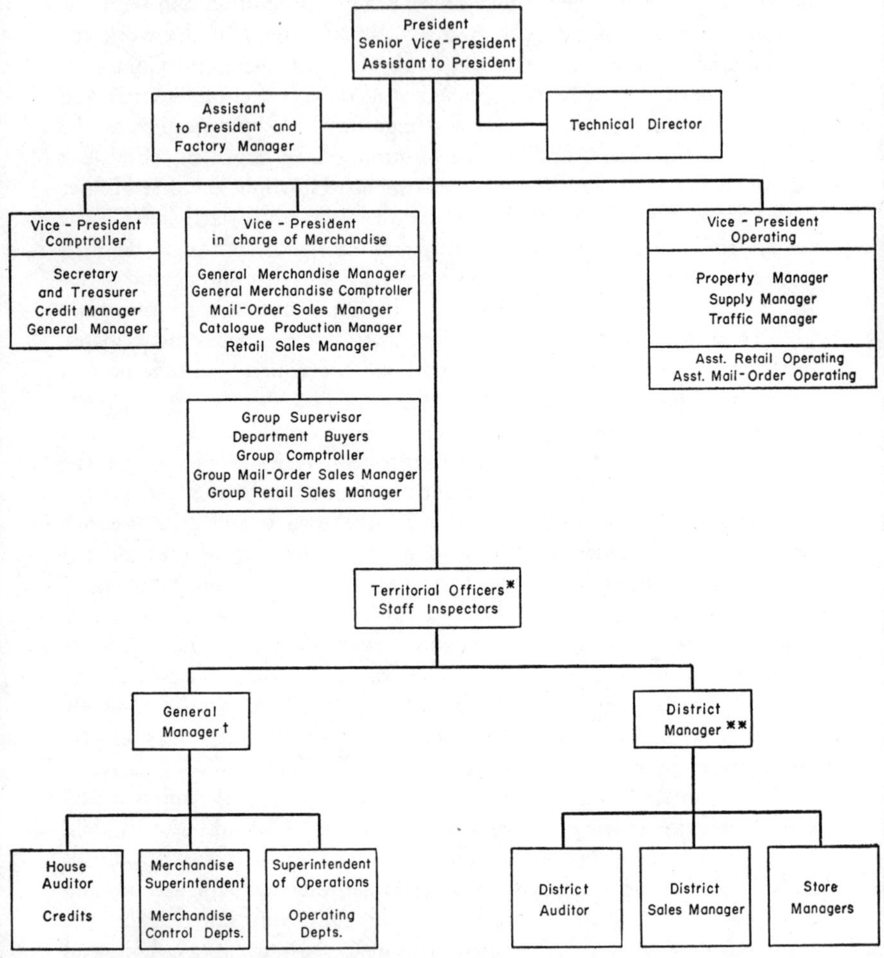

* There will be Territorial Officers located at Philadelphia, Memphis, Chicago, and the Pacific Coast: i.e., four regions in place of the present ten.

† A General Manager for each Mail-Order House.

** A District Manager for each Retail District as established.

recommended. Except for the Merchandise Department, the existing functional structure was only slightly modified. Carney, the new Vice-President in charge of Operating, was given an assistant for the retail as well as one for the mail-order business. Each was to supervise personnel and develop standard methods and procedures in the operations of the two types of business. The chief of the Operating Department also continued to have supervision of the Supply and Traffic Departments and was given jurisdiction over a new officer, the Property Manager.[40] The Vice-President and Comptroller now became responsible for all financial transactions and personnel. He not only supervised the accounting and auditing work and the compilation of statistical data, but he also had the Credit Manager and the Secretary and Treasurer reporting to him. A third senior officer, the executive in charge of factories, continued for the moment as an Assistant to the President.

The Committee proposed more fundamental changes for the Merchandise Department. The staff of the Vice-President in charge not only included a General Merchandise Manager and the General Merchandise Comptroller, but also a Sales Manager for mail-order and another for retail. The primary task of these two new officers was planning sales promotion, for both Houser and Dodd fully realized the critical importance of trying constantly to expand sales. The Mail-Order Sales Manager worked closely with the Catalogue Production Manager, while the Retail Sales Manager was to handle "the preparation and distribution of retail advertising, window displays, and standard manual of sales instructions to retail sales personnel." [41]

Thus the department buyers lost control over sales promotion as they had earlier over inventory. Furthermore, they were now consolidated into administrative departments or Groups. The final decision on the number and make-up of the lines of goods or "commodities" carried by each Group was left to Wood and Nelson, who appear to have followed closely Houser's recommendations to the Frazer Committee. Each had its Group Supervisor, who was responsible for the selection, purchase, and sale of merchandise in its commodity group and who was assisted by a Group Comptroller and Mail-Order and Retail Sales Managers. The Comptroller, beside checking on inventory, was to handle "all matters of office management and routine" in order to "free the department buyers." The Sales Managers were to be the "means of contact" between the unit and the stores or plants and were to concentrate on sales promotion. The Group Comptroller and Sales Managers reported directly to their counterparts at headquarters, and not, as in the manufacturing departments at du Pont or the General Motors' subsidiaries, to the heads of their units, that is, the Group Supervisors. Only the buyers were directly responsible to the Group Supervisor. These men, once among the most powerful executives at Sears now were only buyers, and the situation remains much the same today.

The functional departments at Chicago were to have direct communication with the executives in the ten mail-order houses and the three hundred retail stores. At the same time, the stores and the mail-order houses were part of a regional or territorial organization. A store manager reported to one of thirty-three District Managers who, like the ten Mail-Order House Managers, came under the jurisdiction of one of four Territorial Officers located at either Philadelphia, Memphis, Chicago, or Oakland. The Committee hoped to integrate the territorial divisions and functional departments into a larger over-all structure by defining carefully the duties of each and by indicating explicitly the flow of authority and communication between each. There would be, the Frazer Report pointed out, two lines of authority and communication — the executive line from the President to the retail store managers or mail-order department heads via the District and Mail-Order Managers and the Territorial Officers, and the functional line from the President to the functional men in the stores and mail-order houses via the functional departments in Chicago. "The two principal duties of the Regional [Territorial] Officer," the report explained, "lie in recommendations on matters of personnel and in co-ordination of merchandise supply between the mail order houses and the retail stores." The functional executives at Chicago were, on the other hand, to remain responsible for the carrying out of their respective duties in the stores. They were to have direct contact with the managers of the retail stores and mail-order houses. In the words of the report:

> The plan of organization provides for immediate and constant direct communication between the heads of each function in the business and the functional officers and employees of the business wherever located throughout the country. For illustration, we may say that the Vice-President in Charge of Operating is authorized and directed to give his orders and advices directly to all operating employees of the business, as for example, the operating superintendent of the Kansas City Mail-Order House and each retail store manager. It is expected that each employee of the business will receive and obey instructions communicated to him on the functional line of authority and will be entirely free to report to his superior officer in his functional line. . . .
>
> The territorial organization, including the general managers of the Mail-Order Houses and the District Retail Manager, is likewise authorized and directed to give orders and instructions directly to the members of their respective units. The orders and instructions of the General Manager of the Los Angeles Mail-Order House have full force and authority to all employees located at the Los Angeles Mail-Order House.

To help restrict the Territorial Officers on "the executive line of authority" to their primary task of personnel and service (coordination) of supply, the Committee proposed to keep regional staffs to a minimum. The maximum staff permitted the Territorial Officer was made up of three functional inspectors — a traveling auditor, a merchandise inspector, and an inspector of operations — and these were to be taken from the mail-order and store personnel in his district. At least one prospective Territorial Officer felt that this number was hardly enough. He saw the need for four advertising and a minimum of one personnel man on his staff.[42] But Frazer insisted on a very small staff made up of existing personnel. As he wrote Lessing Rosenwald:

> Human nature is such that each Regional Officer may seek to build up a large ornate staff of his own at a considerable expense to the Company and with the result that the Regional Officer and his staff will be duplicating the work that should be done by the District Retail Managers and by the General Managers of the Mail-Order Houses.[43]

The District Managers and the heads of the mail-order houses who came under the territorial officers were also shown very small staffs. The Mail-Order Managers were to be assisted by an Auditor, a Merchandise Superintendent, and a Superintendent of Operations. The District Manager, despite his critical role, was assigned only an Auditor and a Sales Manager.

Significantly Dodd, the marketing specialist, and Frazer, the expert on organization, viewed the needs for the size of the regional staff differently. And these views reflected their interpretation of the functions of the manager. To Frazer, the District Managers were to do little more than appraise and analyze the performance of the stores and the mail-order houses in his district and to make changes of personnel on the basis of these analyses. To Dodd, the District Manager "has a dual responsibility."[44] Not only was he to see, by constant personal visits and analyses of operating statistics, that "stores in his district are being profitably operated," but he was "secondly, to see that the major merchandise and sales promotion policies of the company are being carried out." His Sales Manager was to have, in Dodd's words, "sales promotion, in the broadest sense, [as] his principal function. He is a sales promoter — not in the sense of merely checking on certain details of store operation — but through actual work in the stores with specific merchandise and operating divisions." Frazer's view won out, for the tasks assigned the District Sales Managers and Auditors were to be only additional part-time jobs for an executive already working in one of the stores. In insisting that the managers have a minimum of staff, Frazer was carrying out his own convictions and also following General Wood's explicit instructions.[45]

The essential weakness in the Committee's recommendations was that the four Territorial Officers and the thirty-three District Managers were all given wide responsibilities. Even though they had almost no staffs and even though the Chicago office was accountable for the functional activities in the stores and mail-order houses, their duties were more than merely supervising personnel and coordinating product flow. Each Territorial Officer would become specifically "responsible to the President and the Senior Vice-President for the activities of the Company in the territory, including assets, profits, expenses, inventories, sales, personnel, and good will of the Company."[46] Moreover, General Managers of the mail-order houses and the retail districts were to report directly to the Territorial Officer "when and as requested" by that officer, even though there was also to be direct communication between the store and plant managers and the functional officers in Chicago.

The Committee hoped to avoid conflicting authority and responsibilities by having the important communications between Chicago and the districts, between stores and plants go also to the Territorial Office for information. That executive could then, at his discretion, veto or suspend an order, giving his reasons to Wood, Rosenwald, and the head of the functional department involved.[47] The Frazer Report spelled out this relationship in the following way:

> In order that both the functional organization and the territorial organization may operate to the fullest efficiency, it is required that instructions given by the functional officer to his functional subordinates in a territorial unit shall be given directly and at the same time that a copy of such instructions shall be given to the territorial officer in charge of the unit affected. For illustration, the Vice-President and Comptroller, will communicate his instructions directly to the Credit Department at the Seattle House and will also send a copy of instructions to the General Manager of the Seattle House and to the territorial executive at Oakland.
>
> The Territorial Officers are on the executive line of authority, reporting directly to the Senior Vice-President. Such officers are authorized and instructed to stop or change any or all orders affecting their territories if, in their judgment, the best interests of the Company are served. For example, the Mail Order Sales Manager may communicate an order directly to the Merchandise Superintendent at the Dallas House. The Regional Assistant Vice-President may either veto or change it, as may the General Manager of the Dallas House. While such cases will be exceptional, each such case will be important.

Here surely were the seeds of discord.

Having outlined the duties of the functional officers at Chicago and the new regional units in the field, the Committee then set up a general over-all policy-formulating and coordinating office. The managers of the major functional departments — Merchandise, Operations, and Finance — and the heads of the four new Territories were to become Vice-Presidents. Lessing Rosenwald, as the new Senior Vice-President, became a general executive in name as well as in fact. He and the other Vice-Presidents and the executive in charge of factories were to meet monthly as the Officers Board to assist "the President on the development of Company policy and in the co-ordination of the functional activities of the Company." As had long been standard procedure in large American business enterprises, the senior executives were responsible individually for the administration of the basic operating units and collectively for the enterprise as a whole. To make sure that the members would devote some of their time to a variety of specific problems, a number of subcommittees were set up to meet and report to Rosenwald at least quarterly. Each subcommittee was chaired by the head of the department most involved and included executives not on the Board. There were committees for factories, advertising, credit policy, merchandise budgets, operating estimates, retail personnel and procedures, and regional organization. Their task, like that of the Officers Board, was only advisory. They were to formulate recommendations for decisions by the President and to check on policies already decided upon.

Carrying Out the Committee's Proposals

Wood and Lessing Rosenwald accepted the Frazer Committee's recommendations with only minor modifications. The most important one accepted was Rosenwald's proposal to set up an Assistant to the President who would handle public relations and recruitment of personnel and also "to analyze reports and recommendations that came to the President."[48] Through creating such a staff office, Rosenwald wrote Wood, he hoped the company "could save Mr. Dodd to the organization," and make the most effective use of his "splendid experience and ability." The Frazer Committee, apparently at Wood's suggestion, had taken Westervelt's Technical Department out of the Merchandise Department so that it became the only other central staff office at Sears.[49]

Wood and Rosenwald next chose the executives to fill the offices of the organization the Committee had fashioned. Rosenwald made the initial recommendations. As he wrote Wood: "These are not to be considered final, by any means, and in some cases I would go so far as to say that they are not desirable. I have gone on the following basis: That each square *must* be filled by a name, even if we make a change later." For the lower echelons, Rosenwald suggested some names, but stressed that department heads and the regional executives must have the final say.

Only about two men did the new Senior Vice-President feel strongly. One was Dodd, and the other was Gilbert E. Humphrey, whom he wanted to take over the post of Assistant to the President for Factories because that department "needs immediate attention and supervision and, furthermore, because there is a tremendous field for this particular activity, at this present time."

In filling in the squares, Rosenwald and Wood tended to rely on Frazer's recommendations on personnel whenever they were uncertain. Both had grave doubts about the possibility of obtaining executives able enough to handle the critical post of Territorial Officer. Because of their hesitancy, only one man, Barker, was made a Vice-President. The other three, Charles B. Roberts, C. A. Woods, and Hiram W. Kingsley, took the title of Territorial Officer rather than of Vice-President or Assistant Vice-President, as the Committee had recommended. For this reason, the regional organization had little representation on the Officers Board, which was made up of Vice-Presidents. Thus the functional officers came to play a larger role in policy making than did the territorial executives.

After the senior officers had been notified of their new jobs, the junior officers were appointed and, finally, all concerned were carefully briefed on the reasons for the change and the nature of each individual's new job. All this was carried out quite smoothly under Carney's supervision.[50] The final meeting of the Frazer Committee was on January 6, 1930, and by February 17, the new structure was in full operation.

Almost at once questions began to be raised concerning the relations between the functional and regional organizations. Late in January Frazer was writing General Wood explaining some of the confusions that had arisen on this point and emphasizing the need to limit the role of the regional officers. One District Manager, for example, had issued instructions that all requisitions for merchandise must be initially written in his office. Frazer insisted that such a step was "absolutely wrong."[51] It violated Wood's original instructions to him and, he added,

> Your plan of organization is a good one, but your expectations under it will be defeated if you permit territorial officers to make themselves into necks of the bottle; or if you permit District Managers to build up extensive overhead; or if you permit a diffusion of functional responsibility between functional officers in Chicago and territorial officers in the field.

The management of the smaller "B" stores created the most difficulties in carrying out the new plan of organization. Their continuing administrative needs brought a constant pressure for enlarging the Territorial and District Offices. "B" stores remained the hardest to stock, the hardest to man, and the ones needing the most attention in display, advertising, and other sales promotion activities. The "A," the full-line department stores carrying almost everything in the catalogue though emphasizing hard lines, had a clear place in Wood's strategy of urban retailing. So did the "C" stores with their concentration on automobile accessories and other hard lines to the almost total exclusion of soft ones. But the "B" stores were, as Emmet and Jeuck phrased it, "a merchandise 'no-man's land.' Their weird assortments included smatterings of many things and full offerings of few lines."[52] Yet, as farm commodity prices plummeted and the mail-order house sales dropped, the "B" stores were becoming an increasingly vital source of revenue for Sears. In 1930 when mail-order sales declined by $56.5 million, sales in the retail stores rose $6.2 million over the previous year. These trends were destined to continue.

By midsummer 1930, Humphrey, who had not yet returned from Los Angeles to take charge of the Factories Department, was insisting that the District Managers' office must be enlarged if the "B" stores were going to carry the right selection of goods and sell them effectively. Under the organization fashioned by the Frazer Committee, Humphrey pointed out:

> All merchandise is in the hands of the [functional] Parent departments and the Heads-of-Stock in the retail stores. The Parent departments select, buy and establish the lines to be sold by the Retail Stores, but have no method of supervision over these lines, this being the function of the Head-of-Stock. In the performance of his functions, the Head-of-Stock is practically independent, being subject only to the general supervision of the Store Manager and receiving no supervision or assistance from anyone who is primarily familiar with his line of merchandise. The results obtained in any line will depend on the individual judgment displayed by the Heads-of-Stock in handling that line, his analysis of sales possibilities of items, his energy in keeping his stocks, his judgment and analysis of price lines to be carried, his shrewdness in sensing popular demand and in estimating possibilities of new items offered him, his judgment in fitting his merchandise to local conditions, his ability to secure sales through proper advertising and display, and his ability to secure the maximum turnover without sacrifice of service, to meet his customer and his ingenuity in taking measures to correct past mistakes and to meet adverse and unlooked-for conditions. . . . The problem is not to find three hundred efficient managers for our stores, but to find three hundred efficient hardware men, three hundred efficient sporting goods men, three hundred efficient paint men, etc. who can perform the intricate duties of retail merchandising under a strange system in which important elements of ordinary commercial procedure are lacking and do it without other guidance than through correspondence with a buyer in Chicago, who, while he is an expert in his line, is thinking

in terms of selecting, buying and pricing, and not of the problems of retail merchandising and selling.[53]

To place so much of the responsibility for sales volume and profits on the various Heads-of-Stock in the retail stores was, Humphrey stressed, "decentralization to the fullest extent." It prevented Sears from taking advantage of the managerial economies of scale. It was not allowing the company to "secure uniform results through established policies"; to employ capable men "in key positions, thus permitting the use of mediocre men in lesser positions"; to develop "new ideas, new policies, new methods [that] may be produced through the interchange of ideas of a number of men better than when limited to the individual," and so to make it possible for "mistakes in merchandising to be corrected by the transfer of goods between stores."

The remedy proposed by Humphrey was to expand the District Managers administrative staff. The Manager should have "a staff of merchandise men, each in charge of related lines, whose duty it would be to supervise and assist the Heads-of-Stock of the stores in that district, to keep the buying organization . . . informed as to conditions in the field and to see that policies and plans of the Parent organization are carefully carried out in detail in the field." After discussing the matter with the other Territorial Officers who supported Humphrey's views, Wood, on August 8, authorized the formation of a merchandising staff in the District Offices.[54]

Frazer Reviews the New Structure

A few weeks later Wood decided to take a second look at the new structure. Not only were the problems of the "B" stores becoming more perplexing as the economic depression deepened, but signs of conflict between functional and regional officers were increasing. At a meeting of the Officers Board on September 30, 1930—also attended by Frazer, Houser, and Dodd—there was general agreement that the underlying problem in retailing work was the need for better personnel at all levels of management.[55] These executives further agreed to have Frazer review the structure he had helped to create.

Frazer's second report, finished a month later, indicated how actual operating conditions were beginning to modify the Committee's carefully drawn plan. Most obvious was the growth of the Territorial and District Offices. Frazer again warned Wood against permitting the Territorial Offices from becoming "the neck of the bottle through which all instructions of every kind and shape had to pass and from which all corrective measures were taken . . . The Territorial Officer under no circumstances should undertake functional work."[56] The consultant was also troubled by the growing tendency for the "A" stores to be administered directly by the Territorial Officer rather than by the District Manager. The danger here, Frazer believed, was that such administration would keep the "B" stores from making full use of the facilities of the "A" stores and therefore would lead to a duplication of facilities in the District Manager's office. He urged both the "A" and "B" Store Managers to make more effective and continuous use of the merchandising experience and facilities in the mail-order houses that were providing them with supplies.

Frazer would approve of the creation of the new merchandising administrative staffs in the District Offices, which Humphrey had first suggested, only after a careful budgetary study had been completed. The appointment of five to ten merchandise supervisors to thirty-three district offices, he pointed out, could increase overhead expenses by over a million dollars a year. "There should not be the slightest fear of doing this," if the enlarged office supplemented the existing resources in the "A" stores and mail-order houses. But if such District Office staffs worked independently of the merchandise control divisions in the mail-order houses and the stock clerks in the "A" stores, Sears would in fact be carrying three separate sets of overhead. Could the company afford that type of expense, Frazer asked?

For the moment at least, the Sears executives were more impressed by the need to improve advertising, display, store design, and other sales promotion activities than by the danger of increasing overhead costs. The district staffs were retained, and both district and store managers were now made even more explicitly responsible for maintaining a satisfactory volume of sales and for making certain that each store carried out its "proper sales promotional work" and that the stores cooperated with the Merchandise Department in Chicago on plans to expand sales.[57]

For more than a year, the structure fashioned late in 1929 and slightly modified in the following autumn continued without a change. For one thing, the problem of supplying the retail stores, one of the three reasons for setting up the Frazer Committee, had been satisfactorily answered.[58] The creation of "pool stocks" or warehouses close to retail stores and the improved control and supervision in Chicago and in the Territories were assuring a smooth flow of supplies to the various stores. The contraction of the market and the small number of new stores being opened had made this problem easier to solve.

Continuing Conflict and Resulting Proposals

By the end of 1931, however, the driving onslaught of the depression again increased the concern over growing administrative costs. At the same time, it intensified the organizational strains resulting from the division of responsibility and authority between the functional departments and the Territories. As profits became harder to obtain, the regional executives responsible for such profits began to interfere more directly with the management of the retail stores and mail-order houses. The store managers in turn looked to the local men rather than to Chicago for assistance on many of their problems. Again, the "B" stores were the seat of most of the difficulties.

To Wood, Sears's difficulties were essentially those of personnel. Improve the caliber and the training of the managers and executives, and the major problems would be overcome. In the fall of 1931, he ordered a careful "inventory of personnel" as a step toward meeting the problems of selection, training, advancement, compensation, appraisal, and disciplining of executive and store personnel.[59] At the same time, following a suggestion Frazer had made in his review of the year before, he set up a Retail Personnel Department under Ira R. Andrews, formerly one of Dodd's assistants. By this time Dodd himself had left Sears to become a vice-president of a large grocery chain, the Kroger Grocery and Baking Company. Andrews was to "handle all policy and planning matters connected with retail personnel." [60] In meeting these problems, his office was also to "act as a clearing house for desirable applicants, employee appeals, requests for men not locally available, etc.," and for information on personnel practices and procedures between the various field offices and Chicago. Its relations to the territorial organizations were not quite clear. The report announcing its formation merely stated: "Contact with the stores will be maintained through the Territorial Officers, each of whom will have a specifically assigned assistant for such work." But who had the final say, the Territorial or the Chicago office?

Next, in mid-December, Wood wrote a memorandum to the Territorial Officers urging them to concentrate on their primary responsibility, that of personnel. This memorandum is worth quoting at some length for in it Wood makes clear some of the basic ideas about management that lay behind the Frazer report and the later organizational changes at Sears:

> In outlining my conception of responsibilities and duties of the Territorial Officer, I am really outlining my conception of my own job, because, in your respective territories, you stand in my place. There is very little that the principal executive of a widely scattered, far-flung organization like Sears, Roebuck can do personally. This applies to me and likewise to you.
>
> As President of the Company, about the most I can hope to do is to select, properly reward, and properly weed out the officers and key men of the Company, besides continuing along the lines of certain fundamental policies. To sum up, my principal job is that of a personnel officer to a limited class

of men, the establishment and maintenance of proper policy and a close watch over the results of policy to the Company.

This again applies to you. In your respective territories your first and most important duty is the proper selection, proper reward and proper elimination of personnel in your territory.

Then Wood added a significant comment.

Standing in my place, you are also there to see that the fundamental policies of the Company are properly carried out, and to watch the policies and the results of all different units in your territory.

When I say that you are there to see that the fundamental policies are carried out, I mean the policies determined by the functional officers of the Company, Mr. Nelson in Merchandising, Mr. Carney in Operating and Mr. Pollock in Accounting. If you feel that these policies are wrong in themselves or that the policies as established by these functional offices are not being properly carried out, it is your duty to call the matter to the attention of the officers, if the policy is wrong, to see if it cannot be changed, or if the policy is correct but execution is bad through misconception or other causes to see that they are informed on the subject.

The greatest danger of any executive — the danger is greater the more active, able and aggressive an executive is — is to surround himself with a staff and to build up a duplicate organization. Personally, I try to avoid this by having only an Office Assistant and a personal secretary. The policies of the business I delegate to the functional officers and the territorial officers.

Again I want to impress you with the vital selection of personnel. Our whole future depends on the proper selection, proper reward and proper elimination of personnel. You cannot personally remedy matters in any unit under your control. You haven't got the time. But you can remedy matters by getting the right men in the right place and I have not seen a single instance in any Territory, Mail Order House, District, or Store where the selection of right men did not almost immediately bring results. Put your personnel work first because it is the most important.[61]

Wood, by placing his faith in personal ability, failed to see the value of systematic organization and therefore to appreciate the fatal flaw in Sears's existing structure. The Territorial Officers had more responsibilities than just that for personnel; they were to carry out the policies set by Chicago. To coordinate and execute those policies was especially difficult since they had no say in their determination. The difficulties increased when the policies were set by executives concerned with one activity and not with the integration of several. The territorial units were specifically responsible for the profit and market performance and for a wide variety of activities within their domains. Moreover, if the Territorial Officers were to select, promote, and drop personnel, they also had to carry out the basic administrative function of appraising operating performance. In other words, Wood was asking the Territorial Officers to administer a multifunction organization while leaving authority over those functions in other hands.

Carney saw the problem more clearly. To the Vice-President in charge of Operations, the problems were more than those of personnel; they resulted from a larger organizational crisis. In fact, the failure to meet effectively personnel needs came in good part from a failure of the existing structure to make clear the responsibility and authority of the functional and territorial offices. The central difficulty, Carney maintained, was that the Territorial Officers were taking on duties that belonged properly to the functional departments. This meant that Territorial Officers had too little time for personnel work and that they and the whole Sears field organization were failing to take advantage of the functional experts in Chicago. On the very day Wood was dictating his memorandum to the Territorial Officers, Carney was drawing up a similar one for Wood, analyzing the reasons of and suggesting solutions to the present difficulties.[62]

Carney began this report by pointing out the continuing pressure on the Territorial Officers to take over the administration of the several different functional activities in their areas:

> While undoubtedly each Territorial Officer appreciated this [the supervision and development of personnel] as the larger responsibility, actually what came to pass — as I see it — was a reference to the Territorial Officer of matters pertaining to operating, accounting, merchandising and last, but not least, sales promotion. It has been our practice to expect a Territorial Officer to be in a position to correct merchandising, operating, and even accounting, as well as sales promotion weaknesses that exist in a particular district or stores. If a poorer class of credits is being accepted in the Stores, the responsibility for correcting this new situation has been put to the Territorial Officer; if a new buying control system is to be installed, the responsibility for making it effective within the Stores is given to the assistants on his staff. If a Store Manager or District Manager wants authority to depart from established methods of sales promotion, outside selling, time payments, or what not, the request for the new ruling is put up to the Territorial Officer.
>
> As I see what is happening: although we have several hundred merchandising, operating, and accounting experts available in the Parent Organization with this knowledge and experience, we have tended more and more to clear all such problems to the Territorial Office, expecting the Territorial Officer and his staff to act as authorities and actually censor the decisions of these experts. Certainly, in many instances, criticisms made by territorial executives have been well-founded, and it has been apparent that field experience has often been of more practical value than the opinion of the

> experts in the Parent offices. This was particularly true during the first year of operation. The very fact that in certain instances the quality of the executive material available on the Territorial staff was such as to permit criticism being made of technical experts' instructions, tended more and more to cause a concentration of such responsibility in the Territorial Office, and there was a greater inclination on the part of the Territorial staff to comment on and criticize the actions of the Functional Executives and their assistants, going so far as to authorize the extension of, or modification of, instructions the latter issued, ofttimes without referring back to the executive who issued and was personally responsible for such instructions.

Because of this "definite tendency to load the Territorial Officer down with responsibility not at first contemplated," Carney continued, personnel training and development "have not received the attention that it was planned they should."

Carney felt that Sears "would be much further along" if the Frazer Committee had originally made the Territorial Officer responsible only for personnel and for the coordination of product flow and had given them no authority to countermand orders of the functional departments. Certainly a clearer definition of responsibility and authority should now be made. The Territorial Officers, Carney insisted, must not concern themselves with interpreting operating, accounting, merchandising, and sales promotion policies. "Only when conflict occurs, when a breakdown is apparent to the Territorial Officer, will he get in on the problem at all, and in such instances he will take the responsibility for seeing that his District Manager gets the best results." By the same token, the functional officers were to keep their hands off personnel problems. "Each Territorial Officer should be told that he is expected and required to handle all matters pertaining to pesonnel, and that he will rise and fall in the organization according to the success he meets in this respect." To Carney, the Territorial Offices should be little units of another functional department, the one for personnel. As he foresaw only constant conflict between the departmental offices in Chicago and the Territorial Offices if both continued to carry on the administration of the several functions, he was in fact essentially advocating a return to a centralized, functionally departmentalized structure.

After discussing the two memoranda with Carney, Wood sent both his report and Carney's to Rosenwald and to the four Territorial Officers.[63] He asked the latter to forward their comments to him prior to a Territorial Officers' meeting to be held early in January, 1932, on the matter of organization. The response of the Territorial Officers should hardly have been a surprise. They felt that, in line with the Frazer Committee's recommendations, they had been given the responsibility and authority to handle broad administrative matters that included more than personnel. They further believed that such broad powers were absolutely necessary if Sears was to meet effectively the changing conditions and challenges in the field.

Barker, the Vice-President in charge of the Eastern Territory, was the most explicit. He reminded Wood that the Frazer Report specifically stated that Territorial Officers were "on the executive line of authority" from the President and Senior Vice-President, that they could countermand orders from the functional departments in Chicago, that the District Manager and the store managers reported to the Territorial Officer, and finally that the Territorial Office had full responsibility for all the activities of the company in the region including "assets, profits, expenses, inventory, sales, personnel, and goodwill," as well as warehousing.[64] Furthermore, the Frazer Report did not give the direct responsibility for profits and sales to the functional officers. Barker failed to mention, however, that Frazer insisted that the regional officers should not concern themselves with functional duties and that they should avoid, as Barker himself had been doing, building up local staffs.

Fowler B. McConnell, who had taken over the Southern Territory from Woods, presented a somewhat weaker stand for territorial autonomy. In "defining field authorities and responsibilities as between the Functional and Territorial Officers," he saw two interpretations, "a literal one" and a "liberal one."[65] The literal one, where the Territorial Officer concerned himself with personnel only, would be a poor solution. "Personnel responsibility, without responsibility for what personnel does, will simply lead to conflict and negative accomplishment." This was all the truer since the development of personnel was tied so intimately to the administration of day-to-day operations and to counseling the managers and appraising their performance. Barker had emphasized this same point.

The more liberal interpretation, whereby responsibility for net profit and customer good will still remained with the Territorial Officer, had "much more merit," in McConnell's opinion. He then attempted to define a specific division of responsibilities between the Territories and Chicago. He would give the functional officers much more authority than Barker deemed advisable. This included control over sales promotion as well as the selection of merchandise and the determination of operating and accounting procedures.[66] But, he maintained, at the very least the Territorial Officer must be responsible for appraisal, supervision, and performance of the stores, particularly the smaller ones. He should also "retain control of the lines carried in 'B' and 'C' Stores because he is closer to the firing line," and should be responsible for inspecting and following up the execution of accounting and operating orders and procedures.

Furthermore, "analyzing store results and acting on these results should remain the duty of the Territorial Officer." Someone beside a functional specialist was needed to appraise "the over-all well-rounded performance of the store."

General Wood agreed with Barker that the Territorial Officer was on the line of executive command and also he approved of McConnell's "liberal" interpretation.[67] Yet, as other executives pointed out, clearly neither of these positions was in line with one basic aim of the original Frazer Report.[68] Both increased the size of the territorial staffs and expanded overhead costs and raised the specter of duplication of effort.

The meeting of the Territorial and functional officers in Chicago on January 15 and 16, 1932, brought out two symptoms of the underlying problem. First, all agreed "that at present a great amount of dammed-up criticism of the Parent exists in the Field, and of the Field in the Parent," with the result that the store and district officers generally turned to the Territorial Officer rather than to Chicago for advice and assistance.[69] Second, there had been genuine confusion as to what was an order and what merely a suggestion. Too often orders from Chicago were disregarded as being mere recommendations.

The results of the two-day conference were essentially a victory for Carney's position. Although the Territorial Officers remained on the ex-executive line of authority and were responsible for profit, they would only have a say in, and in fact would be only informed of, functional activities when an actual conflict between a manager in the field and the Chicago office occurred. Even then the Territorial Officer could do no more than suspend the order until the next meeting of the Officers Board. Besides this change in basic duties, the top executives agreed on some mechanical devices that affected only the symptoms of the conflict between the field and parent offices. New procedures were instituted to ensure that instructions were not mistaken for mere suggestions. Department heads were urged to develop more personal contacts with managers in the field, and the store and District Managers were to be brought regularly to Chicago.[70]

These changes were mere palliatives. The division of responsibility and authority between the Territories and Chicago continued, and so did the controversies. The alternatives were becoming clearer. The Territorial Office must become, as Barker maintained, more autonomous or, as Carney proposed, become little more than sections of a central personnel department. Or else they should be eliminated altogether. Wood's aversion to large staffs and the pressing need to reduce costs as the depression deepened made the choice clear.

The Territorial Organization Scrapped

In May, 1932, the General abolished the Territories.[71] Mail-Order Managers now reported directly to Carney, while the retail Districts came under the jurisdiction of the Vice-President in charge of Retail Administration at Chicago. Barker took over this new post with McConnell as his Assistant. Wood thus put the two strongest and most outspoken Territorial Officers in charge of the new centralized retail organization. Beside the control of retail personnel, the new office, as suggested by McConnell in his memorandum, had responsibility of analyzing and appraising store results and taking executive action on them. The functional officers, however, continued to have direct communication with the store and District Managers on all matters concerning their own activities.

Hard times undoubtedly played a significant role in bringing about the centralization of supervision and the control of the retail stores and mail-order plants in Chicago. As mail-order sales dropped (falling from $266.0 million in 1929 to $209.6 million in 1930 and to $116.8 million in 1932), the Merchandise Department had tightened its control over the Catalogue Department and the buyers.[72] When sales finally fell off in the retail stores (first rising from $174.6 million in 1929 to $185.3 million in 1931 and then dropping in 1932 to $159.0 million), there were similar reasons for centralization. If the market had been expanding rather than contracting, the conflicting issues between the Territorial Officers and the functional officers might have been less acute and possibly there would have been less concern for increasing regional staffs and overhead costs. As it was, the depression only intensified already existing problems. Even with continued prosperity, the "B" stores would have raised difficulties to aggravate the organizational tensions between the Territories and Chicago.

The essential reason for the change in 1932 was the realization by Wood and his colleagues that Sears could no longer operate under a structure that was partly functional and partly regional, a realization that would undoubtedly have come even if there had been no depression. The conflict between Chicago and the regions grew in intensity as the Territorial Officers began to take over the administration of the functions. Business needs rather than drives of human nature stimulated the expansion. As both Carney and McConnell noted, the Territorial Officers were closer to the firing lines. They could meet market changes by adjusting stock, assortments, sales promotion, and other activities much more quickly than could the functional executives in Chicago. So the local managers looked to the Territorial Office rather than to the more distant central office for advice and assistance. The Territorial Officers, too, were the ones responsible for the performance of the stores and mail-order houses in their respective districts. As they increased their administrative load, the size and work of their office expanded accordingly, and the contact with experts in Chicago's functional departments lessened. Thus market needs and administrative responsibilities even more than executive personalities transformed the Territories into *de facto,* multifunction divisions that competed with the functional departments of the central office for the administration of Sears's nationwide marketing empire.

If times had been more prosperous, Wood might have ended the conflict by concentrating administrative control of the functional activities in the Territories rather than in Chicago. Yet there was no indication that anyone, with the possible exception of Barker, the strongest of the Territorial Officers, seriously considered this alternative. In time, however, this was the type of organizational structure Sears would adopt.

Evolutionary Decentralization

Sears was unable to remain long half territorial and half functional. This was the lesson learned from the company's first attempt to fashion an administrative organization for the management of its retail-store network. After the spring of 1932, General Wood tried out other alternatives. First, he centralized the supervision of the retail stores in the Retail Administrative Office in Chicago. Next, early in 1935, he attempted to decentralize the management of the stores completely by abolishing both the local Districts and the Retail Administrative Office. The retail stores and mail-order houses were now to report directly to the President. Then, almost in spite of him, new local administrative organizations, the Group and the Zone, grew up to take the place of the old Districts. By 1940, Wood was once again ready to try a territorial organization to handle the stores and the new local units, and to give the Territorial Officer responsibility for all functions (except the actual buying) as well as for profit. In other words, he was willing to turn the territorial units into multifunction divisions and to transform the Chicago headquarters into a general office. Thus when the company's management structure was completed in the years immediately after World War II, the major task became one of defining the role of the new general or parent office.

The Centralized Retail Organization

When Barker took on his new position as Vice-President in charge of Retail Administration and Personnel in May, 1932, he became responsible for the supervision of 375 retail stores managed through much the same districts as had been set up by the Frazer report. He had to create a headquarters office whose task was, in his words, "two fold: first, administration, with which it was definitely charged, and second, co-ordination of the effort of the Company as a whole on the retail problem."[73] The first task, beside planning and setting procedures for the stores and appraising their performance, was to try to meet the continuing need to recruit, train, and promote competent personnel. The second called for building closer relations between the functional departments and the central retail organization, since each functional officer retained direct contact with and responsibility for his type of activities in the stores. The hoped-for cooperation, Barker was certain, could come only through daily communication with the senior executives in the merchandising, operating, and financial units. Barker had always felt that the weakness of the initial territorial organization had been that, except for himself, the Territorial Officers had not been Vice-Presidents and so "were unable to get important differences between them and the Chicago Vice-Presidents discussed on the basis of give and take."[74] He now worked closely with the other Vice-Presidents, individually on special matters, collectively as chairman of a retail committee.

To help improve the caliber of Sears's retail managers, Barker enlarged the scope of the Personnel Department that Wood had established a few months earlier. To take over that department, he brought with him from Philadelphia F. E. Burrows, whom he had placed as the personnel officer of the Eastern Territory, against the wishes of Chicago.[75] Next, Barker revised the work already begun in systematizing personnel procedures. By the following September, for example, Burrows had distributed a completely new edition of a manual of procedures for retail store managers. Barker also set up personnel offices in the "A" stores and the District Managers' offices. Then, to improve communication between the field and Chicago, he held occasional conferences in that city with the new personnel managers, operating superintendents, and other field executives.

In personnel training, as well as in the executive supervision and appraisal of the stores, Barker relied more on himself and his immediate subordinates than on the printed output of his Chicago office. "Manuals and sales training courses are valuable and vital," he once wrote Wood, "but only effective when the high tension current from the Parent organization dynamos is transformed to the lower and suitable voltage by the transformer — the Manager — in each store."[76] The connection between headquarters and the field should be through the central office executives themselves, for the strength of any large organization, Barker believed, was "to a great extent dependent upon the manager's first-hand acquaintance with conditions on the firing line."

Barker trained and appraised simultaneously. He realized more clearly than had Wood that good managers need good tools. The basic administrative tools that he used and trained his subordinates to use were spot checks and accounting and statistical data. For spot checking, Barker believed in developing a complete and detailed knowledge of a few key items in each and every department. Such knowledge gave to a store manager's subordinates (the men who supervised those who did the actual selling to the customers) an appreciation of the fact that "his Manager *knows* the items checked. He generally imagines that the Manager's range of knowledge of individual items is more extensive than it perhaps actually is."

In his final report as head of the retail organization, Barker indicated how he used statistical information for both supervision and training:

> As a Company, we have worked out and have in effect a comprehensive and satisfactory retail accounting system. The figures presented to the individual Store Manager will give him a picture of almost any phase of the job that he may want. Most Managers have not an adequate comprehension of what they can get from the reports supplied to them. The method which I generally use in looking at the Stores involved, first of all, a review of significant reports in the Manager's office. Incidentally I generally have used his reports because, in that way, I found out whether he had them available and knew what they were. A couple of hours in the office on the reports enable the diagnosis of the Store's case, usually with clarity and definiteness. The time spent in spot-checking actual conditions in the Store after that was efficiently directed through this information and it often seemed almost uncanny to the Manager that the inspection of actual conditions in the Store confirms the diagnosis from figures so accurately. A definite attempt should be made by the Company to teach individual Managers the scope and utility of these reports.[77]

Here Barker was stressing the vital importance of statistical data for efficient administration at every level of operations. With Pollock, the Comptroller, Barker continued to improve these statistical tools and informational controls and to instruct the auditors and other officials to show the store managers how to analyze them properly. In this work, both men received Wood's strong support, for although the General was primarily concerned with obtaining competent managers, he realized that the supervision of their work required some sort of thorough statistical controls. He later pointed out that:

> As a business becomes larger and has branches all over the country, it becomes impossible for the executive to follow it and to control it except by figures. These figures have to be carefully and rapidly compiled, available immediately, and the executive must be able to interpret them properly — read behind the figures.[78]

Second only in importance to the training and appraising of managerial personnel was the planning of what the retail stores should sell. The major problem in the spring of 1932 remained the "B" stores, and it was in trying to meet their difficulties that Barker and his assistants worked most closely with the functional departments. One of the first steps was the classifying of the "B" stores according to the lines carried. The small "B-2" was to concentrate on hard lines, particularly hardware and large appliances. The still smaller "B-3" would, like the "C," focus on automobile supplies and accessories. In fact, it should soon replace the "C," Barker believed, as it had "more complete basic assortments in their lines in place of the 'C' store's smattering." The "B-1" remained the only one of these stores to carry soft goods. Because of the problem of finding satisfactory lines for the small space available in the "B-1" units, Barker was willing to eliminate them and to leave soft lines only in "A" stores.[79] But any such action, he wrote, should await the results of detailed studies then under way on soft lines, as indeed should any decisions on the strategy of store expansion.

To improve Sears's offerings, Barker instituted other reforms. His office worked out a series of assortments, so that a manager in ordering would have at least a minimum line of what a customer might normally expect for a given type of goods. By asking the managers to purchase by specified assortments, Barker hoped to cut out the "smatterings" and odd lots that sold slowly and induced customer dissatisfaction. The Retail Vice-President also further refined and elaborated "unit control" and other statistical procedures to ensure the maintenance and control of inventories so that merchandise would be in stock in the right amounts at the right times. He ordered studies made of district prices and suggested "zone prices . . . for each item in the assortment so that the less merchant-minded managers might have at least hope for a reasonable gross profit if they followed the zone prices, and the more intelligent managers had a guide that aided them in pricing competitively."[80]

By close supervision and discipline in all aspects of the business, by a weeding out of less capable managers, by steady training of the more competent ones, by the planning and development of new marketing procedures and policies, and by achieving closer coordination between the functional departments and retail administrative personnel, Barker had created by the end of 1934 a cohesive and capable retail organization. With the problems of personnel and lines on the way to solution, the most pressing continuing need, according to Barker, had become the improvement of the advertising and sales techniques so essential to the maintaining and expanding of sales volume. The creation of the Store Planning and Display Department within the Merchandise Department in 1932 was a step in that direction, but much more was needed if better sales promotion was to be assured.[81]

Decentralization of the Retail Organization

Barker's success helped Wood to decide that the time had come to turn most of the store management over to their individual managers. Now that these men had learned their tasks, Wood saw few good reasons for maintaining any sort of an elaborate administrative structure. Sears needed little more than himself, competent buyers, and store managers. Late in 1934 he proposed the abolition of the retail districts and the Vice-Presidency for Retail Administration in Chicago.[82] Barker was promoted to be the senior financial officer, and with his departure would come the elimination of the office responsible for planning, appraising, and coordinating the activities of the retail stores. The 400-odd retail-store managers and the heads of the mail-order houses would report directly to the General. The functional departments in Chicago would retain their check on the stores by means of traveling auditors and other liaison men.

Wood's executives opposed this extreme decentralization unanimously.[83] The time had not come, they felt, to permit the store managers so much freedom. The proposed slim structure would not permit Sears to mobilize its total resources effectively. Barker, for one, was certain that the appraisal and analysis of over-all performance would be exceedingly difficult. The merchandising and operating men from Chicago would be able to check only on their own specialties. The traveling auditor might bring to light unsatisfactory conditions, but such men "have generally no adequate background in merchandise or operating experience."[84] Here lay, Barker thought, "one of the dangers of eliminating the Retail Administration Office which, without authority over merchandising, operating, or accounting, except as derived from the goodwill and cooperation of these functional activities, yet had the opportunity to review all phases and thus influence both Parent and Field."

Moreover, this full decentralization would, in the opinion of Barker and the other executives, reduce Sears's ability to make the most of its trained administrative personnel. The smaller "B" and "C" stores particularly needed guidance in sales promotion and advertising, and required a fairly constant appraisal and analysis of their operating performance. "For efficiency," Barker insisted, these stores "must be organized in groups with centralized administrative management and a few low-priced men in charge of each individual store."

Wood's continuing apprehensiveness about bureaucratic growth as well as his lasting belief that individual competence was enough undoubtedly prompted his proposal for a change from a highly centralized to an extremely decentralized structure. He was willing to agree with his subordinates that many managers were not yet ready for autonomy and that Sears might lose some of the advantages of large-scale operations. Yet, as he maintained at about this time:

> While systems are important, our main reliance must always be put on men rather than on systems. If we devise too elaborate a system of checks and balances, it will only be a matter of time before the self-reliance and initiative of our managers will be destroyed and our organization will be gradually converted into a huge bureaucracy.[85]

In spite of his own convictions, Wood heeded the counsel of his managers and so failed to carry decentralization as far as he himself would have liked. He did eliminate the office of Retail Administration as well as the Districts. In theory, all retail store managers were to report directly to the President. In practice, some administrative work continued to be carried on in the field and at Chicago. McConnell, appointed early in 1935 as the Assistant to the President on retail personnel, became responsible for filling all openings in the retail organization, clearing only major appointments with General Wood.[86] On the other hand, no manager could be discharged until his case had been reviewed by a special committee and by Wood himself personally.[87] Nor could a man who was doing satisfactory work be moved from one store to another without his own consent. McConnell had other tasks, too,[88] for he was soon given charge of mail-order and central office personnel and became the company's secretary. So, while he undoubtedly kept an informal check on the performance of the individual stores, he had comparatively little time to analyze the results or to take or suggest action on the basis of the analysis.

This last task was left to the manager of new, local, regionally defined units. For the fact was that, even though the Districts had been abolished, other local administrative organizations developed. Under Barker, several "B" stores in the same area were often grouped together to give uniformity to Sears's prices, goods, and procedures in a single metropolitan region. Such groupings, furthermore, permitted the stores to pool their merchandising talent. These Groups soon came to have their own managers and staffs. After 1935, many "A" stores were added to Groups of "B" 's. Also, with the abolishment of the Districts in 1935, those "B" and "C" stores not yet in Groups were placed in one of five Zones, each headed by an executive who had been a District Manager. These "retail officers were now," Barker wrote in September, 1935, "in a position where they could act incidentally as district manager for the relatively few weak stores in their zones, primarily exercising only an advisory relation to the strong stores which were thus left free from detail supervision." [89]

The Zone Managers were carefully integrated into the existing functional organization. Even though they resided in the field, they were to act "as representatives of the functional officers and form with the senior assistants to the functional vice-presidents a committee which meets at Chicago regularly, discusses retail problems, and presents to the retail policy committee recommendations on basic matters." After 1935 Barker continued to serve as Chairman of this Retail Policy Committee, which included much the same personnel and duties as had the earlier Retail Committee. The responsibilities of "A" group managers to the functional officers in Chicago were probably much the same, although clear evidence is not available on this point.

The Growth of Local Regional Administrative Units

In the years immediately following 1935 the three types of regional administrative units, the Group and Zone offices, and even the administrative staffs of the independent "A" stores not placed in Groups, expanded in much the same way and for much the same reason as had the District and Territorial Offices after 1929. This growth came primarily by the addition of executives, particularly specialists in merchandising, who concentrated their full time and energy on the maintenance and expansion of sales volume by keeping constantly in touch with changing local demands and tastes, by appraising the performance of the stores in their own particular product lines, and by developing advertising and displays in these same specialties. The company's decision to continue and, in fact, to expand its soft lines in the "B" as well as "A" stores increased the need for close contact with the market and for better sales promotion techniques. Therefore that decision may have hastened the addition of these merchandising executives to both the local staffs and the Chicago Merchandise Department.[90] In any case, the regional administrative offices grew for the very reason that Dodd and Humphrey had given for enlarging regional districts when the retail structure was first set up. Only with executives who studied market conditions and sales promotion in order to advise store managers and Chicago buying officers could Sears carry out efficiently its primary economic role of using its vast and widespread resources to lower unit costs and prices by distribution of goods at a high volume and with a rapid turnover.

The "A" store, for example, operating independently of a Group, came to have specialists or Merchandise Managers, as they were called, for hard lines, soft lines, "big tickets," and home furnishings. Such a store soon had its own Advertising and Sales Manager and a Display Manager.[91] The number of managers of Groups of "A" and "B" store staffs grew to be larger than those of a single "A," the major difference in size coming in the number of merchandising departments. The Group Manager had his Personnel, Operating Credit, and Pool Stock Managers, and Group Auditor. He also had a Display Manager. His key assistant, however, was recognized to be the Merchandise and Sales Promotion Manager to whom the various Merchandise Managers reported, and who was assisted by an Advertising Manager. These Merchandise Managers, who helped to keep both store managers and Chicago buyers in close contact with changing regional demands, were staff executives, like the Group Managers's other assistants. They could advise but not order. Of the Group Manager's staff, only the Advertising Manager was directly responsible for his activities at all the stores.

The Zone organization that grew up for the smaller stores after 1935 was quite comparable with that of the Group. The Zone Manager and his Assistant usually had a staff of four men — Sales Promotion, Advertising, Display, and Inventory Managers — and a number of "Merchandise Field Men," staff specialists in the marketing of particular lines who had duties similar to the Merchandise Managers of the Groups. They advised the Division Managers who handled their special lines in the various "B-2," "B-3," and "C" Stores.

By 1939, the retail stores had come to be managed through much the same sort of organization as they had been under Barker. The new structure was more flexible than the earlier one, in that instead of one type of branch administrative office — the District — there were now three, the Zone, the Group, and the independent "A" reporting directly to Chicago. As the number of retail stores grew, from 428 at the end of 1935 to 520 at the end of 1939, and as prosperity returned and the volume of business increased, the need for effective supervision of the stores and for the new regional units became increasingly clear. As a result, the office of Retail Administration was formally revived in 1939, with McConnell as the Vice-President in charge. McConnell now became more than just a personnel officer. As Barker had had before 1935, he now had the responsibility for appraising, analyzing, and taking action on the performance of the store managers, as well as of the executives in charge of the Groups and Zones.

The Return to the Territorial Organization

General Wood was undoubtedly concerned with the growth of the intermediate organization between Chicago and the store managers. Possibly the reason he did little about it was his decision in the summer of 1937 to retire from active command. However, under pressure from Rosenwald he agreed, as he told his executives, "to remain as Chairman of the Board, with responsibilities for policies, the upper personnel of the

Company, but without responsibility as to the active operations of the Company and with my time at my own disposal." [92]

The change in command came early in 1939.[93] Lessing Rosenwald, who since his father's death in 1932 had been Chairman of the Board, retired, and Wood took his place. Carney was promoted to the presidency, and Houser became the new Vice-President in charge of Merchandise. At the same time Wood and Carney selected a new Vice-President in charge of Operations, and a new Comptroller.

As soon as the senior managers were appointed, Wood expressed his concern over the growth of middle management. In his Annual Report dated March 1939, he reminded the senior executive as well as the stockholders, that "this Company has for several years past adopted a policy of decentralization and has given its Mail Order Managers and Store Managers a full measure of authority." [94] A few days later at a conference held in Chicago to introduce the store managers to the new officers, the General was even more explicit:

> You are all familiar with our policy of decentralization. We have deliberately tried to treat you as free, independent merchants and men. We'll try to give you the widest possible authority and scope. We have tried to free you from a hoard of bureaucrats, functionaries, inspectors, who might nag and harass you. We have endeavored in a chain store system to have a cooperative democracy. I think the system has succeeded beyond our best hopes. But I want to remind you of one thing — and that is, if such a system is to remain permanently successful, there must be self-imposed discipline. You as Managers must discipline yourselves, otherwise discipline has to be applied from above. In political and social life the democracies of the world are in retreat today and their principal weakness is their lack of discipline. If they can't get some self-imposed discipline, they will perish.[95]

Yet was discipline enough? With complete decentralization, the company could not take full advantage of its size. The maintenance and expansion of sales volume and the resulting lowering of cost and price were the essential economic justifications for Sears's existence. Experience had clearly shown that increase in volume required constant use of marketing talent and executive direction to plan more effective displays, advertising, use of store space, store planning, and design and choices of assortments, as well as to maintain close touch with the day-to-day changes in the demand for Sears's many, many different products. Devices were needed to keep a continuing check and analysis on store performance and managerial personnel. It was not enough to know that a store was doing poorly; the executives must know why. These appraisals could not be made properly by the functional departments in Chicago, as

McConnell and Barker had pointed out earlier. Effective exploitation of managerial, as well as of the physical economies of scale, called for some type of supervisory or administrative structure.

But was centralization of supervision and control in Chicago the only alternative to the decentralization that General Wood had hoped to achieve in 1935? Certainly a third course was open, a return to the territorial organization. And yet Wood and his executives could hardly have forgotten the conflicts and controversies resulting from the earlier attempt to set up such large regional administrative units. Possibly these same problems were developing again as the local units grew in size. A clear alternative then to overdecentralization or overcentralization would be the creation of Territorial Offices which, unlike those of 1930, would have the authority to administer the functional activities as well as the responsibility for profit and performance.[96]

Not surprisingly, then, Wood and Carney decided to have another try at a territorial organization shortly after the changes in top command had been completed. Not only had Wood's efforts to prevent centralization of decision making at Chicago failed, but the return of good times and the expanding volume of business had increased the number of decisions Chicago had to make. In the five years between 1935 and 1940, sales almost doubled, from $337.2 million to $744.4 million and carried Sears far beyond the predepression peak of $440.7 million in 1929. Moreover, the increase was largely in retail sales, which by 1940 were just under 70 per cent of the total.[97] And if the mail-order business lent itself to a functional organization, the retail store, as the Frazer Committee had realized in 1929, was most easily managed by a territorial one.

This time, Wood and his senior executives agreed to move more slowly. They would start by setting up a Territorial Office on the West Coast, where the lines of communication and supply were geographically the longest.[98] If this new organization proved successful, others would follow. By early 1941, Arthur S. Barrows, one of the company's most competent merchandising executives, had taken charge of the new Pacific Coast Territory. All managers of Group, Zone, independent "A" stores, and mail-order plants in his area were to report to him. He had full responsibility for the functional activities of the company as well as administration of store personnel. Unlike the former Territorial Officers, he had a staff of officers responsible for the performance of the various functional activities. His merchandise was ordered through Chicago, for the Merchandise Department remained the only source of supply for all Sears stores. A close liaison continued between the sales promotion experts at Chicago and the Merchandise Superintendents and field men in the offices of the Group, the Zone, and the independent

"A" stores. Aside from this vital contact, Barrows looked to Chicago only for policy guidance and for a budget under which he had to operate.

The Pacific Coast experiment proved "gratifying beyond our hopes," as General Wood later pointed out.[99] But before the next Territories could be set up, World War II intervened. The postwar plans and expansion, however, were mapped out on the assumption that the organizational framework would be the multifunction Territory with its Groups, Zones, directly reporting "A" stores, and mail-order plants (see Chart 9B). In 1945 Barrows, who had become President on Carney's death in 1942, began to work out the specific organization of two more Territories, one for the South and another for the East.

In outlining the new organization, two types of problems presented themselves. The easiest one to solve was the setting up of the boundaries for the Territories and also for their subunits. Wood, still concerned over the danger of too many large local staffs, wanted the Zone to remain large, with at least forty or fifty stores.[100] The more difficult task was the redefinition of duties of the general or parent office at Chicago.

If the Territorial Officers were to have full autonomy, what should be the role of the functional departments at Chicago? The office that supervised the factories would be little affected. While the Merchandise Department would continue to supply the goods, the exact relation between its large sales promotion offices and the executives handling this critical function in the Territories was still unclear. And what of the powerful and venerable Operating Department and the newer office of Personnel and Retail Administration? As to the former, the answer initially was to abolish it.[101] Its head became the Vice-President of the Eastern Territory. Its Traffic, Property, and Communications Departments were now to report directly to the President. The relations of these three units to the new Territorial Offices and the store and mail-order managers in areas in the central part of the nation, where no territorial organization yet existed, were by no means clear. Some of the accounting activities of the old Operating Department went to the Treasurer's office. The Supplies and Equipment Purchasing Department was turned over to Houser's merchandising organization. The remaining activities were placed under McConnell's Personnel and Retail Administration offices. The duties of these officers were also indefinite. McConnell still administered the local units not yet in Territories, but what was the relation of Retail Administration to the three Territories?

Two weeks after the new Territorial Offices and the altered Chicago office setup went into operation on February 1, 1946, Barrows resigned, and Fowler B. McConnell became Sears's President. McConnell and Wood now decided that, before completing their territorial structure, they would get an outside consulting firm to study the company's organization, to analyze the changes already made, and to suggest answers to the new questions raised. Possibly some unexpected problems had arisen in carrying out the new territorial organization. Undoubtedly, too, the senior executives wished a check on their organizational ideas and concepts.

The consultants completed their report in September, 1947. It was a long, general, and vague document with none of the precision and specifics of the earlier Frazer Report. The consultants had apparently learned little about the company's past organizational history, and were totally unaware of the earlier territorial organization and the conflicts it had generated between Chicago and the field. The report, therefore, is more interesting as a study in general thinking about over-all management structure in the years immediately following World War II than as an analysis of the specific organizational problems of Sears, Roebuck.

Its primary value to Sears's executives was undoubtedly its suggestions in defining the role of the general office. The consultants said very little about the organization or functions of the local units, the independent "A," the Group, or the Zone. They felt that the existing territorial organization was excellent and that the plan to complete it by setting up two more Territories in the Midwest and Southwest should certainly be carried out. Although Midwestern Territory's offices would be in Chicago, it should have its own completely separate organization. The Territorial Officers must operate "in the atmosphere of a chief executive," and should have full responsibility for the establishment of new stores (location, size, and design), personnel, and operations.[102] The consultants however, did not say specifically what they considered the officers' responsibility should be with regard to profit, good will, assets, and over-all performance, nor what title they should hold, nor exactly what should be their relation to the parent office.

In many ways the new general office would be comparable to that of other large decentralized companies. The staff sections would provide special services on an advisory basis and would assist the general officers appraise performance, allocate funds, and formulate long-range policy. Because of the nature of its business, the general office should continue to administer the manufacturing units and, through the Merchandise Department, the buying activities.[103] Aside from continuing to handle the buying function, the Merchandise Department's relations with the Territories were to be solely advisory. It could suggest prices, stock plans, and sales promotion techniques but should have no authority to put them into effect.

The Operating Department ought to be revived as an advisory staff

CHART 9A

Sears Structure, 1948

Charts 9A and 9B are adapted from charts in Boris Emmet and John E. Jeuck, *Catalogues and Counters—A History of Sears, Roebuck and Company* (University of Chicago Press, Chicago, 1950), p. 366 and facing p. 367.

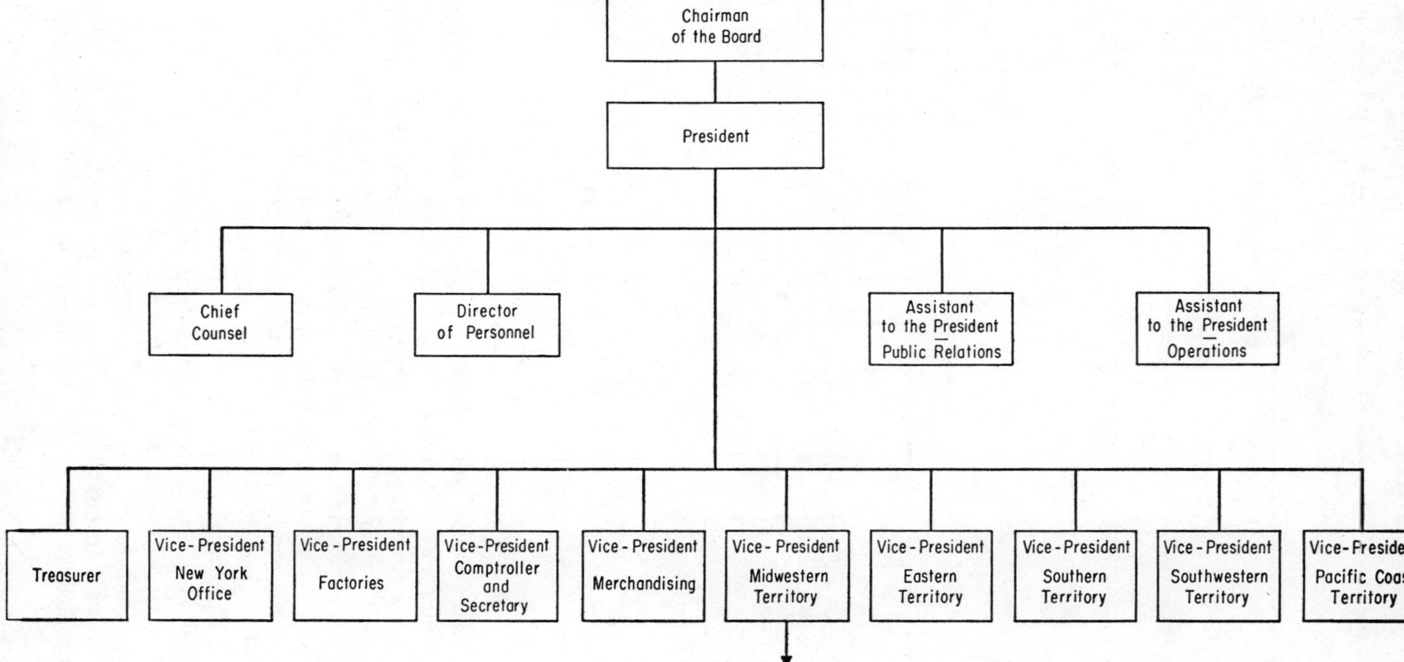

CHART 9B:

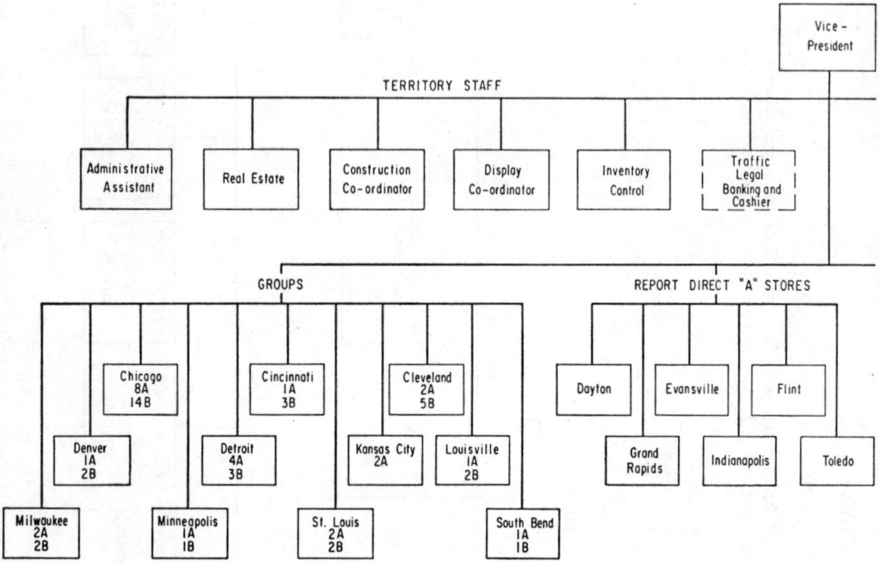

office. Under "an executive of adequate vision and imagination," the consultants' report continued, it could carry on research and develop cost-cutting standards, procedures, and facilities "common to all units of the Company." It could also stimulate a "research point of view" in the Territories, help disseminate ideas and information, work closely with the buying departments on operating problems inherent in their lines of merchandise, and maintain a group of service and consulting specialists. The general office would have similar advisory, coordinating specialists for personnel and public relations. The Treasurer's and the Comptroller's offices were to provide much of the same type of assistance and expertness on tax, insurance, accounting, and other financial matters.

Furthermore, the financial executives should play a key role in the over-all appraising, inspection, and policy planning at Chicago. They should continue, as they had been doing, to collect and compile account-

Organization of Sears Midwestern Territory

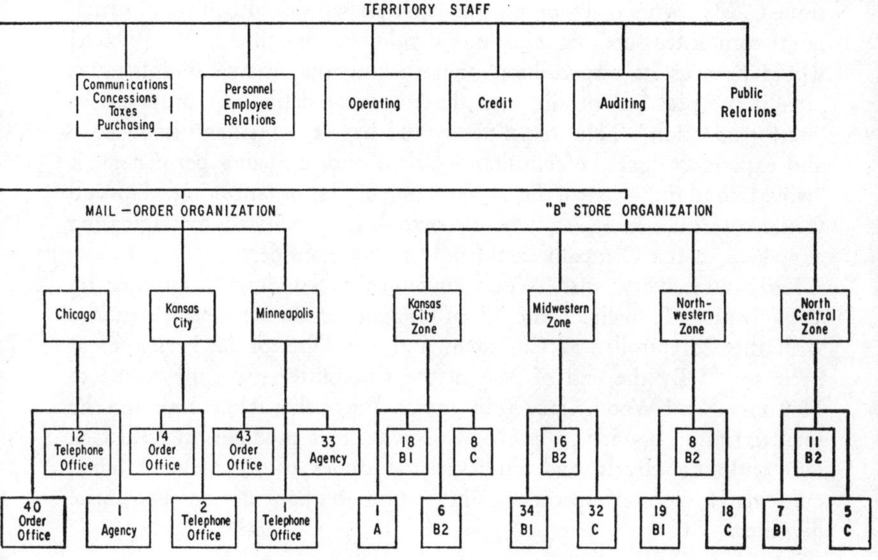

ing and other statistics that would show the day-to-day performance of all Sears's operating units. These offices should review all operating budgets, for both running and capital expenditures, as well as forecasted sales and sales plans of all units before forwarding them to the senior officers for action.

These latter officers, that is the President and Chairman of the Board, working with the financial and Merchandising Vice-Presidents and the heads of the staff units were to plan and decide on broad policy. Theirs would be the impartial over-all view "unencumbered by any particular divisional loyalty or bias." In spite of these recommendations, the report elsewhere suggested the somewhat contradictory proposition that the Territorial Officers should take part in policy making.[104]

The essential message of the consultants' report was that the organizational policy and philosophies of the Sears's executives were correct.

Although some suggestions were made as to the role of the general office, the report gave relatively little help on the specific implementation of these policies. "It is reassuring to have this confirmation of our thinking by outside experts," Barker wrote Wood, "although it is difficult to see how they could arrive soundly at any other conclusion." [105] The next step, the working out of details, must be done from within, he continued. "My own suggestion on this 'next phase,' would be that a permanent committee on organization should be appointed, . . . [which] would have as its responsibility the working out of an administrative plan in its practical details, and the recommendations of proposals to you for adoption." This committee would have the firsthand knowledge and experience that the consultants lacked and, by being permanent, it "would constantly watch the functioning of the organization plan and would constitute an agency where proposals for modifications originating anywhere in the Company could be carefully considered."

Early in January, 1948, Wood appointed a Standing Committee on Organization. It included the Vice-Presidents of the existing Territories with the Comptroller as Chairman and the Director of Personnel as Secretary.[106] By the end of March, the Committee made its report to McConnell and Wood. Once again it was shown that while outlining the final territorial boundaries proved somewhat of a problem, the real task was outlining clearly and explicitly the duties of the general office, particularly the staff specialists, in relation to those of the Territorial divisions.

The Final Structure

On April 26, 1948, the last two Territories, the Midwestern and Southwestern, began operations. Their Vice-Presidents, like those in the other territories, reported directly to the President, and each had "complete charge of operations" in his own area.[107] This included personnel, expenses, inventory, maintenance, operating, banking, and local sales promotion (see Chart 9B).[108] At the same time, the Operations office was revived in the general office on an advisory basis, and the older Retail Administration office was discontinued. Some of the latter's functions, such as real estate, were given to the Territories. Others, like personnel and public relations, were divided between the Territories and the parent office. The sections remaining in Chicago became advisory units concerned with over-all problems and procedures.

The parent office now included, beside Merchandising, Factory Management, and the financial offices, four staff departments — Operations, Personnel, Public Relations, and Chief Counsel (see Chart 9A).[109] The new Operations office had divisions to develop and improve retail and mail-order procedures and included an Operations Research Department. Also it was given charge of the older General Traffic Department, which was responsible for the company-owned "over-the-road" trucking lines as well as rail freight forwarding activities, and for the Communications Department, operating one of the nation's biggest private internal communications networks. The general staff's Personnel Office now concerned itself with developing company-wide procedures in employee recruitment and training, executive development, compensation, labor relations, and other personnel matters.[110] The specific duties of the other staff offices need not be detailed here, but are comparable to ones created at General Motors, du Pont, and Standard Oil in the 1920's.

As in these same companies, the Comptroller's Office at Sears retained a direct line of authority via the Territorial Comptroller to the mail-order plants and retail stores. When the company's Comptroller was asked in 1947 to define the relations of the Territories to the parent, he wrote that the Territorial Comptroller "would be under the control of the chief executive of the territory as to operation, but under the supervision of the corporation's Comptroller as far as accounting policy and practices are concerned."[111] In matters dealing with the latter, the territorial executive would take a hand only when there was a controversy between the local comptroller and Chicago. Then, as was true in the earlier territorial setup, he could countermand the functional officer's orders. If necessary, the problem might go to the President for adjudication, actually a very rare event. A direct line is, Houser pointed out, "a necessary safety measure in a company doing a business in 2,000 locations with a merchandising inventory of $500,000,000 and installment accounts on the books totalling $900,000,000, where uniform accounting practices are essential."[112]

The staff executives at Sears, as in the other decentralized companies, could only advise not order, but they were also given an important appraising or "auditing" responsibility. They had what came to be called the "right of challenge."[113] Executives from headquarters were permitted and expected to challenge line officers in the field as to the results the latter had achieved and the manner in which the results had been accomplished.

Beside auditing and advising, the staff worked closely with the President and Chairman of the Board and the Merchandising and financial Vice-Presidents to plan a broad policy, and to allocate the funds, personnel, and facilities necessary to carry out such plans. Through the control of resources, the general office decided where the company should expand, maintain, or contract its activities. Senior staff and general officers at headquarters also worked together in appraising the activities of the operating units and of the company as a whole. Formal devices, like the Policy Groups at General Motors, were unnecessary at Sears, where the general office was much smaller. Even an Officers Board to assure regular meetings of the general and staff officers in the parent organization proved unnecessary. The Officers Board instituted by the Frazer Committee which had become an informal "Executive Committee" by the mid-1930's was dropped with the creation of the Territories.[114]

Since 1948 the policy initiators at Chicago have discussed their plans with the regional operating officers at the time of Board meetings. Between meetings, they keep in constant touch with the territorial units. To avoid what Barker once called "the tendency that . . . their decisions as to policy will be made in a remote and rarified atmosphere far from the realities of the front-line contact with the public," the general office executives rely, as do those at General Motors, du Pont, and Jersey Standard, on regular inspection tours in the field.[115] Sears's executives also stay in touch through interterritorial committees set up to encourage exchange of information and ideas and carried on under general office supervision. But most important of all, in informing Chicago of territorial activities and performance, is the steady flow of statistics and reports that pour into the parent office. Decisions, including the formulation of the budget, are reviewed but very rarely revised or altered by the Board of Directors.[116]

The structural reorganization at Sears in the 1930's and 1940's required less concentrated effort on the development of statistical and financial controls than on the definition of the lines of communication and authority. The 1921 depression had initially stimulated the development of inventory controls and of estimates of sales for the coming spring and fall buying seasons. At the same time, the Operating Department developed forecasts and budgets of operating and capital expenditures needed for the next two buying seasons. With the move into retailing demanding new types of statistical information and financial controls, Barker and Pollock had worked out, in the early thirties, inventory controls and budgets for the retail stores. These efforts were concentrated primarily on obtaining control over current inventory and current performance. But the stores, the regional organizations, and the functional departments all did develop estimates for the retail stores' expected needs in both goods and money for at least two buying seasons.

Until the mid-thirties, the Chicago office made little effort to provide a check on the sales and expenditure estimates of its stores and buying departments. For one thing, the Merchandise Department had two sources of data, as the estimates from the stores and mail-order houses were carefully compared with those made by the buyers for each of the different lines. In 1935, however, the Merchandise Department set up an Economic Research Office to coordinate and provide an outside review of the data presented by the operating units.[117] The new office also made more detailed estimates of economic conditions and analyzed sales potentials and performances. Such data were as useful to the general office as to the operating units. They helped the top executives plan capital expenditures and the allocation of funds between different units and lines, as well as to define and decide on other financial policies. The company's financial departments began, at about this time, to develop financial forecasts to assist in budgeting and in comparable planning.[118] From the 1920's on, then, the Sears's executives were making their plans on the basis of anticipated as well as past performance, and by the 1930's, such data were becoming more accurate and more sophisticated.

By the summer of 1948, Sears had achieved an organization quite similar to those designed earlier at General Motors, du Pont, and Jersey Standard. This structure, which has remained relatively unchanged, had the same autonomous, self-contained operating divisions and the same general office of functional staff specialists and senior general officers.[119] The process had been slower at Sears because of external circumstances and the convictions of its top executives. But for the depression and General Wood's distrust of bureaucratic procedures, a similar structure might have been worked out in the early 1930's. The conflicts between the regional officers and the functional departments in Chicago could possibly have been solved in 1932 had Wood been willing to transform the territorial units into full-fledged multidepartmental divisions and so create a multidivision decentralized structure. Such an autonomous division might have evolved in any case if strong executives like Barker, who took on authority and created their own staffs, had been permitted to go their own way. However, the depression-created need to cut costs helped force a decision and, given Wood's strong convictions as to the dangers of increased staffs, this decision was the elimination of the territorial organization and the retention of the centralized functional one.

Actually, if General Wood could have had his own way, there would have been only the smallest of intermediate administrative organizations between Chicago and the retail stores and mail-order houses. Yet as the events after 1934 demonstrated, the continuing expansion in the number of stores and particularly the constant pressure to increase sales volume made such a course impractical. Sears simply could not take advantage of its size and its high-volume, low-cost operations unless it had more effective administration of the individual stores, particularly the smaller ones. The need for effective appraisal and, at the same time, the need for a close and constant contact with the ever-changing market led, undoubtedly against Wood's better judgment, to the expansion of administrative offices in the field.

Faced with the continuing centralization of decision making and activities in Chicago, as well as growing administrative branch offices in the field, Sears's senior executive officer decided to return to a territorial type of organization. This time he provided the Territorial Officer with the authority and the functional offices necessary to carry out responsibility for profits and performance. Wood then adjusted the duties of the parent office so that it serviced, appraised, coordinated, and made policy for the territorial divisions and for the company as a whole.

At Sears then, strategic expansion brought structural change. Rapid growth of the activities of the initial Chicago mail-order plant led to the departmentalizing of Sears's major acivities, buying, distributing, and finance. Geographic expansion enlarged departmental activities and brought a definition of the relations between the departmental headquarters and the field. Continued growth also created a greater need for increased central office administrative control of the functional departments. Shortly after the centralized structure necessary to assure full use of Sears's existing resources was completed, the threat of potentially unused plant and personnel turned Wood and his new senior executives to expanding in a new direction in order to obtain a share of the rapidly growing urban and suburban market. The move into direct retailing after 1925 led to the creation of a new structure consisting of District and Territorial Offices for the administration of the recently acquired retail stores. The problem of how to link the new retail administrative units with the older structure, which had been created for the mail-order business, remained unsolved until Wood finally set up several multifunction divisions whose central offices had all the functional activities necessary to administer the units in the field — the Groups, Zones, large "A" stores, and mail-order houses — and whose activities were, in turn, administered in the interest of the enterprise as a whole from the new general office at Chicago.

The experience of Sears, a mass merchandiser, differs from that of the other three companies studied here — all basically manufacturers — in that continued growth rather than vertical integration created the need for central office administration of the functional departments. On the other hand, the Chicago headquarters did take over the primary operating function of coordinating the flow of product from the premanufacturing stage to the ultimate consumer. It acquired this role less from its control over manufacturing (although Sears did purchase stock in manufacturing companies in order to assure itself of supplies) than it did from the careful specifications it set in making high-volume orders from its suppliers. Normally, Sears, rather than the manufacturer, determined the quality of materials and parts that went into the product, as well as how much was to be produced and at what time. In Sears, as at General Motors, the sharp and sudden depression of 1920 made clear the need for closer central office coordination of product flow to changing market demands. Then, much as in the case of du Pont, when Sears moved into a new line of business, the coordination of flow with the market again tended to break down. This failure was a primary reason for initiating the structural changes that, in time, led to the formation of several multifunction divisions.

The differences in Sears's final structure and those of the others also reflect the differences between a mass merchandiser and a large industrial manufacturer. At Sears, the control of some activities, the manufacturing units and the buying, remained centralized. The stores and mail-order houses in the Territories had a wide range of goods to choose from, but they had to be originally purchased by the Sears's buying departments. However, territorial executives had complete responsibility for *how* the selling, sales promotion, and distribution were done. Also Sears developed a policy of supplying the stores, where possible, from local sources.

One other difference between the completed structure at Sears and that in the three other companies was the smaller number of general executives in the parent office. The top administrative team at Sears included the President, a full-time Chairman of the Board, the vice-presidents responsible for merchandising, finance, and manufacturing, and the senior executives in the general staff departments. The heads of the functional units who worked closely with the general officers and the senior staff executives had a large departmental organization to handle operational activities. They had no direct contact with the field units. They were, therefore, in a much better position to maintain the broad strategic outlook of general executives than they had been before the creation of the multidivisional structure. The reason Sears's business requires fewer general officers is that it is less complex than that of du Pont, General Motors, and Jersey. Just because its multifunction divisions carry on the same activities and, except for the new Latin American division, in much the same market, its senior officers have to make relatively fewer and less complex strategic or entrepreneurial decisions. Also the fact that General Wood for so many years made most of the basic entrepreneurial decisions himself may have encouraged his successors to keep the final say in their hands.

If Sears, Roebuck is then considered as a representative of a subspecies of the large American industrial enterprise — its mass-merchandising variation or modification — then its experience fully supports the general propositions outlined in the introduction. Even more clearly than the other three case studies, its story demonstrates the vital need for administrative personnel, for "management in depth," in the large industrial enterprise. Second, it underlines the need for a structure which specifically defines clear, uncrossed lines of authority and communication.

General Wood was surely right when he stressed the importance of having the right man at the right place. Yet, possibly because of his own enormous competence he seemed to forget that good men were often difficult to find, particularly when a great enterprise like his needed literally hundreds of trained and experienced executives. Moreover, as he himself clearly appreciated, the right man was unable to make full use of his talents unless he had a steady flow of accurate "figures" on which to base his action and unless he was certain that his decisions were being carried out. There is no question whatever that competent executives have always been a most vital ingredient in the success of any large enterprise. The lesson General Wood learned was that effective administrators cannot by themselves always assure effective administration.

6 ORGANIZATIONAL INNOVATION—A COMPARATIVE ANALYSIS

The administrative history of Sears, Roebuck, like that of Jersey Standard, General Motors, and du Pont, describes the building of new administrative offices and the refashioning of existing ones to meet the needs created by the growth of the enterprise. By forcing the reorientation of existing resources and the accumulation of more and often quite different types of personnel and facilities, growth brought new problems and new demands at every administrative level. Such needs required the planning and replanning of the design used to administer the resources, old and new, available to the enterprise. Yet, rarely did the building of the necessary structure come immediately. Its construction called for time, thought, and energy. The training, temperament, and daily activities of the executives responsible for the company's basic decisions vitally affected the attention given to and the solutions proposed for these needs. In this way executive experience and personality helped determine the course and rate of structural adaptation and innovation.

In summarizing and analyzing the administrative experiences of these four great industrial enterprises, it seems best first to review the creation of the different types of offices. What were the basic needs at each administrative level? Exactly how did the needs develop and what sort of structure came to meet them most effectively? A comparative analysis of organizational innovation can then be followed by a look at the organizational innovators. Who saw the needs and who did not? And why? Who pushed for reorganization, and why? Once these questions have been considered, then the experience of the four companies must again be compared more specifically with those of many other large industrial enterprises. Which other companies came to have comparable needs and which did not? And why? Of those that did, which came to the same general solution and which did not? And why? How did the personality and experience of their executives affect the pace of organizational change?

The Adaptive Response

In analyzing economic innovation, Joseph A. Schumpeter once made a distinction between a creative innovation and an adaptive response.[1] The first went beyond existing practices and procedures. The second, while involving major changes for the individual or firm making the response, stayed within the range of current custom. In the creation of the "decentralized," multidivisional structure, all four of the firms here studied were making a creative response to new needs and new conditions. On the other hand, in building field units, departmental headquarters, or a central office, they were staying within the bounds of existing business practice. Yet, while the construction of each of these three types of offices was an adaptive response, it was not always merely imitative. The du Ponts and the organization builders of General Motors subsidiaries adapted existing ways to meet their own particular needs, often after carefully observing the experiences of other enterprises. Those at Sears, Roebuck, who considered the experience of governmental as well as business units, also changed accepted procedures to meet their own special needs. At Jersey, on the other hand, where structural change came only as a response to immediate pressures, the executives responsible for reorganization did not consciously borrow their forms from others or even from their own past experience.

These four case studies say very little about the building of the structure to administer the field units that carried out the fundamental economic functions of an enterprise, such as the plant, marketing district office, purchasing unit, laboratory, and the like. The initial expansion at Sears, at the Repauno Chemical Company, at Hyatt, Buick, and other General Motors subsidiaries led to increasing specialization and to the need for coordinating, appraising, and planning systematically for the specialized activities. The organization of such units was usually left to the plant or department manager rather than to the organization builders for the enterprise as a whole. In setting up a structure for a plant or district office, the executives had plenty of information to go on, for it was on this lowest administrative level that Frederick W. Taylor, Frank Gilbreth, Harry Hopf, and other advocates and practitioners of "scientific management" concentrated their energies.[2] As late as World War II, most of the literature on administration still dealt with the management of the individual field unit rather than the larger enterprise. For these reasons, then, this review focuses on the building of the administrative posts at the three higher levels, the departmental headquarters, the central office, and the general office.

Building the Functional Departments

The creation of departmental headquarters for the administration of the field units became necessary when a company had a number of plants or offices scattered throughout the country. This growth, in turn, resulted from a strategy of expansion or of combination and consolidation devised to meet more effectively an increasingly wide demand, both existing and potential, for the company's products. For Sears, the building of the new branch mail-order houses led in 1920 to the first formal definition of the relations between headquarters and the field units of the functional departments. The automobile companies that came to make up General Motors and also the du Pont-financed Repauno Chemical Company expanded both by enlarging the manufacturing facilities and by building up their own sales organizations. The resulting rapid growth brought a formalizing of the relations between headquarters and field. Both Jersey and du Pont had widely scattered manufacturing, marketing, and purchasing units at the time of their rebirth or recreation. Du Pont, after combining and consolidating its holdings, concentrated on carefully defining the structure of its departments as well as of its central office. Jersey, on the other hand, made no comparable reorganization of its existing departments until thirteen years after a new company had risen from the dismemberment of the old. However, where the oil company expanded into new economic functions, such as the producing of crude oil or marine transportation, its executives quickly created departments to administer them.

When the du Ponts re-formed the design by which they mobilized their resources, they were very much aware of the most advanced administrative practices in American industry. Following and improving on the example set by Henry C. Frick in steel and Charles A. Coffin in electricity, they created after 1903 what might be considered an almost "ideal type" of functionally departmentalized, centralized structure. After 1910, the automobile and parts companies that became subsidiaries of General Motors worked out structures quite comparable with those at du Pont. The executives of Sears apparently relied less on outside practices in the reorganization of 1920 than did the automobile and explosives companies in setting up their initial structures, but the resulting organization was, given the differences in Sears's activities, quite comparable. At Jersey, on the other hand, where the executives paid little attention to administrative matters and accepted uncritically traditional ways of management, structural reorganization came only after much stress and strain. Even there, however, the structure of the functional departments and the central office came in time to be quite similar to that of the other three companies.

In fashioning the departmental headquarters, the primary tasks at all four companies were the definition of the lines of authority and communication between headquarters and the field units and the allocation of duties among the different executives at headquarters. The organization designers had to determine how decisions were to be made and how responsibility was to be fixed. In department building, the development of statistics and other information to flow through the lines of communication proved less of a challenge than it did in the setting up of the administrative offices at the next two higher levels. Because the executives at headquarters and those in the field were carrying out the same type of functional activities, uniform accounting and reporting systems were quite easily developed, and both sets of executives could readily interpret and use these data developed as they were in the areas of their own professional specialties. Comparable information was far more difficult to obtain and interpret for units carrying on different functions or handling different lines of business.

In making clear the lines of authority and communication between headquarters and the field, the major problem was the definition of the relation between executives at headquarters and those in the field units who handled the same type of activities. Should the director of an auxiliary or service department, such as personnel, working within a plant or branch office report directly to the personnel manager at headquarters or should he reach him through the plant manager? This sort of problem could arise only when the activities of both headquarters and field became complex enough to require a number of specialists. It hardly existed where the headquarters unit was small with little or no auxiliary or service activities or where the field unit was still managed by two or three executives whose work was not subdivided according to specialties.

But where, as was normally the case, specialized or auxiliary activities did exist at both headquarters and field, the relationship nearly always came to be worked out on a line-and-staff basis. The line-and-staff method of departmental organization was most clearly defined in the manufacturing departments at du Pont and the General Motors subsidiaries. Here the structures used closely paralleled those devised a generation earlier on the Pennsylvania Railroad. The line of authority went from the executive in charge of the department through his immediate assistants to the plant superintendents and then on down to the foremen or supervisors. The plant superintendent and the department head were held fully responsible for the performance of their respective units. They had the authority to give orders and to move and use personnel, funds, and equipment. The executives in charge of the more specialized functions — inspection, personnel, plant layout, purchasing, processes, cost analysis, and so forth — communicated with their subordinates through the line officers at headquarters and at the plant. These men were responsible for developing standards and procedures, but only the line officers could issue orders.

In other departments, it was sometimes more difficult to make the line-and-staff distinction as clear cut. In sales, the general pattern held at du Pont and the automobile companies, except that advertising tended to be centralized at headquarters. That is, the advertising manager had the final say on all matters concerning his activity. The sales departments at du Pont and Jersey had executives at headquarters and in the field for each major product of its basic line. But, in du Pont and in time in Jersey, the lines of communication and authority went from headquarters through the branch or district office manager. The purchasing department of du Pont and apparently those of Jersey and the General Motors subsidiaries had much the same type of organization as the sales departments. At Sears, where purchasing was the company's largest activity, nearly all the responsibility and authority for buying was delegated, until the 1929 changes, to the heads of the buying units. A testing and standards office was the only large staff unit at headquarters.

The other functional departments, such as research, engineering, and personnel, which became in time designated as central office auxiliary or service departments, also developed a line-and-staff structure. At du Pont, well before 1921, the research (Chemical) department had its line units, divisions in charge of laboratories handling research for the major products, and its staff sections, which provided information and set standards. Howard's Development Department at Jersey Standard had much the same structure. So too did the Engineering Departments at du Pont, Jersey, and the General Motors subsidiaries. Incidentally, the du Pont Engineering Department before 1920 had a staff unit that concentrated wholly on studying organization, planning systems, and methods of management for use in the designing and construction of company offices and plants.

In the financial departments of the four companies there was less need for making a line-and-staff distinction. These departments carried on three basic activities. First, they handled the mass of routine financial transactions within all the departments. This included payment of salaries and wages, the approval and payment of vouchers, freight bills, and other accounts payable, and the handling of accounts receivable. Second, they carried out the external financial transactions of the company as a whole. Beside taking care of the routine work of security issues, stock transfers, payment of dividends and interest, and so forth, they invested current cash surpluses in short-term notes or securities. Finally, the financial officers came to provide information essential to planning, coordinating, and appraising the work of other departments and the enterprise as a whole.

Before the 1920's, only the du Pont Company developed this third role for their financial offices. By the time of World War I, the Treasurer's Department had its forecast and analysis section that maintained twelve months' forecasts of probable financial conditions and revised them each month. The Department also provided cost data on all the company's activities, such as manufacturing, sales, construction, and research. In the 1920's the financial departments at the other three companies helped develop comparable data. Thus these departments became increasingly part of the central and even of the general office organizations.

One reason for the fairly general adoption of the line-and-staff type of departmental structure was that it helped make possible the delegation of authority and responsibility to the field units. As the remarks in the Haskell report at du Pont in 1919 and Walter Teagle's comments to the marketing executives in 1925 both stressed, unless the lines of communication and authority between headquarters and the field went through the plant or branch office, the local manager could not reasonably be held responsible for the unit's performance. In that case a great many matters had to be referred back to headquarters for decision.

The experience of both Sears and Jersey emphasizes how the lack of a line-and-staff distinction did result in centralization of decision making. By the 1920 reorganization at Sears, the departmental executives at headquarters became directly responsible for their functions in the branch mail-order plants. As a result, Chicago came to make nearly all the administrative decisions. So too, after 1929, the executives of the auxiliary offices at the Merchandise Department's headquarters had direct contact with their counterparts in the offices of the different Merchandising Groups. Again decisions became centralized at headquarters. When Sears finally settled on the multidivisional structure, it also carried out the line-and-staff concept more explicitly in both the Territories and the buying organization.[3]

The Jersey experience was even more striking, for here the accepted form of departmental organization was the committee or group structure. While the new departments, Production and Marine Transportation, did develop line-and-staff organizations, the Manufacturing Department retained and the Domestic Sales went over to the inherited structure. Even though the committee form died out in the Export Trade Department because competent executives ignored it by creating informally clear-cut lines of communication and authority, the Manufacturing Committee remained the prototype. And it was, as has been stressed, an extreme example of group management of departmental affairs. The plant managers at Jersey did not have their offices in the field but at 26 Broadway. From headquarters, they administered their own refineries individually and managed collectively the Jersey manufacturing activities as a whole. The inevitable result, as Howard's 1924 report so vividly demonstrates, was a complete centralization of all administrative activities at headquarters. The slow and painful shift from a committee-managed department to one administered through a line-and-staff organization with individual responsibility at both department and plant levels was one of the most significant aspects of the Jersey reorganization between 1925 and 1927. Only a new and clearer cut structure made possible the delegation of authority and responsibility for operational decisions from 26 Broadway to the field.

There is a difference, it should be remembered, between group management and consultive management. At du Pont, the General Motors subsidiaries, and Sears, a single individual and not a committee was responsible for the performance of a department and the actions taken within it. In making administrative decisions, the departmental director, manager, or vice-president met with the other executives at the departmental headquarters regularly and often in quite formal committees or "Board" meetings. He often consulted plant superintendents or branch managers from the field. Beside regular sessions with his senior executives, he often called more inclusive departmental meetings to exchange information and to talk over existing problems and new developments. The regular meetings of senior executives and the larger departmental gatherings provided excellent channels of communication. But the committee at du Pont, at the automobile companies, and Sears was not responsible for action and performance. The final decision and responsibility rested with the department head and not of a "Room." As the Haskell report at du Pont stressed, "the principle of individual responsibility and authority" for operational activities had been fundamental to the company's success. Here du Pont was following the accepted practice. As one early writer on industrial organization emphasized in 1913: "Committees are always of an *advisory* character." [4] In time, Jersey's departmental committees also became advisory.

Of course, a change in structure did not necessarily mean that the more routine day-to-day decisions would be taken over by the field, and that the departmental executives could then concentrate more on over-all coordination, appraisal, and planning. The point at which the decisions were actually made depended a great deal on the personality and training of both the executives at headquarters and the field officers. Still, it seems safe to conclude that without a line-and-staff structure decision making tended to be concentrated at headquarters no matter what were the personalities of the executives involved. In any case, the experience of the four companies studied here makes clear that expansion, either by building or obtaining control of geographically dispersed units, called for a clear-cut definition of the lines of authority and communication between the departmental headquarters and its field units. If the responsible executives paid too little attention to clarifying these relationships, confused and inefficient administration resulted.

Building the Central Office

Wherever the departmental headquarters administered units in the field, they in turn, as the enterprise grew, came to be administered by a central office. The executives in the central office had a different set of problems and a different range of activities than those at departmental headquarters. The former had to supervise and allocate resources to several business functions, not merely one. In planning, appraising, and coordinating the use of the enterprise's existing resources and in determining their future allocation and expansion, these executives had to be aware of the impact of changing techniques, demands, financial needs, and legal requirements in manufacturing, marketing, transportation, and in the procurement and often production of raw, semifinished materials or parts and accessories.

In the manufacturing companies, vertical integration, the strategic progenitor of the central office, resulted initially from a combination of marketing with manufacturing. In the 1880's, the original Standard Oil Company had begun to move into its own marketing well before it started to control its own supplies of crude oil. After the dissolution in 1912, marketing remained its second largest activity after refining. For those automobile companies that became part of General Motors, the building of a marketing organization was as essential for the first great growth as was the enlargement of their assembly plants. The du Pont Company in its massive reorganization of 1902 and 1903 followed the example of the most energetic of its predecessors, the Repauno Chemical Company, and created its own sales and distributing organization. Then it no longer needed to rely on wholesalers or other outside middlemen. Sears as a high-volume retailer could not, of course, integrate forward, but it did help finance manufacturing companies or purchase their stock in order to assure itself of adequate supplies.

For the other three companies, integration backward soon followed the marriage of manufacturing and marketing. As in the case of Sears, it was essentially defensive. That is, backward integration resulted from a desire to have an assured stock of supplies at a reasonable price on hand and available whenever the manufacturing plants needed them. At General Motors this strategy led to the purchase of parts and accessories firms, but not to the control of steel, aluminum, tire, or glass works. After 1912, a comparable strategy brought the new Standard Oil Company (New Jersey) into the production of crude oil and marine transportation. After its rebirth, the du Pont Company purchased nitrate sources in Chile. Then with wartime expansion, it developed its own chemicals and other supplies. When diversification followed, it found integration also necessary. Thus du Pont purchased a large plant to manufacture the "gray goods" base for its Fabrikoid production, and at the same time moved forward into the making of finished pyroxylin (Celluloid-type) products as a more certain way to assure outlets for its sheets and other semifinished pyroxylin materials. Finally, after completing the major move into chemicals, it purchased two large companies making basic chemical products, in 1928 the Grasselli Chemical Co., and in 1930 the Roessler & Hasslacher Chemical Co.

Once resources had been accumulated to permit the exploitation of the national market through its own distributing and sales outlets and to assure itself of a fairly sure supply of materials, each of the four companies studied here developed, over time, a central structure to permit the effective administration and presumably the more profitable employment of those resources. Whether planned or not, the new central office eventually developed three types of duties. One critical role became the coordination and integration of the output of the several functional departments to changing market demands, needs, and tastes. This included the coordination of product flow from one functional department to another, an activity whose development is strikingly illustrated in the Jersey Standard case. It also required the maintenance of cooperation between the manufacturing, sales, and development or engineering departments regarding the improvement or redesign of products. Second, expansion and vertical integration encouraged the growth of auxiliary or service departments in the central office which could relieve the administrative load on the functional departments by taking over more specialized activities. Finally, besides coordinating activities with the market and providing specialized services, the central office, of course, allocated the future use as well as appraised the present performance of the resources of the enterprise.

The central office activities that tied the work of the functional departments to the changing market usually came about only after a slowing of market demand. Then, in these four companies, the clear need to coordinate the level of departmental work and the rate of product flow through the departments to market requirements led to the basing of nearly all operational decisions on estimates and forecasts of anticipated conditions rather than on past or even current performance. The more accurately demand could be forecast, the more evenly the flow could be channeled. Before 1920, however, none of these companies except du Pont had begun to correlate production and purchasing schedules systematically with anticipated market demands, and until 1921 du Pont was still feeling its way. By the end of the World War I, its major departments — Sales, Manufacturing, and Purchasing — were making independent quarterly forecasts of sales for their production and volume schedules. As long as the company handled only one line, explosives, the departmental executives had little trouble in correlating these different estimates. Once the three departments had to estimate for new industries in which they had little experience, for which data had never been effectively collected, and whose characteristics were very different from those of explosives, then correlation of departmental information became extremely difficult. At General Motors, little attention had been paid to the coordination of product flow until the sharp postwar depression temporarily punctured the swiftly growing automobile market. In the same year, Sears also learned the value of over-all inventory control. At Jersey, it was the rapid leveling off of demand for gasoline in the summer of 1925 that demonstrated the need to improve techniques to integrate product flow. At Jersey and also at General Motors, the realization of these needs was a significant stimulus for the major organizational changes that re-formed the central office structure as well as set up a general office.

There was another situation that called for careful estimates of market demand. The central office particularly required uniform, accurate, and meaningful data on costs in all the departments if it was to carry out effectively over-all planning and appraisal. While working out techniques for allocating overhead costs and determining variable expenses, the company's executives soon recognized that variable costs, and therefore unit costs, were closely related to volume. Any reliable cost analysis, pricing, or estimating of profits had to be based on accurate forecasts of demand. The supplying of such data was vital to the efficient administration of these large, vertically integrated industrial enterprises.

These four companies initially paid more attention to bringing together the different departments — in order to improve products, to alter their design, or to develop new ones in the face of changing market tastes and needs — than they did to coordinating product flow. At du Pont, the major responsibility for this task belonged at first to the Technical Division of the Sales Department. At Jersey, Howard's Development Department began to take over this role in the 1920's. At General Motors, little was done to coordinate design, manufacturing, and marketing until the 1921 reorganization made such coordination one of the important duties of the interdivisional committees. Finally, at Sears, this type of coordination, initially one of the most significant functions that the buyers performed, began after 1929 to be taken over increasingly by the staff of the Merchandise Department, and then, for the retail stores, by the district or regional administrative offices. In all four companies, the need to relate all activities to market changes brought increasingly intensive studies of present and anticipated demand for existing and potential products.

Finally, the executives at all four companies came to realize, some more slowly than others, that systematic policy formulation and allocation of resources called for carefully defined budgeting and capital appropriations procedures. This planning also required information on future financial and general economic conditions as well as on anticipated market demand. Such data, collected by the du Pont Treasurer's Department by World War I, came to be compiled by the financial sections of both the divisional and general offices at General Motors after the 1921 reorganization, at Jersey by the Budget and Coordination Departments after 1925, and at Sears during the 1920's by the stores and by buyers in the Merchandise Department, and then after 1935 by a staff unit in the Merchandise Department. Thus, in all four of these companies, and certainly also in a great many other American industrial enterprises, tactical and strategic decisions and operational and entrepreneurial activities came to be based on data dealing with anticipated market and economic conditions as well as those concerned with past and current performance. The development of increasingly accurate and precise information for the use of the senior executives in planning, coordinating, and appraising the activities of an enterprise as a whole was a major achievement of the American organization builders.

Even before these large multifunction enterprises began to build offices and techniques for coordinating the use of their plant, facilities, and personnel to the changing market, they started to form auxiliary or service departments to take over specialized activities. In the manufacturing companies, many of the new central staff offices had their beginnings in the manufacturing department. Sears, Roebuck, on the other hand, had no separate central office auxiliary units until 1929, when Lessing Rosenwald set up an office combining public relations, personnel, and the analysis of departmental reports and proposals, and General Wood took Westervelt's testing, standards, and research department out of the Merchandise Department.

At du Pont and Jersey and to some extent apparently at Buick, Cadillac, and the other General Motors subsidiaries, the research, engineering, personnel departments, and the department purchasing supplies and equipment (but not basic materials) were all at first administratively close to manufacturing. Their work soon became valuable for the other departments. Purchasing could buy for district offices as well as for plants. Engineering could design warehouses and laboratories as well as factories. Labor relations programs, welfare plans, medical assistance, and other activities of the personnel office could be carried out for wage earners in all departments. The growth of these newer auxiliary departments raised the question of their relation to the major functional ones. One early answer at both du Pont and Jersey was to return the central office service departments to the control of the manufacturing department. This is what the Haskell Committee proposed at du Pont in 1919 and the Manufacturing Committee at Jersey in 1926. In both cases, however, the units remained in the central office, and their relation to the other major departments became explicitly defined as a staff or advisory one. Their executives could recommend, advise, and suggest, but the actual execution of their ideas was to be carried out on orders from the heads of the functional departments or their line assistants. Unless the lines of authority and communication were defined in this way, the new central office units could easily take over much of the work of the operating departments and so increase the concentration of responsibility and decision making in the central office. Some auxiliary departments, of course, had line duties of their own. Research developed new products or better processes; engineering constructed new facilities or improved existing equipment; while personnel worked out promotion policies, techniques for evaluating performance, and so forth. But when these units were working with one of the major functional line departments, they did so at its request or at least with its approval.

Even more critical for the present health of the enterprise and its future growth than the creation of central staff offices was the clarification of the duties of the senior executives. They had to be encouraged to concentrate on entrepreneurial rather than operational activites. At du Pont, the distinction between these two types of administrative activities came after the 1902–1903 reorganization. Then the reborn explosives company made the distinction, originally introduced by the Pennsylvania Railroad, by which the vice-president in charge of a department should concentrate on broad, long-term planning, appraisal, and coordination, while the department's director should handle the more regular and routine activities necessary to keep it running smoothly. The vice-president, however, was held responsible for the final results. Pierre du Pont made it crystal clear that his Executive Committee should not become directly involved in departmental decision making. Its members could advise department heads, as long as the advice was constructive. The Committee allocated funds and personnel and could remove department heads, but it was not to take an active part in the administrative duties of the departmental headquarters. Yet Pierre's warning often went unheeded and the Executive Committee did become involved in operating duties, although not in any way to the extent that Jersey Standard's Executive Committee did.

At Jersey, a comparable structure developed only over time. Although the Jersey Board included in 1912 a number of executives with broad experience, in the succeeding years nearly all its new members came from the functional departments. Each became individually a Director specifically in charge of the administration of the department handling his specialty. Collectively, as the Board, they determined over-all policy and appraised the activities of the company as a whole. Their tasks thus became similar to those of Vice-Presidents at du Pont. However, Teagle and his colleagues never clearly differentiated between entrepreneurial and operational activities. In the administration of production, for example, Sadler was as much involved in day-to-day administration as he was in long-term planning. In Manufacturing, there were two Directors in charge, and as each worked through the Manufacturing Committee, the duties of the several senior executives and the lines of authority between the Directorate and the department were anything but clear. In Domestic Marketing, much the same situation developed. Only in Foreign Marketing was the distinction between the department heads and the Director in charge clearly drawn and the lines between the central office, the department headquarters, and the field units carefully defined.

At Sears, the pattern was closer to du Pont. But since there were fewer departments and, until the move into retailing, fewer strategic decisions, the relationship between the various senior officers remained on a more informal basis, with Rosenwald, then Loeb, and finally Wood making the major decisions in consultation with the department heads. Walter Chrysler at Buick and the heads of the other automobile subsidiaries at General Motors made their decisions in much the same way as Loeb and Wood, after informal contact with their subordinates. In these new and rapidly expanding automotive enterprises, the President or General Manager tended to become involved in detailed operating duties.

This tendency was, in fact, a basic weakness of the central office structure developed in these several enterprises. Executives responsible for over-all planning, coordination, and appraisal became increasingly enmeshed in operational activities. They had neither the time, the information, nor the inclination necessary to stick to entrepreneurial and strategic decision making. The details of the departmental activities for which they were responsible had priority over what often seemed vague long-term planning and appraisal. Moreover, each was a specialist rather than a generalist. Normally, his whole business career had been in one functional field. Thus he had professional pride as well as institutional responsibility in knowing just how his specialty was being carried on throughout the company. He might become involved in such questions as to what different types of refining machinery were to be sent to Britain or how to set up a branch office in Pittsburgh. Worse yet, just because each such senior officer viewed the company's problems from the point of view of a single function, he tended to reflect, in appraising, planning, and coordinating the activities of the enterprise as a whole, the outlook of one of the parts.

Since these multifunction enterprises were managed by men trained to handle single-function units, the final determination of policy tended to be a result of negotiations between interested parties, rather than of an understanding or an awareness of or even consideration of the best interests of the corporation as a whole. This was particularly true when the decisions involved major allocation of funds and other resources. Such policy making by negotiating seems to have an obvious parallel in the making of military and diplomatic decisions in Washington since World War II.

Management by department heads also hampered sound appraisal and the taking of executive action based on that appraisal. Fletcher Brown made this point forcibly when he described the weakness of the du Pont Executive Committee in 1921:

> The Committee member at the head of any one Department is moreover in no position to investigate or criticize the work of another Department. It has never been found practicable for this Committee to discuss and control the conduct of affairs of any one Department. Furthermore it is unreasonable to expect that a majority of the members will be able to subject their own Departments to such self-examination and criticism so that the Company as a whole will operate efficiently. The various Departments of the Company lack an adequate directing and coordinating force at the present time, without which success is impossible.

To make matters worse, objective data on departmental performance proved hard to devise, if only because profit and loss in one activity depended so much on the work accomplished in another. Moreover, the information on which both appraisal and planning had to be based came largely from the departments involved. Administrative decisions often evolved from the give and take of biased individuals using biased data. At du Pont, the Treasurer's Department began to provide well before World War I, somewhat objective and balanced information which could act as a check on departmental data. At Sears, General Motors, and Jersey, the executives began during the 1920's to get similarly improved data from their financial departments. Those at Jersey did so only after the formation of the Budget and Coordination Committees in 1925.

The lack of time, of information, and of psychological commitment to an over-all entrepreneurial viewpoint were not necessarily serious handicaps if the company's basic activities remained stable, that is, if its sources of raw materials and supplies, its manufacturing technology, its markets, and the nature of its products and product lines stayed relatively unchanged. But when further expansion into new functions, into new geographical areas, or into new product lines greatly increased all types of administrative decisions, then the executives in the central office became overworked and their administrative performance less efficient. These increasing pressures, in turn, created the need for the building or adoption of the multidivisional structure with its general office and autonomous operating divisions.

Prior to the 1920's the closest approximation to this new type of structure occurred in the large holding company that remained administratively wholly or partially a federation. The small, top executive offices in such enterprises had not yet, however, devised the facilities, developed the information, or clearly defined the channels of communication and authority necessary for effective large-scale administration. General Motors under William C. Durant vividly illustrates the administrative weaknesses of an enterprise that, while legally consolidated, remained administratively a decentralized federation.

Durant's office made little effort to exploit the managerial economies of scale by passing around information, ideas, and advice. It developed within the organization no means of coordinating product flow with market demand or of assisting the subsidiaries in carrying out this function more effectively by themselves. Durant failed to work up ways of appraising accurately the performance of his different operating units or even of the enterprise as a whole. He gave little careful and rational attention to the allocation of funds for capital or day-to-day operating expenses. In his Executive Committee, the interested parties — the division managers — negotiated for funds by putting the needs of their separate divisions ahead of those of General Motors as a whole.

Durant and the members of his Executive Committee were never really concerned by this lack of a rational or systematic approach to policy formulation or to the effective mobilization of the existing resources of the great enterprise. The creator of General Motors put his entire faith in the great potential demand for the medium-priced automobile. Given enough dealers, plants, and parts and accessory firms, he was confident that he could sell all the cars he might assemble. Such a sanguine view made cost accounting, forecasting, scheduling, inventory control, and budgeting appear as unnecessary refinements in the booming automobile business of the day. His whole concern was to accumulate the resources necessary to meet the current demand.

Storrow and his banking associates, between 1911 and 1915, made an abortive attempt to create a general office to administer their young, but already huge, automobile empire. They were far more concerned than Durant with the profitable use of existing resources than with the addition of new ones. Their efforts to build offices for providing uniform, centralized purchasing and even technological advice was as ambitious and as well planned as in any such company of that day. But they did not get the data necessary for the effective administration of many subsidiaries nor develop ways of taking any advantage of the economies of size. Nor did Storrow's company appear to have had effective communication with and administrative control over the subsidiaries. The operating units continued to make their products and to spend funds with little oversight from headquarters. Nor was Jersey Standard able to devise, before 1925, much better lines of authority and communication between its parent office and its autonomous integrated affiliates like Louisiana, Imperial, Humble, Gilbert & Barker, and the natural gas companies.

Because of this inability of federated enterprises to achieve effective administration, many firms that began as such combinations quickly consolidated their activities into functionally departmentalized, centralized operating structures. Certainly one major cause for the reorganization of the du Pont Company in 1902 and 1903 was the administrative ineffectiveness of a comparable combination. Only through centralized control did the efficient use of total resources of the enterprise appear possible.

Both the centralized consolidated and the overdecentralized federated organizations had inherent weaknesses for the administration of great industrial enterprises. Where the top managers in the former found themselves involved too much in operating activities, those in the latter were too little aware of what their subsidiaries were doing. Thus in both types, the senior officers were handicapped in carrying out their basic functions of coordination, appraisal, and policy making. As their businesses grew more complex and diversified, a few of these executives became aware of these defects.

The Creative Innovation

The building of the initial structures was significant in itself. In the four cases described here, an examination of the adaptive response to new administrative needs also provides essential background for an analysis of the fashioning of a new structure—of the truly creative response. The inherent weakness in the centralized, functionally departmentalized operating company and in the loosely held, decentralized holding company became critical only when the administrative load on the senior executive officers increased to such an extent that they were unable to handle their entrepreneurial responsibilities efficiently. This situation arose when the operations of the enterprise became too complex and the problems of coordination, appraisal, and policy formulation too intricate for a small number of top officers to handle both long-run, entrepreneurial, and short-run, operational administrative activities. To meet these new needs, the innovators built the multidivisional structure with a general office whose executives would concentrate on entrepreneurial activities and with autonomous, fairly self-contained operating divisions whose managers would handle operational ones.

Complexity in itself, it should be emphasized, did not assure innovation or change; some responsible administrator had to become aware of the new conditions. Furthermore, awareness had to be translated into a plan for meeting the new conditions, and then the plan had to be accepted by most of the senior executives. Since such a program dealt with the relations between persons rather than with technological or mechanical developments, the working out of the plan was more complicated than merely bringing a new product or process into effective use.

Analysis of this basic structural innovation requires examination, first, of the conditions calling for change and, second, of the process of innovation. What created the conditions of complexity in the four companies? Why were these four among the very first large corporations in America to find their existing managements inadequate to carry out the tasks of over-all coordination, appraisal, and policy formulation? And then, why and how did individuals within these companies become aware of these needs, how was this awareness transformed into action, and how were the plans and policies modified once in action?

The Conditions for Innovation

Size, measured by volume of output, capital invested, and men employed, was clearly only one aspect of the new complexity. Growth by diversification into new lines of business and continued vertical integration in widely separated geographical areas proved more significant. The huge expansion of the du Pont Company in World War I created few organizational strains or problems. In fact, the Haskell Committee in recommending postwar organizational changes at du Pont decided that the existing structure had eminently proven its value. The only improvements needed were a more careful definition of the duties and structure of the functional departments, a more explicit placing of authority and responsibility for functional activities on a single individual, and a greater assurance that the Executive Committee would confine itself to "the general supervision of the Company's affairs," and to questions of broad policy.

The inadequacies of the functionally departmentalized structure at du Pont became apparent only as the basic policy of product diversification went into full-scale operation. The need to put to use postwar excess capacity turned the company to making and selling several lines of products. Under the existing management structure, the top executives were unable to give the proper attention to the coordination of product flow and product design with market demand and taste, to the appraisal of current operating performance, or to plan for future allocation of resources in the new businesses as well as the old. As the executives in charge of the final reorganization reminded the Board of Directors in September, 1921: "The Executive Committee is constituted chiefly of heads of Departments, and has found it difficult to coordinate the various functions and to fix properly the due responsibility for results." [5] As long as the company remained in a single line of business, that of explosives, it could be effectively "organized along functional lines with trained specialists in every Department of the Company." But now "our business is so diversified and our experience in the new industries so short that an overwhelming number of problems are clamoring for solution. Each problem requires individual attention and separate treatment and cannot be solved in the same way." Expansion in a single line of business only increased the scale or scope of existing routine and procedures. Diversification into new lines of products with new markets and sources of supplies brought a whole new range of tactical and strategic decisions.

Sears's experience was most like du Pont's. At Sears, the rapid expansion of the mail-order business in the 1920's increased the number of branch plants from three to ten but caused little or no organizational strain. On the other hand, the move into a new line of business, over-the-counter retailing, created a host of new problems of coordination, supervision, and planning which the existing organization found almost impossible to handle.

Jersey's management difficulties resulted from the development of new products created by the coming of the automobile and from the continuing vertical integration in all parts of the world rather than from product diversification. In the years after World War I, the nation's largest petroleum company was opening new oil fields in Europe, Latin America, and Asia, setting up a world-wide shipping system to carry its crude and refined petroleum, constructing refineries here and abroad, and then expanding its marketing in foreign countries and the United States. If Jersey had concentrated, as did most of her American competitors, on production, transportation, refining, and marketing within the United States, its Board would have had far less complicated problems of coordination, appraisal, and planning. There would have been less pressure on Teagle and his associates to set up the general office Coordination and Budget Departments and then to define clearly the separate administrative duties of the parent and of the multifunction operating divisions.

In the case of General Motors, the obvious comparison is with Ford. By concentrating on one model which came to be built largely in one plant, Henry Ford expanded enormously in size without creating many central office management problems. But by the same token Ford found it extremely difficult to develop other products, such as airplanes or tractors, or other cars, like the Lincoln, or even new models of his single product. His whole organization was fashioned rigidly around the Model T.

General Motors, on the other hand, was as diversified as Ford was unified. Where Ford had but one model, General Motors came to have a major line in each price class and a number of models for each line. Moreover, it made and marketed for the national market many more parts and accessories than did Ford. Because of Durant's desire to hold his dealers during World War I, General Motors became one of the largest manufacturers of refrigerators. Kettering had brought with him Delco Light, makers of isolated lighting systems, and an interest in the Dayton-Wright Airplane Company when he joined the corporation. Such a diversity of activities proved almost impossible to manage effectively through the overdecentralized holding company, and made impractical the formation of a centralized, functionally departmentalized structure. The problems of manufacturing, sales, financing, engineering, and purchasing were almost as varied and as technically complicated as those in the recently diversified du Pont Company. Sloan's transformation of Durant's tiny top office into a coordinating, appraising, and policy-making general office made possible the rational and profitable management of such an enterprise. By the same token, such a structure permitted General Motors to diversify with a minimum of strain into other product lines based on the internal-combustion engine when the demand for automobiles leveled off and began to decline in the late 1920's and early 1930's.

If diversity rather than increased size of operations led to organizational inadequacies, then it becomes clearer why these four companies were among the earliest in the United States to consider structural reorganization. Du Pont was the first large chemical company to diversify its products on a major scale. General Motors was far and away the most diversified automobile company of its day. In the 1920's, Jersey's operations were geographically more widely scattered than those of any other American petroleum company. Moreover, the making and selling of chemicals, automobiles, and even petroleum constituted a more complex job in itself than did manufacturing and marketing in such major industries as steel, copper, meat packing, tobacco, and whisky. Sears, although closely followed by Montgomery Ward, pioneered in combining over-the-counter sales with mail-order marketing on a national basis. These four companies were therefore among the earliest to face the complex management problems that came to confront so many large American firms in the post-World War II economic boom.

In these four enterprises, diversity created by the move into new lines of business and by continued expansion of technologically complex existing ones greatly increased the responsibilities of the top administrators. In the case of du Pont, Sears, and to some extent Jersey Standard, the adding of new business activities resulted from the need to assure continuing profitable use of existing plant, equipment, and personnel. In the case of du Pont, the threatened postwar excess capacity turned the executives to looking for new uses for men trained and facilities used in the manufacturing and marketing of a product line based on a nitrocellulose technology. At Sears, the decline of farm income and with it the mail-order company's major market induced General Wood to a search for new employment for his buying and distributing facilities and trained employees. At Jersey, the transferal of existing resources from producing and marketing kerosene to gasoline created as many administrative problems as did its expansion into transportation and crude oil production. Yet at Jersey also the major reorganization was a response to the rapid accumulation of resources necessary to meet the swiftly growing demand for lubricants and fuel oil as well as for gasoline. At General Motors, the administrative problems were those of managing more effectively the vast accumulation of resources Durant had brought together in his efforts to meet the huge demand for the medium-priced car and not, with the exception of a brief period during World War I, of transferring existing resources to new lines.

For the senior executives at du Pont, Sears, and Jersey, expansion into new industries, new lines of business, and new geographical areas broadened the range as well as the complexity of tactical and strategic decisions. Similarly, the rapid growth until 1920 of General Motors' several lines of automobiles, trucks, parts and accessories, electrical machinery, and refrigerators continually increased the administrative load on its executives. These senior officers now had to appraise performance and make basic decisions about starting, maintaining, expanding, or contracting the activities of a number of integrated, multifunction divisions, with each division handling very different lines of goods or operating in quite different areas. The horizons of these officers were no longer those of a single industry but rather of national and international economies. They truly had to be generalists, not functional specialists; and they needed all the time and information they could get for over-all supervision and planning.

The Process of Innovation

While the needs and pressures for structural innovation were much the same in all four companies, the actual working out of the change proved quite different in each case. In transforming the answers to administrative needs into organizational forms, the differing personalities and training of the senior executives in each company and the unique historically determined situation within each played their critical parts. Nevertheless, there were some significant similarities among them in the process of innovation.

At du Pont, General Motors, and Jersey Standard, the initial awareness of the structural inadequacies caused by the new complexity came from executives close to top management, but who were not themselves in a position to make organizational changes. In all three, the president gave no encouragement to the proposers of change. Irénée du Pont strongly resisted the recommendations for a new structure, while Durant and Teagle remained unconcerned about the inadequacies of their existing organizations and the suggestions for their structural improvement. In all three companies, it took a sizable crisis to bring action. Yet all three presidents had received proposals for reorganization before that crisis made their usefulness apparent. Only at Sears did the top policy maker, General Wood, see the organizational needs as they arose and act quickly to meet them.

These comparisons raise two questions: How did the individuals who first proposed reorganization become aware of the structural weaknesses before other executives? Why did the presidents in each of the three cases fail to take immediate action? The innovators appear to have been the executives closest to the problem who were given or took time away from operating duties in order to concentrate on this significant entrepreneurial problem. At du Pont, the plan of reorganization germinated in a committee of young executives who held responsible posts in each of the major functional departments. They became conscious of the inadequacies in their own units and particularly of the difficulties of interdepartmental coordination. Thus, although that special committee was formed to study the marketing problems, it soon became convinced that organizational difficulties transcended and were indeed the underlying cause for the marketing difficulties. The committee then took the time to study thoroughly ways and means to improve the organization in order to meet the problem.

On the other hand, it seems significant that the Haskell Committee, set up specifically to study organization at a time when it did not appear critical, saw no need to reshape the existing structure. The challenge of a real and immediate need as well as an understanding of the nature of the basic difficulties was necessary for the initial innovation at du Pont.

At General Motors after World War I, organization was a clearer and more pressing problem. Yet, except for Sloan, no executive paid real attention to organizational needs. Durant was too busy in building his empire; the executives of the automobile and parts subsidiaries were too engrossed in maintaining and expanding production. The financiers were too occupied in their primary business — the du Ponts in meeting their own war and postwar challenges, and Storrow with those of being the senior partner of one of the nation's largest and best-known investment banking houses. Sloan was as close to the problem as any General Motors executive. He was currently managing a number of operating units and attempting to coordinate the activities of these units, not only with each other, but with the major car assembling and marketing divisions. Because of his concern over the situation, he took the time, apparently on his own initiative, to make a comprehensive study of how to answer these critical needs.

Those executives at Jersey who were initially aware of organizational difficulties were also meeting specific problems. Clark and Howard found the structure of the Manufacturing Committee constantly hampering their day-to-day work. Therefore, Howard, with Clark's blessing, took the time in the fall of 1923 to study carefully the organization of manufacturing units in three other petroleum companies. Later, in 1927, when Howard proposed making a distinction between a holding company and operating activities, he was largely interested in meeting the needs of his Research and Development Department. But because neither Howard nor anyone else at Jersey was given or took the time to make a complete study of Jersey's over-all organizational needs, no detailed design for the company's structure as a whole was worked out.

Sadler, in pointing out the need for better coordination of product flow, had a broader view. And yet to him, the problem was merely one of creating a committee or department to assure the more effective handling of the coordinating function. He failed at that time to concentrate, as Harden would do later, on seeking out the best ways to meet the needs for over-all coordination. Jersey differed from du Pont, General Motors, and Sears in that very few of its executives appreciated the need to study intensively the problems of organization *qua organization*. Furthermore, they were almost always too involved in tactical activities to concentrate on strategic ones.

At Sears, General Wood, the creator of the new strategy, soon became aware of the massive problems created by the move into over-the-counter sales; but, unlike Sloan, he did not have the time to make a proper study of the problem. As President, there were too many other things demanding his attention and action. Because the committee that he set up to investigate the problems included outsiders as well as insiders, the organization builders at Sears had a broader range of general experience than those in the other companies. But they were not necessarily adequately equipped to find solutions to Sears's specific needs. Even to the insiders, the problems of organizing and managing retail stores were quite new. The effectiveness of the results was in direct ratio with the experience of the innovators. In reorganizing the Merchandise Department, where men like Houser and Dodd were very much at home, the Committee's recommendations created a lasting setup. The structure fashioned for the retail operations proved much less satisfactory. There the outside organization expert, Frazer, dominated the planning, and his primary concern was to cut costs, not to sell merchandise.

Thus the manner in which the realization came of organizational inadequacies affected the nature of the resulting proposals. This, in turn, helped to determine the length of time involved in bringing the plan to fruition. At General Motors and du Pont, the initiators of the change created a fairly explicit, detailed over-all plan of reorganization. At Jersey, they developed only piecemeal plans to take care of immediate problems. At Sears, the plan for the retail organization designed by an outsider proved ineffective and inadequate. For these reasons, the time between the initiation of the reorganized structure and its final fruition was relatively short at du Pont and General Motors and comparatively long at Sears and Jersey Standard.

Only at du Pont was there any explicit resistance to the recommendations of the innovators. There the President, Irénée, twice turned down the proposal. He did this partly from a conviction of the value of the functional organization and partly because of the responsibility inherent in his position. If the proposed plan had failed, it would have been considered his mistake rather than that of the men who first recommended it. In his stand, Irénée had the support of his brothers and one or two of the Executive Committee members, particularly Walter Edge, Vice-President in charge of Purchasing. But most of the top management — the two Browns, the Carpenters, Pickard, and Spruance — soon came to favor the reorganization strongly. In contrast, at Jersey and General Motors there was little open opposition to the initial proposals for change. Durant and Teagle were simply not interested.

Possibly just because of Irénée's strong resistance, the initial changes at du Pont were the most clear-cut and required the least subsequent amending of any of the four reorganizations here studied. In the interim period between Irénée's rejection of the proposal in the autumn of 1920 and the final reorganization a year later, the du Pont executives learned several lessons. The compromise structure with its committees representing the major functions for each line of products had proven ineffectual and cumbersome. Clearly day-to-day operating decisions could not be left to committees. This experience, by re-emphasizing the validity of the company's long-held principle of individual responsibility for operations, may have prevented proposals for instituting somewhat comparable interfunctional committees, once the new plan was accepted. It may also have helped the company's chief executives, both junior and senior, to accept the new structure more enthusiastically once it had been agreed upon.

The delay also led to a significant modification of the original reorganization plan. The intervening events convinced H. Fletcher Brown and his colleagues that the general office functions could not be carried out by executives who had operating duties. The top committee must include only general officers who would be able to "give all their time and effort to the business of the Company as a whole. Being connected with no department, they will be able to consider all questions or problems without bias or prejudice." This arrangement would also permit a division manager to "give undivided attention to the details of his own [division]." Thus through rational, careful initial planning and after a brief but useful trial with alternative solutions, the du Pont Company had designed between 1919 and 1921 one of the first and most clear-cut examples of the modern, multidivisional structure.

The final definition of a comparable structure took longer at General Motors, for Sloan, Brown, and Pratt had more creative work to do. They and their assistants had to build a general office almost from scratch. An advisory staff had to be manned and trained. General officers had to be recruited and their duties defined. The problem of working out the relations between the general office and the divisions was particularly difficult, since the latter had always been self-contained units operating with almost complete independence. Moreover, very few of them were using comparable data in calculating their operating costs, and few related either costs or inventories to accurate appraisals of market demand.

One of the most important tasks facing Sloan and Brown in 1921 was the creation of an informational system to provide both the division heads and the general executives with an intelligible picture of present performance and anticipated conditions. By 1924, they had developed these essential data and so made possible the administration of the operating divisions without inhibiting or interfering with the authority and responsibility of the general managers. By this same date, the senior executives at General Motors had become convinced, as had those at du Pont earlier, of the need to have the top executives be truly general officers. They were relieved of operating responsibilities, and each was to have only advisory contact with the division managers, as Sloan had recommended in his original plan. Finally, through the device of the Inter-Divisional Committees formed between 1922 and 1924, Sloan marked out another formal method or channel of communication and authority through which the general executives, staff specialists, and operating managers kept in constant contact with one another. By 1925, the General Motors structure was as clearly outlined as that of du Pont.

At Jersey, this creative innovation was slower in coming. It was worked out in a much more haphazard way, and many years were to pass before it reached as explicitly defined a form as in the other two companies. Just because its executives ignored for so long the problems of organization, their task was even greater than that of the organization builders at du Pont and General Motors. Structural changes, both the shaping and reshaping of the lines of authority and communication and the development of essential data, had to be initiated and carried out on three levels of administration. Between 1925 and 1927, Teagle and his associates outlined the basic structure for the offices at all three levels — departmental headquarters, the central office, and the general office. After 1927, the relations between these offices were readjusted and, at the same time, more and more accurate operating and planning information was developed. The most significant of the later changes came in 1933 when the activities of the general office and the operating affiliates were more explicitly separated by relieving all general officers of operating responsibilities, by removing physically their place of work to another location, and by bringing in several new senior executives. These executives, like those at du

Pont and General Motors, came to have as individuals only an advisory relationship with the operating executives. After wartime expansion brought a return of the multifunction operating affiliates, the structure at Jersey became comparable to that at du Pont and General Motors.

At Sears, the awareness of organization problems came more quickly than in the other three companies, but the development of the necessary structure took longer to achieve. Here the difficulty was not, as at Jersey, of having no over-all plan, but rather of adopting the wrong plan. General Wood, a highly rational administrator with great respect for data, rarely permitted tactical decisions to interfere with strategic ones. When he realized that the move into direct retailing required a new structure, he quickly called together a competent committee to plan it. The resulting structure failed, however, because the lines of authority and communication were conflicting and unclear.

The structure also proved inadequate because it called for too few administrators. A close and intimate relation with military and political organization may have convinced Wood and Frazer that good administration meant little more than putting the right man in the right place. It certainly instilled in both men a dread of bureaucracy that expanded by creating work for itself and not by carrying out any productive economic role. Concerned with this very real, if negative, danger of any administrative organization, they overlooked the positive value to a large business unit of having managers who concentrated on the coordination, planning, and appraisal of their enterprise's many and widespread resources. As one Sears executive quickly reminded them, an adequate administrative organization was absolutely essential if Sears was to carry out its basic economic function of high-volume, low-cost merchandising. Without offices to supervise the store managers, Colonel Gilbert E. Humphrey wrote Wood in June, 1930, Sears needed more than just three hundred highly competent store managers. It also required an able and trained man for each line — hardware, automobile accessories, household appliances, sporting goods, paints, and so forth — in each of the three hundred stores. Under such total decentralization, Humphrey insisted, the company was unable to coordinate and integrate its vast buying and distributing facilities with market demand in order to take full advantage of trained and competent personnel, particularly its merchandising specialists. Valuable ideas and methods already in use in some stores would permeate very slowly through the rest of the organization. The abilities of the most competent men would be confined to a single unit. Nor would there develop "new ideas, new policies, new methods [that] may be produced through the interchange of ideas of a number of men."

After trying a variety of solutions, Wood became convinced by 1940 of the value of the multidivisional structure. The new territorial organization was, in many ways, similar to the one the Frazer Committee had proposed in 1929, but the senior executives had full authority and responsibility for carrying out the several functional activities in their regionally defined divisions. Only the coming of war delayed the creation of five such Territorial Divisions and a parent office with staff specialists and general executives. The final structure varied from that of each of the other three companies, largely because Sears concentrated on the marketing of many lines rather than on manufacturing, marketing, and procuring or producing raw or semifinished materials and other supplies in a few major lines of products.

This brief review of the process of organizational innovation in these four great industrial empires suggests how the attitudes and activities of the different executives affected structural change. The coming of the depression and of World War II most certainly slowed the completion of the new structure at Jersey and Sears. But even with continuing prosperity, the lack of a plan in the first company and the adoption of the wrong plan in the second would undoubtedly have caused much the same delay.

The experience of all four firms makes very clear how concentration on operational activities interfered with and inhibited long-term planning, including the designing of a new structure to meet the administrative needs of a new strategy. Only when the executives withdrew from day-to-day tasks did they produce useful organizational plans or proposals. In the case of planning the multidivisional structure — the creative innovation — the individual innovators needed to have an intimate contact with the problem, and they had to take the time to study it. The question still remains why some executives close to these needs gave the necessary time while others did not. Clearly differences in training, temperament, and business experience played their part.

The Significance of the Innovation

Before examining the impact of these differences in executive personality on organizational change, a final word is needed about the structure which all four companies came to adopt. The basic reason for its success was simply that it clearly removed the executives responsible for the destiny of the entire enterprise from the more routine operational activities and so gave them the time, information, and even psychological commitment for long-term planning and appraisal. Conversely, it placed the responsibility and the necessary authority for the operational administration in the hands of the general managers of the multifunction divisions. At General Motors, Alfred Sloan and Donaldson Brown described this allocation of decision making as one between "policy and administration." In 1937, Sloan succinctly rephrased in the following way what Brown had pronounced publicly ten years earlier:

> By "administration" is meant the daily conduct of the Corporation's affairs. By "formulation of policies" is meant both the establishment of the broad principles by which administration is to be guided and the determination of the fundamental concepts of the business. The prime objectives of the business; the scope of its operation, both as to products and markets, the desirability of expansion, horizontally or vertically or both; the provision of the essential capital for its operations; and the question of distribution of its profits as between the amount paid in dividends and the amount retained in the business — all are problems involving "formulation of policies" and illustrate the principle involved.[6]

Thus the new structure left the broad strategic decisions as to the allocation of existing resources and the acquisition of new ones in the hands of a top team of generalists. Relieved of operating duties and tactical decisions, a general executive was less likely to reflect the position of just one part of the whole, even though old ties and attitudes were often hard to break. Moreover, the top team was now less the captive of its operating organizations than it had been, since it no longer had to base its decisions on information provided by the functional departments. Not only did the financial offices provide more and better data, but the general office advisory staff immediately took on the major task of supplying information of all kinds. In this way it provided an independent check on divisional requests, proposals, and estimates. It also helped the general office to study new areas for development or expansion in which the operating executives would have comparatively little interest or knowledge. In addition, the financial offices and the advisory staff gave the general officers an additional flow of detailed information on past and present performance of the operating units and of the company as a whole. With time and information thus available, the top team was equipped to handle the new range of problems created when the multifunction company became multi-industry or multicontinent in scope.

At the same time, the new structure eased the problems of coordination and appraisal. Coordinating product flow and determining costs in relation to volume as well as adapting product design or make-up to changing demands were all left to the multifunction divisions, each operating in its own clearly defined market. Their estimates of demand, which set the rate of flow through their functional departments and determined per-unit costs, were checked and supplemented by staff specialists in the general office. As methods of forecasting improved, this coordination and cost determination became increasingly routine. Also, through providing a great deal of information, the general staff helped to assure contact between the functional departments regarding changing market tastes and needs. Other types of coordination of activities in the different operating units came through standardizing procedures in personnel regulations, advertising, public relations, and the like. And here, of course, the staff played an important role.

Appraisal of multifunction divisions proved to be more precise than that of single-function departments. Division managers did not depend closely on other units for the sale of their products and their supplies of materials. A steady flow of detailed reports on all aspects of a given division's financial performance and its share of the market provided both its manager and the general officers with a useful and continuing check on operating results and achievements. Comparisons were made with the results of similar units within the enterprise, such as the various automobile divisions of General Motors or the Territories at Sears, or with past performance for similar seasons or with the divisional or general office estimates and forecasts for the same period. At all four companies, visits between the general office and the operating units supplemented the steady flow of reports.

In this way, the new structure left the divisional executives to run the business, while the general officers set the goals and policies and provided over-all appraisal. The division managers, responsible for the functional activities of their units, made decisions about prices charged on specific products, about design and quality of the existing products and the development of new ones, about more immediate markets and marketing, about probable sources of supply, about technological improvements, and finally about the flow of product from supplier to consumer. But these decisions were to be made within the framework set by the broad policy guides and financial budgets through which the general executives determined the present and future allocation of the resources of the enterprise as a whole and within the carefully defined interrelationships between the operating units and the general office as indicated by the company's structure.

Such an allotment of different duties to the outlying parts and to the center brought different methods of decision making. At the operating level, decisions came ultimately to be made by one responsible individual. He might turn to committees from his own staff or to operating managers for advice and information, but the final decisions remained his. At the entrepreneurial level, group action and even group decision became the more usual procedure. Here the problems considered were more complex and less routine, long-term rather than short, more concerned with difficulties to be surmounted and less with specific and immediate demands and requirements to be met. In handling entrepreneurial activities that called for thought, group decisions came to be the practice. In carrying out operational ones where quicker action was demanded, individual decision making predominated.

Beside allocating decision making more effectively and assuring more precise communication and control, the new structure proved to have another advantage over the functionally departmentalized organization. It provided a place to train and test general executives. Under the earlier structure, no one but a president or chairman of the board ever had a continuing, over-all view of the company's affairs. The departmental vice-presidents, as members of an Executive Committee or other senior central office group, might have some experience in over-all coordination, appraisal, and policy making, but even here they tended to be primarily concerned with their own particular functional activity. Now all the division managers had to be generalists rather than specialists, and thus they gained experience in running a complex business. It should be stressed, however, that the value of the structure in preparing, testing, and proving general officers was only a by-product of the change; it had not precipitated it. The reorganizers at du Pont and at Jersey Standard suggested the value of the new structure in developing executive talent but only as an afterthought, once the decision to reorganize had been fully accepted. It was not mentioned by the organizational innovators at General Motors nor at Sears, Roebuck.

In seeking and finding answers to their fundamental problem of assuring the necessary time, information, and psychological commitment to the men who made the critical decisions, the organization builders in these four companies provided useful clues to the scholars anxious to discover exactly who makes some of the most important decisions in the private sector of the American economy.[7] Since many basic industries in America have been dominated by a handful of firms, the identification of the key decision makers in these large enterprises is particularly relevant for an understanding and evaluation of the role of the individual and of decisions by individuals in American industrial growth and change. The men who make the critical decisions in any economy can be defined as those who have the actual or real, rather than merely the legal, power to allocate the resources available to them and who, in fact, determine the basic goals and policies for their enterprises. Clearly the general executive is such a man.

In the large corporation the stockholders, the legal owners, long ago abdicated this function. They had neither the time, information, nor (as long as the enterprise was paying dividends) the interest to make the basic policy decisions. What little they did know about their company was told them by the managers, who spent all their working time administering its affairs. Unless they were also full-time, career executives of the concern, the members of the board of directors had only a little more knowledge and understanding of the workings of their company than the stockholders. To be sure, they met more often and in subcommittees, especially the finance committee, and could obtain more information and take more time to study the condition of the enterprise. Yet they, too, had neither the time nor sources of information independent of the full-time executives. They, too, were occupied with their own business activities. Of course, whenever company's dividends stopped and receivership loomed, the board and the large stockholders came alive. Only then did their ultimate authority, based on the legal sanctions of private property, come into play. But even then, they had little choice except to hire a new set of administrators. Thus the members of the board, unless they were full-time executives of the concern, were as much captives of the professional entrepreneurs as were the stockholders. As the directors of America's largest nineteenth-century business corporation — the Pennsylvania Railroad — noted, as early as 1874: "The present form of organization [part-time directors and full-time officers] makes practical ciphers of the Directors, and this is from no deliberate intention, but from the very necessities of the case."[8] Once a large business had reached a size that required the services of several full-time administrators, the board and the stockholders had only a negative or veto power on the government of their enterprise and on the allocation of its resources. They could say no, but they had neither the information nor the awareness of the company's situation to propose realistic alternative courses of action.

But if the stockholders and the board became captives of the full-time administrators, were not the professional entrepreneurs themselves captives of their subordinates? Were not the information and alternatives available to the top men determined, possibly quite unconsciously, by junior executives down the line? Must not then the enterprise or the organization as a whole be considered responsible for the basic economic decisions? If this is so, then no individual or team of individuals can be identified as the key decision makers in the private sector of the American economy.[9]

The administrative experience of the four companies studied here challenges this last view. The men responsible for the allocation and use of funds, for the transfer of personnel, and for the control and use of equipment can be identified at each administrative level. The department heads in the central office, who made the basic decisions in a large enterprise until the creation of a general office in recent years, may have received their information and the selection of alternative actions from their subordinates in the departments. But unlike the stockholders and board members, they had more opportunity and more technical competence to evaluate the information and the proposals.

Moreover, the basic decisions usually concerned more than one department. Therefore the information and recommendations from one department head could be challenged by others. If the president had the final decision, he need not be the captive of any one group. There was less danger that the executive committee would become a rubber stamp, than there was that its decisions and the resulting allocation of resources would be based on a relatively nonrational negotiated compromise between departments. Nevertheless, the data on which the executive committee in a centralized, functionally departmentalized structure acted did come from biased sources. And two or three biased proposals certainly did not automatically produce a sound unbiased one. Also, as the du Pont and Jersey stories emphasize, such slanted information made objective appraisal of departmental performance difficult. In the centralized, functionally departmentalized structure, therefore, the identification of the actual or real decision makers is often difficult.

The creation of the new structure with its general office and its several multifunction divisions did make identification easier. The executives in the general office, freed from all but the entrepreneurial responsibilities, had full time to spend on planning and appraisal. From the staff they received independent information as a check on data from the divisions and an alternate source for developing policy proposals and recommendations. The reports from the divisions tended to give objective, impersonal data on return on investment and on market performance. The general executives then were relatively independent of their subordinates. And, since they still provided the board and the stockholders and, of course, any government or regulatory agency with whatever detailed data about the company these groups might want, their actions were controlled only negatively by their legal superiors. The general executive of the large corporation is then as crucial and identifiable a figure in mid-twentieth century economy as Adam Smith's capitalist was in the late eighteenth century, and Jean Baptiste Say's entrepreneur in the early nineteenth.

Organizational Innovators

Unless structure follows strategy, inefficiency results. This certainly appears to be the lesson to be learned from the experience of our four companies. Volume expansion, geographical dispersion, vertical integration, product diversification, and continued growth by any of these basic strategies laid an increasingly heavy load of entrepreneurial decision making on the senior executives. If they failed to re-form the lines of authority and communication and to develop information necessary for administration, the executives throughout the organization were drawn deeper and deeper into operational activities and often were working at cross purposes to and in conflict with one another.

Yet, structure often failed to follow strategy. In each of the four companies, there was a time lag between the appearance of the administrative needs and their satisfaction. A primary reason for delay was the very fact that responsible executives had become too enmeshed in operational activities. Nevertheless, some of them did become conscious of the new and growing administrative needs and did take the time away from operational work to study the problems facing the enterprise or appointed others to do so. What, then, caused these executives to be more aware of administrative needs and problems and so turned them to organizational innovation?

An Organization Builder's Personality and Training

The four cases suggest that the empire builder rarely became an organization builder. Coleman du Pont, William C. Durant, and Richard Sears paid very little attention to organizational structure. Of the three, Coleman was most aware of the need for structure, yet even he left its creation and then the management of the enterprise to his younger cousin. These three men were extroverts. Durant and Sears were both brilliant salesmen, and of both Coleman du Pont and Billy Durant, their associates often said that they could charm the birds right out of the trees.

Walter Teagle and Robert Wood were in many ways like those earlier industrial empire builders. Both enlarged their companies' domains greatly. Perhaps if Teagle had been in one of the many newer oil firms rather than in the most venerable of them all, he might have found a still broader scope for his talents. He too was an outstanding salesman, an executive who looked on the whole world as his field of battle, and a man whom others gladly followed. But unlike the makers of new business domains, Teagle became entangled in operating details. He had as little time for planning and carrying out Jersey's strategy of expansion, an activity that he thoroughly enjoyed, as he had for designing her operating structure, a matter that interested him hardly at all.

General Wood, a man of great personal warmth and charm, came closest to being both an empire and an organization builder. His success sprang from his ability to avoid tactical matters and to concentrate on strategic ones. More than any other executive studied here, he kept himself alert to both internal needs and external opportunities. Possibly it was simply because of this superlative competence that Wood was unable to appreciate the need to develop "management in depth" and to define the clear-cut lines of authority and communication that were so necessary if men of somewhat lesser talents were to administer effectively.

The executives who formulated the plans for governing the empires which Coleman du Pont, Durant, and Sears created and those that Teagle and Wood expanded were a different sort. At least they left a different impression on their contemporaries. Pierre du Pont, Harry Haskell, Donaldson Brown, Alfred Sloan, Frank Howard, Edgar Clark, James Barker, and Theodore Houser were more reserved than the empire-builders studied here, and had a more studious approach to business problems. Their range of acquaintances was narrower, and they were less involved in extracurricular activities.

These executives closely resembled the professional administrators of today. With the exception of Pierre du Pont, they did not control or even own large blocks of stock in the company that they managed. Again except for Pierre, his brothers, and brothers-in-law, they had no family ties with the large stockholders. At the same time, their companies became their careers, their callings, and their lives. They did not even have any outside business interests.

Nor had any of the organization builders had very much experience in other companies or industries before joining the company he came to administer. Yet nearly all of them had more outside experience than their successors or the professional executives of today. Pierre du Pont had spent three years in steel and electric railways, and many of his associates had had their start in the steel, electrical, or railway businesses. On the other hand, the executives who engineered the du Pont reorganizations in 1919 and 1921 had spent nearly all their business careers in the explosives industry and in the du Pont Company itself. At General Motors, the organization builders had grown up with the automobile business or had come from the du Pont Company. At Jersey, Howard came to the oil company after practicing patent law, and Clark was recruited from Standard Oil of Indiana. At Sears, more outside talent was involved in the organizational changes than at any of the other companies. Barker, Houser, Dodd, and, of course, Frazer, all had had fairly broad business careers. One other way in which these men differed from the modern professional managers was the shorter length of time they spent in climbing the administrative ladder within their enterprises.

The fact that the organizational changes in the four companies studied here were made by professional administrators rather than by outside owners made those changes more difficult to carry out. Historically, large corporate or bureaucratic hierarchies rarely re-form themselves. The relative ease and speed with which the structural changes came at du Pont and General Motors as compared with Jersey and Sears stressed therefore the value of analyzing the different approaches by which the same breed of professional managers handled the same basic problems of management.

Some correlation seems to exist between the education and training of the executives and their approach to organizational needs. Most of the men who showed the greatest interest in systematizing and explicitly defining organizational relationships had had engineering training. Pierre du Pont, Alfred Sloan, Frank McGregor of du Pont, and James Barker of Sears were all M.I.T. graduates. Barker had even served on the engineering faculty of the Institute. General Wood had had engineering training at West Point. Donaldson Brown, like Sloan, was a trained electrical engineer with a degree from Virginia Polytechnic Institute and graduate work at Cornell. Fletcher Brown began as a scientist rather than as an engineer. He had studied chemistry at Harvard and, before coming to du Pont, had spent several years at the Naval Torpedo Station in Newport, Rhode Island, experimenting with a smokeless powder. Harry Haskell had studied mining engineering at Columbia. Among the other du Pont organization builders, Hamilton Barksdale, John L. Pratt, and Angus Echols were all civil engineers from the University of Virginia.[10] William C. Spruance had graduated from Princeton as an electrical engineer. At Sears, Houser, with a degree in electrical engineering from Iowa, had somewhat the same educational background as Wood and Barker. The two men at Jersey who thought most along organizational lines had both been trained as engineers, Howard at George Washington University and Sadler at the Naval Academy.

The significance of this correlation between education and organizational awareness is uncertain. Possibly the rigor required in working out scientific and engineering problems led these men to approach management needs in somewhat the same way. Also, in these years, engineers were beginning to consider the use of men in working the machines and not just the mechanics of the machines themselves. So it may be that these men learned at their engineering schools something of the value of systematic industrial organization.

In any case, the connection between the engineering profession and the rationalizing and systematizing of industrial administration in the United States has been close. Frederick W. Taylor's scientific management techniques were the best-known example of the introduction of engineering ideas into management. While Taylor dealt primarily with shop organizations and had little concern with the larger structure, he and his disciples certainly showed much the same approach and outlook as many of the organizational innovators studied here. What was new about the scientific management movement, writes Hugh G. J. Aitken:

was the self-conscious and deliberate extension of rationalism to the analysis of industrial work. It is no coincidence that Taylor and most of his immediate disciples were engineers, for it was by way of engineering that scientific analysis had made its most powerful and continuing impact upon industrial production. They accepted without question the engineering approach that had already proved itself in the design of physical objects, and they extended it to the analysis and control of the activities of people.[11]

Engineers were also among the very first to publish analyses of organizational structure for enterprises larger than a factory. In 1911, Charles B. Going, a trained engineer and managing editor of *The Engineering Magazine,* published his *Principles of Industrial Engineering* in New York City. Another pioneer in organizational analysis was Dexter S. Kimball, professor of machine design and construction at Cornell, whose *Principles of Industrial Organization* was published two years later. These books and others by professional engineers suggest the significant role engineering schools and journals played in the early efforts to rationalize management organization. While such writers were fully aware of Taylor's work, they did not borrow or derive many of their ideas directly from him or his disciples any more than did Henry Ford's engineers when they fashioned the assembly line or planned the Highland Park plant.[12] What Taylor, the Ford engineers, the engineering journalists and professors, and the organization builders here studied had in common were not specific ideas, techniques, or methods, but rather the same rational, self-conscious approach to the management of men.

Undoubtedly more important than college training in developing the rational, analytical view of the problems of business and industrial administration were the attitudes existing within the enterprise itself. From the time of its re-formation in 1902 on, the du Pont Company held an engineering approach to management and business problems. These rational and systematic ways were clearly evidenced at the monthly meetings of Barksdale's Smokeless Powder Operating Department, where papers were read that analyzed manufacturing methods carefully by comparative statistics, or discussed the creating of standards, or explained deviations from the standards. By 1911, Barksdale's staff already included a Labor Efficiency Department.[13] This same painstaking approach was used in building the Sales Department or in investigating new fields for the company to enter in its diversification program after 1908. Working in this sort of atmosphere developed in men like Walter Carpenter and Frederick Pickard, who were not engineering-trained, the same rational, systematic approach. On the other hand, Coleman and Alfred du Pont who, although M.I.T. graduates, had not been trained in the new du Pont

Company, did not have this cold, analytical, often impersonal way of going about the company's business.

General Motors did not develop a similar institutional ethos until after Durant had departed and Sloan, Pierre du Pont, and Donaldson Brown had moved in. By the mid-twenties, the approach at General Motors had become much like that of du Pont. And here again, men without engineering training developed an engineering approach. At Sears and particularly at Jersey, the systematic attitude was never so obvious; these companies had fewer engineers in the top ranks. But even after Jersey began to recruit men from M.I.T. and other engineering schools, the more informal, personal approach continued.

Apparently a corporate personality results from the interaction of the nature of the business and the education and personalities of the senior executives. Undoubtedly there was more science and engineering involved in the early years of the chemical and even the automobile industries than in those of the petroleum or volume merchandising trades. Certainly du Pont hired many more trained engineers and used them more in top management than did any of the other three companies studied. Whatever the reason, the differences in the ethos or the personality of each of these companies still persist, as even a short visit to each company does emphasize. Nevertheless, the rational, analytical outlook of the du Pont Company has become, in recent years, the more accepted way in American business.

Our organizational innovators tended to have another common characteristic beside their engineering background or attitudes. They were relatively young and had not been long in the positions they held at the time that they became interested in organizational change. The men who made the initial structural innovations in 1902 and 1903 at du Pont were in their thirties and early forties. This was true, except for Fletcher Brown, of the men who put through the structural reorganization in the same company seventeen and eighteen years later. Sloan was forty-four when he devised his organization study, and his two key assistants in putting the plan into action, Donaldson Brown and John Lee Pratt, were a good bit younger. The Frazer Committee at Sears included men in their late thirties and mid-forties. At Jersey, the Board was older, and it seems significant that the changes there could not really be carried out until the old management was retired and replaced by an almost completely new set of general officers. Moreover, at Sears, du Pont, and General Motors, the organizational changes all came shortly after a sweeping change in top management.

The experience of these innovating firms suggests, then, that organizational changes were most effectively undertaken by men who had not yet identified themselves with one certain pattern or role of action. A redefinition of relationships within the corporate society — even those that define power over the daily work and future destinies of most of the members of that institution — were relatively easy to formulate. The actions and activities of specific individuals proved harder to alter. New structures and new strategies, too, were best built and carried out by younger executives, who had only recently entered top management, but who had had experience in their company's general business, and whose careers had not been wholly confined to work with that one firm. Conversely, one of the primary reasons structure was slow to follow strategy was that the existing management was unable to change its ways. This was not apparently because they felt that their present positions of power were being challenged. Only for a few executives such as the old refiners at Jersey, does this appear to have been the case. Of course such attitudes are not likely to be revealed in company records. Yet the psychological hazards of adjusting to new ways, new tempos, and new duties seem to have been a more significant block to structural change than a concern for diminished power and prestige.

Sources of Information

In reordering the structure of their institutions, what did the young senior professional administrators with their engineering approach bring to the problems of organization beside their own abundant energy and immediate experience? At Jersey and General Motors, the answer seems to have been — very little. Sloan's "Organization Study" was an answer to pressing problems based on his own experience at Hyatt and United Motors. There is nothing in the available evidence to suggest that he borrowed from outside.

Jersey actually did have some direct experience with "the scientific management movement." In 1922, Teagle and the Board hired F. A. Parkhurst, one of the active practitioners of Taylor's methods, to introduce "the system," including time and motion studies, bonuses, and so forth, at the Bayway Refinery.[14] After two years, Teagle decided to drop Parkhurst, largely because of the resistance of the workers. Some of Parkhurst's plans were retained at the great refinery, but the work in scientific management done there appears to have had absolutely no impact on the structural changes that began at Jersey in 1925. Since Teagle did not consider Jersey's difficulties to be organizational, neither he nor, for that matter, his more organization-minded executives like Clark or Howard saw any connection between reorganizing a plant and reshaping the structure of the entire corporation.

For the same reasons, Teagle and his associates appear to have made no use of the existing literature on organization. By the mid-1920's, a great deal was being written on the problems of structure in such periodicals as *Management and Administration* and in the proceedings of the American Management Association, as well as in engineering journals and books. While there was very little specifically on the decentralized type of structure until the publication of the articles by General Motors executives in the spring of 1924 and not really until after Donaldson Brown's article on "Decentralized Operations and Responsibilities with Coordinated Control" in 1927, much information did exist on the organization of individual functional departments.[15] What evidence still exists, all indicates that Teagle and his associates considered most of Jersey's problems to be unique and ones with which outsiders could provide little help.

At du Pont and Sears, there was much more awareness of outside experience, examples, and ideas. The men involved in the re-creation of the du Pont Company in 1903 had had broad experience in the steel, electrical, and mining, as well as explosives, industries. This was undoubtedly one reason why the initial structure at du Pont is such a good example of the organizational form of that period and of an adaptive response to new needs and challenges. The Haskell Committee, in its reorganization plan of 1919, made a careful study of the practices of other companies. Its report also showed a knowledge of the terms and ideas then current in the literature on organizational theory and practice, as spelled out by such writers as Going, Kimball, Hugo Diemer, Lewis H. Haney, Edward D. Jones, A. W. Shaw, and Russell Robb.[16] But both theory and practice only helped to convince the Haskell Committee of the great value of their existing organizational structure.

The later subcommittee's report on "Tonnage versus Merchandising Sales," which presented the first suggestion for a radically new type of structure in du Pont, made no explicit statement of organizational principles. Like Sloan's "Organization Study" at General Motors, it concentrated on the immediate matters at hand. The Committee members did make a wide study of the experience of other firms, but found this of little value since the other companies that were centralized were not so diversified as was du Pont. They did find support for their contention that the basic weakness at du Pont was a lack of responsibility for profit, although they learned little to aid them in setting up a new structure to correct this fault.

The organization builders at Sears drew from an administrative experience that was broader than that tapped by those in the other three companies. In fact, not only did half the members of the Frazer Committee have most of their business experience outside of Sears but also outside the mass-marketing industries. And this was undoubtedly one cause for the continuing problems. Frazer was one of the best-known experts on organization of his day. His efforts had helped in reshaping public bodies — universities and state and municipal governments. Sears was the most important enterprise, he told Wood, that he had ever investigated. Yet, while his report was concise, clear, and specific, developing in many ways an admirable set of recommendations, it did put cutting costs ahead of perfecting Sears's primary aim, the volume sale of merchandise. Here where the relations were clear, the experiences of public and military organizations proved of little specific relevance to the problems of big business.

Actually the management of a private business enterprise and that of a public civil or military organization are fundamentally different. They are, of course, all bureaucracies in Max Weber's sense of the word — hierarchies manned by professional officers — and so have features common to that social form. But the business enterprise has different objectives and functions and far more clear-cut criteria for failure and success. The primary objective of an enterprise is to show a return on investment by the production and sale of goods and services. The continuing profit-and-loss record of a firm provides a fairly precise and objective criterion of its performance and that of its operating divisions and departments. Except in time of war, such impersonal, clear-cut standards for the performance of managers of a military corps or a government bureau are hard to find. Performance in these enterprises, and with it promotion and changes in personnel, must be judged by more subjective standards. Moreover, since these public units do not usually generate the capital to finance their existing and future activities, the legislature provides the funds and appoints the top personnel. Their managers depend far more on the legislature than the executives of an industrial enterprise depend on the board of directors, which theoretically has the same sort of control. The greatest concern of legislators and their advisors has normally been to keep costs as low as possible, as Frazer's attitude suggests. They tend to care not so much for what the unit's staff can do, but rather how little it can do and still meet minimum requirements.

If Frazer's experience in government reorganization provided little of value in reshaping Sears's structure, he might have learned something from the work of Sloan, Bradley, and Brown. These men had all written articles for leading management journals and had delivered papers before the American Management Association on their work at General Motors. Frazer could hardly have avoided knowing about them. If he did read or listen to them, it is significant that he saw no connection whatsoever between his problems and those solved earlier at General Motors and du Pont. Some eighteen years later, when Sears again called in an organization consultant, the reverse was true. The consultants in 1947 kept making too many general comparisons with the decentralized model as worked out at General Motors and du Pont without taking sufficiently into account the differences between Sears's needs and those of the multi-industry automobile and chemical companies.

A comparative analysis of the four enterprises that first created the multidivision structure helps to document the general propositions outlined in the introduction. The conditions for change which led to the adoption of the multidivisional structure came only after an enterprise had expanded its activities into new lines of business or continued its growth on a national or more usually world-wide scale. The new structure met the administrative needs thereby created primarily because it gave to the senior executives who were responsible for the enterprise's health and growth more time and information and a psychological commitment to concentrate effectively on the growing number of strategic decisions resulting from the expansion. And second, because it permitted the executives who were charged with keeping their organization running smoothly to concentrate on their functional activties and on coordinating the flow of goods through these departments to the changing market demand for a single major product line or region.

Delays in initiating or completing the new structure usually resulted from the failure of the senior executives to appreciate the administrative needs created by expansion into new markets. This failure reflected the training and temperament of the individuals involved. Sometimes they were unaware that the problems might be administrative rather than just marketing, finance, manufacturing, or other primarily economic problems. At other times they became too enmeshed in day-to-day operating activities to realize that new needs had arisen or to give proper attention to the building of a structure to meet these needs. Often, it was the rapid increase in the number of administrative decisions resulting from the strategy of expansion that caused the top executives to bog down in tactical detail. This comparative analysis also stresses the fact that men long accustomed to handling administrative matters in one way had difficulty in devising new administrative structures. On the other hand, engineering training, a rational, analytical approach to problems of management, comparative youth, and a relatively short incumbency in any one position, all helped business executives to appreciate the new needs and to become organizational innovators.

7 THE SPREAD OF THE MULTI-DIVISIONAL STRUCTURE

THE comparative analysis of organizational innovation in four pioneers in modern management has made possible a relatively objective evaluation of the performance of executives carrying out some of the most difficult and most important of modern administrative tasks. It suggested how and why some fulfilled their entrepreneurial duties more effectively than others. In providing a more precise evaluation of administration and administrators in these four companies, the analysis also supplied information on the changing methods of management and control in the large American corporation, including such developments as the growth of the line-and-staff concept, the expansion of staff functions, the advances in informational and statistical techniques, and, most important of all, the building of the different offices at the different levels of industrial administration.

The comparison of the administrative experiences of four huge companies based on their internal records tells more about broad changes in the structure of American industrial enterprises than it does about changes in their strategy. The four clearly borrowed from others in building their early structures, and others borrowed from them when they set up the new multidivisional form. But did others come to the new structure for the same reasons as did du Pont, General Motors, Jersey Standard, and Sears? Did structural changes follow strategic ones? Did other firms develop new strategies to assure more efficient and profitable use of their resources? If so, why did they feel the need to turn their resources to new uses? Finally, were executive training and personality significant to the timing and methods of both strategic and structural adjustment? These questions about changing strategy and its impact on administrative structure can be answered only by comparing the experience of the four innovators in the modern "decentralized" form with that of many other great industrial corporations.

This comparison can probably be carried out most efficiently by observing the spread of the new structure through American industry;

that is, by learning which companies adopted and which failed to take on the new structure, and why they have accepted or rejected it. Such a broad comparison can help clarify the relation of structure to strategy and of strategy to the changing nature of the American economy, and so can provide clues to the reasons for the growth of the industrial enterprise in the United States and for the ways in which it has been managed. It can help provide explanations for the patterns of institutional growth and administration which were so briefly outlined in Chapter 1.

This investigation into the spread of the multidivisional structure has relied on the administrative experience of the seventy largest companies listed in Table 2. Besides these seventy, some other important firms on which information was immediately available were also considered. Together they form a sample of large industrial enterprises which seems to be broad as well as neutral. The selection of another set of from 70 to 100 large companies should not greatly alter the basic patterns indicated by the companies studied here, for this latter group includes the leading enterprises in many of the most important American industries. Even if 150 or 200 companies could be examined, the results would be much the same. Also, as a brief review of the 500 largest industrials listed in *Fortune* indicated, if the selection of the 70 largest had been for 1959 instead of for 1948, the major difference would have been the inclusion of more firms that had diversified and decentralized. The review of the administrative history of these many large industrials can touch on the story of the individual companies in only the briefest way. More detailed study and analysis of their experience will certainly modify, but should not basically alter, the underlying pattern shown here as to the ways in which great American industrial corporations have grown and are managed.

A comparative analysis of the adoption of or failure to adopt the new multidivisional form can best be made by grouping the enterprises by industries and by keeping the definition of the multidivisional structure a fairly loose one. An enterprise can be said to have adopted the new form if it came to have a general office with executives whose primary tasks were general rather than functional and if it also had at least two major multidepartmental, relatively autonomous divisions. In some cases, the structure of an enterprise was in 1960 still in need of clear definition. Where this was the case, the direction in which the structure had been moving became critical for understanding the meaning of the enterprise's administrative history. Thus two companies could have developed what appears to be much the same type of mixed or bastard form, but if one had been clearly moving toward a more decentralized, multidivisional structure and the other to a more centralized, functionally departmentalized organization, the significance of the two would clearly differ. Again, the mixed form might have become a permanent one. It is possible, though still rare, for a company to devise a clear-cut, rationally defined structure by which the general office supervises both the single-function and multifunction operating units.

The reason for grouping these enterprises by industries is that those within the same industry normally had to face similar external situations and so could be expected to have met comparable administrative problems and needs. As Table 2 indicates, the seventy companies can be conveniently grouped into nine industrial categories, and for the purposes of this chapter, these nine categories fall into three larger groups. In some industries, such as steel and nonferrous materials, very few firms adopted any variation of the new form. In others, like those that process agricultural products, rubber, and petroleum, some firms accepted the multidivisional structure and others did not. While in a third group, consisting of the electrical (including electronics), power machinery (including automobiles), and chemical industries, nearly all the leading enterprises have turned to it. An examination of the first group reveals the economic conditions that made for little strategic and structural change and so encouraged relative institutional stability and administrative simplicity. The study of the second set of industries shows why administrative needs may vary between enterprises within a single industry. Finally, an analysis of the changes in the third group helps broaden the interpretations developed in the four case studies both as to the nature of the industrial complexity which brought organizational change and, to a lesser extent, the internal factors which inhibited the adjustment to the new needs.

Industries Not Accepting the New Structure

As suggested above, among the more than seventy companies studied, those that were not administering their resources through the new multidivisional structure by 1960 were concentrated in the metals and materials industries. Of these, the copper and nickel companies had paid the least attention to structure. And what thought had been given to organization by executives in such integrated enterprises had turned to tightening their functionally departmentalized structures. The steel companies, on the other hand, had devoted more thought to the lines of authority and communication, and in almost every case this concern had brought increasing centralization. For the makers of other materials, the trend had been the other way. The leading aluminum company, although under pressures for decentralization, retained its old functionally departmentalized form, which has become extremely elaborate and complex. Of the metals and materials firms listed, all three — American Can, International Paper, and Pittsburgh Plate Glass — had accepted the new decentralized, multidivisional form by 1960.

The structural form taken by these enterprises has been closely related to the nature of their markets. As the types of customers became more numerous, the structure tended to become more intricate and more systematized. The copper and nickel companies have concentrated on making semifinished sheets, rods, wire, and extrusions for a relatively few large customers. The steel manufacturers have sold a greater variety of sheet, shapes, and forms to a much larger number of buyers. They have manufactured many standardized products, ahead of specific orders. Also they carry special lines for particular markets like the petroleum industry. The Aluminum Company of America sells to a still wider variety of industries than the steel firms, and has even reached the mass consumer market through its kitchenware line. The other three enterprises in this group have had to satisfy a still larger and more disparate set of customers. In most cases such marketing differences appear to have had a greater effect on the structure of these enterprises than have either differences in their industrial technology or the personalities of their executives.

Copper and Nickel

In the copper, nickel, and zinc industries, the same companies have handled since the early years of the century the greater part of the industry's output in much the same way. Of the nonferrous metals industries, only aluminum has developed new enterprises. Copper's "Big Four" — American Smelting & Refining, Anaconda, Kennecott Copper, and Phelps Dodge — still produce the greatest share of the nation's copper and zinc; while International Nickel, formed in 1902, has a practical monopoly of the free world's nickel supply.[1] Again excepting aluminum, the leaders in the nonferrous metals industries have concentrated on mining, smelting, and refining basic metals. During the 1920's and 1930's, however, all but International Nickel purchased control of fabricating subsidiaries, making sheets, rods, wire, and tubes.[2] By 1950 these subsidiaries manufactured an estimated 65 per cent of the nation's refined copper. As the "Big Four" produced close to 90 per cent of this copper, they also sold to outside fabricators.

Of these integrated firms, two, Kennecott and International Nickel, have a larger investment in mining than in processing. All have small sales organizations to market ore and blister and refined copper to middlemen or to a relatively few large users including their own fabricating subsidiaries. Since orders for these undifferentiated items come in by telephone and telegraph, much of the work of the sales department can be handled by a few men. The fabricating subsidiaries producing relatively few types of wires, cables, rods, and so forth, for industrial customers have somewhat larger sales departments. Since the refining and smelting capacity of the copper companies, except for Kennecott, has been greater than could be supplied by copper ore from their own mines, they sell little ore and purchase a sizable amount of it from outsiders. Yet the purchasing organization has needed to be only a little larger than the sales office. Also, because smelting has been carried on close to the mines, the volume of goods transported has not been large enough to warrant the construction of their own transportation facilities.

Because the copper companies are mining and processing enterprises producing a relatively few types of products for a well-defined market, they have been under less pressure to concern themselves with organizational matters. Their only administrative challenges have been in the improvement of the administrative control of the departmental headquarters and the central office. For standardized, undifferentiated products, the scheduling of production has remained relatively simple. Because these firms have had fewer transportation and storage needs, they have not felt impelled to coordinate product flow as did the oil or steel companies. So, more than most of the enterprises studied here, they have relied on day-to-day fluctuations in prices rather than on forecasts and market analyses to determine when and in what quantities to obtain raw materials and produce their goods.

At both Anaconda and Phelps Dodge, the central office administration of functional activities has been handled informally. Since World War I, the over-all policy making at Anaconda was carried out in weekly meetings of the heads of the functional subsidiaries. Cornelius F. Kelley, as President and Chairman of the Board, dominated the company's affairs from 1918 until 1955, and he gave little thought to building at the central office such staff departments as engineering, research, labor, or public relations, to better the coordination between the functional units or to improve accounting and other financial and administrative data. Nor have the managers at Phelps Dodge attempted to build a sizable central office for the administration of their functional activities.

At American Smelting and Refining and at Kennecott Copper, structure has received more attention. Of the "Big Four," American Smelting and Refining has had the smallest investment in mining, but processes more zinc, lead, and other metals beside copper than do its major competitors. Its central office has long included a vice-president in charge of each of the major functions — mining, smelting and refining, sales, purchasing, research, and finance — as well as a small legal and metallurgical staff. The company, however, has made little effort to extend the control of the central office to include the administration of its fabricating subsidiaries, which it is said, take a relatively small share of its output. However, in the 1930's, it entered the processing of a variety of nonferrous metals from scrap. Because both the purchasing and marketing of these materials were quite different from its primary operations, the company came to form a separate autonomous unit called Federated Metals. However, this venture has not proved very successful, in part because its activities differ from the rest of the larger organization. So, senior executives have seriously considered abandoning this business, which, they feel, has not effectively used its major resources in men, money, and materials nor fitted into the centralized structure.

The Kennecott story has been one of increasing centralized administrative control. Until the retirement in 1933 of Stephen Birch — the man who had, with the backing of the Guggenheims, built this great copper-mining empire — Kennecott was managed as informally as Anaconda and Phelps Dodge have been for so long. Birch's successor, E. T. Stannard, instituted more formal administrative control over mining, smelting, and refining and over the sales and fabricating units by departmentalizing their activities. Stannard also built up the central purchasing and traffic department. After his death in 1949, his successor, Charles Cox, expanded the activities of the central office by adding engineering, public relations, and labor relations staff departments and by enlarging the research organization. Within the mining and fabricating organizations, he instituted more of a line-and-staff structure in order to delegate more authority and responsibility to the field activities. He also concentrated on the development of better cost and performance information in all of the operating departments. Assisted by the heads of the mining, processing, and fabricating units, Cox, with two executive assistants, appraised the activities and made policy for the company as a whole.

Because of the simplicity of operation and the lack of major technological and market changes, administrative decisions in the copper and nickel enterprises have become almost entirely operational ones. Over time, the decisions dealing with the administration of the different functional activities and the coordination of the flow through the functions with the market demand have become quite routinized. Even relatively minor strategic decisions, such as the building of new plants and purchasing of new mining properties, come only occasionally. In fact, administrative needs have not been powerful enough to impel the long-established veteran managements at Anaconda and Phelps Dodge to develop more systematic and rational controls over their functional activities. However, Anaconda recently made a critically important strategic decision to move into the aluminum business. Such a step should certainly create a need for administrative reorganization at that copper company if the experience of the Aluminum Company of America is any criterion.

Administrative experience in the nickel industry has paralleled that of copper. Nickel differs from copper in that its market is smaller and more specialized, and ores come largely from one area in central Canada. Also the nickel industry has been dominated by monopoly rather than oligopoly, and the leading enterprise, International Nickel, has long had a policy of not producing rolled or fabricated goods. Its only rolling mill in America was set up in 1920 to produce rolled bars and sheets of a newly invented metal, Monel. Nickel has been used primarily to make steel alloys or to form such new metals as Monel. Before World War I these alloys and metals were used largely in warships, guns, and other armaments. After the war the automobile, chemical, and electrical industries became the major market. At all times the nickel miners and refiners have sold their products to relatively few customers for further processing.

The International Nickel Company, which became the International Nickel Company of Canada, Ltd. in 1916, began as a combination in 1902. Although its senior executives had worked out an embryonic functional structure by World War I, they did not give serious attention to organization until the postwar depression brought a sharp decline in the demand for nickel. Then a new set of administrators, headed by Robert C. Stanley, a graduate of Stevens Institute of Technology and the Columbia School of Mines, concentrated on cutting costs, improving old and developing new products, and in building a more systematic organizational structure. The resulting centralized, functionally departmentalized organization included a new research and development department that had a technical service unit similar to the one at du Pont and an enlarged sales department that expanded its advertising activities and its marketing areas. At the same time the mining department set up a section devoted to systematic exploration for ores. In 1928 International Nickel's merger with the Mond Nickel Company, Ltd., gave the new combination a virtual monopoly of the industry. Administrative consolidation of these two enterprises came slowly, with the first steps being taken in 1936 and with further centralization in the 1950's.

Steel

In steel, production techniques as well as marketing requirements demanded tight administrative control. Unlike copper and nickel production, steelmaking has long been a closely integrated activity with the refining of ores, the conversion of iron to steel, and the fabrication of steel into semifinished products all being done at the same plant. The big integrated steel works produce a vastly greater amount of a larger variety of products for more types of industries and businesses than do the copper smelters, refineries, and fabricating mills. Not only have the steel companies fashioned rails, structures, plates, sheets, strip, tin plate, bar, rods, nails, wire, pipes, and tubes to the specifications of individual customers for decades, but they have also turned out most of these products in standardized form and in large volume ahead of orders. Such "warehouse stocks" have gone to three sets of customers. Industrial, transportation, and commercial concerns have taken the largest share directly. Some stocks (particularly nails, fencing, pipe, and electrical conduit) went to wholesalers and other large middlemen, while the rest went to meet the more special needs of the oil industry.[3] Finally, the steel companies sold chemicals and by-products of their coke operations to other producers for further processing. Thus the much greater volume of goods and a much larger number of customers, as well as the highly integrated production, have made the scheduling of operations and the coordination of the functional activities far more complicated in steel than in copper enterprises. Also, the production of standard fabricated items on a volume basis ahead of orders has created more of a need to forecast and analyze the future market in order to integrate the activities of the various parts of the enterprise to that market.

As a result of these necessities, most large steel enterprises have long been administered through centralized, functionally departmentalized structures. Of the industry's "Big Eight," five — Bethlehem, Republic, Jones & Laughlin, Inland, and Youngstown — have had for many years such a form. Both Bethlehem and Republic started as combinations early in the century. Before long they consolidated their constituent firms into a single, multidepartmental structure, and as they expanded in later years through purchases, they also placed the newly acquired units within the same basic centralized organization. Armco, National Steel, and United States Steel have been less centralized and have had structures nearer the multidivisional form. Yet even in these companies the trend has been toward centralization rather than decentralization, even though their sales, assets, and volume of output have grown rapidly.

Jones & Laughlin, whose organization was simplified after a careful study in 1951, provides an excellent example of the type of centralized, functionally departmentalized structure with its clear line-and-staff distinctions that is used by leading steel companies. The administrative organizations of Bethlehem, Republic, Inland, and Youngstown Sheet & Tube differ from that of Jones & Laughlin only in detail, and the variations from the standard multidepartmental model come largely from differences in marketing the different types of products.[4] Jones & Laughlin has a major department, headed by a general manager, for ore and quarries and in it an office for exploration. Another general manager supervises coal operations and a third, traffic and transportation. The Vice-President and Assistant Vice-President of the Production Department have administrative control over these general managers as well as over the company's three great steelworks and two staff departments — construction and maintenance, and plant protection.

The Sales Department has an even more complex structure. There are district offices in the field. Headquarters is subdivided with sections for different products and also includes two staff units, commercial research and the sales service office.[5] The latter performs much the same function as did the Technical Division in the old du Pont Company's Sales Department. The office in the Sales Department's headquarters that is responsible for supplying the oil industry with pipe, tubing, drill rods, and similar equipment has more autonomy than the other product units in the same department, for, in order to have a full line of equipment for oil producers, it markets goods made outside of the company as well as inside. Its salesmen, however, work out of the company's branch offices. The warehousing or retailing unit that markets standard items, on the other hand, has its own distributing organization with its own district offices and warehouses. The final functional activity, finance, is divided between the Treasurer's Department and a staff unit, the Accounting Department.

To help administer these functional departments, to coordinate their policies, and to provide them with special assistance, the central office at Jones & Laughlin has developed a large number of staff units including engineering, research, industrial relations, accounting, and general services. The last has a section for organization planning. As is true in most centralized firms, the heads of the departments and the President have become the unit responsible for over-all administration. This central office group has based its decisions on information coming from the staff departments and the financial offices as well as from the line departments themselves.

Beside the major functional departments, there are four smaller autonomous divisions whose managers handle manufacturing as well as sales. Three of them make special products, wire rope, electricweld tube, and containers, and report to a Vice-President in charge of Special Products. A fourth autonomous unit with its own Vice-President is the Stainless and Strip Division, which was purchased by the company in 1948. The existence of these multifunction divisions might indicate that Jones & Laughlin would, in time, turn to a fully decentralized, multidivisional structure. Yet, the available evidence suggests that such a step is unlikely. A large share of Jones & Laughlin's business is still from job orders made to customers' particular specifications calling for intricate centralized scheduling and allocation of the orders to the mills. Moreover, because the ore supply comes primarily from the Lake Superior region, it is cut off during the winter months and careful scheduling of raw materials is required. The managers I talked with at Jones & Laughlin thought the activities of the Stainless and Strip Division would soon be incorporated into those of the other departments, and they expect that the smaller units selling to separate markets will also be integrated into the larger structure. Their view of the proper organization for their company today is strikingly similar to that of Harry Haskell for the du Pont Company in 1919.

The trend towards centralization, which still seems to be going on at Jones & Laughlin, is indicated more clearly by the experience of National Steel and the greatest steel producer of them all, the United States Steel Corporation. The history of the Steel Corporation for the past sixty years has been one of steadily increasing centralization.[6] During the first decades of its existence, United States Steel included many very autonomous, operating divisions that were loosely administered from a small financial office at 71 Broadway in New York City. The holding company's major achievement during its early years was to obtain uniform accounting information from its subsidiaries. In the second decade of its history, the parent company's activities were enlarged. A Vice-President in charge of Purchasing was appointed, and also one for engineering. The task of the first of these officers was to supply ores from foreign sources and then to coordinate their use with the output of the Oliver Mining Company, the Steel Corporation's ore-producing subsidiary. This office began to estimate the ore necessary to meet the operating subsidiaries' production plans, but apparently made no attempt to relate these to estimated long-term market demand. The coordination of product flow remained in the hands of the individual subsidiaries that had little contact with one another. The primary job for the Vice-President in charge of Engineering came to be the reviewing of appropriations and the provision of more systematic information for the current and future allocation of the company's resources. Finally, a third parent-office executive was appointed to maintain contact with major customers. Nevertheless, even though the offices at 71 Broadway were somewhat enlarged, they did not yet have coordinating, appraising, and planning duties comparable with those set up at General Motors and Jersey Standard in the 1920's. United States Steel remained administratively a combination or federation.

The creation of a true general office came as part of the massive reorganization of the Steel Corporation engineered by Myron C. Taylor after he became head of the corporation following Gary's death in 1927. This reorganization, started in a tentative way in 1929 and not completed until 1937, was as thoroughgoing as the changes of 1902 and 1903 were at du Pont. The facilities, activities, and administrative structures of the operating subsidiaries were radically altered and re-formed. New plants and offices were built, others combined, and still others were abandoned.

The major change in over-all administration was the formation of a large general staff very similar to the one Sloan had created earlier at General Motors. The advisory departments with headquarters in Pittsburgh included those for operations, sales, industrial relations, research and metallurgy, and traffic. Each was headed by a Vice-President. The older parent-office units for raw materials, sales, and finance continued on as advisory staff offices. A Production Planning Department was established to furnish the information and channels of communication to guide the flow of product through the company's several subsidiaries. Because the corporation's capacity for making finished products was larger than its steel-producing capacity, this staff planning organization was particularly valuable for coordination of the buying and making of ingots with the needs of the fabricating mills. At the same time, Taylor and his assistants instituted a whole new system of cost accounting and placed forecasting on a more definite and permanent basis. Over-all policy making and appraisal came to be handled by a few full-time executives who divided their time between New York and Pittsburgh. They included Benjamin R. Fairless, Edward R. Stettinius, Jr., and Enders M. Vorhees. Although Stettinius had served in the General Motors general office before coming to United States Steel, Vorhees — a highly rational business school graduate — appears to have been the executive most responsible for putting the new structure into operation.

This multidivisional form continued until 1950, when the corporation developed a structure that resembled more closely the centralized, functionally departmentalized type. In that year, two-thirds of the corporation's steelmaking activities were consolidated into what became known as Central Operations. All activities administered by Central Operations were departmentalized along functional lines. At the same time, this central office began to supervise more closely the functional activities remaining in the multidepartmental divisions that were not directly included within Central Operations. Thus a single set of Executive Vice-Presidents became to a large extent responsible for the administration of their different functions in every part of the corporation. The Executive Vice-President in charge of Production had under him Vice-Presidents for coal, steel, and fabricating in Central Operations, an administrative Vice-President who kept in close contact with Columbia-Geneva (a far western), Tennessee Coal and Iron (the southern), and a third regional division, and another administrative Vice-President to supervise the fabricating divisions including American Steel & Wire, American Bridge, National Tube, and Atlas Cement. The Executive Vice-President in charge of sales had under his command a Vice-President for Central Operations Sales, another who handled the company's warehousing organization and its units supplying the petroleum industry, and a third who had charge of such staff offices as commercial research and sales development and who also maintained close contact with the sales units of the subsidiaries operating outside of Central Operations. The other Executive Vice-Presidents for functional activities — those for Engineering, Personnel Services, Raw Materials, Accounting, and the one for overseas operations — also appear to have a strong voice for carrying out these activities throughout the whole corporation. Collectively, these Executive Vice-Presidents with the President and Chairman of the Board form the Operating Policy Committee that is responsible for over-all appraisal and policy planning. Thus over the years there has been a growing centralization of authority and responsibility at United States Steel, with the functional department becoming the major operating unit. Although a number of integrated divisions still exist, they have been steadily losing their autonomy or freedom of action. The structure of United States Steel is becoming more like that of the du Pont Company prior to 1921 than, as it was before 1950, like that of General Motors or du Pont after 1921.

National Steel, formed in 1929 as a combination of two long-established firms, Weirton Steel Company and the Hanna Iron Ore Company, with the newer Great Lakes Steel Corporation, has recently been moving in the same direction as its largest competitor.[7] It long remained a loose federation whose over-all administration was carried out by its creator, Ernest T. Weir, assisted by the heads of the other two constituent firms and a very small staff. Since 1954 it has consolidated and set up a functionally departmentalized structure that certainly seems as centralized as that of Jones & Laughlin. The sales departments of Weirton and Great Lakes have been combined. A new corporate Research and Development Department has been created. National Steel's central office includes Vice-Presidents in charge of Sales, of Engineering, and of Research. Only manufacturing has not been put under a fully centralized control. However, one autonomous unit, the Stran-Steel Corporation, continues to manufacture and market fabricated specialities for the building and transportation industries. And the old Hanna Furnace Corporation, makers of merchant pig iron, also retains its autonomy.

Armco Steel has not yet moved as far towards centralization as National and United States Steel.[8] Until 1954, its three major operating units were administered as autonomous divisions. These included its major steelmaking operations centered in Ohio, the Sheffield Steel Corporation (largest steelmaker in the Southwest), and a division which manufactured and sold culverts and drainage structures. In that year, its over-all executive offices were enlarged by increasing the staff to include planning and development, research, purchasing, and public and "personal" relations sections. Policy, however, continued to be made by the heads of the leading functional departments together with the President and Chairman of the Board. Whether this step for greater over-all administrative control, like the earlier changes at United States Steel, is one toward further centralization, only time can tell. At the moment, however, Armco's structure is closer to the standard multidivisional type than is that of any of the other metal companies studied here. Its senior officers, however, have functional operating responsibilities and are not general executives like those who guide the fortunes of du Pont, General Motors, Jersey Standard, and even Sears.

Certainly the basic trend in steel has been toward centralization. The complex demands of scheduling and of coordinating departments require close centralized administrative supervision if the great integrated mills, the mines, ore boats, and distributing facilities are to be operated at a fairly even capacity and if loss and waste are to be avoided by piling up inventory in one department or another or through having temporarily idle facilities and other resources. The continuance and growth of the multidepartmental division may have been checked by the fact that the demands of a single market, whether it is in one industry or one region, is not enough to keep a single great mill operating at full capacity. Therefore such mills must draw on the larger national market. Yet it would seem that there are industrial or regional markets, such as the oil industry or the Far West or Southwest, large and diverse enough to take the entire output of a single manufacturing unit. Such markets would mean that the multidepartmental divisions, such as those still functioning at Jones & Laughlin, and United States Steel, Armco, could continue to be operated profitably as autonomous units. Nevertheless, the historical experience at National and United States Steel and the attitudes expressed at Jones & Laughlin indicate clearly that the trend is in the other direction.

If the market, apparently, has not been different enough to bring about the growth of autonomous, integrated divisions, neither have strategic decisions been numerous or complex enough to demand the building of a general administrative office with general executives and staff specialists. The selling of steel as well as the obtaining of ore and its production and fabrication still follows a fairly long-established routine pattern. Decisions about the building of new plants, the opening of new markets, the development of new processes have been so few as to permit senior executives to concentrate on tactics. Most important of all, the production and marketing facilities for ore and semifinished and even finished products cannot be easily transferred to the production and marketing of new and different products. Therefore, the strategy of diversification with its inevitable increase in long-range decision making has not been a tempting one in the expansion of the steel industry.

Aluminum

The largest of the aluminum companies has been under more pressure to decentralize than the leading steel firms. As its markets have been more diverse and have changed more rapidly than those of the steel companies, its executives have had to make both more tactical and more strategic decisions. The Aluminum Company of America (Alcoa) has long had far more administrative complexities and challenges than the other nonferrous enterprises studied here because, from the very start, a much larger portion of its resources was committed to the making and selling of fabricated forms and shapes for many industries and even for the housewife and other final consumers. Alcoa, originally called the Pittsburgh Reduction Co., succeeded in 1888 in commercializing the new metal under the process invented in 1886 by Charles M. Hall.[9] It soon moved into the making and marketing of finished products in order to develop demands for this new metal. Then as demand increased, it integrated backward, obtaining bauxite mines, ore ships, and warehouses. Before World War I, it had become not only an integrated enterprise but the only one in the industry. Not until the sale after World War II of government plants to other aluminum enterprises did Alcoa have to meet competition of other integrated firms. Among its new products, Alcoa early developed its kitchenware line, and thus was the only metals firm studied that sold mass consumer products. Its major growth, however, came from great new industries, particularly automobile, airplane, and missile. By the 1920's, the resources of this rapidly growing enterprise were administered through a centralized, departmentalized structure. As expansion continued in all of its functional activities, Alcoa came to be managed by one of the biggest and most elaborate central offices of any American industrial enterprise.

The Alcoa structure of 1960 is the du Pont structure of 1919 writ large. At the central office, each of three Executive Vice-Presidents has charge of a group of several functional departments. One supervises the legal and financial activities, including the Treasurer's, Comptroller's, Legal, and Secretary's offices, all of which except the last are headed by Vice-Presidents. Under the Second Vice-President come the Vice-Presidents in charge of Raw Materials, of Smelting and Fabricating, of Engineering, of Purchasing, of Personnel and Industrial Relations. As was true of the du Pont Company before 1921, so today most Vice-Presidents in Alcoa have a General Manager to administer day-to-day operations. A key office within this second group is the Production Planning Division, responsible for the scheduling of all orders through the mills. It helps to coordinate, much as Jersey's Coordination Department, the rate and amount of product flow through a large industrial complex. Orders from the Sales Department come to this office, where they are allocated to one of the company's twenty-four fabricating works. The Production Planning Division also provides information that is used to determine schedules for the production and transportation of bauxite and other raw materials.

The Third Executive Vice-President has over-all responsibility for the Sales Department, as well as the activities of the International Division and the Public Relations and Advertising Department. The organization of the Sales Department is geared to four major phases of the company's sales efforts: market planning, industry sales, product sales, and direct or field sales. The fact that these distinct areas are reflected in Alcoa's sales organization emphasizes how much more complex the company's marketing activities are than those of the other nonferrous metals industries, such as copper and nickel.

Each of these four sales activities is headed by a Vice-President who reports to the Vice-President and General Sales Manager. The Vice-President in charge of Commercial Research and Market Planning coordinates the work of specialists in gathering information about estimated product volume, types of products, sales manpower, advertising support, and research and development work. He is primarily concerned with evaluating methods of design, processing, and selling of products in relation to the requirements of new and constantly changing market conditions. The second sales Vice-President is in charge of industry sales. He directs the activities of a group of industry sales managers whose objective is to coordinate and stimulate Alcoa's field sales in six broad industry areas: building products, transportation, aircraft and missiles, consumer durable goods, industrial machinery and equipment, and containers and packaging. These categories have evolved over a period of time and have been modified as market conditions changed.

A third Vice-President is in charge of Product Sales. His department consists of a group of Product Managers, one for each of Alcoa's major products — such as ingot, sheet and plate, foil, extrusions, forgings, and castings. Product Managers help to determine prices for their respective products. They also recommend facilities and work closely with the operating department to help coordinate sales and production. A fourth Vice-President administers field sales and distribution. Reporting to him are the twenty-one district Sales Managers and the Manager of Distribution.

Finally, under this same Executive Vice-President is the President of Wear-Ever Aluminum, Inc., an Alcoa sales subsidiary. Wear-Ever is responsible for aluminum utensils, gift ware, and household foil, three of the major products that the company sells directly to the final consumer. Because the market for these products is so different and because the requirements for coordinating product flow and product development are so unlike that of the rest of the enterprise, this sales organization is the only one at Alcoa that incorporates responsibility for both production and sales. The Vice-President in charge of Smelting and Fabricating has some authority over the plants producing these consumer goods, but it is significant that the only semiautonomous, multifunction division at Alcoa is the one that handles its consumer goods business.

Over-all appraisal and planning are carried on at Alcoa by the three Executive Vice-Presidents, the President, the Chairman of the Board, and the Chairmen of the Executive and Finance Committees. All but the last three meet daily and form what might be considered an executive team, but they have no staff of their own to draw on. Central management at Alcoa includes only these top men and the heads of the functional departments. Even personnel, research, and public relations and advertising are considered line rather than central staff organizations. Interdepartmental coordination, except for that carried out by the Product Managers and by the Production Planning Division, has come to be handled through committees. There are currently close to a *hundred* advisory interdepartmental committees. In addition, there are weekly meetings of the company's departmental Vice-Presidents, as well as many intradepartmental meetings. Such departmental and interdepartmental meetings, company executives stress, are aimed at ensuring adequate communication — a vital need that they feel is best provided in this informal way.

Why then has this increasingly diversified and multiproduct enterprise so long retained a centralized, functionally departmentalized structure? Certainly the lines of communication and authority have become increasingly lengthened and criss-crossed, so that the informal lines of authority and responsibility have become probably more significant than the formal ones. Both the nature of the company's product and its market, as well as the attitudes of its senior executives, have played a part in the continuance of the old structure. The present Chairman of the Board and the President are both men with more than 35 years of Alcoa experience. Roy A. Hunt — son of the company's cofounder, for a long time the President and now Chairman of the Executive Committee — still firmly believes, as did Walter Teagle, in the use of personal, informal methods of management. The advantages of such relationships so valuable to a small family firm, he believes, can be carried on in his present vast industrial empire.

But beside Hunt's strong commitment to informal structure, the need for close coordination between the marketing and production activities provides a powerful pressure for continued centralization. A majority of the company's orders, like those of the steel companies, are made to the specifications of other manufacturers. To assure prompt delivery with specifications exactly filled and, at the same time, to keep the various fabricating plants operating at steady capacity require intricate and complex scheduling of orders and product flow. Nevertheless, the building of plants specialized enough to handle a single major market might make possible the placing of marketing, engineering, and manufacturing for a single line within one autonomous division, in much the same way as has already been done for the Wear-Ever division. In any case, a more rational re-formation of the central office on a line-and-staff basis might well cut down the amount of time now required for committee meetings. Diversity at Alcoa could well bring organizational change after the present veteran management retires. On the other hand, the experience of the steel industry makes clear the difficulty of creating autonomous operating divisions where the resources of the enterprise are concentrated in large-scale operations to produce goods on specification for use in other businesses and industries.

Materials

In the various materials industries, the market demands have been dissimilar enough to counterbalance the centralizing imperatives of volume production. Like the metals companies, the three largest enterprises here — American Can, International Paper, and Pittsburgh Plate Glass — have sold primarily to business and industrial markets rather than to the final consumer. All three, however, have produced and marketed a wide variety of goods that have gone to a larger number of business and industrial firms. Also they have placed a larger proportion of their investment in plant, personnel, and equipment in the marketing of finished goods rather than in the procuring and transportation of raw materials.

American Can and International Paper were both turn-of-the-century combinations that soon consolidated into centralized, functionally departmentalized companies, while Pittsburgh Plate Glass, with its relatively specialized product, developed a similar structure after creating its own marketing organization.[10] Because American Can sold its metal containers and canning machinery to the paint and food industries, which included a large number of small enterprises, it kept its manufacturing operations in many scattered and relatively small mills. In this way, it could more easily meet a wide variety of local demands. As a result it decentralized the administration of its operations into multidepartmental, regionally defined divisions. In the 1930's it set up the Atlantic, Central, Pacific, and Canadian divisions. Even after the company began to move into the making of paper as well as metal containers, this structure served it well. However, as the rate of growth of the metal container business dropped off, and competition as well as costs of materials and labor increased, this company decided to move into the making of paper and plastic containers on a large scale. There it could put its resources, particularly its surplus funds and trained personnel, to more profitable use. Purchases of plastic and paper companies led in 1957 to the formation of three product divisions, with the older metal container organization making up a fourth. The general office was enlarged to include more staff specialists and general executives. So with diversification, a multidivisional structure based on regional boundaries was transformed into one based on product lines.

In the 1920's, International Paper, a combination formed in 1898 which soon consolidated into a centralized, functionally departmentalized structure, decided to apply some of its resources to making heavy kraft paper and bagging as well as to expanding its existing newsprint business. In the late 1930's, it reorganized its structure so that three relatively autonomous multifunction divisions based on both regional and product lines administered its operations. The newsprint division was concentrated in Canada, the kraft division in the South, while the plants and administrative sales offices of the specialties division, which sold to book publishers and other paper users in the Northeast, were located closer to the urban markets.

Unlike International Paper and American Can, Pittsburgh Plate Glass did not come into being through combination, but expanded initially in the 1890's like the meat packers, by building a large marketing organization of warehouses, branch offices, and even retail outlets. Next it integrated backward by producing its own soda ash and other ingredients essential for glass manufacturing. Then, to make fuller use of its marketing resources, the company turned after 1900 to developing a line of paints, brushes, and related items that could be sold through the same channels as window and plate glass. In these years, too, it began to find markets for chemical products based on soda ash. Expansion in the 1920's and again after World War II followed the lines of diversification initially outlined before World War I. More recent growth has brought a clear separation of the company's structure into product divisions and a general office with general executives and staff specialists. By 1960 it had glass, Fiberglas, paint and brush, and chemical divisions. The structure varies from the general pattern only in that while the divisions handle their own industrial sales, the long-established Merchandise Division sells its products to independent dealers, jobbers, distributors, and directly to small customers. Since the chemical unit sells only industrial goods, it has long been almost completely autonomous. Again the market has shaped the structure.

Beside influencing structure, the marketing requirements of these three enterprises encouraged a long-term strategy of expansion which differed from that of the metals companies. Because more of their investment in men, money, and equipment was in marketing facilities than in raw material properties, and even in producing plants and because they had much more extensive distribution and servicing organizations, they were able to transfer their resources more easily into new lines of products when the demand for existing lines fell off. Their senior executives as well as their marketing personnel were well equipped to handle other types of comparable goods. Expansion via diversification was less costly and employed more of their existing resources than would have a similar strategy by metals enterprises. At the same time, markets for the new product lines proved sufficiently different to require these companies to act, as du Pont had acted in 1921, and to set up divisions to coordinate the various functional activities to each new market. For these reasons, the histories of these three enterprises are more similar to those companies considered in the second and even third group of industries studied here than they are to the experiences of the leading enterprises in the basic metals industries.

Industries Partially Accepting the New Structure

The experience of the leading enterprises in the metals and materials industries reinforces the proposition drawn from that of all four of the case studies, namely, that one basic task of a rationally defined structure must be to relate and coordinate the work of the enterprise's different functional activities to market needs and demands. It further indicates that the fewer the markets and the simpler the marketing process, the easier will be the administration and coordination of functional departments. Thus, those companies that sold semifinished products to a relatively few large industrial customers required a comparatively simple type of structure. Those that sold a larger variety of *one major line* of products in much higher volume to a greater number of industries and businesses have consistently centralized the control of their activities through developing and rationalizing their functionally departmentalized structures; while only those making and selling quite *different lines* for increasingly differentiated groups of customers turned to the new multidivisional form. The administrative histories of the largest enterprises in the rubber and petroleum industries and of those that process agricultural products put still greater emphasis on the importance of the market in shaping corporate structure and strategy.

The leading companies in this second cluster of industries (rubber, petroleum, and processing of agricultural products) differed from those in the metals and materials industries in that they sold much more of their output to the mass consumer market than to other business firms for further manufacturing, resale, or other use. And they still so differ. Furthermore, enterprises processing agricultural products grown in the United States purchased their basic materials from a large number of farmers instead of supplying their own raw materials or buying them from a few producers of ore or other primary metals. As long as the large concerns in this second group of industries stuck to one principal line of products for one major set of customers, their administrative problems remained focused, like those of the steel companies, on adjusting and coordinating their activities to the shifting demands of the volume market. So, again like the steel firms, they continued to perfect the centralized, functionally departmentalized structure that nearly all of them had put together after their initial growth. Only when they diversified into new products for new sets of customers or, in the case of the oil companies, when they expanded their activities on a world-wide scale, did the older organizational form prove inadequate. Such expansion into new areas and new products normally came when some of the accumulated resources of these enterprises were not being fully utilized and when their senior executives became convinced that some plant, equipment, personnel, and surplus funds might be more profitably employed in new lines of business.

Processors of Agricultural Products

There are some processers of agricultural products who have not yet attempted to diversify their product line. Although their output has been greatly expanded, their centralized, functionally departmentalized structures, have been little troubled by administrative strains. Others, however, whose expansion came through diversification, turned in every case to the new multidivisional type of administrative structure. These enterprises were able to embark on the new strategy that led to changes in structure because they found it relatively easy to transfer some of their resources to new lines. Either more of their investment was in the marketing than in the producing and purchasing ends of their business, or they handled products like flour that might be still further processed into a number of different end products.

The tobacco industry provides a good illustration of how expansion of volume for the same market raised few new administrative problems. The structures of the three leading tobacco companies — American, R. J. Reynolds, and Liggett & Myers — took their present forms shortly after the Supreme Court decision of 1911 split up the old American Tobacco Company.[11] The present-day centralized, functionally departmentalized structures differ little from the one originally set up for their cigarette business in the 1880's by James B. Duke and his associates. Each of the three companies had its Vice-Presidents in charge of Purchasing, Manufacturing, Marketing, Advertising, and Finance. That advertising has become managed by a separate functional department is easily understood, given the nature of the cigarette market. Although concentrating on marketing, the companies also have a heavy investment in the purchasing and warehouse facilities necessary to re-dry, prize, store, stem, and cure the tobacco leaf.

The only major administrative change in these forms in recent years has been the addition of Assistant Vice-Presidents to handle subactivities of the increasingly expanding business of the growing functional departments. The reorganizations which have occurred here have undoubtedly been more nearly comparable with that of the du Pont Company in 1919 than with that of any others examined in this study. At all three companies, family management has lasted longer than in most large American firms. American Tobacco has among its senior executives two generations of Hills; Liggett & Myers has two of Toms; and the third company, two of Reynolds.

The story is much the same for some of the other enterprises processing agricultural products. For nearly two generations the administration of National Biscuit, American Sugar, United Fruit, and Distillers-Seagrams has changed little.[12] Both American Sugar and United Fruit have had a heavy investment in plantations, shipping, and storage facilities. Although the sugar company has a small sales department, it still relies, much more than do most large enterprises, on brokers and middlemen to handle its marketing. The United Fruit Company has an even greater investment in plantations and steamships. Distillers Corporation-Seagrams, Ltd., a family-managed Canadian maker of whisky which entered the American market after Prohibition, has stayed close to its main lines. It has a centralized, functionally departmentalized structure and is still under family control. In contrast, Schenley Industries has created since the end of Prohibition a much more diversified line of alcoholic beverages and also a line of antibiotics and other pharmaceuticals that used skills and facilities already developed in distilling. While the available data do not make clear the structure of the concern, diversification certainly appears to have brought it toward the multidivisional structure even within its major line. Its beer and pharmaceutical subsidiaries appear to be autonomous. On the other hand, one set of subsidiaries produces the wines and distilled spirits, and another set distributes them.

In the meat-packing industry, only a radical reallocation of an enterprise's resources has brought the attention of administrators to organizational matters and to the adoption of the multidivisional form.[13] Of the two leading packers, Swift has altered little either its structure or its strategy during the past half century, and members of the founder's family have continued to play active parts in the management of the enterprise. At Armour, where the family has had no real voice in administration since 1923, a new set of managers recently turned to a new strategy and a new structure. When these two companies first fashioned their operating organizations more than fifty years ago, they pioneered in the development of systems for coordinating the flow of products from the original purchase of supplies to their sale to the retailer. By 1900, the different branch houses in each concern were telegraphing their orders to the central office in Chicago, which kept in constant touch with its sources of supply at the packing houses and stockyards. The Chicago office then made continuous and almost instantaneous allocations of the output of the packing houses to meet the demands of branches scattered throughout the nation.[14] With this close coordination of supply and demand of their perishable products, the packers did not feel, until very recent years, the need to develop market forecasts and estimates like those worked out at du Pont, General Motors, and Jersey Standard. Also because of their concentration on main product lines, they paid relatively little attention to the by-products, which they administered through their centralized structure, and gave up attempts to market soap, glue, and chemical items on a large scale. Their fertilizer and leather businesses continued to be managed as almost completely independent units with little guidance or administrative control from Chicago.

Not until the 1950's did falling profit margins impel some meat packers to transfer a part of their resources into lines not directly connected with their primary meat and food products and by-products. At Armour, the initial step in this direction was to enlarge the production of soap and allied products. Since the old structure had impeded effective growth, the executives set up a new autonomous division to administer these lines with offices physically separated from the old central office in the stockyards. A major decision to expand chemicals and pharmaceuticals led to an even greater reorganization. The result of a thorough administrative shake-up in 1957 was a multidivisional structure much like that at General Motors. One Group Vice-President was given supervision over the several food divisions, another over the chemical and non-food divisions, and a third over international activities. These Group Vice-Presidents, with the President and Chairman of the Board constituted the company's general executives who, assisted by a general staff, administered the several self-contained operating divisions. At the same time, Regional Vice-Presidents were set up to coordinate purchasing, processing, and sales of different food products. To the outsider, the exact relation between the product divisions and regional offices remains unclear. Possibly the compromise involved in the plan may lead to a conflict like that which occurred at Sears, Roebuck.

Divisions in the chemical group, on the other hand, became fully autonomous. These divisions for fertilizers, pharmaceuticals, industrial chemicals, leather, soaps, and coated abrasives and adhesives are each headed by a Vice-President, and, according to the 1959 annual report, "each is equipped with the staff and managerial functions and facilities to enable it to be a top-flight competitor in its sector of American industry." [15] Since the reorganization, Amour has been placing an increasingly larger share of its funds and personnel into the chemical and pharmaceutical business. Clearly it expects its future growth to be in these lines. In contrast Swift continues to concentrate on its original lines of products, and consequently, its structure has changed little.

The other companies processing agricultural products studied here have diversified more easily than have the meat packers. Although the process of expansion has differed among them, the basic reasons for growth and for structural reorganization appear to have been much the same at General Foods, General Mills, Borden, and Procter & Gamble.[16] All four developed new products initially in order to use existing personnel and facilities more effectively. A fifth, National Dairy Products, was formed in 1928 to give the benefits of economies of scale to several regionally defined dairy-product businesses. At National Dairy, the administrative challenge became the creation of a general office to integrate and supervise the resources of many subsidiaries.

General Foods has concentrated a greater proportion of its resources in marketing than have the meat packers, United Fruit, or American Sugar. In 1928 the Postum Cereal Company, of breakfast cereal fame, merged with a number of other producers of packaged foods, including makers of Jello, chocolate cake, flour, tapioca, salt, syrup, coffee, and sea foods. The purpose of combination was consolidation. A single selling organization would be used in marketing the several product lines, since "the demonstrated economics of selling a line of products through a single sales organization would be increased by the number of items handled by each salesman."[17] To administer the other activities involved in producing such a large line, the company promptly set up a centralized, functionally departmentalized structure. But as the general market expanded in the late 1930's and early 1940's and as General Foods added new lines, like its pioneering Birds Eye quick-freeze goods, the company began to have increasing difficulty in coordinating the purchasing, production, and marketing of its many products through a single functionally defined organization. Before the end of World War II, some of its items, including chocolate, salt, and sea foods, had come to be administered by divisions that controlled both production and sales. Then, a major reorganization in 1946 created sixteen operating divisions grouped under four general executives in a structure quite like that of General Motors. At first the old Sales Division continued to handle those products that could still be efficiently sold through it, much as in the case of Pittsburgh Plate Glass, but in 1955 it too was abolished.[18]

Expansion at General Mills and Borden differed from that at General Foods since the development of new products for new markets came more from the desire to use more fully resources invested in processing and purchasing. But Procter & Gamble's diversification aimed at employing more effectively its marketing as well as producing skills and equipment. General Mills, the successor to James S. Bell's Washburn-Crosby Company, began in the early 1930's to process and distribute prepared breakfast cereals and other packaged foods using the company's flour. In 1937, it carried out a major administrative reorganization, setting up two large autonomous divisions, one for flour and feed and the other for grocery products. In addition, four smaller autonomous divisions were formed, including a Special Commodities Division, which at first manufactured vitamins and soon moved into chemicals. Further diversification into light household appliances so as to use resources developed during World

War II, as well as further expansion in chemicals, led to the building of new divisions after 1945. By that time, General Mills had fashioned a fairly standard multidivisional structure.

Borden's expanded output of condensed and fluid milk led to the creation of an extensive marketing organization before the end of the last century and later to the building of a centralized, multidepartmental structure. In the 1920's and 1930's, diversification into chemicals and animal feeds not only provided new outlets for its basic milk line but also made possible more effective use of existing skills and facilities. By the end of the 1930's, this move had led to the fashioning of a multidivisional form, and some fifteen years later Borden had six product divisions (fluid milk, ice cream, cheese, food products, chemical, and special products) as well as a general office with general executives and staff specialists. In the late 1950's, Borden like Armour put its emphasis on expansion into chemicals.

Procter & Gamble's moves into household tissues, prepared baking mixes, food, toilet goods, and cellulose products came largely after World War II and used even more of its distributing know-how and facilities than of its processing ones. This brought a divisionalizing of the company's activities along product lines in the mid-1950's. In all four food companies, both the administrative problems raised by diversification and their solutions appear to have been very similar to the problems and answers at the du Pont Company.

The organizational necessities of National Dairy Products, on the other hand, were much closer to those of General Motors. The problem was to create a general office and not the product divisions, as in the other food companies. Beginning as a merger of several milk producing and selling companies operating in different areas of the Northeast, National Dairy expanded its activities into somewhat different but allied businesses, such as ice cream and cheese. By the late 1940's, a fairly extensive general office, fashioned to administer many subsidiaries, had come to include staff units for research, quality control, marketing advice, personnel, and management training as well as advertising, purchasing, and accounting. At the same time, more sophisticated statistical and financial controls were developed. The major administrative changes in more recent years have led to the combination of the regionally defined operating subsidiaries into a single larger division for each major product line. Thus, today, National Dairy's primary activities are managed by three divisions — Sealtest (milk), ice cream, and Kraft cheese. In recent years, too, the duties of the general staff and senior officers have been defined more specifically.

Unquestionably, the creation of the multidivisional structure in these enterprises that processed agricultural products sprang only from growth through diversification and not from expansion of volume. Why then have enterprises in flour milling, dairy products, and soap diversified and decentralized while those in tobacco, sugar, and bananas have not? Why has the meat-packing industry moved so hesitantly in this direction? Has not the nature of the company's resources — its equipment and trained personnel — as well as the technological potential of its basic line accounted for the difference? The tobacco companies, the meat packers, United Fruit, and even American Sugar have made huge investments in plant, equipment, and personnel to move vast quantities of one type of goods from the plantation or the farm to the ultimate consumer. This investment in plantations, in refrigerated ships and cars, in specialized warehouses, and in other world-wide distributing as well as processing facilities cannot be used easily for products other than their original lines of goods. On the other hand, General Foods, Borden, National Dairy, and Procter & Gamble have invested much less in nontransferable plant and personnel. Even the resources of General Mills are more mobile than those of the tobacco, banana, and meat-packing companies. Moreover, General Mills and Borden also have had greater opportunity to develop new products that increase the demand for their existing lines. Of course, not all companies with more easily transferable resources necessarily move into new lines of products. National Biscuit, which has had little turnover in its top management since the early 1940's, is still carrying on the same type of business through the same type of centralized, functionally departmentalized organization as it has done for the past sixty years. Nevertheless, the ability to diversify seems to correlate closely with the type of the investment required by the enterprise's original line of business. Resources invested in marketing appear more easily transferable than those invested in obtaining raw materials, in transportation, and even in production.

The specific reasons for diversification and the resulting decentralization in the different enterprises processing agricultural products cannot be determined without a closer study of the experience of each company, based on records and interviews. All that can be definitely said otherwise is that the experiences of the food companies have certain similarities to those of du Pont and Sears, Roebuck. Nevertheless, the underlying motive for diversification certainly appears to be a desire to use existing resources more effectively. In every case, too, the new strategy increased the complexity both of the short-term tactical decisions which had to coordinate the functional activities to current market demand and of long-term strategic ones which had to allocate the resources among the different product lines in view of future market demand and general economic conditions.

Rubber

The rubber industry's "Big Four" illustrate even more clearly the relation between diversification and decentralization. The two that were large enterprises before the coming of the automobile, United States Rubber and B. F. Goodrich, have long sold a variety of products to different markets, and both turned early to the decentralized structure. The other two — Goodyear Tire & Rubber and Firestone Tire & Rubber — that began as tire firms concentrated their resources in obtaining on a massive scale personnel and facilities to procure or produce raw materials, plants, and distributing facilities for a single line of products. They have been slower to diversify and decentralize than their two major competitors.

As early as 1905, the United States Rubber Company became concerned by the leveling off of demand for its major line, boots and shoes, caused by the migration from farm to city and by the increased paving of streets and roads.[19] The growing industrial market for belting, hose, packing, insulated wire, molded, and other rubber products appeared a more promising field for the use of its resources. Shortly after it moved extensively into the industrial rubber business, the automobile suddenly created a great new demand for rubber tires. Then the development of chemical processes initially used in the treatment of rubber brought the company increasingly into the production of anti-oxides, improved acids, and heavy chemicals. In the 1920's, United States Rubber tripled its sale of chemicals. Goodrich's growth followed a pattern similar to that of its largest competitor except that it started in industrial rubber, moved to footwear, clothing, and sundries for the mass consumer markets, and then added tires and chemicals.

Early diversification, which brought it to marketing consumer as well as producers' goods, made United States Rubber one of the very first American industrial enterprises to set up autonomous product divisions. By 1917, on the recommendation of the Development Department, its President, Samuel B. Colt, had separated the company's operations into five divisions (tire, industrial, general, clothing, and chemical), an overseas unit to supervise plantations, and another for foreign sales. Except for the last two, each division handled its own engineering, manufacturing, and sales. However, no general office was created at this time. The Operating Council, which administered the company as a whole, included the Vice-Presidents in charge of the product divisions, those heading the older Legal, Financial, and Development Departments, and the President himself. Before these structural innovations could be fully tested, however, a new management headed by Charles B. Seger, a Wall Street financier with railroad experience, brought back a more centralized, functionally departmentalized organization.

As a result, the final rationalization of the company's administration was more of an adaptive than a creative response. In 1928 as the company approached bankruptcy, the du Ponts purchased 30 per cent of its stock. The new set of senior officers headed by du Pont-trained executives soon adopted the multidivisional structure that had been used so effectively in Wilmington. After 1930, the United States Rubber Company had separate multidepartmental operating divisions for tires, footwear, industrial products, sundries, chemicals, and a department for the sale of crude rubber and liquid latex, another to market finished products overseas, and a third to manage rubber plantations. At the same time, the company instituted a general office with general executives and staff specialists as well as financial and statistical systems and controls similar to those at du Pont and General Motors. The most significant adjustment in this structure came in 1957 when the general executives, including those in charge of groups of divisions, came to have more individual responsibility, and the role of the general staff was enlarged.

Goodrich, which before World War I had developed a highly rational and systematic functionally departmentalized structure, did not turn to the multidivisional form until 1930, when it set up four product divisions.[20] The devastating impact of the depression, and with it retrenchment, brought a return to the earlier structure. The renewed expansion after the depression and continuing product development brought an evolution toward a different type of organization. In 1936, a separate division was formed to manufacture and sell latex products; in 1943 came the formation of the integrated chemical division; and in 1953, the company became fully decentralized. Its completed structure included, beside a general office, six autonomous product divisions — Tire and Equipment, Industrial Products, Footwear, Flooring, Chemical, and Sponge Rubber — and two for foreign activities — the Canadian and the International Divisions.

In the 1920's, while Goodrich and United States Rubber were diversifying, Goodyear and Firestone were expanding, primarily through vertical integration. Concentrating almost wholly on tires, they acquired more textile mills, steel- and rimmaking factories, rubber and cotton plantations, and extensive distributing facilities, including dealers and retail outlets, than did the other two leading rubber companies. Only with the depression and the sudden drop in the demand for tires did Goodyear and Firestone turn hesitantly to developing other lines.

In setting up a line of industrial rubber Goodyear policy concentrated on making a few large-volume items, often only one grade or model which could make the fullest use of the existing plant and continue to be administered through the centralized, functionally departmentalized structure.[21] World War II proved to be a greater force for change. The massive synthetic-rubber program that ensued increased Goodyear's facilities, skills and other resources in chemical production. In 1943, Goodyear opened a large central research laboratory and two years later formed the General Products Division to handle nearly all of its nontire business. The next year an autonomous Chemical Products Division was set up. Then in 1956, after the retirement of Paul W. Litchfield, who had so long dominated the company's affairs, the over-all structure was systematized. Goodyear's nontire business came to be administered by seven product divisions (Chemicals, Industrial Products, Aviation Products, Metal Products, Shoe Products, Foam and Film, and Flooring) with the general manager of each responsible for the major functional activities in his line. Goodyear also had its International Division, while an enlarged general office, consisting of executives without operating responsibilities and a general staff, administered the company as a whole.

Of the leading rubber enterprises, Firestone continues to have the largest concentration of its resources in the tire business.[22] During the depression it took on automobile parts, rubber and plastic items, and other lines that used its marketing organization more than its production facilities. With the postwar boom in tires, it apparently dropped many of these to concentrate once again on its major product. If the demand for tires levels off again, Firestone too may diversify, but even then, with its veteran management which still includes Firestones, it may prefer to stick with a tested strategy. In any case, there seems to be little reason for changing the existing functionally departmentalized, centralized structure until more of its resources are transferred into new products lines.

Petroleum

The changing structure and strategy of large oil enterprises have many parallels to those of the leading tire companies. The oil concerns, too, concentrated the largest part of their resources in marketing, manufacturing, and producing raw materials for a single line of goods for the huge new mass consumer market created by the automobile. With the depression and the consequent decline of demand for gasoline, they began to develop other refined products with a high-volume market, such as oil for household heating, diesel oil for railroads, industrials, and utilities, and high-octane gasoline for aircraft. Since these were all produced through the same refining processes and equipment and all used the same raw materials, the only organizational adjustment called for by their growth was the enlargement of the offices in the sales department headquarters and field units handling them. It was World War II and particularly the war-stimulated synthetic-rubber program that turned the oil as well as the tire companies to chemical production and encouraged broad programs of diversification. Since the war, continued expansion in petrochemicals has provided one powerful pressure for decentralization.

But there was another pressure for setting up a multidivisional structure in the petroleum concerns which was less significant in the tire and other rubber companies. Because the volume of production in the individual oil firms was higher than that of the rubber companies[23] and because their different functional activities — their market facilities and refining and producing operations — were more widely scattered over the globe, the problem of assuring a steady flow from the ground to the customer proved much more difficult. As the largest oil companies expanded the output of their major line, they experienced much the same types of administrative strains as had Jersey Standard before 1925. Following her example, they turned to devising regionally defined, multidepartmental divisions and a general office of general executives and staff specialists. At the same time, many of them were moving into wholly new lines of chemical products which called for the creation of a separate product division. Thus by 1960, with one exception, the Atlantic Refining Company, the twelve oil companies studied here had developed or were beginning to move toward the multidivisional form.

Except for Standard Oil (New Jersey), the histories of all these companies as independent enterprises fall in the twentieth century. During its first twenty-five years, a rapidly changing market, the opening of new sources of crude oil in Texas, California, Oklahoma, and overseas, and the dissolution of the industry's giant in 1911, all stimulated rapid growth. Until the late 1920's, most major oil companies expanded through vertical integration, much like Jersey Standard.[24] Some built or purchased refineries and marketing organizations to assure outlets for their crude; others sought new sources of crude to assure themselves of adequate supplies.[25] After 1925 came the leveling off of the market for gasoline and lubricants following the lessening demand for new automobiles. Very shortly thereafter began that massive overproduction of crude oil which followed the opening of new fields. Then oil executives turned from accumulating more resources to devising ways to employ more efficiently what they already had. Between 1931 and 1936, Gulf Oil, Standard Oil (Indiana), Phillips Petroleum, the Texas Company, Socony Vacuum Oil (now Socony Mobil Oil), Sinclair Oil, Standard Oil of California, Shell Oil, and Continental Oil, all underwent major administrative reorganizations.[26] Only Atlantic Refining and Standard Oil Company (Ohio) waited until the years after World War II to make comparable changes, after they too had completed a program of expansion and integration. Most of these companies combined their activities into a single, centralized, functionally departmentalized structure. But two of the largest, Socony and Standard Oil (Indiana), retained integrated, autonomous, regional units. In both companies, however, the senior executives continued to administer both the functional departments and the autonomous divisions much as the Jersey Directors had done until 1927. In the administrative changes of the 1930's, most of the companies, for the first time, also gave serious attention to coordinating the product flow between the different units within their organizations.

As the country recovered from the depression, the oil companies turned once more to expansion. During World War II and even more in the great postwar boom, the companies enlarged their transportation, refined, and marketing facilities and intensified their search for crude oil. Not only did demand for gasoline grow as the number of automobiles manufactured per year almost doubled, but the call for the newer lines, like household and diesel fuel, increased at an even greater rate. The daily output of gasoline in the United States rose from 1,839,000 barrels in 1941 to 2,473,000 in 1951 or 34.5 per cent while that of distillate fuel rose from 518,000 in 1941 to 1,090,000 in 1951, or 110.2 per cent.[27] Then as demand leveled off in the second half of the 1950's, oil executives began again to concentrate on organizing effectively their accumulated resources. They also sought new customers in order to continue employing their men, money, and materials profitably.

The move into new markets and with it the setting up of new widely scattered refineries to serve these markets brought greater pressure for organizational change than did the opening of new crude oil fields in many parts of the world. Before World War II, many of the oil companies still marketed in only part of the United States. Therefore, one strategy of expansion was to cover the whole American market. Then, particularly in the 1950's, the oil companies concentrated on foreign markets as overseas demand for petroleum products began growing more rapidly than the domestic market. At the same time, they put more emphasis on developing the petrochemical business, where present and future profit margins looked more promising, than in selling petroleum in the domestic market. In nearly all cases, both types of expansion led to structural reorganization.

Standard Oil of California, one of the first to embark on a postdepression strategy of regional expansion, set up integrated divisions for specific geographical areas even before the war. The first division was formed for

Texas and New Mexico in 1937, another for the Canadian Northwest in 1941, and a third for Oklahoma after the war. As early as 1936, the concern joined with the Texas Company to establish a subsidiary, the California Texas Corporation, which combined the production, marketing, and refining activities of the two enterprises in Asia, Africa, and the Pacific areas. The California Company, a subsidiary initially formed to carry out exploration and production outside of the United States, was the instrument that Standard of California used to market company products in the Eastern part of the country. After the war, the California Oil Company, a new division, administered the East Coast refining and marketing activities. As Standard of California was one of the first oil companies to move into petrochemicals, so it had formed by the end of World War II two autonomous petrochemical subsidiaries, one for industrial and the other for agricultural chemicals. In 1954, the company created the Western Division to administer exploring, production, transportation, refining, and marketing in seven western states, Alaska, and Hawaii. With the formation of this division, the parent company was completely divorced from operating activities and became a general office consisting of general executives and staff specialists. By 1954, Standard Oil of California had come to much the same type of structure as Jersey Standard but with product as well as regional divisions.

Even before 1954 the Continental Oil Company, which in the 1940's had expanded both by enlarging its domestic market and by moving rapidly into petrochemicals, had adopted a comparable structure. It included six operating regional divisions, a petrochemical division, and a general office of senior executives and staff specialists. Since the new President, Leonard F. McCollum, who had been responsible for carrying out the reorganization in 1949 and 1950, was a former Jersey executive, he undoubtedly led his company to follow the Jersey pattern even more explicitly than did the other large oil companies.

Standard Oil (Indiana) adjusted its structure more slowly. Undoubtedly because it concentrated almost entirely on the domestic market, it moved toward a more centralized structure. By the end of the 1930's, the parent company was doing its own refining and marketing in the Midwest and obtaining its crude oil from its Stanolind group of producing, purchasing, and transporting subsidiaries. Another subsidiary, Pan American Petroleum produced, refined, and marketed in the Southeast. A third, the Utah Oil Refining Company, did likewise for some of the mountain states. After World War II, the company concentrated on expanding its domestic markets, particularly in the East, so that soon it was selling its products in every state. After some preliminary changes in 1954, a major reorganization took place in 1957, which essentially centralized its administration along functional lines. Producing activities were combined into the Pan American Petroleum Company, which had a separate subsidiary for foreign production. Purchasing was also divided into two companies, a foreign and a domestic one. The American Oil Company now refined and marketed in twenty-eight states, while the Utah company continued the same activities in five mountain ones. And the parent company still refined, transported, and marketed in the fifteen Midwestern states. At the same time, the administration of marketing, processing, and developing petrochemicals was consolidated into the Amoco Chemical Corporation. Company headquarters were enlarged to include functional Vice-Presidents who were still responsible for operations in the Midwest.

At Indiana Standard, consolidation of domestic activities was to be followed by foreign expansion. As the 1958 Annual Report stated: "We intend to develop a substantial foreign position," not only in production of crude but in marketing as well.[28] To develop a European market, it formed a Foreign Market Planning Group under a Vice-President with offices in Paris. If foreign markets grow as Indiana expects, the senior executives will most certainly have to work out an overseas administrative organization. If so, it may develop a multidivisional structure comparable with that fashioned recently by Socony Mobil, Shell, and Texaco.

Until 1958, Socony Mobil's structure was quite similar to that of Jersey Standard before 1927. There were the functional departments — Producing, Domestic Marketing, Foreign Trade, Manufacturing, and Marine Transportation — and two integrated affiliates, Magnolia and General Petroleum, which, like Humble, were primarily producers of crude oil. At headquarters, the Distribution Department had long carried out the role of coordinating the flow of product through the functional activities in much the same way as Jersey's Coordination Department did after 1925. Then the retirement of senior officers, who had played leading executive roles for more than a generation, helped bring a major administrative reorganization. The parent company with general executives and staff specialists, relieved of operating responsibilities, became a general office like that at the Jersey Company. Two new large operating divisions were formed. The Mobil Oil Company had charge of all domestic business. The other, Mobil International Oil Company, administered all foreign activities. Marine transportation remained the only activity managed directly from the general office. The domestic division was divided along functional lines with a separate department for the administration of the development and marketing of petrochemicals and paint. Although General Petroleum and Magnolia retained their separate organizations, company executives indicated that these subsidiaries would probably be incorporated shortly into the new domestic division's functional structure. On the other hand, the Foreign Division included a number of regional administrative units. While the senior officer of each is responsible for all functions in his area, the Middle East department concentrates on production of crude, and the other three — Caribbean and Latin American, Northern and Southeastern Europe, and Africa and Southwestern Europe — are concerned more with sales. Therefore, the Vice-President in charge of Supply and Distribution (that is, of coordination of product flow) heads an important and active organization in the central office of the overseas division.[29] At Socony, the domestic market for petroleum products is considered more homogeneous than the foreign one.

Royal Dutch-Shell in the same year, 1958, reorganized the administration of its business outside of the United States. The result was an over-all structure much like that at Socony. The major difference between the two stems from the fact that Shell had moved much earlier and more extensively into petrochemicals than had the American company. In the United States, Shell's petroleum business had been managed since the 1930's through a centralized, functionally departmentalized structure and its chemical operations through another autonomous division. The latter only recently reorganized its activities into multidepartmental product divisions. By the 1958 reorganization, Shell's activities outside the United States were placed under two general offices, one for the petroleum business and one for chemicals. Each of these two general offices has a fairly large staff with the Supply and Planning Coordinator as a key staff unit in the petroleum division. Like Socony's overseas division, the one that manages Shell's business outside of the United States is divided into at least partially integrated regional divisions. At the very top, Royal Dutch-Shell has sort of a supergeneral office — a seven-man "Managing Directors' Committee" which concentrates its efforts wholly on long-term planning and appraisal of Shell's world-wide activities.[30]

By 1960, both Jersey Standard and Texaco had begun to move toward administering their operating activities through comparable domestic and foreign divisions. The Jersey Company's changes in 1959 have already brought all domestic operations under the administration of a single integrated division. Possibly the next organizational change will be the fashioning of a similar unit or units for Jersey's overseas business and possibly, too, a revamping of the parent company's general office.

Texaco's growth and increased administrative involvement in both overseas activities and petrochemicals have also brought structural changes. Until the mid-1950's, the Texas Company preferred to have its foreign, petroleum, and chemical activities handled through subsidiaries owned jointly with other companies. In 1947, for example, Texaco sold its European subsidiaries, largely marketing organizations, to the subsidiary owned with California Standard, which in 1936 had taken over its facilities in Asia and Africa. By the mid-1950's, it was the joint owner of three petrochemical subsidiaries.[31] The work done by these jointly owned subsidiaries permitted the senior executives at Texaco to concentrate their attention on the administration of their domestic petroleum business. Apparently, however, the Texas Company decided that such indirect control of its overseas and chemical activities hampered the appraisal of the use of its resources in new or distant markets and the planning for future expansion. Since 1954, it has expanded its own overseas marketing as well as production, has built its own research laboratories, and has moved strongly into petrochemicals. As a result, the number of Senior Vice-Presidents without operating duties in the general office has been significantly enlarged. Where in 1956 there were one Executive and one Senior Vice-President, in 1959 there were seven Senior Vice-Presidents. The functional operating Vice-Presidents now handle domestic activities, while a Vice-President for crude oil production outside the United States, one for the Western Hemisphere and West Africa and one for the Eastern Hemisphere, carry on the foreign business. There is also a Vice-President who heads the autonomous Petrochemical Division. It seems that before long Texaco's structure will be very like that of Socony Mobil and Shell.

For Phillips, Sinclair, Standard of Ohio, and Gulf, the move into petrochemicals has been more of a stimulus for reorganizing the centralized, functionally departmentalized structure initially formed in the 1930's than has the expansion of the older lines. Phillips, for example, manufactures and markets carbon-black products in Europe and Africa, but has not attempted to take its gasoline and fuel-oil products overseas. For these companies, then, the move into petrochemicals has increased the central offices' administrative load and so has encouraged the creation of general offices whose executives are relatively free from operating responsibilities.

Up to 1940, nearly all American oil companies stayed close to their primary lines of products, gasoline, lubricants, fuel oil, and kerosene. Their heavy investment in men, money, and materials to produce, move, process, and market petroleum from the well to the customer discouraged them from entering the petrochemical business. As Williams Haynes pointed out in his *American Chemical Industry — A History:*

> Production of chemicals by the petroleum industry appeared to be economically and technically sound, but most petroleum executives could not see what appeared to them to be a tiny market for a multitude of chemicals produced by a complexity of operations and sold to a long and diversified list of customers, tasks for which they had neither the technical nor the sales staffs.[32]

However, in the 1930's and early 1940's, the development of new refinery processes such as catalytic refining and the superfractionating techniques provided new materials as well as technical knowledge and experience in chemical operations. Then the war-engendered artificial rubber program pushed the companies still further into chemistry. The war and postwar industrial boom with its growing demand for basic chemicals created markets, outside of gasoline and oil products for large-scale, low-unit-cost processing operations, and consequently an opportunity for the petroleum companies to apply profitably some of their skills, equipment, and funds to a new line of business. After World War II, nearly all major oil firms moved rapidly into the making and selling of chemicals.

The organizational response to this strategy of diversification has followed a regular pattern. First, the existing functional departments administered the new business. Then a separate marketing organization was formed to operate independently of the sales department. This marketing department came, in time, to be responsible for product development as well as sales. And finally, it took over the refining operations and thus became an autonomous, multifunction division. By the mid-1950's, Shell, Standard of California, Phillips, Texaco, Gulf, Standard (Indiana), Continental Oil, and Standard Oil of Ohio all had integrated chemical divisions. In 1960, the petrochemical departments at Socony Mobil and Sinclair handled development and marketing but not processing. Jersey's Enjay Company still remained primarily a marketing organization. Of the twelve oil companies studied here, only Atlantic Refining continued to administer its petrochemical business through the several functional departments.

While the volume and profits of the petrochemical business are still small in comparison to those of the major lines, diversification has certainly increased the number of strategic decisions senior officers must make. Thus the move into chemicals helped to stimulate administrative reorganization in at least two of the companies that did not turn to expanding overseas markets, Phillips and Gulf. Even though the Gulf Corporation has overseas sources of crude oil, it has made little attempt to market its refined products outside of the Western Hemisphere. While it has been under less pressure to work out a regionally defined structure, its new President has recently tried to improve the existing functional organization so that the senior officers could concentrate on strategic decisions and the departmental heads on tactical ones; or, to say this in a different way, to transform the central office into a more general one although the operating organizations remain functional departments rather than multidepartmental divisions. W. K. Whiteford, the new President who engineered Gulf's reorganization, essayed to achieve this end in two ways. One was to move the departmental headquarters out of Pittsburgh to Houston, Texas, and elsewhere. The other was to insist that the senior officials who stayed in line positions in Pittsburgh were to be "general officers," not functional specialists. Pittsburgh, Whiteford insisted, was to be the place only for "economic planning, long-range planning, policy and objectives. . . . It is the nerve center, the head of communications."[33] Whether these measures will prevent the continuing channeling of operational decisions to the top offices remains to be seen. They are more drastic than those tried by Pierre du Pont and Walter Teagle in their attempts to keep decision making decentralized within a functionally defined structure. Moreover, when Jersey Standard employed a somewhat similar structure for a time after 1933 to administer its domestic business, its senior officers apparently avoided becoming involved in operational activities.

The experience of the oil industry helps make clear that one fundamental purpose of structure is to unite all activities of the enterprise in meeting changing market demand. Where a company's line of end products was produced by the same manufacturing processes from the same supply of raw materials for a relatively few sets of customers, the centralized, functionally departmentalized form provided that essential coordination. But with the development of new lines for new and quite different customers or with the opening of new distant markets, effective interdepartmental coordination became increasingly difficult. For the largest oil companies, the strains usually appeared after expansion in faraway lands led to building refineries and shipping facilities closer to the distant markets. Then these oil companies usually followed the example of the oldest and biggest enterprise in the industry, Standard Oil (New Jersey), by forming integrated regional operating divisions with a general office to coordinate, appraise, and plan the work of the enterprise as a whole. Later, as the domestic market grew more nearly homogeneous and more closely knit, all operational activities again came to be managed by a single autonomous unit. Then these companies, like National Dairy and American Can, dropped their regional divisions within the United States, but overseas activities continued to be managed through geographically defined, integrated divisions.

Rubber, meat-packing, tobacco, and liquor enterprises also developed extensive overseas activities, including processing as well as distributing facilities. Yet these more distant operations failed to exert enough pressure to cause the building of a new structural form. Those concerns decentralized because they diversified. But when they did so, they all set up their "International Division" to administer overseas activities.

When the rubber firms and those processing agricultural products did decentralize, their administrative stories were comparable to those of the oil companies as the latter moved into petrochemicals. The organizational response of the oil industry to diversification illustrates well that the older structure was unable to integrate the resources of the enterprise to the market demands of the new lines and that the requirements for such coordination brought the new structure. The decision to produce petrochemicals, rather than permit the gases or liquids to go to waste or to be sold to a chemical company, first led to the formation of a new organization to market these products. This new organization was soon made independent of the existing sales department, otherwise the older lines continued to receive nearly all the attention. Since effective selling called not only for keeping in close touch with fluctuating demand but also for the continuing improvement and adjustment of products according to changing needs, tastes, and developments by competitors, this marketing unit quickly obtained its own development and research departments. As the nature of the new lines was very different from the older ones, it soon became more practical for the chemical units to build separate plants for their expanded activities than merely to add facilities at the main refineries. Even where processing continued to be carried out at the older works, its control came more and more under the executives in the petrochemical sales and development units. This, then, is the way that the fully integrated division evolved, and in time, the company's top administrative offices and then its whole structure became redefined. The same general patterns developed in rubber and enterprises processing agricultural products as they moved into new lines.

Even though it led to the addition of new resources, the strategy of diversification, which brought decentralization, was usually set up as a way to use existing personnel and facilities. Excess capacity created by the depression and new products demanded by the war helped turn to diversification enterprises in all three sets of industries, rubber, oil, and those processing agricultural products. Most of the resources of these companies remained, it should be stressed, in their original lines. For while they had more resources that were transferable to other types of products than did the steel, copper, or even aluminum firms, their facilities and personnel could not be changed so easily to different end products as could those in chemical, electrical, and even power machinery enterprises. Gasoline, tires, meat, or milk continued to account for the greatest volume of output and share of total profits in the individual enterprises. Normally, however, these older products brought a lower return on investment and lower profit per unit. The newer lines, which were usually more profitable, were therefore those in which the enterprise enlarged as it added or expanded its resources.

Diversification thus brought the new decentralized structure, not because it increased the total output or size of operations, but because it so quickly enlarged the number and complexity of both tactical and strategic administrative decisions. By making the integration of a company's functional activities much more difficult, it led to the creation of a multidepartmental autonomous division for the administration of each major line of products. By forcing senior executives to plan and appraise activities in widely different industries, it encouraged the building of the general office where the men responsible for the destiny of the enterprise could be given the time, information, and psychological commitment necessary to handle these wide-ranging duties.

Even a small amount of diversification in relation to total production raised for these enterprises many of the same problems that the du Pont Company had encountered after embarking on its diversification program. Yet, in the three industries just examined, rubber, gasoline, and processing of agricultural products, the du Pont structure served as a specific model only in the first. Although Jersey Standard had provided the example for regional decentralization, it was slower than some of its competitors to expand petrochemicals and so offered no similar model for product decentralization. The different and evolutionary responses of most companies to the requirements of the new petrochemical lines suggest that no particular example was followed in the setting up of these new product units in the oil industry. Readily available evidence does not indicate what effect either the du Pont or General Motors experience had on the changes in the flour, milk, and meat-packing firms, but the two pioneers, undoubtedly had at least an indirect influence. By the late 1930's, when some companies processing agricultural products first began to set up new structures, the work of du Pont and General Motors had become quite well known.

Industries Widely Accepting the New Structure

In three industries, the electrical and electronics, the power machinery including automobiles, and the chemical, all but two of the twenty leading companies studied here were managed in 1960 through a multidivisional administrative structure. Clearly, in these industries the older centralized, departmentalized form had failed to permit effective coordination and integration of the functional activities with market needs and demands and, as the same time, had prevented the senior executives from finding the time and information necessary to handle an increasing number of strategic decisions. The leading companies in all these industries have increasingly developed new product lines sold in markets quite different from their original one. Only one of the twenty — Deere & Company — has still not moved extensively beyond its initial line of products. This strategy of expansion through diversification brought such powerful demands for administrative readjustment that only the strongest individuals have been able to ignore or resist them. Both of the two companies not adopting the new form, Dow Chemical and Deere & Company, have long been run as family firms.

The motive for the initial diversification by the leading enterprises in these industries again appears to have been, as at du Pont and so many of the firms studied here, that of assuring continuing and fuller use of existing resources. These companies were able to move into new lines of business more readily than most American firms largely because their activities called for a high level of technological skills. Of American industries not primarily involved in making military products, the chemical and electrical have devoted the most resources to systematic research and development.[34] The skills of their highly trained personnel have been based on industrial technologies that can be applied to the development, manufacturing, and marketing of a large number of end products. So, too, have their manufacturing facilities and raw materials been used much more often than those in the steel, copper, aluminum, meat-packing, tire, and gasoline firms to turn out new and different products for quite different sets of customers. It is hardly surprising then that many of these enterprises led the way both in adopting the strategy of diversification and in fashioning the structure necessary to administer diversified lines of business.

In the chemical, power machinery, and automobile industries, the multidivisional form, first fashioned at General Motors and du Pont, served explicitly as a model in the building of the new structures. On the other hand, the leading enterprises in the electrical industry were themselves innovators rather than followers in developing the modern decentralized structure. The administrative reorganization at Westinghouse, started in 1931, began as a creative innovation comparable with those at General Motors and du Pont. At Westinghouse the process of innovation, like its causes, was in many ways strikingly similar to that in all four of the companies studied in detail here. Although General Electric's reorganization was to come later, its senior executives have recently been as innovative in administration as any in American industry.

Electrical and Electronics

Until World War I, both great electrical companies had concentrated their resources in one basic area, the development, manufacturing, and marketing of equipment to provide electric power and light.[35] Because of their industry's technological complexity, their product lines soon came to include a wide variety of items, ranging from huge turbines and electric locomotives to tiny fuses, switches, and electric engine parts. This intricate business was, from the first, successfully administered through a centralized, functionally departmentalized structure. Except for lamps and wiring, most of this machinery and accessories went to other industrial firms for use in furnishing their own goods and services. Moreover, the production, marketing, and obtaining of materials for both the small standardized engines, equipment, and other products and the large nonstandard turbines, generators, and so forth, called for close scheduling and coordination within existing departments. The technological intricacies of this industry, in fact, led to the building of new engineering departments to design both process and product. To meet the continually changing demands for nonstandard products, the closest cooperation between executives in the sales, production, purchasing, and new engineering departments was called for. On the other hand, standard products required, beside estimates of markets, an accurate understanding of the customers' changing and potential needs and also of new machines developed by competitors. The resulting constant pressure for product improvement led these two companies to set up the first research departments in American industry. Also because as the lamp or light bulb was then its only product that went directly to the mass consumer, the differing needs of this market led both companies to set up autonomous division for lamp design, production, and sale. Westinghouse had such a division before World War I. By contrast, because General Electric developed two groups of lamp-making enterprises, it did not come to a single, separate autonomous lamp unit until the 1920's.

When these electrical giants moved into making products other than those used to produce electric power and light, the older structure became increasingly ineffective. At both companies, diversification took two forms. It resulted from the move into electric appliances such as washing machines, refrigerators, vacuum cleaners, hot water heaters, and stoves for the consumer market. Second, it came from commercializing the radio, X rays, alloys, plastics, and electronic devices developed in the companies' research laboratories. These new products were in a sense by-products of research carried on by the laboratories on tubes, wires, and insulation to improve electric lighting and equipment.

In both cases the companies decided to diversify in order to use their existing resources more profitably.[36] If the by-products of research employed enough available equipment, and more importantly the technically trained personnel, and if their production had growth possibilities, then the senior executives usually decided to develop the items commercially themselves. If not, they licensed the patents out to other enterprises. Again, the availability of existing resources helped determine the accumulation of new ones. The motive for the move into consumer appliances was even more explicitly defined as a way to find more employment for existing skills and facilities. According to Gerard Swope, General Electric's President, the move was to increase the need for the company's primary line of products by expanding the demand for electricity. At the same time, the building and selling of appliances meant that current plant, equipment, and personnel could operate at a steadier rate by avoiding or at least counterbalancing the feast-and-famine cycle of the apparatus and heavy electric equipment business. But as at du Pont, diversification used largely engineering and production resources rather than marketing ones. Eventually, the administrative strains it created brought the multidivisional structure.

During the 1920's, both companies made *ad hoc* adjustments in their organizations in order to meet the new administrative pressures. By the beginning of the depression, General Electric had formed a separate subsidiary for the handling of X-ray equipment and another, Carboloy, Inc., to administer its alloy business. It consolidated its chemical activities into a separate, autonomous division in 1930 and set up another for air conditioning shortly thereafter. The severest administrative vexations, however, came from the new appliance business. A Merchandise Department, with headquarters in Bridgeport, Connecticut, was formed in 1928 to market appliances. While independent of the old Sales Department, it remained only a marketing organization until the late 1930's. Refrigerator parts were made at Erie and Schenectady and the finished products assembled at Erie. Flatirons were manufactured in California, stoves and water heaters in Chicago. The older functional departments supervised the designing, manufacturing, and assemblying, but all finished products were sold through Bridgeport. The process of coordinating the flow of product between and within these different parts of the industrial process and of integrating the flow to the market itself became increasingly more difficult and costly. Until 1939, however, General Electric executives did little to relate the work of the Merchandise Department and the other more autonomous new-product divisions with the older functional departments or the company's central offices.

Westinghouse underwent much the same sort of *ad hoc* structural adjustment in the 1920's.[37] Then, in 1931, its senior executives decided to make a thorough investigation of the company's administrative problems and needs. Possibly Westinghouse turned to structural planning and reorganization before General Electric because it felt the profit decline resulting from the depression more sharply. Probably of more significance was the fact that its management was not dominated by a single, brilliant executive like Swope of General Electric who, in much the manner of General Wood at Sears, made most of his company's basic entrepreneurial decisions himself.

The pattern of the resulting reorganization had many similarities to the changes at du Pont and General Motors. In the first place, the senior executives clearly realized that expansion by diversification rather than by volume had created the administrative difficulties. In the words of Westinghouse executives:

> All the activities of the Corporation were divided under the three functions of production, engineering and sales. Each of the three functions was the responsibility of a vice-president, and the responsibility of each of those vice-presidents, so far as his function was concerned, covered the whole diversified and far flung operations of the Corporation. Such an organization of the Corporation's management lacked responsiveness. There was too much delay in the recognition of problems and in the solution of problems after they were recognized. As a result, there was unsatisfactory control over profits and losses.[38]

Moreover, the executives at Westinghouse considered their problems as new and unique: "In 1931 the top management of the Corporation had before it no recognized course to follow. Efforts to reorganize the Corporation's management were necessarily pioneering efforts which involved a certain amount of trial and error and required time for development into final form."[39] While the senior executives at the electrical company were undoubtedly aware of the multidivisional structures that du Pont and General Motors had devised, they probably believed that the organizational form used in a chemical or automobile company had little relevance to their business, just as Frazer and the Sears executives apparently saw little relation between such structures and the needs of their mass-merchandising enterprise.

As had been true at Jersey Standard as well as at du Pont, the initial organizational response was further centralization. The Product Engineering Department was consolidated into the manufacturing organization so that nearly all nonfinancial activities came to be administered through two grand functional departments, Production and Sales. As this step soon proved to be inadequate, the senior officers next decided to set up "a coordinating committee," usually composed of three members representing the engineering, sales, and manufacturing functions, for each major line of products or groups of related products. However, these committees had, as a later report pointed out, "no one person solely responsible for the final operating results."[40] The parallel here to the Divisional Councils at du Pont is striking. And, as at the chemical company, the compromise structure was little more successful than the earlier effort to centralize functional activities.

Then, in 1933, came the decision to experiment with autonomous, integrated operating divisions. First came the Merchandise Division for electric appliances. Unlike its counterpart at General Electric, it included "not only the sales activities of such products as refrigerators, electric ranges, household appliances, etc., but also the related engineering and manufacturing activities, wherever the main outlet for the product involved is through merchandising channels."[41] The success of this experiment led to the creation of a second autonomous, multifunction product unit for what came to be called the steam division. By October, 1934, the senior executives agreed to extend this type of organization to all activities of the company. The new administrative structure included several multifunctional divisions — those for elevators, X ray, lamps, micarta, appliances, steam machinery, electric jobbing, and a division that took over miscellaneous activities. In discussing the proposed structure at a meeting on December 10 and 11, 1934, the executives agreed that: "As far as possible, each division should be self-contained."[42] This should be "not only as to engineering, manufacturing and marketing but also as to accounting." To obtain the necessary coordination and control of the activities of the division, the planners further concurred on the formation of a parent or general office that, "divorced from all its operating activities, . . . would then have only general activities to perform." The parent office would consist of "a General (Coordinating) Committee" and several advisory staff departments. The committee, the organization builders had decided at an early meeting in October, "should be composed of persons not biased through direct connection with any unit division, in order that the necessary impartial view may be obtained. It is suggested that the General Committee be made up of three vice-presidents or men of equivalent abilities — with the Comptroller as assisting member."[43] The terminology in these reports suggests that once Westinghouse had decided on the multidivisional form, it then began to study the experience of other pioneers in decentralization.

Three years were necessary to get the proposed structure into good working order. The executives responsible for carrying out the plan encountered many of the same problems as had those at Jersey and even at General Motors. Developing an effective general headquarters proved even more difficult than adjusting and altering the composition of the divisions. It ultimately became necessary to move both the general and staff offices from the long-established central office in the great manufacturing works outside of Pittsburgh to a downtown office building. Finally, a great deal of attention had to be focused on improving the statistical and informational data that flowed from the divisions to the general office. This information was necessary for carrying on both entrepreneurial and operational activities. It helped, Westinghouse officials noted,

> to enable the Corporation to subject its operations to budgetary control in order to (1) to permit planning by top management with respect to over-all financial policy in the light of anticipated profits at varying sales levels and to provide a gauge by which to judge the operating results of the separate Divisions, and (2) to permit planning by Division Managers with respect to Divisional operations and to direct their attention to any specific aspect of their Divisional operations which was unsatisfactory.[44]

The structural changes at Westinghouse since World War II have modified and adjusted some of the relationships first defined in 1934. The combining of divisions under Group Vice-Presidents has been significant, but the basic structure still remains as outlined in October, 1934. In carrying out the initial and later changes, the engineering-trained Westinghouse executives had much the same rational approach to their administrative problems as had those at du Pont and General Motors.[45]

Major organizational changes at General Electric came only after the retirement in 1939 of its extremely competent President, Gerard Swope, and the Chairman of the Board, Owen D. Young.[46] Swope, with some assistance from Young, administered almost single-handedly his sprawling industrial empire. Shortly after Charles E. Wilson took office as Swope's successor, he began to reshape the company's structure. The war delayed his plans, and in 1946 Wilson turned over the reorganization to Ralph Cordiner. Cordiner's first step was to form six autonomous multifunction divisions. However, the heads of the new divisions and of some of the older functional departments continued to form the top committee that helped the President and Chairman administer General Electric's activities. So no clear-cut general office existed. Meanwhile, war and postwar expansion, by creating new skills and facilities, particularly in the electronics field, by doubling the number of its plants, and by tripling the number of employees, brought increasing pressure for still more structural change.

In 1950, immediately after he became President, Cordiner started a more sweeping reorganization. He broke down the company's activities into twenty operating divisions. These, in turn, administered the work of seventy "departments." By 1960 the number of "departments" had reached 105. Some of these were single-function units, others were multifunction divisions. The general office included a large staff of specialists. The heads of the advisory staff departments assisted the six general officers in over-all administration of the company's affairs. Following the General Motors practice, each general executive, excepting the President, had oversight over one of the five groups of divisions — Apparatus, Industrial Products and Lamps, Appliances and Electronics, Defense Products, and as the fifth, the Associated, Affiliated and Foreign Companies. Cordiner's reorganization went further than those in any other company studied here, both in the creation of a large number of relatively small administrative units and in the methods developed to administer these units. Some executives managed a single integrated multifunction organization with duties very similar to those in the divisions at du Pont or General Motors. But others, particularly those in the apparatus group, supervised a number of what were essentially merely manufacturing departments whose products were sold by still another unit — the Apparatus Sales Division. Still others were responsible for appraising, planning for, and coordinating the activities of several multidepartmental divisions and were, in effect, general executives. In all cases, the staff of the executive in charge was small. For data and assistance, he relied on the staffs of the several departments he managed and the large staff at the general office. He too depended, of course, on the great mass of accounting and statistical data that had been developed through the years at General Electric. Cordiner's imaginative innovations in developing a structure that combined flexibly all three basic types of administrative offices offer an extremely important subject for further research, since they suggest future trends in the organization of the most technologically advanced type of American industrial enterprise.

These changes have undoubtedly facilitated General Electric's recent diversification into nuclear power, jets, computers, industrial automation systems, and other new fields as well as in the expansion of the company's resources abroad. On the other hand, the breaking up of divisions operating in one major line of goods into still smaller units would seem to create new problems of coordination and control, as well as to increase administrative costs. For example, one wonders whether the markets are different enough to warrant the creation of a number of autonomous multifunction units within each of the three larger consumer appliance divisions. The reasons that have brought the oil companies to consolidating their domestic operating divisions and the automobile firms to making and selling the new compact cars through existing rather than new divisions may in time bring General Electric to recombine some of its many autonomous multifunction administrative organizations.

While the other large enterprises in the electrical and electronics field have not gone as far as General Electric in varying the basic multidivisional form, the Radio Corporation of America and the smaller Sylvania Electric had developed decentralized, multidivisional structures by 1950.[47] In fact, by 1953 RCA Victor, RCA's largest division, had itself become a multidivisional organization with a number of product divisions and staff specialists and general executives at its general office. Postwar diversification, particularly in electronics, also led the International Business Machine Corporation, the largest enterprise in its field, to create autonomous divisions and a new general office.[48] Organizational change at IBM came, however, only after the death of Thomas J. Watson, the man who more than any other brought together the resources that had made the company one of America's industrial leaders. By 1959, its divisions included those for data processing, general products, data systems, electric typewriters, supplies, a Federal System Division for the government market, and a World Trade one for the international market.

Power Machinery and Automobiles

The leading power machinery and implement firms were among the first in this country to embark on a policy of diversification in order to assure continuing full use of their resources. Allis-Chalmers, for example, formed as a combination and then as a consolidation of several steam-power machinery companies soon became aware of the challenge of machinery powered by electric and gasoline engines.[49] In 1904, it began to move into the making of both these products, and by 1910 had become the third largest manufacturer of electrical apparatus in the United States. At the end of World War I, it had gone almost as far in creating a line of earth-moving and other construction machinery, including tractors, using the internal-combustion engine. Allis-Chalmers then decided to build tractors for farmers as well as for construction contractors and companies. To meet the competition in this market, it developed a full line of agricultural implements and set up a separate marketing organization with its own branch offices. By 1940, it had become the third largest producer of farm equipment.

International Harvester's story has somewhat of a reverse twist.[50] At first, it applied the internal-combustion engine to its full line of agricultural implements. Then, as the farming depression of the 1920's deepened, it turned some of its facilities, funds, and personnel into the making of trucks and machinery for construction and industrial markets. By 1940, International Harvester was second only to General Motors and Ford in the production of trucks and other commercial vehicles.

Both enterprises first made *ad hoc* adjustments to meet the needs of this expansion in much the same way as did Westinghouse and General Electric. Allis-Chalmers, where the marketing of tractors and implements differed the most radically from that of its other power machinery and equipment, came to have two large operating units, the Tractor Division and the General Machinery Division, well before World War II. The relations of the senior officers, who were also the heads of the functional departments in the General Machinery Division, and of the older central staff to the operating heads of the Tractor Division, were not clearly defined. At International Harvester, it was the truck and industrial machinery business that became increasingly separated from the company's primary activities. Before the 1940's, however, the change had gone no further than the setting up of a separate marketing department for these products.

International Harvester was the first in its industry to adopt a clear-cut multidivisional structure. This reorganization came only after a change in the top command. Unlike his predecessor, Fowler McCormick, who became President in 1941, had a strong interest in organization. After a detailed examination both of the company's needs and of the General Motors experience, International Harvester shifted in 1943 from a centralized, functionally departmentalized organization to a decentralized, multidivisional one. The new general office had its general executives and advisory staff departments. Two of the important new staff departments, each headed by a Vice-President, were Supply and Inventory, which assisted the divisions in coordinating the flow of goods through their several functional activities, and Merchandising Services, which helped to develop policies to improve customer relations, sales operations, and market research.[51] Three of the new divisions — Motor Truck, Industrial Power, and Steel — were fully autonomous, while three others — the Farm Tractor, the Farm Implement, and Fiber and Twine — were primarily engineering and manufacturing organizations that sold their products through a General Line-Sales Department. That department was essentially the same marketing organization that the company had created shortly after its founding in 1902.

One of the participants in the reorganization listed three reasons for "the divisionalizing of the Company."[52] The first was "to reduce the number of burdens our officers and top executives have to carry, and to move the process of making operating decisions further down the line of command and close to the point where operations were actually carried on." The second was for "improving the coordination of the functions," since "men in different functions, who should have worked closely together, were being forced further and further apart." Finally: "We believed the divisional form of organization, by placing more men in positions of sizable responsibility, would yield an increasing number of skilled executives."

Postwar expansion at Allis-Chalmers, particularly in new lines like diesels and industrial machinery, ultimately brought a major reorganization in 1954. The six major product divisions were placed into two groups. One included construction machinery, farm equipment, and diesels and the other power equipment, industrial equipment, and general products. By 1954, other machinery equipment firms, such as Worthington (the successor of International Steam Pump), A. O. Smith, Cherry-Burrell, Thompson Products, and Borg-Warner had adopted the multidivisional form.[53] All but Borg-Warner, which long remained little more than a holding company, shifted to the new structure after carrying out a policy of fairly extensive diversification. For Borg-Warner, as at General Motors and National Dairy, the need was for the creation of a general office to administer its quite different long-established divisions.

Of these implement corporations, only Deere & Company still has the older centralized, functionally departmentalized structure.[54] It has not decentralized because it has not diversified, and it has not diversified because its family management so long preferred to run the company along well-accustomed lines. Only in 1956, with the retirement of the fourth generation of family management, did a new set of executives create the company's first research center, move out of the building that had housed the central office since the 1870's, and enlarge the size of the top management team. Undoubtedly, the new executives will take Deere & Company on the route of development, diversification, and decentralization which so many of its competitors have successfully followed.

Diversification came somewhat later in the automobile business than it did in the power machinery and implement industry. Until the late 1920's, all the leading automobile companies concentrated on the rapidly expanding automobile market for passenger cars. Even at General Motors the general office had most of its personnel and facilities in the automobile business. With the depression, General Motors turned to applying its varied resources to a number of different products. Ford and Chrysler, however, continued to maintain their investment in their single line until wartime conversion to nonautomotive products. World War II thus created a new pool of resources which these two automobile companies found they could profitably use for products other than the passenger car for the mass consumer market.

Before World War II, Henry Ford had actually often tried to build a new line of goods. He developed a cheap tractor at much the same time and for much the same reasons as had William C. Durant.[55] Designed by Ford engineers and manufactured in Ford plants, it proved immediately popular. Yet the Ford tractor failed commercially largely because it was marketed badly. As a competitor, Cyrus McCormick, III, noted:

> But he overran his object when he gave his tractor to his car dealers to sell. . . . Ford dealers in the country were well acquainted with their customers,

but not with their farm needs; and Ford dealers in the city had no sales outlet for farm goods.[56]

Ford built an excellent airplane, but again he was unable to sell it. Although his light truck business, handled through his carmaking and selling organizations, was profitable, he made almost no attempt to develop other types of commercial vehicles. Nor did he build much of a parts and accessories business. Ford, with much the same resources as General Motors, could have as easily developed these businesses. The incredibly bad management of his enormous industrial empire, which was so clearly reflected by the lack of any systematic organizational structure, not only prevented the Ford Motor Company from carrying out a strategy of diversification but also helped cause the rapid drop in Ford's profits and share of the market.

The Chrysler Corporation was under little pressure to diversify until well after World War II.[57] In 1928, Walter P. Chrysler had purchased Dodge and created the De Soto and Plymouth. As he had hardly set up his new enterprise when the depression hit, it remained, until the war, essentially an engine-making and car-assemblying company that was administered through a centralized, functionally departmentalized structure. In these years of declining demand, Chrysler had little difficulty in obtaining all the parts, accessories, and other materials he needed at reasonable prices. Postwar shortages, however, forced the company to integrate vertically in order to gain greater control over its supplies. At the same time, it continued the military lines started during the war and turned some of the resources developed in war work to marine engines and other nonmilitary products. Ford also found use for war-expanded equipment and personnel by developing tractors, farm equipment, commercial vehicles, and other lines.

Both Ford and Chrysler soon adopted the multidivisional structure. Henry Ford II hired Ernest R. Breech and other General Motors executives to manage his company, and one of their very first acts was to clap "the G. M. organization garment onto the Ford manufacturing frame." [58] At Chrysler, comparable changes from the centralized, functionally departmentalized structure to a multidivisional one began with the retirement of K. T. Keller, whom Chrysler had selected as his successor.

Even before World War II, the General Motors structure had come to enjoy the authority of success. Not only had it helped Sloan's company to increase its share of the market from 12 per cent to close to 50 per cent of the automobile market, but also to carry out a brilliant strategy of diversification in the 1930's. Moving into the making of diesels for railroad locomotive power, General Motors acquired almost overnight nearly all the locomotive business in the United States. Its airplane engine was well received. It competed most effectively with other truck and implement firms for the American bus and other commercial vehicle market. At the same time, its Frigidaire, Delco, and its parts and accessories business, all continued to show a fair return on investment. General Motors, too, made the conversion to war work far more easily than Ford. Finally the decentralized structure aided the corporation in establishing, expanding, and systematically managing through its Overseas Group its integrated subsidiaries in Britain, Germany, and Australia.

Possibly Ford and Chrysler may have been too imitative in adopting the multidivisional structure. They needed a general office and new divisions for their nonautomobile products like tractors and marine engines. But they also followed General Motors by setting up separate divisions for each line of cars. When General Motors fashioned its structure in 1920, there was good reason for the separation. At that time each line sold to a different price market. When the low-price market came to dominate during the depression, General Motors permitted the Pontiac, Olds, and even Buick to compete with Chevrolet for this market. Then after the war when the middle-price car attracted the most volume, the divisions continued to compete for much the same customers. The administration of many of the same lines of goods to much the same market through several rather than one integrated divisions may prove to be a fairly expensive luxury. Ford's unhappy experience with the Edsel seems to make this point, as do Chrysler's most recent organizational changes. The introduction of a new model for the middle-price market hardly required the investment involved in creating a wholly new marketing, production, and designing organization. Significantly, when the "Big Three" began to develop the small or "compact" car — the most radical product change since the 1920's — each designed, manufactured, and sold the new lines through existing, not new, divisions. The existence of integrated divisions competing in much the same market greatly complicated the definition and description of divisional boundaries and so must inevitably involve the general office in a large number of tactical decisions. Such decisions arise far less often for the nonautomotive divisions where each administers distinctly different types of businesses.

Chemicals

In the chemical industry, there have been fewer barriers to and more encouragement for diversification than in any other American industry. As both its processes and its products are based on the science of chemistry, systematic research and development have not only rapidly improved existing products but have brought forth a stream of new ones. And since the 1920's, the chemical industry has employed more men and invested more money in research and development than has any other one American industry. From a single specialized technological base, such as cellulose, calcium, or chlorine chemistry, enterprises have quickly developed a wide range of products. Since the development, engineering, and processing of the new items involved much the same technical know-how and equipment as the old, the transfer and application of the company's resources into new lines of products have proved comparatively easy.

Just as du Pont developed artificial leather, rayon and other textiles, paints, varnishes and dyes, cellulose, and plastic products from a nitrocellulose base, so Hercules Powder, once a part of du Pont, developed resins, turpentine, papermaking chemicals, insecticides, and fertilizers by concentrating its expansion on a naval stores base.[59] Dow Chemical's ever-widening line of products has been based on salt chemistry, while Monsanto's lines of fine chemicals initially grew out of the chemistry used to make saccharin. After the latter company integrated vertically to assure a supply of raw materials, it began to build other lines on chlorine and phenol, which brought it into rubber chemicals, benzoates, ethyl alcohols, and a variety of heavy and special chemicals. Tennessee Eastman, originally set up to supply the great photographic equipment firm with its basic film materials, grew in much the same way from a cellulose acetate base. On a similar base, the Celanese Corporation of America added plastic films and chemicals to its original textile lines, but only after its founder, Camille Dreyfus, turned over in 1945 most of the entrepreneurial decision making to his subordinates. Except for a move into making explosives during World War I, American Viscose, the oldest and still the largest producer of rayon, also made relatively little effort to diversify. Then after World War II the increasing competition from other artificial textiles finally turned it to developing other products including new fabrics, cellophane, and plastics.

The companies formed by mergers had even broader bases for diversification. Union Carbide, founded in 1917 as a merger of five companies that supplied one another with raw materials and outlets, moved rapidly in five different directions. From one subsidiary, Electro Metallurgical, came a range of alloys and alloying metals; from a second, Union Carbide, a variety of products based on calcium carbide; from a third, National Carbon, a range of coke-based items; while Linde Air Products and Prest-O-Lite pioneered in the development of many products based on liquid air, acetylene, and natural gas. A sixth division, formed in 1920, Carbide & Carbon Chemical, was one of the very first American enterprises to manufacture petrochemicals. It soon moved into lacquers and nitrocellulose products, while its work in accelerators and rubber vulcanizers and, in the 1930's, in butadiene and other rubber intermediates brought it into the rubber business. Continuing work on plastics led to the purchase of the Bakelite Corporation in 1939. Allied Chemical, formed in 1920 as a combination of complementary chemical companies similar to Union Carbide, failed to diversify until World War II largely because of the conservative policy of its founders, particularly Orlando F. Weber. The Mellon-financed Koppers Company, Inc., of Pittsburgh, while long remaining a holding company, moved faster into a broad range of coke-based chemicals.

While the nature of chemical technology permitted these enterprises to apply their resources to the production of new products with relative ease and low cost, the marketing of these items proved much more difficult. As the company's products went out to a very wide variety of markets, usually to other producers but often also to mass consumer markets, the operational problems of coördinating product flow with market demand and the entrepreneurial problems of allocating the firm's resources to different lines of businesses became increasingly difficult. The almost inevitable result was that many other chemical firms followed du Pont in adopting the multidivisional structure, with a different division to administer each major line of goods. Since rapid growth of the chemical industry in the United States began only in the years after World War I, the depression came before many of the leading companies had begun to diversify seriously. With the return of prosperity and the great expansion of resources during World War II, diversification became an accepted strategy of growth for nearly all the major chemical companies. Thus, while a few firms like Hercules and Monsanto had adopted the multidivisional structure before the war, many more major reorganizations came in the late 1940's and 1950's.[60] For most of them, the du Pont structure served as a model. To be sure, firms like Union Carbide, Allied Chemical, and Koppers, which had started as holding companies, had problems more like those at General Motors, and yet these companies seemed to have looked to du Pont rather than to the automobile company when reorganizing their structures. In any case, only the most powerful executives were able to resist the pressures for decentralization. Even where a veteran management has remained in office, as in the case of Eastman Kodak and American Viscose, the new structure has become accepted.

And there certainly was resistance or at least an indifference to such organizational change. At Allied Chemical, Orlando Weber, who dominated the company from its beginning in 1920 until World War II, paid little attention to organizational matters. A man of many neuroses, he believed in doing everything as secretly as possible and disliked the exchange of information even within his own company. While successful financially, Allied dropped well behind du Pont and Union Carbide in the size of its plant and personnel, in the variety and volume of its products, and in the amount of time and energy spent on research and development. The coming of the new management in the 1950's and with it a program of development and diversification led to the creation of a general office to administer the operating divisions. With these changes, Allied is again moving ahead.

Camille Dreyfus had a somewhat similar though less inhibiting impact on the strategy and structure of the Celanese Corporation that he helped found. So too did a veteran management at American Viscose. The adoption of the multidivisional structure at Celanese had to wait until July, 1956, very shortly after Dreyfus, who had continued on as Chairman of the Board, died. American Viscose, which was the last of the nine chemical companies studied to diversify, was with the exception of Dow also the last to decentralize. It came to a full multidivisional organization in August, 1958. During the preceding year, long-established top executives at Eastman Kodak began to rationalize its complex structure along similar modern lines.

At Dow, where expansion through diversification has been rapid and where resources have been concentrated on research, the senior executives have given little explicit thought to structure. Functional departments, regional offices as well as three autonomous product divisions, administer different parts of the company's varied activities, and a sizable staff had been assembled at the top office. Relations between the departments, the regional offices, the divisions, and the general office and its staff, however, have not been clearly defined but remain on an informal personal basis. As a result, Dow, like Alcoa, has a plethora of coordinating committees. At both Alcoa and Dow, the elder senior executives have liked to think of their enterprises as the relatively small family firms they were when the executives began their own business careers.

In those industries — chemical, power machinery, and electrical — where the new multidivisional structure has been accepted, enterprises have built the most diversified product lines. These are also the industries most closely oriented to modern science. As early as 1938, three-fourths of the personnel working in organized industrial research were in these three industries and in petroleum and rubber.[61] Other basic American businesses, such as steel, nonferrous metals, textiles, food, and other industries processing agricultural products, employed a good deal less than 25 per cent of the trained men in the nation's industrial research laboratories. This pattern has continued since the end of World War II. The only industries beside the five just listed to devote extensive resources to research and development have been those producing aircraft and scientific instruments, both financed largely by military demands. Significantly too, the efforts of the research departments in the nonmilitary enterprises since the war have been concentrated on producers' rather than consumer goods. As a result the leading companies in the chemical, power machinery, and electrical industries are transferring more of their resources to industrial than to consumer products. This trend, which reverses the increasing emphasis on the consumer market between the last decade of the nineteenth century and the third in the twentieth, is clear even in the great mass-consumer enterprises of the rubber and petroleum industries.

Those enterprises whose technological potential rests on modern science, as well as a few food companies, have been able to turn diversification into a highly rational and systematic strategy of growth. Stimulated by institutionalized research, diversification in turn brought decentralization. The distribution of new goods to the different markets and the resulting new need to coordinate different functional activities to assure effective product flow and product development required the building of autonomous product divisions. The increased problems of appraising the activities of a highly diversified enterprise and of planning and supervising its strategy made imperative the creation of a general office where the senior executives had the time and information to work out these complex, long-term decisions. In other words, both the operational activities involved in moving the goods from the producers of the raw materials to the ultimate consumer and the entrepreneurial ones involved in allocating resources to assure their most effective, or at least most profitable use, have called for the adoption of the new structure.

Variations on Structural Change

The Merchandising Enterprises

For the purposes of this chapter, the mass-merchandising enterprises should properly have been described in the second section, for while some of them have adopted the new structure, others have not. However, they must be considered separately. Although they do carry on some manufacturing and transportation, their business, like Sears, Roebuck, is largely the purchasing of a wide variety of goods that are then sold directly to the ultimate consumer. These companies that thus face a differing external situation and somewhat different internal needs must be considered, like Sears, as representatives of a subspecies of the more general industrial enterprises studied here. Where it may be safe to generalize about the comparable activities of more than 65 companies involved in the procuring or producing of raw materials, in manufacturing and distributing to the wholesalers or even to the final customers, it is unsatisfactory to do so for only a half a dozen representatives of this subspecies — the merchandising enterprises. Still, the experience of these few at least helps to document the theses that differences in the market and in methods of marketing brought administrative complexity and that necessary structural changes have often been delayed by the attitudes of senior executives. Here the different developments of Sears, Roebuck and its major competitor parallel closely those of General Motors and Ford.

At Montgomery Ward & Co., Incorporated, the administrative strains raised by the move from mail-order to over-the-counter retailing were undoubtedly similar to those at Sears. To Sewell Avery, who took command of Sears's competitor during the middle of the depression, the therapy was centralization.[62] With renewed growth after the depression, centralized control through a functionally departmentalized structure continued. Avery, like Ford, wanted to run his empire by himself. As a result, former executives of Montgomery Ward became as plentiful in the 1940's as the members of the famous Ford alumni association had been in the 1920's. Once a new management was installed after Avery was finally forced into retirement in the mid-1950's, it quickly copied the structure that had been developed at Sears, just as Ford adopted the one created by General Motors.

Of the other large marketing firms, those in the food business, A. & P., Kroger, and Safeway Stores, have adopted similar structure with autonomous territorial divisions and with a general office with general executives and staff specialists and, of course, a centralized buying organization.[63] On the other hand, those merchandising firms that sell nonperishable goods, such as Woolworth and J. C. Penney, were managed in 1960 much as they had been a generation before. They operated in much the same locations and handled much the same type of merchandise. For these reasons, they were both feeling the major population change — the move to the suburbs — and were also affected by the development of new retail outlets. Nevertheless, their growth, which has not been as rapid as in the food chains, has continued along the same lines in a profitable enough manner. They have not yet felt the need to change their business as radically as Sears did in 1925. Since the products that they market do not require the flexibility and local decision making so necessary in the selling of food and other perishables, these firms will probably continue to retain their older structures. Even so, they might benefit from a structure similar to Sears and Montgomery Ward that would permit operating decisions, based on changing market demand and taste, to be integrated more intimately with local conditions. Veteran top management may have slowed changes at both Woolworth and Penney. But more study is necessary before the experiences of these merchandising companies can be properly compared and analyzed.

Summary of the Process of Structural Change within the Enterprise

This brief review of the administrative history of more than seventy of America's largest industrial enterprises tells much more about why and how they altered their strategy than about how they changed their structures. Only a study of a company's internal business documents and letters can accurately reveal the details of structural reorganization. Nevertheless, this general survey of why some enterprises adopted the new structure and others did not does not appear to contradict or disprove, and often adds positive confirmation to, the generalizations developed in the four case studies based on such records. These points should be covered before reviewing the reasons why these great industrial empires turned to the strategies that necessitated structural change.

This short survey not only stresses that expansion did cause administrative problems which led, in time, to organization change and readjustment, but it further suggests that the essential reshaping of administrative structure nearly always had to wait for a change in the top command. Clearly many empire builders — those industrialists who initially brought vast numbers of men, and amounts of money and of materials, under a single corporate roof — had relatively little interest in devising schemes to assure a more efficient over-all management of these resources. Henry Ford, Walter P. Chrysler, Orlando F. Weber, Herbert H. and Willard H. Dow, Harry F. Sinclair, Captain Alfred E. Hunt and his son Roy A. Hunt of Alcoa, Stephen T. Birch of Kennecott, Cornelius F. Kelley of Anaconda, Elbert H. Gary of United States Steel, Ernest T. Wier of National Steel, Camille Dreyfus of Celanese, and Paul W. Litchfield of Goodyear, all had much the same lack of concern about systematic administration as had William C. Durant, Richard Sears, and Coleman du Pont. The same was true of Sewell Avery, who had helped organize and run the United States Gypsum Company before becoming head of Montgomery Ward.

In general, the few firms among those studied here that remained family held have tended to be slower in changing both structure and strategy than the others. Deere, Distillers-Seagrams, Firestone, Swift, and Singer Sewing Machine as well as Dow and Alcoa long preferred to stick to the old ways. One reason for the lack of change at the tobacco companies may have been the continuing presence of the family in top management. Or what is more likely, the routinization of activities and the lack of strategic decisions in these single-line firms made it easier to keep the family in their top management. Only occasionally have younger members of the original founder's family, like Fowler McCormick and Henry Ford II, encouraged structural reorganization on taking office. The experience of other family-held enterprises stresses the significance of Pierre du Pont's decision to remove or not promote prominent members of the family who were not competent to manage a great industrial enterprise. The broad survey of American industrial companies also reinforces a point suggested in the case studies on General Motors and Sears, Roebuck as well as du Pont. This is that nothing is more crucial to the later history of a firm than the way in which its founders or their families make their terms with the administrative imperatives of large-scale enterprise.

Often, then, organization building has had to wait until the passing of the first generation of administrators. This was not only true at Ford, United States Steel, Sinclair Oil, and the other companies mentioned in the past two paragraphs but also at International Nickel, International Business Machines, Standard Oil of Indiana, and undoubtedly others. Even in those enterprises where professional managers had long been in full charge, necessary organizational changes usually had to wait for the departure of the older executives. New and younger top men have shown more of an interest in and a willingness to alter the ways of their daily work than did their predecessors. This was the case at International Harvester, Chrysler, General Electric, Westinghouse, Armour, Socony-Mobil, Continental Oil, National Dairy, United States Rubber and undoubtedly other companies. In these companies and in those which I have not had the time to study the evidence on the turnover of top personnel in detail — the latter include Standard of California, Shell, Gulf, Hercules, Monsanto, Goodrich, General Foods, General Mills, Borden, Procter & Gamble, and Eastman Kodak — the reorganizers considered their problems as administrative rather than functional ones, to be answered by new organizational structure and practice. Finally, evidence in nearly all these companies indicates that, before the changes came, the senior executives were being increasingly bogged down in operational activities. But it is not detailed enough to make clear whether engineering, business school, or other type of training helped make the younger men more aware of the growing organizational needs.

Nor does this brief review of the experience of these many companies add much to the understanding of the process of organizational change within the enterprise. It tells little about who first suggested, who favored, and who first opposed the changes. The survey is not detailed enough, for example, to point out the very significant role that management consultants, such as McKinsey & Company (a successor to Frazer & Talbot, the consultants in Sears's initial reorganization), Robert Heller & Associates, Cresap, McCormick and Paget, Booz, Allen and Hamilton, and A. T. Kearney and Company have had in bringing about the adoption of the new structure as well as introducing many other administrative innovations and practices.

Only here and there does this summary suggest the important variations in the multidivisional structure. Although all who adopted it have built autonomous multidepartmental divisions and general offices with general executives and staff specialists, the internal arrangements of the general office and the specific relations of the division to the general and staff executives have varied from company to company. In a few, and these are nearly all oil companies, the general office still supervises the functional departments as well as the multifunctional divisions. So also there have been differences in the types of information and statistical data developed to flow through the structure: market and economic forecasts and analyses; return-on-investment and share-of-the-market data; periodic reports and visits to the operating units by executives from the higher administrative offices. A comprehensive analysis of organizational change within the great corporation calls for much more study.

On the other hand, the review of the administrative history of these seventy or more companies indicates even more clearly than the detailed case studies why the large American industrial enterprise developed new strategies of growth. It also strongly reinforces the reasons developed in the four analyses as to why strategic expansion required structural readjustment. Clearly the market was of overwhelming importance to the changing structure and strategy of American industrial enterprise. The changing American market shaped strategic initial growth, integration, and diversification. The coordination of the enterprise's resources, old and new, to the changing market called for the building of the centralized, functionally departmentalized structure. Further expansion on a wide regional scale or into new lines of business led to the construction of different autonomous divisions so that the enlarged functional activities of the enterprise could be closely integrated with differing market demands. An understanding of this intimate relation between the market and the administration of the firm, so strikingly revealed by the administrative history of many great companies, makes possible a more general explanation of how the large American industrial enterprise grew and, in growing, shaped and reshaped its administrative structure.

CONCLUSION—CHAPTERS IN THE HISTORY OF THE GREAT INDUSTRIAL ENTERPRISE

THE COMPARISON of the experience of a sizable sample of large industrial enterprises with that of four pioneers in modern American business administration provides much, though certainly still insufficient, information on which to generalize about the growth and management of this critically important economic institution in the United States. The comparison emphasizes that a company's strategy in time determined its structure and that the common denominator of structure and strategy has been the application of the enterprise's resources to market demand. Structure has been the design for integrating the enterprise's existing resources to current demand; strategy has been the plan for the allocation of resources to anticipated demand. The performance of these companies further suggests that a self-generating force for the growth of the industrial enterprise within a market economy like that of the United States has been the drive to keep resources effectively employed. The same need has shaped the ways, particularly the structure, by which a firm has been managed. Historically then, the role of administration and the function of the administrator in the large American enterprise have been to plan and direct the use of resources to meet the short-term and long-term fluctuations and developments in the market.

Of these resources, trained personnel with manufacturing, marketing, engineering, scientific, and managerial skills often became even more valuable than warehouses, plants, offices, and other physical facilities. Growth and shifts in the location of population, technological developments, and changes in consumer income, all affected the markets to which the administrators applied these resources. Of the two types of administrative decisions, one — the strategic — dealt with the long-term allocation of existing resources and the development of new ones essential to assure the continued health and future growth of the enterprise. The other — the tactical — was more involved in ensuring the efficient and steady use of current resources whose allocation had already been decided.

If the need to use resources provided the dynamic force that changed structure and strategy, the nature of the investment in these resources helped to determine the course and direction of growth and of subsequent structural change. The type of investment, in turn, depended on the technology of production and the techniques of marketing of the individual companies' original product line or lines. Finally, the rate of growth and the effectiveness in the use of the enterprise's resources rested on the ability and ingenuity of its administrators to build, adjust, and apply its personnel and facilities to broad population, technological, and income changes. Although the enterprise undoubtedly had a life of its own above and beyond that of its individual executives, although technological and market requirements certainly set boundaries and limits to growth, nevertheless, its health and effectiveness in carrying out its basic economic functions depended almost entirely on the talents of its administrators.

The market, the nature of their resources, and their entrepreneurial talents have, with relatively few exceptions, had far more effect on the history of large industrial firms in the United States than have antitrust laws, taxation, labor and welfare legislation, and comparable evidences of public policy. Possibly tax regulations have had more of an impact on the strategy of expansion since World War II, but their influence has not appreciably altered broad trends in the structure and strategy of great enterprise. On the other hand, government action such as defense or countercyclical spending that directly affected the market by increasing the national income or by making the government itself a large customer has had a significant effect on the growth of the large enterprise. The changing munitions market was of far more importance, for example, to the history of the du Pont Company than any antitrust action. Antitrust activity has had probably the greatest impact on corporate structure and strategy in those relatively rare cases where it transformed a monopoly into an oligopoly. Yet even in the case of the oil industry, the coming of a huge and entirely new automobile market was as significant as was the breakup of Standard Oil to the strategies and pace of growth of Gulf, Texaco, Shell, Sinclair, Phillips, and other large oil companies.

Historically, the executives administering American industrial enterprises have followed a recognizable pattern in the acquisition and use of resources. The initial acquisition of extensive plant, equipment, and personnel came to meet rapidly growing and often new demands for the products of their company. Or a large enterprise may have come into existence when a number of small firms that had expanded production combined and then consolidated their activities in the face of a temporary decline in demand. To be sure of more certain outlet for their goods, the administrators of enlarged enterprises built their own distributing and marketing (usually wholesaling) organization; to be assured of essential materials, they obtained control over supplies. Once these resources had been acquired, the executives responsible for the destiny of the enterprise began to pay increasing attention to using them more rationally and efficiently. Among other things, this called for the formation of an administrative structure to mobilize systematically the resources within each functional activity and to coordinate with market demand the flow through and to determine the level of activity within the functional departments.

Then came a second period of growth and a second rationalization of the use of the firm's resources. As the enterprise reached the limits of the existing market set by available consumer income, the state of technology, and the location of population, and as it came to the limits of cost reduction through rational and systematic integration and use of its resources, its senior executives began to seek new markets or new lines of business where they might apply some resources only partially used or where existing ones might be employed more profitably. A threatened decline of existing demand even more dramatically increased the pressure to find new markets. Not only did they seek these overseas but they also took their enterprises into new lines of businesses that were similar enough to its existing activities to permit a transfer of resources. The latter type of expansion was practical, however, only if some skills of some of the personnel and the capacity of some of the facilities could be transferred without too great a cost to new lines. Finally, those companies that did develop new markets or new products then had to reshape the channels of communication and authority within the enterprise. Otherwise, the offices managing the several functional activities lost contact with the new and even the old markets, and the senior executives had increasing difficulty in allocating intelligently the expanded and more varied resources at their command.

Thus four phases or chapters can be discerned in the history of the large American industrial enterprise: the initial expansion and accumulation of resources; the rationalization of the use of resources; the expansion into new markets and lines to help assure the continuing full use of resources; and finally the development of a new structure to make possible continuing effective mobilization of resources to meet both changing short-term market demands and long-term market trends. Although each company had a distinct and unique history, nearly all followed along this general pattern. Because all of them operated within the same external environment, these chapters in the collective history of the industrial enterprise or the history of the enterprise considered as an economic institution followed roughly the underlying changes in the over-all American economy.

Of course, the timing of the chapters for the individual companies varied. In the newer industries based on the internal-combustion and electrical engine and on modern chemistry and physics, they came somewhat later than in the older metals or tobacco, sugar, meat packing, and others that processed agricultural products.

In very general terms, then, many of America's largest industrial enterprises initially accumulated their resources in the years between the 1880's and World War I. During the first two decades of the twentieth century, these same firms built their initial administrative structures. For some, continued expansion, largely through diversification, began in the 1920's, but for most it came after the depression of the 1930's. Thus, although the pioneers in the fashioning of a new structural form to manage these expanded resources began their work in the 1920's, most enterprises carried out their major structural reorganizations in the 1940's and 1950's.[1]

The First Chapter — Accumulating Resources

The large American industrial enterprise was born and nurtured in the rapidly industrializing and urbanizing economy of the post–Civil War years. The great railroad construction boom of those years helped swell the population of the agrarian West. It stimulated even more the swift growth of the older commercial centers that serviced the agrarian economy and of the new industrial cities rising to meet the expanding demand for manufactured goods. The railroad itself created a huge new market for the basic iron and steel and machinery industries. The needs of the railroad for vast sums of capital led to the growth of the modern money market in the United States and with it the modern investment banking house, which made it relatively easy later for industrials to tap a wide pool of European and American capital. The construction of the railroads and the rapid urban growth gave work to the unskilled immigrants and farm boys who poured into the larger cities after 1850. The new working force not only provided a supply of labor for the growing industrial enterprises, but also increased the demand for their products. By the 1880's, nearly every existing manufacturing enterprise could reach by railroad a large rural and even more swiftly growing industrial and urban market.

To meet these opportunities, industrial enterprises began to enlarge their productive facilities, labor force, and trained supervisory personnel. Often the new resources were self-generated. The firm's profits provided the funds for further expansion, while the skills of its personnel were developed as the latter carried out their daily tasks. If the enterprise needed outside funds for expansion and combination, it went to the Eastern financial centers. In the 1890's, as railroad expansion leveled off, investment houses that had grown and made their initial reputation in the marketing and handling of railroad securities—firms like J. P. Morgan & Co.; A. M. Kidder & Company; Lee, Higginson & Company; Kuhn, Loeb; Brown Brothers & Company—all began to float and trade in industrial securities. Also as railroad construction declined, the laborers from abroad and from rural America found work in the enlarged steel mills, oil refineries, meat-packing, electrical, farm machinery, and implement plants.

In meeting the new demand, industrialists had more difficulty in obtaining a distribution network than expanding production facilities. The makers of new types of goods, which were often based on technological innovations, created their own distributing and marketing organizations with warehouses, transportation equipment, offices, and even retail outlets. The makers of the older, more staple commodities, however, generally waited until they had combined and consolidated with their fellows before creating marketing organizations. Combination normally proved to be only a temporary expedient, simply because it led to, and indeed demanded, a limited use of the firm's available resources. Consolidation, on the other hand, permitted the lowering of unit costs through high-volume production for the large market. Even so, the need to keep the consolidated production activities working steadily called for closer coordination with the customer demand through the creation of a marketing organization. Conversely, only firms of large capacity could afford to buy or build and to maintain nationwide marketing facilities.

Consolidation, and with it the formation of a marketing department, was usually followed or accompanied by forming purchasing departments and often by obtaining control of raw materials. Beside making possible the economies of large-scale purchasing, the new department made it easier to coordinate supplies with the needs of the mills for materials. Where there was a possibility of a few outsiders or even of competitors obtaining control of a company's basic raw and semifinished materials, the enterprise often moved into the production and transportation of those materials. The main reason for the purchasing of parts and accessories firms was often to assure the close and steady flow of these parts to the primary assemblying or manufacturing activities. Thus, in many key American industries after the 1880's a few great enterprises took over the several different stages of the industrial processes that, up to that time, had always been operated by separate, relatively small wholesalers, manufacturers, transporters, and raw materials producers.

The Second Chapter—Rationalizing the Use of Resources

The creation of these huge new vertically integrated enterprises was the work of the empire builders of American industry. These men, whose names are among the best known in the folklore of American business, usually turned over the administration of the vast resources they had accumulated to other individuals. Their successors had to develop methods for managing rationally the large agglomerations of men, money, and materials. Often in their eagerness to meet the new market, the empire builders in one industry had collected more facilities and personnel than were really necessary to meet the existing demand. Continuing profits depended on the lowering of costs through the systematizing of operations.

In this second period, this pressing task was twofold. First, unit costs had to be reduced by rationalizing the several functional activities and, second, these functional activities had to be closely integrated to market fluctuations. The first task led to the definition of lines of authority and communication within a single functional department; the second brought a structure for the enterprise as a whole. With the first came the systematizing and improving of the processes and techniques of marketing, manufacturing, and the procurement of raw materials. The final form of the second reflected closely the marketing requirements of the firm's products.

For those enterprises that continued to sell ores or primary metals, the task was the least complicated. Here, the market organization remained small, and the flow could be quickly adjusted to current price. But where fabricated shapes and forms made to exact customer specifications were the products, much closer coordination between the selling and manufacturing activities became necessary. To deliver promptly goods made to a bewildering variety of specifications and at the same time to keep large plants operating fairly steadily necessitated scheduling of a high order of skill. When the line of goods became even more technologically complex, as in the case of electrical apparatus, power machinery, and construction equipment companies, then the coordination of production often became even more difficult than in the steel and metal firms. Also the designing of new or improved products to meet customer needs and to counter the offerings of competitors demanded the close cooperation of the marketing, manufacturing, and engineering departments.

For those companies that also manufactured for the producers' market but whose more standardized products were made in advance of orders, the coordination of resources offered somewhat different challenges. In the companies making explosives, chemicals, industrial rubber, glass, paper, metal containers, trucks and farm implements, small engines, and other power machinery and equipment, the scheduling of the flow through the different departments was more routine than it was for nonstandard goods. But because these products were not tailored to specific orders, increasingly accurate estimates of market demand were required so that the different departments would not be caught with either too much or too little inventory of materials, parts, and finished goods. Since the customers' needs varied, technically trained personnel helped coordinate designing, making, and selling so that the standardized product might be made to fit these different needs.

Those enterprises selling products for use by the mass consumer had still another set of problems. Because they tended to have a much larger volume of goods, not based on specific orders, flowing through their various activities than did the enterprises selling to the producers' market, the flow had to be directed still more closely toward the short-term fluctuations of demand if resources were to be used efficiently. Among the first to be faced with this problem of coordinating high-volume flow were the makers of perishable products like meat and fruit. By the turn of the century, the meat packers, with their heavy investment in distributing and purchasing as well as in the processing of all kinds of meats, had pioneered in such coordination by developing telegraphic communications between the branch houses, the packing plants, and the stockyards. Both the branch houses and the buyers in the stockyards were in constant telegraphic communication with the central offices in Chicago. And with such information, the central office could allocate supply to demand almost instantaneously.

The makers of less perishable consumer goods came to require even more than this instantaneous coordination between supply and demand. The processes involved in converting their raw materials into finished goods readily available for customer use were more complex and took more time to accomplish than did those in meat packing and some other food industries. This meant a still larger investment in inventory and greater difficulty in adjusting all activities to short-term shifts in demand. Thus the makers of gasoline, tires, tobacco, and some of the less perishable foods began to rely on long-term as well as short-term estimates of the market in order to coordinate and guide product flow through the several departments, and to determine the use of resources within the functional departments.

For the producers of consumer durables, the need was even more critical. Here the investment was still greater, there were more steps in the process, and each functional activity was more complex. To adjust the flow was more difficult and the failure to adjust more costly. Also, because of the relatively expensive materials involved and the relatively high final unit price, the market changes affected unit cost even more than in other industries; that is, in the automobile and appliance businesses variable unit costs rose and fell more sharply with an increase and decrease of output than in most industries. So it was that General Motors and the electrical companies were among the first to develop statistical methods for estimating long-term and short-term demand on which all current activity became based.

In this way, then, the need to apply resources effectively to changes in short-term demand brought the creation of a centralized, functionally departmentalized administrative structure. The functional activities were departmentalized in order to assure effective and rational coordination, appraisal, and planning in each. The central office, in turn, had to make certain the coordination of these different activities in relation to the market. The resulting structure provided a communication network that linked all the facilities involved in the industrial process with the customer's demand. Such a network rendered easier the accurate compliance with specifications as well as rapid and prompt delivery in the producers' goods industries, and the adjustment of volume of output and the making of minor changes in product necessary to meet the fluctuating demands of the mass-consumer-goods industries.

The senior executives at the central office of the functionally departmentalized structures had to make strategic decisions concerning the future allocation of resources as well as tactical ones to assure their efficient current use. Just as operational activities became tied to the short-term estimates of the market, entrepreneurial ones became increasingly based on estimates and forecasts of long-term changes. As the methods for allotting funds, equipment, and personnel became systematized through the development of formal budgets and capital appropriation procedures, their allocation also came to be based on forecasts of the broader economic and financial conditions as well as of the anticipated performance of the specific market. Through such procedures, these executives were able to review, formulate, and approve plans to maintain and expand their share of the existing market. As the structure was worked out, the allocation of future and the application of present resources became more routinized, and basic entrepreneurial decisions became least frequent. But when the responsible executives decided to move into new markets, the older structure began to hinder the efficient allocation and uses of the firm's resources.

The Third Chapter — Continued Growth

At the end of the first chapter in its history, an enterprise had accumulated enough resources to meet the demands of the national market and often those of foreign ones accessible by steamship and railroad. For the large companies in the older American industries — the metals and foods and some consumer goods like rubber boots and shoes — this period came to an end around the turn of the century. For those in the electrical industry, it lasted somewhat longer; while many large automobile, power machinery, gasoline, tire, and chemical companies were still rounding out this first chapter in the 1920's. At the end of the second chapter, administrators had defined, sometimes with great care and at others in more of an *ad hoc* informal manner, structures to assure more efficient use of the accumulated resources. In the older industries, these structural changes usually came before World War I, for the newer ones in the 1920's and 1930's.

Then, as other firms followed the innovators in developing more efficient purchasing, production, distribution, and above all administrative methods, cost differentials between companies lessened and profit margins droppd. More intensive advertising, product differentiation and improvement, and similar strategies might increase one firm's share of the market, but only major changes in technology, population, and national income could expand the over-all market for a single line of products. As the market became more saturated and the opportunities to cut costs through more rational techniques lessened, enterprises began to search for other markets or to develop other businesses that might profitably employ some of their partially utilized resources or even make a more profitable application of those still being fully employed.

The first step was to develop a "full line" of comparable products.[2] Steel and aluminum firms had "warehouse" lines and special ones for specific industries beside their orders made to customer specifications. The harvester companies built their full line of agricultural implements. The meat packers moved to eggs, poultry, and dairy products to use the refrigerated facilities of their distributing network. The electrical companies developed everything involved in setting up, operating, and maintaining power and light systems. The gasoline companies had their lubricant line. The tire firms made steel rims as well as rubber tires. There are numerous other examples. At the same time, these enterprises intensified their drive to cover the domestic and international market. Expansion overseas often meant the setting up of manufacturing and purchasing as well as marketing facilities. While some companies like International Harvester, Armour, and Swift had invested more than just marketing resources abroad before World War I, many, particularly the chemical firms, only did so after World War II.

More significant than either the filling out of the major line or the move overseas was the development of new products that were often sold to quite different sets of customers. Either new end products might be fashioned from the existing lines or less often wholly new products developed in research laboratories that still employed some of the company's skills and facilities. Sometimes the enterprise began this move by concentrating more on by-products. Often it turned to a brand new field. In either case, the nature of the company's original line and the resulting accumulation of resources determined the extent to which the new products could be developed and new markets captured. In enterprises whose products and processing were based on a highly complex technology, both skills and facilities were most easily transferred to new lines of goods. On the other hand, in those that were less technologically complex and whose resources were concentrated more in raw materials and manufacturing, such a transfer was far more difficult.

Firms whose resources were concentrated in a single function such as transportation had little to transfer besides surplus funds. When a shipping concern, like W. R. Grace & Company, purchased chemical and petroleum companies, it was acting largely as a Wall Street investment house, for it had very few facilities or personnel to re-employ in its new ventures. Many great multifunctional enterprises with vast resources tied up in men and equipment to handle a single line of products have been more reluctant than Grace even to reinvest profits outside of their single major line. They needed funds from their profits to maintain their very large existing investment. When enterprises with few transferable resources, such as the producers and sellers of steel and other metals, and of tobacco, whisky, sugar, and other goods processed from agricultural products, expanded either through merger, or purchase, or the building of new facilities, they usually did so in order to obtain a full line or occasionally to take on allied products for much the same type of market as their own. For comparable reasons, tire and oil companies with huge resources concentrated on a single line have hesitated to embark on a strategy of broad diversification. For some processors of farm products, the task has been easier. A far wider range of products could be made from wheat and milk than from tobacco, bananas, or even meat.

Where a company's resources are invested more in marketing than in raw materials or producing facilities, the opportunity for diversification seems to have been greater. However the enterprises whose resources were the most transferable remained those whose men and equipment came to handle a range of technology rather than a set of end products. In the chemical, electrical and electronic, and power machinery industries, the same personnel using much the same facilities with much the same supplies of raw materials were able to develop new engines, new machines, new household appliances, new synthetic fibers, new films or plastics, or new electrical and electronic devices. Since the enterprises in these industries required the highest of technological skills, their administrators invested increasingly larger amounts of their total resources in research and development. Such resources became less and less tied to any specific product line. As rubber, petroleum, and food companies began to develop technologically advanced skills and facilities, particularly during World War II, they too started to build more of a diversified product line. For all of them, continued growth and with it the accumulation of resources came in their new lines rather than in the old.

The Fourth Chapter—Rationalizing the Use of Expanding Resources

While the strategy of diversification permitted the continuing and expanded use of a firm's resources, it did not assure their efficient employment. Structural reorganization became necessary. If expansion resulted only in the development of a full line of goods that continued to use much the same type of resources, the reorganization of the marketing department so that it had an office for each major type of customer was usually sufficient. But where business diversified into wholly new lines for quite different customers with quite different wants, then more reorganization was needed. It became increasingly difficult to coordinate through the existing structure the different functional activities to the needs of several quite different markets.

Channels of communication and authority as well as the information flowing through these channels grew more and more inadequate. The wants of different customers varied, and demand and taste fluctuated differently in different markets. Such changing market demands and the actions of competitors brought a growing differentiating of the manufacture and procurement of raw materials for the various product lines. Responsibility for maintaining and expanding the enterprise's share of the markets became harder to pin point. In time, then, each major product line came to be administered through a separate, integrated autonomous division. Its manager became responsible for the major operating decisions involved in the coordination of functional activities to changing demand and taste. Expansion into new regions encouraged the formation of comparable divisions for comparable reasons. Yet, as the different geographical markets became more homogeneous (and this occurred as all parts of the United States became more industrial and more urbanized and suburbanized), the regionally defined divisions in petroleum, dairy products, and container enterprises tended to combine into a single unit for one line of products.

Expansion, primarily through diversification, enlarged the range, number, and complexity of the entrepreneurial activities required of the senior executives. The long-term allocation of resources now involved deciding between the expansion, maintenance, and contraction of personnel, plant, and equipment in several different, large-scale, widespread businesses.

The appraisal of existing performance as well as the planning of future uses of resources called for a general office in which the executives were given the time, the information, and the encouragement to develop a broad view, all so necessary for the handling of the new and more complex problems. The multidivisional structure met both the short-term and long-term requirements for the profitable application of resources to the changing markets.

In recent years, the builders of the new organizational structures could look to the model created by du Pont, General Motors, Jersey Standard, and Sears, Roebuck. But before the 1930's, those few firms that had developed lines of business which might have been more effectively administered through a multidivisional structure envisaged only two structural alternatives. To the meat packers, rubber companies, and makers of power machinery, the activities had either to be incorporated into a centralized, functionally departmentalized structure or placed in almost completely independent subsidiaries. In either case, the executives responsible for the destiny of the enterprise had little information about or understanding of how the resources not applied directly to the primary line were being employed. Once the new type of structure became known, as it did during the 1930's, its availability undoubtedly encouraged many enterprises to embark on a strategy of diversification, for the ability to maintain administrative control through such an organizational framework greatly reduced the risks of this new type of expansion.

In fact, the systematizing of strategic decisions through the building of a general office and the routinizing of product development by the formation of a research department have, in a sense, institutionalized this strategy of diversification. Companies whose processes are closely related to the science of chemistry and physics have turned to developing new products steadily in order to assure continuing profitable use of resources that are becoming increasingly based on a technology rather than a product line. The research department develops the products and tests their commercial value. The executives in the general office, freed from all but the most essential entrepreneurial duties, can determine, in something of a rational manner, whether the new product uses enough of the firm's present resources or will help in the development of new ones to warrant its production and sale. If it does and if its market is similar to that of the current line, then its production and sale can be handled through an existing division. If the market is quite different, a new division can and should be formed.

The coming of this new strategy and with it the new structure is of paramount importance to the present health and future growth of the American economy. While some of the new products have been sold in the mass consumer market where, according to some commentators, the technical skills and facilities are sometimes wasted, the largest proportion of the output of the chemical, electronic, electrical, and power machinery enterprises have gone to the producers' market. The industrialist has usually been much more concerned about the performance of what he purchases for his business than the consumer has been in his personal buying, as better performance normally means cutting costs. The institutionalizing of the policy of diversification thus helps to assure continued production of new products to cut costs and raise the efficiency of American industry. Such a development is far more significant to the economy's over-all health than production increases in the older basic industries, such as metals and food. The investment in research and development and in the technical skills and equipment that can handle a range of products within a comparable technology is a far more meaningful index of economic growth in a highly urban and industrial nation than is the output of steel, meat, or even automobiles.

The chapters in the collective history of the American industrial enterprise can be clearly defined. Resources accumulated, resources rationalized, resources expanded, and then once again, resources rationalized. For each individual company, these chapters vary in length, significance, and impact. Some firms never attempted to accumulate the resources essential to meet the demands of a national market. Some of those companies that did expand took longer to rationalize the use of their resources than did others. Some set up new structures very systematically, others more informally. Some began to move into new lines and new markets even before they completed building their initial administrative organization. Again some were much slower than others to join the search for new markets; and again, among those that did, some turned more quickly than others to reshaping the structure necessary for the most profitable employment of the expanded resources. A company like General Motors, by inventing a new type of structure when it first organized its accumulated resources, was able to expand through diversification without requiring further significant structural changes; while Jersey Standard's informal, *ad hoc* mobilization of its resources after 1911 meant that a rapid expansion of facilities and personnel forced a much more difficult and much lengthier reorganization in later years.

Nevertheless, if the great industrial enterprise is considered as a collective entity, then these chapters are more easily identified and examined. And if these chapters have some relation to reality, then they have some significance for the scholar, businessman, and even public officials. However, the data are still too few and the generalizations derived too tenuous and too imprecise to be the basis for suggestions for action. Yet there is some value in presenting even a tentative and partial account of the history of large American industrial enterprise simply because this is a field where myths abound, where more positive generalizations than mine have been made on much less specific data, and where recommendations for action have been seriously proposed on the basis of such generalizations. If it does nothing else, this exploratory study should provide the student of business history and business administration as well as other scholars with some suggestions for significant areas of investigation.

Further researchers in the growth and administration of American industry and business must consider the importance of the market. That the expansion and government of industrial enterprises in a market economy should be closely related to the changing nature of the market seems obvious enough. Yet many writers dealing with principles of business administration, often discuss leadership, communication, and structure with only passing reference to the market. On the other hand, economists, antitrust lawyers, and other experts on market behavior have said little about the impact of the market on corporate administration. The building of the multidivisional structure is, for example, thought to be as feasible in a steel as in a chemical enterprise. Or competition in the steel industry is considered to be comparable with that in the oil or chemical industries, or administrative needs to be much the same in one period of an enterprise's history as in another.

Nor should scholars forget the critical role that the large enterprise in a market economy plays in allocating the nation's economic resources. The success or failure in the allocation of funds, facilities, and skills provides a useful test of the performance and ability of American industrial executives. The criteria for success used by the industrialists themselves — lowering unit costs, increasing output per worker, and long-term return on investment — may by mid-twentieth century, have become too narrow. Yet even if performance is to be evaluated in broader social and human terms, resources can hardly be employed effectively unless the men responsible for their use have relevant information on which to base their decisions and the means to carry them out. Without accurate and meaningful data and without clear-cut lines of communication and authority, they are forced to allocate present and future resources in a haphazard and intuitive way. In all industrial, urban, and technologically advanced societies where the large enterprise, either private or public, has acquired an essential role in planning, coordinating, and appraising economic activities, a lack of systematic structure within these organizations can lead to a wasteful and inefficient use of resources. Further studies of the way in which the great enterprise has grown and become administered have, then, more than mere scholarly value.

NOTES

NOTES

Introduction

1. Alfred D. Chandler, Jr., "Management Decentralization: An Historical Analysis," *Business History Review,* 30:111–174 (June, 1956). After the article was completed, further research indicated that Westinghouse had begun its changes in 1931.
2. The United States Rubber Company's major reorganization in 1929 was completed under du Pont direction; Goodrich quickly abandoned its initial attempt at "decentralization," returning to it only in the 1950's; and by World War II, Union Carbide had made only tentative steps to transform the functions of its headquarters from those of a holding company into those of a modern, policy-making, appraising, and coordinating unit. The reorganization at Westinghouse between 1931 and 1936 began as an independent innovation, but the company's changes were in many ways only a repetition of those that had already been put into effect at du Pont and Jersey Standard. It seemed wise, therefore, merely to outline the Westinghouse story and to broaden the scope of the study by selecting a large merchandise firm with business activities quite different from those of the integrated manufacturing companies already chosen for study.
3. The companies are listed by assets in A. D. H. Kaplan, *Big Enterprise in a Competitive System* (Washington, 1954), pp. 145–155; also *Fortune,* 62:131–150 (July, 1960). I did not include two companies on Kaplan's list, Western Electric and Cities Service Company. The first has been, for all intents and purposes, a part of the American Telephone & Telegraph Company, which takes nearly all its nonmilitary production. The second was a utility as well as an industrial enterprise until 1944. Two other large companies, General Mills and Hercules, were added because of the availability of information about them.
4. For example, the second volume of the history of the Standard Oil Company (New Jersey), George S. Gibb and Evelyn H. Knowlton, *The Resurgent Years, 1911–1927* (New York, 1956), says little about the administrative changes beginning in 1925 and does not give very much information about the history of Jersey's administrative organization. The excellent history of Sears, Boris Emmet and John E. Jeuck, *Catalogues and Counters: A History of Sears, Roebuck and Company* (Chicago, 1950), has an accurate if brief description of the 1929 changes and of the company's organizational structure at the time the book was written, but says almost nothing about the changes between these years. Moreover, by concentrating on a specific activity, I could devote more time to locating documents, and so my chapters on these two companies are based largely on records which the authors of their histories did not use.

5. Werner Sombart, "Capitalism," *Encyclopedia of the Social Sciences* (New York, 1930), III, 200. This form, in turn, is one of the institutional genera that dominate our modern political, military, religious, and educational life as well as the contemporary economic world that Max Weber first delineated as bureaucratic. (H. H. Gerth and C. Wright Mills, *From Max Weber* (New York, 1946), pp. 196–244). Weber stressed:

    It is the peculiarity of the modern entrepreneur that he conducts himself as the 'first official' of his enterprise, in the very same way in which the ruler of a specifically modern bureaucratic state spoke of himself as 'the first servant' of the state. The idea that the bureau activities of the state are intrinsically different in character from the management of private economic offices is a continental European notion and, by way of contrast, is totally foreign to the American way. (*Ibid.*, p. 198)

6. I am greatly indebted to Dr. Fritz Redlich for first pointing out to me this critically important distinction, see his "Unternehmer," *Handworterbuch der Sozialwissenschaften* (Göttingen, 1959), X, 489, and "The Business Leader in Theory and Reality," *American Journal of Economics and Sociology*, 8:223–237 (April, 1949).
7. The distinctions between the duties of the administrative offices at these different levels and the relation of the function of these offices to entrepreneurial activities within the enterprise are worked out in more detail in Alfred D. Chandler, Jr., and Fritz Redlich, "Recent Developments in American Business Administration and Their Conceptualization," *Weltwirtschaftliches Archiv*, 86:103–130 (1961).
8. The companies are listed in Tables 1 and 2. Although the sources of information about many of them will be cited in the next chapter, more historical details and often further citations are given in the preliminary study on "Management Decentralization" (see ftn. 1) and also in my "The Beginnings of 'Big Business' in American Industry," *Business History Review*, 33:1–31 (Spring, 1959), and "Development, Diversification and Decentralization," in Ralph E. Freeman, editor, *Post-War Economic Trends in the United States* (New York, 1960), ch. 7, on which parts of Chapter 1 are based.

Chapter 1

1. Examples of such early personal supervision are numerous: for example, John S. Ewing and Nancy P. Norton, *Broadlooms and Businessmen* (Cambridge, Mass., 1955), especially chs. 1 and 2; Samuel E. Morison, *The Ropemakers of Plymouth* (Boston, 1950), chs. 1–3; Caroline F. Ware, *The Early New England Cotton Manufacture: A Study in Industrial Beginnings* (Boston, 1931), chs. 4 and 7; and Allan Nevins, *Abram S. Hewitt: With Some Account of Peter Cooper* (New York, 1935), chs. 5–7, 9. Among the many studies that indicate how the early American mercantile firm was administered, particularly useful ones are: Kenneth W. Porter, *John Jacob Astor—Business Man* (Cambridge, Mass., 1931), I, especially chs. 2–3, 5–6, II, chs. 12–13; Stuart W. Bruchey, *Robert Oliver—Merchant of Baltimore, 1783–1819* (Baltimore, 1956), especially ch. 3; and Robert G. Albion, *The Rise of New York Port* (New York, 1939), chs. 12–13.
2. Porter, *Astor,* II, ch. 15. The departmental headquarters were at St. Louis

and Mackinac. William B. Astor aided his father in the Fur Company's management, often acting as its president.

3. Fritz Redlich, *The Molding of American Banking—Men and Ideas,* Part I (New York, 1951), pp. 113–126; Reginald C. McGrane, *The Correspondence of Nicholas Biddle* (New York, 1919), pp. 39–40, 67–71.
4. Daniel H. Calhoun, *The American Civil Engineer—Origins and Conflict* (Cambridge, Mass., 1960), pp. 35, 49–50, 54–60.
5. Calhoun, *American Civil Engineer,* pp. 72–78.
6. *Reports of the President and Superintendent of the New York and Erie Railroad to the Stockholders for the Year Ending September 30, 1855* (New York, n.d.) p. 34, quoted in Alfred D. Chandler, Jr., *Henry Varnum Poor—Business Editor, Analyst, and Reformer* (Cambridge, Mass., 1956), p. 146. *Report of the Directors of the New York and Erie Railroad Company to the Stockholders for the Year Ending September 30, 1853* (New York, 1853) indicates some surprisingly advanced ideas about structure (especially pp. 46–48) even before McCallum took the post of general superintendent. In my *Poor* (pp. 144–179) I give consideration to the building of the first administrative structures on American railroads.
7. The development of a systematic administrative structure on the Pennsylvania can be traced in *Pennsylvania Rail Road Company. Organization for Conducting the Business of the Road—Adopted December 26, 1857* (Philadelphia, 1858); *By-Laws and Organization for Conducting the Business of "The Pennsylvania Rail Road Company," as Revised and Approved by the Board of Directors May 13, 1863* (Philadelphia, 1863); *By-Laws and Organization for Conducting the Business of the Pennsylvania Railroad Company as Approved by the Board of Directors May 28, 1873* (Philadelphia, 1873); *By-Laws and Organization for Conducting the Business of the Pennsylvania Railroad Company. Adopted by the Board of Directors March 23, 1893* (Philadelphia, 1893); and *Report of the Investigating Committee of the Pennsylvania Railroad Company Appointed by Resolution of the Stockholders at Annual Meeting Held March 10, 1874* (Philadelphia, 1874), pp. 165–180. The company's annual reports supply additional information, particularly those dated 1849 (pp. 11–16), 1853 (pp. 26 and 48), 1858 (p. 16), 1871 (pp. 27–28 and 45), 1872 (p. 30), and 1873 (pp. 39–40 and 65–66). Ray Morris, *Railroad Administration* (New York, 1910), describes the latter development of the Pennsylvania structure (pp. 63 ff.) and of the "divisional" type of structure in which it pioneered and which became generally accepted on American railroads (ch. 4). See also Henry S. Haines, *American Railway Managemeht, Addresses Delivered before the American Railway Association, and Miscellaneous Addresses and Papers* (New York, 1897), especially pp. 132–138.
8. The statistics are from the United States Department of Commerce, Bureau of the Census, *Historical Statistics of the United States, 1798–1945* (Washington, 1949), pp. 25–29 for population, p. 14 for agricultural income.
9. Swift's story is outlined in Louis F. Swift, *The Yankee of the Yards—the Biography of Gustavus Franklin Swift* (New York, 1927). The United States Bureau of Corporations, *Report of the Commissioner of Corporations on the Beef Industry, March 3, 1905* (Washington, 1905), is excellent on the internal operations and external activities of the large meat-packing firms. There is additional information in the later three-volume *Report of the Federal Trade Commission on the Meat-Packing Industry* (Washington, 1918–1919). Rudolf

A. Clemen, *The American Livestock and Meat Industry* (New York, 1923), has some useful background data. The annual reports, particularly those of Armour, provide further information for the years after 1900.

10. Some information on James B. Duke and the American Tobacco Company can be found in John W. Jenkins, *James B. Duke, Master Builder* (New York, 1927), chs. 5–7, and the company publication, *"Sold American!"—The First Fifty Years* (n.p., 1954), chs. 2–4. More useful was the United States Bureau of Corporations' two-volume *Report of the Commissioner of Corporations on the Tobacco Industry* (Washington, 1909–1911).
11. The story of Bell is outlined in James Gray, *Business Without Boundary, The Story of General Mills* (Minneapolis, 1954), and that of Preston in Charles M. Wilson, *Empire in Green and Gold* (New York, 1947).
12. The early Singer Sewing Machine experience is well analyzed in Andrew B. Jack, "The Channels of Distribution for an Innovation: the Sewing Machine Industry in America, 1860–1865," *Explorations in Entrepreneurial History,* 9:113–141 (Feb., 1957). Eastman Kodak's experience appears to have been similar in many ways to that of Singer Sewing Machine.
13. William T. Hutchinson, *Cyrus Hall McCormick* (New York, 1935), II, 704–712.
14. Harold C. Passer, *The Electrical Manufacturers, 1875–1900* (Cambridge, Mass., 1953), especially chs. 20, 21 and also Harold C. Passer, "Development of Large-Scale Organization—Electrical Manufacturing Around 1900," *Journal of Economic History,* 12:378–395 (Fall, 1952).
15. James H. Bridge, *The Inside History of the Carnegie Steel Company* (New York, 1903), pp. 160–164; Burton J. Hendrick, *Life of Andrew Carnegie* (New York, 1932) I, 310–312; and Victor S. Clark, *History of Manufactures in the United States* (New York, 1929) II, 344–345. The demand for pipe and tubes was increased by the growth of the city and the petroleum industry, while barbed wire for the western plains created another market for the makers of finished iron and steel products.
16. According to company records, Jones & Laughlin had its own "warehousing" office in Chicago as early as 1859. The growth of middlemen who stored and sold standard shapes is indicated in Clark, *History of Manufactures,* II, 305–306, but Clark says nothing as to when manufacturers took over this function. An even more striking growth of a large sales and distributing organization to serve the new urban construction market came in the plate glass industry where the Pittsburgh Plate Glass Company was a pioneer, see pp. 341–342.
17. For details and sources, especially on United States Rubber, Standard Oil, Distillers' Securities Corporation, and National Biscuit, see Chandler, "Beginnings of 'Big Business' in American Industry," pp. 10–18. Hans B. Thorelli, *The Federal Antitrust Policy; Origination of an American Tradition* (Baltimore, 1955), pp. 63–96, 236–308, provides the most satisfactory summary of the extensive literature of the combination movement in the latter part of the nineteenth century.
18. *Annual Report of the National Biscuit Company for the Year Ending December, 1901,* January 3, 1902. References to the centralizing of manufacturing facilities appear in several early reports. As this report was written before Theodore Roosevelt had started to make the Sherman Act an effective antitrust instrument and Ida Tarbell and other journalists had begun to make "muckraking" of big business popular and profitable, the Biscuit Company's shift in policy could hardly have been the result of the pressure of public opinion or

the threat of government action. Ralph M. Hower, *The History of an Advertising Agency: N. W. Ayer & Son at Work, 1869–1939* (Cambridge, Mass., 1939), pp. 115–116, 216, 318, indicates the significance of National Biscuit's policies for the advertising business.

19. Charles R. Flint, "The Gospel of Industrial Steadiness," James H. Bridge, ed., *The Trust: Its Book* (New York, 1902), pp. 87–88, based on a talk Flint gave in Boston, May 25, 1899. Flint has comparable comments on "centralized" and "consolidated" management in his *Industrial Combinations — Address to the Illinois Manufacturers Association . . . Oct. 9, 1900,* (n.p., 1900) pp. 5–6.

20. Ralph W. Hidy and Muriel E. Hidy, *Pioneering in Big Business, 1882–1911* (New York, 1955), pp. 176–188, and Allan Nevins, *Study in Power — John D. Rockefeller, Industrialist and Philanthropist* (New York, 1953), II, 1–3. Nevins adds that another reason for the move into production was "partly to limit the number of active wells and reduce the overproduction of crude oil," II, 2, but he gives no documentation for this statement.

21. *Annual Report of The American Agricultural Chemical Company, August 14, 1907,* also the same company's *Annual Report,* dated August 25, 1902. In addition to the annual reports of the two companies, Clark, *History of Manufactures,* III, 289–291, provides information. There is a brief summary of the story of the International Agricultural Corporation in Williams Haynes, *American Chemical Industry — A History,* vol. III: World War I, 1912–1922 (New York, 1945), p. 173.

22. Hendrick, *Andrew Carnegie,* II, ch. 1; Bridge, *The Inside History of Carnegie Steel Company,* ch. 17; and Nevins, *Rockefeller,* II, 252.

23. Ida M. Tarbell, *The Life of Elbert H. Gary, the Story of Steel* (New York, 1925), pp. 86–97 and *Moody's Manual of Corporation Securities — 1901* (New York, 1901), p. 722.

24. A useful brief summary of these mergers and of those by the steel users, as well as a most concise analysis of the formation of United States Steel, is Eliot Jones, *The Trust Problem in the United States* (New York, 1921), pp. 189–200.

25. Hendrick, *Carnegie,* II, 116–119.

26. The beginnings and the operation of the United States Steel Corporation are outlined in Abraham Berglund, *The United States Steel Corporation: A Study of Growth and Combination in the Iron and Steel Industry* (New York, 1907); Arundel Cotter, *United States Steel: A Corporation With a Soul,* (New York, 1921); and Tarbell, *The Life of Gary.* Some useful new information is presented in John A. Garraty, *Right-Hand Man, The Life of George W. Perkins* (New York, 1960), pp. 93–125.

27. Arthur S. Dewing, *Corporate Promotion and Reorganizations* (Cambridge, Mass., 1914), p. 558. His list given on pp. 557–566 is particularly useful for an appreciation of the challenges facing the organization builders. For a survey of the mergers that proved successful, see Shaw Livermore, "The Success of Industrial Merger," *Quarterly Journal of Economics,* 50:68–96 (Nov., 1935). Such beliefs about the essential inefficiency of large-scale industrial organization became associated in the public mind with the views of Louis D. Brandeis. Brandeis, however, had a much more explicit ideological bias than Dewing and other academic writers. Even if the new great enterprises could be efficiently operated, they remained, in his eyes, a threat to the older values.

In testifying before a Senate Committee in 1911, Brandeis said of United States Steel:

> .... even if it should have been true that as a mere engine of production and distribution this unit would have been more efficient than a smaller one, I am convinced that the inherent, the incidental, social, and political ills which would attend the creation of that huge power would bring about evils to the community which would many times outweigh the advantage, the slight advantage, if any, which would come from an increased efficiency.

Hearings before the Committee on Interstate Commerce, United States Senate, 62nd Congress, 1st Session (1911), cited in Edwin C. Rozwenc, *Roosevelt, Wilson and the Trusts* (Boston, 1950), p. 81.

28. S. F. Van Oss, *American Railroads as Investments* (New York, 1893), p. 235. Van Oss added that the Pennsylvania's equipment, efficiency, and service "are regarded as embodying a state of perfection to equal which should be the highest ambition of every railroad company in the country."
29. These developments are indicated in the reports cited above in ftn. 7.
30. Morris, *Railroad Administration,* ch. 4.
31. Hidy, *Pioneering in Big Business,* p. 329.
32. As the information on the companies in this section will be enlarged in Chapter 7, the citations to the sources will be given there. Parts of this section and of Chapter 7 were based on my "Development, Diversification and Decentralization," in Ralph E. Freeman, editor, *Post-War Economic Trends in the United States* (New York, 1960), ch. 7, which tells of many of these companies in more detail.
33. The rural market, which in 1900 still included 60 per cent of the population, by 1920 had fallen below 50 per cent with 51.6 million of the population listed as rural and 54.2 million as urban. By 1930, these figures stood at 53.8 million and 69.0 million, respectively. Between 1910 and 1930, urban population rose 63 per cent and rural population only 8 per cent. Farm income dropped even faster. In 1919, realized private production income from agriculture was $12.7 billion and in 1929 it was $8.7 billion, *Historical Statistics of United States,* pp. 14, 25, 29.
34. While Eastman Kodak began by assemblying a durable product for the mass consumer market, it soon integrated by obtaining its own supplies of photographic chemicals. In recent years Tennessee Eastman, the chemical subsidiary, has expanded rapidly through diversification of its product line into many nonphotographic chemicals.
35. *Fortune,* 35:88 (May, 1947).
36. Kaplan, *Big Enterprise in a Competitive System,* p. 149, and *Fortune,* 62:131–150 (July, 1960).

Chapter 2

1. The following information on the company and its executives came from: William S. Dutton, *Du Pont — One Hundred and Forty Years* (New York, 1942); Bessie G. du Pont, *E. I. du Pont de Nemours and Company: A History, 1802–1902* (Boston, 1920); Marquis James, *Alfred I. du Pont — the Family Rebel* (New York, 1941); Arthur P. Van Gelder and Hugo Schlatter, *History of the Explosives Industry in America* (New York, 1927); and two antitrust cases, *United States v. E. I. du Pont de Nemours & Company,*

et al. in Circuit Court of the United States, No. 280 in Equity (1909), especially *Defendants' Record Testimony,* vols I and II, and *Petitioner's Record,* vol. II, and *United States v. E. I. du Pont de Nemours & Company, General Motors Corporation,* et al., U.S. District Court for the Northern District of Illinois, Eastern Division. Civil Action No. 49C–1071 (1953). The first case will be cited hereafter as du Pont Antitrust Suit (1909) and the second as the du Pont–General Motors Antitrust Suit.

2. Dutton, *Du Pont,* p. 172. Alfred used the term "birthright" in his description of the events, *ibid.,* p. 169.
3. Tom L. Johnson, *My Story* (New York, 1911), pp. 11–15, 26–36, 91–92.
4. Harold C. Passer, *The Electrical Manufacturers, 1875–1900* (Cambridge, Mass., 1953), pp. 334, 340.
5. Lorain's new owners sold the electric-motor and carmaking part of their business to General Electric, *ibid.,* p. 340.
6. Du Pont, *Du Pont . . . A History,* p. 140. The paragraph referring to Eugene's administration reads in full:

> In one way, however, and that a very important way, the firm's methods were unaltered. The business was entirely managed by the senior partner. It was customary for him to consult the other men in matters that concerned their departments of the industry, but he was in no way bound to accept their advice, and tradition made them hesitate to offer it or to ask questions. The head of the firm was *ex officio* head of the family. The homes of the different partners belonged to the company, and it made any additions or improvements that were necessary and took no rental. For the first sixty years of its existence the individual partners did not even own horses; when a carriage was wanted a message was sent to the office and a vehicle of some sort usually arrived in due time — there were never any too many of them. Checks were cashed at the office and all mail went through the office and was usually sorted by the head of the firm himself. The houses were near together and the partners were men of very simple and domestic tastes, to whom it would never have occurred to want more money than was necessary for the needs of their quiet lives. No one of them ever thought of drawing his full income; they gave their allegiance to the Company and its chief and with it all their ability and confidence.

7. Well described in Dutton, *du Pont,* pp. 119–123.
8. For example, Van Gelder and Schlatter, *History of Explosives,* pp. 609–610.
9. Dutton, *du Pont,* pp. 143–146, and du Pont, *Du Pont . . . A History,* pp. 136–137.
10. Pierre du Pont to Irénée du Pont, Feb. 20, 1902, du Pont-General Motors Antitrust Suit, Defendants' Exhibit DP#2. (The letters DE will be used in citing Defense Exhibits and GE in citing Government Exhibits. Unless otherwise indicated, all exhibits and testimony will be from the du Pont-General Motors Antitrust Suit. In citing the numbers of the exhibits and the pages of the testimony from this suit, those used in *United States Supreme Court Reports, 253, Records and Brief, United States* v. *E. I. du Pont de Nemours & Company, General Motors,* et al., *October Term, 1956* will be given where possible, since these records are more available than those of the District Court.)
11. The events of the purchase and consolidation are covered in detail in the du Pont Antitrust Suit (1909), especially *Defendants' Record Testimony,* I, 484–547, also *Brief for . . . Defendants,* pp. 71–93, and *Defendants' Record*

Testimony, II, 749 ff. Some of this testimony is summarized in James, *Alfred I. du Pont,* pp. 168–182. Also useful is Dutton, *Du Pont,* pp. 179–186. Although the du Pont Company itself in 1902 had manufactured some 36 per cent of the nation's powder, by 1905 the new Powder Company made 64.6 per cent of all soda blasting powder, 80 per cent of all saltpeter and blasting powder, 72.5 per cent of all black sporting powder, 70.5 per cent of all sporting smokeless powder, and, except for a small amount made by the government, 100 per cent of all military smokeless powder.

12. This quotation and the following one are from the du Pont Antitrust Suit (1909), *Defendants' Record Testimony,* I. The first is from p. 488, the second from p. 500.

13. These improvements are described in James H. Bridge, *The Inside History of The Carnegie Steel Company* (New York, 1903), ch. 12. Tom Johnson tells of his close acquaintance with D. A. Morrell, Andrew Carnegie, and other steelmakers in Johnson, *My Story,* pp. 30, 36. Irénée du Pont recalls that when a policy was discussed in the Executive Committee in the early years of the new company, Moxham, who came from Lorain with Coleman, would constantly say: "Now this is the way it was done in steel," (Interview with Irénée du Pont, August 23, 1956). The earlier organization building at General Electric is described in Harold C. Passer, "Development of Large-Scale Organization — Electrical Manufacturing Around 1900," *Journal of Economic History,* 12:378–395 (Fall, 1952).

14. Dutton, *Du Pont,* pp. 146–151. In 1895, Repauno combined with two other explosives firms to form the Eastern Dynamite Company. Each firm continued to be managed separately, with Eastern Dynamite remaining a holding company until 1902. In 1895, Haskell left Repauno to become president of Laflin & Rand.

15. Van Gelder and Schlatter, *History of Explosives,* pp. 211, 597–600, 881–882, indicate some of these changes. In the 1890's the du Pont Company itself, following the example of Repauno, began to set up some district sales offices of its own (du Pont, *Du Pont . . . A History,* p. 140).

16. See citations in ftn. 11.

17. The information on the Operating Departments came from scattered references in Dutton, *Du Pont,* bk. 3, ch. 2; James, *Alfred I. du Pont,* ch. 11; Van Gelder and Schlatter, *History of Explosives,* pt. I. ch. 7, pt. II, ch. 6, pt. III, ch. 9; and du Pont Antitrust Suit (1909), especially *Defendants' Record Testimony,* I and II.

18. These meetings are well described in Ernest Dale, "Du Pont: Pioneer in Systematic Management," *Administrative Science Quarterly,* 2:35–40 (June, 1957). This article and the one Dale wrote on General Motors, cited in the next chapter, have been reprinted in substantially the same form in Ernest Dale, *The Great Organizers* (New York, 1960). Dale has additional information on General Motors as an appendix, *ibid.,* pp. 239–261.

19. The organization of the consolidated Sales Department, completed in July, 1903, is described in the du Pont Antitrust Suit (1909), *Defendants' Record Testimony,* I, 15–33, 128–137, *Petitioner's Record,* II, 694–703; and Van Gelder and Schlatter, *History of Explosives,* pp. 614–617. The latter says the Department's Assistant Directors had charge of products (black powder, dynamite, and smokeless powder), while the testimony in the suit says the organization breakdown was by regions. Apparently the Department started

on a regional basis and shifted to a product basis. Dale ("Du Pont: Pioneer in Systematic Management," p. 44) describes the work of the Trade Record Division. Valuable too is Dale Bumstead to E. C. Ferriday, April 2, 1906, du Pont Antitrust Suit (1909), Defendants' Exhibit #201.

20. Scattered references in Dutton, *Du Pont,* bk. 3, chs. 2, 4, and Du Pont Antitrust Suit (1909), *Defendants' Record Testimony,* II, and *Petitioner's Record,* II. Page 695 of the last indicates that the Accounting Department analyzed monthly reports on sales, prepared by George Kerr's Trade Record Division.
21. *Annual Report of E. I. du Pont de Nemours & Company for 1907,* pp. 1–2; Dutton, *du Pont,* p. 185.
22. *Ibid.,* pp. 184–186.
23. James, *Alfred I. du Pont,* p. 216 and Dutton, *Du Pont* pp. 203–204. The changing relations between the two committees is indicated in a letter from Pierre du Pont to the Board of Directors, Sept. 11, 1914, GE 27.
24 Much of the workings of the initial organizational structure is made clear in the reports on structural reorganization cited below. There were also standing subcommittees of the Executive Committee for service functions like development, purchasing, and construction. The role of the subcommittees is not clear, but they may have checked the Departments' handling of those functions.
25. Dutton, *Du Pont,* pp. 202–204 and James, *Alfred I. du Pont,* pp. 213–216. Coleman was also soon involved in building and real estate activities in New York City and in time became the owner of a large chain of hotels. Beside these outside activities, Coleman had several bouts of illness in these years.
26. Alfred's removal is covered in James, *Alfred I. du Pont,* pp. 233–241. Alfred's divorce and remarriage and its effect on the family and Wilmington society in general are described in detail, *ibid.,* chs. 12–13.
27. These changes can best be seen by reviewing the biographical sketches of these men in Van Gelder and Schlatter, *History of Explosives,* and in Dutton, *Du Pont,* pp. 213–214.
28. *Ibid.,* pp. 195–199.
29. Pierre du Pont to Coleman du Pont, Aug. 28, 1914, GE 26.
30. *Annual Report(s) of E. I. du Pont de Nemours & Company for 1912 and for 1913.* Barksdale signed the first report as Acting President, Coleman the second as President. The earlier ones had been signed by Pierre as Acting President.
31. Pierre du Pont to Coleman du Pont, Aug. 28, 1914, GE 26, and Jan. 4, 1915, DE DP 9; Van Gelder and Schlatter, *History of Explosives,* pp. 541–542.
32. Pierre du Pont to Coleman du Pont, Aug. 28, 1914, GE 26, and testimony of Pierre du Pont, Feb. 25, 1953, pp. 2190–2191. The following quotation is also from the Aug. 28 letter.
33. Pierre du Pont to the Board of Directors, Sept. 11, 1914, GE 27.
34. *Ibid.* The three following quotations are from the same letter.
35. The details of the suit are most succinctly outlined in Dutton, *Du Pont,* bk. III, ch. 4.
36. *Ibid.,* pp. 218, 242–273. The creation and structure of the new chemical department is indicated in "Diagram of Organization of Du Pont Experimental Station," May 1, 1912, DE DP 229. Also wartime expansion led to the formation of departments from what had been smaller offices, such as the mechanical research, medical, and welfare departments, *Annual Report of E. I. du Pont de Nemours & Company for 1919.* The chart attached to a report of the

subcommittee on organization to the Executive Committee, Mar. 31, 1919, diagrams the structure at the war's end.

37. *Annual Report of E. I. du Pont de Nemours & Company for 1919,* p. 15.
38. Dale ("Du Pont: Pioneer in Systematic Management," p. 39) indicates early du Pont appropriations procedures. See also *Annual Report of E. I. du Pont de Nemours & Company for 1918,* pp. 15–16.
39. Information on Brown comes from *"Who's Who in Commerce and Industry* (New York, 1936) and Dale, "Du Pont: Pioneer in Systematic Management," p. 42.
40. *Fortune,* 41:166 (Oct., 1950); and American Management Association, "How the du Pont Organization Appraises its Performance," *Financial Management Series,* No. 94 (1950).
41. Report of Pierre du Pont to the Board of Directors, Apr. 7, 1919.
42. Harry Haskell to Pierre du Pont, Feb. 16, 1919, both a letter and a telegram.
43. This and the two following quotations are from Harry Haskell to Pierre du Pont, Feb. 16, 1919.
44. Report of subcommittee on organization to the Executive Committee, Mar. 31, 1919. The original report was dated Mar. 26, the only change in the first and second was a paragraph added at the end referring to William H. Moore's report.
45. Quoted from a report of Barksdale to the High Explosives Department, in Dale, "Du Pont: Pioneer in Systematic Management," p. 37.
46. This and the following fourteen quotations are from the report of the subcommittee on organization, Mar. 31, 1919. Dale has several long quotations from this report that he dates Mar. 19. He, however, erroneously suggests that it recommended the changes that went into effect in September, 1921, "Du Pont: Pioneer in Systematic Management," pp. 47–52.
47. Report of Pierre du Pont to the Board of Directors, Apr. 14, 1919.
48. Extract from Executive Committee Minutes, Apr. 14, 1919, and "Advice of Action" on that meeting. The six new members were A. Felix du Pont, Charles A. Patterson, William C. Spruance, Walter Edge, C. A. Meade, and W. S. Carpenter, Jr.
49. The Technical Division included Safety, Fire Protection, Planning, Inspection, and Costs offices; the Welfare Division included Housing, Subsistence, Personnel Relations, Sanitation, and Medicine; and the Materials and Products Division included Works Supplies, Orders, Salvage and Reclamation, Finished Products, Works Accounting, and Auditing.
50. As indicated in the later reports on organization.
51. The smaller departments — Personnel, Legal, and Real Estate — all of a staff or service nature, reported to the Chairman of the Executive Committee, whose role was very similar to that outlined for the first Vice-President in the subcommittee's organization report, while over-all supervision of publicity and military sales belonged to the President, in addition to his primary duties.
52. Dutton, *Du Pont,* p. 262.
53. The testimony of Irénée du Pont, p. 1937, also p. 1966.
54. Moxham, as the first head of the Development Department, may have explicitly told his researchers in 1903 to examine new industries into which du Pont might move. See Dutton, *Du Pont,* pp. 185–186. If so, little came from this order, for the documentary evidence presented on both sides in both the du Pont-General Motors Antitrust Suit and the earlier du Pont Antitrust Suit

makes it clear that no steps were taken toward diversification until 1908. See, for example, du Pont Antitrust Suit (1909), *Defendants' Brief*, pp. 266–268.

55. Quoted in *A History of the Du Pont Company's Relations with the United States Government, 1803–1927* (Wilmington, 1928), pp. 68, 71, 97. This book was prepared and published by the Smokeless Powder Department. In 1909, Congress voted appropriations to increase further the capacity of government powder plants.
56. *Annual Report of E. I. du Pont de Nemours & Company for 1908*, p. 2.
57. Quoted from the Executive Committee Minutes of the du Pont Company, Dec. 16, 1908, in an "Advice of Action," dated Dec. 17, 1908, DE DP 69.
58. Pierre S. du Pont to William du Pont, April 20, 1909, DE DP 7.
59. Executive Committee Minutes, Mar. 4, 1909, quoted in an "Advice of Action," dated Mar. 6, 1909, DE DP 70.
60. W. W. Richards to Irénée du Pont, "Artificial Leather — Nitrated Cotton Requirements," Mar. 16, 1909, GE 101, and an interview with Irénée du Pont, Aug. 23, 1956.
61. This and the following quotation are from the "Annual Report of Development Department for the Year 1909," Feb. 9, 1910, DE DP 72. Also useful on the investigation of these industries and its results is the testimony of Irénée du Pont, Feb. 17, 1953, pp. 1916–1931.
62. "Report of the Development Department on Artificial Silk," Feb. 9, 1910, DE DP 72, and "Annual Report of Development Department for the Year 1909," Feb. 9, 1910, DE DP 72. Also testimony for Irénée du Pont, Feb. 18, 1953, pp. 1932–1934.
63. This and the following quotation are from "Annual Report of Development Department for the Year 1909," Feb. 9, 1910, DE DP 72.
64. Report to Finance Committee from Cellulose Products Department, entitled "History and Prospects of Fabrikoid Industry," Nov. 4, 1921, GE 106.
65. In 1913, in order to obtain a foreign outlet and patents, the du Pont Company formed with a British firm — the Pluviusin Company — the du Pont Fabrikoid Co., of which the British company held one-sixth of the stock. The Fabrikoid Company was only a legal organization; no managerial change took place, and Fabrikoid continued to be manufactured and sold by the du Pont Operating and Sales Departments. In 1914, the company purchased an artificial leather manufacturing firm in Canada. By 1920, these companies had been liquidated, "Report of Development Department to Development Committee," Oct. 11, 1912, GE 104, and "History and Prospects of Fabrikoid Industry." Nov. 4, 1921, GE 106.
66. Report of W. W. Richards to R. R. M. Carpenter, Sept. 12, 1913, DE DP 71. Although many years later Lammot du Pont and other company officials claimed that the adverse decision in the antitrust case decided in 1911 turned the company towards diversification, contemporary evidence makes it clear that excess capacity resulting from the loss of government orders, rather than antitrust action, provided the initial motivation to move beyond explosives. The court and the government had, largely at the urging of the Army and Navy, permitted the company to retain all its military powder plants. Neither of the two new companies carved out of du Pont had any smokeless powder operations until after the outbreak of World War I. Du Pont had exactly as much of a monopoly of that business in 1913 as it had had in 1903; and from the first, the diversification program at du Pont was based wholly on finding

uses for nitrocellulose, a material used primarily in smokeless powder rather than high explosives.

67. "Progress Report on Celluloid Investigation," Apr. 17, 1914, GE 108, which includes a summary of an earlier report on this same subject dated Feb. 6, 1914, and testimony of Irénée du Pont, Feb. 17, 1953, pp. 1925–1929.
68. This and the following quotation are from "Progress Report on Celluloid Investigation," Apr. 17, 1914, GE 108.
69. This and the following three quotations are from report of Development Department to the Executive Committee on "Building and Operating a Celluloid Plant," Nov. 11, 1914, DE DP 73.
70. *Ibid.* One reason for deciding on a pilot plant was "The apparent diversity of opinion regarding the most efficient process of operation among the oldest and most experienced manufacturers."
71. "Annual Report of Development Department to Executive Committee," Dec. 31, 1914, DE DP 77, and testimony of Irénée du Pont, Feb. 18, 1953, p. 1934.
72. The information for this paragraph comes from the *Annual Report(s) of E. I. du Pont de Nemours & Company for 1917 and 1918*; Dutton, Du Pont, pp. 226–229; Williams Haynes, *American Chemical Industry — A History,* vol. III: World War I, 1912–1922 (New York, 1945), pp. 192–200.
73. Pierre du Pont to Coleman du Pont, Jan. 14, 1915, DE DP 10.
74. *Annual Report of E. I. du Pont de Nemours & Company for 1918,* especially pp. 3–4, 10, and testimony of Irénée du Pont, Feb. 18, 1953, pp. 1942–1944. According to the annual reports, net earnings rose from $25.2 million in 1914 to $57.4 in 1915 to $82.0 in 1916 and then fell to $49.1 in 1917 and $47.2 in 1918. The dividend record of E. I. du Pont de Nemours & Company for the four years 1915 to 1918 was 30 per cent, 100 per cent, 51 per cent, and 26 per cent, respectively.
75. Memorandum from Irénée du Pont to Development Department, May 3, 1915, DE DP 75; testimony of Irénée du Pont, Feb. 18, 1953, pp. 1947–1948; and Secretary of Executive Committee to P. S. du Pont, "Future Uses of our Smokeless Powder and Guncotton Plants," Jan. 26, 1916, DE DP 82.
76. "Hopewell Plant — Progress Report," Jan. 19, 1916, DE DP 81, and also Hunter Grubb to Irénée du Pont, Nov. 4, 1921, GE 285 (an untitled report on the past conditions and future prospects of the du Pont paint business).
77. "Hopewell Plant — Progress Report," Jan. 19, 1916, DE DP 81. Also Secretary of Executive Committee to P. S. du Pont, "Future Uses of our Smokeless Powder and Guncotton Plants," Jan. 26, 1916, DE DP 82.
78. Report from the Development Department to the Executive Committee on "The Purchase of the Arlington Company," Sept. 12, 1915, prepared by W. S. Carpenter, GE 110; *Annual Report of E. I. du Pont de Nemours & Company for 1915,* p. 3; and testimony of Irénée du Pont, Feb 27, 1953, pp. 2273–2275.
79. The expansion of the Fabrikoid operations as outlined in "History and Prospects of the Fabrikoid Industry," Nov. 4, 1921, GE 106, and report of Development Department to Executive Committee on the purchase of the Fairfield Rubber Company, May 27, 1916, GE 107.
80. Report from W. S. Carpenter to Executive Committee on "Dyestuffs," Dec. 29, 1915, DE DP 85.
81. Testimony of Irénée du Pont, Feb. 18, 1953, pp. 1957–1965 and Dutton, *Du Pont,* pp. 287–291.
82. Report to R. R. M. Carpenter from A. D. Chambers, July 26, 1915, DE DP 78;

"Annual Report of the Development Department," Dec. 31, 1914, DE DP 77; and testimony of Irénée du Pont, Feb. 18, 1953, p. 1948.

83. "Hopewell Plant — Progress Report," Jan. 19, 1916, DE DP 81; report of Development Department to Executive Committee, "Tentative Report on General Utilization of Parlin, Carney's Point and Haskell Plants," May 15, 1916, DE DP 87. This report also considered briefly the future of the Repauno, Deepwater, and Hopewell plants.
84. "Hopewell Plant — Progress Report," Jan. 19, 1916, DE DP 81.
85. Report of Development Department to Executive Committee on "General Utilization of Parlin, Carney's Point and Haskell Plants," May 15, 1916, DE DP 87. The quotation on the Parlin plant is from this report.
86. The May 15, 1916, report noted: "It is not expected that any of the present powder manufacturing machinery could be utilized to any great extent in the manufacture of varnish but portions of the general equipment, such as boiler plant, power plant, store houses, storage tanks, grounds and buildings, as well as railroad sidings could be utilized and the additional equipment required is not too expensive."
87. *Ibid.*
88. This and the following quotation is from the report of the Development Department to the Executive Committee on "The Manufacture of Paints and Varnishes at Parlin," Aug. 11, 1916, GE 111.
89. The reasons for the move into paints are listed in *ibid.* (the two following quotations are from this report), report of the Development Department to the Executive Committee on "Harrison Bros. & Co., Inc.," Nov. 22, 1916, GE 112, and report of Lammot du Pont to Executive Committee, "Purchase of Harrison Bros. & Co., Inc.," Nov. 28, 1916, GE 112. The Department envisioned creating a large consolidated company in the paint industry in much the same way the du Ponts had done in explosives in 1902 and 1903 (Report of H. Grubb to Irénée du Pont on the paint business, Nov. 4, 1921 GE 285). Such plans reveal a lack of appreciation of marketing differences between paint and explosives.
90. As the report on "The Manufacture of Paints and Varnishes at Parlin," Aug. 11, 1916, GE 111 noted: "Furthermore the average maker buys his alcohol in barrels from a denaturing plant. With our large purchases, our own existing denaturing plant and tank-cars, we should have an advantage over *all* other makers, in some cases as much as 5 to 8 cents per gallon of alcohol. As shown the spirit varnishes increased over 100% from 1909 to 1914. Our Company ought to claim at least $1,000,000 of the $3,000,000 total business." The report also added, "our business would be strongly supported by our probable future manufacture of linseed oil and certain chemical colors."
91. Report of R. R. M. Carpenter to Executive Committee on "Excess Plant Utilization and New Industries," DE DP 83.
92. Report of H. Grubb to Irénée du Pont on paint business, Nov. 4, 1921, GE 285; Report from Excess Plant Utilization Division to R. R. M. Carpenter, "Flint Varnish & Color Works," Apr. 17, 1918, prepared by F. S. MacGregor, GE 277; and Report of Lammot du Pont and William Coyne, "Expansion in the Paint Industry," Aug. 14, 1918, GE 278.
93. Report on "Completed Recommendations of Excess Plant Utilization Division," Nov. 23, 1917, DE DP 88, and Excess Plant Utilization Division to R. R. M. Carpenter, Apr. 24, 1918 DE DP 217.

94. Development Department to Executive Committee, Mar. 31, 1917, and Haynes, *American Chemical Industry,* III, 375.
95. There are many contemporary documents on this point in the exhibits of both the defense and the government in the du Pont-General Motors Antitrust Suit. Particularly significant are (1) Treasurer of the du Pont Company to Finance Committee on "The General Motors Stock Investment," Dec. 19, 1917, GE 124 and (2) testimony of Pierre du Pont, Jan. 20, 1953, pp. 1719, 1732, and Feb. 26, 1953, pp. 2215–2220. Neither Irénée nor Lammot du Pont was aware of the scheme prior to Raskob's presentation to the Finance Committee.
96. Dutton, *Du Pont,* pp. 275–276.
97. Haynes, *American Chemical Industry,* III, 220–221.
98. James Lynah to W. S. Carpenter, Jan. 6, 1919, DE GM 142, and W. S. Carpenter to James Lynah, Jan. 7, 1920, DE GM 143. (The date on the first letter was clearly meant to be 1920).
99. Coordination was made more difficult because the subunits within the functional departments were not set up so that each product had its administrative offices in each department. For example, while there was only one Paint and Chemicals Manufacturing Department, its products were sold through three different sales offices, Paints and Pigments, Acids and Heavy Chemicals, and Chemical Products. Research on these same products and their processes was carried out by the Explosives and the "General" units of the Chemical Department. Moreover, the marketing for the new products was not done by the long-established branch offices, which continued to handle only explosives, but by five new consolidated sales offices (see Charts 3A and B).
100. This and the following quotation and also the figures in this paragraph come from the report of H. Grubb to Irénée du Pont on the paint business, Nov. 4, 1921, GE 285. Also especially useful was the report from the Development Department to W. S. Carpenter, Mar 15, 1920, GE 280.
101. "History and Prospects of the Fabrikoid Industry," Nov. 4, 1921, GE 106.
102. This and the ten following quotations are from F. W. Pickard to the Executive Committee on "Merchandising Sales versus Tonnage Sales," Sept. 8, 1919. The initial concern for the sales problem, particularly merchandising, is seen in report to Executive Committee from L. du Pont and F. W. Pickard on the Arlington, Harrison, and Dyestuffs Products, Apr. 19, 1919, and report to the Executive Committee from F. W. Pickard, W. S. Carpenter, and C. A. Meade on "Over-the-Counter Paint and Varnish Business," July 17, 1919. The first mention of the problem in the company paint and varnish business appears in report of Excess Plant Utilization Division to R. R. M. Carpenter, Apr. 24, 1918, DE DP 217.
103. This and the following paragraphs are based on "Report of A. B. Echols (Treasurer's office), W. C. Mathews (Assistant to the President), C. W. Phellis (Sales), A. F. Porter (Production), and F. S. MacGregor (Development), Chairman, to Sub-Committee of Executive Committee on the Question of Merchandising versus Tonnage Sales," Mar. 16, 1920. The following twenty-one quotations are from this report. Also important was report of A. B. Echols on "Merchandising and Tonnage Sales," Nov. 10, 1919. In references to "paints and chemicals" (see Chart 4), chemicals refer to chemicals used in paint manufacturing.
104. The report, like others on the paint industry, made clear the accepted distinction in the business between trade or "over-the-counter" and industrial sales. The most useful summary of the difference in the company's performance in the

field of industrial and in "over-the-counter" sales is in a report from H. Grubb to Irénée du Pont on the paint business, Nov. 4, 1921, cited earlier.

105. Penciled comment on a supplementary report to the subcommittee from sub-subcommittee on "Merchandising versus Tonnage Sales," Mar. 27, 1920.

106. Report to Executive Committee from subcommittee of Executive Committee on "Merchandising versus Tonnage Sales," May 27, 1920.

107. This and the following quotation are given in Dale, "Du Pont: Pioneer in Systematic Management," p. 50. The dates of this report and the second one of Nov. 19, 1920, are given in report to Executive Committee from Subcommittee on "Du Pont Company Organization," Aug. 31, 1921.

108. Irénée's position was made clear in "Notes Taken During Discussion on Report of Sub-Committee on 'Du Pont Company Organization,'" Aug. 31, Sept. 6, 7, 1921. He made the same points in an interview with the author, Aug. 23, 1956. Irénée's vetoes were discussed in the letter to the Executive Committee from H. F. Brown, Aug. 5, 1921.

109. This and the four following quotations are from report to Executive Committee from F. W. Pickard on "Paint and Varnish Business," Dec. 11, 1920. This report summarized the events leading to the appointment of the Paint Steering Committee. The other members of the informal council and the later Steering Committee were, beside MacGregor, S. P. Woodbridge from Sales and E. C. Thompson from Production. The Executive Committee's "Advice of Action," Nov. 23, 1920, authorized a formalizing of the council.

110. Information for the seven following paragraphs and the seven quotations included in them are from report to Executive Committee from the subcommittee on "Control of Business," Dec. 22, 1920.

111. Executive Committee's "Advice of Action," Mar. 1, 1921.

112. Reports to F. W. Pickard from Paint and Varnish Steering Committee, Jan. 1, June 29, and Aug. 5, 1921.

113. H. F. Brown to Executive Committee on "Conditions of the Company—Present and Prospective," Aug. 5, 1921; *Annual Report of E. I. du Pont de Nemours & Company for 1921,* p. 5; and Dale, "Du Pont: Pioneer in Systematic Management," p. 46.

114. This and the three following quotations are from "Notes Taken at Executive Committee Meeting of August 2, 1921."

115. Though Fletcher Brown had officially left the Executive Committee after the 1919 changes, he was sitting in on its meeting. He may have been acting as an alternate for A. Felix du Pont, who in 1919 had taken Brown's place as manager of the Smokeless Powder Department and who was not in Wilmington during most of the summer of 1921. Or Brown may have been made a permanent member of the Committee when the departure of Donaldson Brown for General Motors left a vacancy in December 1920. The following six quotations are from the letter of Fletcher Brown to the Executive Committee, Aug. 5, 1921.

116. Minutes of Joint Meeting of Finance Committee and Executive Committee, Aug. 22, 1921. Donaldson Brown did not leave General Motors to attend. Felix du Pont was at this meeting but left the city shortly thereafter.

117. Report to Executive Committee from subcommittee on "Du Pont Company Organization," Aug. 31, 1921. Information for this and the three following paragraphs and the three quotations in them are from this report.

118. Letter from A. Felix du Pont to Lammot du Pont, Aug. 31, 1921, which was

read at the meeting of Sept. 7 dealing with organization. The information for this paragraph and the next comes from "Notes Taken During Discussion on Report of Sub-Committee on 'Du Pont Company Organization,'" Aug. 31, Sept 7, 1921. Irénée's quotation is from these notes.

119. Successive Presidents have endorsed this principle of majority opinion on matters coming before the Executive Committee.

120. Report of J. B. D. Edge to Executive Committee, Sept. 6, 1921, and W. W. Richards to J. B. D. Edge, Sept. 3, 1921. Richards did not study the experience of General Motors, United States Steel, or several other large, holding-company types of American organizations. Nor did the just-formed Allied Chemical have a central purchasing office until many years after 1921.

121. The Minutes of a meeting of the subcommittee on organization, Sept. 13, 1921. Also "Notes on Meeting to Discuss Organization," Aug. 31 and Sept. 7, 1921. Edge retained the management of Traffic as well as Purchasing. There was some discussion as to the advisability of consolidating all eight Auxiliary Departments into one "Service Department" headed by a single man. Though C. A. Patterson and W. S. Carpenter favored such a consolidation, the senior executives decided to leave each staff department autonomous.

122. Extract from Minutes of Executive Committee, Sept. 8, 1921. The new Executive Committee was to include Irénée and Lammot du Pont, H. F. Brown, Pickard, and Spruance (memorandum to Employees of E. I. du Pont de Nemours & Company, Sept. 25, 1921).

123. This and the following quotation are from a "Report to the Board of Directors from the Executive Committee," Sept. 21, 1921.

124. In 1921, Employee Relations was under the Service Department, and Public Relations was part of the Publicity Office. The International Department has become an operating department, growing out of the older auxiliary Foreign Relations Department.

Chapter 3

1. The information for this paragraph comes largely from P. S. du Pont to I. du Pont, Nov. 26, 1920, Defendants' Exhibit, DP 50 in *United States v. E. I. du Pont de Nemours & Company, General Motors Corporation* et al., U. S. District Court for the Northern District of Illinois, Eastern Division Civil Action No. 49 C–1071 (1953) hereafter cited as du Pont-General Motors Antitrust Suit. The letters DE will be used in citing Defense Exhibits and GE, Government Exhibits. Unless otherwise indicated, all exhibits and testimonies are from this suit. In citing from the case, the numbers of the exhibits and the pages of the testimony are those used in *United States Supreme Court Reports, 253, Records and Brief, United States* vs. *E. I. du Pont de Nemours & Company, General Motors Corporation,* et al., *October Term, 1956,* are given where possible, as these reports are much more readily available than the District Court records. There is more in both the testimony and exhibits concerning the events of November, 1920, but this additional information only fills in details given in Pierre's description of them to Irénée. Lawrence H. Seltzer, *A Financial History of the American Automobile Industry* (Boston, 1928), pp. 202–208, also provides an excellent summary of this episode.

2. Durant received 40 per cent of the common stock of the new company, "Agree-

ment dated November 22, 1920, between du Pont Securities Company, William C. Durant, du Pont American Industries, Inc. and Chevrolet Motor Company," GE 154, and J. J. Raskob to Finance Committee, E. I. du Pont de Nemours & Company, Jan. 17, 1921, GE 156.

3. Durant's early career and his activities in the Durant-Dort Carriage Company are best summarized in Carl Crow, *The City of Flint Grows Up* (New York, 1945), pp. 29–36. John B. Rae gives a good evaluation of Durant's career in his article, "The Fabulous Billy Durant," *Business History Review*, 32:225–271 (Fall, 1958).
4. J. L. Pratt, Direct Testimony, Du Pont-General Motors Antitrust Suit, p. 1406. Hereafter any testimonies cited will be from this suit. As Pratt pointed out, several General Managers at General Motors had their start as farm implement or carriage salesmen. In 1920, these included R. H. Collins, Manager of Cadillac, W. L. Day, Manager of the Truck Division, F. W. Warner, Manager of Oakland, and A. B. C. Hardy, Manager of Oldsmobile.
5. Crow, *Flint*, p. 35.
6. The story of Buick comes from Crow, *Flint*, pp. 54–71; Seltzer, *Financial History*, pp. 145–150; and Arthur Pound, *The Turning Wheel* (Garden City, New York, 1934), pp. 68–90. Pound is good on the early marketing situation (pp. 359–368), as are Ralph C. Epstein, *The Automobile Industry* (Chicago, 1928), ch. 5, and Reginald M. Cleveland and S. T. Williamson, *The Road is Yours* (New York, 1951), p. 53. Pound also mentions the move of Weston-Mott and of Champion to Flint (pp. 111, 456, 490). These moves and the reasons for them are also given in Alfred P. Sloan, Jr., *Adventures of a White-Collar Man* (New York, 1941), pp. 48–49.
7. These statistics are from Seltzer, *Financial History*, pp. 149–150.
8. Pound, *Turning Wheel*, p. 87 and pp. 364–365.
9. The best source on these early years at Buick is Walter P. Chrysler, *Life of an American Working Man* (Philadelphia, 1938), reprinted from *Saturday Evening Post*, pp. 30–34. Pound (*Turning Wheel*, ch. 5) has some additional data.
10. Allan Nevins, *Ford: The Times, the Man, the Company* (New York, 1954), pp. 450, 478–479, 498–511, Russell Robb, *Lectures on Organization* (n.p., 1910), p. 13, and [A. W. Shaw Company], *Executive Control* (Chicago, 1915), pp. 43–45.
11. Durant is said to have told George W. Perkins, a Morgan partner, when Durant and Briscoe were trying to raise funds in 1908: "The time will come when a half a million automobiles a year will be made and sold in this country." To this Perkins reportedly replied, "If that fellow has any sense, he'll keep those observations to himself when he tries to borrow money" (Cleveland and Williamson, *The Road is Yours*, p. 216). Durant's optimism as to the unlimited nature of the market is described in Nevins, *Ford: The Times, the Man, the Company*, p. 386.
12. The story of General Motors' beginning is told in Seltzer, *Financial History*, pp. 32–37, 151–163, and in Pound, *Turning Wheel*, pp. 113–125.
13. *Ibid.*, pp. 93–94. The incorporation of the McLaughlin Motor Company, Ltd., came in 1910. Durant had earlier entered the carriage market in Canada through a profitable alliance with the McLaughlin Carriage Company, headed by R. S. McLaughlin. The new firm, 5,000 of whose 12,000 shares were taken by Buick, would in time become General Motors of Canada, *ibid.*, pp. 124, 235–236.
14. Not that all these purchases were successful. Durant paid over $7 million in

General Motors stock for three electric lamp companies organized by John A. Heany. They proved worthless, since Heany's patents were invalidated (Seltzer, *Financial History,* pp. 158–159).

15. This change in control and command during 1910 is best told in *ibid.,* pp. 160–172, supplemented by Henry G. Pearson, *Son of New England — James Jackson Storrow, 1854–1926* (Boston, 1932), pp. 123–124.
16. The story of the Storrow-Nash regime comes from Pearson, *Storrow,* ch. 7, the company's annual reports, and exhibits in the du Pont-General Motors Antitrust Suit.
17. The organization is best described in *Annual Report of the General Motors Company,* July 31, 1911, pp. 9–10; *Annual Report of the General Motors Corporation,* July 31, 1912, pp. 10–12; and *Annual Report of the General Motors Corporation,* July 31, 1913, p. 10.
18. Pearson, *Storrow,* pp. 129–137, and David F. Edwards, "Delegation and Control by the General Manager in a Textile Machinery Company," in Edward C. Bursk, *The Management Team* (Cambridge, Mass., 1954), pp. 59–60.
19. This and the following quotation are from *Annual Report,* July 31, 1911, p. 9. See also Pearson, *Storrow,* pp. 130–131. Lyons had been the Assistant to the First Vice-President at Westinghouse and the senior executive in Westinghouse's Manufacturing Department (*Annual Report of Westinghouse Electric Manufacturing Company for 1910*). Pound tells of A. D. Little's contribution in *Turning Wheel,* p. 269.
20. "General Motors Company Meeting of Purchasing Agents, May 7, 1913," DE GM 37. Details of other meetings are suggested in the minutes of the meetings for June 4, July 30, Nov. 5, 1913, Aug. 19, 1914, and Aug. 20, 1915, DE GM 38–42. These exhibits also indicate the role of the Board of Managers.
21. Pearson, *Storrow,* p. 130.
22. Edwards, "Delegation and Control," p. 59, and a conversation with Mr. Edwards, who in 1960 was Chairman of the Board, Saco-Lowell Shops.
23. See Seltzer, *Financial History,* pp. 172–182, and Pound, *Turning Wheel,* chs. 10–12. There is much significant information on the change in the testimony and exhibits of the du Pont-General Motors Antitrust Suit.
24. "One of his associates recalled," Ernest Dale has written, "that he [Durant] appeared to think of volume of sales as an end in itself, more important than profits," Dale, "Contributions to Administration by Alfred P. Sloan, Jr. and GM," *Administrative Science Quarterly* 1:33 (June, 1956). The scope and nature of Durant's program can be most easily seen by comparing the list of active operating units or subsidiaries in *Annual Report of the General Motors Corporation,* July 31, 1913, p. 10, with the *Annual Report of the General Motors Corporation,* Dec. 31, 1918, p. 7, and that of Dec. 31, 1919, pp. 7–8. Sheridan, one of the two carmaking units, is mentioned in J. L. Pratt, Direct Testimony, pp. 1415, 1418.
25. In 1920, Durant's three assistants included Karl M. Zimmerschied (General Manager of Chevrolet, 1920–1922), P. D. Wagoner, and a personal secretary, W. W. Murphy. Their names are listed on the organization chart attached to A. P. Sloan's "General Motors Corporation—Organization Study," DE GM 1. J. L. Pratt (Direct Testimony, p. 1394) also mentions Durant's small personal staff.
26. The central staff offices existing under Durant are indicated in "Communication dated September 5, 1917, from T. S. Merrill (GMC) to Pierre S. du Pont transmitting list of Directors and Officers of General Motors Corporation," GE

123, and the chart accompanying "General Motors Corporation—Organization Study," DE GM 1. L. Blackmore headed the Patent Department. The outside legal consultants were from the firm of Stevenson, Carpenter, Butzel, and Bacchus. Testimony in the General Motors-du Pont Antitrust Suit emphasizes the lack of systematic cost and accounting data. See, for example, A. P. Sloan, Direct Testimony, p. 973.

27. Seltzer, *Financial History,* pp. 183–188. The major operations of these companies were, respectively, at Harrison, N. J., Bristol, Conn., Anderson, Ind., Dayton, Ohio, and Jackson, Mich.
28. Pound, *Turning Wheel,* ch. 12. Also an "Unsigned Letter dated June 29, 1918, to H. M. Barksdale" (P. S. du Pont's initials and those of his secretary are at the lower left of the last page), GE 133, suggests Durant's concern over the determination of Washington to cut off the steel supply for automobiles and other nonessential products.
29. Direct Testimony of J. L. Pratt, p. 1403.
30. There is much on the du Pont Company's investment in General Motors in the du Pont-General Motors Antitrust Suit. The best summary is in a memorandum entitled "History of the du Pont Company's Investment in the General Motors Corporation," dated Aug. 17, 1921, GE 166. Also useful is the "Memorandum dated December 12, 1918 to Finance Committee from Chairman," GE 134.
31. Pound, *Turning Wheel,* ch. 13, supplemented by the annual reports of these years. "Memorandum dated December 12, 1918 to Finance Committee from Chairman," GE 134 gives a good indication of Durant's strategy as its outlines estimated postwar capital expenditures.
32. Direct Testimony of J. L. Pratt, pp. 1392–1396, and Pound, *Turning Wheel,* p. 183.
33. *Ibid.,* pp. 381–382. Ford chose not to follow Raskob's innovation, with unhappy results for his dealers. Allan Nevins and Frank E. Hill, *Ford: Expansion and Challenge: 1915–1933* (New York, 1957), pp. 267–269.
34. Pound, *Turning Wheel,* pp. 165, 173–175, and *Automotive Industries,* 37:390 (Aug. 30, 1917).
35. J. L. Pratt, Direct Testimony, pp. 1405–1406, and A. P. Sloan, Direct Testimony, pp. 969–974.
36. *Annual Report of General Motors Corporation for 1918,* pp. 7–8.
37. "Excerpts from meeting of Board of Directors of General Motors Corporation of March 21, 1918," GE 131, also "Excerpts from meeting of Board of Directors of General Motors Corporation of February 21, 1918," GE 130; "Communication dated March 8, 1918 from Treasurer to Finance Committee" (both of du Pont) GE 128; and an agreement between W. C. Durant and the du Pont Company to form the Motor Securities Company, undated, DE DP 45. This last item stressed that General Motors was to have appropriations procedures similar to those at du Pont.
38. "Excerpts from meeting of Board of Directors of General Motors Corporation of March 21, 1918," GE 131.
39. "Communication dated March 8, 1918 from Treasurer to Finance Committee," GE 128, lists the membership of both the Executive and Finance Committees. Hamilton M. Barksdale, like Haskell, a retired du Pont official, was expected to serve in much the same capacity; but he did little because of illness. He died in October, 1918. (P. S. du Pont to H. M. Barksdale, June 29, 1918, GE

133, and *Annual Report of E. I. du Pont de Nemours & Company for 1918,* p. 18).

40. Chrysler, "Life of an American Working Man," p. 37, and J. L. Pratt, Direct Testimony, pp. 1405, 1417.
41. *Ibid.,* pp. 1402–1403.
42. *Ibid.,* pp. 1391–1398. Pratt emphasized Durant's concern over the availability of supplies if General Motors was to achieve successfully a massive output. Beside making general studies on the availability of aluminum, petroleum, plate glass, and housing, Pratt investigated the value of various parts and assembly companies, such as the Hayes Wheel Company and manufacturers of storage batteries.
43. "Memorandum dated February 18, 1919, from R. R. M. Carpenter to P. S. du Pont," DE GM 195, and R. R. M. Carpenter to Executive Committee (du Pont Company) Mar. 19, 1919, GE 557. The latter mentions the work of the Engineering Company.
44. J. L. Pratt, Direct Testimony, p. 1397.
45. R. R. M. Carpenter wrote in a letter to the Executive Committee, Mar. 19, 1919, GE 557:

    Personally, I think that both this arrangement and the Engineering Department arrangement should be considered as more or less temporary, and I gather this is the general idea of the Executive Committee.

    When Pratt did go to General Motors in December, 1919, he went more as a personal assistant and trouble shooter for Durant than as a staff expert.
46. This and the following two quotations are from J. L. Pratt, Direct Testimony, pp. 1402–1403. Alfred Sloan commented on accounting weaknesses in Direct Testimony, p. 970. By the agreement made between Durant and the du Pont Company, General Motors was to have appropriations procedures similar to those at du Pont, DE DP 45.
47. T. A. Boyd, *Professional Amateur — The Biography of Charles Franklin Kettering* (New York, 1957), pp. 117–119; K. W. Zimmerschied, Assistant to the President, to C. M. Stine, Oct. 28, 1919, GE 599; and *Automotive Industries,* 42:980 (Apr. 22, 1920). Kettering's original connection with the General Motors group through the sale of Delco to United Motors is described by Boyd in pp. 84–85. One result of this appointment may have been the construction of a "Laboratory Building" attached to the central office building at Detroit, which was "five stories high, built in four wings of re-enforced concrete construction . . . and is designed for research work along mechanical, electrical and chemical lines," *Annual Report of General Motors Corporation for 1921,* p. 7.
48. E. D. Kennedy, *The Automobile Industry* (New York, 1941), p. 123.
49. Pratt describes the pressures for buying inventory in his Direct Testimony, pp. 1405, 1414–1415.
50. "Memorandum dated March 19, 1920 from J. J. Raskob to Finance Committee, du Pont Company," GE 140, and "History of the du Pont Company's Investment in the General Motors Corporation dated August 17, 1921," GE 166. The views and actions of Durant and Raskob in raising funds are covered in GE 141 through 144.
51. *Annual Report of General Motors Corporation for 1922,* Mar. 19, 1923, p. 9.
52. Nevins and Hill, *Ford: Expansion and Challenge,* pp. 151–152; *Automotive Industries,* 42:784, 926, 985, 1036, 1074, 1084, 1093–1094, and 1129 (Mar. 25,

Apr. 15, 22, 29, May 6, 13, 19, and 20, 1920); and "History of the du Pont Company's Investment in the General Motors Corporation dated August 17, 1921," GE 166.

53. This and the following data on inventories came from *Annual Report of General Motors Corporation for 1922,* pp. 9–10.

54. J. L. Pratt, Direct Testimony, p. 1405, Seltzer, *Financial History,* pp. 198–199, and Direct Testimony of A. P. Sloan, p. 972.

55. The drop in the automobile market is indicated in *Automotive Industries,* 43:36–37, 101, 145, 195, 237, 486, and 636 (July 1, 15, 22, Sept. 2 and 23, 1920), and J. L. Pratt, Direct Testimony, pp. 1404–1405.

56. *Ibid.,* pp. 1416–1418.

57. *Annual Report of General Motors Corporation for 1922,* p. 10. The figures in this sentence and the ones just before and after it are from the Annual Report. Loans outstanding during this period are given in "General Motors Corporation — Bank Loans Outstanding, end of each month, 1920 and 1921, and first five months 1922," DE DP 51.

58. Nevins and Hill, *Ford: Expansion and Challenge,* pp. 152–154, and *Automotive Industries,* 43:636 (Sept. 23, 1920).

59. *Ibid.,* 43:639, 644, 684, and 786 (Sept. 23 and 30, Oct. 7 and 14, 1920).

60. *Ibid.,* 43:1044 (Nov. 18, 1920), and Seltzer, *Financial History,* pp. 10–212. Pratt emphasized the need for cash at General Motors in his Direct Testimony, p. 1405.

61. *Annual Report of General Motors Corporation for 1922,* p. 9.

62. "Communication dated November 22, 1920 from Secretary, Finance Committee (du Pont) to P. S. du Pont," GE 179, and Sloan, *Adventures of a White-Collar Man,* pp. 131–132.

63. For example, "Excerpts from Memorandum re Meeting between President and Plant Managers, December 1, 1920 (GMC)," DE GM 196.

64. "Communication dated December 29, 1920 from P. S. du Pont (GMC) to Officers, Directors and Heads of Department," with accompanying organization chart, GE 178.

65. Rae, "Fabulous Billy Durant"; Chrysler, "American Workingman," pp. 32–37; and Pound, *Turning Wheel,* pp. 77–78. In the letters used as exhibits in the General Motors-du Pont Antitrust Suit, Sloan is addressed and referred to usually as "Mr. Sloan" and occasionally by such men as Lammot du Pont and Walter Carpenter as "Alfred."

66. Sloan's early years are described by him in *Adventures of a White-Collar Man,* Part I, and are summarized by John B. Rae, *American Automobile Manufacturers — The First Fifty Years* (New York, 1959), pp. 192–193.

67. Sloan, *Adventures of a White-Collar Man,* Parts II and III; Alfred P. Sloan, "The Most Important Thing I Ever Learned About Management," *System — the Magazine of Business,* 44:137 (Aug., 1924); Direct Testimony, A. P. Sloan, pp. 956–958, 1299–1300; Nevins, *Ford: The Times, the Man, the Company,* pp. 215, 398.

68. Direct Testimony, A. P. Sloan, pp. 959–967. Deposition of A. P. Sloan, Apr. 28, 1925, pp. 11–13, is an even better source on his work at United Motors. The quotation in this paragraph is from p. 12. The Deposition, not forwarded to the Supreme Court, is in the District Court records. Also useful was Sloan, *Adventures of a White-Collar Man,* Part IV, and Seltzer, *Financial History,* pp. 183–187.

69. Direct Testimony, A. P. Sloan, pp. 969–971.
70. A. P. Sloan to J. A. Haskell, July 16, 1918, DE GM 27.
71. Direct Testimony, A. P. Sloan, pp. 980–981 and 1344, and Sloan, *Adventures of a White-Collar Man,* pp. 118–119.
72. Direct Testimony, A. P. Sloan, p. 974.
73. Sloan was close enough to Storrow to be asked to join Lee, Higginson & Company. Nor is there any reason to think that Sloan looked outside of industry to the Army and the government for models or that, if he did, he could have learned anything of value from them.
74. "General Motors Corporation — Organization Study," DE GM 1. Unless otherwise indicated, all the following quotations in this section are from this study.
75. The changes are most clearly seen by comparing Sloan's chart in DE GM 1 with that of the organization adopted by Pierre in GE 178. See also Direct Testimony, A. P. Sloan, pp. 984–985.
76. *Ibid.,* p. 982. Deposition of A. P. Sloan, Apr. 28, 1952, p. 32.
77. "Communication dated December 29, 1920 from P. S. du Pont (GMC) to Officers, Directors and Heads of Department," GE 178.
78. General Motors organization chart, Jan. 3, 1921, GE 178, and J. L. Pratt, Direct Testimony, p. 1418. E. F. Johnson, who was at one time a du Pont manager, became the executive who supervised the Parts Group.
79. John D. Mooney supervised this group, *Automotive Industries,* 47:1026 and 1045 (Nov. 15 and 23, 1922). *Annual Report of General Motors Corporation for 1922,* p. 10.
80. The Treasurer was M. L. Prensky and the Comptroller, Frank Turner, General Motors organization chart, Jan. 3, 1921, GE 178.
81. Pound, *Turning Wheel,* pp. 129, 150.
82. H. L. Barton headed the Manufacturing Section and L. Blackmore the Patent Department (General Motors Corporation organization chart, Jan. 3, 1921). Pound (*Turning Wheel,* pp. 126, 150, and 233) tells of Hardy. Hardy and J. H. Main, who took his place, are mentioned in A. P. Sloan, Direct Testimony, pp. 1041–1042, while Hawkins is referred to in *Printers' Ink,* 116:3 (Sept. 29, 1921), and in Nevins and Hill, *Ford: Expansion and Challenge — 1915–1933,* pp. 146 and 169.
83. A. P. Sloan, Direct Testimony, p. 989.
84. *Ibid.,* pp. 987–988.
85. A. P. Sloan, Direct Testimony, pp. 970–971 and 987, and *Annual Report of General Motors Corporation for 1923,* Mar. 24, 1924, p. 6. For prices see Kennedy, *Automobile Industry,* pp. 130–132.
86. The figures for cars sold in 1919 and 1921 are given in Seltzer, *Financial History,* p. 213; Federal Trade Commission, *Report on Motor Vehicle Industry* (Washington, 1939), pp. 29, 31; and "General Motors Corporation — Comparison of Numbers and Proportion of Motor Vehicles (Passenger and Truck) Sold by Ford, General Motors and Other Manufacturers, 1921," DE GM 35. A. P. Sloan (Direct Testimony, pp. 970–971) succinctly described the quality of the corporation's different cars in 1920.
87. *Annual Report of General Motors Corporation for 1923,* Mar. 24, 1924, p. 6.
88. A. P. Sloan, Direct Testimony, pp. 970–971 and 987.
89. *Annual Report of General Motors Corporation for 1923,* p. 6; *Printers Ink,* 116:3 (Sept. 29, 1921), 125:17–19 (Dec. 13, 1923).

90. *Annual Report of General Motors Corporation for 1925,* Feb. 24, 1926, p. 7. The Oakland Division marketed and sold the Pontiac and in time dropped the Oakland and concentrated wholly on the Pontiac.
91. *Annual Report of General Motors Corporation for 1920,* Mar. 26, 1921, p. 8.
92. Donaldson Brown describes interdivisional price and policies in "Decentralized Operations and Responsibilities with Coordinated Control," American Management Association, *Annual Convention Series,* No. 57 (Feb., 1927), p. 10.
93. "Extracts from Executive Committee Minutes for Meeting, March 30, 1926," GE 903. At the meeting the Committee modified the older policy by requiring the approval of the Group Executives before making outside purchases.
94. J. L. Pratt, Direct Testimony, pp. 1404–1405. The following quotation is from p. 1405.
95. The Committee's new duties are described in the "Excerpts from Memorandum re Meeting between President and Plant Managers, December 1, 1920 (GMC)," DE GM 196, and J. L. Pratt, Direct Testimony, p. 1414.
96. *Ibid.,* pp. 1416–1417.
97. Donaldson Brown, "Pricing Policy in Relation to Financial Control," *Management and Administration,* 7:196 (Feb., 1924), and C. S. Mott, "Organizing a Great Industrial," *Management and Administration,* 7:527 (May, 1924). Mott wrote:

> Inventory, production, and sales forecasts are presented every 30 days, on a blank which covers a period of 90 days. In the case of a report made on October 25, 1923, for example, the blank shows actual inventory at October 1, with estimates for November 1, December 1 and January 1, which of course include commitments already made or to be made within the period. Production and sales forecasts are given in the same manner and all of the information given as of October 25 is compared with similar information given as of the 25th, one, two, and three months previous. The actual results are compared automatically with previous forecasts; and this tends to secure accuracy in forecasting.
>
> These data are given for the vehicle divisions and for the intercompany parts group as well. On another portion of the blank are set down actual production by months for November and December, 1923 and January and February, 1924. Data are also furnished, showing the total estimated for four months, in all vehicles and parts plants, both in the United States and Canada. Each month, therefore, opportunity is given to the executives to observe the closeness of relation between forecasts and actual results. The figures as they stand are reported by the president to the Executive Committee. The report in the form outlined brings clearly forward the conditions of the individual plant, inventories, and so on.

The detailed working-out of purchasing and the use and day-to-day control of inventory are well described in E. Carl Wennerlund, "Quality Control of Inventories — Physical Regulation Contrasted with Mere Financial Information," *Management and Administration,* 7:677–682 (June, 1924). Wennerlund was the head of the Factory Organization Section, formerly the Manufacturing Section, of the advisory staff.

98. Pratt mentions "ten-day reports" as being worked out in early 1921. They were probably operating reports (J. L. Pratt, Direct Testimony, p. 1416).
99. These procedures are carefully described in Mott, "Organizing a Great Industrial," pp. 526–527.

100. These procedures are described in Alfred H. Swayne, "Mobilization of Cash Reserves," *Management and Administration,* 7:21–23 (Jan., 1924). The system had such additional advantages as those of making available more bank credit to General Motors and of rendering it possible to invest excess cash so that it earned interest.
101. General Motors Corporation organization chart, Jan. 3, 1921, GE 178. Sloan describes the financial organization of a division in his Deposition, Apr. 28, 1952, pp. 48–50.
102. These procedures are indicated in Thomas B. Fordham and Edward H. Tingley, "Applying the Budget to Industrial Operations — Control through Organization and Budget," *Management and Administration,* 7:57–62, 205–208, and 291 (Jan., Feb., and Apr., 1924), and in the articles by Donaldson Brown in the same volume of *Management and Administration,* especially pp. 283–286.
103. This and the following quotation are from Donaldson Brown, "Pricing Policy in Relation to Financial Control," p. 283.
104. Albert Bradley, "Setting up a Forecasting Program," American Management Association, *Annual Convention Series,* No. 41 (Mar., 1926), p. 8.
105. Donaldson Brown, "Pricing Policy in Relation to Financial Control," p. 285.
106. See particularly *ibid.,* pp. 417–422.
107. This and the following quotation are from *ibid.,* p. 196.
108. *Annual Report of the General Motors Corporation for 1924,* Mar. 23, 1925, p. 8. Figures on production are in Seltzer, *Financial History,* pp. 212–216, and F.T.C., *Motor Vehicle Industry,* pp. 22–24.
109. Dale ("Contributions to Administration," p. 45) describes Sloan's trip west.
110. "Excerpts — General Purchasing Committee re Production Schedule Forecasts from Minutes of Committee for April 18, July 2, Sept. 5, 1924, and Feb. 6, 1925," DE GM 125.
111. Testimony of A. P. Sloan, p. 988.
112. Bradley, "Setting up a Forecasting Program," p. 13.
113. This quotation is from *ibid.,* pp. 6–7, and the two following are from pp. 12–13. By this time the Financial Staff had begun, as Bradley indicated, to use more sophisticated methods in computing selling costs than Donaldson Brown had used two years earlier, pp. 8–9.
114. Bradley, "Setting up a Forecasting Program," p. 3.
115. The buyers at General Motors realized that the leveling of demand would please their suppliers, so that the General Purchasing Committee "agreed that a letter from Mr. Sloan dealing with the plan for controlling production which manifestly would control the demand upon suppliers for their products and materials, which our Purchasing Agents could refer to in conversation on negotiations with suppliers, might strengthen our buying position by conveying to the suppliers our efforts toward scientifically preventing wide fluctuations in demand resulting from drastic adjustments of Schedules," Minutes of General Purchasing Committee, Sept. 25, 1924, DE GM 125. For figures on improvement in steadying seasonal fluctuations in employment and on the improvement in the turnover of productive inventory, see Bradley, "Setting up a Forecasting Program," pp. 15–18, and Dale, "Contributions to Administration," pp. 51–52.
116. *Ibid.,* p. 47.
117. The role of Kettering's section is indicated in Boyd, *Professional Amateur,*

pp. 117–126, and "Meeting of Car Division Managers with Executive Committee December 1, 1921," DE GM 104. The work of the Sales and Factory Sections is indicated in Mott, "Organizing a Great Industrial," pp. 524–526, in *Printers Ink,* 116:3 ff., (Sept. 29, 1921), 125:17–19 (Dec. 13, 1923). The initial duties of the Purchasing Section are spelled out in letter from A. P. Sloan to all General Officers and General Managers of Divisions, Jan. 25, 1921, DE GM 43. As this letter stressed: "The use of such general contracts [are] to be entirely at the option of the Operating Divisions and, when used, all dealings to be directly between the Seller and the Purchasing Division."

118. *Annual Report of General Motors Corporation for 1922,* pp. 15–16. The story of the copper-cooled engine and the resulting line-and-staff conflict is briefly covered in Boyd, *Professional Amateur,* pp. 119–123. See also *Automotive Industries,* 48:1253 (June 7, 1923).

119. "Memorandum dated December 1, 1924 from Alfred P. Sloan, Jr. to Members of General Purchasing Committee," DE GM 65.

120. A. P. Sloan, Letter No. 25 to General Managers of Divisions and other Officers, May 8, 1922 and attached memorandum entitled "Proposal for Coordination of General Motors Purchases," DE GM 49. See also A. P. Sloan to J. H. Main, Feb. 9, 1922, DE GM 48, A. P. Sloan, Direct Testimony, p. 1032, and "Meeting of Car Division Managers with Executive Committee, Nov. 3, 1921," DE GM 45.

121. The replies of the General Managers and their purchasing agents are given in several exhibits in the General Motors-du Pont Antitrust Suit, DE GM 50–60.

122. A. P. Sloan to Division Managers and other Officers, Nov. 28 and 29, 1922, DE GM 61 and 62. A. P. Sloan to J. Lynch (Feb. 6, 1923, DE GM 328) shows that Sloan was Chairman and Lynch Secretary of the Committee.

123. Memorandum from A. P. Sloan to P. S. du Pont, J. Raskob, C. F. Kettering, and Fred B. Fisher, August 6, 1923, GE 904 (D.C.). At General Purchasing Committee meeting on August 2, 1923, Sloan outlined the functions of a "proposed Works Engineers Committee." This is possibly what became of the General Technical Committee, General Purchasing Committee Minutes, Aug. 2, 1923, DE GM 152. The committees are described in Mott, "Organizing a Great Industrial," p. 526; Donaldson Brown, "Decentralized Operations and Responsibilities with Co-ordinated Control," p. 15; and A. P. Sloan, Direct Testimony, p. 994, and indicated in "Chart showing General Motors Corporation Organization, January, 1925," DE GM 2. The make-up of the General Technical Committee is given in *Automotive Industries,* 51:531–532 (Sept. 18, 1924).

124. Compare Mott, "Organizing a Great Industrial," pp. 524–525, which includes an organization chart of General Motors for 1924 (see Chart 7) with General Motors Corporation — Organization Charts — Jan., 1925, and April, 1927, DE GM 2 and 3. The following names of members are from the 1927 chart.

125. General Motors Corporation — Organization Charts, Jan. 1925 and Apr. 1927, DE GM 2 and 3.

126. *Ibid.,* and Donaldson Brown, "Decentralized Operations and Responsibilities with Co-ordinated Control," pp. 15–16.

127. A. P. Sloan to C. F. Kettering, July 25, 1924, GE 666.

128. For example, the General Sales Committee, in a meeting in May, 1925, defined the corporation's policy on trade-in and resale of used cars. The members agreed that Ford's policy of insisting that the dealers make a profit on used cars was unrealistic. The basic aim of the dealer should be to sell as many

new cars as possible and to profit on the over-all transaction rather than merely make a profit on the used car sales. Then on Oct. 8, 1925, the Committee spelled out in detail just what the corporation's policy for all divisions would be on used cars, F.T.C., *Motor Vehicle Industry,* pp. 215–216. The Federal Trade Commission's report, quoting from the General Sales Committee Minutes, then describes later modifications and adjustments of the policy. On pp. 255–258, the report cites the Minutes of the Committee on the formulation of the corporation's policy concerning exclusive dealerships.

129. Donaldson Brown, "Decentralized Operations and Responsibilities with Coordinated Control," p. 16. The General Purchasing Committee also set up standards and specifications for parts and equipment for all divisions. (Minutes of General Purchasing Committee, DE GM 152, and A. P. Sloan, Direct Testimony, p. 994.)
130. *Annual Report of General Motors Corporation for 1922,* p. 3; *Annual Report of General Motors Corporation for 1924,* Mar. 23, 1925, p. 3; and General Motors Organization Charts, Jan., 1925, and Apr., 1927, DE GM 2 and 3.
131. The initial make-up of the Operations Committee is indicated in the chart showing the organization of the company, Jan. 3, 1921, GE 178. Its later make-up is indicated in Mott, "Organizing a Great Industrial," p. 526.
132. Donaldson Brown, "Pricing Policy in Relation to Financial Control," p. 195, and A. P. Sloan, Direct Testimony, p. 997.
133. In 1925 Harry H. Bassett, General Manager of Buick, was on the Committee as was Lawrence P. Fisher, head of Cadillac, in 1927, General Motors Organization Charts, Jan., 1925, and Apr., 1927, DE GM 2 and 3.
134. F.T.C., *Motor Vehicle Industry,* pp. 29–31. This rapid rise was partly because of the Ford shift from the "T" to the "A," but in 1931 General Motors' share was 41.8 per cent.
135. Kennedy, *Automobile Industry,* p. 211, claims that this was the largest net profit yet made by an American corporation.
136. F.T.C., *Motor Vehicle Industry,* p. 29.
137. Edward L. Allen, *Economics of American Manufacturing* (New York, 1952), p. 293.
138. *Automotive Industries,* 69:532 and 536–537 (Oct. 28, 1933).
139. *Fortune,* 17:73 ff. (Apr. 19, 1938); *Annual Report of the General Motors Corporation for 1937,* Mar. 31, 1938, pp. 37–38; "Report to the Stockholders of General Motors Corporation, May 17, 1937," pp. 2–5; and testimony and exhibits in the du Pont Antitrust Suit. F.T.C., *Motor Vehicle Industry* (pp. 527–529), indicates that the General Sales Committee lasted until September, 1933.
140. Donaldson Brown, "Decentralized Operations and Responsibilities with Coordinated Control," pp. 7–8. Most of the other articles by senior General Motors executives have been cited earlier in this chapter.

Chapter 4

1. George S. Gibb and Evelyn H. Knowlton, *History of Standard Oil Company (New Jersey), The Resurgent Years, 1911–1927* (New York, 1956), pp. 668–669.
2. Ralph W. Hidy and Muriel E. Hidy, *History of Standard Oil Company (New*

Jersey), *Pioneering in Big Business, 1882–1911* (New York, 1955), pp. 324–325.

3. The committees included one each for export trade, domestic marketing, the marketing of lubricants, manufacturing, crude oil, production, pipe lines, and transportation, and two for purchasing supplies, Hidy, *Pioneering in Big Business,* pp. 55–68. When these committees were started, they were, the Hidys have pointed out: "vested largely, though not exclusively, with advisory powers," (*ibid.,* p. 55). However, the continuing history of Standard Oil, as described by the Hidys, indicates that before long these committees and not department heads or chiefs of subsidiaries carried out most of the administrative activities. In any case, by the time of the dissolution of the company in 1911, the Manufacturing Committee clearly administered a large number of the companies refineries.
4. Gibb and Knowlton, *Resurgent Years,* pp. 598, 678, also pp. 3–14 (especially pp. 7–10), and 31–33.
5. The Rumanian affiliate, the only one among the Jersey European companies to produce, refine, and market, came under the supervision of the Export Trade Committee. From 1916 to the end of World War I, the Rumanian fields were under the control of the German government. After the war, production in Rumania was supervised by Sadler's new Foreign Producing Department and its marketing and refining by the Export Trade Department.
6. For Teagle and Imperial, see Gibb and Knowlton, *Resurgent Years,* pp. 195 ff.; for Weller, *ibid.,* p. 34; and for Moffett, *The Lamp,* 7(1):6 (June, 1924).
7. *Ibid.,* 1(4):21–22 (Nov., 1918).
8. Gibb and Knowlton, *Resurgent Years,* p. 172. The Tuscarora Company had its operating offices in Pittsburgh; the Oklahoma Pipeline Company, its in Tulsa.
9. The Jersey Marketing Department's organization is described in detail in *The Lamp,* 1(3):20–26 (Sept., 1918) and Louisiana's Department in *ibid.,* 1(5):4 (Jan., 1919) and 2(1):35 (Jan., 1920). T. J. Williams headed the Jersey department.
10. Correspondence in the Jersey files and comments by Gibb and Knowlton (*Resurgent Years,* chs. 8, 16) show that Harper, Asche, and Teagle handled nearly all the administration of foreign trade. See also *Resurgent Years,* pp. 28–29 and 497.
11. G. W. McKnight to E. M. Clark and C. G. Black, Jan. 29, 1926. The information on the manufacturing organization came largely from the reports on its operations and suggestions for its improvement. These reports will be considered later in this chapter. The most valuable were E. M. Clark to G. W. McKnight, Jan. 7, 1924, and to F. A. Howard, Jan. 14, 1924; G. W. McKnight to E. M. Clark and C. G. Black, Jan. 29, 1926; and E. M. Clark to W. C. Teagle, Apr. 2, 1928. In my interviews with F. A. Howard, O. Harden, and F. W. Abrams, these men all stressed that the refineries, especially the large New York ones, competed with each other for money, men, materials, supplies, and outlets.

    Unless otherwise indicated, all letters cited in this chapter are from the files of Standard Oil Company (New Jersey). Where a letter is also quoted by Gibb and Knowlton, a reference will be made to the page where they use it. The great majority of the records used here came from the E. M. Clark files, which were not located when Gibb and Knowlton did their study.
12. Gibb and Knowlton, *Resurgent Years,* pp. 26–31 and 259–260.
13. The shift in the market and the increase in total demand are most clearly seen

in the table on "Delivery of Refined Products," Gibb and Knowlton, *Resurgent Years,* p. 681. Also Federal Trade Commission, *Petroleum Industry — Prices, Profits and Competition* (Washington, 1929), pp. 148–149. This latter report (pp. 139–140) also emphasizes the continuing large volume of petroleum used for fuel oil in industrial power as well as in ships and locomotives. Fuel oil was sold, from the first, in bulk to large industrial users, Hidy, *Pioneering in Big Business,* pp. 452 and 737.

14. W. C. Teagle to Board of Directors, June 4, 1927.
15. Gibb and Knowlton, *Resurgent Years,* pp. 44, 187, and 678.
16. As one executive pointed out: "Prior to the dissolution, the South Penn, Ohio Oil, and Prairie Oil & Gas . . . protected the refinery investment of this company, while today we have no claim on them nor in shaping their policies," memorandum of E. J. Sadler, Sept. 22, 1919, cited in Gibb and Knowlton, *Resurgent Years,* pp. 56 and 108, and Sadler memorandum of March 5, 1919, partly quoted in *ibid.,* pp. 107–108.
17. Expansion of production of crude oil to 1917 is described in *ibid.,* chs. 3 and 4.
18. Memorandum of E. J. Sadler, March 5, 1917. See also reference in Gibb and Knowlton, *Resurgent Years,* pp. 107–108.
19. *Ibid.,* p. 412.
20. Jersey executives continued to look on Humble in this light until very recently. The investment was increased from time to time and by 1958 represented more than 98 per cent of Humble's capital stock. In 1959, Jersey decided to merge most of its domestic affiliates into a single legal entity with Humble as perhaps the most important participant in the merger (see ftn. 155).
21. Memorandum of E. J. Sadler, March 5, 1917.
22. Memorandum of E. J. Sadler, Aug. 6, 1920.
23. *The Lamp,* 1(4):21–22 (Nov., 1918).
24. Memoranda of E. J. Sadler, July 23, August 6, 1920. The quotation is from the July 23 memorandum.
25. Gibb and Knowlton, *Resurgent Years,* pp. 153–165 and 472–481.
26. *Ibid.,* pp. 454–456 and 676–679. Shipping figures are on p. 481.
27. *Ibid.,* p. 187.
28. *The Lamp* 3(4):7 (Dec., 1920) and *ibid.,* 7(1):6 (June, 1924).
29. Gibb and Knowlton, *Resurgent Years,* p. 681
30. O. Harden, memorandum on the Coordination Department, Oct. 28, 1927, and forwarding letter from E. M. Clark to W. C. Teagle, April 2, 1928, and memorandum from E. J. Sadler to the Board of Directors, June 27, 1924.
31. Gibb and Knowlton, *Resurgent Years,* pp. 115–117. The use of the Burton Process is told in ch. 5, and the bringing of Clark and Howard to Jersey Standard and later developments are described in ch. 17.
32. The story of the beginnings of the Development Department is described in *ibid.,* pp. 520–531. Howard added information in a letter to the author, May 26, 1959.
33. W. C. Teagle to A. C. Bedford, June 5, 1919, quoted in Gibb and Knowlton, *Resurgent Years,* p. 524.
34. Howard's Department included five units — the General Laboratory; the Research Laboratory, headed by C. O. Johns "to carry on the research directed toward the solution of important chemical and physical problems involved in our business"; the Experimental Division (the "connecting link between the Laboratory and Practical Operations") under N. H. Loomis, with respon-

sibility for "the development of new processes, equipment, and products"; the Patent Division, under C. A. Straw; and a Library and Technical Information Service (Annual Report of Development Department, Nov. 24, 1920). Although, as Gibb and Knowlton state (*Resurgent Years,* p. 529), the old Standard Inspection Laboratory was not placed under Howard's department until 1922, the General Laboratory headed by C. I. Robinson, the Company's Chief Chemist, which "serves as a central, analytical, general chemical and oil refining laboratory of the Company," was under Howard from the start.

35. Frank A. Howard, *Organizing for Technical Progress* (New York, 1957), p. 2, and his first Annual Report (Nov. 24, 1920). In this long and detailed document he explained to Teagle, much as Sadler had in his first report in the same year, why such a formal document appeared necessary:

> Through your own activities in the work of the Department, you are doubtless familiar with all the foregoing. It was thought desirable, however, to render a formal report on the first year's activities of the Department in order that you might have the opportunity of getting a bird's-eye view of the whole situation with respect to this Department, to determine to what extent and at what cost, it is doing the things it was expected to do.

Also Howard's detailed organizational charts of his Department were among the first such charts seen at Standard Oil.

36. Gibb and Knowlton, *Resurgent Years,* p. 124.
37. Hick's work is outlined in *ibid.,* ch. 18. By 1923, the Personnel and Training Department had its own set of offices on the sixth floor at 26 Broadway (G. L. Olney to E. M. Clark, Dec. 3, 1923).
38. Roy S. Bonsib became head of the new Safety Division in January, 1921. *The Lamp,* 3(5):11 (Feb., 1921). For the Medical Department, see Gibb and Knowlton, *Resurgent Years,* pp. 394–395 and 577. Another important development in the field of employee relations was the publication of *The Lamp,* which came to be edited by Northrup Clarey. The editor considered that his job included public as well as employee relations. He appears to have reported directly to Teagle (Gibb and Knowlton, *Resurgent Years,* pp. 577–578 and 613). For Purchasing, see *The Lamp,* 3(6):27 (April, 1921).
39. *The Lamp,* 3(5):9–10 (Feb., 1921).
40. Their backgrounds are briefly described in *The Lamp,* 8(3):9 (Oct., 1925) and *ibid.,* 8(4):3 (Dec., 1925). Other Directors in 1925 included Walter Jennings and Frederick H. Bedford. The former took no part in company affairs. The latter concerned himself only with his specialty — the marketing of lubricating oil, especially abroad. Gibb and Knowlton, *Resurgent Years,* p. 26.
41. *Ibid.,* p. 608.
42. Teagle's attitude toward formal organization was quite clear. He would not allow his executives to draw up organization charts, diagrams, or manuals for the company as a whole. Such forms created more problems, he insisted, than they solved. In later years when asked whether he considered the 1927 reorganization as a major incident in the company's history, he replied: "Hell no. That wasn't anything at all. That kind of thing you'd have to do anyway." Teagle made this comment to George S. Gibb, coauthor of the *Resurgent Years.* Every executive I talked to emphasized Teagle's distaste for organization charts and manuals.
43. Gibb and Knowlton, *Resurgent Years,* p. 537.
44. E. M. Clark to G. W. McKnight, Jan. 7. 1924.

45. This and the five following quotations are from the report of F. A. Howard to G. W. McKnight, January 14, 1924.
47. This and the following quotations are from a memorandum of E. J. Sadler to Board of Directors, June 27, 1924.
47. This and the following quotations are from a memorandum of E. J. Sadler to the Board, July 8, 1924.
48. "Table X — Delivery of Refined Products," in Gibb and Knowlton, *Resurgent Years,* p. 681. The deliveries abroad are both from American and foreign refineries, and total deliveries were as follows:

Years	*Deliveries Abroad*	*Total*
1922	39.8 (millions of bls.)	88.5 (millions of bls.)
1923	45.8	114.3
1924	59.4	144.9
1925	64.1	142.5
1926	76.1	157.3
1927	82.5	172.1

49. W. C. Teagle to E. M. Clark, July 31, 1925. Sadler was even more concerned over the possibility that demand for refined might outrun the supply of crude (E. J. Sadler to W. C. Teagle, Feb. 4, 1924).
50. *The Lamp,* 8(1):26 (June, 1925), interview with Orville Harden June 24, 1957. Harden said he went in Black's place, because Black, who preferred New York to the field and disliked answering Teagle's questions, could always find excuses to stay home. The trip extended from June 2 to June 25.
51. W. C. Teagle to E. M. Clark, August 7, 1925, and E. M. Clark to J. A. Moffett, September 16, 1925.
52. The quotation is from O. Harden, "Memorandum on Marketing Analysis," March, 1929, where he is referring to the 1925 situation.
53. Gibb and Knowlton, *Resurgent Years,* pp. 488–489; also Marketing Conference memorandum, July, 1925; and F.T.C., *Petroleum Industry — Prices, Profits and Competition,* p. 56. In January, 1926, Jersey Standard was only twelfth among the large oil companies in the number of its retail service stations, although fourth in the number of its bulk stations. By 1926, it had, according to the Federal Trade Commission, 381 retail stations. In 1919, it had 11, and in 1924, 87.
54. Gibb and Knowlton, *Resurgent Years,* pp. 598–599.
55. This and the following quotation are from W. C. Teagle to E. M. Clark, August 7, 1925. The recommendations on marketing policy approved by the Board, August 7, 1925, attached to this letter of Teagle to Clark, and the memorandum of the Marketing Conference held in the last week of July, 1925, are also valuable.
56. W. C. Teagle to E. M. Clark, July 31, 1925. The next paragraph, the last in the letter, emphasizes that overproduction of crude was not yet a problem: "We want to stop anticipating Crude oil shortage," Teagle wrote, "and run our business without this constant bugaboo hanging over us."
57. No such reports could be found in the Jersey files. Nor is there any mention of such reports in the rather voluminous available correspondence, memoranda, and other business files of this period. Nor are there any reports of the discussions of the Board as no records were kept of its meetings. A letter from

W. C. Teagle to E. J. Sadler, October 16, 1926, does review the decisions about organization made at that time.

58. Jersey Standard, Circular Letter #159, Sept. 3, 1925, and *The Lamp,* 8(4):18 (Dec., 1925).

59. This and the following five quotations are from a memorandum of Orville Harden on "Responsibilities and Duties of the Co-ordination Committee Department," October 28, 1927. In this memorandum Harden was generally excluding Humble, which continued to operate quite independently of Jersey.

60. E. M. Clark to W. C. Teagle, Apr. 2, 1928, with which Clark forwarded Harden's memorandum. The more detailed data included the statistics on "Crude production, available Crude supplies, the stock situation, Crude purchases and sales, pipeline runs, Crude cost and yield and other pertinent data." Particularly important were improved marketing forecasts. The Committee began to get combined monthly estimates or "requirement figures" for the next six months as well as actual monthly deliveries for the past six months, these deliveries being compared to the past estimates (Memorandum on "Sales Research and Market Analysis" by O. Harden forwarded by E. M. Clark to W. C. Teagle, March 20, 1929).

61. This and the following quotation are from Harden's memorandum on the Coordination Department, Oct. 28, 1927. Letters from E. M. Clark to W. C. Teagle on Dec. 31, 1926, and Jan. 4, 1927, show how quickly those data and with them the Committee itself began to be used for long-range planning. The question to be discussed by the Coordination Committee, mentioned in these letters, was future refinery construction.

62. E. M. Clark to W. C. Teagle, Apr. 2, 1928.

63. Memorandum of E. J. Sadler to the Board, June 27, 1924.

64. This and the following quotation are from Jersey Standard, Circular Letter #160, Sept. 4, 1925.

65. This and the following quotation are from S. B. Hunt to E. M. Clark, Nov. 30, 1925. Other letters concerning the new budget are from E. M. Clark to G. W. McKnight, Dec. 2, 1925, and from G. W. McKnight to E. M. Clark, Jan. 8, 1926.

66. Jersey Standard, Circular Letter #179, Jan. 21, 1926. New budgets were being sent to Zane's office before this date (E. M. Clark to G. H. Jones, Jan. 8, 1926).

67. Jersey Standard, Circular Letter #77, Feb. 15, 1923. The Efficiency Committee appointed on Apr. 7, 1922 (Circular Letter #47) was, like the earlier Statistical Committee, to study what reports might be discontinued. They were known in the company as the "carbon removal committees." C. T. White to L. E. Freeman, Apr. 4, 1922, and Circular Letter #77, cited above, indicate that they had little or no connection with organizational changes to improve coordination, as Gibb and Knowlton have suggested in *Resurgent Years,* pp. 617–618.

68. Interview with Wesley Zane, June 24, 1957.

69. Data on the functioning of Zane's department come from the interview with Zane, just cited, and letters in the Clark file, including E. M. Clark to G. H. Jones, Jan. 8, 1926; E. M. Clark to G. W. McKnight, Mar. 5, 12, 1926; and especially W. Zane to E. M. Clark, May 29, 1929.

70. This and the following quotation are from "Memorandum on Sales Research and Market Analysis," Mar., 1929.

71. The changes in the marketing organization are outlined in *The Lamp,* 8(4):15–15 (Dec., 1925), and *ibid,* 8(5):12–13 (Feb., 1926).
72. Memorandum of E. G. Barber, A. C. Bedford, R. A. Holbein, and J. A. Van Wynan, on "Marketing Organization," Dec. 4, 1925. The opening sentence refers to the November 25 conference.
73. W. C. Teagle to Barber, Bedford, Holbein, and Van Wynan, Dec. 9, 1925.
74. W. C. Teagle to James A. Moffett, Dec. 9, 1925.
75. This and the two following quotations are from E. G. Barber, A. C. Bedford, E. A. Holbein, and J. A. Van Wynan to J. A. Moffett, Dec. 21, 1925.
76. W. C. Teagle to G. H. Jones, Jan. 3, 1926.
77. *The Lamp,* 9(2):20 (Aug., 1926). C. O. Scholder, head of the Louisiana sales unit, kept his permanent office in Louisiana. Sheffield also took charge of marketing specialty products as well as fuel oil. At this time, asphalt sales were centralized under J. S. Helm in New York.
78. The major issue between the two groups was the batch versus the continuous-process refining (Gibb and Knowlton, *Resurgent Years,* pp. 536–537; interview with F. W. Abrams, June 5, 1957; and E. M. Clark to C. H. Graff, undated, but referring to a letter of W. C. Teagle to G. W. McKnight, June 7, 1927). In Clark's letter to Graff, he writes that he believes Teagle is not fully aware of the recent changes made in continuous-process refining.
79. These included Frank W. Abrams, Thomas R. Parker, George Gordon, and P. P. Perkins, the last of whom became Secretary of the Manufacturing Committee after Harden left to organize the Coordination Department.
80. As indicated in G. W. McKnight and C. E. Graff to E. M. Clark and C. G. Black, Jan. 29, 1926; and E. M. Clark to W. C. Teagle, Nov. 11, 1925.
81. E. M. Clark to G. W. McKnight, Jan. 11, 1926.
82. G. W. McKnight and C. E. Graff to E. M. Clark and C. O. Black, Jan. 29, 1926.
83. The report did request that a higher limit be placed on the amounts the Manufacturing Committee could approve without requiring further approval by the Board. The Board did not grant this request.
84. W. C. Koehler to E. M. Clark and C. G. Black, Mar. 1, 1926, indicates the objections, and G. W. McKnight to E. M. Clark and C. G. Black, Mar. 18, 1926, on "Manufacturing Committee Organization," gives the final decisions. The second letter begins: "Referring to the Conference of the Manufacturing Committee with the Board of Directors yesterday morning; as a matter of record this will confirm the conclusions reached and which we will arrange to put into effect."
85. C. E. Graff to E. M. Clark and C. G. Black, Sept. 17, 1926.
86. W. C. Teagle to C. E. Graff telling of the Board's approval of the Sept. 17 recommendations; and E. M. Clark to S. B. Hunt, Sept. 24, 1926.
87. *The Lamp,* 9(3):5 (Oct., 1926). George S. Weddon and T. R. Armstrong were the general assistants for foreign producing.
88. *The Lamp,* 9(2):17 (Aug., 1926).
89. E. J. Sadler to W. C. Teagle, Apr. 27, 1926, gives a good example of Sadler's activities. Howard recalls that Sadler preferred to do much of his own departmental work rather than delegate it to others (interview with F. A. Howard, June 28, 1957).
90. E. J. Sadler to E. M. Clark, July 9, 1924; E. M. Clark to W. C. Teagle, July 10, 1924; E. M. Clark to F. H. Bedford, Jan. 9, 1925; and Gibb and Knowlton, *Resurgent Years,* pp. 277, 497–498. A report of the meeting of the European

Committee on Dec. 12, 1924, shows that it discussed the use of Gilbert & Barker equipment (Jersey's affiliate that manufactured and sold stoves and pumps), the elimination of specific gravity specification for one grade of gasoline, changing export quotations from f.o.b. New York to an f.o.b. Gulf basis, trademarks, and policies as to the purchases of Russian products and the disposal of old tankers. At the meeting McKnight and Clark discussed European refining problems and developments.

91. E. J. Sadler to E. M. Clark, July 9, 1924, and E. M. Clark to W. C. Teagle, July 10, 1924.
92. E. M. Clark to W. C. Teagle, July 1, 19, 1925; to G. W. McKnight, July 1, 1925; to J. A. Moffett, Aug. 3, 1925; and W. C. Teagle to H. Riedemann, July 16, 1925.
93. E. M. Clark to G. H. Jones, Aug. 27, 1927; memorandum of C. E. Graff on "Annual Review of Manufacturing Department Activities for 1926," undated; and *The Lamp,* 9(3):5 (Oct., 1926).
94. *Ibid.,* 8(5):14 (Feb., 1926).
95. W. C. Teagle to E. J. Sadler, Oct. 16, 1926.
96. Memorandum of C. E. Graff on "Annual Review of Manufacturing Departments' Activities for 1926," undated.
97. W. C. Teagle to E. M. Clark, C. G. Black, and D. R. Weller, Feb. 15, 1927.
98. J. M. Moffett in a letter to F. A. Howard, undated, in answer to Howard's letter of March 23, 1928, outlines earlier policies. C. G. Sheffield to C. G. Black, May 16, 1929 also reviews policies prior to 1927 changes.
99. Report of committee "to investigate the possibility of the formation of a separate company to handle service stations of the Jersey and Louisiana companies," Aug. 19, 1926, and Teagle's reply to the committee's report, Aug. 22, 1926.
100. W. C. Koehler to G. W. McKnight, Oct. 26, 1926; J. R. Carringer to F. W. Abrams, Dec. 2, 1926, Jan. 4, 1927; F. W. Abrams to G. W. McKnight, Jan. 3, 1927; and E. M. Clark to W. C. Teagle, Jan. 20, 1927. Clark noted:

> I cannot believe, however, that it would be beneficial to refer to the old haphazard type of organization. I think that Mr. Abrams is looking at it correctly and that the minor changes he has suggested should be made. At the same time, I believe that much of Parkhurst's [the consultant] methods should be retained, that we should find the extension of many of them to the Bayonne plant of decided value. I believe we can safely leave this in the hands of Mr. Abrams, as from my talks with him I am sure that he will carry it through to the right conclusion.

See also Minutes, Annual Conference of the Manufacturing Department, Jan. 27, 28, 1927.

101. G. W. McKnight to E. M. Clark, undated, enclosing a letter dated Oct. 17, 1926, describing means agreed upon "to improve contact between the Manufacturing Department and the Bayway Laboratories of the Development Department." See also F. A. Howard to W. C. Teagle, "Annual Report of the Development Department," Feb. 17, 1927.
102. Memorandum of C. E. Graff, on "Annual Review of Manufacturing Department Activities for 1926," undated.
103. An emphasis on more careful cost analysis, particularly in overhead costs, is indicated in Minutes, Annual Conference of Manufacturing Department, Jan. 27–28, 1927; W. C. Teagle to E. M. Clark, Jan. 21, 1927; O. Harden to

G. W. McKnight, undated (early 1927); and W. C. Teagle to E. M. Clark, June 1, 1927.

104. Gibb and Knowlton, *Resurgent Years,* pp. 598–599. The figure is a total for Jersey, Louisiana, and Humble.

105. W. C. Teagle to H. Riedemann, Nov. 26, 1924, quoted in *ibid.,* p. 347.

106. H. Riedemann to W. C. Teagle, Sept. 2, 1925 quoted in *ibid.,* p. 349.

107. W. C. Teagle to P. Hurll, Nov. 27, 1925, quoted in *ibid.,* pp. 350–351.

108. The broad story is covered in *ibid.,* ch. 14, particularly pp. 445–453. Also useful is Federal Trade Commission, *Report on Panhandle Crude Petroleum, February 3, 1928* (Washington, D. C., 1928). The specific responses of Teagle and the Board are indicated in E. M. Clark to W. C. Teagle, Feb. 16, 1927; W. C. Teagle to E. M. Clark, Apr. 18, 1927; and W. C. Teagle to the active Directors (Black, Clark, Hunt, Jones, Moffett, Sadler, and Weller), June 4, 1927.

109. Minutes, Annual Conference of Manufacturing Department, Jan. 27–28, 1927, W. C. Teagle to E. M. Clark, June 8, 1926; E. M. Clark to W. C. Teagle, Nov. 29, 1926; W. C. Teagle to C. G. Black, July 20, 1927, and W. C. Teagle to G. H. Jones, July 20, 1927.

110. Gibb and Knowlton, *Resurgent Years,* pp. 598–599. A breakdown of earnings by functional activities was as follows: production, $2.2 million (including $422,000 loss in the United States); transportation, $37.8 million, marketing $32.6; natural gas, $10.2; and refining and manufacturing, a loss of $37.1 million. Miscellaneous charges outbalanced income from interest to add an additional loss of $5.3 million. In 1926 the figures had been $20.6, $28.7, $30.8, $14.6, and $23.4, respectively, and for Miscellaneous a loss of $0.4 million.

111. W. C. Teagle to active Directors June 4, 1927; W. C. Teagle to G. H. Jones, E. M. Clark, and E. J. Sadler, June 16, 1927; W. C. Teagle to E. M. Clark, Oct. 17, 1927; and W. C. Teagle to D. R. Weller, Oct. 13, 1927.

112. E. M. Clark mentioned "the proposed plans for reorganization" to W. C. Teagle in a letter referring to questions Teagle had raised about reductions in personnel in a letter to Clark, Black, and Weller, May 26, 1927. Once these plans are made effective, Clark continued, "it will be then possible to very materially reduce the General Engineering and Research, Development Departments, by combining and changing their present form or organization." *Fortune* gives Teagle and Sadler the credit for the 1927 changes. *Fortune,* 44:102 (Oct., 1950).

113. W. C. Teagle to E. J. Sadler, Oct. 16, 1926. In this letter, Teagle turned down Sadler's suggestion to put a marketer on the Coordination Committee. Clark's earlier proposal to put Howard on the new Marketing Committee is suggested in E. M. Clark to W. C. Teagle, December 4, 1925. As late as 1933, Clark wanted to get a marketer on the Coordination Committee, and again Teagle refused (E. M. Clark to W. C. Teagle, April 13, 1933, and Teagle's reply, April 18, 1933).

114. For comparative profit record see Gibb and Knowlton, *Resurgent Years,* pp. 598–599.

115. E. M. Clark to W. C. Teagle, Apr. 2, 1928.

116. Teagle's concern for cutting down office personnel at 26 Broadway and its relation to the 1927 changes are emphasized in W. C. Teagle to E. M. Clark, C. G. Black, and D. R. Weller, May 26, 1927, and E. M. Clark to W. C. Teagle, undated, answering that letter of Teagle. See also E. M. Clark to

W. C. Teagle, Apr. 22, 1927; O. Harden to E. M. Clark, May 2, 1927; E. M. Clark to G. W. McKnight, undated (the latter was filed in with May 1927 letters); and W. C. Teagle to E. M. Clark, Nov. 7, 1927.

117. W. C. Teagle to C. G. Black and E. M. Clark, Mar. 31, 1922.

118. This and the following two quotations are from F. A. Howard to W. C. Teagle, "Annual Report of the Development Department," Feb. 17, 1927.

119. Interview with Frank A. Howard, June 28, 1957. Tax considerations seem to be the reason why the new units became affiliates rather than divisions as at du Pont and General Motors.

120. The organization and personnel of the Delaware Company are described in detail in *The Lamp,* 10(3):3–4, 7–15 (Oct., 1927). The lead article in that issue which commented on the changes concluded with:

> Each of the departments which is attaining the new status of a separate entity will represent a business of considerable magnitude. It is the confident expectation that these businesses will gain in efficiency by reason of the increased responsibility and authority placed in their executives and that overhead and operating costs will be reduced. Of possibly greater value is the broadening of the field for the training of executives in all phases of the business of each unit, the advantage of which will be apparent when the necessity arises for matured and experienced recruits for the board of the holding company.

As the value of the new organization for executive recruitment is not mentioned in available internal correspondence, this reasoning may have been a rationalization rather than a basic cause for the change.

121. *Ibid.*, 10(5):10–12 (Feb., 1928). See also E. M. Clark to F. H. Bedford, Nov. 14, 1928. Bedford, the organizer of the Nujol Department and its manager since 1916 and the head of the Lubricating Oil Department in 1917, had become a Director in October 1927.

122. *The Lamp,* 10(1):26 (June, 1927).

123. The over-all manufacturing setup including European and Latin American operations after the 1927 reorganization is described in a memorandum attached to a letter from W. C. Colby to E. M. Clark, Feb. 14, 1928. Senior's marketing organization is described in Jersey Standard Circular Letter #J-38, Mar. 31, 1931.

124. The organization and personnel of the Standard Shipping Company are described in *The Lamp,* 10(3):7–15 (Oct., 1927). The status of Gilbert & Barker, like that of pipe-line subsidiaries, remained relatively unchanged.

125. The reasons for creating the 1922 company are given in F. A. Howard to W. C. Teagle, Aug. 18, 1922, and C. A. Straw to E. M. Clark, Nov. 23, 1922. The name was changed because the old one was the same as that of a real estate company in New Jersey.

126. G. W. McKnight to E. M. Clark, Sept. 15, 1927; E. M. Clark to R. T. Haslam, Oct. 3, 1927; R. T. Haslam to E. M. Clark, Oct. 8, Nov. 2, 1927; and E. M. Clark to W. Zane, Dec. 20, 1927. The details of the organization and personnel of the new Development department, whose creation had to wait until Clark returned from a tour of the European refineries in August, 1927, are given in *The Lamp,* 10(4):11, 14 (Dec., 1927).

127. *Ibid.,* 10(4):11 (Dec., 1927).

128. Memorandum attached to letter of W. C. Colby to E. M. Clark, Feb. 14, 1928. A good example of coordination between the subsidiaries and the central

office in the development of new products and processes is suggested in E. M. Clark to W. C. Teagle, May 2, 1928, and E. M. Clark to D. R. Weller, Jan. 21, 1929.

129. *The Lamp,* 16(1):10 (June, 1933); *ibid.,* 16(6):7 (Apr., 1934), and Building Directory, 26 Broadway, June 28, 1929.

130. *The Lamp,* 16(1):15 (June, 1933), and Building Directory, 26 Broadway, June 28, 1929.

131. Building Directory, 26 Broadway, June 28, 1929. Also these same officers moved uptown with the parent company in 1933, *The Lamp,* 16(1):1 (June, 1933).

132. Until 1933 the Jersey and Delaware Companies had the same identical financial, legal, and secretarial offices, *The Lamp* (3):7 (Oct., 1927).

133. *Ibid.,* 15(1):12 (June, 1932).

134. *Ibid.,* 10(1):26 (June, 1927); and *ibid.,* 10(5):10–12 (Feb., 1928). Peter Hurll joined the Board in 1929 as representative for activities in England and France, *The Lamp,* 17(3):7 (Oct., 1934).

135. As Clark wrote R. W. Hanna on Nov. 25, 1927, not only "will our work be rather definitely designated as compared with the past," but also "we all hope to have more time to ourselves."

136. *Fortune,* 44:102 (Oct., 1950).

137. The third volume of the *History of the Standard Oil Company (New Jersey),* which is to be published shortly.

138. The changes are described in much detail in *The Lamp,* vol. 16, issues of June and August, 1933.

139. *Ibid.,* 16(1):24 (June, 1933). The same issue (p. 22) tells of Abrams' new duties. The personnel and positions of the new sales department are listed on p. 24.

140. *Ibid.,* 16(1):22–23 (June, 1933); *ibid.,* 16(5):5 (Feb., 1934); and *ibid.,* 17(1):4 (June, 1934).

141. *The Lamp* reported: "In order to facilitate action, the Executive Committee of the company now convenes daily," 16(2):22 (Aug., 1933).

142. As *Fortune* pointed out: "The job of Farish, as he himself defines it, is to consolidate Jersey's position and to concentrate on operations," *Fortune,* 21:160 (April, 1940).

143. *Ibid.,* 21:62 (June, 1940).

144. *The Lamp,* 16(2):22 (Aug., 1933), describes the functions and the personnel of the Coordination Committee. H. L. Shoemaker was the Committee's Secretary.

145. *Fortune,* 21:63 (June, 1940).

146. The changes can be most clearly seen by comparing the organization as described in the *Fortune* articles of the spring of 1940 with those of the October, 1950, issue.

147. *Fortune,* 44:104–105 (Oct., 1950).

148. *The Lamp,* 26(4):10–12 (June, 1944), and *Fortune,* 44:104 (Oct., 1950).

149. *Ibid.,* 44:101–103, 174 (Oct., 1950).

150. After Harper, Harry G. Siedel and then Emil E. Soubry headed the Foreign Trade Department. Siedel's title had been, according to *The Lamp,* "coordinator of marketing activities outside of the United States." *The Lamp,* 25(4):16 (Dec., 1942); and *ibid.,* 25(5):4, 26 (Feb., 1943).

151. *Ibid.,* 25(7):21 (July, 1943).

152. *The Annual Report of the Standard Oil Company (New Jersey) for 1945,* p. 9.
153. *Fortune,* 44:174 (Oct., 1950). There is a useful detailed analysis of the operations of the Coordination Committee and its relation to the Executive Committee and the general staff departments in Henry Ozanne, "The Jersey Standard Plan — Decentralization for Efficiency," *World Oil* (March, 1949).
154. *Fortune,* 44:103 (Oct., 1950).
155. *Annual Report of the Standard Oil Company (New Jersey) for 1959,* pp. 12, 16.

Chapter 5

1. The following summary of Sears's history came largely from Boris Emmet and John E. Jeuck, *Catalogues and Counters — A History of Sears, Roebuck and Company* (Chicago, 1950), chs. 1–18. Some additional information was from Louis E. Asher and Edith Heal, *Send No Money* (Chicago, 1942), and M. R. Werner, *Julius Rosenwald* (New York, 1939).
2. *National Cyclopedia of American Biography* (New York, 1953), XXXVIII, 390, gives a better summary of Asher's career than does his own book.
3. These procedures are well described in Emmet and Jeuck, *Catalogues and Counters,* pp. 134–136, and in Asher and Heal, *Send No Money,* pp. 124–126. John Meier, Doering's able assistant, may have been even more responsible than Doering for their development.
4. Report of Committee on Reorganization, dated Jan. 6, 1930, hereafter cited as the Frazer Committee Report. Unless otherwise indicated, all unpublished materials are from Sears, Roebuck and Company's files. In 1930, the Traffic Manager was responsible for the movement of goods and storage. The Supply Manager became "responsible for the purchase, storage, and distribution of expendable supplies." (Frazer Committee Report.)
5. These two top company executives were John Higgins, who became Secretary, and Walker O. Lewis, who in time became Treasurer. At the same time, an Executive Committee of the Board was formed. ("Sears, Roebuck & Company — Certificate of Incorporation and By-Laws, 1906," p. 11, Baker Library, Harvard Graduate School of Business Administration.) The Committee does not seem to have played a significant role in policy formulation.
6. Emmet and Jeuck, *Catalogues and Counters,* p. 244. The lists of factories, wholly or partly owned, are given on pp. 241–243. E. P. Brooks, for many years the Vice-President in charge of Sears's factories, stressed that the purchase of factories or stock in manufacturing companies resulted from a need to be secure in obtaining goods at a reasonable price and even more of its proper quality (interview with E. P. Brooks, September 21, 1959).
7. This and the following quotation are from Emmet and Jeuck, *Catalogues and Counters,* pp. 217–218. The new manager who instituted these changes was L. H. Crawford.
8. Theodore V. Houser, "The Sears Organization — Past and Present," an address to the National Conference Board, 1956, p. 6.
9. Emmet and Jeuck, *Catalogues and Counters,* p. 382.
10. Inventory values are given in *ibid.,* pp. 201–202.
11. This and the following quotation are from the Frazer Committee Report.

12. The Merchandise Vice-President still had ultimate, over-all control of inventories (Emmet and Jeuck, *Catalogues and Counters,* p. 376); but the Comptroller was "responsible for the procedures, records and forms used throughout the organization." He also had "charge of all statistics of the organization as well as all accounts and is the officer responsible to the President for the preparation of all budgets and estimates affecting any department, division or territory of the business." (Both quotations are from the Frazer Committee Report.)
13. This memorandum is quoted in Emmet and Jeuck, *Catalogues and Counters,* pp. 339–340. Wood stressed that, except for the long-established grocery chains like the Great Atlantic & Pacific Tea Co., the chains had no distributing warehouse system.
14. *Fortune,* 17:106 (May, 1938).
15. Houser had gone on to Montgomery Ward in 1915 after graduating from Iowa State with a degree in engineering. He had worked closely with Wood during the latter's tenure there, *Fortune,* 50:13 (Dec., 1954), and *Who's Who in America.*
16. The "B" stores grew from 8 to 150 in 1928. Emmet and Jeuck (*Catalogues and Counters,* pp. 341–379) give the details of retail store expansion at both Sears and Ward.
17. Interview with R. E. Wood, July 30, 1958.
18. This and the five following quotations are from R. E. Wood, "Mail Order Retailing — Pioneered in Chicago," Newcomen Address, Nov. 4, 1948 (mimeographed). This address gives the best concise summary of Wood's strategy of retailing.
19. According to *Fortune,* only 1 per cent of the company's gross sales came from cities over 100,000, *Fortune,* 17:106 (May, 1938).
20. Both the Frazer Committee Report of Jan. 6, 1930, and a long report submitted by J. M. Barker to R. E. Wood, Jan. 2, 1935, suggest this basic strategy, as do Wood's own public statements in the 1930's. A good example of the latter is Wood's speech at the Conference on Distribution at Boston, Sept. 20, 1937. See also *Annual Report of Sears, Roebuck & Company for the year ending Jan. 31, 1941.*
21. The continuing problem of the location of the "B" stores is indicated in a report of F. M. Gibian, "Problem — Down Town vs. Outlying Locations," July 9, 1943. The problem of lines is mentioned in reports discussed later in this chapter and in Emmet and Jeuck, *Catalogues and Counters,* especially pp. 351 and 386.
22. *Fortune,* 17:108 (May, 1938).
23. J. M. Barker, in an interview, July 28–29, 1958, pointed out that W. H. Alexander came to have a sort of general supervision over the "A" stores and a Mr. Trimble over the "B" stores. Emmet and Jeuck (*Catalogues and Counters,* p. 352) say that Alexander was first appointed "Acting Manager of the Retail Stores" on May 27, 1925. See also p. 358.
24. The personnel, merchandising, and supply problems are indicated in Emmet and Jeuck, *Catalogues and Counters,* ch. 21, and in *Annual Report of Sears, Roebuck & Company for the year ending Jan. 31, 1941.* They were also discussed in interviews with J. M. Barker and R. E. Wood.
25. Interview with R. E. Wood, July 30, 1958.

26. "Letter to Stockholders", signed by R. E. Wood, Jan. 29, 1931, in Baker Library, Harvard Graduate School of Business Administration.
27. These statistics are from Emmet and Jeuck, *Catalogues and Counters,* pp. 649–650, 653.
28. The quotation is from *ibid.*, p. 548.
29. After teaching manual training in Massachusetts schools, Dodd became the principal of the leading industrial arts school in Boston in 1908. In 1912, he took the position of Director of The National Society for the Promotion of Industrial Education. Five years later he became a member of the United States Army Board of Classification of Personnel, where he may have met Wood. In the next year, Dodd was the head of the War Service Committee of the Retail Dry Goods Industry. From 1917 until 1921, he was Director of the Retail Research Association and the Associated Merchandising Corporation. Then, until 1927, he was Manager of the Distribution Department of the United States Chamber of Commerce. His knowledge of retailing may have been increased because of his marriage in 1921 to Catherine Filene of the highly successful Boston retailing family. *Who's Who in Commerce and Industry* (New York, 1948).
30. Emmet and Jeuck, *Catalogues and Counters,* pp. 377–378.
31. These objectives are listed in *ibid.,* p. 359.
32. Interview with J. M. Barker, July 28–29, 1958.
33. This information comes largely from George E. Frazer, *First Forty Years* (n.p., 1957), pp. 7–18, supplemented by *Who's Who in Industry and Commerce* (New York, 1948). When Frazer set up his own consulting firm in 1917, his announcement stated that his firm "has been organized for practice as counsel in business organization, accounting and industrial management," (*ibid.,* p. 7). During the 1920's, his firm sponsored a number of books on industrial organization and management. From 1917 on, he held a lectureship in accounting at the University of Chicago. One of the firm's earlier associates and partners, James O. McKinsey, became a leading American management consultant.
34. This and the following quotation are from G. E. Frazer to R. E. Wood, Jan. 6, 1930.
35. Barker and Carney continued to work out of Philadelphia.
36. Memorandum from T. V. Houser on "Classification of Lines of Merchandise," Dec. 14, 1929.
37. G. E. Frazer to the Committee, Dec. 14, 1929, and G. E. Frazer to T. V. Houser, Dec. 18, 1929.
38. Two undated and unsigned memoranda to the Frazer Committee, one on "the Organization of Regions and the Retail Districts," and the other on the responsibilities and types of men required for District Manager, District Sales Manager, and store manager, enclosed with a letter of G. E. Frazer to Committee, Dec. 14, 1929. The second of these memoranda, Frazer wrote, was specifically prepared by Dodd.
39. G. E. Frazer to the Committee, Dec. 14, 1929; L. Rosenwald to R. E. Wood, Dec. 26, 1929; and G. E. Frazer to R. E. Wood, Jan. 6, 1930.
40. The Property Manager became "responsible for the purchase, sale and maintenance of land, buildings and equipment," and for the preparation of plans and budgets for building construction and repairs. This quotation is from the Frazer Committee Report, Jan. 6, 1930.

41. This and the following six quotations are from the Frazer Committee Report.
42. C. B. Roberts to R. E. Wood, Dec. 30, 1929.
43. G. E. Frazer to L. Rosenwald, Jan. 14, 1930. Frazer used the words "Regional" and "Territorial" interchangeably.
44. This and the following quotations are from the memorandum prepared by Dodd for the Frazer Committee on responsibilities and types of men required for District Manager, District Sales Manager, and store manager.
45. G. E. Frazer to R. E. Wood, Jan. 28, 1930.
46. This and the following three quotations are from the Frazer Committee Report.
47. The Managers of the mail-order houses were given the same power of veto, although the District Managers were not.
48. This and the following four quotations are from L. Rosenwald to R. E. Wood, Dec. 26, 1929.
49. Emmet and Jeuck (*Catalogues and Counters,* pp. 377–381) describe the activities of this Department. In 1932, it was placed under the supervision of the Merchandise Department, where it had been before 1929.
50. T. J. Carney to L. Rosenwald, Dec. 31, 1929, and a supplementary note attached to that memorandum; also a memorandum from C. B. Roberts to R. E. Wood, Dec. 30, 1929.
51. This and the following quotation are from G. E. Frazer to R. E. Wood, Jan. 28, 1930. In this same letter Frazer pointed out two other illustrations of the problems that had arisen. First was the question of whether four clothing experts could be sent into the field as advisors to the retail stores. The question involved related to the status of these men when they were working in the field. Frazer said they were still members of the General Merchandise Department and completely under its control. The other case concerned the responsibility for placing retail advertising throughout the country. This responsibility, Frazer insisted, was clearly that of the Retail Sales Manager and his staff at Chicago.
52. Emmet and Jeuck, *Catalogues and Counters,* p. 386. At the end of 1929, Sears had 48 "A" stores, 237 "B" stores, and 34 "C" stores, *ibid.,* p. 345. The sales figures for retail and mail-order sales are on the same page.
53. This and the six following quotations are from a Memorandum of G. E. Humphrey, June 26, 1930.
54. R. E. Wood to H. W. Kingsley, J. M. Barker, C. B. Roberts, and C. A. Woods, June 27, 1930; H. W. Kingsley to R. E. Wood, July 12, 1930; and G. E. Humphrey to R. E. Wood, July 17, 1930. While there were differences of opinion on the type of staff necessary, all agreed on its need.
55. W. H. Alexander, who was asked at the last moment to attend the meeting, felt that the greatest difficulty was in the caliber of the top personnel in the Territorial Office. "This subject, of course," he told Wood, "I could not discuss, and undoubtedly it is the most important subject," W. H. Alexander to R. E. Wood, Sept. 30, 1930; also R. E. Wood to L. Rosenwald, Sept. 24, 1930.
56. This and the following quotation are from G. E. Frazer and A. W. Torbet to R. E. Wood, Oct. 29, 1930.
57. "Suggested Revisions and Eliminations" to the Frazer Committee's "Definitions of Responsibilities," undated.
58. Described in T. J. Carney to R. E. Wood, Dec. 16, 1931.
59. *Ibid.*

60. This and the two following quotations are from a memorandum of T. J. Carney, Oct. 1, 1931, cited in Emmet and Jeuck, *Catalogues and Counters,* p. 549. Following a recommendation made by Frazer in his second report, a personnel office was set up in each territory under an executive who reported to Andrews. Andrews himself reported to Carney. Dodd's move is indicated in *Who's Who in Commerce and Industry* (New York, 1948). He would, in 1934, leave Kroger to become Executive Vice-President and then President of the American Management Association.
61. R. E. Wood to the Territorial Officers, Dec. 21, 1931. Wood sent a draft of this memorandum to Carney on Dec. 15, R. E. Wood to T. J. Carney, Dec. 15, 1931.
62. Three items from T. J. Carney to R. E. Wood, Dec. 16, 1931 — a long memorandum, a forwarding letter, and a letter commenting on Wood's memorandum to the Territorial Officers. In the forwarding letter, Carney said: "I dictated the attached memorandum to you before receiving a copy of the letter you proposed sending to each Territorial Officer." The following five quotations are from Carney's memorandum.
63. R. E. Wood to L. Rosenwald, Dec. 21, 1931, and R. E. Wood to the Territorial Officers, Dec. 21, 1931.
64. J. M. Barker to R. E. Wood, Dec. 31, 1931. Barker concluded his letter by saying:

> Whether or not such centralization is desirable can best be judged by the experience of other great organizations which have tried it. Personally I cannot see that it will work as well as our present plan. In any case, the Territorial Officer, responsible for personnel, but not for profits, would undoubtedly find it difficult to fit personnel into a scheme when his choice of individuals would be judged by profit results over which he had no control.

65. This and the five following quotations are from F. B. McConnell to R. E. Wood, Jan. 5, 1932.
66. McConnell would leave the selection of store sites, store design, and equipment to the central office but subject to the approval of the Territorial Officer.
67. R. E. Wood to T. J. Carney, Jan. 15, 1932.
68. C. A. Woods to R. E. Wood, Jan. 7, 1932.
69. Memorandum by T. J. Carney on the meeting of Jan. 16, forwarded to the Territorial Officers for comment on Jan. 20, with the revised version being sent to Wood on Jan. 29. McConnell in his letter of Jan. 5 stressed that "the lack of mutual understanding" between Chicago and the field had inhibited effective use of "the reservoir of experts" in Chicago.
70. The first large formal meeting of the Store Managers in Chicago was on Feb. 8, 1932. These meetings became periodic affairs (R. E. Wood, "On to Chicago" speech at Stevens Hotel Conference, Mar. 30, 1939).
71. Emmet and Jeuck, *Catalogues and Counters,* pp. 362–363, also memorandum of J. M. Barker to R. E. Wood, Jan. 2, 1935.
72. The data in this and the following sentence are from Emmet and Jeuck, *Catalogues and Counters,* p. 653.
73. Memorandum of J. M. Barker to R. E. Wood, Jan. 2, 1935, a memorandum written at Wood's request, "intended to summarize the basic principles in line with which the effort of the Retail Administration Office has been directed, together with a statement of some of the major problems which confront Sears, Roebuck & Company at present and for the future in the development of retail

stores." Also useful on this point is J. M. Barker, "Administration in an Extensive Retail Organization," a paper presented before the Boston Conference on Distribution, Sept. 23, 1935, p. 8.

74. J. M. Barker to R. E. Wood, Dec. 15, 1947.
75. Emmet and Jeuck, *Catalogues and Counters,* pp. 548–551, and interview with J. M. Barker, July 29–30, 1958. The manual is mentioned in Emmet and Jeuck, *Catalogues and Counters,* p. 548. A conference of field and parent personnel men is described on p. 555.
76. This and the three following quotations are from J. M. Barker to R. E. Wood, Jan. 2, 1935. Caldwell, Baker's retail personnel assistant, recalls that "virtually all his time was spent inspecting stores and appraising the quality of the personnel," Emmet and Jeuck, *Catalogues and Counters,* p. 559.
77. These major reports included: Profit and Loss, Balance Sheet, Merchandise Condition, Item Report on Old Merchandise, Age of Inventory by Season Letter, Inventory Shrinkage Report, Period and Seasonal Mark-Down Classification, Cumulative Daily Record Report, Divisional Pay-Roll Report, File of Auditor's Reports, Latest Report of Daily Stores, and Henry Rose Sales Report.
78. Quoted in David G. Moore, "Managerial Strategies and Organization Dynamics in Sears Retailing," a doctoral dissertation submitted at the University of Chicago, 1954, p. 77.
79. The problem of how much and what kind of soft lines to carry in the "B-1" was much like that of the "A" — one of space. The "A," with its 60,000 to 100,000 square feet, was small in size as department stores went. Moreover, one-third of its area was given over to hard lines. So as Barker wrote, in comparison with the offerings of "competitive department stores, the disparity of the relation between the soft line areas . . . is striking." The problem of the "B," with its 20,000 square feet, was even more difficult.
80. J. M. Barker to R. E. Wood, Jan. 2, 1935.
81. Emmet and Jeuck, *Catalogues and Counters,* p. 357.
82. From an interview with R. E. Wood, July 30, 1958; J. M. Barker to R. E. Wood, Jan. 2, 1935; and Barker, "Administration in an Extensive Retail Organization," Sept. 23, 1935.
83. Interview with R. E. Wood, July 30, 1958.
84. This and the two following quotations are from J. M. Barker to R. E. Wood, Jan. 2, 1935.
85. Quoted in Emmet and Jeuck, *Catalogues and Counters,* p. 371.
86. Information on the 1935 changes are from J. M. Barker, "Administration in an Extensive Retail Organization," Sept. 23, 1935, and comments by F. B. McConnell sent to the author by J. C. Worthy, Dec. 1, 1959. McConnell said that he needed to clear only the "A" store and Group appointments with Wood.
87. R. E. Wood, "On to Chicago," speech at Stevens Hotel Conference, Mar. 30, 1939.
88. Emmet and Jeuck, *Catalogues and Counters,* p. 553, and *Annual Report for Sears, Roebuck & Company for year ending January 29, 1935.* The personnel manager for Factory Personnel also reported to McConnell after the post was founded in 1938.
89. This and the following quotation are from J. M. Barker, "Administration in an Extensive Retail Organization," Sept. 23, 1935.
90. *Fortune,* 17:108 (May, 1938) tells of the expansion in soft lines. The Merchandise Department in time came to have its special offices for soft lines, hard

lines, home furnishings, and advertising as well as for store planning and display. *Printers Ink Monthly,* 41:6–7 (July, 1940) describes well the relations between the Group and Zone managers and Chicago in carrying out sales promotion activities.

91. The following information on the organization of independent "A" stores, Groups, and the Zones comes from Emmet and Jeuck, *Catalogues and Counters,* pp. 368–371 and 482–487. Beside the sales promotion officers, an "A" store staff included an Operating Superintendent and his assistants—Personnel, Customer Service, and Installation Service.

92. R. E. Wood, "On to Chicago," Mar. 30, 1939.

93. *Annual Report(s) for Sears, Roebuck & Company for the year(s) ending Jan. 31, 1939 and Jan. 31, 1940;* and R. E. Wood, "On to Chicago," Mar. 30, 1939. Barker became Treasurer and Comptroller in early 1939. He retired in April, 1940, with Humm becoming Comptroller and R. J. De Motte, Treasurer. E. P. Brooks became Vice-President in charge of Factories at the same time that McConnell took the position of Vice-President in charge of Retail Administration and Personnel. Nelson was made an Executive Vice-President in early 1939, but served only a little over a year before going to Washington to become Director of Purchases in the Office of War Production.

94. *Annual Report of Sears, Roebuck & Company for the year ending Jan. 31, 1939.*

95. R. E. Wood, "On to Chicago," Mar. 30, 1939.

96. Wood had kept in mind another alternative. When the Company was under attack with other retail chains during the mid-30's, Wood proposed to the Attorney General's Office that the Company might be divided into six separate regional corporations having a central purchasing unit organized as a nonprofit corporation. *Fortune,* 17:110 (May, 1938). In other words, Wood, under the pressure of government intervention, was willing to accept the alternative of strong autonomous divisions and practically no general office except for the essential central buying organization.

97. Emmet and Jeuck, *Catalogues and Counters,* p. 653. The exact figure was 69.2 per cent.

98. *Annual Report of Sears, Roebuck & Company for the year ending Jan. 31, 1941.*

99. From a speech at Atlanta, Georgia, Jan. 15, 1946. "Preliminary Report on Survey of Organization, Sept. 25, 1947 for Sears, Roebuck & Company," submitted by an outside consultant firm, hereafter cited as Consultant's Report, Sept. 25, 1947, indicated that the Pacific Coast Territory was considered to be a "general model" for later territorial units. This report suggests the amount of autonomy given to the new territorial organization.

100. R. E. Wood to A. S. Barrows, Dec. 18, 1945.

101. Memorandum of A. S. Barrows, "Changes in Organization, 1946," Dec., 1945.

102. This and the following four quotations are from the Consultant's Report, Sept. 25, 1947.

103. These factories were managed along the same basic policies of the delegation of authority as was the rest of the organization. E. P. Brooks, Vice-President in charge of Factories, recalls that his tasks were to check over the factory managers' reports on personnel and their financial accounts, and that the rest of his job was trouble shooting (interview with E. P. Brooks, Sept. 21, 1959).

104. The authority of the parent office, the Consultant's Report, Sept. 25, 1947, continued:

> should be exercised largely in the atmosphere of counselling and guiding and should be concerned primarily with matters of a long-range nature. It should control the activities of subordinate units only in the broadest sense and should be the rallying point for the development and coordination of major policies affecting the business as a whole.

What the consultants may have been saying here was that the senior executives would use their line authority only in emergency and rely on reason, persuasion, and tact to get the Territorial Officers committed to their broad plans. The Report also advised that most legal problems should be handled in the Territories and that those of a more general nature could be carried on by an outside consulting law firm on a fee basis. The Report makes no mention of McConnell's Retail Administration Office, except possibly when its organization chart shows a senior officer in Chicago to whom apparently all Territorial Officers were to report.

105. This and the two following quotations are from J. M. Barker to R. E. Wood, Dec. 15, 1947.

106. E. Gudeman, Jr., was also a member (R. E. Wood to Humm, Hattersley, Moore, Kingsley, Gudeman, and Caldwell, Jan. 13, 1948). The Vice-Presidents of the new Territories were appointed in June, 1948 (F. B. McConnell to R. E. Wood, June 3, 1948, and Wood's reply).

107. Memorandum from F. B. McConnell on "Changes in Organization," Apr. 26, 1948.

108. T. V. Houser, "The Sears Organization, Past and Present," an address to the National Industrial Conference Board, 1956.

109. Described briefly in Houser, "The Sears Organization." Moore, "Sears Retailing," has a good analysis of the changing relationships of buyers of the Merchandise Department and the stores, pp. 243–248.

110. For example, Houser, in an address on "Personnel Policies and Techniques," delivered at New York University (undated), pointed out that "Our Headquarters Personnel Department is organized in the following units:

> 1. Personnel planning and research
> 2. Salary and wage research and administration
> 3. Psychological testing, including employee attitude surveys
> 4. Employee education and development
> 5. Employee policies and benefits
> 6. Employee relations involving our activities with outside groups
> 7. A separate unit which handles personnel administration for our Headquarters offices . . ."

Moore, "Sears Retailing," pp. 255–260, analyzes the impact of decentralization on Sears's personnel activities.

111. Memorandum of C. E. Humm on "Organization of Vice-President's–Comptroller's Function," Oct. 16, 1947.

112. Houser, "The Sears Organization," and an interview with Crowdus Baker, then Sears's Vice-President and Comptroller, Aug. 13, 15, 1957, also Moore, "Sears Retailing," pp. 251–252.

113. Houser, "The Sears Organization."

114. *Fortune,* 17:104 (May, 1938).

115. The quotation is from J. M. Barker to R. E. Wood, Dec. 15, 1947. Barker also mentions the interterritorial committee.
116. In the late 1950's, the Board included the general officers, retired executives, two members of the Rosenwald family, and four outsiders, three active businessmen and the President of Northwestern University. Its Finance Committee reviews expenditures over $500,000.
117. Arthur Rosenbaum ("The Economic Outlook," a presentation to the California Personnel Management Association, Apr. 21, 1953) provides an excellent summary of forecasting procedures at Sears. Some of the basic data he used had been recorded continuously since 1935. This was the approximate date of the forming of Rosenbaum's department, according to Barker and other executives.
118. Barker recalls that he did "a great deal of this [developing financial forecasts] either as the Financial Vice-President, or as the chairman of a succession of ad hoc finance committees," J. M. Barker to author, May 12, 1959.
119. Beside the adjustment of the boundaries of the Territories, the most important change since 1948 has been the creation of what amounts to a sixth territory for the new Latin American activities, which was formed in 1955 with headquarters at Chicago. Also the Property Department was separated from Operations. The period after the adoption of the new organization was one of great growth. From 1946 to 1955, for example, the number of "A" and "B-1" stores increased over 40 per cent. (F. B. McConnell, "A Report on Sears, Roebuck," Feb. 2, 1956).

Chapter 6

1. Joseph A. Schumpeter, "The Creative Response in Economic History," *Journal of Economic History,* 7:149–159 (Nov., 1947). By Fritz Redlich's more precise definitions, the formation of the multidivisional structure by du Pont and General Motors was a genuine, primary innovation, while its creation by Jersey Standard, Sears (and Westinghouse) was closer to a primary reinnovation. Those of du Pont, the General Motors divisions, and Sears, which set up the departmental and central offices, were derivative innovations, while that at Jersey Standard might even be classified as primary reinnovation. Fritz Redlich, "Innovation in Business," *American Journal of Economics and Sociology,* 10:285–291 (Apr., 1951).
2. Leland H. Jenks, "Early Phases of the Management Movement," *Administrative Science Quarterly,* 5:421–447 (Dec., 1960), provides an excellent introduction to the beginnings of rational, carefully planned organization of work in factories and plants. Herman J. Hagedorn, "The Management Consultant as Transmitter of Business Techniques," *Explorations in Entrepreneurial History,* 7:164–173 (Feb., 1955), indicates something of comparable beginnings in office work.
3. See charts of Merchandise Department in Boris Emmet and John E. Jeuck, *Catalogues and Counters: A History of Sears, Roebuck and Company* (Chicago, 1950) opposite p. 380. The citations for facts or quotations in this chapter will be given only when they have not been specifically cited in an earlier chapter.
4. Dexter S. Kimball, *Principles of Industrial Organization* (New York, 1913), p. 89. The italics are Kimball's. Similar views are expressed in [A. W. Shaw Company] *Executive Control* (New York, c. 1915), pp. 41–42. Information on

departmental organization in other large companies is sparse, but the evidence seems to show that individuals rather than committees remained responsible for decisions. For example, there is nothing in Harold Passer's study of General Electric's early administration to suggest that the functional committees rather than the functional vice-presidents had the final responsibility, "Development of Large Scale Organization—Electrical Manufacturing Around 1900," *Journal of Economic History,* 12:384–387 (Fall, 1952). Charles U. Carpenter of The National Cash Register Company, one of the earliest advocates of the committee system in factory management, stressed that committees must not interfere with individual authority and responsibility. He proposed the setting up of a committee or "board" to decide on the practicality of new ideas concerning inventions, designs, and products, and to handle complaints and suggestions. On these matters, he wrote:

> This board must be the supreme and final power in the factory, the only official in the organization ranking it in authority being the general manager. . . . This board should have a permanent chairman selected by the company, and all orders emanating from it should be issued in his name. The chairman of this board should be the person highest in authority in the factory. . . . Each member of the board should have certain departments allotted to him according to his particular ability and experience, over which departments his authority should be complete.

This quotation comes from Charles U. Carpenter, "Money-Making Management for Workshop and Factory," *Engineering Magazine,* 22:699–700 (Feb., 1902). See also Jenks, "Early Phases of the Management Movement," p. 441. This proposal is surprisingly similar to the one Howard advocated for Jersey's Manufacturing Committee in 1924. John H. Patterson, President of The National Cash Register Company, a pioneer in rationalizing management and sales methods and an articulate exponent of the delegation of decision making, was even clearer on this point than his subordinate. The first on his long list of the principles of management was "An organization should have but one head. Centralized authority means no red tape, no delay in making decisions. An army cannot win victories with divided authority. The same thing is true in business." Samuel Crowther, *John H. Patterson, Pioneer in Industrial Welfare* (Garden City, New York, 1923), pp. 247–248. In time committees at General Electric and possibly other large firms came to have group responsibilities for operational activities. This development came not through any specific decision but by unplanned evolutionary process. At General Electric, such committee management was only finally completely eliminated with Cordiner's post-World War II organization changes.

5. This and the two following quotations are from a report to the Board of Directors [of du Pont] from the Executive Committee, Sept. 21, 1921.
6. *Annual Report of General Motors Corporation for 1937,* Mar. 31, 1938, pp. 37–38.
7. There is more detailed discussion relating changes in organization structure to the theory of entrepreneurship in Alfred D. Chandler, Jr., and Fritz Redlich, "Recent Developments in American Business Administration and their Conceptualization," *Weltwirtschaftliches Archiv,* 86:103–130 (1961).
8. *Report of the Investigating Committee of the Pennsylvania Railroad Company Appointed by Resolution of the Stockholders at the Annual Meeting Held March 10, 1874* (Philadelphia, 1874), p. 169. The Pennsylvania's answer was

to have full-time, paid directors, which meant, in fact, only appointing some of the senior executives as directors.

9. For example, Frederick Harbison, "Entrepreneurial Organization is a Factor in Economic Development," *Quarterly Journal of Economics,* 70:364–379 (Aug., 1956).

10. Echols was the representative of the Treasurer's Department on the sub-subcommittee that first proposed the new multidivisional structure for du Pont.

11. Hugh G. J. Aitken, *Taylorism at Watertown Arsenal: Scientific Management in Action, 1908–1915* (Cambridge, 1960), pp. 15–16, also Jenks, "Early Phases of the Management Movement," pp. 442–443.

12. While Kimball drew on Taylor and Emerson in his *Principles of Industrial Organization,* see especially ch. 8, many of his ideas were developed quite independently from Taylor's group. The lack of any direct connection between the Ford engineers and Taylor is clearly indicated in Allan Nevins, *Ford, The Times, the Man, the Company* (New York, 1954), pp. 468–469.

13. Earnest Dale, "Du Pont: Pioneer in Systematic Management," *Administrative Science Quarterly,* 2:37 (June, 1957).

14. W. C. Teagle to C. G. Black and E. M. Clark, Mar. 31, 1922; E. M. Clark to C. J. Hicks, Jr., June 1, 1922; G. W. McKnight to E. M. Clark, June 6, 1922; E. M. Clark to W. C. Teagle, Apr. 16, 1924; and W. C. Teagle to F. A. Parkhurst, Apr. 19, 1924. F. A. Parkhurst, *Applied Methods of Scientific Management* (New York, 1912), indicates his connection with that movement.

15. At Jersey, Howard at least was aware of the du Pont experience. He went abroad in the winter of 1924–1925 with Frederick Pickard in connection with the Ethyl Corporation, which was jointly owned by Jersey, du Pont, and General Motors. Recalling discussions with Pickard over organizational management, he remembered that he was most impressed by what he learned of the du Pont scheme of management. Probably these discussions gave Howard the idea of the value of distinguishing clearly between parent and operating company activities, a distinction that Teagle adopted as a basis for his 1927 changes. But it is clear that any relation between the two reorganizations was indeed tenuous. For one thing, Howard was not specifically consulted on the 1927 changes outside of his own Development Department. Neither he nor anyone else made even the briefest formal study of the du Pont organization. More significant to the changes at Jersey were the visits of Howard and McKnight to other oil companies.

16. Beside the books by Kimball and the A. W. Shaw Company cited earlier, there were Charles B. Going, *Principles of Industrial Engineering* (New York, 1911); Edward B. Jones, *Business Administration* (New York, 1914), and *The Administration of Industrial Enterprises* (New York, 1916); Russell Robb, *Lectures on Organization* (n.p. 1910); Hugo Diemer, *Industrial Organization and Management* (Chicago, 1915); and Lewis H. Haney, *Business Organization and Combination* (New York, 1913), especially ch. 17. A chart outlining organizational structure very similar to the one prepared by the Haskell Committee appeared in the periodical, *Industrial Management,* in 1920. It has been reprinted in Leon C. Marshall, *Business Administration* (Chicago, 1921), p. 606.

CHAPTER 7

1. The information for these companies came from their annual reports and from articles in *Fortune,* including 14:83 ff. (Dec., 1936), 15:71 ff. (Jan., 1937), and 51:89 ff. (Jan., 1955) for Anaconda; 1:73 ff. (Apr., 1930), 44:84 ff. (Nov., 1951) for Kennecott; 6:40 ff. (July, 1932) for Phelps Dodge, and 42:93 ff. (Nov., 1950) for International Nickel. Also valuable were two books by Isaac F. Marcosson, *Magic Metal—the Story of American Smelting and Refining Company* (New York, 1949), and *Anaconda* (New York, 1957); and Robert G. Cleland, *A History of Phelps Dodge, 1834–1950* (New York, 1952); and John F. Thompson and Norman Beasley, *For the Years To Come: A Story of International Nickel of Canada* (New York and Toronto, 1960).
2. American Smelting and Refining obtained financial control of General Cable Corp. and Revere Copper & Brass, Inc.; Anaconda, of American Brass Co. and Anaconda Wire & Cable Co.; Kennecott, of Chase Brass & Copper Co.; and Phelps Dodge, of National Electric Products Corp. and Harbishaw Cable & Wire Corp. Phelps Dodge has recently consolidated its fabricating subsidiaries into the Phelps Dodge Company Products Corporation. For these purchases and their place in the industry, see Edward L. Allen, *Economics of American Manufacturing* (New York, 1952), pp. 114–115.
3. For example, the American Steel Warehouse Association reports that during 1951 independent warehouse distributors shipped 8.5 million tons to the first group, 3.5 million tons to the second, and 2.0 million tons to the third, *This is Your American Steel Warehouse Association* (Cleveland, n.d.), p. 7. The ratio must have been much the same for warehousing units of the large integrated enterprises.
4. Gertrude G. Schroeder, *The Growth of the Major Steel Companies* (Baltimore, 1953), gives brief but useful information on these companies. For Jones & Laughlin, annual reports and interviews with executives provided additional information, as did the company-published *"J & L"—The Growth of American Business (1853–1953)* (Pittsburgh, 1953). Arundel Cotter, *The Story of Bethlehem Steel* (New York, 1916); the company-written *50 Years on Inland Steel, 1893–1943* (Chicago, 1943); and for Youngstown Sheet and Tube, *50 Years in Steel* (Youngstown, 1950), provide further information on these steel firms. The more useful *Fortune* articles include 23:61 ff. (Apr., 1941) and 47:101 ff. (March, 1953) for Bethlehem; 8:52 ff. (Sept., 1933) for Republic; 3:30 ff. (June, 1932) for National; 16:174 ff. (Nov. 1937) for Youngstown; and 58:95 ff. (July, 1958) for Inland.
5. There were separate units in the Sales Department for mill products, sheet mill products, hot-rolled bars and shapes, cold-finished bars, tubular products, wire products, and coal chemicals.
6. Beside Schroeder, *Growth of the Major Steel Companies,* interviews with executives, and annual reports, information on the changing structure of the Steel Corporation came from *Fortune,* 13:59 ff. (Mar., 1936), 13:113 ff. (June, 1936), 21:64 ff. (Mar.. 1940), and 44:89 ff. (Jan., 1956). Myron C. Taylor summarized the mammoth reorganization that he engineered in *Annual Meeting of the Stockholders of the United States Steel Corporation, April 6, 1938. Remarks of Myron C. Taylor* (New York, 1938), pp. 8–22. Also useful in indicating increased centralization was A. D. H. Kaplan, Joel B. Dirlam, and

Robert F. Lanzelotti, *Pricing in Big Business—A Case Approach* (Washington, D. C., 1958), p. 244.

7. Schroeder, *Growth of the Major Steel Companies,* pp. 59–60; annual reports, especially 1954, pp. 8–9; *Fortune,* 3:31 ff. (June, 1932) and 35:219 (May, 1947); and Kaplan, Dirlam, and Lanzelotti, *Pricing in Big Business,* p. 236. Ernest Dale, *The Great Organizers* (New York, 1960), ch. 4, has an excellent description of the personal and informal administration of Ernest T. Weir, the empire builder who created National Steel.
8. *Fortune,* 60:129 ff. (Nov., 1959), has a good description of Armco's past and present activities.
9. The data on Alcoa came from annual reports, interviews with executives, and *Fortune,* 1:68 ff. (Mar., 1930), 10:46 (Sept, 1934), 33:103 ff. (May, 1946), and 52:114 (Oct., 1955). Charles C. Carr, *Alcoa, an American Enterprise* (New York, 1952), adds almost nothing, but Kaplan, Dirlam, and Lanzelotti, *Pricing in Big Business,* pp. 220–229, do.
10. The information on these three companies came primarily from annual reports. For Pittsburgh Plate Glass, the "Brief History of the Company" in the 1952 annual report and the fairly extended description of the present organization in the 1959 report were particularly valuable. There is some additional information in *Fortune* 9:42 ff. (Jan., 1934). Recent changes in American Can Company, including diversification and the shift from regional to product divisions, are covered in the 1956, 1957, and 1959 reports. Also useful are comments in Kaplan, Dirlam, and Lanzelotti, *Pricing in Big Business,* pp. 222, 245, and *Fortune,* 2:39 ff. (Nov., 1930). For the third enterprise, a company publication, *International Paper Company, 1898–1948,* (n.p., 1948), and *Fortune,* 1:65 (May, 1930) and 16:13 ff. (Dec., 1937), provided additional data.
11. The information for the tobacco companies came from their annual reports, with some additional data from *Fortune,* 14:97 ff. (Dec., 1936), on American Tobacco Company; and *Fortune,* 3:54 ff. (Jan., 1931), 18:25 ff. (Aug., 1938), and 56:128 ff. (Dec., 1957), on R. J. Reynolds Tobacco Company. The last of these articles has a section entitled "open nepotism." *Sold American!—The First Fifty Years* (n.p., 1954) provides a little more information on the oldest of the Big Three.
12. This can be seen by examining the annual reports of these four companies. Also *Fortune,* 13:99 ff. (May, 1936), has additional information on Schenley. The organization of the United Fruit Company is described in detail in the company-written *The United Fruit Company—General Instructions for the Information and Guidance of All Employees* (Boston, 1929).
13. Beside the company's quite full annual reports and interviews with executives, information on Swift came from *Fortune,* 46:102 ff. (Sept., 1952), and on Armour from *Fortune,* 3:49 ff. (Apr., 1931), 9:59 ff. (June, 1934), 51:129 ff. (May, 1955), and 60:117 ff. (Oct., 1959).
14. The United States Bureau of Corporations, *Report of the Commissioner of Corporations on the Beef Industry, March 3, 1905* (Washington, 1905), especially p. 21.
15. *Annual Report of Armour & Company for 1959,* p. 11, and the report for 1960, pp. 13–18. The 1960 report, pp. 2, 13–16, also stressed the shifting of resources to chemicals. The 1959 annual report emphasized that an intensive

research effort was "exploring the merits of entering into production chemistry as contrasted to the chemistry of additives which is largely the nature of its current products."

16. Much of the information on these four companies and National Dairy came from their annual reports. James Gray, *Business without Boundaries—the Story of General Mills* (Minneapolis, 1954), especially ch. 15, is very good on changes in the structure of that company. The company-sponsored *General Foods, Family Album* (n.p., 1948) and *Into a Second Century with Procter & Gamble* (Cincinnati, 1944) have some additional information on those firms, as has *Fortune* 5:20 ff. (Feb., 1932), 10:69 ff. (Oct., 1934). National Industrial Conference Board, *Company Organization Charts, Studies in Personnel Policy,* No. 139 (1953), p. 67, has an organization chart of General Foods and on pp. 68–69 one of General Mills. National Dairy's annual reports were supplemented by interviews with senior executives, and *Fortune,* 46:144 (Dec., 1952). *Fortune,* 56:160 (Nov., 1957), has a little on Procter & Gamble's recent developments and 4:92 ff. (Dec., 1931) and 19:77 ff. (Apr., 1939) on earlier ones. *Fortune,* 2:81 ff. (Nov., 1930), gives a little background on General Mills.
17. *Annual Report of General Foods Corporation for 1929,* p. 15.
18. *Annual Report(s) of the General Foods Corporation for 1943,* p. 17, and *for 1946,* p. 9; National Conference Board, *Company Organization Charts,* p. 67, and Kaplan, Dirlam, and Lanzelotti, *Pricing in Big Business,* p. 231.
19. The annual reports of the United States Rubber Company have much detailed information; especially useful were those dated 1894, 1895, 1896, 1904, 1906, 1910–1914, 1917, 1918, 1921, 1929, 1957, and 1960. Constance McL. Green, *History of Naugatuck, Connecticut* (New Haven, 1948), pp. 193–198, 201–204, 215–220, and 232–237; Williams Haynes, *American Chemical Industry—A History,* vol. VI: The Chemical Companies (New York, 1949), pp. 452–455; *United States of America* v. *E. I. du Pont de Nemours & Company, General Motors Corporation* et al., United States District Court for the Northern District of Illinois, Eastern Division, Civil Action No. 49 C-10 71 (1953), and *Fortune,* 9:52 ff. (Feb., 1934), provided additional information on the United States Rubber Company.
20. Information on Goodrich comes from its annual reports and from Haynes, *American Chemical Industry,* VI, 190–195.
21. Information on Goodyear came from Paul W. Litchfield, *Industrial Voyage* (Garden City, N. Y., 1954); Hugh Allen, *The House of Goodyear* (Cleveland, 1949), especially chs. 7 and 9; Haynes, *American Chemical Industry,* VI, 195–197; David Dietz, *Harvest Research, the Story of the Goodyear Chemical Division* (Akron, 1955); *Fortune,* 54:95 (July, 1956); 62:162 ff. (Oct., 1960); and annual reports.
22. The company's annual reports tell little. Alfred Lief, *The Firestone Story* (New York, 1951), has a little more information as has Haynes, *American Chemical Industry,* VI, 163–165.
23. In 1941, for example, the estimated amount of new rubber consumed in the United States was 202,000 long tons, and in 1949 it was 329,370; while in the petroleum industry the average *daily* capacity rose from 4.1 million barrels in 1939 to 6.9 million in 1951, Allen, *Economics of American Manufacturing,* pp. 130, 185.
24. These very general trends are indicated by the annual reports of the large oil

companies listed here and analyzed in part by John G. McLean and Robert W. Haigh, *The Growth of Integrated Oil Companies* (Boston, 1954).

25. The defensive search for crude has continued up to the present. In 1958, Standard of Indiana, which had been concentrating its activities within the United States, began a large-scale exploration program for overseas crude. As the company's annual report for 1958 explained: "As our business grows, the needs for our own production become ever more important. Currently our Company's requirements for crude oil substantially exceed our own production. In the long range, we believe it is essential for our Company to own or control the major part of its crude resources so that it will not be dependent on competitors for raw material," pp. 5–6.

26. A major source of data for all these companies was their annual reports. Additional information on Standard Oil Company (Indiana) came from Paul H. Giddens, *Standard Oil Company (Indiana): Oil Pioneer of the Middle West* (New York, 1955); on Shell Oil, from Kendell Beaton, *Enterprise in Oil: A History of Shell in the United States* (New York, 1957), and *Fortune,* 56:138 ff. (Sept., 1957), 56:138 (Oct., 1957); on the Texas Company, from Marquis James, *The Texaco Story: the First Fifty Years, 1902–1952* (n. p., 1952); on Sinclair Oil, *Fortune,* 6:56 ff. (Nov. 1932), and 53:117 ff. (Apr., 1956); on Socony Vacuum Oil, *ibid.,* 26:111 ff. (Nov. 1942), and 27:117 ff. (Feb., 1943); on Phillips Petroleum, *ibid.,* 50:72 ff. (Aug., 1954); on Atlantic Refining, *ibid.,* 48:128 ff. (Aug., 1953); on the Gulf Oil, *ibid.,* 16:79 ff. (Oct., 1937), and 49:132 ff. (Feb., 1954), Sidney Swensrud, *Gulf Oil Company: the First Fifty Years, 1901–1951* (New York, 1951), and Craig Thompson, *Since Spindletop* (n.p., c. 1951); on Continental Oil, *Fortune,* 46:126 (Sept., 1952): Standard Oil Company (Ohio), *ibid.,* 59:61 (Apr., 1959); and on Standard of California, *ibid.,* 58:113 ff. (Nov., 1958). National Conference Board, *Company Organization Charts* (pp. 43 and 121), gives organization charts for Continental Oil and Shell Oil, respectively. For Socony-Mobil, Shell, Gulf, as well as Jersey Standard, this information was supplemented by interviews with executives.

27. Allen, *Economics of American Manufacturing,* p. 132.

28. *The Annual Report of the Standard Oil Company (Indiana)* for 1958, pp. 5 and 8.

29. The management of Socony overseas also includes an Executive Vice-President who is responsible for liaison with Standard-Vacuum (the subsidiary jointly owned with Jersey Standard formed in 1933 to administer the Far Eastern properties and activities of both companies), a Vice-President in charge of International Sales (Aviation, Marine, Bunker, and Wholesale Sales), and the Vice-President in charge of Finance.

30. *Petroleum Week* (April 10, 1959), pp. 30–31, briefly summarizes these changes.

31. These were the Jefferson Chemical Company owned jointly with American Cyanamid, the Coltex Corporation with Columbia Carbon, and Texas-U.S. Chemical Corporation with U.S. Rubber.

32. Williams Haynes, *American Chemical Industry — A History,* vol. V: Decade of New Products (New York, 1954), p. 211.

33. These quotes are from Alan Rosensweet, "Reorganizing an Industrial Giant," *Pittsburgh Post-Gazette,* Mar. 21, 22, 1960, which provides the best summary of the Gulf reorganization. Whiteford, who used the term "general officers," insisted that the committees set up in the general office were only to be used

for advice and information, "'I hate committee decisions,' Mr. Whiteford says . . . 'If something goes wrong, nobody remembers who made the decision but if it's successful everybody takes the credit. Now, an order must carry the signature of the individual officer responsible for making it. This way, the men on the firing line can always get decisions. And our top people — the board chairman and president and vice-presidents — have the authority to make decisions.'" Apparently Whiteford and others at Gulf took a look at the du Pont organizational experience, for Donaldson Brown has long been one of the few outside Directors on its Board.

34. Valuable facts on this point are provided in the National Research Council's survey by George Perazich and Philip M. Field, *Industrial Research and Changing Technology* (Philadelphia, 1940), especially chs. 2 and 3 and Tables A-13, A-15, A-17, and D-1; Howard R. Bartlett, "The Development of Industrial Research in the United States," and Franklin S. Cooper, "Location and Extent of Industrial Research Activity in the United States," both in National Resources Planning Board, *Research — A National Resource* (Washington, D. C., 1941), II; U.S. Bureau of Labor Statistics, Department of Labor, and Research and Development Board, Department of Defense, *Industrial Research and Development — A Preliminary Report* (Washington, D. C., 1953), pp. 4–20; National Science Foundation, *Science and Engineering in American Industry — A Final Report on the 1953–54 Survey* (Washington, 1954), especially Charts 5, 8, and 11, and National Science Foundation, "Research and Development Costs in American Industry, 1956," *Reviews of Data on Research and Development* (May, 1958).

35. Harold C. Passer, *The Electrical Manufacturers, 1875–1900* (Cambridge, Mass., 1953), gives the best analysis of Westinghouse and General Electric in the early period. Also useful were *Thirty Year Review of General Electric Company, 1892–1922* (Schenectady, N. Y., 1923); John W. Hammond, *Men and Volts, the Story of General Electric* (Philadelphia, 1941); John T. Broderick, *Forty Years with General Electric* (Albany, N. Y., 1929); Paul W. Keating, *Lamps for a Brighter America: A History of the General Electric Lamp Business* (New York, 1954); Arthur A. Bright, *The Electric Lamp Industry* (New York, 1948); Benjamin G. Lamme, *Benjamin G. Lamme, Electrical Engineer: An Autobiography* (New York, 1926); and Henry G. Prout, *A Life of George Westinghouse* (New York, 1922).

36. *Fortune,* 21:102 (Jan., 1940), and Kent Sangendorph, *Charles Edward Wilson, American Industrialist* (New York, 1949). Kendall Birr, *Pioneering in Industrial Research — The History of the General Electric Research Laboratory* (Washington, D. C., 1957), analyzes the diversification through product development in the laboratory. David Loth, *Swope of G. E. — The Story of Gerard Swope and General Electric in American Business* (New York, 1958); *Fortune,* 3:31 ff., 89 ff. (Jan., Feb., 1931) and 25:65 ff. (Mar., 1942); and the company's annual reports provided additional data on General Electric.

37. While annual reports and *Fortune,* 3:85 ff. (Feb., 1931), provide background information for Westinghouse's organizational changes in the 1930's, the primary source of information was the corporation's *Application for Relief Under Section 722 of the Internal Revenue Code of 1939,* Feb. 11, 1952, in which the company had compiled a large number of valuable internal reports, memoranda, and correspondence. In citing from this document, I have substituted the word Corporation for that of Taxpayer. Dale, *The Great Organ-*

izers, ch. 5, has a useful analysis of the later stages of the reorganization but says nothing about the developments between 1931 and 1935.

38. Westinghouse, *Application for Relief,* p. 50.
39. *Ibid.,* p. 17.
40. *Ibid.,* p. 17.
41. *Annual Report of the Westinghouse Electric Company for 1934,* p. 10.
42. This and the following quotation are from the memorandum of Operating Heads' meeting, East Pittsburgh, December 10 and 11, 1934, on the unit structure of the company, an exhibit in Westinghouse, *Application for Relief.*
43. Memorandum on "Unit Divisions for Diversified Products with Centralized Servicing, Coordination and Control," Oct. 20, 1934, exhibit in *ibid.*
44. *Ibid.,* p. 27.
45. According to L. E. Osborne, the most influential of the organizational planners at Westinghouse was Ralph Kelley, a technically trained engineer who had been in the Sales Department and then in the Statistical Department. He played the leading role in the reorganization in his capacity as the corporation's "Budget Manager," interview with L. E. Osborne, June 17, 1959. Postwar changes are indicated in annual reports, especially for 1954 and 1957, and *Fortune,* 46:119 ff. (Dec., 1952), 48:152 (July, 1953), and 58:87 ff. (Aug., 1958).
46. Information on the reorganization of General Electric comes from *Fortune,* 35:121 ff. (May, 1947), 48:142 (July, 1953), and 52:110 ff. (Dec., 1955); *60th Annual Report of the General Electric Company for 1951,* pp. 11, 14–19; Lawrence M. Hughes, "G. E. Seeks Conquest of Business Through Fanned-Out Management," *Sales Management,* 69:26 ff. (Oct. 1, 1952); Ralph Cordiner, *The Implications of Decentralization,* General Management Series, No. 113 (New York, 1945), pp. 24–32; and *Problems of Management at a Large Decentralized Organization,* same series, No. 159 (1952), pp. 3–17, both published by the American Management Association.
47. RCA Victor's organization can be seen most clearly in National Conference Board, *Company Organization Charts,* pp. 114–117. A company publication, *33 Years of Pioneering and Progress in Radio and Television* (New York, 1953), provides some background information on RCA. Sylvania's experience is summarized in Alfred D. Chandler, Jr., "Management Decentralization: An Historical Analysis," *Business History Review,* 30:126–127 (June, 1960), based on data from annual reports, and from Don G. Mitchell, "Big Business in Small Plants," *Advanced Management,* 15:2–5 (Dec., 1950).
48. The changes in IBM's organization are indicated in its annual reports, especially 1956, pp. 5–6, and 1959, p. 11, also *Fortune,* 54:113 ff. (Sept., 1956), especially p. 104.
49. The information on Allis-Chalmers came from its annual reports and also the company-sponsored *1847–1947; A Story of Men . . . and of a Great Industrial Era* (Milwaukee, 1947), which provides a good brief summary of the company's history. See also *Economic Concentration and World War II,* Report of the Small War Plants Corporation to the Special Committee to Study Problems of American Small Business, United States Senate (Washington, 1946), p. 137. Although Allis-Chalmers began building its first tractors in 1914, not until the 1920's did it establish new Tractor Division branch offices throughout the country. With the appointment of H. C. Merritt as manager of the division in 1926, operations were expanded and new factories built or purchased.
50. Cyrus McCormick, *The Century of the Reaper* (Boston, 1931), especially

chs. 7–13; Forrest Crissey, *Alexander Legge, 1866–1933* (Chicago, 1936); and the company's annual reports. Interviews with executives were also most helpful.

51. The Supply and Inventory Department was divided into three departments, Estimate Order and Review, Materials Control, and Order and Distribution. Merchandising Services included offices for customer relations, sales operations, market research, and credit collections. The organization is summarized in the *Annual Report of International Harvester Company for 1943,* pp. 14–15. Kaplan, Dirlam, and Lanzelotti, *Pricing in Big Business,* pp. 232–233, suggest that in coordinating pricing between divisions the staff has taken over this critical type of operating decision.

52. This and the four following quotations are from Christian E. Jarchow, "Harvester's Divisional Organization — A Decade of Experience," an address before the New Orleans chapter, Society for Advancement of Management, Dec. 8, 1953.

53. Information on these companies came from annual reports, and National Conference Board, *Company Organization Charts,* pp. 36–37, 126–127, as well as a conversation with a senior executive of the A. O. Smith Corporation, and *Fortune,* 51:102 ff. (May, 1955), on Borg-Warner.

54. The information on Deere & Company came from its annual reports.

55. These generalizations about Ford and his company are based largely on Allan Nevins, *Ford: The Times, The Man, The Company* (New York, 1954), and Allan Nevins and Frank E. Hill, *Ford: Expansion and Challenge, 1915–1933* (New York, 1957); Federal Trade Commission, *Report on Motor Vehicle Industry* (Washington, 1939); and *Fortune,* 35:82 ff. (May, 1947), 45:97 ff. (Mar., 1952), and 50:123 ff. (Sept., 1954).

56. McCormick, *Century of the Reaper,* p. 198.

57. Information on Chrysler came from the F.T.C., *Report on Motor Vehicle Industry,* Walter P. Chrysler, *Life of an American Workman,* (Philadelphia, 1938), reprinted from *Saturday Evening Post,* the company's annual reports, and *Fortune,* 12:30 ff. (Aug., 1935), 22:57 ff. (Dec., 1940), 38:103 ff. (Oct. 1948), 49:127 ff. (Apr., 1954), 57:129 (June, 1958).

58. *Fortune,* 35:88 (May, 1947).

59. Excellent brief summaries of the history of all these chemical concerns can be found in Haynes, *American Chemical Industry,* VI. These summaries were supplemented by annual reports and, at Union Carbide and Allied Chemical, with interviews with executives. Some of the more valuable *Fortune* articles are 60:124 ff. (Dec., 1959) on Celanese; 16:83 ff. (Dec., 1937), 23:61 ff. (June, 1941), 24:49 ff. and 57 ff. (July, Sept., 1941), and 55:123 ff. (Feb., 1957) on Union Carbide; 1:81 ff. (June, 1930), 16:83 ff. (Dec., 1937), 20:44 ff. (Oct., 1939), and 50:119 ff. (Oct., 1954) on Allied Chemical; 45:67 ff. (Jan., 1952) on Koppers; 50:73 ff. (July, 1954) on Eastman; and 3:58 ff. (April, 1931), 16:83 ff. (Dec., 1937), 26:110 ff. (Dec., 1942), and 45:104 ff. (May, 1952) on Dow. Murray Campbell and Harrison Hatton, *Herbert H. Dow, Pioneer in Creative Chemistry* (New York, 1951), provide background for that company. Edith T. Penrose, "The Growth of the Firm — A Case Study: The Hercules Powder Company," *Business History Review,* 34:1–23 (Spring, 1960), is excellent. Kaplan, Dirlam, and Lanzelotti, *Pricing in Big Business,* pp. 241–242, provide useful data for Union Carbide. The current organization of most of these companies can be

found in Kenneth R. Kern, ed., *Corporate Diagrams & Administrative Personnel of the Chemical Industry* (Princeton, 1960).

60. See Chapter 1, p. 44.
61. See citations in ftn. 34.
62. Information on Montgomery Ward came from its annual reports and from *Fortune,* 11:69 ff. (Jan., 1935), 33:111 ff. (May, 1946), 53:122 (May, 1956), and 62:138 ff. (Nov., 1960). The *Annual Report of Montgomery Ward & Company for 1957,* pp. 8–9, provides a detailed chart of the company's structure after its reorganization in 1956. The 1956 annual report noted: "Every major officer of the Company, with a single exception, has been elected to his present responsibilities within the past two years," p. 4.
63. For A. & P., see Morris A. Adelman, *A & P; A Study in Price—Cost Behavior and Public Policy* (Cambridge, 1959), pp. 27–36, 110–112. The information on Kroger and Safeway came from their annual reports. The annual reports of Penney and Woolworth can be supplemented by Norman Beasley, *Main Street Merchant: The Story of J. C. Penney and Company* (New York, 1948); *Fortune,* 42:101 ff. (Sept., 1950); and the company-sponsored *Woolworth's First 75 Years* (n.p. 1954), and *Fortune,* 8:63 ff. (Nov., 1933), 49:150 (Apr., 1954), and 61:92 ff. (Jan., 1960).

Conclusion

1. I did not have the opportunity to read Edith T. Penrose, *The Theory of the Growth of the Firm* (Oxford, 1959), until I had completed my manuscript. While using somewhat different data and asking somewhat different questions, Dr. Penrose's findings have many similarities with mine. Her superlative study focuses on the economics of growth and not on structure and on its relation to strategy. My empirical data, however, certainly do help to support her theoretical concepts about the growth of the firm which are defined more rigorously than the more impressionistic generalizations developed here. Particularly relevant to my generalizations are her Chapter 5, "Inherited Resources and the Direction of Expansion," and Chapter 7, "The Economics of Diversification."
2. These developments are suggested in somewhat more detail in Alfred D. Chandler, Jr., "Integration and Diversification as Business Strategies—A Historical Analysis," a paper given before the Business History Conference at the University of Illinois, February 14, 1959 (mimeographed).

INDEX